T0212988

Lecture Notes in Computer Science 9796

Commenced Publication in 1973
Founding and Former Series Editors:
Gerhard Goos, Juris Hartmanis, and Jan van Leeuwen

More information about this series at http://www.springer.com/series/7412

Bodo Rosenhahn · Bjoern Andres (Eds.)

Pattern Recognition

38th German Conference, GCPR 2016
Hannover, Germany, September 12–15, 2016
Proceedings

 Springer

Editors
Bodo Rosenhahn
University of Hannover
Hannover
Germany

Bjoern Andres
Max Planck Institute for Informatics
Saarbrucken
Germany

ISSN 0302-9743   ISSN 1611-3349   (electronic)
Lecture Notes in Computer Science
ISBN 978-3-319-45885-4   ISBN 978-3-319-45886-1   (eBook)
DOI 10.1007/978-3-319-45886-1

Library of Congress Control Number: 2016950420

LNCS Sublibrary: SL6 – Image Processing, Computer Vision, Pattern Recognition, and Graphics

Printed on acid-free paper

This Springer imprint is published by Springer Nature
The registered company is Springer International Publishing AG
The registered company address is: Gewerbestrasse 11, 6330 Cham, Switzerland

Preface

It was a pleasure to organize the 38th German Conference on Pattern Recognition (GCPR) in Hannover during September 12–15, 2016.

This year's call for papers resulted in 84 submissions from institutions of 21 countries. Each paper underwent a rigorous double-blind reviewing procedure by at least three Program Committee (PC) members, sometimes with support from additional experts. Afterwards, one of the involved PC members served as moderator for a discussion among the reviewers and prepared a consolidation report that was also forwarded to the authors in addition to the reviewers. The final decision was made during a PC meeting held in Hanover based on all reviews, discussions, and, if necessary, additional reviewing. As a result of this rigorous reviewing procedure, 36 of the 84 submissions were accepted, which corresponds to an acceptance rate of 43 %. Finally, from these accepted papers the organizers chose 20 for oral presentation in a single-track program and 16 for poster presentation. In accordance with the conference tradition, we organized a Young Researchers Forum to promote scientific interaction between outstanding young researchers and our community. The work of 5 selected students was presented at the conference and included in these proceedings. The accepted papers cover the entire spectrum of pattern recognition, machine learning, image processing, and computer vision. We thank all authors for their submissions to GCPR 2016 and all reviewers for their valuable assessment.

In addition to the presentations from the technical program we were also happy to welcome three internationally renowned researchers as our invited speakers to give a keynote lecture at GCPR 2016: Patrick Perez (Technicolor France), Thomas Wiegand (HHI Berlin, Germany), and David Fleet (University of Toronto, Canada). The technical program was complemented by a workshop on New Challenges in Neural Computation and by two tutorials: one on *Embeddings and Metric Learning* and the other on *CNNs*.

The success of GCPR 2016 would not have been possible without the support of many institutions and people. We would like to thank MVTec Software GmbH, Viscom Vision Technology, Robert Bosch GmbH, and DAGM (Deutsche Arbeitsgemeinschaft für Mustererkennung e.V.) for their sponsorship. Special thanks goes to the members of the Technical Support and the Local Organizing Committees. Finally, we are grateful to Springer for giving us the opportunity of continuing to publish GCPR proceedings in the LNCS series.

This year's conference city, Hannover, was founded in 1150 and was once the family seat of the Hanoverian Kings of Great Britain. Since then it has evolved into one of the 15 largest cities in Germany with 523 642 inhabitants. The Hannover Fair is the largest in the world, due to numerous extensions especially for the Expo 2000. The Hanover Fair and the CeBIT are counted among the most important fairs in Hannover. The city is of national importance because of its universities and medical school, its international airport, and its large zoo. With its many parks and its large municipal woods, Hannover is the second most green city in Europe. It was an honor to host the GCPR this year and to witness animated scientific discussions.

July 2016

Bodo Rosenhahn
Bjoern Andres

Organization

Conference Committee

Conference Chair

Bodo Rosenhahn   University of Hannover, Germany

Program Chair

Bjoern Andres   MPI for Informatics, Germany

Program Committee

Andreas Maier	University of Erlangen-Nürnberg, Germany
Andreas Bruhn	University of Stuttgart, Germany
Angela Yao	University of Bonn, Germany
Bastian Goldlücke	University of Konstanz, Germany
Björn Menze	TU Munich, Germany
Carsten Rother	TU Dresden, Germany
Carsten Steger	MVTec Munich, Germany
Christian Bauckhage	Fraunhofer IAIS, Germany
Christian Heipke	LU Hannover, Germany
Christoph Lampert	IST, Austria
Daniel Cremers	TU Munich, Germany
Fred Hamprecht	University of Heidelberg, Germany
Helmut Mayer	Bundeswehr University Munich, Germany
Horst Bischof	Graz University of Technology, Austria
Joachim Denzler	University of Jena, Germany
Josef Pauli	University of Duisburg-Essen, Germany
Jürgen Gall	University of Bonn, Germany
Laura Leal-Taixé	ETH Zürich, Switzerland
Mario Fritz	MPI for Informatics, Germany
Martin Welk	UMIT Hall, Austria
Olaf Hellwich	TU Berlin, Germany
Olaf Ronneberger	University of Freiburg, Germany
Peter Gehler	MPI Intelligent Systems, Germany
Reinhard Koch	Universität Kiel, Germany
Rudolf Mester	University of Frankfurt, Germany
Simone Frintrop	University of Hamburg, Germany

Thomas Pock	Graz University of Technology, Austria
Ullrich Köthe	University of Heidelberg, Germany
Volker Roth	University of Basel, Switzerland
Walter Kropatsch	Vienna University of Technology, Austria

Additional Reviewers

C. Bauckhage	A. Geiger	S. Nowozin
H. Bischof	B. Goldlücke	B. Ommer
T. Brox	F. Hamprecht	J. Pauli
A. Bruhn	C. Heipke	T. Pock
J. Buhmann	O. Hellwich	O. Ronnenberger
D. Cremers	S. Jegelka	B. Rosenhahn
A. Dengel	X. Jiang	S. Roth
J. Denzler	R. Klette	V. Roth
P. Favaro	R. Koch	C. Rother
G. Fink	U. Köthe	H. Scharr
B. Flach	W. Kropatsch	B. Schiele
W. Förstner	C. Lampert	K. Schindler
J.-H. Frahm	L. Leal-Taixé	C. Schnörr
U. Franke	B. Leibe	B. Schuller
S. Fintrop	E. Levinkov	C. Steger
M. Fritz	A. Maier	R. Stiefelhagen
A. Fuksova	H. Mayer	P. Sturm
J. Gall	B. Menze	M. Welk
P. Gehler	R. Mester	A. Yao

Technical Support, Conference Management System and Proceedings

Timo von Marcard	University of Hannover, Germany
Roberto Henschel	University of Hannover, Germany
Marco Munderloh	University of Hannover, Germany
Holger Meuel	University of Hannover, Germany
Oliver Müller	University of Hannover, Germany
Hendrik Hachmann	University of Hannover, Germany
Bastian Wandt	University of Hannover, Germany
Petrissa Zell	University of Hannover, Germany

Local Organizing Committee

| Silke Kenzler | Kenzler Conference Management |

Sponsoring Institutions

MVTec Software GmbH, Munich, Germany
Viscom Vision Technology, Hannover, Germany
Robert Bosch GmbH, Gerlingen, Germany
DAGM Deutsche Arbeitsgemeinschaft für Mustererkennung e.V., Germany
Technicolor, France

Awards 2015

German Pattern Recognition Award

The *Deutscher Mustererkennungspreis 2015* was awarded to Stefanie Jegelke for her outstanding work on *Submodular Functions in Machine Learning and Computer Vision*.

DAGM MVTec Award

The DAGM MVTec Award 2015 was received by Marcus Rohrbach for his dissertation *Combining Visual Recognition and Computational Linguistics*.

GCPR Awards 2015

The GCPR Best Paper 2015 was awarded to

Andreas Geiger and Chaohui Wang
Joint 3D Object and Layout Inference from a Single RGB-D Image

GCPR 2015 Honorable Mention:

Johannes L. Schönberger, Alexander C. Berg, and Jan-Michael Frahm
Efficient Two-View Geometry Classification

Anna Rohrbach, Marcus Rohrbach, and Bernt Schiele
The Long-Short Story of Movie Description

Contents

Poster Session

Image Processing

Precise and Robust Line Detection for Highly Distorted and Noisy Images

Dominik Wolters[✉] and Reinhard Koch

Department of Computer Science, Kiel University, Kiel, Germany
dwol@informatik.uni-kiel.de

Abstract. This article presents a method to detect lines in fisheye and distorted perspective images. The detection is performed with subpixel accuracy. By detecting lines in the original images without warping the image with a reverse distortion, the detection accuracy can be noticeably improved. The combination of the edge detection and the line detection to a single step provides a more robust and more reliable detection of larger line segments.

1 Introduction

The purpose of this research is the development of a line detector which can handle highly distorted images, in particular fisheye images, without undistorting these images. This should lead to greater accuracy since the detection takes place in the original image and no warping is necessary. In addition, the entire image area can be used. The focus is on the detection of line segments that are suitable for use in line-based structure from motion (SfM).

To achieve a high accuracy in the reconstruction, the lines should be detected with subpixel accuracy. Furthermore, a complete, fast and robust detection of the entire line without interruptions is important, even if the background changes or the surfaces are heavily textured. In the reconstruction short line segments often lead to inaccurate triangulation results and multiple edges. In addition, the matching of many small line segments is time-consuming and error-prone.

1.1 Related Work

Line Detection. Accurate detection of lines is relevant for many areas of image processing. Lines are an important low-level feature, especially in man-made environments. They are used e.g. to describe the objects in images, pose estimation [19], structure from motion [16,18] and stereo matching [3] but also for object detection [10] or camera calibration [17].

The aim of the line detection is to find edge pixels belonging to the same straight line segments. Edges are contours or borders of different image regions. A classical approach to edge detection is the Canny edge detector [8].

Simple approaches to detect lines are RANSAC [13] or the Hough transform [2]. There are many improved and optimized variants which use the Hough

© Springer International Publishing AG 2016
B. Rosenhahn and B. Andres (Eds.): GCPR 2016, LNCS 9796, pp. 3–13, 2016.
DOI: 10.1007/978-3-319-45886-1_1

transform, e.g. [12]. However, these approaches usually require a binary edge map and detect infinitely long lines, that need to be split into line segments. To obtain good results, the parameters have to be adjusted for each scene.

First attempts at line segment detection by grouping pixel based on the gradient magnitude and gradient direction were described by Burns et al. [7]. The line segment detector presented by Gioi et al. [14] enables detection of lines in images without tuning parameters. The EDLine detector [1] presented by Akinlar and Topal uses the Edge Drawing algorithm instead of a classical edge detector, e.g. Canny edge detector, to find edges in the image. The detector is capable of real time and also requires no parameter tuning.

The condition for the application of these algorithms is the presence of perspective input images without distortion.

Some works deal with the detection of lines in fisheye images. Examples are e.g. [4,5]. They detect great circles on the equivalence sphere. Other approaches detect arcs in fisheye images [6,20].

Fisheye Camera Model. In this work the fisheye camera model from OpenCV is used for the calibration of the fisheye cameras. It is based on the generic camera model proposed by [15]. The model, however, can easily be replaced by any other distortion model.

Contribution. In this paper, we propose a line detector, which is capable of processing both distorted perspective images and fisheye images, without requiring them to be undistorted. The detection is done with subpixel accuracy. We combine the edge and line detection to a single detection step. The advantage of this approach is that the line is already used as a model for the detection. In this way a reliable and robust detection is achieved, which makes it possible to detect continuous line segments, that usually were fragmented in current approaches.

2   Methods

2.1   Line Detection on Fisheye Images

Approach. The standard methods used for detecting lines in images expect undistorted images as input. Therefore, the conventional approach to detect lines in distorted perspective or fisheye images is to correct those distortions by warping the image with a reverse distortion and use this software-corrected images as input (Fig. 1).

To use a software-corrected image instead of the original image for the line detection has many disadvantages and should be avoided. The reason for this is on the one hand the performance, because the image has to be warped, and on the other hand, the accuracy because the original image is transformed e.g using a bilinear interpolation. Without adjusting the focal length, the software-corrected fisheye image either gets very large or large parts of the images are cut. An adjustment of the focal length means that the image center, which usually

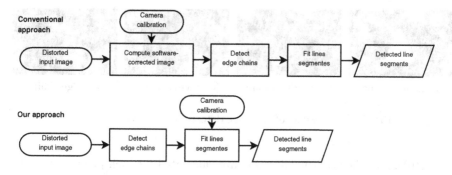

Fig. 1. Application of line detection for fisheye images

contains the relevant image content, is scaled down, so that information is lost here. Another aspect is that errors in the calibration directly affect the detection accuracy of the lines, if the image is warped with a inaccurate reverse distortion. If the intrinsic camera parameters are corrected in a later processing step, for example, by a bundle adjustment, the complete detection including the software correction of all images and the calculation of the descriptors must be performed again.

For these reasons we do not use a software-corrected image but use the original image as input to the line detection (Fig. 1).

Algorithms. Our approach is based on the EDLines algorithm [1]. Its advantages over other line-segment detectors are that it provides robust and accurate results and is also very fast. Unlike classical edge detectors, the Edge Drawing step produces contiguous and exactly one pixel wide, well localized edges.

The EDLines algorithm consists of three sub-steps: First, edge detection is done with Edge Drawing (ED) algorithm. This generates continuous chains of pixels. Line segments are then extracted from the generated pixel chains. The line candidate are finally validated by the Helmholtz principle [11].

In order to perform the approach to fisheye images, some adjustments are needed. The Edge Drawing step detects edges that do not necessarily correspond to straight lines so it can also be used for fisheye images. But for the line fitting step undistorted pixel coordinates are needed.

We undistort the edge coordinates for the line-fit instead of fitting circle arcs. We do this because in our case the calibrations of the cameras are already known and so any distortions can be considered. The approach can be used both for perspective images as well as fisheye images and it is ensured that only straight line segments are detected.

Adjustments to the Line Detection Process. The edge detection with Edge Drawing consists of several steps. First, the image is smoothed with a Gaussian filter to reduce noise (Fig. 2(a)). Subsequently, the gradient magnitude

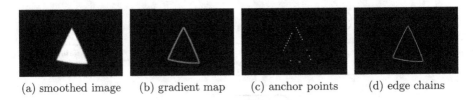

(a) smoothed image   (b) gradient map   (c) anchor points   (d) edge chains

Fig. 2. Process flow of the edge detection with edge drawing

(Fig. 2(b)), and the gradient direction are calculated for each pixel. In the gradient image anchor points are extracted (Fig. 2(c)), which are pixels with high probability of being edge elements. Specifically, these are the peaks in the gradient image. The anchor points are connected with smart routing (Fig. 2(d)). The gradient magnitude and gradient direction are used in this step. This produces a set of edge segments, which are connected chains of edge pixels.

The edge segments obtained are the input to the line extraction step. Here, the edge segments are split into one or more line segments. The basic idea is to run along the chain of edge pixel and fit line segments using a least-squares line fitting method. If the deviation of the pixels of the line is below a threshold value, the line is extended. If the threshold is exceeded, the line segment is terminated and the remaining pixels of the chain are then processed to extract further line segments. We choose the parameters according to the recommendations for the EDLines algorithm [1].

To enable line detection for fisheye images, in our approach, the pixel coordinates are undistorted during the line extraction step (Listing 1.1). In order to increase the robustness and prevent the premature breaking off of line segments, we allow some outlier pixels during the line fitting step in addition. Outliers are pixels that are connected to the chain, but do not fit to the line. Up to 3 pixels are skipped if thereafter again are pixels in the chain, which can be added to the line.

Listing 1.1. Pseudocode for the adjusted line extraction step

```
ExtractLineFisheye:
  undistort edge pixels
  while number of edge pixels greater than or equal n
    fit line to first n pixels
    if residual of fit greater than threshold
      remove first edge pixel
    else
      set first n edge pixels as line pixels
      while number of edge pixels greater than 0 and max. of iterations not reached
        fit line to line pixels
        set number of outliers to 0
        while number of edge pixels greater than 0
          if distance between next edge pixel and line greater than threshold
            increment number of outliers
            if number of outliers greater than outlier threshold
              break
          else
            add pixel to line
          remove first edge pixel
      store line
```

2.2   Line Detection with Subpixel Accuracy

So far, the detection of the line pixel is only done with pixel accuracy. The line equation is, however, set as the best-fit line through all discrete pixel positions so that the start and the end of the line can be specified with subpixel positions.

In the detection step only the pixels with the maximum gradient in the local environment are considered. If the local environment of the line is taken into account, a higher detection accuracy could be achieved. Possible approaches include an analysis of the distribution of the gradient magnitude perpendicular to the line or a subpixel localization of each line pixel before the line fit. We use the second approach, since in this case the rotation can be corrected and no warping of the line environment is required.

For each pixel of a line, the local environment (4-neighborhood or 8-neighborhood) is considered. The subpixel position is the average of the positions of the pixels in the neighborhood weighted by the gradient magnitude of the pixels.

2.3   Optimized Line Detection

Problems with High-Resolution Images. In high-resolution images, the lines often split into several individual segments. These short line segments have numerous disadvantages, especially for use in SfM: A triangulation of short line segments is more susceptible to noise, so that the position of the triangulated lines is inaccurate. A real line is described by a plurality of segments in the image, which are triangulated individually by line-based structure from motion applications. This leads to redundant lines in the reconstruction.

The Causes of Fragmented Lines. The fragmentation of the lines is caused by the Edge Drawing step. Here, contiguous pixel chains are formed starting from anchor points. The edge always follows the strongest gradient magnitude. By doing so, the edge chain kinks in the case of irregularities along the line and the pixel chains tear off. The reasons for such irregularities can be e.g. a junction of two lines, structured surfaces such as wood, but also noise. In the subsequent line-fitting step only short pixel chains are available. The result is that only short line segments are extracted.

Figure 3(a) shows the gradient map of a junction of two lines. The intersecting edge has a stronger gradient magnitude, therefore the pixel chain (red) kinks at the junction and does not form a continuous line.

Through gaps in the gradient (Fig. 3(b)), the pixel chains tear off and the lines fragment into several pieces.

An additional problem occurs with closed contours. The detection of edges starts from the anchor point in one direction and as long as pixels can be added, and then in the opposite direction. For closed contours the starting point is also the end point. If the start point is in the middle of a line, this line is unnecessarily divided into two parts.

Our goal to use lines for the reconstruction requires a reliable detection of lines. The lines should be detected without interruptions, even with a change of

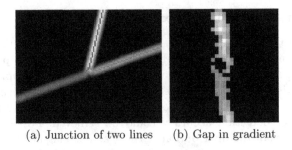

(a) Junction of two lines   (b) Gap in gradient

Fig. 3. Gradient map of challenging locations for the line detection (Color figure online)

the background or along heavily textured surfaces, which have a strong influence on the gradient magnitude and the gradient direction along the edge.

Our Optimized Detection Approach. To solve these problems, we developed a method that combines the detection of edge pixels and lines to one step (Fig. 4). This makes it possible that only the relevant edges, i.e. lines, are detected. At the same time the approach prevents the premature chipping of the pixel chains and thus the fragmentation of the lines.

In the first step, the gradient magnitude and the gradient direction per pixel are calculated and the anchor points are determined as in the Edge Drawing method. Starting from the anchor points, chains of edge pixels are determined. Once a minimum length (e.g. 15 pixels) is achieved, the fitting of an initial line is attempted.

If an initial line is found, the next step is the extension of the line (Listing 1.2). For this purpose, the linear equation of the initial line segment is determined. The linear equation is used to predict the search directions. The extension of the line is performed simultaneously at both ends of the line segment. The pixel with the strongest gradient is selected from the neighboring pixels in the search direction. Subsequently, the linear equation is updated. If all neighboring pixels are below the threshold for an edge or if an already detected edge is reached, up to 3 pixels can be skipped in line direction, to bridge gaps or intersections in the gradient map. Thus, the line is detected continuously. The advantage of this approach is that the line is already used as a model for the detection.

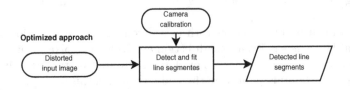

Fig. 4. Optimized line detection approach

Listing 1.2. Pseudocode for the optimized line detection

```
ExtendInitialLineSegments:
  fit line to line pixels
  if line has a slope between +1 and -1
    while extension of the line possible
      calculate next y-value at end of line segment, based on line equation
      if gradient magnitude at [x, floor(y)] greater than value at [x, ceil(y)]
        set y to floor(y)
      else
        set y to ceil(y)
      calculate distance between [x, y] and line
      if gradient magnitude at [x, y] equal 0 or distance greater than threshold
        increment number of outliers
        if number of outliers greater than outlier threshold
          stop extending the end of the line
        fit line to line pixels
      else
        add [x, y] to line pixels
        set number of outliers to 0
      [...] // the beginning of the line segment is extended analogously
  else
    [...] // similar: use equation x = my + c
```

3 Evaluation

3.1 Evaluation of Detection Accuracy on Fisheye Images

To examine the detection and localization accuracy, synthetic test data were generated that contain simple geometric shapes, e.g. triangles and rectangles (Fig. 5). The configuration of the scene corresponds to images of 3 m large objects from different positions from a distance of 5 m to 7 m. The camera has a fisheye lens with an aperture angle of 120°. Apart from a slight smoothing (5×5 Gaussian filter, $\sigma = 1$) the data contains no errors except from the discretization. For each distance 50 images were generated.

The edges of the objects were detected by the proposed method. To evaluate the detection accuracy, the points of intersection of the detected lines are calculated, and the residuals to the real corner points are determined.

The evaluation is performed on the generated fisheye images without and with the additional subpixel localization. Furthermore, the conventional approach is used for comparison. Software-corrected images are calculated for that

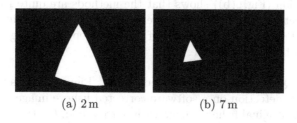

(a) 2 m   (b) 7 m

Fig. 5. Two examples of the generated images from different distances

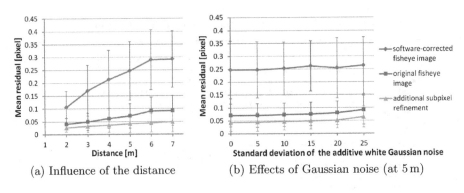

(a) Influence of the distance   (b) Effects of Gaussian noise (at 5 m)

Fig. 6. Detection accuracy (in pixel) of the methods in comparison

and used as input for the normal EDLines algorithm. The software-corrected images are calculated by warping the generated fisheye image with a reverse distortion. Here, the same distortion model is used as for the generation of the fisheye images. This way, no calibration error occurs in the evaluation.

The results (Fig. 6(a)) show that the mean residual is significantly larger on the software-corrected image data. The causes of the rather large deviation in the software-corrected images are partly due to the fact that the focal length is adjusted during the warping to get a large part of the fisheye image without the image size increasing excessively. Thus, the resolution is reduced in the center of the image.

The detection accuracy is less precise at increasing distances, i.e for shorter lines, especially for the software-corrected images.

The localization accuracy can be further improved by the additional subpixel refinement. In particular, at large distances, i.e. for shorter lines, the improvement is bigger. The precise localization of each pixel is important in this case to achieve a high accuracy because the line is not fitted over many pixels.

A precise detection is important for a reconstruction of the lines with SfM, because the detection error greatly affects the accuracy of triangulated lines, since there is a quadratic relationship.

To analyze the effects of noise on the line detection, another synthetic data set was generated. The distance is fixed at 5 m, but we add different levels of additive white Gaussian noise. The standard deviation of the noise is varied from 0 to 25. We use 8-bit images, i.e. the pixel values are between 0 and 255.

The evaluation (Fig. 6(b)) shows that the methods are quite robust against noise. The detection accuracy hardly deteriorates even with a high level of noise. This is partly due to the fact that one of the first steps of the algorithms is the Gaussian smoothing of the image.

Number and Quality of the Detected Lines. Figure 7 shows the difference between the line detection on a software-corrected fisheye image and the direct detection on the original fisheye image with our method. On the cabinet and on the rear wall of the room significantly more lines are detected. In total 81 lines are found on the software-corrected image. With our approach 165 lines can be found.

(a) Software-corrected image   (b) Our approach

Fig. 7. Qualitative results of the line detection on a real fisheye image

3.2 Qualitative Evaluation of the Optimized Line Detection

For the evaluation of the optimized line detection, we proposed in Sect. 2.3, we use the public data set from [9]. It contains 9 sets of perspective images of building facades. We use one image from each sequence. Figure 8(a) shows the detected lines on one image from the data set.

For comparison, we use the EDLines algorithm again. With both methods, lines are detected in similar areas. A detailed view of a part of the image shows the differences. At intersections lines are often divided in two line segments by the EDLines algorithm (mark A in Fig. 8(b)). With our approach, these lines are detected as one continuous line segment (Fig. 8(c)). The reason for the splitting of the lines is that the edge detector follows the locally strongest gradient magnitude and not the direction of the line. Our approach prevents this by predicting the search direction. Another difference is recognizable in areas of low contrast (mark B). In these areas lines often break because of gaps in the gradient. With our approach, gaps can be bridged. So, the lines are more reliably and robustly detected over the entire length.

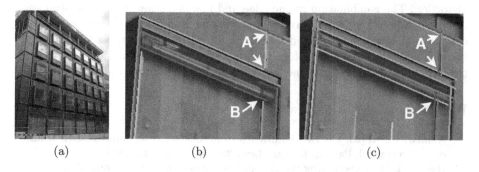

(a)   (b)   (c)

Fig. 8. Qualitative results of the line detection on one image from the dataset from [9]. (a) Entire Image. (b) Detail view (marked in (a)) of the detected lines with the EDLines algorithm. (c) Detail view of the detected lines with our approach

Table 1. Evaluation of the number and the average length of the detected lines on the data set of [9] and the ratio of the average lengths between our approach and EDLines

	EDLines		Our approach		Ratio of avg. lengths
Building	Number	Avg. length [pixel]	Number	Avg. length [pixel]	
1	2582	93.65	1761	168.41	1.80
2	2011	79.66	1133	170.59	2.14
3	2365	86.24	1209	186.68	2.16
4	2214	83.39	1380	158.39	1.90
5	3335	63.08	1238	180.62	2.86
6	7037	47.29	1603	174.08	3.68
7	1772	81.48	991	170.27	2.09
8	1044	93.00	537	208.56	2.24
9	2461	95.10	1247	201.42	2.12
Mean	2758	80.32	1233	179.89	2.24

For a statistical analysis, we have determined the number and the average length of the detected lines for all buildings of the data set. The results are shown in Table 1. With our approach, the number of detected lines is lower, but the average lengths are almost twice as long. As seen already in the images, the lines are detected reliably and fragmented significantly less into several sub-segments.

4   Conclusion

In this paper we have presented a method to detect lines in fisheye and distorted perspective images. The detection accuracy can be significantly improved by detecting lines in the original images without warping the image with a reverse distortion. The combination of the edge and line detection to a single step and the prediction of the search direction, provides a more robust and more reliable detection of larger line segments. This is an advantage in the reconstruction because short line segments often lead to inaccurate triangulation results and the matching of many small line segments is time-consuming and error-prone.

References

1. Akinlar, C., Topal, C.: EDLines: a real-time line segment detector with a false detection control. Pattern Recogn. Lett. **32**(13), 1633–1642 (2011)
2. Ballard, D.H.: Generalizing the Hough transform to detect arbitrary shapes. Pattern Recogn. **13**(2), 111–122 (1981)
3. Bay, H., Ferrari, V., Van Gool, L.: Wide-baseline stereo matching with line segments. In: IEEE Computer Society Conference on Computer Vision and Pattern Recognition, CVPR 2005, vol. 1, pp. 329–336. IEEE (2005)

4. Bazin, J.C., Demonceaux, C., Vasseur, P.: Fast central catadioptric line extraction. In: Martí, J., Benedí, J.M., Mendonça, A.M., Serrat, J. (eds.) IbPRIA 2007. LNCS, vol. 4478, pp. 25–32. Springer, Heidelberg (2007). doi:10.1007/978-3-540-72849-8_4
5. Boutteau, R., Savatier, X., Bonardi, F., Ertaud, J.Y.: Road-line detection and 3d reconstruction using fisheye cameras. In: 2013 16th International IEEE Conference on Intelligent Transportation Systems-(ITSC), pp. 1083–1088. IEEE (2013)
6. Bukhari, F., Dailey, M.N.: Automatic radial distortion estimation from a single image. J. Math. Imaging Vis. **45**(1), 31–45 (2012)
7. Burns, J.B., Hanson, A.R., Riseman, E.M.: Extracting straight lines. IEEE Trans. Pattern Anal. Mach. Intell. PAMI **8**(4), 425–455 (1986)
8. Canny, J.: A computational approach to edge detection. IEEE Trans. Pattern Anal. Mach. Intell. PAMI **8**(6), 679–698 (1986)
9. Ceylan, D., Mitra, N.J., Zheng, Y., Pauly, M.: Coupled structure-from-motion and 3D symmetry detection for urban facades. ACM Trans. Graph. (TOG) **33**(1), 2 (2014)
10. David, P., DeMenthon, D.: Object recognition in high clutter images using line features. In: Tenth IEEE International Conference on Computer Vision, ICCV 2005, vol. 2, pp. 1581–1588 (2005)
11. Desolneux, A., Moisan, L., Morel, J.M.: From Gestalt Theory to Image Analysis, Interdisciplinary Applied Mathematics, vol. 34. Springer, New York (2008)
12. Fernandes, L.A.F., Oliveira, M.M.: Real-time line detection through an improved hough transform voting scheme. Pattern Recogn. **41**(1), 299–314 (2008)
13. Fischler, M.A., Bolles, R.C.: Random sample consensus: a paradigm for model fitting with applications to image analysis and automated cartography. Commun. ACM **24**(6), 381–395 (1981)
14. von Gioi, R.G., Jakubowicz, J., Morel, J.M., Randall, G.: LSD: a line segment detector. Image Process Line **2**, 35–55 (2012)
15. Kannala, J., Brandt, S.S.: A generic camera model and calibration method for conventional, wide-angle, and fish-eye lenses. IEEE Trans. Pattern Anal. Mach. Intell. **28**(8), 1335–1340 (2006)
16. Taylor, C.J., Kriegman, D.J.: Structure and motion from line segments in multiple images. IEEE Trans. Pattern Anal. Mach. Intell. **17**(11), 1021–1032 (1995)
17. Wang, L.L., Tsai, W.H.: Camera calibration by vanishing lines for 3-D computer vision. IEEE Trans. Pattern Anal. Mach. Intell. **13**(4), 370–376 (1991)
18. Zhang, L., Koch, R.: Structure and motion from line correspondences: representation, projection, initialization and sparse bundle adjustment. J. Vis. Commun. Image Represent. **25**(5), 904–915 (2014)
19. Zhang, L., Xu, C., Lee, K.-M., Koch, R.: Robust and efficient pose estimation from line correspondences. In: Lee, K.M., Matsushita, Y., Rehg, J.M., Hu, Z. (eds.) ACCV 2012, Part III. LNCS, vol. 7726, pp. 217–230. Springer, Heidelberg (2013)
20. Zhang, M., Yao, J., Xia, M., Li, K., Zhang, Y., Liu, Y.: Line-based multi-label energy optimization for fisheye image rectification and calibration. In: 2015 IEEE Conference on Computer Vision and Pattern Recognition (CVPR), pp. 4137–4145, June 2015

Pixel-Level Encoding and Depth Layering for Instance-Level Semantic Labeling

Jonas Uhrig[1,2(✉)], Marius Cordts[1,3], Uwe Franke[1], and Thomas Brox[2]

[1] Daimler AG R&D, Stuttgart, Germany
jonas.uhrig@daimler.com
[2] University of Freiburg, Freiburg im Breisgau, Germany
[3] TU Darmstadt, Darmstadt, Germany

Abstract. Recent approaches for instance-aware semantic labeling have augmented convolutional neural networks (CNNs) with complex multi-task architectures or computationally expensive graphical models. We present a method that leverages a fully convolutional network (FCN) to predict semantic labels, depth and an instance-based encoding using each pixel's direction towards its corresponding instance center. Subsequently, we apply low-level computer vision techniques to generate state-of-the-art instance segmentation on the street scene datasets KITTI and Cityscapes. Our approach outperforms existing works by a large margin and can additionally predict absolute distances of individual instances from a monocular image as well as a pixel-level semantic labeling.

1 Introduction

The task of visual semantic scene understanding is mainly tackled from two opposing facets: pixel-level semantic labeling [4,21,22] and bounding-box object detection [11,12,23,24]. The first assigns each pixel in an image with a semantic label segmenting the semantically connected regions in the scene. Such approaches work well with non-compact (*background*) classes such as buildings or ground, yet they do not distinguish individual object instances. Object detection aims to find all individual instances in the scene and describes them via bounding boxes. Therefore, the latter provides a rather coarse localization and is restricted to compact (*object*) classes such as cars or humans.

Recently, instance-level semantic labeling gained increasing interest [8,19,34, 35]. This task is at the intersection of both challenges. The aim is to combine

Fig. 1. Example scene representation as obtained by our method: instance segmentation, monocular depth estimation, and pixel-level semantic labeling.

© Springer International Publishing AG 2016
B. Rosenhahn and B. Andres (Eds.): GCPR 2016, LNCS 9796, pp. 14–25, 2016.
DOI: 10.1007/978-3-319-45886-1_2

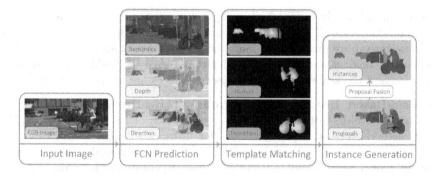

Fig. 2. From a single image, we predict 3 FCN outputs: semantics, depth, and instance center direction. Those are used to compute template matching score maps for semantic categories. Using these, we locate and generate instance proposals and fuse them to obtain our instance segmentation.

the detection task with instance segmentation. Such a representation allows for a precise localization, which in turn enables better scene understanding. Especially in the domain of robotics and autonomous vehicles, instance-level semantic segmentation enables an explicit occlusion reasoning, precise object tracking and motion estimation, as well as behavior modeling and prediction.

Most state-of-the-art methods build upon a fully convolutional network (FCN) [21]. Recent approaches typically add post-processing, for example, based on conditional random fields (CRFs) [34,35]. Other methods score region proposals for instance segmentation [7,14] or object detection [11,12,23,24], or use a multi-stage neural network for these tasks [8,19].

In this work, we focus on street scene understanding and use a single monocular image to simultaneously obtain a holistic scene representation, consisting of a pixel-level semantic labeling, an instance-level segmentation of traffic participants, and a 3D depth estimation for each instance. We leverage an FCN that yields powerful pixel-level cues consisting of three output channels: a semantic class, the direction to the object center (where applicable) and the object distance (where applicable). Scene understanding is mainly due to the network and post-processing with standard computer vision methods is sufficient to obtain a detailed representation of an instance-aware semantic segmentation, *c.f.* Figs. 1 and 2. Our method significantly outperforms state-of-the-art methods on the street scene datasets KITTI [10] and Cityscapes [6].

2   Related Work

For the task of instance-level semantic labeling, there exist two major lines of research. The first leverages an over-complete set of object proposals that are either rejected, classified as an instance of a certain semantic class, and refined to obtain an instance segmentation. Common to all such methods is that the performance is depending on the quality of these proposals, since they cannot recover from missing instances in the proposal stage. Generally, such approaches tend to be slow since all proposals must be classified individually. These properties cause inaccurate proposals to limit the performance of such methods [6,16]. Our method belongs to the category of proposal-free methods, where the segmentation and the semantic class of object instances are inferred jointly.

Proposal-Based Instance Segmentation. Driven by the success of deep learning based object detectors such as R-CNN [12] or its variants [11,24,25], recent methods rely on these detections for instance segmentation. Either the underlying region proposals, such as MCG [2], are directly used as instance segments [6,7,14], or the bounding boxes are refined to obtain instance masks [5,13]. Instead of bounding boxes, [18] uses a layered pictorial structure (LPS) model, where shape exemplars for object parts are mapped to the image in a probabilistic way. This yields an initial proposal for the object's pose and shape, which is refined using appearance cues. Using a bank of object detectors as proposals, [32] infers the instance masks via occlusion reasoning based on discrete depth layers. In [30], pixel-level semantic labels are used to score object candidates and vice versa in an alternating fashion, while also reasoning about occlusions and scene geometry. Based on proposals that form a segmentation tree, an energy function is constructed in [29] and its solution yields the instance segmentation.

Recently, [8] extended the R-CNN for instance segmentation with a multi-task network cascade. A fully convolutional network combined with three classification stages produces bounding-box proposals, refines these to segments, and ranks them to obtain the final instance-level labeling. They achieve excellent performance on PASCAL VOC [9] and MS COCO [20].

Proposal-Free Instance Segmentation. Pixel-level semantic labeling based on neural networks has been very successful [4,17,21,33,36]. This triggered interest in casting also instance segmentation directly as a pixel labeling task. In [27], the network predicts for each pixel, whether it lies on an object boundary or not, however, requiring a rather delicate training. Using a long short-term memory (LSTM) network [15], instance segmentations can be sequentially sampled [26].

In [34,35], instances are encoded via numbers that are further constrained to encode relative depth ordering in order to prevent arbitrary assignments. An FCN predicts these IDs at each pixel and a subsequent Markov Random Field (MRF) improves these predictions and enforces consistency. However, such a method is limited to scenes, where a clear depth ordering is present, *e.g.* a single row of parking cars, and the maximum number of instances is rather low.

The proposal-free network (PFN) [19] is a CNN that yields a pixel-level semantic labeling, the number of instances in the scene, and for each pixel the parameters of a corresponding instance bounding box. Based on these predictions, instances are obtained by clustering. The network has a fairly complex architecture with many interleaved building blocks, making training quite tricky. Further, the overall performance highly depends on the correct prediction of the number of instances in the scene. In street scenes, there can be hundreds of instances per image [6]. Thus, the number of training samples per number of instances is low, mistakes in their estimation can be critical, and the available cues for clustering might not correlate with the estimated number of instances.

In this work, we focus on urban street scenes. Besides each pixel's semantic class, our network estimates an absolute depth, which is particularly useful for instance separation in street scenes. We encode instances on a pixel-level by the direction towards their center point. This representation is independent of the number of instances per image and provides strong signals at the instance boundaries.

3   Method

3.1   FCN Feature Representation

Our network extends the FCN-8s model [21] with three output channels that together facilitate instance segmentation. All channels are jointly trained as pixel-wise discrete labeling tasks using standard cross-entropy losses. Our proposed representation consists of (1) a semantic channel that drives the instance classification, (2) a depth channel to incorporate scale and support instance separation, and (3) a 2D geometric channel to facilitate instance detection and segmentation.

We chose the upscaling part of our FCN such that we can easily change the number of classes for each of the three proposed channels without re-initializing all upsampling layers. To this end, after the largest downsampling factor is reached, we use Deconvolution layers together with skip layers [21] to produce a representation of $\frac{1}{8}$ of the input resolution with a depth of 100 throughout all intermediate layers. The number of channels of this abstract representation is then reduced through 1×1 convolutions to the proposed semantic, depth, and instance center channels. To reach full input resolution, bilinear upsampling is applied, followed by a separate cross-entropy loss for each of our three output channels.

Semantics. To cope with different semantic classes, we predict a semantic label for each input pixel, *c.f.* Fig. 3a. These predictions are particularly important as they are the only source of semantic information in our approach. Further, the predicted semantic labels allow us to separate objects from background as well as objects of different classes from each other.

| (a) Semantic label. | (b) Depth class. | (c) Instance direction. |

Fig. 3. Ground truth examples of our three proposed FCN channels. Color overlay (a) as suggested by [6], (b) represents depth per object from red (close) to blue (distant), (c) represents directions towards corresponding instance centers. (Color figure online)

Depth. Urban street scenes typically contain objects at various distances [6]. To guide the post-processing in terms of objects at different scales, we predict a depth label for each object pixel. We assign all pixels within an object instance to a constant depth value, e.g. the median over noisy measurements or the center of a 3D bounding box, *c.f.* Fig. 3b. These depth estimates also support instance separation, which becomes apparent when considering a row of parking cars, where the depth delta between neighboring cars is a full car length instead of a few centimeters in continuous space. The depth values are discretized into a set of classes so that close objects have a finer depth resolution than distant objects.

Direction. Object instances are defined by their boundary and class. Therefore, it seems natural to train an FCN model to directly predict boundary pixels. However, those boundaries represent a very delicate signal [1] as they have a width of only one pixel, and a single erroneously labeled pixel in the training data has a much higher impact compared to a region-based representation.

We introduce a class-based representation which implicitly combines information about an instance's boundary with the location of its visible center. For each object pixel we compute the direction towards its corresponding center and discretize this angle to a set of classes, *c.f.* Fig. 3c. This information is easier to grasp within a local region and is tailored for an FCN's capability to predict pixel-wise labels. Especially for pixels on the boundary between neighboring objects, our representation clearly separates the instances as predictions have nearly opposite directions. Since we predict the center of the visible area of an object and not its physical center, we can handle most types of occlusions very well. Furthermore, instance centers have a distinct pattern, *c.f.* Fig. 3c, which we exploit by applying template matching, as described in Sect. 3.2. Even though our proposed representation does not directly yield instance IDs, it is well defined even for an arbitrary number of instances per image.

To obtain an accurate direction estimation for each pixel, we assign the average direction by weighting all direction vectors with their respective FCN score (after softmax normalization). This allows us to recover a continuous direction estimation from the few discretized classes.

3.2   Template Matching

To extract instance centers, we propose template matching on the direction predictions, where templates are rectangular and contain the distinct pattern visible in Fig. 3c. We adjust the template's aspect ratio depending on its semantic class, so we can better distinguish between pedestrians and vehicles. In order to detect also distant objects with consistent matching scores, we scale the size of the templates depending on the predicted depth class.

To reduce induced errors from confusions between objects of similar semantic classes, we combine multiple semantic classes into the categories *human*, *car*, *large vehicle*, and *two wheeler*.

Normalized cross-correlation (NCC) is used to produce a score map for each category by correlating all pixels with their respective template. These maps indicate the likelihood of pixels being an instance center, *c.f.* Fig. 2. In the following, we predict instances for each category separately. After all instances are found, we assign them the majority semantic class label.

3.3   Instance Generation

Instance Centers. To determine instance locations, we iteratively find maxima in the generated template matching score maps via non-maximum suppression within an area that equals the template size. This helps avoid multiple detections of the same instance while incorporating typical object sizes. Those maxima represent our *temporary instance centers*, which are refined and merged in the following steps.

Instance Proposals. Each pixel with a predicted direction from the FCN is assigned to the closest temporary instance center where the relative location and predicted direction agree. Joining all assigned pixels per instance hypothesis yields a set of *instance proposals*.

Proposal Fusion. Elongated objects and erroneous depth predictions cause an over-segmentation of the instances. Thus, we refine the generated instances by accumulating estimated directions within each proposal. When interpreting direction predictions as vectors, they typically compensate each other within instance proposals that represent a complete instance, *i.e.* there are as many predictions pointing both left and right. However, incomplete instance proposals are biased to a certain direction. If there is a neighboring instance candidate with matching semantic class and depth in the direction of this bias, the two proposals are fused.

To the remaining instances we assign the average depth and the most frequent semantic class label within the region. Further, we merge our instance prediction with the pixel-level semantic labeling channel of the FCN by assigning the argmax semantic label to all non-instance pixels. Overall, we obtain a consistent scene representation, consisting of object instances paired with depth estimates and pixel-level labels for background classes.

4   Experiments

4.1   Datasets and Metrics

We evaluated our approach on the KITTI object detection dataset [10] extended with instance-level segmentations [3,35] as well as Cityscapes [6]. Both datasets provide pixel-level annotations for semantic classes and instances, as well as depth information, which is essential for our approach. For the ground truth instance depths we used the centers of their 3D bounding box annotation in KITTI and the median disparity for each instance in Cityscapes based on the provided disparity maps. We used the official splits for training, validation and test sets.

We evaluated the segmentation based on the metrics proposed in [35] and [6]. To evaluate the depth prediction, we computed the mean absolute error (MAE), the root mean squared error (RMSE), the absolute relative difference (ARD), and the relative inlier ratios (δ_1, δ_2, δ_3) for thresholds $\delta_i = 1.25^i$ [31]. These metrics are computed on an instance level using the depths in meters. We only considered instances that overlap by more than 50 % with the ground truth.

4.2 Network Details

For Cityscapes, we used the 19 semantic classes and combined the 8 object classes into 4 categories (*car, human, two-wheeler,* and *large vehicle*). For KITTI, only *car* instance segmentations are available. For both datasets, we used 19 depth classes and an explicit class for background. We chose ranges for each depth class and template sizes differently for each dataset to account for different characteristics of present objects and used camera settings [6]. This is necessary as distances and semantic classes of objects differ remarkably. Details are provided in the supplementary material. The instance directions were split into 8 equal parts, each covering an angle of 45° for both datasets.

We use the 8-stride version of an FCN, which is initialized using the ImageNet dataset [28]. After initializing the upsampling layers randomly, we fine-tune the network on KITTI and Cityscapes to obtain all three output channels.

4.3 Ablation Studies

We evaluated the influence of each proposed component by leaving out one or more components from the complete processing pipeline (*Ours*). The performance was evaluated on the respective validation sets and is listed in Tables 1 and 2 (top) for both datasets.

For *Ours-D*, we removed the depth channel and chose the template size scale-agnostic. It turned out that a rather small template size, which leads to a large number of instance proposals, produces the best results. This is possible when post-processing heavily relies on correct direction predictions, which induces successful instance fusion. However, the performance is significantly worse in most

Table 1. Evaluation of our variants on KITTI *val* (top) and comparison with baselines (*Best* [34]/[35]) on KITTI *test* (bottom) using metrics from [35]. For AvgFP and AvgFN lower is better, all other numbers are in percent and larger is better. *Mix* [35] shows the best results per metric from all baseline variants.

Method	Set	IoU	MWCov	MUCov	AvgPr	AvgRe	AvgFP	AvgFN	InsPr	InsRe	InsF1
Ours-D-F	val	79.4	41.5	43.4	**92.8**	54.4	0.042	1.33	16.6	29.8	21.4
Ours-F	val	82.2	35.9	35.7	83.6	**86.7**	0.158	**0.100**	31.4	69.5	43.3
Ours-D	val	79.6	**82.4**	**79.9**	89.9	54.6	**0.017**	1.33	**96.0**	42.8	59.2
Ours	val	82.2	80.7	76.3	83.7	**86.7**	0.100	**0.100**	91.8	**82.3**	**86.8**
Best [34]	test	77.4	67.0	49.8	82.0	61.3	0.479	0.840	48.9	43.8	46.2
Best [35]	test	77.0	69.7	51.8	83.9	57.5	0.375	1.139	65.3	50.0	56.6
Mix [35]	test	77.6	69.7	53.9	83.9	63.4	0.354	0.618	65.3	52.2	56.6
Ours	test	**84.1**	**79.7**	**75.8**	**85.6**	82.0	0.201	0.159	**86.3**	**74.1**	**79.7**

Table 2. Evaluation on Cityscapes *val* (top) and *test* (center) using metrics in [6]. Further, we compare the performance for the most frequent label *car*, where we include KITTI *test* (bottom). All numbers are in percent and larger is better.

Variant	Dataset	Labels	AP	$AP^{50\%}$	AP^{100m}	AP^{50m}
Ours-D-F	CS val	all	2.4	5.7	3.6	4.9
Ours-F	CS val	all	7.0	17.5	11.1	12.8
Ours-D	CS val	all	6.8	15.8	10.9	14.2
Ours	CS val	all	**9.9**	**22.5**	**15.3**	**17.5**
MCG+R-CNN [6]	CS test	all	4.6	12.9	7.7	10.3
Ours	CS test	all	**8.9**	**21.1**	**15.3**	**16.7**
MCG+R-CNN [6]	CS test	car	10.5	26.0	17.5	21.2
Ours	CS test	car	22.5	37.8	36.4	40.7
Ours	KITTI test	car	41.6	69.1	49.3	49.3

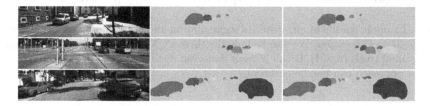

Fig. 4. Example results of our instance segmentation (right) and corresponding ground truth (middle) on KITTI. We even detect objects at very large distances.

metrics on both datasets compared to our full system, which shows that the depth information is an essential component of our approach. When the fusion component was also removed (*Ours-D-F*), a larger template size was needed to prevent an over-segmentation. However, performance dropped by an even larger margin than for *Ours-D*. In our last variant we kept the depth information but directly used the instance proposals as final instance predictions (*Ours-F*). The performance was even slightly worse than *Ours-D*, which shows that all our components are important to obtain accurate object instances. These observations are consistent on both datasets.

4.4 Instance Evaluation

KITTI. We clearly outperform all existing works on KITTI (*Best* [34]/[35]), *c.f.* Table 1 (bottom). Compared to the better performing work *Best* [35], we achieve a margin of 37 % relative improvement averaged over all metrics. Even when comparing our single variant with the best numbers over all existing variants for each metric individually (*Mix* [35]), we achieve a significantly better performance. We also evaluated our approach using the metrics introduced in [6] to enable comparisons in future publications, *c.f.* Table 2 (bottom). Qualitative results are shown in Fig. 4.

(a) Input Image   (b) Instance Ground Truth   (c) Instance Prediction

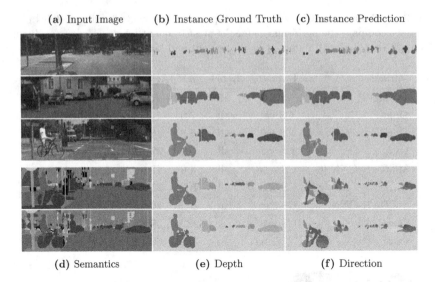

(d) Semantics   (e) Depth   (f) Direction

Fig. 5. Example results of our instance segmentation and corresponding ground truth (rows 1–3) on Cityscapes. We also include the three FCN output channels (row 5) and their ground truth (row 4). It can be seen that even distant objects are segmented well and the approach can handle occlusions.

Cityscapes. On the Cityscapes dataset, our approach outperforms the baseline *MCG+R-CNN* [6] in all proposed metrics as evaluated by the dataset's submission server, *c.f.* Table 2 (center). We nearly double the performance in terms of the main score AP. Compared to the performance on KITTI, *c.f.* Table 2 (bottom), the numbers are significantly lower, indicating the higher complexity of scenes in Cityscapes. Qualitative results are shown in Fig. 5.

4.5   Depth Evaluation

As shown in Table 3, the average relative and mean absolute error of our predicted instances are as low as 7.7 % and 1.7m, respectively, on the KITTI dataset. On the Cityscapes dataset, which contains much more complex scenes, with many and distant object instances, we achieve 11.3 % and 7.7m, respectively. These results are particularly impressive, since we used only single monocular

Table 3. Instance-based depth evaluation on KITTI test and Cityscapes validation. MAE and RMSE are in meters, the others in percent. MAE, RMSE, and ARD denote error metrics, where smaller is better, δ_i represent accuracy, where higher is better.

Dataset	MAE	RMSE	ARD	δ_1	δ_2	δ_3
KITTI (test)	1.7	2.8	7.7	95.1	99.3	99.8
Cityscapes (val)	7.7	24.8	11.3	86.2	95.1	97.7

Table 4. Semantic pixel-level evaluation on Cityscapes test compared to baselines and using the corresponding metrics [6]. All values are in percent and larger is better.

Method	IoU_{class}	$iIoU_{class}$	$IoU_{category}$	$iIoU_{category}$
FCN 8s [6]	65.3	41.7	85.7	70.1
Dilation10 [33]	**67.1**	**42.0**	**86.5**	71.1
Ours	64.3	41.6	85.9	**73.9**

images as input for our network. We hope that future publications compare their depth estimation performance using the proposed metrics.

4.6 Evaluation of Semantic Class Labels

Our method also yields a pixel-level semantic labeling including background classes that we evaluate on Cityscapes, *c.f.* Table 4. We compare to two baselines, *FCN 8s* [21] that uses the same FCN architecture as our approach and *Dilation10* [33], which is the currently best performing approach on Cityscapes [6]. It can be seen that our approach is on par with the state-of-the-art although this work focuses on the harder instance segmentation task.

5   Conclusion

In this work, we present a fully convolutional network that predicts pixel-wise depth, semantics, and instance-level direction cues to reach an excellent level of holistic scene understanding. Instead of complex architectures or graphical models for post-processing, our approach performs well using only standard computer vision techniques applied to the network's three output channels. Our approach does not depend on region proposals and scales well for arbitrary numbers of object instances in an image.

We outperform existing works on the challenging urban street scene datasets Cityscapes [6] and KITTI [34, 35] by a large margin. On KITTI, our approach achieves 37 % relative improvement averaged over all metrics and we almost double the performance on Cityscapes. As our approach can reliably predict absolute depth values per instance, we provide an instance-based depth evaluation. Our depth predictions achieve a relative error of only a few meters, even though the datasets contain instances in more than one hundred meters distance. The main focus of this work is instance segmentation, but we also achieve state-of-the-art performance for pixel-level semantic labeling on Cityscapes, with a new best performance on an instance-based score over categories.

References

1. Arbelaez, P., Maire, M., Fowlkes, C., Malik, J.: Contour detection and hierarchical image segmentation. Trans. PAMI **33**(5), 898–916 (2011)
2. Arbelez, P., Pont-Tuset, J., Barron, J., Marques, F., Malik, J.: Multiscale combinatorial grouping. In: CVPR (2014)
3. Chen, L.C., Fidler, S., Urtasun, R.: Beat the MTurkers: automatic image labeling from weak 3d supervision. In: CVPR (2014)
4. Chen, L., Papandreou, G., Kokkinos, I., Murphy, K., Yuille, A.L.: Semantic image segmentation with deep convolutional nets and fully connected CRFs. In: ICLR (2015)
5. Chen, Y.T., Liu, X., Yang, M.H.: Multi-instance object segmentation with occlusion handling. In: CVPR (2015)
6. Cordts, M., Omran, M., Ramos, S., Rehfeld, T., Enzweiler, M., Benenson, R., Franke, U., Roth, S., Schiele, B.: The Cityscapes Dataset for semantic urban scene understanding. In: CVPR (2016)
7. Dai, J., He, K., Sun, J.: Convolutional feature masking for joint object and stuff segmentation. In: CVPR (2015)
8. Dai, J., He, K., Sun, J.: Instance-aware semantic segmentation via multi-task network cascades. In: CVPR (2016)
9. Everingham, M., Gool, L., Williams, C.K.I., Winn, J., Zisserman, A.: The pascal visual object classes (VOC) challenge. IJCV **88**(2), 303–338 (2009)
10. Geiger, A., Lenz, P., Urtasun, R.: Are we ready for autonomous driving? The KITTI vision benchmark suite. In: CVPR (2012)
11. Girshick, R.: Fast R-CNN. In: ICCV (2015)
12. Girshick, R., Donahue, J., Darrell, T., Malik, J.: Rich feature hierarchies for accurate object detection and semantic segmentation. In: CVPR (2014)
13. Hariharan, B., Arbelez, P., Girshick, R., Malik, J.: Hypercolumns for object segmentation and fine-grained localization. In: CVPR (2015)
14. Hariharan, B., Arbeláez, P., Girshick, R., Malik, J.: Simultaneous detection and segmentation. In: Fleet, D., Pajdla, T., Schiele, B., Tuytelaars, T. (eds.) ECCV 2014, Part VII. LNCS, vol. 8695, pp. 297–312. Springer, Heidelberg (2014)
15. Hochreiter, S., Schmidhuber, J.: Long short-term memory. Neural Comput. **9**(8), 1735–1780 (1997)
16. Hosang, J., Benenson, R., Dollr, P., Schiele, B.: What makes for effective detection proposals? Trans. PAMI **38**(4), 814–830 (2016)
17. Kirillov, A., Schlesinger, D., Forkel, W., Zelenin, A., Zheng, S., Torr, P.H.S., Rother, C.: Efficient likelihood learning of a generic CNN-CRF model for semantic segmentation. In: [cs.CV] (2015). arXiv:1511.05067v2
18. Kumar, M.P., Ton, P.H.S., Zisserman, A.: Obj Cut. In: CVPR (2005)
19. Liang, X., Wei, Y., Shen, X., Yang, J., Lin, L., Yan, S.: Proposal-free network for instance-level object segmentation. In: [cs.CV] (2015). arXiv:1509.02636v2
20. Lin, T.-Y., Maire, M., Belongie, S., Hays, J., Perona, P., Ramanan, D., Dollár, P., Zitnick, C.L.: Microsoft COCO: common objects in context. In: Fleet, D., Pajdla, T., Schiele, B., Tuytelaars, T. (eds.) ECCV 2014, Part V. LNCS, vol. 8693, pp. 740–755. Springer, Heidelberg (2014)
21. Long, J., Shelhamer, E., Darrell, T.: Fully convolutional networks for semantic segmentation. In: CVPR (2015)
22. Papandreou, G., Chen, L., Murphy, K., Yuille, A.L.: Weakly- and semi-supervised learning of a DCNN for semantic image segmentation. In: ICCV (2015)

23. Redmon, J., Divvala, S.K., Girshick, R.B., Farhadi, A.: You only look once: Unified, real-time object detection. In: CVPR (2016)
24. Ren, S., He, K., Girshick, R., Sun, J.: Faster R-CNN: Towards real-time object detection with region proposal networks. In: NIPS (2015)
25. Ren, S., He, K., Girshick, R.B., Zhang, X., Sun, J.: Object detection networks on convolutional feature maps. In: [cs.CV] (2015). arXiv:1504.06066v1
26. Romera-Paredes, B., Torr, P.H.S.: Recurrent instance segmentation. In: [cs.CV] (2015). arXiv:1511.08250v2
27. Ronneberger, O., Fischer, P., Brox, T.: U-Net: convolutional networks for biomedical image segmentation. In: Navab, N., Hornegger, J., Wells, W.M., Frangi, A.F. (eds.) MICCAI 2015. LNCS, vol. 9351, pp. 234–241. Springer, Heidelberg (2015)
28. Russakovsky, O., Deng, J., Su, H., Krause, J., Satheesh, S., Ma, S., Huang, Z., Karpathy, A., Khosla, A., Bernstein, M., Berg, A.C., Fei-Fei, L.: ImageNet large scale visual recognition challenge. IJCV **115**(3), 211–252 (2015)
29. Silberman, N., Sontag, D., Fergus, R.: Instance segmentation of indoor scenes using a coverage loss. In: Fleet, D., Pajdla, T., Schiele, B., Tuytelaars, T. (eds.) ECCV 2014, Part I. LNCS, vol. 8689, pp. 616–631. Springer, Heidelberg (2014)
30. Tighe, J., Niethammer, M., Lazebnik, S.: Scene parsing with object instances and occlusion ordering. In: CVPR (2014)
31. Wang, P., Shen, X., Lin, Z., Cohen, S., Price, B., Yuille, A.: Towards unified depth and semantic prediction from a single image. In: CVPR (2015)
32. Yang, Y., Hallman, S., Ramanan, D., Fowlkes, C.: Layered object models for image segmentation. Trans. PAMI **34**(9), 1731–1743 (2012)
33. Yu, F., Koltun, V.: Multi-scale context aggregation by dilated convolutions. In: ICLR (2016)
34. Zhang, Z., Schwing, A.G., Fidler, S., Urtasun, R.: Monocular object instance segmentation and depth ordering with cnns. In: ICCV (2015)
35. Zhang, Z., Fidler, S., Urtasun, R.: Instance-level segmentation with deep densely connected MRFs. In: CVPR (2016)
36. Zheng, S., Jayasumana, S., Romera-Paredes, B., Vineet, V., Su, Z., Du, D., Huang, C., Torr, P.H.S.: Conditional random fields as recurrent neural networks. In: ICCV (2015)

Artistic Style Transfer for Videos

Manuel Ruder[✉], Alexey Dosovitskiy, and Thomas Brox

Department of Computer Science, University of Freiburg,
Freiburg im Breisgau, Germany
{rudera,dosovits,brox}@cs.uni-freiburg.de

Abstract. In the past, manually re-drawing an image in a certain artistic style required a professional artist and a long time. Doing this for a video sequence single-handed was beyond imagination. Nowadays computers provide new possibilities. We present an approach that transfers the style from one image (for example, a painting) to a whole video sequence. We make use of recent advances in style transfer in still images and propose new initializations and loss functions applicable to videos. This allows us to generate consistent and stable stylized video sequences, even in cases with large motion and strong occlusion. We show that the proposed method clearly outperforms simpler baselines both qualitatively and quantitatively.

1 Introduction

There have recently been a lot of interesting contributions to the issue of style transfer using deep neural networks. Gatys et al. [3] proposed a novel approach using neural networks to capture the style of artistic images and transfer it to real world photographs. Their approach uses high-level feature representations of the images from hidden layers of the VGG convolutional network [10] to separate and reassemble content and style. This is done by formulating an optimization problem that, starting with white noise, searches for a new image showing similar neural activations as the *content image* and similar feature correlations (expressed by a Gram matrix) as the *style image.*

The present paper builds upon the approach from Gatys et al. [3] and extends style transfer to video sequences. Given an artistic image, we transfer its particular style of painting to the entire video. Processing each frame of the video independently leads to flickering and false discontinuities, since the solution of the style transfer task is not stable. To regularize the transfer and to preserve smooth transition between individual frames of the video, we introduce a temporal constraint that penalizes deviations between two frames. The temporal constraint takes the optical flow from the original video into account: instead of penalizing the deviations from the previous frame, we penalize deviation along the point trajectories.

This work was supported by the ERC Starting Grant VideoLearn.

Electronic supplementary material The online version of this chapter (doi:10.1007/978-3-319-45886-1_3) contains supplementary material, which is available to authorized users.

B. Rosenhahn and B. Andres (Eds.): GCPR 2016, LNCS 9796, pp. 26–36, 2016.
DOI: 10.1007/978-3-319-45886-1_3

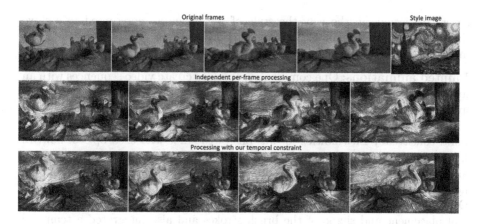

Fig. 1. Scene from *Ice Age* (2002) processed in the style of *The Starry Night*. Comparing independent per-frame processing to our time consistent approach, the latter is clearly preferable. Best observed in the supplemental video, see Sect. 8.1.

Disoccluded regions as well as motion boundaries are excluded from the penalizer. This allows the process to rebuild disoccluded regions and distorted motion boundaries while preserving the appearance of the rest of the image, see Fig. 1.

In addition, we present two extensions of our approach. The first one aims on improving the consistency over larger periods of time. When a region that is occluded in some frame and disoccluded later gets rebuilt during the process, most likely this region will have a different appearance than before the occlusion. To solve this, we make use of long term motion estimates. This allows us to enforce consistency of the synthesized frames before and after the occlusion.

Secondly, the style transfer tends to create artifacts at the image boundaries. For static images, these artifacts are hardly visible, yet for videos with strong camera motion they move towards the center of the image and get amplified. We developed a multi-pass algorithm, which processes the video in alternating directions using both forward and backward flow. This results in a more coherent video.

We quantitatively evaluated our approach in combination with different optical flow algorithms on the Sintel benchmark. Additionally we show qualitative results on several movie shots. We were able to successfully eliminate most of the temporal artifacts and can create smooth and coherent stylized videos.

2   Related Work

Style transfer using deep networks: Gatys et al. [3] showed remarkable results by using the VGG-19 deep neural network for style transfer. Their approach was taken up by various follow-up papers that, among other things, proposed different ways to represent the style within the neural network. Li et al. [5] suggested an approach to preserve local patterns of the style image. Instead of using a global representation of the style, computed as Gram matrix, they used patches of the neural activation from the style image. Nikulin et al. [7] tried the style transfer algorithm by Gatys et al. on other nets than VGG and proposed several variations in the way the style of the image is represented to archive different goals like illumination or season transfer. However, we are not aware of any work that applies this kind of style transfer to videos.

Painted animations: One common approach to create video sequences with an artistic style is to generate artificial brush strokes to repaint the scene. Different artistic styles are gained by modifying various parameters of these brush strokes, like thickness, or by using different brush placement methods. To achieve temporal consistency Litwinowicz [6] was one of the first who used optical flow. In his approach, brush strokes were generated for the first frame and then moved along the flow field. Later, this approach was refined. Hays et al. [4] proposed new stylistic parameters for the brush strokes to mimic different artistic styles. O'Donovan et al. [8] formulated an energy optimization problem for an optimal placement and shape of the brush strokes and also integrated a temporal constraint into the optimization problem by penalizing changes in shape and width of the brush strokes compared to the previous frame. These approaches are similar in spirit to what we are doing, but they are only capable of applying a restricted class of artistic styles.

3   Style Transfer in Still Images

In this section, we briefly review the style transfer approach introduced by Gatys et al. [3]. The aim is to generate a stylized image x showing the content of an image p in the style of an image a. Gatys et al. formulated an energy minimization problem consisting of a *content loss* and a *style loss*. The key idea is that features extracted by a convolutional network carry information about the content of the image, while the correlations of these features encode the style.

We denote by $\Phi^l(\cdot)$ the function implemented by the part of the convolutional network from input up to the layer l. The feature maps extracted by the network from the original image p, the style image a and the stylized image x we denote by $P^l = \Phi^l(p)$, $S^l = \Phi^l(a)$ and $F^l = \Phi^l(x)$ respectively. The dimensionality of these feature maps we denote by $N_l \times M_l$, where N_l is the number of filters (channels) in the layer, and M_l is the spatial dimensionality of the feature map, that is, the product of its width and height.

The content loss, denoted as $\mathcal{L}_{content}$, is simply the mean squared error between $P^l \in \mathbb{R}^{N_l \times M_l}$ and $F^l \in \mathbb{R}^{N_l \times M_l}$. This loss need not be restricted to only one layer. Let $L_{content}$ be the set of layers to be used for content representation, then we have:

$$\mathcal{L}_{content}(p, x) = \sum_{l \in L_{content}} \frac{1}{N_l M_l} \sum_{i,j} \left(F_{ij}^l - P_{ij}^l\right)^2. \tag{1}$$

The style loss is also a mean squared error, but between the correlations of the filter responses expressed by their Gram matrices $A^l \in \mathbb{R}^{N_l \times N_l}$ for the style image a and $G^l \in \mathbb{R}^{N_l \times N_l}$ for the stylized image x. These are computed as

$A_{ij}^l = \sum_{k=1}^{M_l} S_{ik}^l S_{jk}^l$ and $G_{ij}^l = \sum_{k=1}^{M_l} F_{ik}^l F_{jk}^l$. As above, let L_{style} be the set of layers we use to represent the style, then the style loss is given by:

$$\mathcal{L}_{style}(\boldsymbol{a}, \boldsymbol{x}) = \sum_{l \in L_{style}} \frac{1}{N_l^2 M_l^2} \sum_{i,j} (G_{ij}^l - A_{ij}^l)^2 \tag{2}$$

Overall, the loss function is given by

$$\mathcal{L}_{singleimage}(\boldsymbol{p}, \boldsymbol{a}, \boldsymbol{x}) = \alpha \mathcal{L}_{content}(\boldsymbol{p}, \boldsymbol{x}) + \beta \mathcal{L}_{style}(\boldsymbol{a}, \boldsymbol{x}), \tag{3}$$

with weighting factors α and β governing the importance of the two components.

The stylized image is computed by minimizing this energy with respect to $\boldsymbol{x}$ using gradient-based optimization. Typically it is initialized with random Gaussian noise. However, the loss function is non-convex, therefore the optimization is prone to falling into local minima. This makes the initialization of the stylized image important, especially when applying the method to frames of a video.

4   Style Transfer in Videos

We use the following notation: $\boldsymbol{p}^{(i)}$ is the ith frame of the original video, $\boldsymbol{a}$ is the style image and $\boldsymbol{x}^{(i)}$ are the stylized frames to be generated. Furthermore, we denote by $\boldsymbol{x}'^{(i)}$ the initialization of the style optimization algorithm at frame i. By x_j we denote the jth component of a vector $\boldsymbol{x}$.

4.1   Short-term Consistency by Initialization

When the style transfer for consecutive frames is initialized by independent Gaussian noise, two frames of a video converge to very different local minima, resulting in a strong flickering. The most basic way to yield temporal consistency is to initialize the optimization for the frame $i + 1$ with the stylized frame i. Areas that have not changed between the two frames are then initialized with the desired appearance, while the rest of the image has to be rebuilt through the optimization process.

If there is motion in the scene, this simple approach does not perform well, since moving objects are initialized incorrectly. Thus, we take the optical flow into account and initialize the optimization for the frame $i + 1$ with the previous stylized frame warped: $\boldsymbol{x}'^{(i+1)} = \omega_i^{i+1}(\boldsymbol{x}^{(i)})$. Here ω_i^{i+1} denotes the function that warps a given image using the optical flow field that was estimated between image $\boldsymbol{p}^{(i)}$ and $\boldsymbol{p}^{(i+1)}$. Clearly, the first frame of the stylized video still has to be initialized randomly.

We experimented with two state-of-the-art optical flow estimation algorithms: DeepFlow [12] and EpicFlow [9]. Both are based on Deep Matching [12]: DeepFlow combines it with a variational approach, while EpicFlow relies on edge-preserving sparse-to-dense interpolation.

4.2   Temporal Consistency Loss

To enforce stronger consistency between adjacent frames we additionally introduce an explicit consistency penalty to the loss function. This requires detection of disoccluded regions and motion boundaries. To detect disocclusions,
we perform a forward-backward consistency check of the optical flow [11]. Let
$\mathbf{w} = (u, v)$ be the optical flow in forward direction and $\hat{\mathbf{w}} = (\hat{u}, \hat{v})$ the flow in
backward direction. Denote by $\widetilde{\mathbf{w}}$ the forward flow warped to the second image:

$$\widetilde{\mathbf{w}}(x, y) = \mathbf{w}((x, y) + \hat{\mathbf{w}}(x, y)). \tag{4}$$

In areas without disocclusion, this warped flow should be approximately the
opposite of the backward flow. Therefore we mark as disocclusions those areas
where the following inequality holds:

$$|\widetilde{\mathbf{w}} + \hat{\mathbf{w}}|^2 > 0.01(|\widetilde{\mathbf{w}}|^2 + |\hat{\mathbf{w}}|^2) + 0.5 \tag{5}$$

Motion boundaries are detected using the following inequality:

$$|\nabla\hat{u}|^2 + |\nabla\hat{v}|^2 > 0.01|\hat{\mathbf{w}}|^2 + 0.002 \tag{6}$$

Coefficients in inequalities (5) and (6) are taken from Sundaram et al. [11].

The temporal consistency loss function penalizes deviations from the warped
image in regions where the optical flow is consistent and estimated with high
confidence:

$$\mathcal{L}_{temporal}(\boldsymbol{x}, \boldsymbol{\omega}, \boldsymbol{c}) = \frac{1}{D} \sum_{k=1}^{D} c_k \cdot (x_k - \omega_k)^2. \tag{7}$$

Here $\boldsymbol{c} \in [0, 1]^D$ is per-pixel weighting of the loss and $D = W \times H \times C$ is
the dimensionality of the image. We define the weights $c^{(i-1,i)}$ between frames
$i-1$ and i as follows: 0 in disoccluded regions (as detected by forward-backward
consistency) and at the motion boundaries, and 1 everywhere else. Potentially
weights between 0 and 1 could be used to incorporate the certainty of the optical
flow prediction. The overall loss takes the form:

$$\mathcal{L}_{shortterm}\left(\boldsymbol{p}^{(i)}, \boldsymbol{a}, \boldsymbol{x}^{(i)}\right) = \alpha\mathcal{L}_{content}\left(\boldsymbol{p}^{(i)}, \boldsymbol{x}^{(i)}\right) + \beta\mathcal{L}_{style}\left(\boldsymbol{a}, \boldsymbol{x}^{(i)}\right)$$
$$+ \gamma\mathcal{L}_{temporal}\left(\boldsymbol{x}^{(i)}, \omega_{i-1}^{i}(\boldsymbol{x}^{(i-1)}), \boldsymbol{c}^{(i-1,i)}\right). \tag{8}$$

We optimize one frame after another, thus $\boldsymbol{x}^{(i-1)}$ refers to the already stylized
frame $i-1$.

Furthermore we experimented with the more robust absolute error instead
of squared error for the temporal consistency loss; results are shown in Sect. 8.

4.3   Long-term Consistency

The short-term model has the following limitation: when some areas are occluded
in some frame and disoccluded later, these areas will likely change their appearance in the stylized video. This can be counteracted by also making use of long-
term motion, i.e. not only penalizing deviations from the previous frame, but also

from temporally more distant frames. Let J denote the set of indices each frame should take into account, relative to the frame number. E.g. $J = \{1, 2, 4\}$ means frame i takes frames $i-1$, $i-2$ and $i-4$ into account. Then, the loss function with long-term consistency is given by:

$$\mathcal{L}_{longterm}\left(\boldsymbol{p}^{(i)}, \boldsymbol{a}, \boldsymbol{x}^{(i)}\right) = \alpha \mathcal{L}_{content}\left(\boldsymbol{p}^{(i)}, \boldsymbol{x}^{(i)}\right) + \beta \mathcal{L}_{style}\left(\boldsymbol{a}, \boldsymbol{x}^{(i)}\right)$$
$$+ \gamma \sum_{j \in J : i-j \geq 1} \mathcal{L}_{temporal}\left(\boldsymbol{x}^{(i)}, \omega_{i-j}^{i}(\boldsymbol{x}^{(i-j)}), \boldsymbol{c}_{long}^{(i-j,i)}\right)$$

$$(9)$$

It is essential how the weights $\boldsymbol{c}_{long}^{(i-j,i)}$ are computed. Let $\boldsymbol{c}^{(i-j,i)}$ be the weights for the flow between image $i-j$ and i, as defined for the short-term model. The long-term weights $\boldsymbol{c}_{long}^{(i-j,i)}$ are computed as follows:

$$\boldsymbol{c}_{long}^{(i-j,i)} = \max\left(\boldsymbol{c}^{(i-j,i)} - \sum_{k \in J : i-k > i-j} \boldsymbol{c}^{(i-k,i)}, \boldsymbol{0}\right), \quad (10)$$

where max is taken element-wise. This means, we first apply the usual short-term constraint. For pixels in disoccluded regions we look into the past until we find a frame in which these have consistent correspondences. An advantage over simply using $\boldsymbol{c}^{(i-j,i)}$ is that each pixel is connected only to the closest possible frame from the past. Since the optical flow computed over more frames is more erroneous than over fewer frames, this results in nicer videos. An empirical comparison of $\boldsymbol{c}^{(i-j,i)}$ and $\boldsymbol{c}_{long}^{(i-j,i)}$ is shown in the supplementary video (see Sect. 8.1).

4.4   Multi-pass Algorithm

We found that the output image tends to have less contrast and is less diverse near image boundaries than in other areas of the image. For mostly static videos this effect is hardly visible. However, in cases of strong camera motion the areas from image boundaries move towards the center of the image, which leads to a lower image quality over time when combined with our temporal constraint. Therefore, we developed a multi-pass algorithm which processes the whole sequence in multiple passes and alternating directions. The basic idea is that we progressively propagate intermediate results in both forward and backward direction, avoiding an one-way information flow from the image boundaries to the center only.

Every pass consists of a relatively low number of iterations without full convergence. At the beginning, we process every frame independently based on a random initialization. After that, we blend frames with non-disoccluded parts of previous frames warped according to the optical flow, then run the optimization algorithm for some iterations initialized with this blend. The direction in which the sequence is processed is alternated in every pass. We repeat this blending and optimization to convergence.

Formally, let $x'^{(i)(j)}$ be the initialization of frame i in pass j and $x^{(i)(j)}$ the corresponding output after some iterations of the optimization algorithm. When processed in forward direction, the initialization of frame i is created as follows:

$$
x'^{(i)(j)} = \begin{cases} x^{(i)(j-1)} & \text{if } i = 1, \\ \delta c^{(i-1,i)} \circ \omega_{i-1}^{i}\big(x^{(i-1)(j)}\big) + \big(\overline{\delta}1 + \delta\overline{c}^{(i-1,i)}\big) \circ x^{(i)(j-1)} & \text{else.} \end{cases}
$$

$$(11)$$

Here $\circ$ denotes element-wise vector multiplication, δ and $\overline{\delta} = 1-\delta$ are the blend factors, 1 is a vector of all ones, and $\overline{c} = 1 - c$.

Analogously, the initialization for a backward direction pass is:

$$
x'^{(i)(j)} = \begin{cases} x^{(i)(j-1)} & \text{if } i = N_{\text{frames}} \\ \delta c^{(i+1,i)} \circ \omega_{i+1}^{i}\big(x^{(i+1)(j)}\big) + \big(\overline{\delta}1 + \delta\overline{c}^{(i+1,i)}\big) \circ x^{(i)(j-1)} & \text{else} \end{cases}
$$

$$(12)$$

The multi-pass algorithm can be combined with the temporal consistency loss described above. We achieved good results when we disabled the temporal consistency loss in several initial passes and enabled it in later passes only after the images had stabilized.

5   Experiments

In this section, we briefly describe implementation details and present experimental results produced with different versions of our algorithm. While we did our best to make the paper self-contained, it is not possible to demonstrate effects like video flickering in still images. We therefore advise the readers to watch the supplementary video, which is available at https://youtu.be/vQk_Sfl7kSc.

5.1   Implementation Details

Our implementation[1] is based on the Torch [2] implementation called *neural-style*[2]. We used the following layers of the VGG-19 network [10] for computing the losses: *relu4_2* for the content and *relu1_1,relu2_1,relu3_1,relu4_1,relu5_1* for the style. The energy function was minimized using L-BFGS. For precise evaluation we incorporated the following strict stopping criterion: the optimization was considered converged if the loss did not change by more than 0.01 % during 50 iterations. This typically resulted in roughly 2000 to 3000 iterations for the first frame and roughly 400 to 800 iterations for subsequent frames when optimizing with our temporal constraint, depending on the amount of motion and the complexity of the style image. Using a convergence threshold of 0.1 % cuts the number of iterations and the running time in half, and we found it still produces reasonable results in most cases. However, we used the stronger criterion in our experiments for the sake of accuracy.

---

[1] GitHub: https://github.com/manuelruder/artistic-videos.
[2] GitHub: https://github.com/jcjohnson/neural-style.

For videos of resolution 350×450 we used weights $\alpha = 1$ and $\beta = 20$ for the content and style losses, respectively (default values from *neural-style*), and weight $\gamma = 200$ for the temporal losses. However, the weights should be adjusted if the video resolution is different. We provide the details in Sect. 7.2.

For our multi-pass algorithm, we used 100 iterations per pass and set $\delta = 0.5$, but we needed at least 10 passes for good results, so this algorithm needs more computation time than our previous approaches.

We used DeepMatching, DeepFlow and EpicFlow implementations provided by the authors of these methods. We used the "improved-settings" flag in DeepMatching 1.0.1 and the default settings for DeepFlow 1.0.1 and EpicFlow 1.00.

Runtime. For the relaxed convergence threshold of 0.1 % with random initialization the optimization process needed on average roughly eight to ten minutes per frame at a resolution of 1024×436 on an Nvidia Titan X GPU. When initialized with the warped previous frame and combined with our temporal loss, the optimization converges 2 to 3 times faster, three minutes on average. Optical flow computation runs on a CPU and takes roughly 3 minutes per frame pair (forward and backward flow together), therefore it can be performed in parallel with the style transfer. Hence, our modified algorithm is roughly 3 times faster than naive per-frame processing, while providing temporally consistent output videos.

5.2 Short-term Consistency

We evaluated our short-term temporal loss on 5 diverse scenes from the MPI Sintel Dataset [1], with 20 to 50 frames of resolution 1024×436 pixels per scene, and 6 famous paintings (shown in Sect. 7.1) as style images. The Sintel dataset provides ground truth optical flow and ground truth occlusion areas, which allows a quantitative study. We warped each stylized frame i back with the ground truth flow and computed the difference with the stylized frame $i-1$ in non-disoccluded regions. We use the mean square of this difference (that is, the mean squared error) as a quantitative performance measure.

On this benchmark we compared several approaches: our short-term consistency loss with DeepFlow and EpicFlow, as well as three different initializations without the temporal loss: random noise, the previous stylized frame and the previous stylized frame warped with DeepFlow. We set $\alpha = 1$, $\beta = 100$, $\gamma = 400$.

A qualitative comparison is shown in Fig. 2. Quantitative results are in Table 1. The most straightforward approach, processing every frame independently, performed roughly an order of magnitude worse than our more sophisticated methods. In most cases, the temporal penalty significantly improved the results. The *ambush* scenes are exceptions, since they contain very large motion and the erroneous optical flow impairs the temporal constraint. Interestingly, on average DeepFlow performed slightly better than EpicFlow in our experiments, even through EpicFlow outperforms DeepFlow on the Sintel optical flow benchmark.

5.3 Long-Term Consistency and Multi-pass Algorithm

The short-term consistency benchmark presented above cannot evaluate the long-term consistency of videos (since we do not have long-term ground truth flow available) and

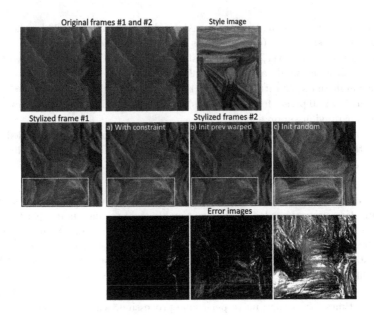

Fig. 2. Close-up of a scene from Sintel, combined with *The Scream* painting. **(a)** With temporal constraint **(b)** Initialized with previous image warped, but without the constraint **(c)** Initialized randomly. The marked regions show most visible differences. *Error images* show the contrast-enhanced absolute difference between frame #1 and frame #2 warped back using ground truth optical flow, as used in our evaluation. The effect of the temporal constraint is very clear in the error images and in the corresponding video.

Table 1. Short-term consistency benchmark results. Mean squared error of different methods on 5 video sequences, averaged over 6 styles, is shown. Pixel values in images were between 0 and 1.

	alley_2	ambush_5	ambush_6	bandage_2	market_6
DeepFlow	**0.00061**	**0.0062**	**0.012**	0.00084	0.0035
EpicFlow	0.00073	0.0068	0.014	**0.00080**	**0.0032**
Init prev warped	0.0016	0.0063	**0.012**	0.0015	0.0049
Init prev	0.010	0.018	0.028	0.0041	0.014
Init random	0.019	0.027	0.037	0.018	0.023

their visual quality (this can only be judged by humans). We therefore excluded the long-term penalty and the multi-pass approach from the quantitative comparison and present only qualitative results. Please see the supplementary video for more results.

Figure 3 shows a scene from Miss Marple where a person walks through the scene. Without our long-term consistency model, the background looks very different after the person passes by. The long-term consistency model keeps the background unchanged. Figure 4 shows another scene from Miss Marple with fast camera motion. The multi-pass algorithm avoids the artifacts introduced by the basic algorithm.

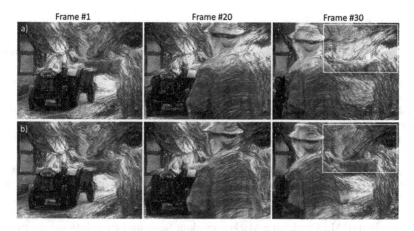

Fig. 3. Scene from Miss Marple, combined with The Starry Night painting. **(a)** Short-term consistency only. **(b)** Long-term consistency with $J = \{1, 10, 20, 40\}$. Corresponding video is linked in Sect. 8.1.

Fig. 4. The multi-pass algorithm applied to a scene from Miss Marple. With the default method, the image becomes notably brighter and loses contrast, while the multi-pass algorithm yields a more consistent image quality over time. Corresponding video is linked in Sect. 8.1.

6   Conclusion

We presented a set of techniques for style transfer in videos: suitable initialization, a loss function that enforces short-term temporal consistency of the stylized video, a loss function for long-term consistency, and a multi-pass approach. As a consequence, we can produce stable and visually appealing stylized videos even in the presence of fast motion and strong occlusion.

References

1. Butler, D.J., Wulff, J., Stanley, G.B., Black, M.J.: A naturalistic open source movie for optical flow evaluation. In: Fitzgibbon, A., Lazebnik, S., Perona, P., Sato, Y., Schmid, C. (eds.) ECCV 2012, Part VI. LNCS, vol. 7577, pp. 611–625. Springer, Heidelberg (2012)
2. Collobert, R., Kavukcuoglu, K., Farabet, C.: Torch7: A matlab-like environment for machine learning. In: BigLearn, NIPS Workshop (2011)
3. Gatys, L.A., Ecker, A.S., Bethge, M.: A neural algorithm of artistic style (2015). CoRR abs/1508.06576. http://arxiv.org/abs/1508.06576
4. Hays, J., Essa, I.: Image and video based painterly animation. In:Proceedings of the 3rd International Symposium on Non-photorealistic Animation and Rendering, NPAR 2004, pp. 113–120. ACM, New York, NY, USA (2004). http://doi.acm.org/10.1145/987657.987676
5. Li, C., Wand, M.: Combining Markov random fields and convolutional neural networks for image synthesis (2016). CoRR abs/1601.04589. http://arxiv.org/abs/1601.04589
6. Litwinowicz, P.: Processing images and video for an impressionist effect. In: Proceedings of the 24th Annual Conference on Computer Graphics and Interactive Techniques, SIGGRAPH 1997, pp. 407–414. ACMPress/Addison-Wesley Publishing Co., New York, NY, USA (1997). http://dx.doi.org/10.1145/258734.258893
7. Nikulin, Y., Novak, R.: Exploring the neural algorithm of artisticstyle (2016). CoRR abs/1602.07188. http://arxiv.org/abs/1602.07188
8. O'Donovan, P., Hertzmann, A.: Anipaint: interactive painterly animation from video. IEEE Trans. Vis. Comput. Graph. **18**(3), 475–487 (2012)
9. Revaud, J., Weinzaepfel, P., Harchaoui, Z., Schmid, C.: EpicFlow: edge-preserving interpolation of correspondences for optical flow. In: CVPR2015 - IEEE Conference on Computer Vision & Pattern Recognition, Boston, United States, June 2015. https://hal.inria.fr/hal-01142656
10. Simonyan, K., Zisserman, A.: Very deep convolutional networks for large-scale image recognition (2014). CoRR abs/1409.1556. http://arxiv.org/abs/1409.1556
11. Sundaram, N., Brox, T., Keutzer, K.: Dense point trajectories by GPU-accelerated large displacement optical flow, September 2010. http://lmb.informatik.uni-freiburg.de//Publications/2010/Bro10e
12. Weinzaepfel, P., Revaud, J., Harchaoui, Z., Schmid, C.: DeepFlow: Large displacement optical flow with deep matching. In: ICCV 2013 - IEEE International Conference on Computer Vision, pp. 1385–1392. IEEE, Sydney, Australia, December 2013. https://hal.inria.fr/hal-00873592

Semantically Guided Depth Upsampling

Nick Schneider[1,3(✉)], Lukas Schneider[1,2], Peter Pinggera[1], Uwe Franke[1],
Marc Pollefeys[2], and Christoph Stiller[3]

[1] Environment Perception, Daimler R&D, Sindelfingen, Germany
{nick.schneider,lukas.schneider}@daimler.com
[2] ETH Zurich, Zurich, Switzerland
[3] Karlsruhe Institute of Technology, Karlsruhe, Germany

Abstract. We present a novel method for accurate and efficient upsampling of sparse depth data, guided by high-resolution imagery. Our approach goes beyond the use of intensity cues only and additionally exploits object boundary cues through structured edge detection and semantic scene labeling for guidance. Both cues are combined within a geodesic distance measure that allows for boundary-preserving depth interpolation while utilizing local context. We model the observed scene structure by locally planar elements and formulate the upsampling task as a global energy minimization problem. Our method determines globally consistent solutions and preserves fine details and sharp depth boundaries. In our experiments on several public datasets at different levels of application, we demonstrate superior performance of our approach over the state-of-the-art, even for very sparse measurements.

1 Introduction

Many computer vision applications benefit from high resolution dense depth maps, e.g. image segmentation, scene flow computation, object detection and tracking, as well as 3D reconstruction and mapping. Traditionally, stereo vision has been the method of choice for obtaining per pixel depth estimates. However, accurate and dense state-of-the-art stereo algorithms[1] suffer from high computational complexity and distance-dependent measurement noise. In recent years, Light Detection and Ranging (LIDAR) sensors have become increasingly popular in the robotics domain due to their supreme range accuracy and constant improvements in size and cost. At the same time, compact and inexpensive Time of Flight (ToF) cameras have become key for indoor range sensing, providing per-pixel depth information at high frame rates. They however suffer from acquisition noise due to limited illumination energy and a comparatively low resolution compared to stereo camera systems. LIDAR sensors provide range measurements with very high accuracy in both indoor and outdoor scenarios, but only with a sparse and non-uniform sampling pattern.

The first two authors contributed equally to this work.
[1] http://www.cvlibs.net/datasets/kitti/.

© Springer International Publishing AG 2016
B. Rosenhahn and B. Andres (Eds.): GCPR 2016, LNCS 9796, pp. 37–48, 2016.
DOI: 10.1007/978-3-319-45886-1_4

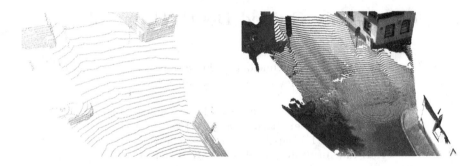

Fig. 1. Example output of the proposed method. The result is smooth and accurate, while fine structures, e.g. the pole and the sign, are preserved.

Sophisticated upsampling to a target resolution is a common method to address the sparseness of the measured depth data. Typically, a high resolution camera image is registered to the low resolution data and used to guide the upsampling process giving significant improvements, c.f. [10,19,25,29]. The key assumption of such approaches is that depth boundaries coincide with intensity edges. We have however observed that actual object boundaries are more likely to induce depth discontinuities than plain intensity gradients. Hence, we aim to additionally exploit object boundary information as a guidance for upsampling.

In this paper, we present a novel image guided depth upsampling approach which utilizes both, object-based edge information as well as pixel-wise semantic class labels. For both cues, we leverage state-of-the-art approaches, i.e. structured edge detection [6] and pixel-wise semantic scene labeling [4]. The cues define a geodesic distance measure, allowing for boundary-aware distance computation between image pixels and sparse data samples. We model the observed scene structure as a set of locally planar elements and formulate the upsampling task as a global energy minimization problem. A thorough evaluation on several public datasets and different application levels demonstrates the benefits of our approach, particularly in terms of computing globally consistent solutions while preserving fine structures and sharp depth boundaries, c.f. Fig. 1.

2   Related Work

Upsampling of sparse information through high resolution imagery is an active area in optical flow, stereo, and Time of Flight (ToF) research. All applications share two key assumptions: (1) the observed scenes consist of piecewise smooth surfaces, (2) depth and flow discontinuities tend to coincide with image edges. We identify four lines of related work:

First, many upsampling approaches apply an interpolation filter to the low resolution data. Since the filter is supposed to be guided by an associated high resolution image, the appropriate design of the filter kernel and its support is crucial. A popular approach involves bilateral filtering to combine sparse measurement data with ab high resolution guidance image [1,7,19,36]. In [17], the guided filter is proposed as an efficient and improved alternative to bilateral upsampling. [26] exploit geodesic distances to define the filter support, achieving improvements at fine image details. Other methods rely on a previous segmentation of the image coupled with sophisticated smoothing operations [29, 30].

The second line of work formulates the upsampling task as a global optimization problem. [5] define a Markov Random Field (MRF), with the sparse depth measurements representing the data fidelity and the high resolution image serving as smoothness term. [32] incorporate adaptive multi-cue neighborhood weighting and nonlocal means regularization into the MRF to better preserve fine local details. [10] formulate a convex optimization problem with higher order regularization and an anisotropic diffusion tensor to handle fine structure. The higher order term enforces piecewise affine solutions and is modeled as a second order Total Generalized Variation (TGV) regularization. [9] compute geodesic neighborhoods and fit affine models to the low resolution data, with a subsequent greedy optimization scheme promoting global consistency. For optical flow upsampling [33] also use a geodesic distance representation to estimate the influence of sparse flow matches on an image pixel, followed by an energy minimization.

Third, a few approaches employ sparse signal representations for guided upsampling making use of the wavelet domain [16], learned dictionaries [23] or co-sparse analysis models [14, 18].

Finally, there are methods that estimate a dense depth representation leveraging pixel-level semantic cues as obtained by deep neural networks [2, 8, 24, 27, 28, 37]. Such methods either perform a joint inference on pixel-level using stereoscopic image data [3, 22], or operate on 3D reconstructed point clouds [11, 15, 20]. In this work, we also leverage semantic input through fully convolutional networks (FCNs) [28], but operate in the image domain and take sparse depth measurements as input. Our approach avoids common shortcomings such as oversmoothing and surface-flattening by combining a geodesic distance formulation with meaningful local geometric models and efficient global optimization.

Our main contributions are: (1) a novel energy formulation for depth upsampling that takes global image context into account, is robust to outliers and is optimized efficiently; (2) an extension of the well known geodesic distance to leverage probabilistic pixel-level semantic cues; (3) superior accuracy and computational requirements to state-of-the-art baselines.

3   Method

The goal of this work is to estimate a depth value for each pixel in a high resolution image, given sparse measurements. To describe an observed scene we infer planes, constrained to be consistent with their local context in the image. This formulation is driven by the observation that most object surfaces are intrinsically smooth and can thus be well approximated by local planes. We treat this task as a novel optimization problem of a global energy function, c.f. Sect. 3.1. In order to acquire meaningful context for each pixel, we leverage geodesic distances that respect image and semantic boundaries, c.f. Sect. 3.2.

By approximating the geodesic distance, c.f. Sect. 3.3, we can drop most of the free parameters of the energy function and optimize it efficiently, c.f. Sect. 3.4.

3.1 Energy Formulation

Given a set $\mathcal{M}$ of pixels i with sparse depth measurements z_i and weights $w_{i,j}$ between i and j, we formulate an energy function in order to estimate one plane $\theta_i \in \theta$ per pixel in the $u, v, \frac{1}{z}$ space as well as binary outlier indicators $\mathbf{o}$ for all measurements and co-planarity indicators $\mathbf{c}$ between all pairs of planes:

$$E(\theta, \mathbf{o}, \mathbf{c}, \mathbf{z}) = \sum_i E_{una}(\theta_i(i), o_i, z_i) +$$
$$\sum_{i,j} w_{i,j} \cdot E_{pair}(\theta_i(i), \theta_j(i), c_{i,j}) + E_o(o_i, \theta, z_i, \mathbf{c}) . \tag{1}$$

If a measurement is marked as outlier, it is discarded in the unary that otherwise enforces consistency to its measurement:

$$E_{una}(\theta_i(i), o_i, z_i) = w_{una} \cdot \begin{cases} \left(\theta_i(i) - z_i^{-1}\right)^2 & , \text{ if } i \in \mathcal{M} \wedge o_i = 0 \\ 0 & , \text{ otherwise.} \end{cases} \tag{2}$$

The function $\theta_j(i)$ evaluates the inverse depth at pixel i via $\theta_j \cdot [u_i, v_i, 1]^T$. In the pairwise term, the consistency of connected planes is reflected via

$$E_{pair}(\theta_i(i), \theta_j(i), c_{i,j}) = w_c \cdot \begin{cases} (\theta_i(i) - \theta_j(i))^2 & , \text{ if } c_{i,j} = 1 \\ \lambda_c & , \text{ otherwise,} \end{cases} \tag{3}$$

with a penalty λ_c for non-consistent planes. Finally, the outlier formulation is kept as generic as possible by employing a probabilistic model taking the inferred planes into account:

$$E_o(o_i, \theta, z_i, \mathbf{c}) = \begin{cases} 0 & , \text{ otherwise} \\ -log\left(p(o_i|\theta, z_i, \mathbf{c})\right) & , \text{ if } i \in \mathcal{M}. \end{cases} \tag{4}$$

This potential is conveniently adaptable to the actual application demands and sensor properties. In this work, we opt for a simple outlier probability function that rates the measurement z_i by judging its deviation from connected planes.

3.2 Geodesic Distance

The proposed energy formulation depends on pairwise weights that control the influence of the pairwise energies. We define $w_{i,j} = -log\left(D_{i,j}\right)$ by means of a distance function $D_{i,j}$ between pixels in the image. With the intention of preserving depth discontinuities and tiny structures, we introduce an edge- and semantics-aware geodesic distance. It is defined as the costs along the minimal path π from pixel i to j. These costs are calculated as a weighted mean considering edge costs

$s_I(\pi)$, semantic costs $s_S(\pi)$ as well as costs $s_l(|\pi|)$ which penalize the length of a considered path:

$$D_g(i,j) = \min_{\pi} \frac{w_I * s_I(\pi) + w_S * s_S(\pi) + s_l(|\pi|)}{w_I + w_S + w_D}. \tag{5}$$

The edge term increases by traversing pixels with high edge scores $s_I(\pi) = \prod_{i \in \pi} s_I(i)$. Pixels along a path are more likely to be connected if they share the same semantic class. Therefore, we search for the label $l \in L$ which aggregates high scores $s_L(l,i)$ over all pixels i along π. Since $s_L(l,i)$ increases with more certainty of label l, we define $s_S(\pi) = 1 - \underset{l}{\text{maximize}} \prod_{i \in \pi} s_L(l,i)$. Note that we expect normalized costs, thus $D_g(i,j) \in (0,1] \Rightarrow w_{i,j} = -log(D_g(i,j)) \in \mathbb{R}^+$.

3.3 Approximation

We follow [33] and approximate the geodesic distance from Eq. 5 with $\hat{D}_g(i,j)$. This allows us to efficiently compute the distances between all pixels in the image and simplifies the energy function. For each pixel i we therefore firstly compute the nearest pixel $n_i \in \mathcal{M}$ with a valid measurement with respect to the original distance D_g [33]. Using the measurement pixels as seeds, this step results in Voronoi cells $\mathcal{V}_i$, as shown in Fig. 2. Now, we define $D_g^g(i,j) \approx D_g(i,j)$ by restricting the paths to contain the seeds in the traversed cells. This leads to $\hat{D}_g(i,j) = D_g(i,n_i) + D_g^g(n_i,n_j) + D_g(j,n_j)$. The distances to the closest pixel with valid measurement $D_g(i,n_i)$ are very small (assuming a reasonable number of measurements). Thus, we approximate them with a small constant ϵ:

$$\hat{D}_g(i,j) \approx D_g^g(n_i,n_j) + \epsilon. \tag{6}$$

$D_g^g(n_i,n_j)$ can be computed efficiently using Dijkstra's algorithm, we refer to [33] for more details. The main advantage of the proposed approximation, however, lies in a significant reduction of the parameters necessary to optimize as we will show in the following. Let i,j be pixels in the same cell $\mathcal{V}_k$. The approximated geodesic distance $\hat{D}_g(i,j) = \epsilon$ is very small leading to large pairwise weights $w_{i,j} = -log(\epsilon)$. The weights control the influence of the pairwise energy of Eq. (1), thus forcing a solution of the energy function to satisfy $(\theta_i(i) \approx \theta_j(i))^2$. This leads to the observation that $\theta_i(i), \theta_j(i)$ have to intersect at $[u_i, v_i, \theta_i(i)]$. Since this observation holds for all pixel combinations in the cell, the plane parameters have to be equal: $\theta_i = \theta_j$ and we can replace all θ_i with θ_{n_i}. In the following we denote the pixels with a valid measurement and their cell index as n, m. For pixels i, j in two different cells with their corresponding measurement pixels n, m, the pairwise weights are constant and can be rewritten as $w_{n,m}$. We can thus reorder the summation and write

$$\sum_{i,j} w_{i,j} E_{pair}(\theta_i(i), \theta_j(i), c_{i,j}) = \sum_{n,m \in \mathcal{M}} w_{n,m} \sum_{p \in \mathcal{V}_n} E_{pair}(\theta_n(p), \theta_m(p), c_{n,m}) \tag{7}$$

| input | SED | semantics | voronoi cells | connected cells |

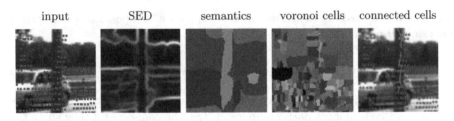

Fig. 2. The properties of the geodesic distance given the three inputs. The geodesic distance respects object boundaries as visible in the Voronoi and connected cells.

Combining Equation (7) with the unary and outlier terms that evaluate to zero at pixels without valid measurements yields

$$E(\theta, \mathbf{o}, \mathbf{c}, \mathbf{z}) = \sum_{n \in \mathcal{M}} E_{una}(\theta_n(n), o_n, z_x) +$$
$$\sum_{n,m \in \mathcal{M}} w_{n,m} \cdot \sum_{p \in \mathcal{V}_n} E_{pair}(\theta_n(p), \theta_m(p), c_{n,m}) + \sum_{n \in \mathcal{M}} E_o(o_n, \theta, z_n, \mathbf{c}) . \tag{8}$$

This new energy is effectively defined over cells instead of pixels reducing the number of free parameters in the optimization. However, given the reasonable approximation of the distance (and small ϵ), both are essentially equivalent. In practice, we apply pairwise costs only to the N nearest measurements with a maximal distance $\hat{D}_g < D_{max}$ by setting $w_{n,m} = 0$ otherwise. This results in a consistent set of cells allowing for robust depth optimization.

3.4   Optimization

Optimizing the energy function of Eq. (8) is difficult, as it contains a large set of discrete and continuous variables. We adapt an iterative scheme from [35], repeatedly optimizing the coplanarity flags, outlier flags and plane parameters one after another. The energy is convex in θ and can efficiently be solved in closed form. It is carried out in parallel for all planes, assuming the rest of the planes and parameters as given, using polynomial coefficients to evaluate the unary and pairwise potentials in constant time. Although there is no guarantee for the energy to decrease in each iteration, in our experiments the measured depth error decreases consistently with an increasing number of iterations, c.f. Sect. 4. In such an iterative optimization scheme, good results are often extremely sensitive to the initialization. Throughout our experiments, however, we opt for a simple initialization by $o_i = 0, c_{i,j} = 1$ and $\theta_i = [0, 0, z_i^{-1}]$. With available label input, we greedily decide if a cell is dominated by ground or object pixels independently. In the former cases, we initialize the planes with upright normals instead.

4   Evaluation

We evaluate our approach on three different application levels. First, we use
the sampled groundtruth of the Middlebury 2014 stereo dataset [34]. Second, we
evaluate our algorithm on two real-world datasets: the indoor dataset introduced
by Ferstl [10] and the KITTI dataset ([12,13,31]). We opt for a generic and
efficient edge detector [6] that uses trained structured forests to predict edge
scores for each pixel.

4.1   Middlebury Benchmark Evaluation

To test the performance of our algorithm on almost noise-free input data, we
make use of the recent Middlebury 2014 Stereo Benchmark [34]. The dataset
contains high resolution images and corresponding groundtruth generated by
structured lighting. Previous depth super resolution methods [10,32] used Bicu-
bic or Bilinear downsampling to simulate the input. As this distorts the input
data especially at depth edges and blurs tiny structures, we simply sample data
at equidistant points. We compare to a state state-of-the-art method of [10] and
three additional upsampling approaches. The parameters of our and Ferstl's [10]
algorithm were empirically determined for each upsampling factor. Quantitative
results in terms of the Mean Absolute Error (MAE) are shown in Table 1. All
baselines are significantly outperformed on all three images and all strides, particularly for highly sparse inputs. The runtime of our algorithm, visualized in
Fig. 3, strongly depends on the number of input depth points. While [10] report
moderate runtimes of their algorithm (318.2 ms for upsampling 0.8 megapixel
images and 1900 ms for 1.4 megapixel images), the speed depends on the resolution of the image instead. Thus, our algorithm is best suited for real-world
depth sensors, which so far have a very limited resolution. Figure 3 visualizes the
performance and runtime of our method in comparison to the number of input
measurements.

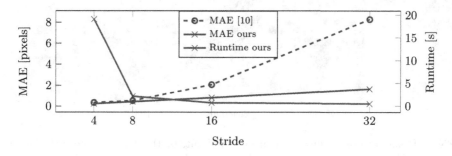

Fig. 3. Comparison of runtime and MAE (in pixel) for different strides on the Middlebury 2014 Benchmark [34].

Table 1. MAE for Middlebury 2014 dataset for four chosen images.

	Backpack				Sword1				Umbrella			
	4x	8x	16x	32x	4x	8x	16x	32x	4x	8x	16x	32x
Nearest	2.65	3.95	5.24	6.74	1.72	2.94	4.65	7.16	0.77	1.26	2.18	4.06
Bicubic	2.22	3.44	4.76	<u>6.07</u>	1.44	2.56	4.23	<u>6.65</u>	0.67	1.10	1.90	3.64
Bilinear	1.95	3.21	4.56	6.20	1.28	2.40	4.12	6.75	0.56	0.94	1.69	<u>3.37</u>
Ferstl	<u>0.50</u>	<u>0.79</u>	<u>3.37</u>	11.54	<u>0.49</u>	<u>0.75</u>	<u>2.61</u>	9.43	<u>0.15</u>	<u>0.22</u>	<u>1.37</u>	9.10
OURS	**0.15**	**0.27**	**0.47**	**0.90**	**0.34**	**0.61**	**1.07**	**2.22**	**0.09**	**0.16**	**0.27**	**0.53**

4.2 Results for ToF Data Upsampling

The Middlebury dataset is popular for the evaluation of depth upsampling methods but does not reflect real acquisition setups. Therefore, we further carry out an exhaustive evaluation on two real-world datasets. The first is provided by [10] and consists of three different scenes captured by a 120×160 pixel wide ToF camera and a 810×610 pixel wide greyscale CMOS camera. Groundtruth for these scenes was generated using a structured light scanner with a high-speed projector as well as two 2048×2048 pixel wide high-speed intensity cameras (with a depth uncertainty of 1.2 mm). We compare our results to three upsampling algorithms: joint bilateral upsampling [19], guided image filtering [17] and anisotropic total generalized variation [10]. A quantitative comparison of the results is shown in Table 2, qualitative results in Fig. 4. We demonstrate that our method produces smooth surfaces while preserving sharp depth edges and thin elements. The runtime for a single frame is 107 ms on the given input data and was measured as an average over 1000 runs (Ferstl [10] reports an average of 318.2 ms).

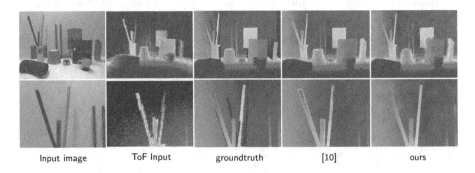

| Input image | ToF Input | groundtruth | [10] | ours |

Fig. 4. Result for upsampling the Time of Flight data on the 'books' scene of the Ferstl dataset [10]. In the second row a zoomed-in view is shown for better visual comparison. Although input data is noisy, our algorithm preserves sharp edges.

Table 2. Results on the Ferstl dataset [10] by means of MAE error in depth [mm].

	Books	Shark	Devil
Kopf [19]	16.03	18.79	27.57
He [17]	15.74	18.21	27.04
Ferstl [10]	12.36	**15.29**	14.68
OURS	**12.12**	15.46	**14.03**

4.3   Results for LIDAR Upsampling

The KITTI Vision Benchmark Suite [13] was created to fill the gap of demanding benchmarks for visual systems in the context of autonomous driving. The dataset provides depth data from a Velodyne HDL-64E LIDAR as well as RGB images with a resolution of 1392×512 pixels which were recorded from a moving platform. With the help of a highly accurate inertial measurement unit (IMU) LIDAR depth data is accumulated while driving and serves as groundtruth for stereo vision methods. In [31], a novel dataset was presented in which also frames with moving objects are considered. The dynamic objects are first removed and then re-inserted by fitting CAD models to the point cloud. Furthermore, occlusions due to sensor displacement are manually removed, resulting in a clean and dense ground truth for depth evaluation. We use the raw LIDAR measurements as input to our algorithm. It is apparent from Fig. 6 that the groundtruth differs extremely from raw input in terms of both, outlier frequency and density. We traced the raw LIDAR data associated to the training images of the 2015 Stereo Benchmark and found 82 corresponding frames from the raw dataset, which we will make publicly available to allow for future evaluation on this data. The raw LIDAR points projected into the image (u, v, d) contain many errors due to the large displacement between the LIDAR and the camera especially at

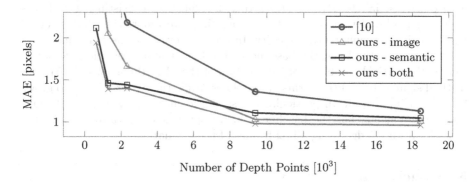

Fig. 5. Quantitative results on the Kitti dataset for varying number of input measurements. Results in terms of disparity MAE depending on the number of input points are reported for a baseline [10] and three input configurations (image only, semantic only, both inputs) of the proposed method.

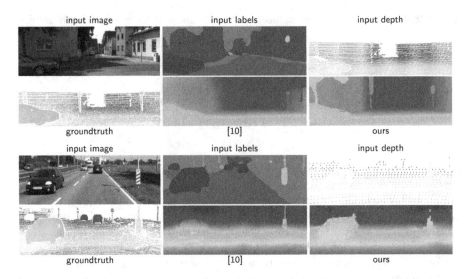

Fig. 6. Example outputs of the proposed algorithm compared to our baseline, ground-truth and the inputs for two cases with all (top) respectively $\frac{1}{12}$ (bottom) measurements. The semantic input guides our upsampling to respect object boundaries as can be seen at the objects, e.g. car, signed and poles, in the lower example. The 3D reconstruction using the inferred depth is presented in Fig. 1. Note that the sign on the right (top) is correctly represented without available depth measurements, by propagating the depth along the sign and pole.

top borders of objects. Instead of heuristically removing measurements, we aim for an outlier rejection in the proposed optimization, c.f. Sect. 3. We tackle this challenge by leveraging pixel-level semantic information in addition to the sparse depth measurements. Therefore, we use a FCN [28] trained on the Cityscapes Dataset [4] and fine-tune it on a disjunct part of the KITTI images annotated with pixel-wise labels [21]. It is trained with a label set consisting of 11 labels including road, sidewalk, car, pole and building. We report the MAE over all pixels having a groundtruth disparity. In order to evaluate the performance of the proposed method and the baseline with different input densities, we down-sample the vertical and horizontal resolution of the LIDAR output (Fig. 5). Our method significantly outperforms all baselines, while the performance gap grows for sparser input data. In particular the semantic cues play a greater role with less measurements. For the baseline [10], we optimized the parameters to the best of our knowledge using all 82 frames of the evaluation.

5   Conclusion

In this paper, we presented a novel approach for the challenging problem of accurate depth upsampling. Our proposed method exploits boundary cues and pixel-wise semantic class labels obtained via a high resolution guidance image and fully convolutional networks. In order to preserve depth boundaries and fine structures, we combine those cues in a geodesic distance measure. We formulate the upsampling task as a pixel-wise global energy minimization problem and apply a suitable approximation which allows to reduce the number of parameters for a real-time optimization. A thorough evaluation on three different public datasets is carried out at different application levels. Compared to a state-of-the-art method, we achieve significantly better results. The proposed method can particularly exploit its strength at very sparse depth measurements or a high target resolution. Here, the performance gap to the baselines increases in terms of both, computational demands and depth accuracy. Furthermore, the experiments demonstrated robustness of our approach to noise and false depth measurements.

References

1. Chan, D., Buisman, H., Theobalt, C., Thrun, S.: A noise-aware filter for real-time depth upsampling. In: ECCV Workshops (2008)
2. Chen, L.C., Papandreou, G., Kokkinos, I., Murphy, K., Yuille, A.L.: Semantic image segmentation with deep convolutional nets and fully connected CRFs. In: ICLR (2015)
3. Chen, W., Hou, J., Zhang, M., Xiong, Z., Gao, H.: Semantic stereo: integrating piecewise planar stereo with segmentation and Classification. In: ICIST (2014)
4. Cordts, M., Omran, M., Ramos, S., Rehfeld, T., Enzweiler, M., Benenson, R., Franke, U., Roth, S., Schiele, B.: The cityscapes dataset for semantic urban scene understanding. In: CVPR (2016)
5. Diebel, J., Thrun, S.: An application of markov random fields to range sensing. In: NIPS (2005)
6. Dollar, P., Zitnick, C.L.: Fast edge detection using structured forests. TPAMI **37**(8), 1558–1570 (2015)
7. Dolson, J., Baek, J., Plagemann, C., Thrun, S.: Upsampling range data in dynamic environments. In: CVPR (2010)
8. Everingham, M., Eslami, S.M.A., Van Gool, L., Williams, C.K.I., Winn, J., Zisserman, A.: The PASCAL Visual object classes challenge: a retrospective. IJCV **111**, 98–136 (2015)
9. Facciolo, G., Caselles, V.: Geodesic neighborhoods for piecewise affine interpolation of sparse data. In: ICIP (2009)
10. Ferstl, D., Reinbacher, C., Ranftl, R., Ruether, M., Bischof, H.: Image guided depth upsampling using anisotropic total generalized variation. In: ICCV (2013)
11. Floros, G., Leibe, B.: Joint 2D-3D temporally consistent semantic segmentation of street scenes. In: CVPR (2012)
12. Geiger, A., Lenz, P., Stiller, C., Urtasun, R.: Vision meets robotics: the KITTI dataset. IJRR **32**, 1231–1237 (2013)
13. Geiger, A., Lenz, P., Urtasun, R.: Are we ready for autonomous driving? the KITTI vision Benchmark Suite. In: CVPR (2012)
14. Gong, X., Ren, J., Lai, B., Yan, C., Qian, H.: Guided depth upsampling via a cosparse analysis model. In: CVPR Workshops (2014)
15. Häne, C., Zach, C., Cohen, A., Angst, R., Pollefeys, M.: Joint 3D scene reconstruction and class segmentation. In: CVPR (2013)
16. Hawe, S., Kleinsteuber, M., Diepold, K.: Dense disparity maps from sparse disparity measurements. In: ICCV (2011)

17. He, K., Sun, J., Tang, X.: Guided image filtering. In: Daniilidis, K., Maragos, P., Paragios, N. (eds.) ECCV 2010, Part I. LNCS, vol. 6311, pp. 1–14. Springer, Heidelberg (2010)
18. Kiechle, M., Habigt, T., Hawe, S., Kleinsteuber, M.: A bimodal co-sparse analysis model for image processing. IJCV **114**, 233–247 (2014)
19. Kopf, J., Cohen, M.F., Lischinski, D., Uyttendaele, M.: Joint bilateral upsampling. ACM Trans. Graph. (TOG) **26**(3), 96 (2007). ACM
20. Kundu, A., Li, Y., Dellaert, F., Li, F., Rehg, J.M.: Joint semantic segmentation and 3D reconstruction from monocular video. In: Fleet, D., Pajdla, T., Schiele, B., Tuytelaars, T. (eds.) ECCV 2014, Part VI. LNCS, vol. 8694, pp. 703–718. Springer, Heidelberg (2014)
21. Ladický, L., Shi, J., Pollefeys, M.: Pulling things out of perspective. In: CVPR (2014)
22. Ladický, L., Sturgess, P., Russell, C., Sengupta, S., Bastanlar, Y., Clocksin, W., Torr, P.H.S.: Joint optimization for object class segmentation and dense stereo reconstruction. IJCV **100**, 122–133 (2011)
23. Li, Y., Xue, T., Sun, L., Liu, J.: Joint example-based depth map super-resolution. In: ICME (2012)
24. Lin, G., Shen, C., Reid, I., van dan Hengel, A.: Efficient piecewise trainingof deep structured models for semantic segmentation. Arxiv (2015)
25. Liu, J., Gong, X.: Guided depth enhancement via anisotropic diffusion. In: Huet, B., Ngo, C.-W., Tang, J., Zhou, Z.-H., Hauptmann, A.G., Yan, S. (eds.) PCM 2013. LNCS, vol. 8294, pp. 408–417. Springer, Heidelberg (2013)
26. Liu, M.Y., Tuzel, O., Taguchi, Y.: Joint geodesic upsampling of depth images. In: CVPR (2013)
27. Liu, Z., Li, X., Luo, P., Change, C., Tang, L.X.: Semantic image segmentation via deep parsing network. In: ICCV (2015)
28. Long, J., Shelhamer, E., Darrell, T.: Fully convolutional networks for semantic segmentation. In: CVPR (2015)
29. Lu, J., Forsyth, D.: Sparse depth super resolution. In: CVPR (2015)
30. Matsuo, K., Aoki, Y.: Depth image enhancement using local tangent plane approximations. In: CVPR (2015)
31. Menze, M., Geiger, A.: Object scene flow for autonomous vehicles. In: CVPR (2015)
32. Park, J., Kim, H., Tai, Y.-W., Brown, M.S., Kweon, I.: High quality depth map upsampling for 3D-TOF cameras. In: ICCV (2011)
33. Revaud, J., Weinzaepfel, P., Harchaoui, Z., Schmid, C.: EpicFlow: edge-preserving interpolation of correspondences for optical flow. In: CVPR (2015)
34. Scharstein, D., Hirschmüller, H., Kitajima, Y., Krathwohl, G., Nešić, N., Wang, X., Westling, P.: High-resolution stereo datasets with subpixel-accurate ground truth. In: Jiang, X., Hornegger, J., Koch, R. (eds.) GCPR 2014. LNCS, vol. 8753, pp. 31–42. Springer, Heidelberg (2014)
35. Yamaguchi, K., McAllester, D., Urtasun, R.: Efficient joint segmentation, occlusion labeling, stereo and flow estimation. In: Fleet, D., Pajdla, T., Schiele, B., Tuytelaars, T. (eds.) ECCV 2014, Part V. LNCS, vol. 8693, pp. 756–771. Springer, Heidelberg (2014)
36. Yang, Q., Yang, R., Davis, J., Nister, D.: Spatial-depth super resolution for range images. In: CVPR (2007)
37. Zheng, S., Jayasumana, S., Romera-Paredes, B., Vineet, V., Su, Z., Du, D., Huang, C., Torr, P.H.S.: Conditional random fields as recurrent neural networks. In: ICCV (2015)

Learning I

Chimpanzee Faces in the Wild:
Log-Euclidean CNNs for Predicting Identities
and Attributes of Primates

Alexander Freytag[1,2(✉)], Erik Rodner[1,2], Marcel Simon[1], Alexander Loos[3],
Hjalmar S. Kühl[4,5], and Joachim Denzler[1,2,5]

[1] Computer Vision Group, Friedrich Schiller University Jena, Jena, Germany
[2] Michael Stifel Center Jena, Jena, Germany
[3] Fraunhofer Institute for Digital Media Technology, Ilmenau, Germany
[4] Max Planck Institute for Evolutionary Anthropology, Leipzig, Germany
[5] German Centre for Integrative Biodiversity Research (iDiv), Leipzig, Germany
alexander.freytag@uni-jena.de

Abstract. In this paper, we investigate how to predict attributes of
chimpanzees such as identity, age, age group, and gender. We build
on convolutional neural networks, which lead to significantly superior
results compared with previous state-of-the-art on hand-crafted recognition pipelines. In addition, we show how to further increase discrimination abilities of CNN activations by the Log-Euclidean framework on
top of bilinear pooling. We finally introduce two curated datasets consisting of chimpanzee faces with detailed meta-information to stimulate
further research. Our results can serve as the foundation for automated
large-scale animal monitoring and analysis.

1 Introduction

In 2009, a detailed report came to the conclusion that the global biodiversity
is severely threatened [31]. While the report is admiringly detailed, the assessment only represents the snapshot of a single date. However, dense information
regarding the development of biodiversity over time would be highly valuable,
e.g., for assessing whether new political actions are required or whether previous
ones have been successful. A major difficulty is the necessity of analyzing large
amounts of recorded data, which often needs to be done manually. Hence, reliable quantitative insights into the status of eco systems and animal populations
are difficult to obtain and expensive. In direct consequence, keeping biodiversity
assessments up-to-date is rarely possible although highly needed.

While analyzing large amounts of data manually is not feasible, recording
such large datasets is easily possible, *e.g.,* using camera traps [21,23]. Hence,
the gap between data recording and data analysis can only be closed using reliable automated techniques. Fortunately, computer vision researchers developed

Electronic supplementary material The online version of this chapter (doi:10.
1007/978-3-319-45886-1_5) contains supplementary material, which is available to
authorized users.

B. Rosenhahn and B. Andres (Eds.): GCPR 2016, LNCS 9796, pp. 51–63, 2016.
DOI: 10.1007/978-3-319-45886-1_5

Fig. 1. We investigate attribute predictions for chimpanzees based on cropped faces. Results have been obtained using ground truth head regions and learned attribute predictions. *Left:* expert annotations are (Dorien-30y-Adult-Female), (Kofi-5y-Infant-Male), and (Bangolo-1y-Infant-Male). *Right:* expert annotations are (Robert-35y-Adult-Male) and (Corrie-34y-Adult-Female).

a multitude of algorithms for these scenarios over the past years. Techniques of fine-grained recognition allow for visually discriminating among highly similar object categories, *e.g.*, among different birds [25], sharks [13] or flowers [15]. In consequence, we are in the perfect position for transferring our solutions to biologists to amplify their research.

Our first contribution is to provide such a transfer into the area of mammal investigation. More precisely, we provide an in-depth study of how to apply deep neural networks to scenarios where chimpanzees need to be analyzed. Our analysis reveals that activations of deep neural networks substantially improve recognition accuracy over established pipelines for chimpanzee identification. Moreover, they are highly useful for additional attribute prediction which allows for detailed analysis and large-scale animal monitoring. A result of our learned attribute prediction models is shown in Fig. 1.

In addition, we present how the matrix logarithm transformation can further increase discrimination abilities even on top of state-of-the-art bilinear pooling in convolutional neural networks [17]. Our technique is inspired by [4,30], where authors demonstrated its advances when using handcrafted features. The benefit in terms of recognition performance can not only be seen in our real-world application but also in a straightforward synthetic experiment that reveals the benefits of this transformation especially for fine-grained scenarios. As noise signals in low-quality images are thereby amplified as well, we found that the operation is especially helpful if the image data is of high quality.

The focus of this paper can be summarized as follows:

1. We show that deep-learned image representations significantly outperform the current state-of-the-art pipeline for chimpanzee identification,
2. We apply the LOGM-operation as post-processing on top of bilinear pooling of CNN activations and present an in-depth study of the resulting benefits, and
3. We release curated versions of the datasets presented in [19] of cropped chimpanzee faces with detailed meta information for public use.

We review related work (Sect. 2) and convolutional neural networks (Sect. 3) before introducing the matrix logarithm transform in detail (Sect. 4).

2   Related Work

Fine-grained Recognition. Over the past decade, fine-grained recognition received increasing attention within the computer vision community due to the challenging nature of the task [3,8,9,25,34]. In contrast to classification of coarse object categories, fine-grained recognition needs to identify localized patterns, *e.g.*, striped wings or a dotted neck. A recent technique is bilinear pooling on top of CNN activations proposed by Lin et al. [17]. Furthermore, Tuzel et al. [30] and later on Carreira et al. [4] proposed the LOGM operation as post-processing of bilinear pooled handcrafted features. We combine both ideas to tackle the task of differentiating among individuals of a single species which is related to but still different from fine-grained recognition.

Identification of Human Faces. Eigenfaces, one of the earliest and perhaps the most famous approach for face recognition, was presented by Turk and Pentland and is based on PCA projections of cropped face images [29]. He et al. presented Laplacianfaces, which rely on a more sophisticated projection [11]. Later on, Wright et al. reported benefits for face recognition using sparse representation models [32]. Following that line of work, Yang and Zhang improved the efficiency of sparse representation by using responses of Gabor-filters as representations [33]. Simonyan et al. transferred the idea of Fisher vector encoding to face recognition [26]. However, all of these methods rely on hand-crafted image representations which need to be optimized independently.

Recently, deep neural networks trained with millions of face images significantly improved the recognition accuracy for human faces by directly learning appropriate representations and metrics from data. One of the first networks was Deepface by Taigman et al. trained from 4M face images [27]. Even more powerful is the VGG-faces network by Parkhi et al. [22] trained from 2.6M face images. Hence, our first contribution is to adapt these models to the task of chimpanzee identification. A major difference is the comparatively small amount of training data in our application domain.

Identification of Chimpanzees. To the best of our knowledge, Loos et al. [18,19] presented the only published pipeline so far for the identification of chimpanzees Inspired by results from human face recognition, a central part is the alignment of faces to guarantee that extracted visual descriptors are semantically comparable. To this end, an affine transformation is applied using facial features such as eyes and mouth and the resulting image is cropped and scaled to standard size. Aligned faces are fed into a three step pipeline which consists of feature extraction, feature space transformation, and classification. For image description, extended local ternary patterns [28] are extracted on spatially divided Gabor magnitude pictures (GMPs). Finally, the dimensionality is reduced using locality preserving projections [10] and a sparse representation classification [33] serves as classification model. Due to the implemented alignment step, the entire pipeline is restricted to near-frontal face recordings. In this work, we show how to improve accuracy by using learned image representations without the necessity of aligned face images.

3   Convolutional Neural Networks in a Nutshell

Deep (convolutional) neural networks. Computer vision systems of the last decades were commonly well-designed pipelines consisting of feature extraction, post-processing, and classification. Since all stages were developed and specified separately, this plug-and-play principle allowed for easily exchanging individual modules. In contrast, recent architectures are designed end-to-end without a clear separation of feature extraction and classification which allows for jointly optimizing all involved parameters. An example are deep neural networks which are concatenations of several processing stages f_i, $i = 1, \ldots, L$ that are tightly connected. These stages are referred to as layers and are parameterized with $\boldsymbol{\theta}_i$:

$$f(\mathbf{x}_i; \boldsymbol{\theta}) = f_L \left(\ldots \left(f_2 \left(f_1 \left(\mathbf{x}_i; \boldsymbol{\theta}_1 \right); \boldsymbol{\theta}_2 \right) \ldots \right); \boldsymbol{\theta}_L \right). \tag{1}$$

When operating on image data, location invariance of learnable patterns should be explicitly incorporated into the network layout as done in Convolutional Neural Networks (CNNs) [16]. In consequence, some layers are evaluated as convolutions between learnable filter masks and outputs of the previous layer.

Optimization. Based on collected training data $\mathcal{D} = (\mathbf{x}_i, y_i)_{i=1}^{N}$, parameter values of all layers can be estimated by jointly optimizing a single loss function:

$$\bar{\mathcal{L}}(\boldsymbol{\theta}; \mathcal{D}) = \frac{1}{N} \sum_{i=1}^{N} \mathcal{L}(f(\mathbf{x}_i; \boldsymbol{\theta}), y_i) + \omega(\boldsymbol{\theta}). \tag{2}$$

where $\omega(\cdot)$ servers as regularizer [35]. The resulting optimization problem is usually hard and the most commonly used optimization technique is stochastic gradient descent (SGD) [2] with mini-batches [20]:

$$\boldsymbol{\theta}^{t+1} = \boldsymbol{\theta}^t - \gamma \cdot \tilde{\nabla}_{\boldsymbol{\theta}} \bar{\mathcal{L}}(\boldsymbol{\theta}^t; \mathcal{S}_{\text{sgd}}^t). \tag{3}$$

SGD is an iterative technique where the parameter γ controls the impact of individual steps. Furthermore, the term $\tilde{\nabla}_{\boldsymbol{\theta}} \bar{\mathcal{L}}(\boldsymbol{\theta}^t; \mathcal{S}_{\text{sgd}}^t)$ represents the approximated gradient of the loss function with respect to the current estimate $\boldsymbol{\theta}^t$ and the currently drawn mini-batch $\mathcal{S}_{\text{sgd}}^t$:

$$\tilde{\nabla}_{\boldsymbol{\theta}} \bar{\mathcal{L}}(\boldsymbol{\theta}; \mathcal{S}_{\text{sgd}}^t) = \frac{1}{\left| \mathcal{S}_{\text{sgd}}^t \right|} \sum_{i \in \mathcal{S}_{\text{sgd}}^t} \nabla_{\boldsymbol{\theta}} \mathcal{L}(f(\mathbf{x}_i; \boldsymbol{\theta}), y_i) + \nabla_{\boldsymbol{\theta}} \omega(\boldsymbol{\theta}). \tag{4}$$

Gradients of intermediate layers can be computed using backpropagation [24].

Fine-tuning. Training millions of parameters is an ill-posed problem if labeled data is rare. Fortunately, large labeled datasets exist in other application domains (*e.g.*, ImageNet [6]). The process of fine-tuning refers to using the pretrained network weights as initialization for a novel task. Running only a limited number of optimization steps on the small data set is sufficient in practice.

4   Log-Euclidean Convolutional Neural Networks

One of the current state-of-the-art approaches on fine-grained recognition by Lin et al. [17] uses bilinear pooling to transform the outputs of convolutional layers in a CNN. Bilinear pooling has been developed by Tuzel et al. [30] and Carreira et al. [4] and computes second-order statistics of features within a spatial region. We briefly review this approach and present how the matrix logarithm on top of CNN bilinear pooling can further increase discrimination abilities.

Second-order Statistics. Given the output tensor $g_{i,j,k}$ of a CNN layer with $1 \leq k \leq K$ filters, the second-order transformation is computed as pooling result over outer products of channel responses for every spatial field:

$$M = \sum_{i,j} g_{i,j,\cdot} \; g_{i,j,\cdot}^T. \tag{5}$$

Here, the suffix $\cdot$ denotes the vectorization of the respective component. We specified the pooling operation over spatial responses in Eq. (5) as sum-pooling, however, other pooling operations are equally possible [4].

Matrix Logarithm of Second-order Statistics. The matrix M is an arbitrary symmetric positive semi-definite (PSD) matrix and therefore embedded on a Riemannian manifold but not in a (Euclidean) vector space. This implies that a function that separates the manifold into two regions (binary classification) is not just a simple hyperplane as in the Euclidean case. Whereas this is ignored in [17], it was already argued by Tuzel et al. [30] and Carreira et al. [4] that the bilinear pooling matrix should be first transformed to a vector space with proper Euclidean metric and scalar product for further processing. A straightforward option for this transformation is the matrix logarithm as used in the Log-Euclidean framework of [1], which directly maps PSD matrices to a vector space [4,30].

The matrix logarithm is computed using the eigendecomposition $M = U D U^T$ and performing a logarithmic transformation on the eigenvalues $D = \mathrm{diag}(\lambda_1,...,\lambda_K)$. Therefore, our Log-Euclidean layer performs the following operation:

$$\textsc{logm}(M) = U \; \mathrm{diag}(\log(\lambda_1),\ldots,\log(\lambda_K)) \; U^T. \tag{6}$$

Note that this information does not lead to any loss in information. We follow [4] and add a constant ϵ to all eigenvalues to ensure their positiveness.

Understanding the Effectiveness of the Matrix Logarithm. As we will see in our experiments, the LOGM-transformation can increase accuracy in animal identification tasks. The field of topology already delivers a clear mathematical motivation. In the following, let us additionally analyze the effectiveness of LOGM from a pure machine learning point of view.

As can be seen from Eq. (6), the matrix logarithm transforms the axes length of the ellipsoid spanned by the local descriptors $\mathbf{f}_{i,j,\cdot}$. Small axes (eigenvalues) below $\alpha \approx 0.567$ get a larger absolute value. Similarly, long axes above α are

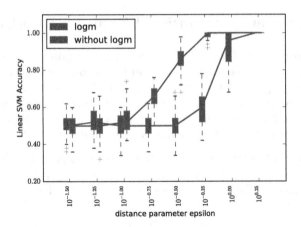

Fig. 2. Synthetic experiment comparing standard second-order pooling with LOGM-transformation of the matrices.

shrunken with respect to their absolute value. However, the absolute value of the axes influences the impact of the axes on the matrix and also on the resulting feature vectors. Therefore, the LOGM-transformation can be seen as amplifying axes with small variances in data. Intuitively, this is ideal for identification tasks where small parts of the image are supposed to be discriminative. To verify this intuition, we performed a small synthetic experiment where we sampled matrices M for two classes as follows: the first class generates matrices by sampling 30 feature descriptors $g_{i,j,.}$ from a bi-variate normal distribution $\phi_1 = \mathcal{N}(\mathbf{0}, \mathrm{diag}(10^{-2}, 10))$. The second class is generated by sampling feature vectors from ϕ_1 with probability $1 - p$ and from $\phi_2 = \mathcal{N}([0, \epsilon], \mathrm{diag}(10^{-2}, 10))$ with probability p. To establish a scenario that corresponds to challenging identification tasks, we use $p = 0.1$ (*i.e.*, only 10 % of the feature descriptors are discriminative before bilinear pooling). We then train a linear SVM with 25 sampled matrices and evaluate the accuracy on 25 hold-out samples.

The results after 50 repetitions for various values of the distance ϵ are given in Fig. 2. As can be seen, the LOGM-transformation leads to a higher accuracy compared to standard bilinear pooling for a wide range of ϵ values (x-axis is in log-scale). In the following, we investigate the effect on real-world data.

5   Datasets for Chimpanzee Identification and Beyond

For our experiments, we assembled two datasets of cropped ape faces (denoted as C-Zoo and C-Tai). The datasets are based on previously published chimpanzee datasets by Loos and Ernst and have been extended and specifically curated for the task of attribute prediction for chimpanzee faces. We released all data as well as train-test splits at http://www.inf-cv.uni-jena.de/chimpanzee_faces.html. In the following, we briefly describe both datasets regarding content and quality. A detailed analysis is given in Sect. S1 of the supplementary material.

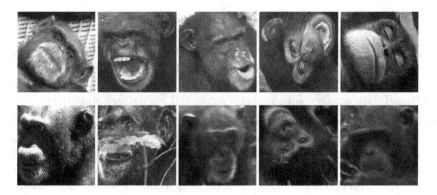

Fig. 3. Example images of the datasets C-Zoo (*top*) and C-Tai (*bottom*).

The C-Zoo Dataset. Loos and Ernst introduced a chimpanzee dataset in [19] which originated from a collaboration with animal researchers in Leipzig. We build on an extension of their dataset which covers 24 individuals that have been manually labeled by experts. Provided images are of high quality, are well exposed, and are taken without strong blurring artifacts. The final C-Zoo dataset consists of 2,109 faces which are complemented by biologically meaningful keypoints (centers of eyes, mouth, and earlobes). Each individual is assigned into one out of four age groups. In addition, the gender and current age of each individual is provided as meta-information. The visual variation of contained faces is shown in the top row of Fig. 3.

The C-Tai Dataset. Loos and Ernst presented a second dataset which consists of recordings of chimpanzees living in the Taï National Park in Côte d'Ivoire. The image quality differs heavily, *e.g.*, due to strong variations in illumination and distance to recorded objects. Again, we build on an extension of their data collection and obtain 5,078 chimpanzee faces which forms our second dataset. We refer to it as C-Tai and show the visual variation in the lower part of Fig. 3. In total, 78 individuals are recorded from 5 age groups. Unfortunately, the annotation quality of additional information is not as high as for the first dataset (*i.e.*, not every face is complemented with all attributes). In our evaluations, we therefor use only those 4,377 faces where identity, age, age group, and gender are provided which results in 62 different individuals.

6   Experiments

For both datasets, we were interested in the accuracy for identification of individual chimpanzees as well as for prediction of attributes age, gender, and age group. In the following, we analyze identification and gender estimation in detail for various variants of CNN codes, fine-tuning, and post processing. Due to the lack of space, we present evaluations regarding the estimation of age and age groups only in the supplementary material. The developed source code for identification and attribute prediction including a demo-pipeline is available at https://github.com/cvjena.

6.1   Experiments of Chimpanzee Identification

Setup – Data. For each dataset, we generate five random splits using stratified sampling with 80 % for training and hold-out 20 % for testing. Trained models are evaluated using averaged class-wise recognition rates to reflect the potentially imbalanced datasets (see supplementary material for dataset statistics).

Setup – Face Recognition Baselines. The approach of Loos and Ernst [19] resembles the current state-of-the-art for chimpanzee recognition. We additionally follow by Parkhi et al. [22] who presented a state-of-the-art network for human face recognition. Since the network with weights trained on the Labeled Faces in the Wild (LFW) dataset [12] is publicly available, we use activations of the network for the task of chimpanzee identification (denoted with VGGFaces).

Setup – Investigated Approaches. Our first question was whether CNNs for identification of human faces are better suited for the task of chimpanzee identification than other networks. Hence, we apply the Caffe BVLC reference model (denoted as BVLC AlexNet) which was originally trained for differentiating among object categories from the ImageNet challenge ILSVRC. For BVLC AlexNet and VGGFaces, we extract activations from the layers `pool5` (last layer before fully-connected layers) and `fc7` (last layer before ImageNet or LFW scores) on the cropped face regions (denoted as CNN codes). As suggested in [5], we L_2-normalize activations before passing them to the final classifier.

In addition, we were interested in the effect of post processing of CNN activations. Hence, we apply the bilinear pooling and optionally the LOGM-operation. We further increase numerical stability by normalizing the second order matrix similar to the suggestion in [17] (denoted with "+ norm", see Sect. S3 in the supplementary material). On top of extracted representations, we train linear SVMs using LibLinear [7]. The regularization parameter C is found by ten-fold cross validation in $10^{-5} \ldots 10^5$.

Furthermore, we analyze the effect of fine-tuning with little data. To prevent over-fitting, we experiment with freezing lower layers. We follow recommendations of the Caffe toolbox and apply a weight decay of 0.0005 as well as a momentum of 0.9. On C-Zoo, we fine-tune for 2,000 iterations, whereas we conduct 8,000 iterations on C-Tai to reflect the difficulty of the dataset. The learning rate for the last layer is set to 0.001 and to 0.0001 for all remaining non-frozen layers. Training of CNNs is done using the Caffe framework [14]. During fine-tuning, we either follow the Caffe suggestions and use random crops of 227 px × 227 px after scaling training images to 256 px × 256 px or we directly scale images to 227 px × 227 px (denoted as "random crops" and "no random crops"). Results for all settings are shown in Table 1.

Results – Application-specific Feature Design or Feature Learning. Our first question was whether representations learned from millions of images can improve over well-designed recognition pipelines based on expert domain knowledge. Comparing the state-of-the-art system by Loos et al. (1-a) against CNN codes (1-d) already shows a noticeable increase in accuracy. Hence, learned

Table 1. Identification results on C-Zoo and C-Tai. We report mean and standard deviation of avg. class-wise recognition rates (ARR) from 5 random splits (given in %).

Approach	C-Zoo	C-Tai
Baseline: state-of-the-art		
(1-a) Loos and Ernst [19]	82.88 ± 01.52	64.35 ± 01.39
CNN codes + SVM		
(1-b) VGGFaces `pool5`	82.73 ± 00.69	67.96 ± 01.06
(1-c) VGGFaces `fc7`	66.34 ± 02.36	53.33 ± 01.04
(1-d) BVLC AlexNet `pool5`	89.17 ± 01.07	$\mathbf{76.60 \pm 01.25}$
(1-e) BVLC AlexNet `fc7`	81.06 ± 01.33	67.07 ± 01.58
CNN Finetuning (BVLC AlexNet)		
(1-f) `fc7-fc8`, random crops	85.57 ± 05.81	51.08 ± 03.60
(1-g) `fc7-fc8`, no random crops	91.89 ± 06.58	49.82 ± 03.58
(1-h) `conv1-fc8`, no random crops	90.21 ± 01.66	70.22 ± 01.71
CNN codes (BVLC AlexNet) + Pooling +SVM		
(1-i) `pool5` + bilinear	89.21 ± 01.59	76.13 ± 00.31
(1-j) `pool5` + bilinear + norm	89.81 ± 01.25	76.22 ± 00.66
(1-k) `pool5` + bilinear + norm + LOGM	$\mathbf{91.99 \pm 01.32}$	75.66 ± 00.86

representations lead to clear benefits for chimpanzee identification even without further fine-tuning or post-processing.

Results – Faces or Objects Network. When comparing CNN codes from VGGFaces (1-b and 1-c) and BVLC AlexNet (1-d and 1-e), we observe that the faces net is clearly outperformed. This is somewhat surprising, since we expected that the VGGFaces network could have learned typical human facial features which should also be important to distinguish between Chimpanzee faces.

Results – Fine-tuning. On the C-Zoo dataset, we observe that using no random sub-crops clearly improves accuracy (1-f to 1-h). Tuning all layers slightly reduces accuracy due to overfitting to the relatively small dataset. In contrast, fine-tuning is hardly possible on the C-Tai dataset. We attribute this observation to the strong variations in pose, lighting, and occlusion which would require more data to learn a representative model.

Results – Bilinear Pooling. Regarding bilinear pooling, we observe a significant increase in accuracy for the Zoo dataset when the LOGM-operation is applied (1-k). In contrast, results for the Tai dataset are not improved which we again attribute to the strong image variations in the dataset. Thereby, non-discriminative artifacts are eventually amplified by the LOGM transformation. We conclude that our transformation is well suited for identification scenarios where data is of sufficiently high quality. On C-Zoo, bilinear pooling without the LOGM transformation does not lead to a performance benefit compared to using the CNN activations directly (1-d), which we attribute to a missing vector space embedding. Finally, we observe that the LOGM-results are only marginally above results from fine-tuning on C-Zoo. However, fine-tuning requires dedicated hardware (*e.g.*, GPUs) to conduct backward passes through the network. Instead, bilinear pooling and LOGM only compute forward passes and post-processing which can efficiently be performed on low-budget standard hardware.

6.2 Evaluation of Chimpanzee Gender Estimation

Setup – Data. For each dataset, we split the 2,109 and 4,377 face images by selecting 80 % of each gender for training and all remaining data for model evaluation. Results are averaged over five random splits.

Setup – Baselines, Approaches, and Generalization. Since Loos et al. [18,19] did not tackle attribute prediction, there is no obvious baseline for this task. Nonetheless, a naive baseline arises by predicting the majority of all genders in data ("baseline naive"). Furthermore, we can rely on the identification models of Sect. 6.1 and use the age of the predicted individual averaged over all its recordings during training ("Identification + attribute query"). In addition, we apply CNN codes of both networks by following the same experimental setup as in Sect. 6.1. Furthermore, we evaluate the effect of bilinear pooling and the LOGM-operation for the task of gender prediction. We are finally interested in

Table 2. Gender estimation results on C-Zoo and C-Tai. Results are averaged over five random splits. We report areas under ROC curves (AUC in %).

Approach	C-Zoo	C-Tai
Baseline: naive		
(2-a) majority gender	50.00 ± 0.00	50.00 ± 0.00
Identification + attribute query		
(2-b) using (1-k)	97.61 ± 0.94	89.60 ± 0.53
CNN codes + SVM		
(2-c) VGGFaces pool5	94.77 ± 1.38	79.78 ± 1.94
(2-d) VGGFaces fc7	89.32 ± 1.00	88.00 ± 0.55
(2-e) BVLC AlexNet pool5	96.61 ± 1.07	90.49 ± 1.23
(2-f) BVLC AlexNet fc7	95.61 ± 1.39	86.97 ± 0.62
CNN codes (BVLC AlexNet) + Pooling +SVM		
(2-g) pool5 + bilinear	97.60 ± 00.48	$\mathbf{92.97 \pm 0.42}$
(2-h) pool5 + bilinear + norm	97.81 ± 00.36	92.83 ± 0.35
(2-i) pool5 + bilinear + norm + LOGM	$\mathbf{98.16 \pm 00.35}$	90.86 ± 0.74
Cross-Dataset		
(2-j) using (2-i)	70.48 ± 3.39	66.17 ± 2.73

the generalization abilities across datasets. Hence, we train models on LOGM-transformed features using all images from one dataset and evaluate these models on the five splits of the other dataset.

Results. Results are shown in Table 2. Again, we obtain inferior results of the faces network compared to the object categorization net. Nonetheless, we observe that CNN codes on their own are already well suited for gender estimation (2-c to 2-f). The strong results are partly due to the sophisticated identification capabilities (2-a). However, bilinear pooling and the LOGM-operation can further improve results (2-g to 2-i). We finally observe that the generalization across datasets is partly possible. The clear drop in accuracy can be attributed to the different dataset characteristics (see supplementary material).

7 Conclusions

In this paper, we investigated several tasks which arise in animal monitoring for biological research. More precisely, we tackled chimpanzee identification, gender prediction, age estimation, and age group classification and provided an in-depth study of the applicability of recently popular deep neural network architectures. Furthermore, we applied the LOGM-operation as post-processing step on bilinear CNN activations which further improved accuracy when training data is sufficiently representative. Our results clearly demonstrate the effectiveness of latest vision algorithms for zoological applications, $e.g.$, with an identification accuracy of $\sim 92\,\%$ ARR or a gender estimation accuracy of $\sim 98\,\%$ AUC.

Acknowledgements. The authors thank Dr. Tobias Deschner for providing the images which were used to build the C-Tai dataset, Laura Aporius and Karin Bahrke for collecting and annotating the images which were used to build the C-Zoo dataset, and the Zoo Leipzig for providing permission for image collection. The images used for creating the C-Zoo dataset were collected as part of the SAISBECO project funded by the Pact for Research and Innovation between the Max Planck Society and the Fraunhofer-Gesellschaft. Part of this research was supported by grant RO 5093/1-1 of the German Research Foundation (DFG) and by a grant from the Robert-Bosch-Stiftung.

References

1. Arsigny, V., Commowick, O., Pennec, X., Ayache, N.: A log-Euclidean framework for statistics on diffeomorphisms. In: Larsen, R., Nielsen, M., Sporring, J. (eds.) MICCAI 2006. LNCS, vol. 4190, pp. 924–931. Springer, Heidelberg (2006)
2. Bottou, L.: Stochastic gradient descent tricks. In: Montavon, G., Orr, G.B., Müller, K.-R. (eds.) Neural Networks: Tricks of the Trade, 2nd edn. LNCS, vol. 7700, pp. 421–436. Springer, Heidelberg (2012)
3. Branson, S., Van Horn, G., Belongie, S., Perona, P.: Improved bird species categorization using pose normalized deep convolutional nets. In: British Machine Vision Conference (BMVC) (2014)

4. Carreira, J., Caseiro, R., Batista, J., Sminchisescu, C.: Free-form region description with second-order pooling. IEEE Trans. Pattern Anal. Mach. Intell. (TPAMI) **37**(6), 1177–1189 (2015)
5. Chatfield, K., Simonyan, K., Vedaldi, A., Zisserman, A.: Return of the devil in the details: delving deep into convolutional nets. In: British Machine Vision Conference (BMVC) (2014)
6. Deng, J., Dong, W., Socher, R., Li, L.J., Li, K., Fei-Fei, L.: Imagenet: a large-scale hierarchical image database. In: IEEE Conference on Computer Vision and Pattern Recognition (CVPR), pp. 248–255 (2009)
7. Fan, R.E., Chang, K.W., Hsieh, C.J., Wang, X.R., Lin, C.J.: Liblinear: a library for large linear classification. J. Mach. Learn. Res. (JMLR) **9**, 1871–1874 (2008). http://www.csie.ntu.edu.tw/~cjlin/liblinear/
8. Freytag, A., Rodner, E., Darrell, T., Denzler, J.: Exemplar-specific patch features for fine-grained recognition. In: Jiang, X., Hornegger, J., Koch, R. (eds.) GCPR 2014. LNCS, vol. 8753, pp. 144–156. Springer, Heidelberg (2014)
9. Göring, C., Rodner, E., Freytag, A., Denzler, J.: Nonparametric part transfer for fine-grained recognition. In: IEEE Conference on Computer Vision and Pattern Recognition (CVPR), pp. 2489–2496 (2014)
10. He, X., Niyog, P.: Locality preserving projections. In: Neural Information Processing Systems (NIPS), vol. 16, p. 153 (2004)
11. He, X., Yan, S., Hu, Y., Niyogi, P., Zhang, H.J.: Face recognition using laplacianfaces. IEEE Trans. Pattern Anal. Mach. Intell. (TPAMI) **27**(3), 328–340 (2005)
12. Huang, G.B., Ramesh, M., Berg, T., Learned-Miller, E.: Labeled faces in the wild: A database for studying face recognition in unconstrained environments. Technical report, pp. 07–49. University of Massachusetts, Amherst (2007)
13. Hughes, B., Burghardt, T.: Automated identification of individual great white sharks from unrestricted fin imagery. In: British Machine Vision Conference (BMVC), pp. 92.1–92.14 (2015)
14. Jia, Y., Shelhamer, E., Donahue, J., Karayev, S., Long, J., Girshick, R., Guadarrama, S., Darrell, T.: Caffe: convolutional architecture for fast feature embedding. In: ACM International Conference on Multimedia, pp. 675–678 (2014)
15. Kumar, N., Belhumeur, P.N., Biswas, A., Jacobs, D.W., Kress, W.J., Lopez, I.C., Soares, J.V.B.: Leafsnap: a computer vision system for automatic plant species identification. In: Fitzgibbon, A., Lazebnik, S., Perona, P., Sato, Y., Schmid, C. (eds.) ECCV 2012, Part II. LNCS, vol. 7573, pp. 502–516. Springer, Heidelberg (2012)
16. LeCun, Y., Bottou, L., Bengio, Y., Haffner, P.: Gradient-based learning applied to document recognition. Proc. IEEE **86**(11), 2278–2324 (1998)
17. Lin, T.Y., RoyChowdhury, A., Maji, S.: Bilinear CNN models for fine-grained visual recognition. In: IEEE International Conference on Computer Vision (ICCV), pp. 1449–1457 (2015)
18. Loos, A.: Identification of great apes using gabor features and locality preserving projections. In: ACM International Workshop on Multimedia Analysis for Ecological Data, pp. 19–24. ACM (2012)
19. Loos, A., Ernst, A.: An automated chimpanzee identification system using face detection and recognition. EURASIP J. Image Vid. Process. **2013**(1), 1–17 (2013)
20. Ngiam, J., Coates, A., Lahiri, A., Prochnow, B., Le, Q.V., Ng, A.Y.: On optimization methods for deep learning. In: International Conference on Machine Learning (ICML), pp. 265–272 (2011)
21. O'Connell, A.F., Nichols, J.D., Karanth, K.U.: Camera Traps in Animal Ecology: Methods and Analyses. Springer, Japan (2010)

22. Parkhi, O.M., Vedaldi, A., Zisserman, A.: Deep face recognition. In: British Machine Vision Conference (BMVC) (2015)
23. Rowcliffe, J.M., Carbone, C.: Surveys using camera traps: are we looking to a brighter future? Anim. Conserv. **11**(3), 185–186 (2008)
24. Rumelhart, D.E., Hinton, G.E., Williams, R.J.: Learning representations by back-propagating errors. Nature **323**, 533–536 (1986)
25. Simon, M., Rodner, E.: Neural activation constellations: unsupervised part model discovery with convolutional networks. In: IEEE International Conference on Computer Vision (ICCV) (2015)
26. Simonyan, K., Vedaldi, A., Zisserman, A.: Learning local feature descriptors using convex optimisation. IEEE Trans. Pattern Anal. Mach. Intell. (TPAMI) **36**(8), 1573–1585 (2014)
27. Taigman, Y., Yang, M., Ranzato, M., Wolf, L.: Deepface: closing the gap to human-level performance in face verification. In: IEEE Conference on Computer Vision and Pattern Recognition (CVPR), pp. 1701–1708 (2014)
28. Tan, X., Triggs, B.: Enhanced local texture feature sets for face recognition under difficult lighting conditions. IEEE Trans. Image Process. (TIP) **19**(6), 1635–1650 (2010)
29. Turk, M.A., Pentland, A.P.: Face recognition using eigenfaces. In: IEEE Conference on Computer Vision and Pattern Recognition (CVPR), pp. 586–591 (1991)
30. Tuzel, O., Porikli, F., Meer, P.: Pedestrian detection via classification on riemannian manifolds. IEEE Trans. Pattern Anal. Mach. Intell. (TPAMI) **30**(10), 1713–1727 (2008)
31. Vié, J.C., Hilton-Taylor, C., Stuart, S.N.: Wildlife in a changing world: an analysis of the 2008 IUCN Red List of threatened species. IUCN (2009)
32. Wright, J., Yang, A.Y., Ganesh, A., Sastry, S.S., Ma, Y.: Robust face recognition via sparse representation. IEEE Trans. Pattern Anal. Mach. Intell. (TPAMI) **31**(2), 210–227 (2009)
33. Yang, M., Zhang, L.: Gabor feature based sparse representation for face recognition with gabor occlusion dictionary. In: Daniilidis, K., Maragos, P., Paragios, N. (eds.) ECCV 2010, Part VI. LNCS, vol. 6316, pp. 448–461. Springer, Heidelberg (2010)
34. Zhang, N., Donahue, J., Girshick, R., Darrell, T.: Part-based R-CNNs for fine-grained category detection. In: Fleet, D., Pajdla, T., Schiele, B., Tuytelaars, T. (eds.) ECCV 2014, Part I. LNCS, vol. 8689, pp. 834–849. Springer, Heidelberg (2014)
35. Zou, H., Hastie, T.: Regularization and variable selection via the elastic net. J. Roy. Stat. Soc. Ser. B (Stat. Methodol.) **67**(2), 301–320 (2005)

Convolutional Scale Invariance for Semantic Segmentation

Ivan Krešo[✉], Denis Čaušević, Josip Krapac, and Siniša Šegvić

Faculty of Electrical Engineering and Computing,
University of Zagreb, Zagreb, Croatia
`ivan.kreso@fer.hr`

Abstract. We propose an effective technique to address large scale variation in images taken from a moving car by cross-breeding deep learning with stereo reconstruction. Our main contribution is a novel scale selection layer which extracts convolutional features at the scale which matches the corresponding reconstructed depth. The recovered scale-invariant representation disentangles appearance from scale and frees the pixel-level classifier from the need to learn the laws of the perspective. This results in improved segmentation results due to more efficient exploitation of representation capacity and training data. We perform experiments on two challenging stereoscopic datasets (KITTI and Cityscapes) and report competitive class-level IoU performance.

1 Introduction

Semantic segmentation is an exciting computer vision task with many potential applications in robotics, intelligent transportation systems and image retrieval. Its goal is to associate each pixel with a high-level label such as the sky, a tree or a person. Most successful approaches in the field rely on dense strongly supervised multi-class classification of the image window centered at the considered pixel [28]. Such pixel-level classification of image windows resembles the localization task [30], which is also concerned with finding objects in images. However, the two tasks are trained in a different manner. Positive object localization windows have a well-defined spatial extent: they are tightly aligned around particular instances of the considered class. On the other hand, the class of a semantic segmentation window is exclusively determined by the kind of the object which projects to the central pixel of the window. Thus we see that the window size does not affect semantic segmentation outcome, which poses contrasting requirements. In cases of featureless or ambiguous texture, large windows have to be considered in order to squeeze information from the context [7]. In cases of small distinctive objects one has to focus onto a small neighborhood, since off-object pixels may provide misleading classification cues. This suggests that a pixel-level classifier is likely to perform better if supplied with a local image representation at multiple scales [4,11,21] and multiple levels of detail [22,24].

We especially consider applications in intelligent transportation systems and robotics. We note that images acquired from vehicles and robots are quite different from images taken by humans. Images taken by humans always have a purpose:

ⓒ Springer International Publishing AG 2016
B. Rosenhahn and B. Andres (Eds.): GCPR 2016, LNCS 9796, pp. 64–75, 2016.
DOI: 10.1007/978-3-319-45886-1_6

the photographer wants something to be seen in the image. On the other hand, a vehicle-mounted camera operates independently from the pose of the objects in the scene: it simply acquires a fresh image each 40 milliseconds. Hence, the role of the context [7] in car-borne datasets [6,12] will be different than in datasets acquired by humans [9]. In particular, objects in car-borne datasets (cars, pedestrians, riders, etc.) are likely to be represented at a variety of scales due to forward camera motion. Not so in datasets taken by humans, where a majority of objects is found at particular scales determined by rules of artistic composition. This suggests that paying a special attention to object scale in car-borne imagery may bring a considerable performance gain.

One approach to address scale-related problems would be to perform a joint dense recovery of depth and semantic information [8,20]. If the depth recovery is successful, the classification network gets an opportunity to leverage that information and improve performance. However, these methods have limited accuracy and require training with depth groundtruth. Another approach would be to couple semantic segmentation with reconstructed [23] or measured [2] 3D information. However, the pixel-level classifier may not be able to successfully exploit this information. Yet another approach would be to use the depth for presenting better object proposals [2,5]. However, proposing instance locations in crowded scenes may be a harder task than classifying pixels.

In this paper we present a novel technique for scale-invariant training and inference in stereoscopic semantic segmentation. Unlike previous approaches, we address the scale-invariance directly, by leveraging the reconstructed depth information [13,32] to disentangle the object appearance from the object scale. We realize this idea by introducing a novel scale selection layer into a deep network operating on the source image pyramid. The resulting scale-invariance substantially improves the segmentation performance with respect to the baseline.

2   Related Work

Early semantic segmentation work was based on multi-scale hand-crafted filter banks [26,28] with limited receptive fields (typically less than 50×50 pixels). Recent approaches [3,4,21,22] leverage amazing power of GPU [11] and extraordinary capacity of deep convolutional architectures [19] to process pixel neighborhoods by ImageNet-grade classifiers. These classifiers typically possess millions of trainable parameters, while their receptive fields may exceed 200×200 pixels [29]. The capacity of these architectures is dimensioned for associating an unknown input image with one of 1000 diverse classes, while they typically see around million images during ImageNet pre-training plus billions of patches during semantic segmentation training. An architecture trained for ImageNet classification can be transformed into a fully convolutional form by converting fully-connected layers into equivalent convolutional layers with the same weights [15,22,27]. The resulting fully convolutional network outputs a dense $W/s \times H/s \times 1000$ multi-class heat map tensor, where $W \times H$ are input dimensions and s is the subsampling factor due to pooling. Now the number of outputs of the last layer can be redimensioned to whatever is the number of classes in the specific application and the network is ready to be fine-tuned for the semantic segmentation task.

Convolutional application of ImageNet architectures typically results in considerable downsampling of the output activations with respect to the input image. Some researches have countered this effect with trained upsampling [22] which may be reinforced by taking into account switches from the strided pooling layers [16,25]. Other ways to achieve the same goal include interleaved pooling [27] and dilated convolutions [22,31]. These approaches typically improve the baseline performance in the vicinity of the object borders due to more accurate upsampling of the semantic maps. We note that the system presented in our experiments does not feature any of these techniques, however it still succeeds to deliver competitive performance.

As emphasized in the introduction, presenting a pixel-level classifier with a variety of local image representations is likely to favor the semantic segmentation performance. Previous researchers have devised two convolutional approaches to meet this idea: the skip architecture and the shared multi-class architecture. The shared multi-class architectures concatenate activations obtained by applying the common pixel-level classifier at multiple levels of the image pyramid [4,11,20, 21,29]. The skip architectures concatenate activations from different levels of the deep convolutional hierarchy [22,24]. Both architectures have their merits. The shared multi-scale architecture is able to associate the evaluated window with the training dataset at unseen scales. The skip architecture allows to model the object appearance [30] and the surrounding context at different levels of detail, which may be especially appropriate for small objects. Thus it appears that best results might be obtained by a combined approach which we call a multi-scale skip architecture. The combined approach concatenates pixel representations taken at different image scales and at different levels of the deep network. We note that this idea does not appear to have been addressed in the previous work.

Despite extremely large receptive fields, pixel-level classification may still fail to establish consistent activations in all cases. Most problems of this kind concern smooth parts of very large objects: for example, a pixel in the middle of a tram may get classified as a bus. A common approach to such problems is to require pairwise agreement between pixel-level labels, which leads to a global optimization across the entire image. This requirement is often formulated as MAP inference in conditional random fields (CRF) with unary, pairwise [3,18, 21] and higher-order potentials [1]. Early methods allowed binary potentials exclusively between neighboring pixels, however, this requirement has later been relaxed by defining binary potentials as linear combinations of Gaussian kernels. In this case, the message passing step in approximate mean field inference can be expressed as a convolution with a truncated Gaussian kernel in the feature space [3,18]. Recent state of the art approaches couple the CRF training and inference in custom convolutional [21] and recurrent [1] deep neural networks. We note that our present experiments feature a separately trained CRF with Gaussian potentials while our future work shall include joint CRF training [21].

We now review the details of the previous research which is most closely related to our contributions. Banica et al. [2] exploit the depth sensed by RGBD sensors to improve the quality of region proposals and the subsequent region-level classification on indoor datasets. Chen et al. [4] propose a scale attention mechanism to combine classification scores at different scales. This results in soft pooling of the classification scores across different classes. Ladicky and Shi [20] propose to train binary pixel-level classifiers which detect semantic labels at some canonical depth by exploiting the depth groundtruth obtained by LIDAR. Their inference jointly predicts semantic segmentation and depth by processing multiple levels of the monocular image pyramid. Unlike all previous approaches, our technique achieves efficient classification and training due to scale-invariant image representation recovered by exploiting reconstructed depth. Unlike [4], we perform hard scale selection at the representation level. Unlike [20], we exploit the reconstructed instead of the groundtruth depth.

3   Fully Convolutional Architecture with Scale Selection

We integrate the proposed technique into an end-to-end trained fully convolutional architecture illustrated in Fig. 1. The proposed architecture independently feeds images from an N-level image pyramid into the shared feature extraction network. Features from the lower levels of the pyramid are upsampled to match the resolution of features from the original image. We forward the recovered multi-scale representation to the pixel-wise scale selection multiplexer. The multiplexer is responsible for establishing a scale-invariant image representation in accordance with the reconstructed depth at the particular pixel. The back-end classifier scores the scale-invariant features with a multi-class classification model. The resulting score maps are finally converted into the per-pixel distribution over classes by a conventional softmax layer.

3.1   Input Pyramid and Depth Reconstruction

The left image of the input stereo pair is iteratively subsampled to produce a multi-scale pyramid representation. The first pyramid level contains the left input image. Each successive level is obtained by subsampling its predecessor with the factor α. If the original image resolution is W × H, the resolution of the l-th level is $W/\alpha^l \times H/\alpha^l$, $l \in [0..N-1]$ ($\alpha = 1.3$, N = 8). We reconstruct the depth by employing a deep correspondence metric [32] and the SGM [13] smoothness prior. The resolution of the disparity image is W × H.

3.2   Single Scale Feature Extraction

Our single scale feature extraction architecture is based on the feature extraction front-end of the 16-level deep VGG-D network [29] up to the relu5_3 layer (13 weight layers total). In order to improve the training, we introduce a batch normalization layer [14] before each non-linearity in the 5th group: relu5_1,

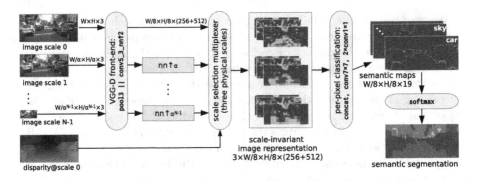

Fig. 1. A convolutional architecture with scale-invariant representation.

`relu5_2` and `relu5_3`. This modification helps the fine-tuning by increasing the flow of the gradients during backprop. Subsequently we perform a 2×2 nearest neighbor upsampling of `relu5_3` features and concatenate them with `pool3` features in the spirit of skip architectures [22,24] (adding `pool4` features did not result in significant benefits). In comparison with `relu5_3`, the representation from `pool3` has a 2×2 higher resolution and a smaller receptive field (40×40 vs 185×185). We hypothesize that this saves some network capacity because it relieves the network from propagating small objects through all 13 convolutional and 4 pooling layers.

The described feature extraction network is independently applied at all levels of the pyramid, in the spirit of the shared multi-class architectures [4,11,20,21,29]. Subsequently, we upsample the representations of pyramid levels 1 to N−1 in order to revert the effects of subsampling and to restore a common resolution across the representations at all scales. We perform the upsampling by a nearest neighbor algorithm in order to preserve the sparsity of the features. After upsampling, all N feature tensors have the resolution $W/8 \times H/8 \times (512 + 256)$. The 8×8 subsampling is due to three pooling levels with stride 2. Features from `relu5_3` have 512 dimensions while features from `pool3` have 256 dimensions.

The described procedure produces a multi-scale convolutional representation of the input image. A straight-forward approach to exploit this representation would be to concatenate the features at all N scales. However, that would imply a huge computational complexity which would make training and inference infeasible. One could also perform such procedure at some subset of scales. However, that would require a costly validation to choose the subset, while providing less information to the back-end classification network. Consequently, we proceed towards achieving scale-invariance as the main contribution of our work.

3.3 Scale Selection Multiplexer

The responsibility of the scale selection multiplexer is to represent each image pixel with scale-invariant convolutional features extracted at exactly $M = 3$ out of

N levels of the pyramid. The scale invariance is achieved by choosing the pyramid levels in which the apparent size of the reference metric scales are closest to the receptive field of our features.

In order to explain the details, we first establish the notation. We denote the image pixels as p_i, the corresponding disparities as d_i, the stereo baseline as b, and the reconstructed depths as Z_i. We then denote the width of the receptive field for our largest features (conv5_3) as $w_{rf} = 185$, the metric width of its back-projection at distance Z_i as W_i and the three reference metric scales in meters as $W_R = \{1, 4, 7\}$. Finally, we define s_{mi} as the ratio between the m-th reference metric scale W_{Rm} and the back projection W_i of the receptive field:

$$s_{mi} = \frac{W_{Rm}}{W_i} = \frac{W_{Rm}}{\frac{b}{d_i} w_{rf}} = \frac{d_i \cdot W_{Rm}}{b \cdot w_{rf}} . \tag{1}$$

The ratio s_{mi} represents the exact image scaling factor by which we should downsample the original image to attain the reference scale m at pixel i. Now we are able to choose the representation from the pyramid level l_{mi} which has a downsampling factor closest to the true factor s_{mi}:

$$\hat{l}_{mi} = \operatorname*{argmin}_{l} \left| \alpha^l - s_{mi} \right|, \quad l \in \{0, 1, ..., N-1\} . \tag{2}$$

The multiplexer determines the routing information at pixel p_i, by mapping each of the M reference scales to the corresponding pyramid level l_{mi}. We illustrate the recovered l_{mi} in Fig. 2 by color coding the computed pyramid levels at three reference metric scales. Note that in case when $s_{mi} < 1$ we simply always choose the first pyramid level ($l = 0$). We have not experimented with upsampled levels of the pyramid mostly because of memory limitations. The output of the multiplexer is a scale-invariant image representation which is stored in M feature tensors of the dimension $W/8 \times H/8 \times (512 + 256)$.

Fig. 2. Visualization of the scale selection switches. From left to right: original image, switches for the three reference metric scales of 1 m, 4 m and 7 m.

3.4   Back-End Classifier

The scale-invariant feature tensors are concatenated and passed on to the classification subnetwork which consists of one 7×7 and two 1×1 convolution+ReLU layers. The former two layers have 1024 maps and batch normalization before non-linearities. The last 1×1 convolutional layer is configured in a way that the number of feature maps corresponds to the number of classes. The resulting class scores are passed to the pixel-wise softmax layer to obtain the distribution across classes for each pixel.

4   Experiments

We evaluate our method on two different semantic segmentation datasets containing outdoor traffic scenes: Cityscapes [6] and KITTI [12]. The Cityscapes dataset [6] has 19 classes recorded in 50 cities during several months. The dataset features good and medium weather conditions, large number of dynamic objects, varying scene layout and varying background. It consists of 5000 images with fine annotations and 20000 images with coarse annotations (we use only the fine annotations). The resolution of the images is 2048×1024. The dataset includes the stereo views which we use to reconstruct the depth.

The KITTI dataset [12] provides a large collection of 1241×376 traffic videos with LIDAR reconstruction groundtruth. Unfortunately, there are no official semantic segmentation annotations for this dataset. However, a collection of 150 images annotated with 11 object classes has been published [26]. We expand that work by annotating the same 11 classes in another 299 images from the same dataset, as well as by fixing some inconsistent annotations in the original dataset. The combined dataset with 399 training and 46 test images is freely available for academic research[1].

We train our networks using Adam SGD [17] and batch normalization [14] without learnable parameters. Due to memory limitations we only have one image in a batch. The input images are zero-centered and normalized. We initialize the learning rate to 10^{-5}, decrease it to $0.5 \cdot 10^{-5}$ after 2nd epoch and again to 10^{-6} after 10th epoch. Before each epoch, the training set is shuffled to eliminate the bias. The first 13 convolutional layers are initialized from VGG-D [29] pretrained on ImageNet and fine tuned during training. All other layers are randomly initialized. In all experiments we train our networks for 15 epochs on Cityscapes dataset and 30 epochs on KITTI dataset. We use the softmax cross-entropy loss which is summed up over all the pixels in a batch. In both datasets the frequency of pixel labels is highly unevenly distributed. We therefore perform class balancing by weighting each pixel loss with the true class weight factor w_c. This factor can be determined from class frequencies in the training set as follows: $w_c = \min(10^3, p(c)^{-1})$, where $p(c)$ is the frequency of pixels from the class c in the batch. In all experiments the three reference metric scales were set to equidistant values $W_R = \{1, 4, 7\}$ which were not cross-validated but had a good coverage over the input pixels (cf. Fig. 2). A Torch implementation of this procedure is freely available for academic research[2].

In order to alleviate the downsampling effects and improve consistency, we postprocess the semantic map with the fully-connected CRF [18]. The negative logarithms of probability distributions across classes are used as unary potentials, while the pairwise potentials are based on a linear combination of two Gaussian kernels [18]. We fix the number of mean field iterations to 10. The smoothness kernel parameters are fixed at $w^{(2)} = 3, \theta_\gamma = 3$, while a coarse grid

---

[1] http://multiclod.zemris.fer.hr/kitti_semseg_unizg.shtml.
[2] https://github.com/ivankreso/scale-invariant-cnn.

Table 1. Individual class results on the Cityscapes validation and test sets (IoU scores). Last row represents a fraction by which each class is represented in the training set.

method	road	sidewalk	building	wall	fence	pole	traffic light	traffic sign	vegetation	terrain	sky	person	rider	car	truck	bus	train	motorcycle	bicycle	mean
Validation set																				
Single5	93.0	64.6	80.6	28.7	37.5	30.4	38.5	43.6	81.9	42.3	81.5	57.2	37.3	83.4	36.0	43.9	37.1	38.6	58.8	53.4
Single3+5	93.8	67.9	83.2	30.1	37.4	37.8	45.3	55.5	86.3	49.3	85.9	63.8	40.9	87.0	32.7	50.5	31.7	37.1	63.5	56.8
FixedScales	94.6	70.9	85.5	42.5	42.4	39.6	46.2	55.3	86.5	50.3	86.4	64.4	45.4	88.3	47.2	60.8	54.0	43.1	63.9	61.4
ScaleInvariant	95.1	72.4	86.6	45.3	47.3	42.0	50.6	56.3	87.2	52.7	86.1	69.8	51.1	89.0	55.3	70.8	54.0	46.8	64.1	64.4
Test set																				
ScaleInvariant	95.3	73.5	86.4	36.8	42.7	45.5	56.6	57.8	89.5	63.6	90.3	73.5	53.1	90.3	30.8	48.2	39.6	52.2	62.7	62.5
ScaleInvariant+CRF	96.3	76.8	88.8	40.0	45.4	50.1	63.3	69.6	90.6	67.1	92.2	77.6	55.9	90.1	39.2	51.3	44.4	54.4	66.1	66.3
% in train	33.5	6.3	24.0	0.7	1.0	1.4	0.2	0.6	16.9	1.2	4.0	1.4	0.2	7.6	0.3	0.3	0.3	0.1	0.5	

search on 200 Cityscapes images is performed to optimize $w^{(1)} \in \{5, 10\}, \theta_\alpha \in \{50, 60, 70, 80, 90\}, \theta_\beta \in \{3, 4, 5, 6, 7, 8, 9\}$.

The segmentation performance is measured by the intersection-over-union (IoU) score [10] and the pixel accuracy [22]. We first evaluate the performance of two single scale networks which are obtained by eliminating the scale multiplexer layer and applying our network to full resolution images (cf. Fig. 1). This network is referred to as Single3+5. Furthermore, we also have the Single5 network which is just Single3+5 without the representation from pool3. The label ScaleInvariant shall refer to the full architecture visualized in Fig. 1. The label FixedScales refers to the similar architecture with fixed multi-scale representation obtained by concatenating the pyramid levels 0, 3 and 7.

First, we show results on the Cityscapes dataset. We downsample original images and train on smaller resolution (1504 × 672) due to memory limitations. Table 1 shows the results on the validation and test sets. We can observe that our scale invariant network improves over the single scale approach across all classes in Table 1. We can likewise notice that the concatenation from pool3 is important as Single3+5 produces better results then Single3 and that improvement is larger for smaller classes like poles, traffic signs and traffic lights. That supports our hypothesis that the representation from pool3 helps to better handle smaller objects. Furthermore, the scale invariant network achieves significant improvement over multi-scale network with fixed image scale levels (FixedScales). This agrees with our hypothesis that the proposed scale selection approach should help the network to learn a better representation. The table also shows results on the test set (our online submission is entitled Scale invariant CNN + CRF).

The last row in Table 1 represents a proportion by which each class is represented in the training set. We can notice that the greatest contribution of our approach is achieved for classes which represent smaller objects or objects that we see less often like buses, trains, trucks, walls etc. This effect is illustrated in Fig. 3 where we plot the improvement of the IoU metric with respect to the training set proportion for each class. Likewise we achieve improvement in pixel accuracy from 90.1 % (Single3+5) to 91.9 % (ScaleInvariant).

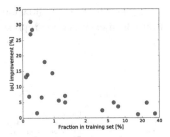

Fig. 3. Improvement of the IoU metric between Single3+5 and ScaleInvariant architecture with respect to the proportion inside training set for each class.

Figure 4 shows examples where the scale-invariant network produces better results. The improvement for big objects is clearly substantial. We often observe that the scale-invariant network can differentiate between road and sidewalk and person and rider, especially when they assume a rare appearance as in the last row with cobbled road which is easily mistaken for sidewalk.

Table 2 shows results on the KITTI test set. We notice a significant improvement in mean IoU class metric, which is, however, smaller than on Cityscapes. The main reason is that KITTI has much less smaller classes (only pole, sign and cyclist). Furthermore, it is a much smaller dataset which explains why the

Fig. 4. Examples where scale invariance helps the most. From left to right: input, groundtruth, baseline segmentation (Single3+5), scale invariant segmentation.

Table 2. Individual class results on the KITTI test set (IoU scores).

Method	Sky	Building	Road	Sidewalk	Fence	Vegetation	Pole	Car	Sign	Pedestrian	Cyclist	Mean
Single3+5	82.1	82.1	89.5	71.8	37.1	**80.7**	27.4	79.7	32.6	41.9	**14.3**	58.1
ScaleInvariant	**84.1**	**83.9**	**91.4**	**73.1**	**43.2**	79.2	**33.6**	**82.0**	**44.7**	**57.3**	12.8	**62.3**

performance is so low on classes like cyclist and pole. Here we again report an improvement in pixel accuracy from 87.63 (Single3+5) to 88.57 (ScaleInvariant).

5   Conclusion

We have presented a novel technique for improving semantic segmentation performance. We use the reconstructed depth as a guide to produce a scale-invariant representation in which the appearance is decoupled from the scale. This precludes the necessity to recognize objects at all possible scales and allows for an efficient use of the classifier capacity and the training data. This trait is especially important for navigation datasets which contain objects at a great variety of scales and do not exhibit the photographer bias.

We have integrated the proposed technique into an end-to-end trainable fully convolutional architecture which extracts features by a multi-scale skip network. The extracted features are fed to the novel multiplexing layer which carries out dense scale selection at the pixel level and produces a scale-invariant representation which is scored by the back-end classification network.

We have performed experiments on the novel Cityscapes dataset. Our results are very close to the state-of-the-art, despite the fact that we have trained our network on reduced resolution. We also report experiments on the KITTI dataset where we have densely annotated 299 new images, improved 146 already available annotations and release the union of the two datasets to the community. The proposed scale selection approach has consistently contributed substantial increases in segmentation performance. The results show that deep neural networks are extremely powerful classification models, however, they are still unable to learn geometric transformation better than humans.

Acknowledgement. This work has been fully supported by Croatian Science Foundation under the project I-2433-2014. The Titan X used for this research was donated by the NVIDIA Corporation.

References

1. Arnab, A., Jayasumana, S., Zheng, S., Torr, P.H.S.: Higher order potentials in end-to-end trainable conditional random fields. CoRR abs/1511.08119 (2015)
2. Banica, D., Sminchisescu, C.: Second-order constrained parametric proposals and sequential search-based structured prediction for semantic segmentation in RGB-D images. In: IEEE Conference on Computer Vision and Pattern Recognition, CVPR 2015, Boston, MA, USA, pp. 3517–3526, 7–12 June 2015
3. Chen, L., Papandreou, G., Kokkinos, I., Murphy, K., Yuille, A.L.: Semantic image segmentation with deep convolutional nets and fully connected crfs. In: International Conference on Learning Representations, ICLR 2015, San Diego, California (2014)
4. Chen, L., Yang, Y., Wang, J., Xu, W., Yuille, A.L.: Attention to scale: scale-aware semantic image segmentation. In: IEEE Conference on Computer Vision and Pattern Recognition, CVPR, Las Vegas, Nevada (2016) (to appear)
5. Chen, X., Kundu, K., Zhu, Y., Berneshawi, A., Ma, H., Fidler, S., Urtasun, R.: 3d object proposals for accurate object class detection. In: NIPS (2015)
6. Cordts, M., Omran, M., Ramos, S., Scharwächter, T., Enzweiler, M., Benenson, R., Franke, U., Roth, S., Schiele, B.: The cityscapes dataset. In: CVPR Workshop on the Future of Datasets in Vision (2015)
7. Divvala, S.K., Hoiem, D., Hays, J., Efros, A.A., Hebert, M.: An empirical study of context in object detection. In: 2009 IEEE Computer Society Conference on Computer Vision and Pattern Recognition (CVPR 2009), Miami, Florida, USA, pp. 1271–1278, 20–25 June 2009
8. Eigen, D., Fergus, R.: Predicting depth, surface normals and semantic labels with a common multi-scale convolutional architecture. In: 2015 IEEE International Conference on Computer Vision, ICCV 2015, Santiago, Chile, pp. 2650–2658, 7–13 December 2015
9. Everingham, M., Eslami, S.M.A., Gool, L.V., Williams, C.K.I., Winn, J.M., Zisserman, A.: The pascal visual object classes challenge: a retrospective. Int. J. Comput. Vis. 111(1), 98–136 (2015)
10. Everingham, M., Gool, L., Williams, C.K., Winn, J., Zisserman, A.: The pascal visual object classes (voc) challenge. Int. J. Comput, Vis. 88(2), 303–338 (2010)
11. Farabet, C., Couprie, C., Najman, L., LeCun, Y.: Learning hierarchical features for scene labeling. IEEE Trans. Pattern Anal. Mach. Intell. 35(8), 1915–1929 (2013)
12. Geiger, A., Lenz, P., Stiller, C., Urtasun, R.: Vision meets robotics: the kitti dataset. Int. J. Robot. Res. (IJRR) (2013)
13. Hirschmüller, H.: Stereo vision in structured environments by consistent semi-global matching. In: 2006 IEEE Computer Society Conference on Computer Vision and Pattern Recognition (CVPR 2006), New York, NY, USA, pp. 2386–2393, 17–22 June 2006
14. Ioffe, S., Szegedy, C.: Batch normalization: Accelerating deep network training by reducing internal covariate shift. In: Proceedings of the International Conference on Machine Learning, ICML 2015, Lille, France, pp. 448–456, 6–11 July 2015
15. Jia, Y., Shelhamer, E., Donahue, J., Karayev, S., Long, J., Girshick, R.B., Guadarrama, S., Darrell, T.: Caffe: Convolutional architecture for fast feature embedding. In: Proceedings of the ACM International Conference on Multimedia, MM 2014, Orlando, FL, USA, 03–07 November 2014, pp. 675–678 (2014)
16. Kendall, A., Badrinarayanan, V., Cipolla, R.: Bayesian segnet: model uncertainty in deep convolutional encoder-decoder architectures for scene understanding. CoRR abs/1511.02680 (2015)

17. Kingma, D.P., Ba, J.: Adam: a method for stochastic optimization. CoRR abs/ 1412.6980 (2014)
18. Krähenbühl, P., Koltun, V.: Efficient inference in fully connected crfs with gaussian edge potentials. In: Advances in Neural Information Processing Systems 24: 25th Annual Conference on Neural Information Processing Systems 2011, Proceedings of a meeting held 12–14, Granada, Spain, pp. 109–117, December 2011
19. Krizhevsky, A., Sutskever, I., Hinton, G.E.: Imagenet classification with deep convolutional neural networks. In: Annual Conference on Neural Information Processing Systems, Lake Tahoe, Nevada, United States, pp. 1106–1114 (2012)
20. Ladicky, L., Shi, J., Pollefeys, M.: Pulling things out of perspective. In: 2014 IEEE Conference on Computer Vision and Pattern Recognition, CVPR 2014, Columbus, OH, USA, 23–28 June 2014, pp. 89–96 (2014)
21. Lin, G., Shen, C., van dan Hengel, A., Reid, I.: Efficient piecewise training of deep structured models for semantic segmentation. In: IEEE Conference on Computer Vision and Pattern Recognition, CVPR, Las Vegas, Nevada (2016) (to appear)
22. Long, J., Shelhamer, E., Darrell, T.: Fully convolutional networks for semantic segmentation. In: IEEE Conference on Computer Vision and Pattern Recognition, CVPR 2015, Boston, MA, USA, 7–12 June 2015, pp. 3431–3440 (2015)
23. Martinovic, A., Knopp, J., Riemenschneider, H., Gool, L.V.: 3d all the way: semantic segmentation of urban scenes from start to end in 3d. In: IEEE Conference on Computer Vision and Pattern Recognition, CVPR 2015, Boston, MA, USA, 7–12 June 2015
24. Mostajabi, M., Yadollahpour, P., Shakhnarovich, G.: Feedforward semantic segmentation with zoom-out features. In: IEEE Conference on Computer Vision and Pattern Recognition, CVPR 2015, Boston, MA, USA, 7–12 June 2015, pp. 3376–3385 (2015)
25. Noh, H., Hong, S., Han, B.: Learning deconvolution network for semantic segmentation. In: 2015 IEEE International Conference on Computer Vision, ICCV 2015, Santiago, Chile, 7–13 December 2015, pp. 1520–1528 (2015)
26. Ros, G., Ramos, S., Granados, M., Bakhtiary, A., Vázquez, D., López, A.M.: Vision-based offline-online perception paradigm for autonomous driving. In: 2015 IEEE Winter Conference on Applications of Computer Vision, WACV 2014, Waikoloa, HI, USA, 5–9 January 2015, pp. 231–238 (2015)
27. Sermanet, P., Eigen, D., Zhang, X., Mathieu, M., Fergus, R., LeCun, Y.: Overfeat: integrated recognition, localization and detection using convolutional networks. In: International Conference on Learning Representations, ICLR 2014, Banff, Canada, pp. 1–16 (2014)
28. Shotton, J., Winn, J.M., Rother, C., Criminisi, A.: Textonboost for image understanding: multi-class object recognition and segmentation by jointly modeling texture, layout, and context. Int. J. Comput. Vis. $81(1)$, 2–23 (2009)
29. Simonyan, K., Zisserman, A.: Very deep convolutional networks for large-scale image recognition. In: International Conference on Learning Representations, ICLR 2015, San Diego, California, pp. 1–16 (2014)
30. Viola, P.A., Jones, M.J.: Robust real-time face detection. Int. J. Comput. Vis. $57(2)$, 137–154 (2004)
31. Yu, F., Koltun, V.: Multi-scale context aggregation by dilated convolutions. In: International Conference on Learning Representations, ICLR 2016, San Juan, Puerto Rico, pp. 1–9 (2016)
32. Zbontar, J., LeCun, Y.: Stereo matching by training a convolutional neural network to compare image patches. CoRR abs/1510.05970 (2015)

Optimization

Convexification of Learning from Constraints

Iaroslav Shcherbatyi[1,2] and Bjoern Andres[1(✉)]

[1] Max Planck Institute for Informatics, Saarbrücken, Germany
andres@mpi-inf.mpg.de
[2] Saarland University, Saarbrücken, Germany

Abstract. Regularized empirical risk minimization with constrained labels (in contrast to fixed labels) is a remarkably general abstraction of learning. For common loss and regularization functions, this optimization problem assumes the form of a mixed integer program (MIP) whose objective function is non-convex. In this form, the problem is resistant to standard optimization techniques. We construct MIPs with the same solutions whose objective functions are convex. Specifically, we characterize the tightest convex extension of the objective function, given by the Legendre-Fenchel biconjugate. Computing values of this tightest convex extension is NP-hard. However, by applying our characterization to every function in an additive decomposition of the objective function, we obtain a class of looser convex extensions that can be computed efficiently. For some decompositions, common loss and regularization functions, we derive a closed form.

1 Introduction

We study an optimization problem: Given a finite set $S \neq \emptyset$ whose elements are to be labeled as 0 or 1, a non-empty set $Y \subseteq \{0,1\}^S$ of *feasible labelings*, $x : S \to \mathbb{R}^m$ with $m \in \mathbb{N}$, called a *feature matrix*, $l : \mathbb{R} \times [0,1] \to \mathbb{R}_0^+$ with $l(\cdot, 0)$ convex, $l(\cdot, 1)$ convex, $l(r, 1) \to 0$ as $r \to \infty$ and $l(-r, 0) \to 0$ as $r \to \infty$, called a *loss function*, $\Theta \subseteq \mathbb{R}^m$ convex, called the set of *feasible parameters*, $\omega : \Theta \to \mathbb{R}_0^+$ convex, called a *regularization function*, and $C \in \mathbb{R}_0^+$, called a *regularization constant*, we consider the optimization problem

$$\inf_{(\theta,y) \in \Theta \times Y} \varphi(\theta, y) \tag{1}$$

with

$$\varphi(\theta, y) := \omega(\theta) + \frac{C}{|S|} \sum_{s \in S} l_s(\theta, y_s) \tag{2}$$

$$l_s(\theta, y_s) := l(\langle x_s, \theta \rangle, y_s) . \tag{3}$$

A minimizer $(\hat{\theta}, \hat{y})$, if it exists, defines a *classifier* $c : \mathbb{R}^m \to \{0,1\} : x \mapsto \frac{1}{2}(1 + \mathrm{sgn}\,\langle \hat{\theta}, x \rangle)$ and a feasible labeling $\hat{y} \in Y$. The optimization problem (1)

© Springer International Publishing AG 2016
B. Rosenhahn and B. Andres (Eds.): GCPR 2016, LNCS 9796, pp. 79–90, 2016.
DOI: 10.1007/978-3-319-45886-1_7

is a remarkably general abstraction of learning. On the one hand, it generalizes supervised, semi-supervised and unsupervised learning:

- If the labeling y is fixed by $|Y| = 1$ to precisely one feasible labeling, (1) specializes to *regularized empirical risk minimization with fixed labels* and is called *supervised*.
- If Y fixes the label of at least one but not all elements of S, (1) is called *semi-supervised*.
- If Y constrains the joint labelings of S without fixing the label of any single element of S, (1) is called *unsupervised*. For example, consider $Y = \{y \in \{0,1\}^S \mid \sum_{s \in S} y_s = \lfloor |S|/2 \rfloor\}$.

On the other hand, the optimization problem (1) generalizes classification, clustering and ranking:

- If $S = A \times B$ and Y is the set of characteristic functions of *maps* from A to B, (1) is an abstraction of *multi-label classification*, as discussed, for instance, in [9–12, 20, 21, 39].
- If $S = A \times A$ and Y is the set of characteristic functions of *equivalence relations* on A, (1) is an abstraction of *clustering*, as discussed in [15, 38]. For fixed parameters θ, it specializes to the NP-hard minimum cost clique partition problem [13, 16] that is also known as correlation clustering [3, 14].
- If $S = A \times A$ and Y is the set of characteristic functions of *linear orders* on A, (1) is an abstraction of *ranking*. For fixed parameters θ, it specializes to the NP-hard linear ordering problem [28].

The set Y of feasible labelings, a subset of the vertices of the unit hypercube $[0,1]^S$, is a non-convex subset of $\mathbb{R}^S$ iff $2 \le |Y|$. Typically, one considers a relaxation $y \in P$ of the constraint $y \in Y$ with P a convex polytope such that $\operatorname{conv} Y \subseteq P \subseteq [0,1]^S$ and $P \cap \{0,1\}^S = Y$. In practice, one considers an intersection of half-spaces, i.e., $n \in \mathbb{N}$, $A \in \mathbb{R}^{n \times S}$ and $b \in \mathbb{R}^n$ such that $P = \{y \in \mathbb{R}^S \mid Ay \le b\}$. Also typically, the set $\Theta \subseteq \mathbb{R}^m$ of feasible parameters is a convex polyhedron and is described also as an intersection of half-spaces, i.e., by $n' \in \mathbb{N}$, $A' \subseteq \mathbb{R}^{n' \times m}$ and $b' \in \mathbb{R}^{n'}$ such that $\Theta = \{\theta \in \mathbb{R}^m \mid A'\theta \le b'\}$. Hence, the optimization problem (1) assumes the form of a mixed integer program (MIP):

$$\inf_{(\theta, y) \in \mathbb{R}^m \times [0,1]^S} \varphi(\theta, y) \tag{4}$$

$$\text{subject to} \quad A'\theta \le b' \tag{5}$$

$$Ay \le b \tag{6}$$

$$y \in \{0,1\}^S \tag{7}$$

For *convex* loss functions l_s such as the squared difference loss (Table 1), the objective function φ is convex on the domain $\mathbb{R}^m \times [0,1]^S$. Thus, the continuous relaxation (4)–(6) of the problem (4)–(7) is a convex problem. Its solutions $(\hat{\theta}', \hat{y}')$, although possibly fractional in the coordinates of y', can inform a search

Table 1. Loss functions

Loss	Form of $l_s(\theta, y_s)$	Function $l_s : \mathbb{R}^m \times [0,1] \to \mathbb{R}_0^+$
Squared difference	$(\langle \theta, x_s \rangle - y_s)^2$	convex
Logistic	$\log(1 + \exp(-(2y_s - 1)\langle \theta, x_s \rangle))$	non-convex
Hinge	$\max\{0, 1 - (2y_s - 1)\langle \theta, x_s \rangle\}$	non-convex
Squared Hinge	$\max\{0, 1 - (2y_s - 1)\langle \theta, x_s \rangle\}^2$	non-convex

for feasible solutions of (4)–(7) with certificates [6,10,11]. See also [7] for a recent survey of convex mixed-integer non-linear programming. For *non-convex* loss functions l_s such as the logistic loss, the Hinge loss and the squared Hinge loss (Table 1), φ is non-convex on the domain $\mathbb{R}^m \times [0,1]^S$. In this case, (4)–(7) is resistant to standard optimization techniques. See [4,25,36] for an overview of non-convex mixed-integer non-linear programming.

1.1   Contribution

We construct, for the MIP (4)–(7) whose objective function is non-convex, MIPs with the same solutions whose objective functions are convex. Our approach is illustrated in Fig. 1 and is summarized below. In Sect. 3, we consider the restriction ϕ of φ to the feasible set $\Theta \times Y$ and characterize the tightest convex extension ϕ^{**} of ϕ to $\Theta \times \text{conv } Y$. This tightest convex extension ϕ^{**} is mostly of theoretical interest as computing its values is NP-hard. In Sect. 4, we consider a decomposition of the function ϕ into a sum of functions. By applying our characterization of tightest convex extensions to every function in this sum, we construct a convex extension ϕ' of ϕ to $\Theta \times [0,1]^S$ which is not generally tight but whose values can be computed efficiently. For common loss and regularization functions, we derive a closed form. For every convex extension ϕ' we construct, including ϕ^{**}, the MIP (9)–(11) written below has the same solutions as (4)–(7). Like (4)–(7),

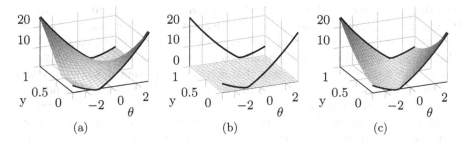

(a)   (b)   (c)

Fig. 1. Depicted above in (a) is the non-convex objective function φ of the optimization problem (1) for $Y = \{0,1\}$, $\Theta = \mathbb{R}$, the Hinge loss (Table 1) and $\omega(\cdot) = \|\cdot\|_2^2$. Its restriction ϕ to the feasible set $\Theta \times \{0,1\}$ is depicted in black. As the goal is to minimize φ over the feasible set, one can replace the values of φ for $y \in (0,1)$ without affecting the solution, for instance, by zero, as depicted in (b). In this paper, we characterize the tightest convex extension of ϕ to $\Theta \times \text{conv } Y$, which is depicted in (c).

it is NP-hard, due to the integrality constraint (11). Unlike (4)–(7), its objective function and polyhedral relaxation (8)–(10) are convex. Thus, unlike (4)–(7), it is accessible to a wide range of standard optimization techniques.

$$\inf_{(\theta,y)\in\mathbb{R}^m\times\mathbb{R}^S} \phi'(\theta,y) \tag{8}$$

$$\text{subject to} \quad A'\theta \leq b' \tag{9}$$

$$Ay \leq b \tag{10}$$

$$y \in \{0,1\}^S \tag{11}$$

2   Related Work

Convex Extensions. For large classes of univariate and bivariate functions, tightest convex extensions are characterized in [27,34]. Convex envelopes of multivariate functions that are convex in all but one variable are characterized in [19]. For functions of the form $f(x,y) = g(x)h(y)$ and with g and h having additional properties, e.g., g being component-wise concave and submodular, and h being univariate convex, tightest convex extensions are characterized in [23,24]. For functions $f : A \times B \to \mathbb{R}$ with $A, B \subseteq \mathbb{R}^n$ and $f(a, \cdot)$ being either convex or concave and $f(\cdot, b)$ being either convex or concave for any $a \in A$ and $b \in B$, tightest convex extensions are characterized in [2]. Tightest convex extensions of pseudo-Boolean functions $f : \{0,1\}^n \to \mathbb{R}$ are known as convex closures [1]. Convex closures of submodular functions are Lovász extensions. The characterization of tightest convex extensions of functions $f : \Theta \times Y \to \mathbb{R}$ with $f(\cdot, y)$ convex for all $y \in Y$ that we establish is consistent with results of [19] for functions $f : \mathbb{R}^n \times \{0,1\} \to \mathbb{R}$. It extends some results of [19] to non-differentiable $f(\cdot, 0)$ and $f(\cdot, 1)$. The local envelope relaxations we construct in Sect. 4 resonate with local envelope relaxations of the Mumford-Shah functional and the spatially continuous Potts model studied in a series of papers by Pock et al. [8,29–31] and Strekalovskiy et al. [33].

Regularized Empirical Risk Minimization with Constrained Labels. Regularized empirical risk minimization with constrained labels has been studied intensively in the special case of semi-supervised learning for 01-classification. Algorithms that find feasible solutions efficiently are defined in [9,10,12,20,21, 32]. A branch-and-bound algorithm that solves the problem to optimality was suggested already by Vapnik [37] and has been implemented and applied to data by Chapelle, Sindhwani and Keerthi [10,11], with the result that optimal solutions can generalize better than feasible solutions found by approximate algorithms. An approach to the problem by convex optimization, specifically, by a semi-definite relaxation of the dual problem, is proposed in [5]. Similar relaxations are studied in the context of semi-supervised learning for multi-label classification [18,39], correlation clustering [38,40] and latent variable estimation [17]. For maximum margin clustering, a convex relaxation tighter than the SDP relaxation is constructed in [26]. For multi-label classification with a softmax loss function, a tight SDP relaxation is proposed in [22].

3   Tightest Convex Extensions

In this section, we consider the restriction ϕ of φ to the feasible set $\Theta \times Y$, i.e., the function

$$\phi: \quad \Theta \times Y \to \mathbb{R}_0^+: \quad (\theta, y) \mapsto \varphi(\theta, y) . \tag{12}$$

We characterize the tightest convex extension ϕ^{**} of ϕ to $\Theta \times \operatorname{conv} Y$ in Theorem 1.

Definition 1. *[35] For any $n \in \mathbb{N}$, any $A \subseteq \mathbb{R}^n$ and any $\phi: A \to \mathbb{R}$, a function $\phi': \operatorname{conv} A \to \mathbb{R}$ is called a* convex extension *of ϕ iff ϕ' is convex and $\forall a \in A: \phi'(a) = \phi(a)$. Moreover, a function $\phi^{**}: \operatorname{conv} A \to \mathbb{R}$ is called the* tightest convex extension *of ϕ iff ϕ^{**} is a convex extension of ϕ and, for every convex extension ϕ' of ϕ and for all $a \in \operatorname{conv} A: \phi'(a) \le \phi^{**}(a)$.*

Lemma 1. *A (tightest) convex extension ϕ^{**} of ϕ exists.*

Theorem 1. *For every finite $S \ne \emptyset$, every $Y \subseteq \{0, 1\}^S$ with $|Y| > |S|$, every $m \in \mathbb{N}$, every convex $\Theta \subseteq \mathbb{R}^m$ and every $\phi: \Theta \times Y \to \mathbb{R}_0^+$ such that $\phi(\cdot, y)$ is convex for every $y \in Y$, the tightest convex extension $\phi^{**}: \Theta \times \operatorname{conv} Y \to \mathbb{R}_0^+$ of ϕ is such that for all $(\theta, y) \in \Theta \times \operatorname{conv} Y$:*

$$\phi^{**}(\theta, y) = \min_{Y' \in \mathcal{Y}(y)} \inf_{\theta': Y' \to \Theta} \left\{ \sum_{y' \in Y'} \lambda_{yY'}(y') \, \phi(\theta'(y'), y') \ \middle| \ \sum_{y' \in Y'} \lambda_{yY'}(y') \, \theta'(y') = \theta \right\} \tag{13}$$

where

$$\mathcal{Y}(y) := \left\{ Y' \in \binom{Y}{|S|+m+1} \ \middle| \ y \in \operatorname{conv} Y' \right\} \tag{14}$$

is the set of $(|S| + m + 1)$-elementary subsets Y' of Y having y in their convex hull, and, for every $y \in \operatorname{conv} Y$ and every $Y' \in \mathcal{Y}(y)$: $\lambda_{yY'}: Y' \to \mathbb{R}_0^+$ are the coefficients in the convex combination of y in Y', i.e.

$$\sum_{y' \in Y'} \lambda_{yY'}(y') \, y' = y \tag{15}$$

$$\sum_{y' \in Y'} \lambda_{yY'}(y') = 1 . \tag{16}$$

Remarks are in order:

- $|\mathcal{Y}(y)|$ can be strongly exponential in $|S|$. This is expected, given that the complexity of computing the value of a convex extension is NP-hard.
- Given a polynomial-time oracle for the outer minimization in (13), the tightest convex extension can be computed in polynomial time.
- Conceivable in special cases is a polynomial-time oracle for constraining $\mathcal{Y}(y)$ to a strict subset, without compromising optimality in (13).
- An upper bound on the tightest convex extension can be obtained by considering any subset of $\mathcal{Y}(y)$.

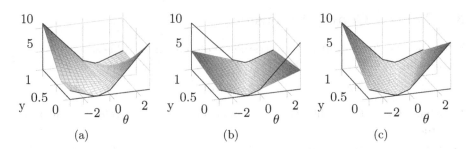

Fig. 2. Depicted above in (a) is the non-convex objective function φ of the optimization problem (1) for $Y = \{0, 1\}$, $\Theta = \mathbb{R}$, the Hinge loss (Table 1) and $\omega(\cdot) = \| \cdot \|_1$. Its restriction ϕ to $\Theta \times \{0, 1\}$ is depicted in black. Depicted in (b) is the tightest convex extension of ϕ to $\Theta \times [0, 1]$. Depicted in (c) is the tightest convex extension of ϕ to $[-b, b] \times [0, 1]$, for $b \in \mathbb{R}_0^+$. It can be seen that, for bounded θ, the tightest convex extension is continuous.

4   Efficient Convex Extensions

In this section, we characterize, for common loss and regularization functions, convex extensions ϕ' of ϕ that are not necessarily tight but can be computed efficiently in general. The construction is in two steps:

Firstly, we consider an additive decomposition of ϕ. Specifically, we consider a convex function $c : \Theta \to \mathbb{R}_0^+$ and, for every $s \in S$, a function $d_s : \Theta \times \{0, 1\} \to \mathbb{R}_0^+$ such that $d_s(\cdot, 0)$ and $d_s(\cdot, 1)$ are convex. These functions are chosen such that, for all $(\theta, y) \in \Theta \times Y$:

$$\phi(\theta, y) = c(\theta) + \frac{1}{|S|} \sum_{s \in S} d_s(\theta, y_s) \ . \tag{17}$$

One example is given by $c := \omega$ and, for every $s \in S$, $d_s := C l_s$. Another example is given by $c := 0$ and, for every $s \in S$, every $\theta \in \Theta$ and every $y_s \in \{0, 1\}$: $d_s(\theta, y_s) := \omega(\theta) + C l_s(\theta, y_s)$.

Secondly, we characterize, for each d_s, its tightest convex extension d_s^{**} : $\Theta \times [0, 1] \to \mathbb{R}$, by a specialization of Theorem 1 stated as Corollary 1. A convex extension ϕ' of ϕ to $\Theta \times [0, 1]^S$ is then given by

$$\phi' : \quad \Theta \times [0, 1]^S \to \mathbb{R}_0^+ : \quad (\theta, y) \mapsto c(\theta) + \frac{1}{|S|} \sum_{s \in S} d_s^{**}(\theta, y_s) \ . \tag{18}$$

Corollary 1. *For every* $d : \Theta \times \{0, 1\} \to \mathbb{R}_0^+$ *such that* $d_0(\cdot) := d(\cdot, 0)$ *and* $d_1(\cdot) := d(\cdot, 1)$ *are convex, the tightest convex extension* $d^{**} : \Theta \times [0, 1] \to \mathbb{R}_0^+$ *of* d *is such that for all* $(\theta, y) \in \Theta \times Y$:

$$d^{**}(\theta, y) = \begin{cases} d(\theta, y) & \text{if } y \in \{0, 1\} \\ \Psi(\theta, y) & \text{if } y \in (0, 1) \end{cases} \tag{19}$$

with

$$\Psi(\theta, y) = \inf_{\theta^0, \theta^1 \in \Theta} \left\{ (1-y) d_0(\theta^0) + y d_1(\theta^1) \mid (1-y)\theta^0 + y\theta^1 = \theta \right\} . \quad (20)$$

The solutions of the optimization problem (20) are characterized in Lemma 2. Subgradients are given in Lemma 3.

Lemma 2. *For every solution* $(\hat{\theta}^0, \hat{\theta}^1) \in \Theta^2$ *of* (20)*, there exists a* $G \neq \emptyset$ *such that, for* $\xi_{\theta,y} : \Theta \to \Theta : t \mapsto (\theta - (1-y)t)/y$:

$$(\delta d_0)(\hat{\theta}^0) \cap (\delta d_1)(\xi_{\theta,y}(\hat{\theta}^0)) = G \quad (21)$$

$$(\delta d_0)(\xi_{\theta,1-y}(\hat{\theta}^1)) \cap (\delta d_1)(\hat{\theta}^1) = G . \quad (22)$$

Lemma 3. *If a solution* $(\hat{\theta}^0, \hat{\theta}^1) \in \Theta^2$ *of* (20) *exists, then* $\binom{v}{w} \in (\delta d^{**})(\theta, y)$ *iff* $v \in G$ *with* G *defined equivalently in* (21) *and* (22) *and* $w = v^T \hat{\theta}^0 - v^T \hat{\theta}^1 + d_1(\hat{\theta}^1) - d_0(\hat{\theta}^0)$. *Otherwise,* $y \in \{0, 1\}$ *and:*

$$y = 0 \quad \Rightarrow \quad \forall v \in (\delta d(\cdot, 0))(\theta) : \binom{v}{\infty} \in (\delta d^{**})(\theta, y) \quad (23)$$

$$y = 1 \quad \Rightarrow \quad \forall v \in (\delta d(\cdot, 1))(\theta) : \binom{v}{-\infty} \in (\delta d^{**})(\theta, y) . \quad (24)$$

We proceed as follows: In Sect. 4.1, we consider two decompositions of the class (17) for which the tightest convex extension of any d_s is easy to characterize but the resulting convex extension of ϕ is rather loose. In Sects. 4.2 and 4.3, we consider decompositions of the class (17) with $c = 0$. These yield the tightest convex extension of ϕ of any decomposition of the class (17). For any combination of the logistic loss, the Hinge loss and the squadred Hinge loss (Table 1) with either L1 regularization $\omega(\cdot) = \| \cdot \|_1$ or L2 regularization $\omega(\cdot) = \| \cdot \|_2^2$, we characterize the convex extension explicitly and, in some cases, in closed form. Examples of all combinations are depicted in Fig. 3.

4.1 Instructive Examples

The first convex extension we characterize is for the decomposition (17) with $c := \omega$ and $\forall s \in S : d_s := Cl_s$.

Corollary 2. *For any* $d : \Theta \times \{0, 1\} \to \mathbb{R}_0^+$ *such that* $d_0(\cdot) := d(\cdot, 0)$ *and* $d_1(\cdot) := d(\cdot, 1)$ *are convex and for which* $d_0(-r) \to 0$ *and* $d_1(r) \to 0$ *as* $r \to \infty$, *the convex extension* $d^{**} : \Theta \times [0, 1] \to \mathbb{R}$ *of* d *has the form*

$$d'(\theta, y) = \begin{cases} d(\theta, y) & \text{if } y \in \{0, 1\} \\ 0 & \text{if } y \in (0, 1) \end{cases} . \quad (25)$$

The second convex extension we characterize is for the logistic loss $l_s(\theta, y) = -\langle x, \theta \rangle y + \log(1 + e^{\langle x, \theta \rangle})$, for $\omega(\cdot) = \| \cdot \|_2^2$ and for the decomposition (17) such that, for every $s \in S$, $d_s(\theta, y) := \|\theta\|_2^2 - C \langle x, \theta \rangle y$.

Corollary 3. *The tightest convex extension* $d^{**} : \Theta \times [0, 1] \to \mathbb{R}_0^+$ *of* $d : \Theta \times \{0, 1\} \to \mathbb{R}_0^+$ *with* $d(\theta, y) = \|\theta\|_2^2 - C \langle x, \theta \rangle y$ *has the form* $d^{**}(\theta, y) = \|\theta - y\frac{C}{2}x\|_2^2 - y\|\frac{C}{2}x\|_2^2$.

4.2 L2 Regularization

We now consider $\omega(\cdot) = \frac{1}{2}\|\cdot\|_2^2$ and decompositions (17) such that, for every $s \in S$: $d_s(\theta, y) = \omega(\theta) + C\, l_s(\theta, y)$.

Corollary 4. *The tightest convex extension* $d^{**} : \Theta \times [0,1] \to \mathbb{R}_0^+$ *of* $d : \Theta \times \{0,1\} \to \mathbb{R}_0^+$ *with* $d(\theta, y) = \frac{1}{2}\|\theta\|_2^2 + Cl(\langle x, \theta\rangle, y)$ *is given by* (19) *and* (20). *Moreover, the solution of* (20) *is given by* $\hat{\theta}^0 = \theta - yCxz$ *with*

$$z \in (\delta l_0)(x^T(\theta - yCxz)) - (\delta l_1)(x^T(\theta + (1-y)Cxz)) \subseteq \mathbb{R} . \qquad (26)$$

Although this characterization is not a closed form, values of d^{**} can be computed efficiently using the bisection method. For specific loss functions, closed forms are derived below.

Corollary 5. *The tightest convex extension* $d^{**} : \Theta \times [0,1] \to \mathbb{R}_0^+$ *of* $d : \Theta \times \{0,1\} \to \mathbb{R}_0^+$ *with* $d(\theta, y) = \frac{1}{2}\|\theta\|_2^2 + Cl(\langle x, \theta\rangle, y)$ *and* $l : \mathbb{R} \times \{0,1\} \to \mathbb{R}_0^+$ *of the form*

$$l(r, y) = (C_0(1-y) + C_1 y)\max\{0, 1 - (2y-1)r\} \qquad (27)$$

where $C_0, C_1 \in \mathbb{R}_+$ *define weights on the two values of* y, *is given by Corollary 4. Moreover, every* z *satisfying* (26) *holds*

$$z \in \left\{0,\ C_0,\ C_1,\ C_0 + C_1,\ \frac{1 + x^T\theta}{yCx^Tx},\ \frac{1 - x^T\theta}{(1-y)Cx^Tx}\right\} . \qquad (28)$$

Corollary 6. *The tightest convex extension* $d^{**} : \Theta \times [0,1] \to \mathbb{R}_0^+$ *of* $d : \Theta \times \{0,1\} \to \mathbb{R}_0^+$ *with* $d(\theta, y) = \frac{1}{2}\|\theta\|_2^2 + Cl(\langle x, \theta\rangle, y)$ *and* $l : \mathbb{R} \times \{0,1\} \to \mathbb{R}_0^+$ *of the form*

$$l(r, y) = \frac{C_0(1-y) + C_1 y}{2}(\max\{0, 1 - (2y-1)r\})^2 \qquad (29)$$

where $C_0, C_1 \in \mathbb{R}_+$ *define weights on the two values of* y, *is given by Corollary 4. Moreover, every* z *satisfying* (26) *holds*

$$z \in \left\{0,\ \frac{C_0 + C_0 x^T\theta}{1 + C_0 yCx^Tx},\ \frac{C_1 - C_1 x^T\theta}{1 + C_1(1-y)Cx^Tx},\ \frac{C_0 + C_1 + (C_0 - C_1)x^T\theta}{1 + (C_0 y + C_1(1-y))Cx^Tx}\right\} . \qquad (30)$$

4.3 L1 Regularization

We now consider $\omega(\cdot) = \|\cdot\|_1$ and decompositions (17) such that, for every $s \in S$: $d_s(\theta, y) = \omega(\theta) + C\, l_s(\theta, y)$. We focus on a special case where θ is bounded. This is necessary in order for the convex extension to be continuous; see Fig. 2.

Corollary 7. *For $b, t \in (\mathbb{R} \cup \{-\infty, \infty\})^m$ and $\Theta = \{\theta \in \mathbb{R}^m : b \leq \theta \leq t\}$, the tightest convex extension $d^{**} : \Theta \times [0, 1] \to \mathbb{R}_0^+$ of $d : \Theta \times \{0, 1\} \to \mathbb{R}_0^+$ with $d(\theta, y) = \|\theta\|_1 + Cl(\langle x, \theta \rangle, y)$ is given by (19) and (20). Moreover, the solution of (20) is given by*

$$
\hat{\theta}^0 = \begin{cases} \theta' & \text{if } \exists r \in a(x^T \theta') : \|rCx\|_\infty \leq 2 \\ \text{aux}(\theta', x, a, b, t) & \text{otherwise} \end{cases} \tag{31}
$$

with $a : \mathbb{R} \to 2^{\mathbb{R}} : p \mapsto (\delta l_0)(p) - (\delta l_1)((x^T \theta - (1 - y)p)/y)$ and

$$
\forall i \in \{1, \ldots, m\} : \quad \theta_i' = \begin{cases} \min\limits_{r \in [b_i', t_i']} |r| & \text{if } \theta_i > 0 \Leftrightarrow x_i > 0 \\ \min\limits_{r \in [b_i', t_i']} \left| \dfrac{\theta_i}{(1 - y)} - r \right| & \text{otherwise} \end{cases} . \tag{32}
$$

The function "aux" is defined in terms of Algorithm 1 in Appendix B of the supplement. At its core, this algorithms solves, for fixed $k \in [m]$ and fixed $V \in \Theta$, the equation (33) for the unknown $z \in \mathbb{R}$. For specific loss functions, closed forms are derived in Corollaries 8 and 9.

$$
\left| a \left(x^T V - z x_k \right) C x_k \right| = 2 \tag{33}
$$

Corollary 8. *The tightest convex extension $d^{**} : \Theta \times [0, 1] \to \mathbb{R}_0^+$ of $d : \Theta \times \{0, 1\} \to \mathbb{R}_0^+$ with $d(\theta, y) = \|\theta\|_1 + Cl(\langle x, \theta \rangle, y)$ and $l : \mathbb{R} \times \{0, 1\} \to \mathbb{R}_0^+$ of the form*

$$
l(r, y) = (C_0(1 - y) + C_1 y) \max\{0, 1 - (2y - 1)r\} \tag{34}
$$

where $C_0, C_1 \in \mathbb{R}_+$ define weights on the two values of y, is given by Corollary 7. Moreover, every solution $z \in \mathbb{R}$ of (33) holds

$$
z \in \left\{ \frac{1 + x^T V}{x_k^2}, \frac{y + x^T(\theta - (1 - y)V)}{(1 - y)x_k^2} \right\} . \tag{35}
$$

Corollary 9. *The tightest convex extension $d^{**} : \Theta \times [0, 1] \to \mathbb{R}_0^+$ of $d : \Theta \times \{0, 1\} \to \mathbb{R}_0^+$ with $d(\theta, y) = \|\theta\|_1 + Cl(\langle x, \theta \rangle, y)$ and $l : \mathbb{R} \times \{0, 1\} \to \mathbb{R}_0^+$ of the form*

$$
l(r, y) = \frac{C_0(1 - y) + C_1 y}{2} (\max\{0, 1 - (2y - 1)r\})^2 \tag{36}
$$

where $C_0, C_1 \in \mathbb{R}_+$ define weights on the two values of y, is given by Corollary 7. Moreover, every solution $z \in \mathbb{R}$ of (33) holds (37) with $v_0 := x^T V$ and $v_1 := -x^T \xi_{\theta, y}(V)$.

$$
z \in \left\{ \frac{1 + v_0 - 2(C|x_k|C_0)^{-1}}{x_k^2}, \frac{1 + v_1 - 2(C|x_k|C_1)^{-1}}{x_k^2}, \right.
$$
$$
\left. \frac{y(C_0(1 + v_0) + C_1(1 + v_1) - 2(C|x_k|)^{-1})}{(yC_0 + (1 - y)C_1)x_k^2} \right\} \tag{37}
$$

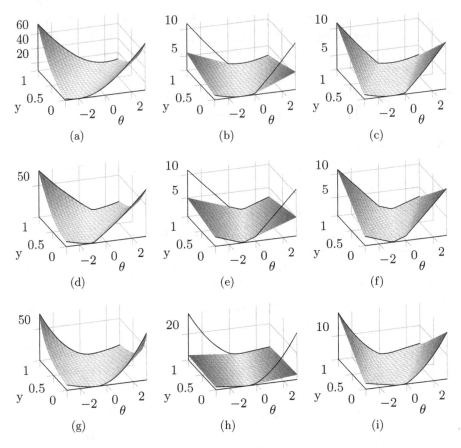

Fig. 3. Depicted above are tightest convex extensions of the logistic loss (first row), the Hinge loss (second row) and the squared Hinge loss (third row), in conjunction with L2 regularization (first column), L1 regularization (second column) and L1 regularization with θ constrained to $[-3.1, 3.1]$ (third column). Values for $y \in \{0, 1\}$ are depicted in black. Note that the convex extensions of L1-regularized loss functions for unbounded θ are discontinuous. Parameters for these examples are $x = 1$ and 3(a): $C = 16$, 3(b): $C = 5$, 3(c): $C = 5$, 3(d): $C = 16$, 3(e): $C = 5$, 3(f): $C = 5$, 3(g): $C = 4$, 3(h): $C = 4$. 3(i): $C = 4$.

5   Conclusion

We have characterized convex extensions, including the tightest convex extension, of functions $f : \Theta \times Y \to \mathbb{R}_0^+$ with $\Theta \subseteq \mathbb{R}^m$ convex, $Y \subseteq \{0, 1\}^n$ and $f(\cdot, y)$ convex for every $y \in \{0, 1\}^n$. This has allowed us to state regularized empirical risk minimization with constrained labels as a mixed integer program whose objective function is convex. Convex extensions that strike a practical balance between tightness and computational complexity are a topic of future work.

References

1. Bach, F.: Learning with submodular functions: a convex optimization perspective. Found. Trends Mach. Learn. **6**(2–3), 145–373 (2013)
2. Ballerstein, M.: Convex relaxations for mixed-integer nonlinear programs. Dissertation, Eidgenössische Technische Hochschule ETH Zürich, Nr. 21024 (2013)
3. Bansal, N., Blum, A., Chawla, S.: Correlation clustering. Mach. Learn. **56**(1–3), 89–113 (2004)
4. Belotti, P., Kirches, C., Leyffer, S., Linderoth, J., Luedtke, J., Mahajan, A.: Mixed-integer nonlinear optimization. Acta Numerica **22**, 1–131 (2013)
5. Bie, T.D., Cristianini, N.: Semi-supervised learning using semi-definite programming. In: Chapelle, O., Schölkopf, B., Zien, A. (eds.) Semi-Supervised Learning, pp. 119–135. MIT Press, Cambridge (2006)
6. Bojanowski, P., Bach, F., Laptev, I., Ponce, J., Schmid, C., Sivic, J.: Finding actors and actions in movies. In: ICCV (2013)
7. Bonami, P., Kilinç, M., Linderoth, J.: Algorithms and software for convex mixed integer nonlinear programs. In: Lee, J., Leyffer, S. (eds.) Mixed Integer Nonlinear Programming, pp. 1–39. Springer, New York (2012)
8. Chambolle, A., Cremers, D., Pock, T.: A convex approach to minimal partitions. SIAM J. Imag. Sci. **5**(4), 1113–1158 (2012)
9. Chapelle, O., Chi, M., Zien, A.: A continuation method for semi-supervised SVMs. In: ICML (2006)
10. Chapelle, O., Sindhwani, V., Keerthi, S.S.: Branch and bound for semi-supervised support vector machines. In: NIPS (2006)
11. Chapelle, O., Sindhwani, V., Keerthi, S.S.: Optimization techniques for semi-supervised support vector machines. J. Mach. Learn. Res. **9**, 203–233 (2008)
12. Chapelle, O., Zien, A.: Semi-supervised classification by low density separation. In: AISTATS (2005)
13. Chopra, S., Rao, M.R.: The partition problem. Math. Programm. **59**(1–3), 87–115 (1993)
14. Demaine, E.D., Emanuel, D., Fiat, A., Immorlica, N.: Correlation clustering in general weighted graphs. Theoret. Comput. Sci. **361**(2), 172–187 (2006)
15. Finley, T., Joachims, T.: Supervised clustering with support vector machines. In: ICML (2005)
16. Grötschel, M., Wakabayashi, Y.: A cutting plane algorithm for a clustering problem. Math. Programm. **45**(1), 59–96 (1989)
17. Guo, Y., Schuurmans, D.: Convex relaxations of latent variable training. In: NIPS (2008)
18. Guo, Y., Schuurmans, D.: Adaptive large margin training for multilabel classification. In: AAAI (2011)
19. Jach, M., Michaels, D., Weismantel, R.: The convex envelope of (n-1)-convex functions. SIAM J. Optim. **19**(3), 1451–1466 (2008)
20. Joachims, T.: Transductive inference for text classification using support vector machines. In: ICML (1999)
21. Joachims, T.: Transductive learning via spectral graph partitioning. In: ICML (2003)
22. Joulin, A., Bach, F.: A convex relaxation for weakly supervised classifiers. In: ICML (2012)
23. Khajavirad, A., Sahinidis, N.V.: Convex envelopes of products of convex and component-wise concave functions. J. Global Optim. **52**(3), 391–409 (2012)

24. Khajavirad, A., Sahinidis, N.V.: Convex envelopes generated from finitely many compact convex sets. Math. Programm. **137**(1–2), 371–408 (2013)
25. Lee, J., Leyffer, S.: Mixed Integer Nonlinear Programming. Springer, Heidelberg (2011)
26. Li, Y.F., Tsang, I.W., Kwok, J.T., Zhou, Z.H.: Tighter and convex maximum margin clustering. In: AISTATS (2009)
27. Locatelli, M.: A technique to derive the analytical form of convex envelopes for some bivariate functions. J. Global Optim. **59**(2–3), 477–501 (2014)
28. Martí, R., Reinelt, G.: The Linear Ordering Problem: Exact and Heuristic Methods in Combinatorial Optimization. Springer, Heidelberg (2011)
29. Pock, T., Chambolle, A., Cremers, D., Bischof, H.: A convex relaxation approach for computing minimal partitions. In: CVPR (2009)
30. Pock, T., Cremers, D., Bischof, H., Chambolle, A.: An algorithm for minimizing the mumford-shah functional. In: ICCV (2009)
31. Pock, T., Schoenemann, T., Graber, G., Bischof, H., Cremers, D.: A convex formulation of continuous multi-label problems. In: Forsyth, D., Torr, P., Zisserman, A. (eds.) ECCV 2008, Part III. LNCS, vol. 5304, pp. 792–805. Springer, Heidelberg (2008)
32. Sindhwani, V., Keerthi, S.S., Chapelle, O.: Deterministic annealing for semi-supervised kernel machines. In: ICML (2006)
33. Strekalovskiy, E., Chambolle, A., Cremers, D.: A convex representation for the vectorial mumford-shah functional. In: CVPR (2012)
34. Tawarmalani, M., Richard, J.P.P., Xiong, C.: Explicit convex and concave envelopes through polyhedral subdivisions. Math. Programm. **138**(1–2), 531–577 (2013)
35. Tawarmalani, M., Sahinidis, N.V.: Convexification and Global Optimization in Continuous and Mixed-integer Nonlinear Programming: Theory, Algorithms, Software, and Applications. Springer, New York (2002)
36. Tawarmalani, M., Sahinidis, N.V.: Global optimization of mixed-integer nonlinear programs: a theoretical and computational study. Math. Programm. **99**(3), 563–591 (2004)
37. Vapnik, V.N., Chervonenkis, A.J.: Theory of pattern recognition: Statistical problems of learning. Nauka, Moscow (1974)
38. Xu, L., Neufeld, J., Larson, B., Schuurmans, D.: Maximum margin clustering. In: NIPS (2005)
39. Xu, L., Schuurmans, D.: Unsupervised and semi-supervised multi-class support vector machines. In: AAAI (2005)
40. Zhang, K., Tsang, I.W., Kwok, J.T.: Maximum margin clustering made practical. IEEE Trans. Neural Netw. **20**(4), 583–596 (2009)

FSI Schemes: Fast Semi-Iterative Solvers for PDEs and Optimisation Methods

David Hafner[1(✉)], Peter Ochs[1], Joachim Weickert[1], Martin Reißel[2], and Sven Grewenig[1]

[1] Mathematical Image Analysis Group, Faculty of Mathematics and Computer Science, Campus E1.7, Saarland University, 66041 Saarbrücken, Germany
{hafner,ochs,weickert,grewenig}@mia.uni-saarland.de
[2] Fachbereich Medizintechnik und Technomathematik, Fachhochschule Aachen, Heinrich-Mußmann-Straße 1, 52428 Jülich, Germany
reissel@fh-aachen.de

Abstract. Many tasks in image processing and computer vision are modelled by diffusion processes, variational formulations, or constrained optimisation problems. Basic iterative solvers such as explicit schemes, Richardson iterations, or projected gradient descent methods are simple to implement and well-suited for parallel computing. However, their efficiency suffers from severe step size restrictions. As a remedy we introduce a simple and highly efficient acceleration strategy, leading to so-called *Fast Semi-Iterative* (FSI) schemes that extrapolate the basic solver iteration with the previous iterate. To derive suitable extrapolation parameters, we establish a recursion relation that connects box filtering with an explicit scheme for 1D homogeneous diffusion. FSI schemes avoid the main drawbacks of recent Fast Explicit Diffusion (FED) and Fast Jacobi techniques, and they have an interesting connection to the heavy ball method in optimisation. Our experiments show their benefits for anisotropic diffusion inpainting, nonsmooth regularisation, and Nesterov's worst case problems for convex and strongly convex optimisation.

1 Introduction

In the present paper we propose efficient numerical solvers for three problem classes in image processing and computer vision: *(i)* diffusion evolutions, *(ii)* variational models leading to elliptic partial differential equations (PDEs), *(iii)* constrained convex optimisation problems.

Diffusion processes have applications e.g. as linear or nonlinear scale-spaces [8,11,21]. In the space-discrete case, they are given by dynamical systems of type

$$\partial_t \boldsymbol{u} = \boldsymbol{A}(\boldsymbol{u})\,\boldsymbol{u}\,, \tag{1}$$

where the vector $\boldsymbol{u} \in \mathbb{R}^N$ contains the grey values in N different pixel locations, $t \in (0, \infty)$ denotes the diffusion time, and $\boldsymbol{A} \in \mathbb{R}^{N \times N}$ is a symmetric negative semi-definite matrix that may depend in a nonlinear way on the evolving image $\boldsymbol{u}$. This abstract model holds in any dimension and includes isotropic

© Springer International Publishing AG 2016
B. Rosenhahn and B. Andres (Eds.): GCPR 2016, LNCS 9796, pp. 91–102, 2016.
DOI: 10.1007/978-3-319-45886-1_8

as well as anisotropic diffusion models with differential operators of second or higher order.

Elliptic problems frequently arise as steady states of diffusion evolutions or as Euler-Lagrange equations of variational models [2]. Space-discrete formulations lead to systems of equations in the form of

$$\boldsymbol{B}(\boldsymbol{u})\,\boldsymbol{u} \;=\; \boldsymbol{d}(\boldsymbol{u})\,, \tag{2}$$

where $\boldsymbol{B} \in \mathbb{R}^{N \times N}$ is symmetric positive definite, and $\boldsymbol{d} \in \mathbb{R}^N$ is the known right hand side. In case of nonlinear evolutions or nonquadratic variational models, the system matrix $\boldsymbol{B}$ and the vector $\boldsymbol{d}$ may depend on the evolving image $\boldsymbol{u}$.

Constrained convex optimisation problems appear e.g. in dual formulations of certain nonsmooth minimisation tasks such as total variation (TV) regularisation [1,14]. A general framework can be cast as

$$\min_{\boldsymbol{u}\in\mathcal{C}} F(\boldsymbol{u})\,, \tag{3}$$

where $F\colon \mathbb{R}^N \to \mathbb{R}$ is a smooth convex function, and $\mathcal{C}$ denotes a convex set that models the constraint. Such constrained optimisation methods are flexible modelling tools that have a broad range of applications.

For all three problem classes there exist basic iterative schemes, namely *(i)* explicit finite difference schemes, *(ii)* Richardson iterations, and *(iii)* projected gradient descent methods. These schemes are easy to implement and well-suited for parallel architectures such as GPUs. Unfortunately, severe restrictions of the time step sizes or the relaxation parameters render such algorithms rather inefficient. Hence, it would be highly desirable to find acceleration strategies that improve the efficiency of those basic schemes while preserving their advantages.

Our Contributions. We propose an acceleration strategy that consists of a semi-iterative approach in the sense of Varga [19]. It computes the new iterate $\boldsymbol{u}^{k+1}$ by applying the basic iterative scheme to $\boldsymbol{u}^k$ and extrapolating the result by means of $\boldsymbol{u}^{k-1}$. Here, the extrapolation step is responsible for a substantial acceleration. We call such techniques *Fast Semi-Iterative* (FSI) schemes. In contrast to classical semi-iterative approaches from the numerical literature, we obtain different extrapolation parameters that can be derived in an intuitive way from box filter recursions. Box filters are known to give a good compromise between efficiency and numerical stability [22]. On top of that, we uncover theoretical connections of our FSI schemes to well-performing iterative procedures such as Fast Explicit Diffusion (FED) [22] or Polyak's heavy ball method [12].

Paper Organisation. After a discussion of related work, we review 1D linear diffusion and expose its relation to box filtering in Sect. 2. Subsequently, we transfer this concept to iterative schemes and present our novel FSI techniques for diffusion evolutions (Sect. 3), elliptic problems (Sect. 4), and constrained optimisation (Sect. 5). Our experiments in Sect. 6 illustrate the benefits of our algorithms. Finally, we conclude our paper with a summary and outlook in Sect. 7.

Related Work. Our schemes are closely related to nonstationary iterative schemes, where the algorithmic parameters vary from iteration to iteration. In this context, already in 1911, Richardson discussed possible benefits of varying relaxation parameters in his iterative scheme [13]. Later, based on Chebyshev polynomials of the first kind, cyclic parameter choices were proposed that allow substantial speed-ups; see e.g. [24]. Inherently, the Richardson method in [13] is closely related to gradient descent schemes, and thus to the solution of parabolic PDEs. In this context, similar ideas have been proposed by Yaun'Chzhao-Din [25] and Saul'yev [16]. They are known under the name super time stepping [4]. Recently, motivated by box filter factorisations, Weickert et al. [22] propose cyclically varying parameters that substantially improve the damping properties of the resulting schemes. Additionally, the authors introduce a Jacobi-like scheme for elliptic problems. Setzer et al. [17] base on the work of [22] and provide an extension to projection methods with application to nonsmooth optimisation. Furthermore, we can relate such cyclic Richardson approaches to so-called semi-iterative procedures that rely on Chebyshev recursion formulas [5,19]. Interestingly, these semi-iterative schemes additionally share similarities with Polyak's heavy ball method [12], where Ochs et al. [10] recently proposed an extension that includes proximal mappings. Similarly, our technique relates to the so-called momentum method that is frequently applied in machine learning approaches; see e.g. [15,18].

2 How to Benefit from Box Filtering

2.1 Explicit Scheme for 1D Linear Diffusion

As starting point of our work we consider linear diffusion of a 1D signal $u(x,t)$:

$$\partial_t u \;=\; \partial_{xx} u\,. \tag{4}$$

With grid size h and time step size τ, an explicit scheme for (4) is given by

$$u_i^{k+1} \;=\; (I + \tau\,\Delta_h)\,u_i^k\,, \tag{5}$$

where I denotes the identity operator, $\Delta_h := (1,-2,1)/h^2$ the discrete Laplacian, and u_i^k approximates u in pixel i at time level k. For stability reasons, all stencil weights should be nonnegative. This implies that the time step size must satisfy $\tau \leq h^2/2$. Obviously, this restriction makes such an explicit scheme inefficient: With n explicit diffusion steps, we can only reach a stopping time of $\mathcal{O}(n)$.

2.2 Box Filtering via Iterative Explicit Diffusion

In order to use explicit schemes more efficiently, let us make a didactic excursion to box filters. A box filter B_{2n+1} of length $(2n+1)h$ is given by

$$[B_{2n+1}\,u]_i \;=\; \frac{1}{2n+1}\sum_{j=-n}^{n} u_{i+j}. \tag{6}$$

It is well-known [6] that linear diffusion with stopping time T is equivalent to a convolution with a Gaussian of variance $\sigma^2 = 2T$. Moreover, the central limit theorem tells us that iterated box filtering approximates Gaussian convolution. Indeed, an m-fold iteration of a box filter B_{2n+1} with variance σ_n^2 approximates a Gaussian with variance $m\sigma_n^2$. The variance of B_{2n+1} is given by (cf. also [23])

$$\sigma_n^2 = \frac{1}{2n+1} \sum_{j=-n}^{n} (jh-0)^2 = \frac{2h^2}{2n+1} \frac{n(n+1)(2n+1)}{6} = \frac{n(n+1)}{3}h^2. \quad (7)$$

This implies that a single application of a box filter B_{2n+1} approximates linear diffusion with stopping time $T_n = \sigma_n^2/2 = \frac{n(n+1)}{3}\frac{h^2}{2}$. Note that this stopping time is $\mathcal{O}(n^2)$. Hence, if we were able to implement B_{2n+1} by means of n explicit linear diffusion steps, we could accelerate the explicit scheme from $\mathcal{O}(n)$ to $\mathcal{O}(n^2)$. To this end, we introduce the following theorem which can be proven by induction:

Theorem 1 (Connection of Box Filters and Explicit Diffusion). *A box filter B_{2n+1} of length $(2n+1)h$ can be constructed iteratively by n explicit linear diffusion steps:*

$$B_{2k+3} = \alpha_k \cdot (I + \tau\Delta_h) B_{2k+1} + (1-\alpha_k) \cdot B_{2k-1} \qquad (k = 0, \ldots, n-1)$$

with $\tau := h^2/2$, $\alpha_k := (4k+2)/(2k+3)$, and $B_{-1} := I$.

Note that for $k = 0$ we have $B_3 = I + \frac{h^2}{3}\Delta_h$, which is a single diffusion step with time step size $\frac{2}{3}\tau$.

2.3   Accelerating the Explicit Scheme for 1D Linear Diffusion

To apply Theorem 1 for accelerating the explicit diffusion scheme (5), let us first rewrite it in matrix-vector notation:

$$u^{k+1} = (I + \tau L) u^k, \qquad (8)$$

where the vector $u \in \mathbb{R}^N$ contains the discrete entries of u, $I \in \mathbb{R}^{N \times N}$ is the identity matrix, and the symmetric negative semi-definite matrix $L \in \mathbb{R}^{N \times N}$ implements the Laplacian. The box filter relation in Theorem 1 suggests the following scheme to accelerate the explicit diffusion scheme (8) such that u^k corresponds to an application of a box filter B_{2k+1}:

$$u^{k+1} = \alpha_k \cdot (I + \tau L) u^k + (1-\alpha_k) \cdot u^{k-1} \qquad (9)$$

with $\tau = h^2/2$, $\alpha_k = (4k+2)/(2k+3)$, and $u^{-1} := u^0$. As we have seen, n iterations of this scheme implement a box filter B_{2n+1} of length $(2n+1)h$. However, a single box filter might be a poor approximation for the actual linear diffusion process that is equivalent to Gaussian convolution. To improve the approximation quality, we should iterate the box filter. Hence, we propose a *cyclic* application of (9), where the m-th cycle with cycle length n is given by

$$
\boxed{
\begin{aligned}
\boldsymbol{u}^{m,k+1} &= \alpha_k \cdot \left(\boldsymbol{I} + \tau\,\boldsymbol{L}\right) \boldsymbol{u}^{m,k} + (1 - \alpha_k) \cdot \boldsymbol{u}^{m,k-1} \\
&\text{with } \boldsymbol{u}^{m,-1} := \boldsymbol{u}^{m,0} \text{ and } \alpha_k = (4k+2)/(2k+3) \text{ for } k = 0,\dots,n-1.
\end{aligned}
}
\tag{10}
$$

Here, the number of cycles is responsible for the accuracy, while the cycle length n accounts for the $\mathcal{O}(n^2)$ efficiency. For the next cycle, we set $\boldsymbol{u}^{m+1,0} := \boldsymbol{u}^{m,n}$.

3   FSI Schemes for Diffusion Evolutions

Our discussion so far was for didactic reasons only, since linear diffusion can be implemented directly as an efficient box filter without explicit iterations. However, it suggests how we could generalise these ideas to arbitrary isotropic or anisotropic nonlinear diffusion processes (1) that have explicit schemes of type

$$
\boldsymbol{u}^{k+1} = \left(\boldsymbol{I} + \tau\,\boldsymbol{A}(\boldsymbol{u}^k)\right)\boldsymbol{u}^k \,.
\tag{11}
$$

Since $\boldsymbol{A}$ is negative semi-definite, stability in the Euclidean norm requires the time step size restriction $0 < \tau < 2/\rho(\boldsymbol{A}(\boldsymbol{u}^k))$, where ρ denotes the spectral radius. Obviously, there is a strong similarity of (11) to the linear diffusion scheme in (8). Hence, it appears to be natural to formulate, in analogy to (10), the following *Fast Semi-Iterative* (FSI) scheme:

$$
\boxed{
\begin{aligned}
\boldsymbol{u}^{m,k+1} &= \alpha_k \cdot \left(\boldsymbol{I} + \tau\,\boldsymbol{A}(\boldsymbol{u}^{m,k})\right) \boldsymbol{u}^{m,k} + (1 - \alpha_k) \cdot \boldsymbol{u}^{m,k-1} \\
&\text{with } \boldsymbol{u}^{m,-1} := \boldsymbol{u}^{m,0} \text{ and } \alpha_k = (4k+2)/(2k+3) \text{ for } k = 0,\dots,n-1.
\end{aligned}
}
\tag{12}
$$

This scheme describes the m-th cycle with length n of our FSI algorithm. We repeat it several times to reach a specific stopping time. Similar to [7], one can conduct an analysis of the internal stability of this iterative scheme. This way, one can show that for every iteration our scheme is stable in a suitable norm. This stability analysis requires the symmetry of $\boldsymbol{A}$.

Connection to Fast Explicit Diffusion (FED). As discussed in Sect. 2, we base on the connection between box filtering and explicit schemes. This was inspired by the cyclic FED approach of Weickert et al. [22] which demonstrates the benefits of a reliance on box filters. More specifically, they exploit a factorisation of a box filter into several explicit diffusion steps to construct their algorithms. In case of linear problems, one can even show that FED and FSI schemes yield identical results after each cycle. However, in case of nonlinear problems, the discussed semi-iterative structure of our FSI scheme is highly beneficial since it allows to perform nonlinear updates within one cycle. We illustrate this by means of our experiments in Sect. 6. Moreover, FED schemes are highly sensitive to numerical inaccuracies. Thus, sophisticated rearrangements of possibly unstable time steps are required to avoid the explosion of rounding errors; see e.g. [22] and references therein. We eliminate this drawback by our FSI technique.

4 FSI Schemes for Elliptic Problems

So far, we have considered diffusion-like processes that correspond to parabolic PDEs. Next we explain how to transfer this concept to discretised elliptic PDEs, or more generally to the solution of equation systems in the form of (2). In the linear case, formulating (2) as $u = u - \omega(Bu - d)$ gives rise to the Richardson scheme [13]

$$u^{k+1} = (I - \omega B) u^k + \omega d. \tag{13}$$

Choosing $0 < \omega < 2/\rho(B)$ guarantees stability in the Euclidean norm, since the eigenvalues of $I - \omega B$ lie in $(-1, 1]$. Considering the error vector $e^k = u^k - u^*$ between the current estimate u^k and the unknown exact solution u^* yields

$$e^{k+1} = (I - \omega B) e^k. \tag{14}$$

We observe a strong similarity of (14) to the explicit diffusion scheme in (8). Hence, we propose the following FSI scheme for elliptic problems:

$$\boxed{\begin{aligned} u^{m,k+1} &= \alpha_k \cdot \big((I - \omega B) u^{m,k} + \omega d\big) + (1 - \alpha_k) \cdot u^{m,k-1} \\ \text{with } u^{m,-1} &:= u^{m,0} \text{ and } \alpha_k = (4k+2)/(2k+3) \text{ for } k = 0, \ldots, n-1. \end{aligned}} \tag{15}$$

To extend (15) to nonlinear systems of equations in the form of (2), we replace B and d by their nonlinear counterparts $B(u^{m,k})$ and $d(u^{m,k})$, and choose $0 < \omega < 2/L$, where $L > 0$ is the Lipschitz constant of $B(u)u - d(u)$.

Preconditioning. The discussed FSI method yields fast convergence for problems where the coefficients of the equation system have a similar value of magnitude. However, in case of strongly differing coefficients a preconditioning or, in other words, a different splitting of the system matrix B, is highly beneficial. As an example, we consider the Jacobi overrelaxation splitting $B = \frac{1}{\omega} D + (B - \frac{1}{\omega} D)$, where D denotes a positive definite diagonal matrix. This leads to

$$u^{m,k+1} = \alpha_k \cdot \big((I - \omega D^{-1} B) u^{m,k} + \omega D^{-1} d\big) + (1 - \alpha_k) \cdot u^{m,k-1}. \tag{16}$$

Assuming a symmetric positive definite matrix B, this process is stable with a suitable ω such that the eigenvalues of $I - \omega D^{-1} B$ lie in $(-1, 1]$.

Connection to Fast Jacobi. Similar to the connection to FED in the parabolic case, we can show a relation of our FSI scheme to the recent Fast Jacobi solver of Weickert et al. [22] for elliptic problems. As before, we eliminate the drawback of rearranging the relaxation parameters and provide an internal stability that allows for intermediate nonlinear updates.

5 FSI Schemes for Constrained Optimisation

Often, the elliptic problem from the previous section can be interpreted as the minimality condition of a suitable optimisation problem. In fact, the gradient descent scheme to compute a minimiser of the optimisation problem (3) without side-constraints is given by

$$u^{k+1} = u^k - \omega \nabla F(u^k).$$ (17)

This scheme is stable for $0 < \omega < 2/L$, where $L > 0$ is the Lipschitz constant of ∇F. Again, the structural similarity to (8) suggests the following FSI iteration:

$$u^{m,k+1} = \alpha_k \cdot (u^k - \omega \nabla F(u^{m,k})) + (1 - \alpha_k) \cdot u^{m,k-1}.$$ (18)

Adaptation to Constrained Problems. As it turns out, the provided internal stability of our algorithm enables us to perform projections onto convex sets in every iteration step. Thus, our technique is additionally well-suited for constrained optimisation problems in the form of (3), where the solution u is constrained to some convex set $\mathcal{C}$. With the corresponding orthogonal projection operator $P_{\mathcal{C}}$, our FSI scheme for constrained optimisation is given by

$$\boxed{\begin{array}{l} u^{m,k+1} = P_{\mathcal{C}}\Big(\alpha_k \cdot (u^k - \omega \nabla F(u^{m,k})) + (1 - \alpha_k) \cdot u^{m,k-1}\Big) \\ \text{with } u^{m,-1} := u^{m,0} \text{ and } \alpha_k = (4k+2)/(2k+3) \text{ for } k = 0,\ldots,n-1. \end{array}}$$ (19)

Adaptation to Strongly Convex Problems. So far, we have considered the case where the Lipschitz constant L is assumed to be known. However, strongly convex problems additionally provide information about the strong convexity parameter ℓ. To make use of this additional knowledge, we propose the following recursive parameter choice to accelerate our iterative scheme:

$$\alpha_k = \frac{1}{1 - \frac{\alpha_{k-1}}{4} \cdot \left(\frac{L-\ell}{L+\ell}\right)^2} \qquad (k = 1,\ldots,n-1),$$ (20)

where $\alpha_0 = 2(L+\ell)/(3L+\ell)$ and $\omega = 2/(L+\ell)$. It can be derived using classical Chebyshev reasonings. With $\ell = 0$, these parameters come down to (18). We present a full description of our FSI method in Algorithm 1. Also in the elliptic case (Sect. 4) we can apply such a parameter choice. Here, ℓ and L correspond to the smallest and largest eigenvalues of the positive definite system matrix B.

Connection to Heavy Ball Method. Let us now derive a close relation of the proposed FSI scheme to Polyak's heavy ball method [12]

$$u^{k+1} = u^k - \tilde{\alpha} \cdot \nabla F(u^k) + \tilde{\beta} \cdot (u^k - u^{k-1}).$$ (21)

The first part of this iterative scheme can be seen as a gradient descent step, while the second part represents an inertial term. It relates the current iterate u^k to the old time step u^{k-1}. This allows significant speed-ups. Interestingly, we can connect (21) to our FSI approach by applying *cyclically varying* parameters $\tilde{\alpha}_k = \omega \alpha_k$ and $\tilde{\beta}_k = \alpha_k - 1$ with α_k given by (18), combined with a restart $u^{m,-1} := u^{m,0}$ after each cycle. We illustrate benefits of our approach in Sect. 6.

Algorithm 1. FSI scheme with projection operator P_C and $0 \leq \ell < L$.

input : $\nabla F, P_C, L, \ell, n, u^0$

1 $\omega = \frac{2}{L+\ell}$, $\alpha_0 = 2(L+\ell)/(3L+\ell)$, $\alpha_k = 1 \Big/ \Big(1 - \frac{\alpha_{k-1}}{4} \cdot \big(\frac{L-\ell}{L+\ell} \big)^2 \Big)$

2 $u^{0,-1} = u^{0,0} = u^0$

3 **for** $m = 0, 1, \ldots$ **do**

4   **for** $k = 0, 1, \ldots, n-1$ **do**

5          $u^{m,k+1} = P_C \Big(\alpha_k \big(u^k - \omega \, \nabla F(u^{m,k}) \big) + (1 - \alpha_k) \, u^{m,k-1} \Big)$

6      $u^{m+1,-1} = u^{m+1,0} = u^{m,n}$

---

6 Experiments

6.1 Inpainting with Edge-Enhancing Anisotropic Diffusion

In our first experiment, we consider image inpainting by means of edge-enhancing anisotropic diffusion [20]:

$$\partial_t u = (1 - c(\boldsymbol{x})) \cdot \mathrm{div} \left(\boldsymbol{D}(\nabla u_\sigma) \, \nabla u \right) - c(\boldsymbol{x}) \cdot (u - f), \qquad (22)$$

where $c \colon \Omega \to [0,1]$ is a binary mask that indicates known data, and $\Omega \subset \mathbb{R}^2$ denotes the rectangular image domain. Furthermore, $\boldsymbol{D}(\nabla u_\sigma) := \mu_1 \cdot \boldsymbol{v}_1 \boldsymbol{v}_1^\top + \mu_2 \cdot \boldsymbol{v}_2 \boldsymbol{v}_2^\top$ is the so-called *diffusion tensor*, where the first eigenvector $\boldsymbol{v}_1 \parallel \nabla u_\sigma$ points across image edges, and the second one $\boldsymbol{v}_2 \perp \nabla u_\sigma$ along them. Here, u_σ denotes convolution of u with a Gaussian of standard deviation σ. Since we want to perform full diffusion along edges but reduced smoothing across them, we set $\mu_2 = 1$ and determine μ_1 by means of the Charbonnier diffusivity with a contrast parameter $\lambda > 0$, i.e. $\mu_1 = 1 / \sqrt{1 + |\nabla u_\sigma|^2 / \lambda^2}$.

Figure 1 depicts the sparse input data as well as our inpainting results. First, the provided speed-up by our FSI technique compared to the baseline explicit diffusion (ED) scheme is obvious. Moreover, we perform nonlinear updates after *each* iteration step. As discussed in [22], FED schemes inherently do not allow for such intermediate updates within one cycle. Hence, we offer more flexibility in this regard which further allows for a better performance.

6.2 Total Variation Regularisation

In this experiment, we consider image regularisation by means of the following energy functional [1,14]:

$$E(u) = \frac{1}{2} \int_\Omega (u - f)^2 \, \mathrm{d}\boldsymbol{x} + \gamma \, \mathrm{TV}(u), \qquad (23)$$

where $f \colon \Omega \to \mathbb{R}$ represents a noisy input image, and the parameter $\gamma > 0$ steers the amount of smoothness. The regulariser $\mathrm{TV}(u) := \sup_{\|\boldsymbol{p}\|_\infty \leq 1} \int_\Omega u \, \mathrm{div} \, \boldsymbol{p} \, \mathrm{d}\boldsymbol{x}$

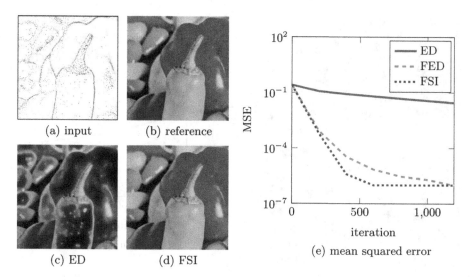

(a) input   (b) reference

(c) ED   (d) FSI

(e) mean squared error

Fig. 1. Inpainting with edge-enhancing anisotropic diffusion, initialised with a black image. (a) Input with inverted colours for visibility reasons. (b) Converged reference result of a standard explicit diffusion (ED) scheme. (c) Result of ED after 600 iterations. (d) Result of FSI after three cycles with length $n = 200$. (e) Mean squared error (MSE) between current estimates and reference solution. The grey value range is $[0, 1]$.

penalises the total variation of u, and $\boldsymbol{p} \colon \Omega \to \mathbb{R}^2$ is a smooth vector field with compact support on Ω. To compute the minimiser of (23), we solve the dual problem [3]

$$\min_{\|\boldsymbol{p}\|_\infty \leq \gamma} \frac{1}{2} \int_\Omega (f - \operatorname{div} \boldsymbol{p})^2 \, \mathrm{d}\boldsymbol{x} . \tag{24}$$

We discretise this constrained optimisation problem and solve it with the proposed FSI scheme in Algorithm 1. In this example, the projection operator is given point-wise by $P_C(\boldsymbol{p}) = \boldsymbol{p}/\max\{1, |\boldsymbol{p}|/\gamma\}$.

Figure 2 shows the noisy input image and our smoothed results. Also here, the provided acceleration of the baseline projected gradient (PG) scheme by our FSI approach is obvious. The comparison to the cyclic FED-like projection method by Setzer et al. [17] (CPG) demonstrates that our FSI scheme is stable under the applied projections within each iteration, while the standard CPG approach without backtracking does not converge properly for such large cycle lengths.

6.3   Performance on Nesterov's Worst Case Problems

In our last experiment, we evaluate the performance of our FSI techniques w.r.t. related iterative schemes on Nesterov's worst case problems for smooth convex and strongly convex optimisation [9]. These are quadratic minimisation problems which are difficult for any algorithm that can solve all instances of the respective

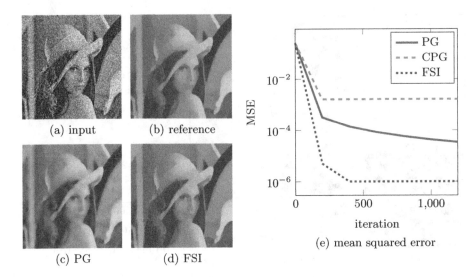

Fig. 2. Total variation (TV) regularisation. (a) Input with white Gaussian noise. (b) Converged reference result of standard projected gradient (PG) approach. (c) Result of PG after 200 iterations. (d) Result of FSI after one cycle with length $n = 200$. (e) Mean squared error (MSE) between current estimates and reference solution.

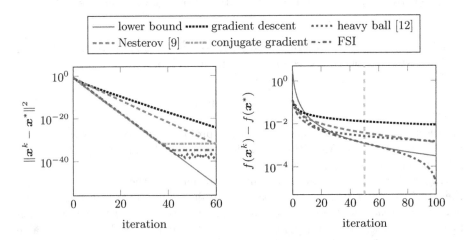

Fig. 3. Numerical comparisons by means of worst case functions of Nesterov [9]. *Left*: Strongly convex optimisation. *Right*: Convex optimisation. Here, the lower bound only holds for $k = 50$ (grey line). In both cases, the problem dimension is $N = 10^5$.

class of problems. In [9, Thm. 2.1.13], Nesterov provides a lower bound for all iterations and predicts a linear convergence rate on the class of *smooth strongly convex* problems. The lower bound for *smooth convex* problems derived in [9, Thm. 2.1.7] is only valid for one specific iteration count $k \in \mathbb{N}$ (here: $k = 50$). Nothing is said about the error before and after the k-th iteration.

Figure 3 plots for both problems the resulting error curves of different solvers. While our FSI scheme offers state-of-the-art performance for the strongly convex problem, it even outperforms competing methods in case of convex optimisation. In particular, this illustrates the benefits of our non-stationary cyclic parameter choice compared to Polyak's heavy ball method.

7   Conclusions and Future Work

We have presented *Fast Semi-Iterative* (FSI) schemes that offer efficient solutions for diffusion evolutions, elliptic problems, and constrained optimisation. The proposed schemes are simple to implement and well-suited for parallel implementations. Hence, they are applicable for a wide range of image processing and computer vision tasks. More specifically, we investigated the relation between box filtering and explicit schemes. It is fascinating to see how this simple concept generalises to flexible and highly efficient algorithms. In contrast to FED-like approaches, the provided internal stability of our techniques allows for performing nonlinear updates and projections within each iteration. Our experiments demonstrate these benefits w.r.t. related iterative procedures. In future work, we plan to conduct a deeper theoretical analysis of the presented approaches which may allow us to state precise convergence rates. Furthermore, we plan to extend and generalise our schemes, e.g. to general non-expansive proximal operators and nonsymmetric system matrices.

Acknowledgements. Our research has been partially funded by the *Deutsche Forschungsgemeinschaft* (DFG) through a Gottfried Wilhelm Leibniz Prize for Joachim Weickert and by the Graduate School of Computer Science at Saarland University. This is gratefully acknowledged.

References

1. Acar, R., Vogel, C.R.: Analysis of bounded variation penalty methods for ill-posed problems. Inverse Prob. **10**, 1217–1229 (1994)
2. Bertero, M., Poggio, T.A., Torre, V.: Ill-posed problems in early vision. Proc. IEEE **76**(8), 869–889 (1988)
3. Chambolle, A.: An algorithm for total variation minimization and applications. J. Math. Imaging Vis. **20**(1), 89–97 (2004)
4. Gentzsch, W., Schlüter, A.: Über ein Einschrittverfahren mit zyklischer Schrittweitenänderung zur Lösung parabolischer Differentialgleichungen. Zeitschrift für Angewandte Mathematik und Mechanik **58**, T415–T416 (1978). in German
5. Golub, G.H., Varga, R.S.: Chebyshev semi-iterative methods, successive overrelaxation iterative methods, and second order Richardson iterative methods. Part I. Numerische Mathematik **3**(1), 147–156 (1961)
6. Hellwig, G.: Partial Differential Equations. Teubner, Stuttgart (1977)
7. van der Houwen, P.J., Sommeijer, B.P.: On the internal stability of explicit, m-stage Runge-Kutta methods for large m-values. Zeitschrift für Angewandte Mathematik und Mechanik **60**(10), 479–485 (1980)

8. Iijima, T.: Basic theory on normalization of pattern (in case of typical one-dimensional pattern). Bull. Electrotech. Lab. **26**, 368–388 (1962). in Japanese

9. Nesterov, Y.: Introductory Lectures on Convex Optimization: A Basic Course, Applied Optimization, vol. 87. Kluwer, Boston (2004)

10. Ochs, P., Brox, T., Pock, T.: iPiasco: inertial proximal algorithm for strongly convex optimization. J. Math. Imaging Vis. **53**(2), 171–181 (2015)

11. Perona, P., Malik, J.: Scale space and edge detection using anisotropic diffusion. IEEE Trans. Pattern Anal. Mach. Intell. **12**(7), 629–639 (1990)

12. Polyak, B.T.: Some methods of speeding up the convergence of iteration methods. USSR Comput. Math. Math. Phys. **4**(5), 1–17 (1964)

13. Richardson, L.F.: The approximate arithmetical solution by finite differences of physical problems involving differential equation, with an application to the stresses in a masonry dam. Philos. Trans. R. Soc. A **210**, 307–357 (1911)

14. Rudin, L.I., Osher, S., Fatemi, E.: Nonlinear total variation based noise removal algorithms. Physica D **60**, 259–268 (1992)

15. Rumelhart, D.E., Hinton, G.E., Williams, R.J.: Learning internal representations by error propagation, chap. 8. In: Rumelhart, D.E., McClelland, J.L. (eds.) Parallel Distributed Processing: Explorations in the Microstructure of Cognition, vol. 1, pp. 318–362. MIT Press, Cambridge (1986)

16. Saul'yev, V.K.: Integration of Equations of Parabolic Type by the Method of Nets. Elsevier, Pergamon, Oxford (1964)

17. Setzer, S., Steidl, G., Morgenthaler, J.: A cyclic projected gradient method. Comput. Optim. Appl. **54**(2), 417–440 (2013)

18. Sutskever, I., Martens, J., Dahl, G., Hinton, G.: On the importance of initialization and momentum in deep learning. In: Proceedings of 30th International Conference on Machine Learning, pp. 1139–1147. Atlanta, GA, June 2013

19. Varga, R.S.: A comparison of the successive overrelaxation method and semi-iterative methods using Chebyshev polynomials. J. Soc. Ind. Appl. Math. **5**(2), 39–46 (1957)

20. Weickert, J.: Theoretical foundations of anisotropic diffusion in image processing. Comput. Suppl. **11**, 221–236 (1996)

21. Weickert, J.: Anisotropic Diffusion in Image Processing. Teubner, Stuttgart (1998)

22. Weickert, J., Grewenig, S., Schroers, C., Bruhn, A.: Cyclic schemes for PDE-based image analysis. Int. J. Comput. Vis. **118**(3), 275–299 (2016)

23. Wells, W.M.: Efficient synthesis of Gaussian filters by cascaded uniform filters. IEEE Trans. Pattern Anal. Mach. Intell. **8**(2), 234–239 (1986)

24. Young, D.M.: On Richardson's method for solving linear systems with positive definite matrices. J. Math. Phys. **32**(1), 243–255 (1954)

25. Chzhao-Din, Y.: Some difference schemes for the solution of the first boundary value problem for linear differential equations with partial derivatives. Ph.D. thesis, Moscow State University (1958). in Russian

Segmentation

Automated Segmentation of Immunostained Cell Nuclei in 3D Ultramicroscopy Images

Aaron Scherzinger[1(✉)], Florian Kleene[1], Cathrin Dierkes[2], Friedemann Kiefer[2], Klaus H. Hinrichs[1], and Xiaoyi Jiang[1]

[1] Department of Mathematics and Computer Science,
University of Münster, Münster, Germany
scherzinger@wwu.de

[2] Max Planck Institute for Molecular Biomedicine, Münster, Germany

Abstract. Detection, segmentation, and quantification of individual cell nuclei is a standard task in biomedical applications. Due to the increasing volume of acquired image data, it is not possible to rely on manual labeling and object counting. Instead, automated image processing methods have to be applied. Especially in three-dimensional data, one of the major challenges is the separation of touching cell nuclei in densely packed clusters. In this paper, we propose a method for automated detection and segmentation of immunostained cell nuclei in ultramicroscopy images. Our algorithm utilizes interactive learning and voxel classification to obtain a foreground segmentation and subsequently performs the splitting process for each cluster using a multi-step watershed approach. We have evaluated our results using reference images manually labeled by domain experts and compare our approach to state-of-the art methods.

1 Introduction

Detection and segmentation of individual cell nuclei is a standard procedure in many biomedical applications as it is often essential for the quantitative analysis of biological processes. Due to the increasing amount of accumulated image data, manual labeling is usually not a viable option in practice. This problem is aggravated even more due to the difficulty of segmenting three-dimensional data as well as cases of closely juxtaposed or touching cell nuclei, which may form densely packed clusters that can be difficult to separate even for experts. Despite the large body of work and vast methodological diversity (see Sect. 2), no general approach for tackling the segmentation of cell nuclei seems to be available, which is likely due to the variation among different cell types regarding shape and size, as well as the diverse characteristics of the available imaging techniques.

Our images have been obtained using ultramicroscopy, which is based on the principle of light sheet fluorescence microscopy. In this imaging technique the specimen, in our case optically cleared murine fetal tissue, is illuminated by a thin sheet of light, which may be generated by a scanned laser beam or cylinder lenses [12]. This light sheet is projected into the focal plane of an orthogonally

B. Rosenhahn and B. Andres (Eds.): GCPR 2016, LNCS 9796, pp. 105–116, 2016.
DOI: 10.1007/978-3-319-45886-1_9

 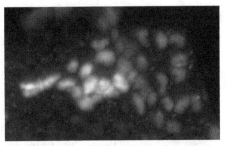

(a) This 2D slice view shows an example of the large variation in fluorescence intensity within ultramicroscopy images. Regions containing cell nuclei have been exemplarily marked using the red ellipses.

(b) This image shows a 3D rendering using maximum intensity projection (MIP). Cell nuclei can form dense clusters which have to be separated to segment and quantify individual cell nuclei in the tissue.

Fig. 1. Example images of immunostained cell nuclei in ultramicroscopy images

oriented detection objective which collects fluorescence signals from the specimen. Moving the sample through the light sheet in a stepwise fashion allows to generate image stacks from which high resolution 3D data sets can be reconstructed [17]. In contrast to confocal laser scanning microscopes, the light sheet setup uncouples the illumination from the detection light path which allows nearly isotropic resolution while keeping the illumination intensity of the sample minimal [22]. Light sheet microscopes can be realized with low magnification lenses, allowing the inspection of large samples with volumes of up to $1\,cm^3$ at still subcellular resolution. In our samples, mouse embryo wholemount preparations were immunostained using an antiserum against a homeobox transcription factor to identify expressing cells. For subsequent light sheet imaging the specimen were optically cleared using the BABB protocol [26].

Several challenges arise in the segmentation of cell nuclei in ultramicroscopy image data which are due to the properties of the imaging modality and the biological samples. The images often suffer from a large variation of fluorescence intensity both in the labeled objects as well as the background (see Fig. 1(a)), which prohibits the application of global thresholding approaches, especially since the background intensity in dense regions is higher than foreground intensities in other regions. Moreover, foreground objects usually have fuzzy or blurry contours. One of the largest challenges, however, is the separation of touching cell nuclei of seemingly arbitrary orientation which form dense clusters extending in all directions within the three-dimensional data (see Fig. 1(b)).

Our main contribution is a pipeline specifically designed for ultramicroscopy images which combines machine learning and watershed segmentation as well as the integration of a geometric marker extension into the cluster splitting.

In the remainder of this paper, we first give an overview of existing methods for three-dimensional segmentation of clustered cell nuclei, followed by the workflow of our method. Next, we focus on the main part of our algorithm, the cluster splitting step, and subsequently evaluate the performance of our algorithm.

2   Related Work

Cell nuclei segmentation and quantification is one of the fundamental problems in biomedical image processing. The large diversity of imaging modalities and cell types as well as the complexity of the task have led to a large body of work and a tremendous variety of approaches for over more than ten years.

One of the most basic methods for segmentation is thresholding which is usually based on the intensity histogram of the image. An overview of thresholding techniques is given by Sezgin and Sankur [19]. Often, thresholding is applied to obtain an initial foreground segmentation which is followed by further refinement and cluster splitting computations. Lin et al. [10] have proposed an algorithm which relies on thresholding followed by several post-processing steps. Afterwards, they apply a 3D watershed segmentation on the gradient-weighted distance transform of the thresholded image. To compensate for over-segmentation of the cell nuclei clusters, this is followed by a model-based merging step relying on *a priori* knowledge about the size and shape of the cell nuclei. Wählby et al. [24] have also proposed a method which is based on watershed segmentation. Initially, they detect foreground seeds in the original image by applying a h-maxima transform. The watershed segmentation is then performed on the gradient magnitude image of the data. To improve the cluster separation results, they perform an additional watershed segmentation step on the distance transform of the previous result. Gertych et al. [7] have recently proposed an algorithm which combines a 3D radial symmetry transform for seed detection with a watershed-based segmentation after an initial background removal step.

Another approach for cell nuclei segmentation is the application of machine learning techniques. Fehr et al. [5] have proposed a method for segmentation and classification of cell nuclei in 3D fluorescence microscopy data which performs a voxel-wise classification on gray scale invariant features using a support vector machine (SVM). Tek et al. [23] have applied an interactively trained random forest classifier to perform a voxel-wise foreground segmentation, which is afterwards improved by morphological post-processing and the application of a size filter for the connected components.

Another class of cell nuclei segmentation methods is based on graph cuts. Daněk et al. [4] have proposed a two-stage graph cut method which performs the foreground segmentation using a two-terminal graph cut where initial seed labels are determined using histogram analysis. Afterwards, each connected component of the binary image is processed separately using a multi-terminal graph cut where seeds are identified by computing local maxima in the distance transform. Al-Kofahi et al. [2] have proposed an approach which utilizes a graph cut relying on initial foreground class probabilities computed by bimodal histogram analysis to perform the foreground segmentation. Afterwards, for each connected component in the binary image a multi-scale Laplacian-of-Gaussian (LoG) filter is applied to obtain seed points for the individual nuclei and perform a clustering step. The result of this step is then refined using a multi-terminal graph cut.

There are also several methods for cell nuclei segmentation that are based on level set active contours. Harder et al. [8] have proposed an approach which initializes the contours using local adaptive thresholding followed by a distance transform and a 3D watershed segmentation. Bergeest and Rohr [3] have proposed a method based on minimizing a convex energy functional using a level set representation and applying the 3D Laplacian operator for the cluster splitting.

The problem of separating densely packed cell nuclei has also been addressed using geometric approaches, usually based on a convexity-concavity analysis of the binary image obtained by applying one of the various foreground segmentation methods. Such approaches rely on the fact that cell nuclei, although not necessarily round, can be considered approximately convex. However, often these methods are based on analyzing two-dimensional contours to find concave splitting points (e.g., [16,25]) and are not directly applicable to three-dimensional images. Indhumathi et al. [9] have applied this principle to 3D images by performing the concavity analysis and detection of splitting paths slice-wise while taking into account the relationship with the previous slice as a reference. Mathew et al. [11] have proposed a different approach for three-dimensional data which performs an approximate convex decomposition of a cluster of cell nuclei. Their method detects local maxima in the distance transform to establish the number k of components in the cluster. Afterwards, a set of line segments between sampled surface points is defined and *Lines of Sight* (LoS), i.e., line segments which do not leave the foreground component, are selected from this set. The LoS are then clustered into k clusters which are used to label the surface points. Afterwards, the label of each voxel is chosen by majority voting of the nearest surface points.

In our proposed method, we combine machine learning by interactively training a voxel classifier to obtain a binary image with a multi-step watershed approach which consists of a seed detection step, a geometric component involving the distance transform of the binary image, and a marker-based watershed segmentation step to compute the final labeling for each individual voxel.

3   Workflow Overview

Our approach uses a well-established workflow consisting of three basic steps. First, foreground segmentation is performed to obtain a binary image. Next, a connected component labeling is computed on the binary image. In the last step, the cell nuclei cluster splitting is applied separately for each component.

As outlined above, global thresholding does not perform well on ultramicroscopy images due to the intensity inhomogeneities in the fluorescence signal. Moreover, the histograms of our images do not show a bimodal distribution. This prohibits the use of several methods relying on modeling the histogram using a mixture of Gaussian or Poisson distributions such as in [4] or [2] to conveniently initialize more sophisticated methods segmentation algorithms like

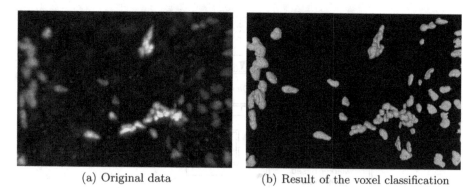

(a) Original data   (b) Result of the voxel classification

Fig. 2. 3D rendering example of the foreground segmentation.

graph cuts. Instead, we perform the foreground segmentation step using voxel classification by interactively training a random forest classifier, which has been shown to be among the classifiers with the best overall performance [6]. For the interactive training, we use the open source tool Ilastik [21], which has already been applied in a similar way (although on different data) by Tek et al. [23]. We set up a binary (foreground vs. background) classification problem and interactively label voxels in a training data set while inspecting the intermediate results. Since Ilastik provides the option to visualize regions of high uncertainty in the classification, an expert performing the labeling can directly locate such regions of interest in the training data. After finishing the interactive training phase, the classifier can be used for batch processing of the actual data sets. We use a set of rotation-invariant features (smoothed raw data, gradient magnitude, and Hessian eigenvalues) at three-different Gaussian scales with $\sigma_1 = 1.0, \sigma_2 = 1.6$, and $\sigma_3 = 3.5$. An example of the foreground segmentation is depicted in Fig. 2.

After foreground segmentation, we apply a median filter on the binary image as a post-processing step. Then, we perform connected component analysis on the result. We discard components below a size threshold of 200 voxels which might originate from staining artifacts or false positives output by the voxel classifier. The choice of this threshold results from a size distribution of cell nuclei derived from a test data set which has been labeled voxel-wise by a domain expert (see Sect. 5). Each of the resulting connected components corresponds to either a single cell nucleus or a cluster of touching cell nuclei. The cluster splitting is then computed separately for each of the connected components, which will be outlined in detail throughout the following section.

4   Cluster Splitting

Our cluster splitting consists of three basic steps. First, we detect seeds which correspond to local maxima in the fluorescence intensities within the cluster. In the next step, the seeds are extended geometrically to spheres before labeling the

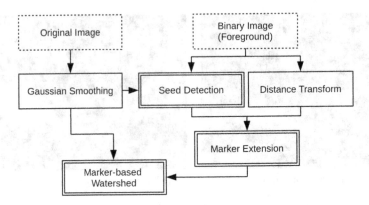

Fig. 3. Workflow of our proposed cluster splitting approach. The original image and the binary image obtained from foreground segmentation are depicted using the stippled boxes. The key steps of our method are indicated by the double borders of the boxes.

remaining voxels of the cluster using a marker-based watershed segmentation. The complete workflow of our proposed cluster splitting method is depicted in Fig. 3. In the following, the three key steps will be discussed in detail.

4.1 Seed Detection

In the first step, seeds for the individual nuclei in the cluster are detected. Due to the (approximative) convexity of cell nuclei, this is often done by finding local maxima in the distance transform of the binary image. Unfortunately, this method did not perform well on our images, which is due to the relatively small radius of the nuclei as well as the blurry contours of the foreground which might significantly influence the result of the foreground segmentation and thus modify the convexity and concavity properties of the cluster. Moreover, the clusters are often very dense so that convex subsets can not be identified anymore.

Since fluorescence intensity in our images increases towards the centers of cell nuclei, we detect local maxima in the original image intensities instead of applying the distance transform. After smoothing the image with a 3D Gaussian filter kernel, we apply watershed by rainfall simulation [15] to the three-dimensional image. This method is based on the idea of rain falling on terrain and flowing along the path of steepest descent until reaching a *catchment basin* corresponding to a local minimum. In our case, we invert the flow direction of the algorithm. For each voxel in the smoothed image masked by the foreground segmentation, we start a path which will always flow to the neighbor voxel with the highest intensity value of its three-dimensional 26-neighborhood until reaching a local maximum (see Fig. 4(a)). Each of the detected local maxima is then considered a seed point. In contrast to the common application of this procedure, we do not label any of the start voxels to create a segmentation, but only use the method for detecting the local maxima. Moreover, for each maximum m we can easily compute the number s_m of start voxels with a flow path ending in m.

0	0	0	2	5	3	0	0
0	0	4	11	14	10	0	0
0	6	16→(25)		15	8	0	0
5	12	15	19	18	7	0	0
5	7	8	9	15	20	12	0
0	0	0	8	24	(30)	20	0
0	0	0	6	12	15	17	0
0	0	0	0	7	8	6	0

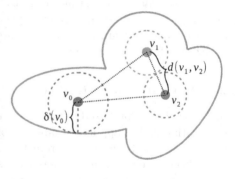

(a) Two-dimensional example of the watershed by rainfall computation. The background voxels are masked (and set to zero) by the foreground segmentation. For two voxels, the path to the local maximum is depicted using arrows.

(b) Example of the spherical marker extension for three seed points v_0, v_1, v_2. For v_0, the radius r_0 of the sphere corresponds to the distance to the background $\delta(v_0)$, for v_1 and v_2, it is restricted to half of their Euclidean distance $d(v_1, v_2) = d(v_2, v_1)$.

Fig. 4. Schematic examples of the seed detection and marker extension steps.

This information can then be used to remove m from the list of seeds if s_m is below a threshold t_s, e.g., if the local maximum results from an artifact in the foreground segmentation. Since the local maxima correspond to the centers of cell nuclei, the number k of seed points corresponds to the number of detected cell nuclei within the cluster.

4.2 Marker Extension

For each seed point $v_i, 0 \leq i < k$ detected in the previous step, the label i should be assigned to all of the voxels within the cluster which belong to the corresponding cell nucleus. Before assigning all of the voxels to a seed, we perform a geometric marker extension which is based on the fact that cell nuclei are approximately convex. For each seed v_i, we compute a sphere c_i with center v_i which contains voxels that can unquestionably be assigned the label i. The radius r_i of the sphere c_i is given by

$$r_i = \min\left\{\delta(v_i), \frac{1}{2}\min\{d(v_i, v_j)\}\right\}, 0 \leq i, j < k, i \neq j, \tag{1}$$

where $\delta(v_i)$ is the Euclidean distance of v_i to the background, and $d(v_i, v_j)$ is the Euclidean distance between v_i and v_j. For the first part, we compute the distance transform of the binary image obtained in the foreground segmentation, and compute $\delta(v_i)$ by sampling the distance transform at v_i. The second term is a constraint which accounts for the fact that, depending on the density of the cluster and orientation of the nuclei, spheres centered in the seed points with just the distance to the background might overlap and in such cases restricts the radius to half of the distance of v_i to its nearest neighbor in the set of seed points. Figure 4(b) illustrates an example of the marker extension computation. All of the voxels within the sphere c_i are assigned the label i and act as an initialization for the next step.

4.3   Marker-Based Watershed

Using the spheres computed in the previous step, a marker-controlled watershed segmentation [20] is applied to label all of the remaining voxels in the cluster. This method floods the image from the markers (i.e., the spheres which have already been labeled) using the intensity values of the smoothed image. In each step, we select the voxel with the highest intensity value from the set of unlabeled voxels and assign a neighboring label to it. When viewed topologically, the markers derived from the local maxima correspond to hills from which the labels flow down while the boundaries between the labels (i.e., cell nuclei) correspond to basins. Some examples of the cluster splitting results are shown in Fig. 5.

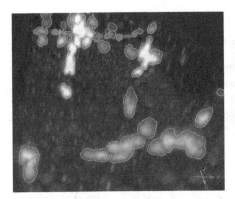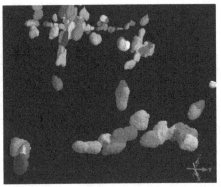

Fig. 5. 3D examples of cluster splitting results. Left: original image with silhouettes of the foreground segmentation, right: resulting segmentation.

5   Performance Evaluation

We have evaluated the performance of our segmentation approach using two reference data sets which have been manually labeled by domain experts, which took an effort of several weeks. The first data set with a size of $195 \times 168 \times 129$ voxels containing 139 cell nuclei has been labeled voxel-wise, while in the second data set with a size of $425 \times 276 \times 129$ voxels containing 190 cell nuclei the centroids of the nuclei have been marked. All of the data sets are 16-bit images and have a resolution of $1\,\mu$m in $x-, y-$, and $z-$direction. In all tests, the Gaussian smoothing of the original data in the cluster splitting step has been performed using a $5 \times 5 \times 5$ filter kernel with $\sigma = 0.6$. For the post-processing step of the foreground segmentation, two successive median filter operations using a

$3 \times 3 \times 3$ kernel have been used. The threshold t_s in the seed detection has been set to 1 so that no filtering of local maxima was applied.

From the voxel-wise labeled cell nuclei we have calculated the mean volume in voxels as well as the standard deviation. We have only incorporated nuclei which do not contain any border voxels to avoid cases where nuclei are only partially visible. Additionally, we have excluded one outlier with a volume of 3339 voxels which had been identified to include a lot of background at its boundary. From the remaining 105 nuclei we have calculated the mean volume of 1094 voxels and the standard deviation of 533 voxels. Since the smallest cell nucleus in the manual labeling had a volume of 266 voxels, we conservatively chose a size threshold of 200 voxels for the connected components in the foreground segmentation.

Unfortunately, no definitive ground truth can be generated for the data, since even manual segmentation is a very time-consuming and error-prone task due to the three-dimensional nature of the images, a certain amount of ambiguity, and the overall complexity of the cluster splitting task, especially for a voxel-wise labeling. Outliers in the size distribution of the nuclei might thus indicate cases of over- and under-segmentation in the manual labeling.

For the quantitative performance evaluation we adopt the method of [11] which is based on the well-established metrics *Recall*, *Precision*, *Accuracy*, and *F-measure*. To calculate the metrics, we match the centroids of the cell nuclei in the manual reference segmentation (RS) to the centroids computed by the automated segmentation (AS). For each centroid in the RS, a spherical neighborhood of 9 voxels was considered. If a single centroid of the AS was found within the radius, it is counted as a *true positive* (TP) and removed from the list. For multiple matches, the closest is counted as a TP. Based on those matches, the *false negatives* (FN), i.e., centroids in the RS for which no match was found, and *false positives* (FP), i.e., centroids in the AS which have not been selected as a TP, are computed. The four metrics can then be calculated as follows:

$$\text{Recall} = \frac{\text{TP}}{\text{TP} + \text{FN}} \qquad \text{Precision} = \frac{\text{TP}}{\text{TP} + \text{FP}}$$

$$\text{F-Measure} = 2 \cdot \frac{\text{Precision} \cdot \text{Recall}}{\text{Precision} + \text{Recall}} \qquad \text{Accuracy} = \frac{\text{TP}}{\text{TP} + \text{FN} + \text{FP}}$$

We compare our method to three different state-of-the art approaches, a 3D watershed algorithm proposed by Ollion et al. [14] which is available as a Fiji plugin [18], the Lines-of-Sight (LoS) decomposition method by Mathew et al. [11], and the graph-cut based method proposed by Al-Kofahi et al. [2] which has been implemented in the FARSight toolkit [1]. Where required, the best parameter sets for the methods have been determined by parameter scanning. For the FARSight implementation, the images had to be converted to 8-bit. For the first data set, the voxel-wise manual segmentation was used as a foreground segmentation (except for the FARSight implementation of the method of Al-Kofahi) to solely evaluate the cluster splitting. For the LoS method, this foreground segmentation was additionally processed using a $3 \times 3 \times 3$ median filter to improve the results. On this data set, our cluster splitting method achieved an accuracy of

Table 1. Quantitative evaluation of our proposed method in comparison to three state-of-the-art methods on two data sets (DS). For DS 1, the manual labeling was used as a foreground segmentation except for FARSight (*). The second column shows the number of cell nuclei in the reference segmentation (RS). The metrics Recall, Precision, Accuracy, and F-measure range from 0 (worst performance) to 1 (best performance).

Data set	#cells (RS)	Algorithm	#cells	TP	FP	FN	Recall	Prec.	Acc.	F-Measure
DS 1	139	Proposed	116	111	5	28	0.80	0.96	0.77	0.87
		LoS	68	57	11	82	0.41	0.84	0.38	0.55
		FARSight$^{(*)}$	92	70	22	69	0.50	0.76	0.43	0.60
		3D Watershed	154	117	37	22	0.84	0.76	0.66	0.80
DS 2	190	Proposed	145	143	2	47	0.75	0.99	0.75	0.85
		LoS	68	67	1	123	0.35	0.99	0.35	0.52
		FARSight	106	87	19	103	0.46	0.82	0.42	0.59
		3D Watershed	192	155	37	35	0.82	0.81	0.68	0.81

0.77 and an F-measure of 0.87 and considerably outperformed all of the other algorithms. On the second data set, we have computed the foreground segmentation using our voxel classification method. For both the LoS method as well as the 3D watershed, we have used the foreground segmentation computed by our random forest classifier since using the proposed thresholding approaches further diminished the performance. Again, our method outperformed all of the other approaches. On the second data set, we achieved an accuracy of 0.75 and an F-measure of 0.85. All of the results of our quantitative evaluation are listed in Table 1. It should be noted that in contrast to other approaches our method generally produces almost no false positives.

We have also tested the influence of the marker extension in the cluster splitting workflow on the second data set. When leaving out the marker extension, the accuracy slightly decreases to 0.73 and the F-measure decreases to 0.84. Moreover, while the mean volume of the segmented cell nuclei in both variants of our methods is 1205 voxels, without the marker extension step the standard deviation increases from 848 to 876.

6   Conclusion

We have proposed a method for automated detection and segmentation of clustered immunostained cell nuclei in three-dimensional ultramicroscopy images. Our approach yields good overall results and outperforms several other state-of-the art algorithms on our images, which we have evaluated using reference data that has been manually labeled by domain experts. Our method produces almost no false positives, so that errors in the segmentation are almost exclusively due to cases of under-segmentation. To improve the applicability of the algorithm in quantification applications, an additional uncertainty computation could be derived from the size distribution of the cell nuclei by analyzing the number of detected cell nuclei in relation to the total volume of a cluster. This information could then be integrated into the workflow in form of a guided manual correction.

Acknowledgments. This work has been partly supported by the Deutsche Forschungsgemeinschaft, CRC 656 "Cardiovascular Molecular Imaging". The images in this paper have been rendered using the framework *Voreen* [13].

References

1. The FARSight toolkit. http://www.farsight-toolkit.org
2. Al-Kofahi, Y., Lassoued, W., Lee, W., Roysam, B.: Improved automatic detection and segmentation of cell nuclei in histopathology images. IEEE Trans. Biomed. Eng. **57**(4), 841–852 (2010)
3. Bergeest, J.P., Rohr, K.: Segmentation of cell nuclei in 3D microscopy images based on level set deformable models and convex minimization. In: 11th IEEE International Symposium on Biomedical Imaging (ISBI), pp. 637–640 (2014)
4. Daněk, O., Matula, P., Ortiz-de-Solórzano, C., Muñoz-Barrutia, A., Maška, M., Kozubek, M.: Segmentation of touching cell nuclei using a two-stage graph cut model. In: Salberg, A.-B., Hardeberg, J.Y., Jenssen, R. (eds.) SCIA 2009. LNCS, vol. 5575, pp. 410–419. Springer, Heidelberg (2009)
5. Fehr, J., Ronneberger, O., Kurz, H., Burkhardt, H.: Self-learning segmentation and classification of cell-nuclei in 3D volumetric data using voxel-wise gray scale invariants. In: Kropatsch, W.G., Sablatnig, R., Hanbury, A. (eds.) DAGM 2005. LNCS, vol. 3663, pp. 377–384. Springer, Heidelberg (2005)
6. Fernández-Delgado, M., Cernadas, E., Barro, S., Amorim, D.: Do we need hundreds of classifiers to solve real world classification problems? J. Mach. Learn. Res. **15**(1), 3133–3181 (2014)
7. Gertych, A., Ma, Z., Tajbakhsh, J., Velásquez-Vacca, A., Knudsen, B.S.: Rapid 3-D delineation of cell nuclei for high-content screening platforms. Comput. Biol. Med. **69**, 328–338 (2016)
8. Harder, N., Bodnar, M., Eils, R., Spector, D.L., Rohr, K.: 3D segmentation and quantification of mouse embryonic stem cells in fluorescence microscopy images. In: IEEE International Symposium on Biomedical Imaging: From Nano to Macro, pp. 216–219 (2011)
9. Indhumathi, C., Cai, Y., Guan, Y., Opas, M.: An automatic segmentation algorithm for 3D cell cluster splitting using volumetric confocal images. J. Microsc. **243**(1), 60–76 (2011)
10. Lin, G., Adiga, U., Olson, K., Guzowski, J.F., Barnes, C.A., Roysam, B.: A hybrid 3D watershed algorithm incorporating gradient cues and object models for automatic segmentation of nuclei in confocal image stacks. Cytometry Part A **56**(1), 23–36 (2003)
11. Mathew, B., Schmitz, A., Muñoz-Descalzo, S., Ansari, N., Pampaloni, F., Stelzer, E., Fischer, S.: Robust and automated three-dimensional segmentation of densely packed cell nuclei in different biological specimens with lines-of-sight decomposition. BMC Bioinform. **16**(1), 1–14 (2015)
12. Mertz, J.: Optical sectioning microscopy with planar or structured illumination. Nat. Methods **8**(10), 811–819 (2011)
13. Meyer-Spradow, J., Ropinski, T., Mensmann, J., Hinrichs, K.H.: Voreen: a rapid-prototyping environment for ray-casting-based volume visualizations. IEEE Comput. Graphics Appl. (Appl. Dept.) **29**(6), 6–13 (2009)

14. Ollion, J., Cochennec, J., Loll, F., Escudé, C., Boudier, T.: TANGO: a generic tool for high-throughput 3D image analysis for studying nuclear organization. Bioinformatics **29**(14), 1840–1841 (2013)

15. Osma-Ruiz, V., Godino-Llorente, J.I., Sáenz-Lechón, N., Gómez-Vilda, P.: An improved watershed algorithm based on efficient computation of shortest paths. Pattern Recogn. **40**(3), 1078–1090 (2007)

16. Qi, J.: Dense nuclei segmentation based on graph cut and convexity-concavity analysis. J. Microsc. **253**(1), 42–53 (2014)

17. Reynaud, E.G., Peychl, J., Huisken, J., Tomancak, P.: Guide to light-sheet microscopy for adventurous biologists. Nat. Methods **12**(1), 30–34 (2015)

18. Schindelin, J., Arganda-Carreras, I., Frise, E., Kaynig, V., Longair, M., Pietzsch, T., Preibisch, S., Rueden, C., Saalfeld, S., Schmid, B., Tinevez, J.Y., White, D.J., Hartenstein, V., Eliceiri, K., Tomancak, P., Cardona, A.: Fiji: an open-source platform for biological-image analysis. Nat. Methods **9**(7), 676–682 (2012)

19. Sezgin, M., Sankur, B.: Survey over image thresholding techniques and quantitative performance evaluation. J. Electron. Imaging **13**(1), 146–168 (2004)

20. Soille, P.: Morphological Image Analysis: Principles and Applications, 2nd edn. Springer, Heidelberg (2003)

21. Sommer, C., Straehle, C.N., Köthe, U., Hamprecht, F.A.: Ilastik: interactive learning and segmentation toolkit. In: 8th IEEE International Symposium on Biomedical Imaging (ISBI), pp. 230–233. IEEE (2011)

22. Stelzer, E.H.K.: Light-sheet fluorescence microscopy for quantitative biology. Nat. Methods **12**(1), 23–26 (2015)

23. Tek, F.B., Kroeger, T., Mikula, S., Hamprecht, F.A.: Automated cell nucleus detection for large-volume electron microscopy of neural tissue. In: 11th IEEE International Symposium on Biomedical Imaging (ISBI), pp. 69–72 (2014)

24. Wählby, C., Sintorn, I.M., Erlandsson, F., Borgefors, G., Bengtsson, E.: Combining intensity, edge and shape information for 2D and 3D segmentation of cell nuclei in tissue sections. J. Microsc. **215**(1), 67–76 (2004)

25. Wienert, S., Heim, D., Saeger, K., Stenzinger, A., Beil, M., Hufnagl, P., Dietel, M., Denkert, C., Klauschen, F.: Dense nuclei segmentation based on graph cut and convexity-concavity analysis. Sci. Rep. **2**, 503–510 (2012)

26. Yokomizo, T., Yamada-Inagawa, T., Yzaguirre, A.D., Chen, M.J., Speck, N.A., Dzierzak, E.: Whole-mount three-dimensional imaging of internally localized immunostained cells within mouse embryos. Nat. Protoc. **7**(3), 421–431 (2012)

Robust Interactive Multi-label Segmentation with an Advanced Edge Detector

Sabine Müller[1,2(✉)], Peter Ochs[2], Joachim Weickert[2], and Norbert Graf[1]

[1] Department of Pediatric Oncology and Hematology, Saarland University Hospital,
66421 Homburg, Germany
smueller@mia.uni-saarland.de
[2] Mathematical Image Analysis Group, Saarland University, Campus E1.7,
66041 Saarbrücken, Germany

Abstract. Recent advances on convex relaxation methods allow for a flexible formulation of many interactive multi-label segmentation methods. The building blocks are a likelihood specified for each pixel and each label, and a penalty for the boundary length of each segment. While many sophisticated likelihood estimations based on various statistical measures have been investigated, the boundary length is usually measured in a metric induced by simple image gradients. We show that complementing these methods with recent advances of edge detectors yields an immense quality improvement. A remarkable feature of the proposed method is the ability to correct some erroneous labels, when computer generated initial labels are considered. This allows us to improve state-of-the-art methods for motion segmentation in videos by 5–10 % with respect to the F-measure (Dice score).

1 Introduction

Image segmentation is a highly ambiguous task. By definition, the goal is a partitioning of an image into a finite number of meaningful regions. Unless there is a clear specification of the word "meaningful", the quality of a segmentation cannot be measured. Usually a "meaningful" segmentation refers to a separation of the visible objects in an image. However, even this task can be ambiguous. Consider for instance a fruit bowl with many apples. Should we consider each apple as an individual object, or the collection of apples in the fruit bowl as a single object?

In this paper, we argue that this distinction is important even when user input is provided. Assume the user seeds a label on a single apple. If only the seeded apple is to be segmented, the label can be propagated until the closest visual edge of the apple. Strong prior assumptions like the grouping of points that have a similar texture or colour can counteract the goal of segmenting a single apple. Similar structures are connected across edges and the label spreads to other apples as well. This is beneficial when the collection of apples is to be segmented. Nevertheless, in any of the two cases edge information is essential for achieving the desired segmentation.

© Springer International Publishing AG 2016
B. Rosenhahn and B. Andres (Eds.): GCPR 2016, LNCS 9796, pp. 117–128, 2016.
DOI: 10.1007/978-3-319-45886-1_10

The goal of our paper is to complement a segmentation method that uses some user input with results from a sophisticated edge detector. The challenge for the segmentation method is to align the segments' boundaries with the "right" edges. Since the edge detector does not know what object the user is interested in, many edges are generated that are unimportant for the segmentation method. Moreover, often edges are not closed contours, hence selecting the right edges is not enough. The segmentation method needs to extend the proposed edges and close gaps. These challenges are by no means trivial. Additionally, the perception of important edges can vary significantly from image to image. While in a low contrast recording—for example taken at night—a weak change of colour is important, the same variation of colours is negligible in a high contrast recording. The proposed segmentation method deals with these challenges and shows a favourable performance on several semi-supervised segmentation benchmarks.

We apply our method also to video segmentation where many ambiguities are resolved by considering motion. Current state-of-the-art methods in motion segmentation in videos cluster a sparse set of point trajectories into similarly moving groups. Their output is an object-oriented sparse labelling of each video frame (more or less evenly distributed). We take these labellings as "user input" and turn the sparse labels into dense segmentations. A major challenge in this task is the ability to correct a moderate amount of these input labels. They are automatically generated labels and are often erroneous close to object boundaries. We significantly improve on the state-of-the-art method in this challenge.

Last but not least, we show that our method is also interesting for medical applications, where for example a clinician roughly marks a kidney tumour in a single slice of a volumetric MRI recording and receives a segmentation of the tumour in all slices.

2   Related Work

We propose a method for interactive segmentation. The "object" that is to be segmented in the image is seeded with labels. In the context of interactive segmentation these labels are often called scribbles and are set by a user. However, labels can also be generated automatically by an algorithmic method. In this paper, we consider both scenarios, which are fundamentally different. While user scribbles are usually assumed to be correct, i.e., the segmentation method needs to fill in labels between the given ones, automatically generated labels can be erroneous and need to be corrected partially.

Most of the available literature deals with the former scenario. A successful idea is the estimation of statistical features from given scribbles in order to define likelihoods for each label, e.g. mean value [9], colour/intensity histograms [4,13, 18,23], or texture [1,19,24,25]. As a regulariser usually the boundary length in the image metric is minimised. In [28] the boundary length is penalised in the metric induced by the image gradients, which aligns the segmentation boundaries to image edges. In [29] the boundary length is measured in a non-local metric, which achieves good results for small details, but suffers from expensive non-local computations.

Of course, the image metric can be induced by more sophisticated edge indicators such as the traditional ones [6,22], which are based on colour and intensities, or more recent ones that include also texture information. We propose to induce the image metric by one of the state-of-the-art trained edge detectors by Dollár and Zitnick [11,12]. Besides having better information about edges in the image, much fewer edges are detected compared to the simple gradient magnitude measure. This has also a positive effect on the computation time, as the propagation of labels is hampered less by unimportant structures.

A flexible framework for multi-label segmentation is the formulation as a minimal partitioning problem [15,17], which can be solved via convex relaxation methods [7]. This framework, which is sometimes referred to as Potts multi-label segmentation model, is very flexible, since all the above data likelihoods can be incorporated. The boundary length is represented using the total variation of the label indicator functions, and is easily adjusted to a modification of the image metric. This convex relaxation framework is used for example in [18–20,28,29] for the task of interactive segmentation. In [27] it has been extended to a non-metric prior, in [26] to generalised ordering constraints, which constraints labels appearing adjacent to each other in a certain direction, in [10] to RGB-D data, and in [3] to the context of semantic segmentation. All these models can be easily complemented in the way we propose by a sophisticated edge detector.

The second scenario where automatically generated labels must be corrected has been considered in [20,21], which is also formulated in the convex relaxation framework mentioned above. We propose a generalisation of their method to an arbitrary edge indicator function, and this extension has a strong impact on practical results. On the FBMS-59 benchmark [21] we improve their method by about 5–10 %. For recent works on interactive segmentation on medical images, we refer to [2,14] and the references therein.

3   Method

In this section, we discuss a generic multi-label segmentation model. Based on this model, we recapitulate the interactive segmentation method proposed in [18] and our improvements: We take erroneous user scribbles into account and introduce a new regularisation term with an advanced edge detector.

3.1   A Multi-label Segmentation Model

Following Chambolle et al. [7], we consider a minimal partitioning problem of the rectangular image domain $\Omega \subset \mathbb{R}^2$ into $\Omega_1, \ldots, \Omega_n \subset \mathbb{R}^2$ non-overlapping regions. The generic variational problem is

$$\min_{\Omega_1,\ldots,\Omega_n \subset \Omega} \frac{1}{2} \sum_{i=1}^{n} \mathrm{Per}(\Omega_i; \Omega) + \sum_{i=1}^{n} \int_{\Omega_i} h_i(\mathbf{x})\, d\mathbf{x},$$

$$\text{s.t.} \quad \Omega = \bigcup_{i=1}^{n} \Omega_i, \quad \Omega_i \cap \Omega_j = \emptyset, \quad \forall\, i \neq j \tag{1}$$

where $h_i \colon \mathbb{R} \to \mathbb{R}_+$ are potential functions reflecting the cost for each pixel being assigned to a certain label $i = 1, \ldots, n$, and $\mathrm{Per}(\Omega_i; \Omega)$ denotes the perimeter of region Ω_i inside Ω. A weighting parameter $\lambda > 0$ is not required, as it can be absorbed in the functions h_i. In order to improve the alignment of region boundaries with image edges the perimeter is usually measured in a metric that is induced by the underlying image $f \colon \Omega \to \mathbb{R}^d$. A common choice is a weighting with the image gradient with $\exp(-\gamma|\nabla f(\mathbf{x})|)$, where ∇f denotes the Jacobian of f and $|\nabla f|$ is its Frobenius norm. This reduces the measure of the boundary length where the image gradient magnitude is high. As the middle column of Fig. 1 demonstrates, this choice is suboptimal when we seek for segmentations of objects. The image gradient magnitude shows clutter, i.e., it is high for unimportant edges. In this paper, we propose to use a sophisticated edge detector instead. We built on the fast structured edge detector [11,12], which in contrast to traditional edge detectors, incorporates texture, colour, and brightness. The right column of Fig. 1 shows that this state-of-the-art edge detector is well-suited to identify also texture edges and illusory contours. Let $\mathcal{E} \colon \Omega \to \mathbb{R}$ be the output of this edge detector, i.e., $\mathcal{E}(\mathbf{x})$ is large on edges and low otherwise. We weight the perimeter of region boundaries with the function

$$g(\mathbf{x}) = \exp(\mathcal{E}(\mathbf{x})^\beta / \bar{\mathcal{E}}), \tag{2}$$

where $\bar{\mathcal{E}} := \frac{2}{\Omega} \int_\Omega |\mathcal{E}(\mathbf{x})|\, d\mathbf{x}$ and β is a positive parameter.

Let us now turn our attention to the potential functions in the second term of (1). Any method that proposes a new way to estimate these potential functions may be combined with the perimeter regularisation discussed above. In the following, we recap the model proposed by Nieuwenhuis et al. [18].

Spatially Varying Colour Distributions. Assume the user provides a (measurable) set of scribbles $\mathcal{S}_i \subset \Omega$ for each label i. Nieuwenhuis and Cremers [18] suggest to define the potential function $h_i(\mathbf{x})$ in (1) as the negative logarithm of the linearly to $[0, 1]$-scaled function $\tilde{h}(\mathbf{x})$ of[1]

$$\frac{1}{|\mathcal{S}_i|} \int_{\mathcal{S}_i} k_{\rho_i(\mathbf{x})}(\mathbf{x} - \mathbf{y})\, k_\sigma(f(\mathbf{x}) - f(\mathbf{y}))\, d\mathbf{y}, \tag{3}$$

where $|\mathcal{S}_i|$ denotes the area that is occupied by ith label, k_σ and k_{ρ_i} are Gaussians with standard deviation σ in colour space and adaptive standard deviation $\rho_i(\mathbf{x}) = \alpha \inf_{\mathbf{y} \in \mathcal{S}_i} |\mathbf{x} - \mathbf{y}|$ in the spatial domain, respectively. The idea of this spatially adaptive standard deviation is to reduce the influence of the colour

---

[1] Instead of integrating over the set of scribbles they sum over all scribbled pixels.

Fig. 1. Exemplary results for edge detection. From left to right: input image. Gradient magnitude image. Result of structured edge detector. Edge maps are inverted and gamma corrected for visualisation. The structured edge detector shows more object edges and less clutter for unimportant structures.

distribution from scribbles that are far away. This influence is reduced proportionally to distance from $\mathbf{x}$ to the closest scribble location.

In our opinion, a major drawback of this model is the assumption that all labels are correct. Formally, $h_i(\mathbf{x})$ must be set to $+\infty$ for $\mathbf{x} \in \mathcal{S}_i$, since (3) does not make sense for $\rho_i(\mathbf{x}) = 0$. Therefore, we propose to use potential functions that allow the segmentation method to correct possibly wrong scribbles/labels— this issue arises for instance when scribbles are provided automatically by a computer. This is achieved by setting for scribble positions $\mathbf{x} \in \mathcal{S}_j$ the function values $\tilde{h}_i(\mathbf{x}) = 1 - \zeta$ if $i = j$ and $\tilde{h}_i(\mathbf{x}) = \zeta/(n-1)$ otherwise, where $1 - \zeta$ is the assumed probability for the scribble being correct.

The variational minimization problem (1) can be solved efficiently after a convex relaxation [7]. The regions $\Omega_1, \ldots, \Omega_n$, their non-overlapping and covering criterion can be easily represented by label indicator functions, whose ranges get relaxed to $[0, 1]$. In this representation, the perimeter of the regions is measured by the weighted total variation. Using the dual definition of the total variation makes the application of the efficient primal–dual algorithm in [8] straightforward.

4 Experimental Evaluation

We evaluated our approach on the GRAZ benchmark [24], the FBMS-59 [21] data sets, and MRI data sets from patients with kidney tumours. We show results in terms of the metrics suggested in [18,19,21,24]: *precision* and *recall* are computed as

$$
P_{\hat{\Omega}_i, \Omega_i} := \frac{|\hat{\Omega}_i \cap \Omega_i|}{|\Omega_i|}, \qquad R_{\hat{\Omega}_i, \Omega_i} := \frac{|\hat{\Omega}_i \cap \Omega_i|}{|\hat{\Omega}_i|}, \tag{4}
$$

where $\hat{\Omega}_i$ is the ground truth labelling, and Ω_i the result of our algorithm for label i. The harmonic mean of precision and recall, the *F-measure* or *Dice-score* relates the area of a cluster to its overlap with the ground truth:

$$F_{\hat{\Omega}_i,\Omega_i} = \frac{2P_{\hat{\Omega}_i,\Omega_i}R_{\hat{\Omega}_i,\Omega_i}}{P_{\hat{\Omega}_i,\Omega_i} + R_{\hat{\Omega}_i,\Omega_i}} \ . \tag{5}$$

Finally, the average F-measure determines the overall segmentation accuracy.

4.1 Multi-label Segmentation of Colour Images

The GRAZ benchmark dataset [24] consists of 262 seed-ground-truth pairs from 158 natural images for interactive multilabel segmentation. We use the following manually tuned parameters for experiments with space-variant colour distributions: $\alpha = 15$, $\beta = 2$, $\sigma = 3$, and $\zeta = 0.05$.

We compare our results in Table 1 to the original approach by Nieuwenhuis et al. [18], as well as their advanced method that incorporates texture information [19]. The results indicate that using an advanced edge detector textural information in the data term can be neglected. Figure 2 shows an exemplary result from our evaluation. The information from an advanced edge detection is sufficient for segmentations of high quality.

Table 1. Comparison to spatially variant approaches by Nieuwenhuis et al. [18,19].

Method	Dim	Dice score
Nieuwenhuis/Cremers, spatially constant [18]	3	0.89
Nieuwenhuis/Cremers, space-variant [18]	5	0.92
Nieuwenhuis/Cremers, space-variant [18]	13	0.93
Nieuwenhuis et al., space-variant + texture [19]	13	0.94
Our approach, spatially constant, no colour	5	0.77
Our approach, spatially constant, colour	5	0.90
Our approach, space-variant, no colour	5	0.80
Our approach, space-variant, colour	5	0.93
Our approach, space-variant, colour	13	0.94

Decreasing the diameter of user scribbles leads to slightly worse approximations of the colour distributions. However, our model can compensate this lack of information since textural and colour information are also included in the edge detector. In fact, the texture based model [19] seems to rely on a large diameter.

The creators of the GRAZ benchmark made an important contribution towards evaluation of interactive multi-label segmentation, but current state-of-the-art segmentation reached the limit of these data sets. Small details are very important, and not all ground truth labellings are optimal, see Fig. 3. Overall, the results on this data set are very close to the optimum. Therefore it might not be desirable to further improve the Dice score on this data set.

Fig. 2. Exemplary segmentation result exclusively based on colour variation and the structured edge detector. From left to right: scribble image, dim = 5. Ground truth labelling. Our result.

Fig. 3. Limitations of GRAZ benchmark. From left to right: scribble image. Ground truth label image. Our result. It is clearly visible, that the quality of image labels is limited and the segmentation outcome can not reflect the user intention. Dice score: 0.86

4.2 Video Segmentation

The FBMS-59 [21] data set, an extended version of [5], contains 29 video sequences for training and 30 video sequences for testing. We used minimum cost multicuts [16] as well as [21] to generate and automatically label point trajectories. Ideally, they provide sparse, and temporally consistent labels for each frame in a video. In contrast to interactive or supervised segmentation, trajectory labels are single pixels spread over the whole image domain and tend to be erroneous. Video segmentation is a challenging task. Even the considered state-of-the-art methods [16,21] provide erroneous trajectories. Therefore, methods that turn the sparse labels into dense segmentations, such as our method, must be able to correct some of the wrong labels. We incorporate this prior knowledge by increasing the uncertainty parameter ζ. The manually tuned parameters we used for all video frames are $\alpha = 30$, $\beta = 2$, $\sigma = 3$, and $\zeta = 0.2$.

We compare our approach to the recent approach [21] that densifies the sparse labels from the trajectories in each frame based on image gradients. We stick to point trajectories generated by [21] for the sake of comparability. Table 2 states our benchmark results for two variants of our model: In the first version, we include exclusively information about label position and rely on information already contained in our edge detector (SPT-C, NC). This version coincides with [21] except for the edge detection. In the second variant, we include all available information for segmentation and use spatially variant colour distributions

Table 2. Results on the video segmentation benchmark FBMS-59.

Method	Density	Dice	Precision	Recall	F≥ 75%
Training set					
Ochs et al., MoSegDense [21]	100%	0.69	0.84	0.59	15/65
Ochs et al., MoSegSparse [21]	0.87%	0.72	0.85	0.62	17/65
Our approach, SPT-C, NC (SC [21])	100%	0.79	0.83	0.75	18/65
Our approach, SPT-V, C (SC [21])	100%	0.81	0.84	0.78	20/65
Keuper, MCe sparse, prior 0.5 (MT [16])	0.86%	0.79	**0.87**	0.73	31/65
Our approach, SPT-V, C (MT [16])	100%	**0.82**	0.85	**0.80**	24/65
Test set					
Ochs et al., MoSegDense [21]	100%	0.66	0.78	0.57	17/69
Ochs et al., MoSegSparse [21]	0.92%	0.69	0.80	0.61	24/65
Our approach, SPT-C, NC (SC [21])	100%	0.71	0.75	0.68	18/65
Our approach, SPT-V, C (SC [21])	100%	0.74	0.76	**0.72**	21/69
Keuper, MCe sparse, prior 0.5 (MT [16])	0.87%	**0.76**	**0.88**	0.68	25/69
Our approach, SPT-V, C (MT [16])	100%	0.75	0.81	0.71	23/69

(SPT-V, C). Though the edge detector should already contain all relevant color and texture information in the image, favouring slightly color similarity improves the results. This is due to a suboptimal performance of the edge detector. We clearly outperform [21] on all error metrics.

Moreover, we complement the sparse labels of the state-of-the-art in motion segmentation from Keuper et al. [16] with our approach. The ability to correct also erroneous labels (see Fig. 4) allows us to even improve the results in the dense segmentation. Note that the difference in performance on test and training set is due to different challenges and the (still limited) number of video sequences rather than over-fitting.

4.3   Volumetric MRI Data

Additionally, we evaluate the performance of our method on MRI data of unilateral kidney tumours and rely on image data of 12 nephroblastoma-patients before and after chemotherapy. This encompasses in total 24 pre- and post-chemotherapeutic monomodal volumetric images of T_2 modality (inslice-sampling ranges from 0.4 mm to 0.6 mm, across-slice sampling from 1 mm to 7 mm). The (pre- and post-chemotherapy) ground truth of the tumour's outline was defined by manual expert segmentation of two human expert raters. A clinician, familiar with tumours, draw user scribbles in a single depth slice for each data set. We use the following parameters for our experiments on MRI data: $\alpha = 15$, $\beta = 2$, $\sigma = 5$, and $\zeta = 0.05$. We compare the results of our approach for several kind of information in Table 3. Our method does not perform well when no intensity information is included as only two labels are provided - tumour and not tumour. Incorporating intensity information dramatically improves the

Fig. 4. Exemplary results on FMBS-59 [21] data sets. From top to bottom: labels from SC-point trajectories [21]. Segmentation results of Ochs et al., MoSegDense [21]. Our segmentation result, no colour, spatially constant. Trajectory labels are enhanced for visualisation. Our method is able to correct a significant amount of labels.

Table 3. Evaluation for unilateral nephroblastoma patients.

Method	Dim	Dice	Precision	Recall
Our approach, SPT-C, no intensity	5	0.76	0.79	0.74
Our approach, SPT-C, intensity	5	0.77	0.80	0.75
Our approach, SPT-V, no intensity	5	0.79	0.83	0.75
Our approach, SPT-V, intensity	5	0.90	0.92	0.89
Our approach, SPT-V, intensity	13	0.91	0.92	0.91

result, but similar to our results on the GRAZ benchmark in Table 1, few user scribbles are sufficient for highly accurate segmentation results (Fig. 5).

4.4 Runtimes

We conducted our experiments on a desktop PC with 3.4 GHz Intel Core i7 CPU, 16 GB RAM, and a NVidia GeForce GTX 970 graphics card with 4 GB RAM and 1664 CUDA cores. The edge maps [12] for all benchmarks were precomputed with an average computation time of 0.9 s. The average computation time for an image of size 625×391 was 1.08 s. This is comparable to [18,19,24].

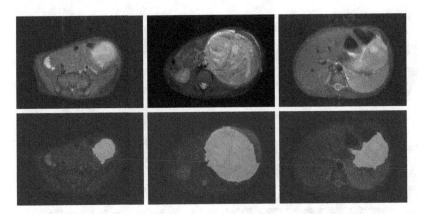

Fig. 5. Example results for 3D medical image segmentation. From left to right: slice 2, slice 7, slice 19. User scribbles are set for one slice. Cost volume computation, as well as optimisation are conducted in 3D.

5 Summary

We proposed a robust algorithm for interactive multi-label segmentation based on a sophisticated edge detector that includes texture, colour, and brightness. As interaction, we considered two scenarios: The labels are set by a user and are always correct, and the labels are computed by an algorithm and are likely to be erroneous. Especially the second setting is rarely considered. However, a common methodology for motion segmentation in videos is to cluster a sparse set of point trajectories. These trajectories can be considered as the (erroneous) user scribbles in each frame and can be made dense by our approach. For this problem, we improve on state-of-the-art by about 5–10 % in the Dice score. In our ongoing research, we are also considering extensions of our approach that allow uncertainty quantification labellings of other computer vision tasks.

Acknowledgements. This work was partially funded by the European Union's FP7 under the project Computational Horizons in Cancer (grant agreement No. 600841).

References

1. Arbelaez, P., Maire, M., Fowlkes, C., Malik, J.: Contour detection and hierarchical image segmentation. IEEE Trans. Pattern Anal. Mach. Intell. **33**(5), 898–916 (2011)
2. Bauer, S., Porz, N., Meier, R., Pica, A., Slotboom, J., Wiest, R., Reyes, M.: Interactive segmentation of MR images from brain tumor patients. In: Proceedings of the 11th International Symposium on Biomedical Imaging, Beijing, China, pp. 862–865 (2014)
3. Bergbauer, J., Nieuwenhuis, C., Souiai, M., Cremers, D.: Proximity priors for variational semantic segmentation and recognition. In: ICCV Workshop on Graphical Models for Scene Understanding, Sydney, Australia, pp. 15–21 (2013)

4. Boykov, Y.Y., Jolly, M.P.: Interactive graph cuts for optimal boundary & region segmentation of objects in N-D images. In: Proceedings of the 2001 IEEE International Conference on Computer Vision, Vancouver, Canada, pp. 105–112 (2001)

5. Brox, T., Malik, J.: Object segmentation by long term analysis of point trajectories. In: Daniilidis, K., Maragos, P., Paragios, N. (eds.) ECCV 2010, Part V. LNCS, vol. 6315, pp. 282–295. Springer, Heidelberg (2010)

6. Canny, J.: A computational approach to edge detection. IEEE Trans. Pattern Anal. Mach. Intell. **8**, 679–698 (1986)

7. Chambolle, A., Cremers, D., Pock, T.: A convex approach to minimal partitions. SIAM J. Appl. Math. **5**(4), 1113–1158 (2012)

8. Chambolle, A., Pock, T.: A first-order primal-dual algorithm for convex problems with applications to imaging. J. Math. Imaging Vision **40**(1), 120–145 (2011)

9. Chan, T.F., Vese, L.A.: Active contours without edges. IEEE Trans. Image Process. **10**(2), 266–277 (2001)

10. Diebold, J., Demmel, N., Hazırbaş, C., Moeller, M., Cremers, D.: Interactive multi-label segmentation of RGB-D images. In: Aujol, J.-F., Nikolova, M., Papadakis, N. (eds.) SSVM 2015. LNCS, vol. 9087, pp. 294–306. Springer, Heidelberg (2015)

11. Dollár, P., Zitnick, C.L.: Structured forests for fast edge detection. In: Proceedings of the 2013 IEEE International Conference on Computer Vision, Washington, DC, USA, pp. 1841–1848 (2013)

12. Dollár, P., Zitnick, C.L.: Fast edge detection using structured forests. IEEE Trans. Pattern Anal. Mach. Intell. **37**(8), 1558–1570 (2015)

13. Felzenszwalb, P.F., Huttenlocher, D.P.: Efficient graph-based image segmentation. Int. J. Comput. Vision **59**(2), 167–181 (2004)

14. Feng, C., Zhao, D., Huang, M.: Segmentation of stroke lesions in multi-spectral MR images using bias correction embedded FCM and three phase level set. In: MICCAI Ischemic Stroke Lesion Segmentation, p. 3 (2015)

15. Geman, S., Geman, D.: Stochastic relaxation, Gibbs distributions, and the Bayesian restoration of images. IEEE Trans. Pattern Anal. Mach. Intell. **6**, 721–741 (1984)

16. Keuper, M., Andres, B., Brox, T.: Motion trajectory segmentation via minimum cost multicuts. In: Proceedings of the 2015 IEEE International Conference on Computer Vision, Santiago, Chile, pp. 3271–3279 (2015)

17. Mumford, D., Shah, J.: Optimal approximation of piecewise smooth functions and associated variational problems. Commun. Pure Appl. Math. **42**, 577–685 (1989)

18. Nieuwenhuis, C., Cremers, D.: Spatially varying color distributions for interactive multilabel segmentation. IEEE Trans. Pattern Anal. Mach. Intell. **35**(5), 1234–1247 (2013)

19. Nieuwenhuis, C., Hawe, S., Kleinsteuber, M., Cremers, D.: Co-sparse textural similarity for interactive segmentation. In: Fleet, D., Pajdla, T., Schiele, B., Tuytelaars, T. (eds.) ECCV 2014, Part VI. LNCS, vol. 8694, pp. 285–301. Springer, Heidelberg (2014)

20. Ochs, P., Brox, T.: Object segmentation in video: a hierarchical variational approach for turning point trajectories into dense regions. In: Proceedings of the 2011 IEEE International Conference on Computer Vision, Barcelona, Spain, pp. 1583–1590 (2011)

21. Ochs, P., Malik, J., Brox, T.: Segmentation of moving objects by long term video analysis. IEEE Trans. Pattern Anal. Mach. Intell. **36**(6), 1187–1200 (2014)

22. Perona, P., Malik, J.: Scale space and edge detection using anisotropic diffusion. IEEE Trans. Pattern Anal. Mach. Intell. **12**, 629–639 (1990)

23. Rother, C., Kolmogorov, V., Blake, A.: "GrabCut": interactive foreground extraction using iterated graph cuts. In: Proceedings of the SIGGRAPH 2004, New York, NY, USA, pp. 309–314, August 2004

24. Santner, J., Pock, T., Bischof, H.: Interactive multi-label segmentation. In: Kimmel, R., Klette, R., Sugimoto, A. (eds.) ACCV 2010, Part I. LNCS, vol. 6492, pp. 397–410. Springer, Heidelberg (2011)

25. Santner, J., Unger, M., Pock, T., Leistner, C., Saffari, A., Bischof, H.: Interactive texture segmentation using random forests and total variation. In: Proceedings of the 2009 British Machine Vision Conference, London, UK, pp. 66.1–66.12 (2009)

26. Strekalovskiy, E., Cremers, D.: Generalized ordering constraints for multilabel optimization. In: Proceedings of the 2011 IEEE International Conference on Computer Vision, Barcelona, Spain, pp. 2619–2626 (2011)

27. Strekalovskiy, E., Nieuwenhuis, C., Cremers, D.: Nonmetric priors for continuous multilabel optimization. In: Fitzgibbon, A., Lazebnik, S., Perona, P., Sato, Y., Schmid, C. (eds.) ECCV 2012, Part VII. LNCS, vol. 7578, pp. 208–221. Springer, Heidelberg (2012)

28. Unger, M., Pock, T., Trobin, W., Cremers, D., Bischof, H.: TVSeg - interactive total variation based image segmentation. In: Proceedings of the 2008 British Machine Vision Conference, Leeds, UK, pp. 40.1–40.10 (2008)

29. Werlberger, M., Unger, M., Pock, T., Bischof, H.: Efficient minimization of the non-local potts model. In: Bruckstein, A.M., ter Haar Romeny, B.M., Bronstein, A.M., Bronstein, M.M. (eds.) SSVM 2011. LNCS, vol. 6667, pp. 314–325. Springer, Heidelberg (2012)

Applications

Contiguous Patch Segmentation in Pointclouds

William Nguatem$^{(\boxtimes)}$ and Helmut Mayer$^{(\boxtimes)}$

Institute of Applied Computer Science,
Bundeswehr University Munich, Neubiberg, Germany
{william.nguatem,helmut.mayer}@unibw.de

Abstract. An algorithm for **C**ontiguous **PA**tch **S**egmentation (CPAS) in 3D pointclouds is proposed. In contrast to current state-of-the-art algorithms, CPAS is robust, scalable and provides a more complete description by simultaneously detecting contiguous patches as well as delineating object boundaries. Our algorithm uses a voxel grid to divide the scene into non-overlapping voxels within which clipped planes are fitted with RANSAC. Using a Dirichlet process mixture (DPM) model of Gaussians and connected component analysis, voxels are clustered into contiguous regions. Finally, we use importance sampling on the convex-hull of each region to obtain the underlying patch and object boundary estimates. For urban scenes, the segmentation represents building walls, ground and roof elements (Fig. 1). We demonstrate the robustness of CPAS using data sets from both image matching and raw LiDAR scans.

1 Introduction

Due to emerging applications in the game industry, urban planning, and virtual environments, the generation of 3D models from pointclouds is an active field of research in computer graphics, computer vision and photogrammetry [22–24,27,31,40,42]. However, fully automatic modelling of large scenes from noisy 3D pointclouds is a difficult task. For urban scenes, the difficulties exacerbate. As urban scenes are largely planar, means towards solving this problem is the automatic segmentation of planar patches. There has been significant interest in object segmentation in 3D data [12,14,24,28,34,43]. The main focus of these works has been to achieve (a) data reduction, (b) automatic object recognition and reconstruction from unstructured 3D pointclouds, and (c) integration of semantics into the construction of 3D models. These efforts have partially addressed our goal whilst using raw LiDAR scans. The major reasons for this state of affairs are (1) the maturity of the LiDAR technology and (2) the resulting high accuracy of the obtained 3D data. Meanwhile, in recent years, 3D point-cloud acquisition through image matching – Structure-from-Motion (SfM) and Multi-View Stereo (MVS) – has made tremendous progress by the development of new algorithms [11,13,16,19,20,26], and the availability of (cheap) dedicated hardware (GPUs). Though 3D pointclouds from SfM/MVS can have significant point density variations as well as accuracy issues, the ease of data acquisition using standard consumer cameras compared to LiDAR technology is invincible

© Springer International Publishing AG 2016
B. Rosenhahn and B. Andres (Eds.): GCPR 2016, LNCS 9796, pp. 131–142, 2016.
DOI: 10.1007/978-3-319-45886-1_11

Fig. 1. We present the Contiguous **PA**tch **S**egmentation (CPAS) algorithm for unstructured and noisy 3D pointclouds. In this example, CPAS is used to segment building walls, roof elements, and the non-planar ground from a raw pointcloud (left: 46M points) from Multi-View Stereo (MVS) reconstruction. Classical approaches for object segmentation in noisy 3D pointclouds – RANSAC, energy minimization, Mean-Shift, Markov Random Field – are error prone and not reliable for large-scale noisy environments. Instead, CPAS employs a probabilistic inference formulation, that robustly segments all patches (right) with estimates of the object boundaries. Contiguous patches are represented with randomly chosen colors.

Fig. 2. In addition to accurate segmentation of contiguous patches at different sizes, CPAS is robust against noise e.g. trees or reconstruction artifacts from SfM/MVS and estimates accurate boundaries for each patch. Here, the data (left: 7.6M points) is from SfM/MVS. Segmented patches are randomly colored (middle, right).

for certain applications. Thus, there is a need for robust algorithms for large-scale semantic segmentation of scenes which are independent of the data acquisition technology.

1.1   Related Work

RANSAC-Based Methods. The RAndom SAmple Consensus (RANSAC) [3,9,35,37] family of algorithms has been widely used for object segmentation in pointclouds. The algorithm is stochastic and generates many object hypotheses minimum sets, and then selects the most probable. In its most vanilla form, the number of inliers to the model is used as a selection criteria, however, spatial proximity is also often used [39]. RANSAC is robust against noise and easy to implement. However, a major drawback is that one has to know a-priori the number of objects, k, to segment. For an agent exploring the real world, it is hardly possible to know the number of walls, roof elements balconies, table tops etc. present in the scene a-priori. Also, as k increases, RANSAC tends to fail due to being data driven coupled with uniform random sampling in environments of non-uniform point density.

Energy-Based Methods. Energy based approaches to data fitting and segmentation have been widely used in computer vision [5,17,34]. An energy is defined which measures the quality of the segmentation of the objects with respect to the data. Usually, a combination of terms is used to account for the consistency of the objects with the data, e.g., spatial proximity, and other terms taking into account the interaction between the objects in some context. Most often, a Markovian context is assumed. Though these approaches produce consistent results for most indoor scenes, they are highly error prone for urban scenes due to the artifacts present in these environments (high noise level, highly variable point density). Also, these algorithms aren't scalable even when using dedicated hardware for acceleration such as GPUs [32].

Region Growing and Clustering Based Methods. These are unsupervised labelling techniques in computer vision to build consistent partitions from 2D or 3D data. In contrast to RANSAC, a major advantage of these approaches is that a-priori knowledge of k, the number of object instances in the scene, is not required. In region growing, the idea is to start at an initial seed point and grow connections to neighboring points according to some well defined criteria, e.g., smoothness, spatial proximity. Through this propagation the underlying object shapes emerge. It stops when the given criteria are violated [6,33,41]. However, region growing is highly sensitive to noise and thus would clearly fail for large-scale urban scenes. Recently, a Bayesian non-parametric (BNP) clustering-based approach using a DPM model of Gaussians has been proposed [2,38]. Here, normal vectors of every single 3D point are projected on the unit sphere and clustered. For indoor scenes acquired by LiDAR, consistency in normal estimations can be assumed. Yet, this assumption completely breaks down when moving to large-scale urban scenes from SfM/MVS. Also, as the number of 3D points increases, normal computation becomes a very computationally intensive task. Other probabilistic approaches commonly used for data segmentation in computer vision are Mean-Shift [4] and Markov Random Field [23].

Therefore, the current state-of-the-art approaches to patch segmentation have three major deficits: lack of scalability as well as robustness and that they are tailored only for raw LiDAR scans.

1.2 Contributions

We propose a large-scale **C**ontiguous **PA**tch **S**egmentation (CPAS) algorithm for noisy 3D pointclouds, which not only detects the location of contiguous patches e.g., table tops, roofs elements, walls and the ground, in pointclouds, but also estimates their boundaries (see Figs. 1 and 2). The method divides the scene into non-overlapping voxels and samples a clipped plane within each voxel using

RANSAC. Clusters of neighbouring voxels are build using a DPM model of Gaussians coupled with connected component analysis (CCA) into contiguous regions. These regions are then smoothed using Important Sampling (IS) as an optimization to produce the final contiguous patch. The main contributions of this paper are (1) a scalable framework for contiguous patch segmentation in noisy 3D pointclouds through a probabilistic inference formulation for consistent clustering (2) and smoothing of regions integrating uncertainty and producing object boundary estimates.

2   Dirichlet Process Mixture Model Based Clustering

In order to describe our probabilistic inference formulation, we define some basic concepts related to clustering using DPM.

The **Dirichlet Process (DP)** introduced by Ferguson [8] is a probability measure on the space Θ, of discrete probability distributions. It is parameterized by α, the concentration parameter and G_0, the base measure. Realizations of the DP on the space Θ are given by

$$G \sim DP\left(\alpha, G_0\right). \tag{1}$$

Since samples from a DP are discrete, they are usually convolved with a smoothing kernel. The resulting model is a (non-parametric) prior over smooth probability densities (the kernel) and is called a Dirichlet process mixture (DPM) model [25]. It is represented by the following hierarchical equations

$$\begin{aligned} x_i &\sim f\left(x, \theta_i\right), \quad i = 1 \cdots n \\ \theta_i &\sim G \\ G &\sim DP\left(\alpha, G_0\right) \end{aligned} \tag{2}$$

where $f\left(x, \theta_i\right)$ is a non-negative smoothing kernel on the space $\mathcal{X} \times \Theta$, with $\int_{\mathcal{X}} f\left(x, \theta\right) dx = 1$ for all θ. The base measure, G_0, is usually chosen to be the conjugate prior of the kernel in order to simplify the mathematics. DP induces a clustering effect on data points, with the data points in the eth cluster having parameter θ_e. The cluster parameters defines central tendency values (e.g., location, spread, skewness) of the kernel and are themselves independent and identically distributed (i.i.d.) samples drawn from G_0, which characterises the spread of the clusters in parameter space. Figure 3 shows a simple example of the clustering effect for 1000 data points in $\mathbf{R}^2$ using two samples (left and right plot) of a DP. Gaussian kernels have been used, thus, a DPM model of Gaussians. The five clusters of the left plot have zero covariance. Therefore, the latent variable (the cluster parameter) for each cluster is the mean. Thus, both Θ and $\mathcal{X}$ are the 2D Euclidean space, $\mathbf{R}^2$. The right plot shows three clusters and the covariance matrix varies across clusters. Therefore, $\Theta = \mathbf{R}^2 \times \mathcal{S}_2^+$, where $\mathcal{S}_2^+$ is the space of positive definite 2D symmetric matrices. Here, it is common to use the conjugate normal-inverse Wishart (NIW) distribution as G_0, the base measure [15]. In this work, we use the NIW as G_0 to cluster surface normals

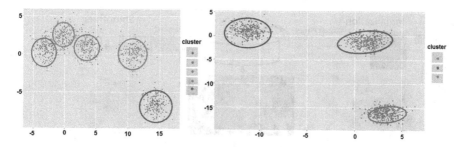

Fig. 3. Two samples from a DPM model of Gaussians in $\mathbf{R}^2$. The latent variables are the means (left), and the means and the covariances (right).

(our data points) in $\mathbf{R}^3$. Furthermore, we use the Chinese Restaurant Process (CRP) [1] representation of a DP. This is a procedure which assigns data points to clusters. Mathematically, this assignment is given by

$$p\left(z_n = e \,|\, z_{1:n-1}\right) = \begin{cases} \frac{m_e}{n-1+\alpha} & \text{if } m_e > 0 \quad (\text{i.e., } e \text{ is old}) \\ \frac{\alpha}{n-1+\alpha} & \text{if } m_e = 0 \quad (\text{i.e., } e \text{ is new}) \end{cases}, \tag{3}$$

where m_e is the number of data points assigned to cluster θ_e, $\alpha \geq 0$ the concentration parameter of the DP and n the total number of data points present. The latent variable z_i defines our cluster assignment. Since we assume that our data points (surface normals) are from a multivariate normal distribution with mean μ, and covariance matrix Σ, the data generation process is defined as follows

$$\begin{aligned} \theta_{1,2,\ldots} &\sim G_0 = NIW\left(\mu_0, \kappa_0, \Psi_0, \upsilon_0\right) \\ z_{1:n-1} &\sim CRP\left(\alpha\right) \\ x_{i=1,2,\ldots n-1} &\sim \mathcal{N}\left(\mu, \Sigma\right), \end{aligned} \tag{4}$$

where $NIW\left(\mu_0, \kappa_0, \Psi_0, \upsilon_0\right)$ is the NIW distribution with its four parameters. To infer the cluster assignments given the data and parameters of the NIW, $p\left(z_{i:n} \,|\, x_{i:n}, \mu_0, \kappa_0, \Psi_0, \upsilon_0\right)$, we use Gibbs sampling [30]. The algorithm updates each variable in turn by sampling from its posterior predictive distribution conditional on all other variables and is presented in Algorithm 1.

3 Contiguous Patch Segmentation (CPAS)

Starting from an unstructured 3D pointcloud, $\mathcal{D}$, our goal is to segment $\mathcal{D}$ into a set of contiguous patches with associated object boundary estimates. Here, patches are areas of $\mathcal{D}$ which are planar within a local neighborhood e.g., roof elements, walls, table tops, the ground. As part of the input, we assume that $\mathcal{D}$ has a known metric scale. The proposed algorithm is shown in Fig. 4 and composed of three main stages: (i) Initialization, (ii) Clustering, and (iii) Smoothing.

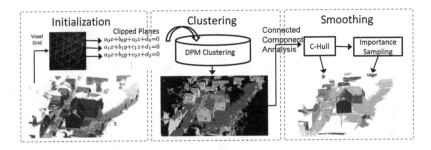

Fig. 4. Algorithm overview. CPAS segments a raw pointcloud by extracting contiguous patches along with the object boundaries. It works in three main stages: (i) Initialization, (ii) Clustering, and (iii) Smoothing.

3.1 Initialization

The goal of this stage is to generate consistent surface normals for $\mathcal{D}$ whilst avoiding normal estimation for every single point which is a computationally expensive task and produces normals which are not a good representation of the underlying surfaces. To this end, we make use of the fact that most man-made scenes are planar within a local neighborhood. We divide $\mathcal{D}$ into non-overlapping voxels using a voxel grid and fit a plane within every voxel using RANSAC. These planes have finite support, i.e., are clipped at voxels bounds. The voxel leaf size, l, is chosen such that the dimension of the smallest patch of interest is greater than l. This ensures that every patch of interest is captured by at least one voxel. The result of the initialization are a set of unit vectors, one for every voxel. Figure 5 shows this form of surface representation for two data sets revealing the clusters formed by clipped plane normals on the unit sphere.

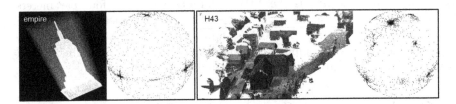

Fig. 5. In contrast to the normals of individual points, clipped plane normals do not suffer from "overfitting". They form consistent clusters on the unit sphere. Left, the "Empire" data set from [21] and right, a self acquired data set "H43" from SfM/MVS.

3.2 Clustering

The aim of this stage is to partition the voxels into contiguous regions using the normals of the clipped planes and voxel adjacency information. Unit vectors in $\mathbf{R}^3$ are directional data. Probabilistic modelling of directional data should employ some form of directional statistics [7,10,18,38]. To reduce the computational complexity, we convert the normals of the clipped planes to unit vectors in $\mathbf{R}^3$ and cluster them using the DPM model of Gaussians without taking into account the directionality of the data points. The clustering is presented in Algorithm 1. The resulting clusters have ambiguities, e.g., parallel surfaces will belong to the same cluster (see Fig. 6b, parallel surfaces have the same color). We build a voxel adjacency graph of all voxels maintaining 26-adjacency i.e., neighboring voxels can share a face, vertex, or an edge, and use spatial proximity as a metric to denote connectivity. Then we perform connected component analysis (CCA) [41] within every cluster and resolve these ambiguities. This two step approach has two main benefits: It provides a clear distinction between the stochastic and deterministic part of the clustering and speeds up the clustering as a whole, since all parallel surfaces in the scene will have the same θ (cf. Eq. (4)), i.e., the effective sample space of θ will be smaller compared to modelling with directional statistics [38]. The output of the clustering are a set of contiguous regions, see Fig. 6c.

Input: $x_{i:n}$, $G_0 = NIW(\mu_0, \kappa_0, \Psi_0, \upsilon_0)$
Output: $p(z_{i:n} | x_{i:n}, \mu_0, \kappa_0, \Psi_0, \upsilon_0)$, a set of new cluster parameters $\hat{\theta}^*$
initialize $z_{1:n-1}$, i.e., assign the data points to some initial clusters θ^*
foreach *Gibbs sampling iteration j* **do**
    foreach *data point i* **do**
        Discard the cluster assignment z_i of the ith data point
        If i belongs to its own cluster, discard θ_{z_i} from θ^*
        Sample a new assignment for i using CRP prior (cf. Eq. (3)) as follows
$$p(z_i = e \,|\, \theta^*) = \begin{cases} \frac{m_e}{n-1+\alpha} f(x_i, \theta_e^*) & \text{if } m_e > 0 \ \ (\text{i.e., } e \text{ is old}) \\ \frac{\alpha}{n-1+\alpha} \int f(x_i, \theta) G_0(\theta) \, d\theta & \text{if } m_e = 0 \ \ (\text{i.e., } e \text{ is new}) \end{cases}$$
        If i is assigned to a new cluster, sample this cluster's parameters from
$$p(\hat{\theta}_{z_i}^* \,|\, x_{i:n}) \propto G_0\left(\hat{\theta}_{z_i}^*\right) f\left(x_i \,\big|\, \hat{\theta}_{z_i}^*\right)$$
    end
end

Algorithm 1. Gibbs sampling using CRP Representation.

3.3   Smoothing

Dividing the scene into non-overlapping voxels leads to smoothness issues along object boundaries (cf. Fig. 6c). We solve this problem using the following procedure: Let convex-hull-voxels for the jth region collected after CCA be defined as the set of voxels which lines connecting the elements of the convex hull pass through. The importance of the cth voxel in this set is given by the likelihood function $\mathcal{L}(\pi_c)$ which is the MSAC score of the clipped plane for the cth voxel. The aim of the smoothing is to get a better estimate of the underlying object boundary. For the jth region,

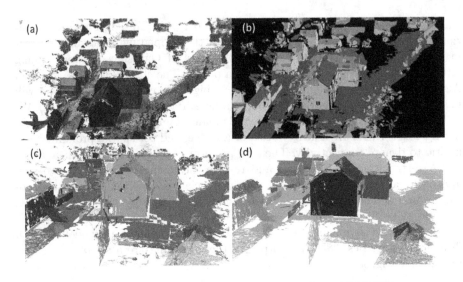

Fig. 6. The input data in (a) contains 47M 3D points from SfM/MVS reconstruction. Clustering ambiguity without using the directionality can be seen in (b). Parallel surfaces belong to the same cluster and have the same color. Connected component analysis resolves this ambiguity (c). Finally, the resulting regions are smoothed (d).

– compute the convex-hull-voxels
– repeat N times
  – randomly perturbate the normals of the clipped planes
  – compute the sum of $\mathcal{L}(\pi_c)$ for these voxels
– select inliers of planes with the best score, i.e., smallest MSAC score

The convex hull of the inliers is the estimate of the object boundary.

4   Experiments

Data Set: We performed experiments on pointclouds from LiDAR and SfM/MVS. The sizes of the clouds range between 1.2M points for the "Empire" and "Lans" data sets (courtesy of [21]), and self acquired 107M 3D points from SfM/MVS from an urban settlement, "Bonnland" (see Fig. 7(a)). Obtaining ground-truth from large-scale urban data sets is difficult. Thus, we conducted (for now) all our experiments without quantitative evaluations.

Parameters: CPAS requires several parameters for the three stages Initialization, Clustering and Smoothing. The two parameters required during the initialization are voxel leaf size l and RANSAC inlier threshold t for plane fitting within voxels. Since $\mathcal{D}$ have a metric scale, we set both l and t as constant to 2.0 m and 0.25 m respectively, for all our experiments. We set the four parameters of NIW during clustering as follows: $\mu_0 = (0,0,0)$, $\kappa_0 = 1$, $\Psi_0 = \mathbf{I}_3$, $v_0 = 4$, where $\mathbf{I}_3$ is the identity matrix in $\mathbf{R}^3$. The concentration parameter α is crucial

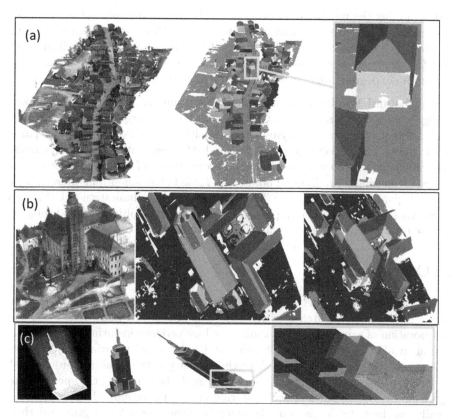

Fig. 7. Output of CPAS for three data sets. Data sets "Bonnland", (a) and "Adelsbach", (b) are from SfM/MVS with 107M and 50M 3D points, respectively. The "Empire" data set (c) is courtesy of [21]. Segmented patches are randomly colored.

Table 1. Runtime analysis of normal estimation for individual 3D points and clipped planes (CP) for four data sets. For individual 3D points, we used the optimized OpenMP-based implementation presented in [36] and compared CP against two neighborhood search modes within an efficient data structure (kd-tree): Radius search at radii $r = 0.05$ m and $r = 0.1$ m, and k-nearest neighbor search at $k = 15$ and $k = 25$. All execution times (columns 4–8) are measured in seconds using an Intel Xeon E5507 2.26 GHz processor with 96 GB RAM. Bold entries indicate best runtime performance for each data set. We also report the number of CP clustered by CPAS compared to the number of 3D points for each data set. Highlighted columns are produced by CPAS.

Dataset	Num. Points ($\times10^6$)	Num. CP	$r = 0.05m$	$r = 0.1m$	$k = 15$	$k = 25$	CP
Bonnland	107	74942	240	672	310	470	**18**
H43	47	6402	172	201	51	81	**8**
Adelsbach	50	25168	125	310	70	160	**10**
Empire	1.2	2606	4	6	2	4	

in determining the number of clusters [29]. The higher the value of α, the more clusters are found. We used two values for α, $\alpha = 15$ for the "Bonnland" data set and $\alpha = 8$ for the rest. 3000 iterations of the Gibbs sampling algorithm were used for all experiments. For smoothing, $N = 100$ and uniform sampling was used with six degrees angular tolerance during perturbation.

Strengths and Weaknesses of CPAS: The results of our experiments shown in Fig. 7 reveal the strengths of CPAS in segmenting large-scale urban scenes from different origin, with varying point densities and noise without any parameter tuning. Larger contiguous patches are better segmented than smaller ones. Clipped plane (CP) normal estimation is several orders of magnitude faster than normal estimation for individual points (cf. Table 1) and smoothing independent regions is parallelizable, making CPAS scalable. A major limitation of CPAS are its weaknesses when segmenting scenes with many little objects. Also problematic are objects which are non-planar within the voxel.

5   Conclusion

We have presented the CPAS algorithm to segment noisy unstructured 3D point-clouds by contiguous patches with their boundaries. The main novelty is the incorporation of sample space division to reduce variance in surface normal estimation in 3D pointclouds due to noise and point density variations in large-scale scenes avoiding overfitting. A further novelty is the combination of DPM model clustering with connected component analysis increasing the speed of the algorithm by solving parts of the clustering problem deterministically. Algorithmically, we first divide the sample space by means of a voxel grid and then we generate robust surface normals using RANSAC. Voxels are clustered into regions using a DPM model of Gaussians combined with connected component analysis and refined. The resulting algorithm works independently of the origin of the input data (LiDAR, or image matching) as well as the point density. The robustness and scalability of the algorithm is demonstrated for several test scenarios for which high quality results have been obtained without parameter fine tuning. An obvious next step is to model the extracted patches by polygons to produce a fully watertight CAD-like model. Also, the fixed size voxelization could be extended to variable size to enable the proper segmentation of scenes with large object size variations.

References

1. Aldous, D.J.: Exchangeability and related topics. In: Hennequin, P.L. (ed.) École d'Été de Probabilités de Saint-Flour XIII – 1983. Lecture Notes in Mathematics, pp. 1–198. Springer, Heidelberg (1985)
2. Cabezas, R., Straub, J., Fisher III., J.W.: Semantically-aware aerial reconstruction from multi-modal data. In: ICCV, pp. 2156–2164 (2015)
3. Chum, O., Matas, J.: Matching with PROSAC - progressive sample consensus. In: CVPR, pp. 220–226 (2005)

4. Comaniciu, D., Meer, P.: Mean shift: a robust approach toward feature space analysis. PAMI **24**(5), 603–619 (2002)
5. Delong, A., Osokin, A., Isack, H.N., Boykov, Y.: Fast approximate energy minimization with label costs. IJCV **96**(1), 1–27 (2012)
6. Demir, I., Aliaga, D.G., Benes, B.: Coupled segmentation and similarity detection for architectural models. SIGGRAPH **34**(4), 104:1–104:11 (2015)
7. Evans, M., Hastings, N., Peacock, B.: von mises distribution. In: Statistical Distributions, pp. 189–191 (2000). Chap. 41
8. Ferguson, T.S.: A bayesian analysis of some nonparametric problems. Ann. Statist. **1**(2), 209–230 (1973)
9. Fischler, M.A., Bolles, R.C.: Random sample consensus: a paradigm for model fitting with applications to image analysis and automated cartography. Commun. ACM **24**(6), 381–395 (1981)
10. Fisher, R.: Dispersion on a sphere. Proc. R. Soc. Lond. A: Math. Phys. Eng. Sci. **217**(1130), 295–305 (1953)
11. Frahm, J.-M., Fite-Georgel, P., Gallup, D., Johnson, T., Raguram, R., Wu, C., Jen, Y.-H., Dunn, E., Clipp, B., Lazebnik, S., Pollefeys, M.: Building Rome on a cloudless day. In: Daniilidis, K., Maragos, P., Paragios, N. (eds.) ECCV 2010, Part IV. LNCS, vol. 6314, pp. 368–381. Springer, Heidelberg (2010)
12. Fransens, J., Van Reeth, F.: Hierarchical PCA decomposition of point clouds. In: Proceedings of the Third International Symposium on 3D Data Processing, Visualization, and Transmission (3DPVT 2006), pp. 591–598 (2006)
13. Furukawa, Y., Ponce, J.: Accurate, dense, and robust multi-view stereopsis. PAMI **32**(8), 1362–1376 (2010)
14. Golovinskiy, A., Funkhouser, T.: Min-cut based segmentation of point clouds. In: IEEE Workshop on Search in 3D and Video (S3DV) at ICCV, September 2009
15. Görür, D., Rasmussen, C.E.: Dirichlet process gaussian mixture models: choice of the base distribution. J. Comput. Sci. Technol. **25**(4), 653–664 (2010)
16. Hirschmüller, H.: Stereo processing by semiglobal matching and mutual information. PAMI **30**(2), 328–341 (2008)
17. Isack, H., Boykov, Y.: Energy-based geometric multi-model fitting. IJCV **97**(2), 123–147 (2011)
18. Kent, T.J.: The fisher-bingham distribution on the sphere. J. Roy. Stat. Soc.: Ser. B (Methodol.) **44**(1), 71–80 (1982)
19. Kuhn, A., Hirschmüller, H., Mayer, H.: Multi-resolution range data fusion for multi-view stereo reconstruction. In: Weickert, J., Hein, M., Schiele, B. (eds.) GCPR 2013. LNCS, vol. 8142, pp. 41–50. Springer, Heidelberg (2013)
20. Kuhn, A., Mayer, H., Hirschmüller, H., Scharstein, D.: A TV prior for high-quality local multi-view stereo reconstruction. In: Proceedings of the 2014 2nd International Conference on 3D Vision, vol. 01, pp. 65–72 (2014)
21. Lafarge, F., Alliez, P.: Surface reconstruction through point set structuring. In: Proceedings of Eurographics, Girona, Spain (2013)
22. Lafarge, F., Keriven, R., Bredif, M., Vu, H.H.: A hybrid multi-view stereo algorithm for modeling urban scenes. PAMI **35**(1), 5–17 (2013)
23. Lafarge, F., Mallet, C.: Creating large-scale city models from 3D-point clouds: a robust approach with hybrid representation. IJCV **99**(1), 69–85 (2012)
24. Lin, H., Gao, J., Zhou, Y., Lu, G., Ye, M., Zhang, C., Liu, L., Yang, R.: Semantic decomposition and reconstruction of residential scenes from lidar data. SIGGRAPH 32(4) (2013)
25. Lo, A.Y.: On a class of bayesian nonparametric estimates: I. density estimates. Ann. Statist. **12**(1), 351–357 (1984)

26. Mayer, H., Bartelsen, J., Hirschmüller, H., Kuhn, A.: Dense 3D reconstruction from wide baseline image sets. In: Real-World Scene Analysis 2011, pp. 285–304 (2012)
27. Meixner, P., Leberl, F.: 3-dimensional building details from aerial photography for internet maps. Remote Sens. **3**, 721–751 (2011)
28. Monszpart, A., Mellado, N., Brostow, G., Mitra, N.: RAPter: rebuilding man-made scenes with regular arrangements of planes. SIGGRAPH (2015)
29. Müller, P., Andrs Quintana, F., Jara, A., Hanson, T.: Bayesian nonparametric data analysis. Springer, Switzerland (2015). Springer Series in Statistics
30. Neal, R.M.: Markov chain sampling methods for dirichlet process mixture models. Journal of Comput. Graph. Stat. **9**(2), 249–265 (2000)
31. Nguatem, W., Drauschke, M., Mayer, H.: Roof reconstruction from point clouds using importance sampling. Ann. Photogrammetry, Remote Sens. Spat. Inf. Sci. **II–3/W3**, 73–78 (2013). City Models, Roads and Traffic (CMRT)
32. Oesau, S., Lafarge, F., Alliez, P.: Planar shape detection and regularization in tandem. Comput. Graph. Forum **35**(1), 14 (2015)
33. Papon, J., Abramov, A., Schoeler, M., Wörgötter, F.: Voxel cloud connectivity segmentation - supervoxels for point clouds. In: CVPR, pp. 2027–2034 (2013)
34. Pham, T., Chin, T., Yu, J., Suter, D.: The random cluster model for robust geometric fitting. PAMI **36**(2), 1658–1671 (2014)
35. Raguram, R., Chum, O., Pollefeys, M., Matas, J., Frahm, J.M.: Usac: a universal framework for random sample consensus. PAMI **35**(8), 2022–2038 (2013)
36. Rusu, R.B., Cousins, S.: 3D is here: point cloud library (pcl). In: 2011 IEEE International Conference on Robotics and Automation (ICRA), pp. 1–4. IEEE (2011)
37. Schnabel, R., Wahl, R., Klein, R.: Efficient RANSAC for point-cloud shape detection. Comput. Graph. Forum **26**(2), 214–226 (2007)
38. Straub, J., Chang, J., Freifeld, O., Fisher III, J.W.: A dirichlet process mixture model for spherical data. In: AISTATS (2015)
39. Torr, P.H.S., Zisserman, A.: Mlesac: a new robust estimator with application to estimating image geometry. CVIU **78**, 2000 (2000)
40. Verdie, Y., Lafarge, F., Alliez, P.: LOD generation for urban scenes. SIGGRAPH **34**(3), 15 (2015)
41. Vosselman, G.: Point cloud segmentation for urban scene classification. Int. Arch. Photogrammetry, Remote Sens. Spatial Inf. Sci. **XL–7/W2(2)**, 257–262 (2013)
42. Wahl, R., Schnabel, R., Klein, R.: From detailed digital surface models to city models using constrainted simplification. Photogrammetrie-Fernerkundung-Geoinformation **2008**(3), 207–215 (2008)
43. Zhang, X., Li, G., Xiong, Y., He, F.: 3D mesh segmentation using mean-shifted curvature. In: Chen, F., Jüttler, B. (eds.) GMP 2008. LNCS, vol. 4975, pp. 465–474. Springer, Heidelberg (2008)

Randomly Sparsified Synthesis for Model-Based Deformation Analysis

Stefan Reinhold$^{(\boxtimes)}$, Andreas Jordt, and Reinhard Koch

Department of Computer Science, University of Kiel, Kiel, Germany
sre@informatik.uni-kiel.de

Abstract. The tracking of deformation is one of the current challenges in computer vision. Analysis by Synthesis (AbS) based deformation tracking provides a way to fuse color and depth data into a single optimization problem very naturally. Previous work has shown that this can be done very efficiently using sparse synthesis. Although sparse synthesis allows AbS-based tracking to perform in real-time, it requires a great amount of problem specific customization and is limited to certain scenarios. This article introduces a new way of randomized adaptive sparsification of the reference model that adjusts the sparsification during the optimization process according to the required accuracy of the current optimization step. It will be shown that the efficiency of AbS can be increased significantly using the proposed method.

1 Introduction

Pose estimation and 3D object tracking are major research areas in computer vision for more than 40 years. Traditionally a two-stage approach is applied, where first images are analyzed using edges, features, or optical flow, and next the features are used to calculate a result. The benefit of this two-stage approach is a mathematically sound formulation since the problem is reduced to aligning corresponding feature locations within the image.

However, if the reconstruction task is extended to the non-rigid case, the fundamental constraint allowing such a sound formulation is often removed. The continuous improvement of depth cameras in the last 20 years and especially the appearance of the Microsoft Kinect in 2010 has enriched the family of reconstruction algorithms by depth-image based approaches, which in many cases differ significantly from color image based reconstruction. Although for the rigid case mature reconstruction [12] and people tracking [22] techniques are available, generic deformation reconstruction still remains subject to research. Since depth images provide dense distance information, and color images allow to deduce lateral movements, a combination of both sensor types yields a powerful tool to allow ambiguity free deformation reconstruction.

Color and depth information are not easily combined, hence a joint problem formulation is difficult when following the traditional two-stage reconstruction using features. A class of algorithms bypassing the fusion problem is Analysis by Synthesis [14] (AbS, sometimes also referred to as "direct methods"). Instead of

B. Rosenhahn and B. Andres (Eds.): GCPR 2016, LNCS 9796, pp. 143–154, 2016.
DOI: 10.1007/978-3-319-45886-1_12

deducing a solution in multiple stages from the input image, the optimization problem is formulated as finding parameters for a scene model that generates artificial sensor images, which fit the real input images best. A lot of inherent reconstruction problems are circumvented this way, including the fusion of various input entities. As long as input data of a sensor can be synthesized, the joint problem formulation is straight forward. A disadvantage of AbS is the increased computational work, since the evaluation of the objective function implies a rendering process for every sensor involved and a global search, in many cases without available derivatives[1], whereas feature correspondences allow local optimization on a function with known derivatives. The key to efficient AbS is the combination of a fast synthesis, based on partial, 'sparse' synthesis [13], and an efficient global optimization scheme. Such a system can even track deforming objects in real-time [23].

In this article, a new way of synthesis sparsification for AbS system is introduced that circumvents the need for manual reference object sparsification, provides automatic adjustment of the synthesis implicitly regarding the reference object complexity, and improves the overall AbS performance significantly. Experiments show a potential speed up of factor 8 and more compared to the established sparse synthesis.

1.1   Related Work

Deformation tracking in combined depth and color (RGB-D) video is a research area that has not been investigated as much as deformation tracking in color video or depth video alone. A lot of research has been carried out on color-based deformation tracking using Non-Rigid Structure from Motion (NRSfM), which was introduced by Bregler et al. [3] as an extension to Structure from Motion (SfM) [24] by a set of deformation spaces, and it has been extended over the years [5,6,25]. Like the original SfM, NRSfM utilizes 2D feature movements to formulate a convex minimization problem which is solved using local (least-squares) optimization methods. This allows to simultaneously recover camera position, object shape, and deformation. If the initial object shape is already known, Salzmann et al. [20] proposed a method that utilizes the object geometry as a deformable triangle mesh, rather than relying on linear deformation spaces. For the multi-camera case, Cagniar et al. [4] introduced a method that is able to track complex human deformation spaces if the background can be subtracted in the input footage. Similar to the multi-camera tracking of Rosenhahn [19], it utilizes the object contour in the input data as well as feature movements to align the tracking target with the input image.

The problem of deformation tracking in depth data is handled in a very different way by most algorithms, as depth images provide less information that can be used to generate correspondences, such as features. Hence, algorithms relying on depth features do only provide good results for small deformations [16].

---

[1] One exception can be found in [7], where the derivatives of the reprojection error are calculated for a multi-view stereo setting.

The main advantage of range data over color is its ability to reconstruct a 3D model of the observed scene for every frame, allowing it to directly track deformations in 3D space. Algorithms like [17] perform local, ICP-like [2] shape fitting combined with global smoothness enforcement. Tracking human poses in a depth camera is already well understood and can be solved by machine learning approaches [22]. For many specialized tasks, e.g., skeleton based tracking [10], hand tracking [18,21] real-time solutions are available, as well as for generic models and deformations if they are small enough such that a local, hierarchical optimization can be applied [27]. Xu et al. [26] expressed non-rigid object tracking in RGB-D video as an inference problem in a Conditional Markov Random Field using deformable patches to represent the observed surface. This way they removed the requirement of the tracking target to be completely visible in the first frame. In [11] Innmann et al. combine color feature tracking with a depth-based constraint formulation to dynamically reconstruct geometric shapes from a single RGB-D sensor at real-time.

The remainder of this article is organized as follows: Sect. 2 summarizes the AbS tracking approach and the sparse synthesis as introduced in [13,14], Sect. 3 proposes the new adaptive sparsification method and introduces an approximation algorithm to estimate the inaccuracy induced by sparsification. Section 4 evaluates the proposed method on real data with known ground-truth and Sect. 5 concludes this article.

2   Analysis by Synthesis

The AbS concept is a generative, model-driven approach that differs from traditional reconstruction problem formulations in many key aspects. Input images are not analyzed and processed, instead, a parameter space is established that allows to express the solution as a parameter vector within this search space. A solution guess (model parameters) can be evaluated by synthesizing the input images given the solution candidate and comparing it to the real input (see Fig. 1). This approach can be efficient, if the synthesis is not performed by standard rendering, but in a sparse way [23]. An in-depth introduction to AbS used for deformation reconstruction can be found in [14].

Let M be a textured triangle mesh serving as a reference object for the AbS tracking. Sparse synthesis reduces the triangle mesh information given by M to the indexed set of vertices $V = \{v_i\} \subset \mathbb{R}^3$ and their corresponding texture color $C = \{c_i\} \subset [0, 255]^3$. A deformation parameter Θ is evaluated as follows:

Given a set of Sensors $\mathcal{S}$, let the input image be given as a function $I_c^{in} : \mathbb{R}^2 \rightarrow [0, 255]$ and $I_d^{in} : \mathbb{R}^2 \rightarrow \mathbb{R}$ for each color sensor $c \in \mathcal{S}$ and depth sensor $d \in \mathcal{S}$, respectively. Let further $\mathcal{P}_s : \mathbb{R}^3 \rightarrow \mathbb{R}^2$ denote the projection function for sensor s, mapping 3D points to the image plane. Let $\mathcal{D}_\theta : \mathbb{R}^3 \rightarrow \mathbb{R}^3$ be a deformation function parameterized by θ. Then the RMS error for a color sensor s_c is

$$e_{s_c}(\theta) = \left(|V|^{-1} \sum_{(v,c) \in V \times C} \|(I_{s_c}^{in} \circ \mathcal{P}_{s_c} \circ \mathcal{D}_\theta)(v) - c\|_2^2 \right)^{-\frac{1}{2}}, \tag{1}$$

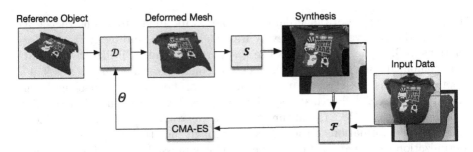

Fig. 1. Overview of the Analysis by Synthesis approach. A reference object is deformed by a deformation function $\mathcal{D}$ using a estimated parameter vector Θ. The sensor set $\mathcal{S}$ synthesizes artificial images which are compared to the input images by a fitness function $\mathcal{F}$. The fitness value is used by the optimizer (CMA-ES) to generate a refined Θ.

where $\circ$ denotes function composition. The depth error can be defined accordingly. But since using an absolute depth error would make the error measure dependent on the scene scale, we define the relative RMS depth error for a depth sensor s_d as follows:

$$e_{s_d}(\boldsymbol{\theta}) = \left(|V|^{-1} \sum_{v \in V} \frac{\left((I_{s_d}^{in} \circ \mathcal{P}_{s_d} \circ \mathcal{D}_{\boldsymbol{\theta}})(\boldsymbol{v}) - \|\mathcal{D}_{\boldsymbol{\theta}}(\boldsymbol{v}) - \mathcal{O}_{s_d}\|_2 \right)^2}{\|\mathcal{D}_{\boldsymbol{\theta}}(\boldsymbol{v}) - \mathcal{O}_{s_d}\|_2^2} \right)^{-\frac{1}{2}}, \quad (2)$$

where $\mathcal{O}_{s_d}$ is the camera center of sensor s_d. In addition to providing invariance to scene scale, this error formulation implicitly regards the accuracy of depth sensors, which usually decreases with distance. A more sophisticated error formulation, exploiting an explicit noise model can be found in [15].

The error sum of all sensors can be defined as a fitness function

$$\mathcal{F}(\boldsymbol{\theta}) = \sum_{s \in \mathcal{S}} \lambda_s e_s(\boldsymbol{\theta}) \quad (3)$$

using weights $\lambda_s \in \mathbb{R}_{>0}$ for each sensor s, which can either be found manually, by automatic adjustment [14], or by deriving them from the probability distribution of the measurements of each sensor [15]. Additional constraints or regularization terms can be added to the fitness function depending on the task at hand.

The tracking can now be formulated as an optimization problem: $\boldsymbol{\theta}^{\star} = \text{argmin}\,\mathcal{F}(\boldsymbol{\theta})$, which is solved using the Covariance Matrix Adaptation - Evolution Strategy (CMA-ES) optimization scheme [9]. It proved to be very suitable for this class of problems, since it is coordinate system independent, derivation free, very economical with respect to the number of necessary fitness function evaluations, while still being able to find global optima in noisy and non-convex environments [1]. The optimization scheme falls into the class of distribution-based optimizers. For every iteration, a set of samples (parameter vectors $\boldsymbol{\theta}$) is distributed with respect to a multivariate Gaussian distribution and evaluated by the fitness function $\mathcal{F}$. Using the fitness of each parameter vector $\mathcal{F}(\boldsymbol{\theta})$, the Gaussian distribution is updated such that it maximizes the probability of producing higher fitness values in the next iteration.

The combination of a fast implementation of $\mathcal{F}$ and the efficient CMA-ES optimization allows to track deformations in real-time. A crucial parameter when tuning the AbS framework for a real-time tracking task is the degree of sparsification, as the evaluation time of each iteration has a linear relationship to the number of vertices used in the sparse synthesis. Too few vertices will cause the optimization to loose accuracy, while too many vertices cause long optimization times.

In each iteration i of the CMA-ES, a new population of parameter vectors $\{\boldsymbol{\theta}_{i,j}\}_{j=0,...,\lambda-1}$ is sampled, so that $\boldsymbol{\theta}_{i,j} \sim \mathcal{N}(\overline{\boldsymbol{\theta}}_{i-1}, \sigma_{i-1}^2 C_{i-1})$, for all $j = 0, ..., \lambda - 1$, where $\overline{\boldsymbol{\theta}}_{i-1}$, σ_{i-1}^2 and C_{i-1} are the population mean, variance and normalized covariance matrix (i.e. $\det C = 1$) of the last iteration, respectively and $\lambda \in \mathbb{N}_{>1}$ is the population size. The fitness function is then evaluated for each individual and the parameter vectors are sorted with respect to their fitness values. For easier notation (w.l.o.g), let the parameter vector indices match their fitness rank, that is $\mathcal{F}(\boldsymbol{\theta}_{i,0}) \geq \mathcal{F}(\boldsymbol{\theta}_{i,1}) \geq \cdots \geq \mathcal{F}(\boldsymbol{\theta}_{i,\lambda-1})$. To calculate a new mean, the sorted parameter vectors are weighted by a weight vector $\boldsymbol{w} \in [0,1]^\lambda$, with $w_0 \leq w_1 \leq \cdots \leq w_{\lambda-1}$ and $\|\boldsymbol{w}\|_1 = 1$. Evolutionary selection is implemented by setting the first $\mu \in \mathbb{N}$ weights to zero. The selection index μ is usually set to $\mu = \frac{\lambda}{2}$ and the non-zero weights are chosen in a linear or logarithmic fashion [8]. The new population mean is then computed as $\overline{\boldsymbol{\theta}}_i = \sum_j w_j \boldsymbol{\theta}_{i-1,j}$. The new covariance matrix C_i is compiled from the old covariance C_{i-1}, the sample covariance of the current distribution and the distribution C_i^1 along the recent path of movements in the parameter space. For further details refer to [9].

3   Adaptive Sparsification

The idea of adaptive sparsification is to exploit an important property of the CMA-ES: The distribution at iteration i around a mean $\overline{\boldsymbol{\theta}}_i$ is completely calculated from ordered sample positions and the update $\overline{\boldsymbol{\theta}}_{i-1} \rightarrow \overline{\boldsymbol{\theta}}_i$ and therefore solely depends on the order induced by the fitness function $\mathcal{F}$ and not by the fitness values themselves.

Now let $\mathcal{F}_s$ be a sparsified version of $\mathcal{F}$, in which only a random subset V_s of V is regarded, with $|V_s| = s|V|$, $s \in (0,1]$. The larger the sparsification rate s^{-1}, the likelier it is that $\mathcal{F}_s$ deviates from $\mathcal{F}$ introducing a sparsification error. But if s is chosen in a way that induces a sparsification error small enough such that it does not change the order of the samples induced by $\mathcal{F}_s$ in each iteration, the sparsification does not affect the optimization at all. Although in practice the missing knowledge about $\mathcal{F}$ and the random selection of V_s does not allow to provide a guaranteed preservation of order between $\mathcal{F}$ and $\mathcal{F}_s$, it is expedient to investigate the probability of an order change happening and how to maintaining a low probability throughout the optimization.

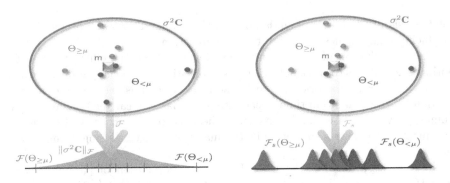

Fig. 2. Left: The fitness function $\mathcal{F}$ calculates a scalar fitness value $\mathcal{F}(\Theta)$ (lower part) for every individual $\Theta \sim \mathcal{N}(m, \sigma^2 C)$ (upper part). The image $\|\sigma^2 C\|_{\mathcal{F}}$ of the distribution in parameter space is visualized in blue. Right: In contrast to $\mathcal{F}$ (left), the sparsified fitness function $\mathcal{F}_s$ introduces an uncertainty to the results, which is modeled as a Gaussian distribution (lower part) for every $\mathcal{F}_s(\Theta)$. (Color figure online)

For the following derivation we assume that the images of the $\mathcal{N}(\overline{\theta}, \sigma^2 C)$ distributed parameter vectors in $\mathcal{F}$ also follow a gaussian distribution (cf. Fig. 2 left). In general this assumption does not hold since $\mathcal{F}$ depends on the input images and is often neither monotone nor continuous. However, since we are only interested in investigating the probability of an order change of two parameter vectors θ_i, θ_{i+1}, with $\mathcal{F}(\theta_i) > \mathcal{F}(\theta_{i+1})$, it is sufficient to investigate $\mathcal{F}$ in a local neighborhood of θ_i, in which we can approximate $\mathcal{F}$ linearly. Therefore, let $\|\sigma^2 C\|_{\mathcal{F}}^2$ denote the covariance of the image distribution in $\mathcal{F}$.

For sake of simplicity, let $\lambda = 2$ and $\mu = 1$, so that θ_0, θ_1, with $\mathcal{F}(\theta_0) > \mathcal{F}(\theta_1)$, are the only individuals of the population. Let $d = \mathcal{F}(\theta_0) - \mathcal{F}(\theta_1)$ and $d_s = \mathcal{F}_s(\theta_0) - \mathcal{F}_s(\theta_1)$ be the distances of the projections under the original and the sparse fitness function, respectively. If $\mathcal{F}(\theta)$ and $\mathcal{F}_s(\theta)$ are gaussian, then d and d_s are also gaussian with $d \sim \mathcal{N}(0, \|\sigma^2 C\|_{\mathcal{F}}^2)$ and $d_s \sim \mathcal{N}(0, \|\sigma^2 C\|_{\mathcal{F}_s}^2)$. It can be seen easily, that the probability p of an order change between $\mathcal{F}(\theta_0), \mathcal{F}(\theta_1)$ and $\mathcal{F}_s(\theta_0), \mathcal{F}_s(\theta_1)$ is equal to the probability that d and d_s have different signs. This can be visualized by the intersecting Integrals of the probability density functions (Fig. 2 right). To calculate the integral, it is convenient to rewrite d_s as $d_s = d + \Delta_s$ with $\Delta_s \sim \mathcal{N}(0, 2\sigma_s^2)$. With this we can write

$$p = P(|\Delta_s| > |d|) P(\mathrm{sign}(\Delta_s) \neq \mathrm{sign}(d)) \tag{4}$$

$$= \frac{1}{2} P\left(\frac{|\Delta_s|}{|d|} > 1\right) \tag{5}$$

$$= \frac{1}{2} \int_1^\infty \mathcal{N}\left(0, \frac{\sigma_s^2}{\|\sigma^2 C\|_{\mathcal{F}}^2}\right), \tag{6}$$

where $P(A)$ denotes the probability of the event A to occur. Although the integral in Eq. 6 cannot be calculated directly, known discrete evaluations (e.g., σ-bounds) of the distribution integral can be used as upper limits for an estimation (e.g. $p < 0.01$). The 2σ-bound of the normal distribution yields a probability of about 0.03. Using

$$0.03 \approx 1 - \int_{-2}^{2} \mathcal{N}(0,1) = 2 \int_{0}^{\infty} \mathcal{N}(0,1), \tag{7}$$

the requested probability $p < 0.01$ is given if $\sigma_s^2 \|\sigma^2 C\|_{\mathcal{F}}^{-2} = \frac{1}{2}$. During the optimization $\|\sigma^2 C\|_{\mathcal{F}}^2$ is provided by the variance of the calculated fitness values in every iteration, therefore to suffice $p < 0.01$, s should be choose such that σ_s^2 satisfies

$$\sigma_s^2 = \frac{\|\sigma^2 C\|_{\mathcal{F}}^2}{2}. \tag{8}$$

For CMA-ES to work properly, more than two individuals are required. To account for that, the probability of an order change has to be evaluated for every pair of individuals, except for the combinations in which both individuals are weighted zero. As the probabilities are equal for each combination of individuals, the extensions to more than two individuals can be done by making use of the number of pairwise comparisons

$$n = \left(\sum_{j=1}^{\lambda-1} j - \sum_{j=1}^{\mu-1} j \right) = \sum_{j=\mu}^{\lambda-1} j, \tag{9}$$

which leads to an overall probability of

$$p_n = \sum_{k=0}^{n-1} (1-p)^k p^k, \tag{10}$$

that can be approximated by $p_n \approx np$ for small p. For example with a population of size eight, the probability of an order change is approximately 6 % when choosing σ_s^2 according to (8). To change this probability, the σ-bounds need to be chosen accordingly.

The relationship between s and σ_s^2 depends on the input images and therefore is very complex. Since evaluating σ_s^2 by discrete probes in every iteration to estimate s is computational very expensive, we developed a heuristic to adapt s to the current requirement of the optimization by choosing s such that $s \propto \frac{1}{\sigma}$. In the next section we show that we can obtain a speedup of eight and higher using this heuristic as compared to a static sparse synthesis.

4   Evaluation

To analyze the potential of adaptive sparsification, practical tests have been performed using a publicly available 313 frame RGB-D input sequence[2] with ground-truth data (see Fig. 3). The input sequence comes with a set of a few

---

[2] RGB-D sequence available at http://cvlab.epfl.ch/data/dsr.

Fig. 3. Color input data of the deformation tracking method (top row) along with the deformed referenced model from a rotated point of view (bottom row).

hundreds 3D-to-2D correspondences between points inside a reference mesh and the input image for each frame. By deforming the reference mesh using the deformation function resulting from the tracking and by using the 2D image coordinates to obtain the true camera measurements, the absolute tracking error in mm can be computed. A NURBS-based deformation function was used as described in [14] such that the parameter space of $\mathcal{D}$ contains the control point positions in mm.

4.1   Induced Inaccuracy

When the adaptive sparsification is applied in practice, the rate of induced order changes is not necessarily a good way to analyze the possible benefits, also because low order change probabilities can only be obtained for high σ or a large number of individuals, which in turn increases the workload.

The far more interesting question is, to what extend does a sparsification induced order change influence the overall optimization process. Figure 4 (left) depicts the fitness values during the optimization, performed using different sparsification rates, averaged over all frames of the input sequence. It shows that even high sparsification rates (i.e. small s) do not influence the optimization process in the early and middle stages much. However, in the final optimization process the lack of accuracy clearly prevents the sparse fitness function from reaching a precise optimization goal (see Fig. 4 left, zoomed area).

The benefit of sparsification becomes more visible when the optimization process is plotted over equivalent computational work rather than iteration counts. As a fitness function evaluation of $\mathcal{F}_{0.01}$ only takes 1 % of the computational work compared to $\mathcal{F}$, this sparse optimization can perform 100 iterations in the same time as one full synthesis iteration is performed. Figure 4 (right) depicts the same data but plotted over actual computational work, equivalent to one iteration with the full vertex set. Hence, to exploit high precision and efficient evaluation, the sparsification rate should be adapted during the optimization process. Equation (8) motivated the linear coupling of the sparsification rate s to σ. Figure 4 (dashed orange) shows the fitness function for the case that the sparsification rate is chosen such that $s \propto \frac{1}{\sigma}$. This online adaptation of the

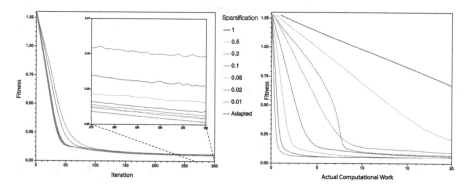

Fig. 4. The optimization process averaged over the complete 313 frame sequence depicted in Fig. 3. Left: the fitness value for the sparse vertex set during the optimization for various sparsification rates, plotted over the number of iterations. The last 25 iterations are zoomed to better visualize the differences between the sparsification rates at the late optimization stage. Right: the same fitness values as on the left but plotted over the actual computational work instead of iterations. (Colour fig online)

sparsification rate s provides an optimization result as accurate as the synthesis using the full vertex set, but using less than 10 % of the computational work.

Besides from lowering the number of vertices that are evaluated in each iteration, low sparsification rates also act as a damping factor for the search range σ: In each iteration a new subset of vertices is randomly chosen. Therefore, if CMA-ES discovers a local minimum of the fitness function in one iteration, it might not be a minimum in the following iteration, where a different subset is evaluated. If in one iteration of CMA-ES two or more individuals with non-neglectable distances in the parameter space have equally low fitness values, the population search range σ increases. Therefore, an increasing σ indicates that the optimization process hit several local minima, whereas a decreasing σ indicates that it converges into a single minimum. Figure 5 (right) depicts the progress of σ over the optimization process for various sparsification rates, averaged over all frames of the input sequence. The search range rapidly increases in the first optimization stage for all sparsification rates and then converges until the end of the optimization. The peak for low sparsification rates is significantly lower than for the higher ones, resulting in a narrower search space. As a consequence the global minimum is not found and therefore the optimization process becomes less accurate (cf. Fig. 4 left). For the adaptive sparsification this is not the case. The coupling $s \propto \frac{1}{\sigma}$ prevents the optimization to converge prematurely to a local minimum.

4.2   Results

Figure 4 (right) already shows the effectiveness of adaptive sparsification during the optimization on real data. Figure 5 (left) illustrates the tracking error

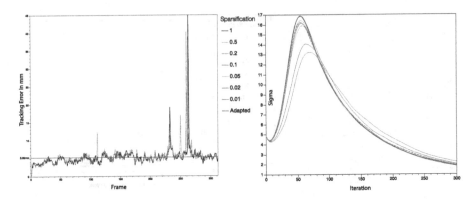

Fig. 5. Left: Tracking error for each frame in the input sequence in mm for 100 %, 1 % and adaptive sparsification. Right: σ_s during the optimization process, averaged over all frames, depicted for various sparsification rates.

for each frame of the input sequence, for the full vertex set synthesis, for a 1 % sparsification and for the adaptive sparsification. In average all three variants perform equally well: (full vertex set: 5.23 mm ± 2.67 mm, 1 % sparsification: 5.37 mm ± 2.55 mm, adaptive sparsification: 5.28 mm ± 1.83 mm), but the adaptive sparsification has the lowest standard deviation. To compare our results with the approach in [26], we also computed the depth and the 2D-displacement[3] errors separately[4]. The mean depth errors are 3.38 mm ± 0.091 mm, 3.48 mm ± 1.03 mm and 3.42 mm ± 0.91 mm, for the full vertex set, for the 1 % sparsification and for the adaptive sparsification, respectively. The 2D-displacement errors are 3.28 mm ± 2.63 mm, 3.35 mm ± 2.40 mm and 3.29 mm ± 1.71 mm. As a comparison[5] Xu et al. in [26] achieved higher mean depth and displacement errors of over 5 mm.

5   Conclusion

This article introduced a novel approach to increase the effectiveness of the sparse synthesis used in AbS deformation tracking. The method uses random adaptive sparsification to adjust the number of reference model vertices to the optimization status of the tracking algorithm. By coupling the sparsification rate to the distribution size, the accuracy of the synthesis is adapted to the current requirement of the optimizer. Tests on publicly available real data have been presented, showing large speed up capabilities (factor 8 and more) while maintaining the accuracy of a full synthesis and also increasing the robustness.

---

[3] Called registration error in [26].

[4] Plots are available as supplementary materials.

[5] Since there were no definite numbers in [26] available, we roughly estimated a lower bound based on the given Figs. 5 and 6.

References

1. Auger, A., Brockhoff, D., Hansen, N.: Benchmarking the (1,4)-CMA-ES with mirrored sampling and sequential selection on the noisy BBOB-2010 testbed. In: The 12th Annual Conference Companion on Genetic and Evolutionary Computation, pp. 1625–1632, July 2010

2. Besl, P.J., McKay, N.D.: A method for registration of 3-D shapes. IEEE Trans. Pattern Anal. Mach. Intell. **14**(22), 239–256 (1992)

3. Bregler, C., Hertzmann, A., Biermann, H.: Recovering non-rigid 3D shape from image streams. In: CVPR, vol. 2, pp. 2690–2696 (2000)

4. Cagniart, C., Boyer, E., Ilic, S.: Iterative mesh deformation for dense surface tracking. In: 2009 IEEE 12th International Conference on Computer Vision Workshops, ICCV Workshops, pp. 1465–1472, January 2009

5. Del Bue, A., Agapito, L.: Non-rigid stereo factorization. Int. J. Comput. Vis. **66**(22), 193–207 (2006)

6. Fayad, J., Agapito, L., Del Bue, A.: Piecewise quadratic reconstruction of non-rigid surfaces from monocular sequences. In: Daniilidis, K., Maragos, P., Paragios, N. (eds.) ECCV 2010, Part IV. LNCS, vol. 6314, pp. 297–310. Springer, Heidelberg (2010)

7. Gargallo, P., Prados, E., Sturm, P.: Minimizing the reprojection error in surface reconstruction from images. In: 2007 IEEE 11th International Conference on Computer Vision, pp. 1–8. IEEE (2007)

8. Hansen, N.: The CMA evolution strategy: a comparing review. In: Lozano, J.A., Larrañaga, P., Inza, I., Bengoetxea, E. (eds.) Towards a New Evolutionary Computation. Studies in Fuzziness and Soft Computing, vol. 192, pp. 75–102. Springer, Heidelberg (2006)

9. Hansen, N., Ostermeier, A.: Completely derandomized self-adaptation in evolution strategies. Evol. Comput. **9**(2), 159–195 (2001)

10. Helten, T., Baak, A., Bharaj, G., Müller, M., Seidel, H.P., Theobalt, C.: Personalization and evaluation of a real-time depth-based full body tracker. In: 3DV, pp. 279–286 (2013)

11. Innmann, M., Zollhöfer, M., Nießner, M., Theobalt, C., Stamminger, M.: VolumeDeform: real-time volumetric non-rigid reconstruction, January 2016. CoRR abs/1603.08161v2 [cs.CV]

12. Izadi, S., Kim, D., Hilliges, O., Molyneaux, D., Newcombe, R.A., Kohli, P., Shotton, J., Hodges, S., Freeman, D., Davison, A.J., et al.: KinectFusion: real-time 3D reconstruction and interaction using a moving depth camera. In: UIST, pp. 559–568, January 2011

13. Jordt, A., Koch, R.: Fast tracking of deformable objects in depth and colour video. In: BMVC, pp. 1–11, January 2011

14. Jordt, A., Koch, R.: Direct model-based tracking of 3D object deformations in depth and color video. Int. J. Comput. Vis. **102**(11), 239–255 (2012)

15. Jordt, A., Koch, R.: Reconstruction of deformation from depth and color video with explicit noise models. In: Grzegorzek, M., Theobalt, C., Koch, R., Kolb, A. (eds.) Time-of-Flight and Depth Imaging. LNCS, vol. 8200, pp. 128–146. Springer, Heidelberg (2013)

16. Kambhamettu, C., Goldgof, D., He, M., Laskov, P.: 3D nonrigid motion analysis under small deformations. Image Vis. Comput. **21**(33), 229–245 (2003)

17. Li, H., Adams, B., Guibas, L.J., Pauly, M.: Robust single-view geometry and motion reconstruction. ACM Trans. Graph. **28**(5), 175:1–175:10 (2009)

18. Qian, C., Sun, X., Wei, Y., Tang, X., Sun, J.: Realtime and robust hand tracking from depth. In: CVPR, pp. 1106–1113, January 2014
19. Rosenhahn, B., Kersting, U.G., Powell, K., Klette, R., Klette, G., Seidel, H.P.: A system for articulated tracking incorporating a clothing model. Mach. Vis. Appl. **18**(1), 25–40 (2007)
20. Salzmann, M., Hartley, R.I., Fua, P.: Convex optimization for deformable surface 3-D tracking. In: ICCV, pp. 1–8, January 2007
21. Sharp, T., Keskin, C., Robertson, D., Taylor, J., Shotton, J.: Accurate, robust, and flexible real-time hand tracking. In: Proceedings of CHI 2015, January 2015
22. Shotton, J., Fitzgibbon, A.W., Cook, M., Sharp, T., Finocchio, M., Moore, R., Kipman, A., Blake, A.: Real-time human pose recognition in parts from single depth images. In: CVPR, pp. 1297–1304, January 2011
23. Steimle, J., Jordt, A., Maes, P.: Flexpad: highly flexible bending interactions for projected handheld displays. In: Proceedings of the SIGCHI Conference on Human Factors in Computing Systems, pp. 237–246, January 2013
24. Tomasi, C., Kanade, T.: Shape and motion from image streams under orthography: a factorization method. Int. J. Comput. Vis. **9**(22), 137–154 (1992)
25. Torresani, L., Hertzmann, A.: Learning non-rigid 3D shape from 2D motion. In: Advances in Neural Information Processing Systems, January 2003
26. Xu, W., Salzmann, M., Wang, Y., Liu, Y.: Nonrigid surface registration and completion from RGBD images. In: Fleet, D., Pajdla, T., Schiele, B., Tuytelaars, T. (eds.) ECCV 2014, Part II. LNCS, vol. 8690, pp. 64–79. Springer, Heidelberg (2014)
27. Zollhöfer, M., Theobalt, C., Stamminger, M., Nießner, M., Izadi, S., Rehmann, C., Zach, C., Fisher, M., Wu, C., Fitzgibbon, A., et al.: Real-time non-rigid reconstruction using an RGB-D camera. ACM Trans. Graph. **33**(44), 1–12 (2014)

Depth Map Based Facade Abstraction from Noisy Multi-View Stereo Point Clouds

Andreas Ley[✉] and Olaf Hellwich

Computer Vision and Remote Sensing Group, TU Berlin, Berlin, Germany
{andreas.ley,olaf.hellwich}@tu-berlin.de

Abstract. Multi-View Stereo offers an affordable and flexible method for the acquisition of 3D point clouds. However, these point clouds are prone to errors and missing regions. In addition, an abstraction in the form of a simple mesh capturing the essence of the surface is usually preferred over the raw point cloud measurement. We present a fully automatic pipeline that computes such a mesh from the noisy point cloud of a building facade. We leverage prior work on casting the computation of a 2.5D depth map as a labeling problem and show that this formulation has great potential as an intermediate representation in the context of building facade reconstruction.

1 Introduction and Related Work

Multi-View Stereo (MVS) has become a viable tool for the 3D reconstruction of objects. In the context of 3D city modeling, the relative affordability and ease of use makes MVS an interesting choice for the reconstruction of building facades. Due to lack of texture, however, the point clouds produced by MVS often contain holes and outliers. In addition to those issues, a form of abstraction is usually desired which removes clutter and noise as well as irrelevant details. Such an abstraction provides the essence of the surface, usually in polygonal form rather than as points or voxels.

Both aspects, noise removal and abstraction, require strong priors as well as a geometric representation of the facade that supports them. We focus on the use of depth maps cast as Markov Random Fields for cleaning as well as abstracting building facade reconstructions. Based on this concept, we demonstrate a fully automatic pipeline, point cloud to mesh (see Fig. 1), which offers many opportunities for additional semantic priors. Our approach is heavily inspired by prior work which we summarize in this section. We describe the individual steps of our processing chain in Sect. 2 and show results and comparisons in Sect. 3. Additional results can be found in the supplementary material. We close with a conclusion and discussion of future work in Sect. 4.

The idea to use MVS methods in conjunction with strong priors for building facade reconstruction is by no means new. The prior work in this field is too

Electronic supplementary material The online version of this chapter (doi:10.1007/978-3-319-45886-1_13) contains supplementary material, which is available to authorized users.

© Springer International Publishing AG 2016
B. Rosenhahn and B. Andres (Eds.): GCPR 2016, LNCS 9796, pp. 155–165, 2016.
DOI: 10.1007/978-3-319-45886-1_13

Fig. 1. We present a method to compute simple but concise meshes (shown with ambient occlusion in the middle and textured on the right) from noisy Multi-View Stereo point clouds (left) of building facades by using a depth map as an intermediate representation and using a Markov Random Field based formulation to incorporate strong regularization. Green lines, where visible, highlight geometric edges between planar regions. Based on the Herz-Jesu-P25 dataset of [15]. (Color figure online)

extensive to cover it here in its entirety. Instead we discuss a representative subset to sketch the extend of the different approaches.

Works explicitly targeting building facades range in their expressive power from ruled vertical surfaces [5] over flat facades with parameterized windows and doors [18] to arbitrary but axis aligned and facade-parallel rectangles [19]. We lend the idea of using an orthographic depth map from [19], but are less restrictive in our choice of further regularization, allowing shapes other than rectangles. Similarly, we are not limited to a set of handcrafted shapes as in [18].

When extending the scope from building facades to man made structures in general, the wealth of explored regularizations is even more extensive. A recurring theme, however, is the use of Markov Random Field (MRF) formulations. The methods in [6,14] compute a dense depth map for one of the input images by assigning labels to pixels. Each label corresponds to a plane which is aligned to one of the three main directions in man made structures [6] or derived from intersecting lines [14]. To promote large, homogeneous areas, a smoothness constraint is used in both cases. We adopt the MRF formulation but apply it not in the image space of one of the input images but instead in a coordinate system embedded into the facade. We also restrict the planes' orientations to be parallel to the facade. This is similar to the modeling of wall details in [10] but without the rank reduction which enforces axis aligned rectangular shapes.

The image space depth map of [6] is extended to a full 3D model in [7] by fusing the individual depth maps. Another full 3D representation is proposed in [3] which splits the space into convex volumes based on extracted planes and then labels the volumes as solid or free based on a graph cut formulation. The expressive power of both cases is obviously higher than in our 2.5D approach. For most building facades, however, a 2.5D representation is sufficient if not even better suited.

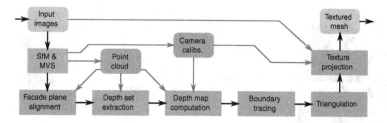

Fig. 2. Overview of the proposed processing chain. Orange: Input and output. Green: Stock SfM/MVS pipeline which produces the input to our method (blue). Red: Our method. Black arrow: Processing flow. Gray arrows: Additional data flow. (Color figure online)

2 Methodology

Our approach is summarized in Fig. 2. In the default case, the only input are images of the facade. We use standard SfM and MVS [8] pipelines to estimate the camera parameters and the point cloud of the surface. Not unlike [19] and many others, we use a depth map as an intermediate representation even though the final result is a mesh.

Using a depth map requires an accurate estimation of the facade's orientation (see Sect. 2.1). This includes the orientation of the facade plane as well as an appropriate in plane rotation to align horizontal and vertical directions with the axes of the depth map. The depth map is filled with depth values by first compiling a set of discrete depth hypotheses and then labeling the pixels of the depth map with those hypotheses (see Sect. 2.2). The depth map is converted back into a mesh by tracing the boundaries between depth segments and performing a constrained Delaunay triangulation (see Sect. 2.3). Finally a texture map is computed from the input images (see Sect. 2.4).

2.1 Plane Alignment

The estimation of the depth map as well as future additional semantic processing require an accurate estimation of the facade orientation. In addition, a rotation within the facade plane needs to be estimated to align horizontal and vertical directions in the facade with the coordinate axes of the depth map. Figure 3 summarizes our facade orientation estimation approach.

We run a modified version of PEaRL [11] to fit planes to the point cloud. PEaRL alternates between a labeling phase and a model fitting phase. In the labeling phase, data points are assigned to models (planes) under a smoothness constraint that promotes equal labels for neighboring data points. In the model fitting phase, the models (planes) are readjusted to fit the corresponding data points as closely as possible. To circumvent the problem of defining neighborhoods in a point cloud, we replace the MRF based alpha expansion of the labeling phase in PEaRL with the dense conditional random field (dCRF)

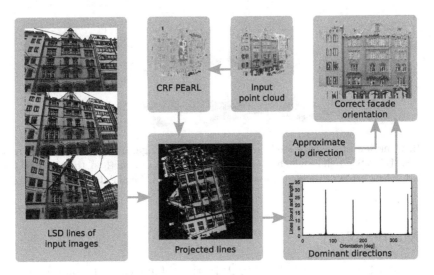

Fig. 3. Automatic computation of the facade orientation. See text for details.

formulation of [12]. A dCRF simply connects all nodes with each other with weights computed from Gaussian kernels applied to the nodes' feature vectors. Similarly to [12] we use position and color as features, with the minor difference that our points have 3D positions.

The plane with the most support is extracted as the main facade plane. It usually fits the facade very closely as the points in windows and balconies are explained away with secondary planes. Nonetheless, we use an additional clutter model in PEaRL to soak up spurious outliers.

With the facade plane at hand, the facade still needs to be rotated such that the roof points up in the depth map. This is beneficial to the grid structure of the depth map and will facilitate future semantic analysis. We make the common assumption that for man made structures such as facades, most lines are either horizontal or vertical and can be used to align the facade rotation. We extract LSD line segments [9] from the input images and project them onto the facade plane. Computing the histogram of line directions yields four very clear spikes from which the facade rotation can be judged up to an ambiguity of multiples of 90 ° (see Fig. 3). An approximate up direction from each input image in the form of the average blue gradient is used to resolve this ambiguity. Another possibility is to use the orientation meta data in the jpeg exiv tags which might provide a more reliable hint.

2.2 Orthographic Depth Map

Since the facades that we are interested in are mostly flat, we adopt the assumption laid out in [19] that the facade geometry can be described in a 2.5D fashion by the depth map of an orthographic projection of the facade. This description

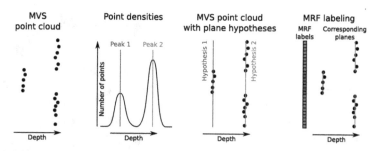

Fig. 4. Overview of the MRF approach to the depth map computation. From left to right: (1) Point cloud projected into the coordinate system of the facade. (2) Histogram of occurring depths. (3) Depth hypotheses extracted from the histogram. (4) MRF based labeling of the depth map pixels, each label of which corresponds to a depth.

has the elegant property that surfaces parallel to the facade plane, which are well exposed to the camera and thus well supported by the data, are explicitly modeled while the surfaces perpendicular to the facade plane, which are often missing in the data, are modeled implicitly by depth jumps in the depth maps.

We embed the depth map in the coordinate system of the facade and limit it horizontally and vertically to the extend of the central 98 % of the input points on the facade plane. The depth map must be filled with depth values based on the input data as well as possible regularizations. In [19], the (primary) regularization is to enforce rectangular regions of equal depth. The same prior, although realized by different means, can be found in [10] as well where it is applied to wall details inside rooms. Since most surfaces of a building facade are either perpendicular or parallel to the main facade plane, this restriction to regions of homogeneous depth performs quite well in practice. The rectangular outlines however, while working great with most windows and doors, are too restrictive for our purposes as we seek to reconstruct curved structures such as arched windows as well.

Instead we adapt the pixel labeling approach of [6,14] to operate directly within the orthographic projection. We project the input point cloud into the facade-aligned coordinate system and compute a histogram of depth values (see Fig. 4). A limited set of depth hypotheses is then extracted from this histogram. They represent possible depths that the pixels of the depth map can adopt. This step is very similar to [6] except that we limit the depth hypotheses to one axis instead of all three. The actual filling of the depth map with depth values is cast as a labeling problem of the depth map pixels where the individual labels are the depth hypotheses. Just like [6], we formulate this problem as the minimization of the following energy:

$$E = \sum_{p} E_d(h_p) + \sum_{p,q \in \mathcal{N}(p)} E_s(h_p, h_q). \tag{1}$$

The unary data term $E_d(h_p)$ represents the cost of assigning a specific hypothesis h_p to depth map pixel p and the binary smoothness term $E_s(h_p, h_q)$ models

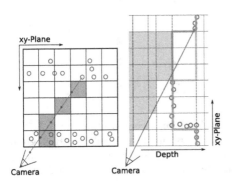

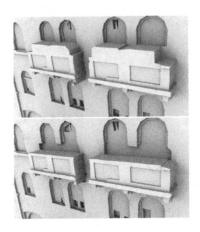

Fig. 5. Accumulation of free space votes. For each point, the depth map pixels towards all its observing cameras are considered in turn (left side) and all hypotheses that would block the view ray recieve a data term penalty for that pixel (right side). (Color figure online)

Fig. 6. Impact of the free space votes on occluded regions. Top without and bottom with free space votes. The two cases correspond to the pink and blue lines on the right side of Fig. 5.

the cost of assigning (possibly differing) hypotheses h_p and h_q to neighboring pixels p and q. When interpreted as a Markov Random Field (MRF), the solution to this energy minimization can be approximated through repeated graph cuts via alpha expansion [2].

The cost of data term $E_d(h_p)$ is computed from (a) the distances between the depth hypothesis h_p and the point cloud points that fall onto pixel p and (b) the number of free space votes. The free space votes represent the knowledge that the view rays between point cloud points and their observing cameras must be unobstructed (amongst others see [6,14]). We accumulate those votes up front by walking the path from each point cloud point to all of its observing cameras through the depth map. For each covered pixel, votes are accumulated for all hypotheses that would occlude the view ray (see Fig. 5). We found this to be extremely helpful in resolving ambiguities at occlusion boundaries like balconies (see Fig. 6).

The cost of the smoothness term $E_s(h_p, h_q)$ is zero for equal labels $h_p = h_q$ and always greater than zero for differing labels to enforce large, uniform depth regions. Similarly to [6], we assume that geometric edges often coincide with visual edges in the images and thus modulate the cost with the strength of edge gradients in the input images. Contrary to the image space based depth map in [6], where a direct mapping between depth map locations and image locations exists, our depth map does not live in the same coordinate system as one of the input images. Instead the depths of the depth hypotheses and the camera

Fig. 7. Left to right: Point cloud (for reference), initial depths (based solely on $E_d(h_p)$), final depths.

calibrations are used to find the correct location of the front and back edge of a depth jump in the input images.

Figure 7 shows the results that can be achieved with the described approach. Note that the regularization removes most of the outliers while retaining to a large degree the (subjectively) important structures such as windows, balconies, columns, and arches. Also note that a reasonable, albeit primitive inpainting of holes in the point cloud is achieved as well. Contrary to the approaches outlined in [10,19], we are not restricted to axis aligned rectangles and thus recover arches and round windows as well, although at the cost of more "wobbly" windows.

2.3   Meshing

After the computation of the depth map, we seek to create a low poly mesh of the facade. We first trace and simplify the boundary curves between the depth segments with an approach similar to Variational Shape Approximation (VSA) [4] only operating on lines instead of triangles.

The boundaries between differing depth labels in the depth map are cast as a graph of connected line segments. Straight lines are fitted to larger, junction free stretches of line segments by alternating between model assignment and model fitting. During model assignment, line segments are assigned to one of the straight lines (models) through a greedy region/line growing process along the graph starting from seeds. During the model fitting, the straight lines (models) are adjusted to fit as closely as possible to the assigned line segments. Additional straight lines (models) are added and optimization is performed until the set of straight lines approximates the underlying depth boundaries sufficiently. Anchor vertices are placed automatically between connected straight lines and at junctions, yielding simplified and smoothed segment boundaries. Figure 8 shows the result of this contour extraction.

With the boundary curves represented as a set of connected (anchor) vertices, the individual facade elements are meshed with a constrained Delaunay triangulation. Finally, the faces perpendicular to the facade plane are added.

Fig. 8. Simplified contour lines. Notice that the simplified contour lines smooth out the round boundaries of the arches while retaining sharp window corners.

2.4   Texturing

Finally, we create a texture by projecting the input images onto the mesh. Since we do not want the balconies to bleed onto the facade, or the facade to bleed onto the windows, occlusions have to be taken into account. We use the pose of the facade as well as the camera parameters to render a depth map for each input image which contains in each pixel the distance of the closest intersection with the surface along the corresponding view ray. This map is easily obtained through rasterization of the mesh in the input image space.

The 3D mesh is unfolded into the 2D texture space using the automatic UV layouting tool in Blender [1]. Using those 2D texture coordinates, we then rasterize the mesh into the texture. For each texel and each camera, the depth in the camera's view space is computed and compared to the depth stored in the camera's depth map to determine if the camera actually observes that part of the surface or whether it is occluded. In the unoccluded case, the color is sampled from the input image and the colors from all (unoccluded) cameras are averaged and stored in the texture. Occlusions from objects not present in the mesh, such as street lights, land lines, and passing cars, are presently not handled.

3   Evaluation

Abstractions, as in reduction to the essence, always contain a certain subjective and artistic aspect. This makes quantitative evaluations rather complicated and the method presented here is no exception. For reference we show the precision of the produced mesh in Fig. 9 alongside the precision of the input point cloud. The images and reference data are the Herz-Jesu-P8 dataset of [15]. As expected, the abstraction results in an increased error.

Nonetheless, in less forgiving datasets with more outliers, our approach compares favorably to a baseline poisson mesh of the input point cloud (see Fig. 10). Some remaining errors are visible in the right cut-out of Fig. 10 which can be further suppressed by additional constraints like symmetry.

Depending on the actual use case, however, those remaining errors might actually be tolerable or hidden when a texture is applied to the mesh. For point

0cm   1cm   2cm   3cm   4cm   5cm

Fig. 9. Precision as distance from reference data, color coded from zero to five centimeters as blue through red. Top: PMVS point cloud. Bottom: Ours. (Color figure online)

Fig. 10. Comparison with a baseline poisson mesh. Top to bottom: Poisson, ours, ours with manually specified symmetries (additional links in the MRF).

Fig. 11. Top: Input point cloud. Bottom: Textured mesh with highlighted seams.

clouds with gross errors as well as missing regions, Fig. 11 demonstrates aesthetically pleasing meshes. Note that essential structures like balconies, windows, doors, rain pipes, etc. are reconstructed well while otherwise keeping the geometry to a minimum. Additional reconstructions can be found in the supplementary material.

4   Conclusion and Future Work

We leverage the prior work of casting dense depth map estimation as a labeling problem and apply it to building facade reconstruction. It performs well in this context and presents a multitude of options for further regularization. A method to extract a simplified mesh from this depth map is described as well, which makes the depth map a viable intermediate representation even if a mesh is desired as the final result.

We demonstrate our method on noisy and incomplete MVS point clouds and compare it to a baseline poisson mesh. The proposed approach creates visually pleasing abstractions of facades, retaining the major geometric entities while removing clutter and noise alike.

In the future we seek to experiment with various additional priors, such as automatic detection of symmetries and repetitions. Inferring such semantic data, usually supported by shape grammars, has been demonstrated for 2D and 3D input (for example, see [16] and [13] respectively). Semantic input in the form of detected windows can help remove regions where the MVS pipeline reconstructed the curtains or other interior surfaces. Such constraints must be included in the energy formulation of Eq. (1). The data and smoothness terms provide a wealth of opportunities in that regard. The smoothness cost can be reduced along lines that should be favored for depth jumps. This can be used to guide edges along dominant lines or to restrict the borders of semantic objects. The data cost can also be modified in favor of certain labels in specific depth map regions, for example to favor a certain depth for windows. To encourage symmetries, additional links can be added to the MRF formulation between pixels that should have the same label (see bottom of Fig. 10 for an example).

Right now, the only "primitive type" are facade parallel planes. However, sloped planes as in [14] or axis aligned cylinders are also conceivable within this framework. Alternating between pixel labeling and readjusting the hypotheses in a fashion similar to PEaRL [11] might further increase the precision. Proper sky detection as in [19] is another avenue worth exploring as it can provide an upper boundary for the facade.

Even though texturing is not the central focus of our attention, some simple improvements are of interest. Street lights and cars sometimes leave faint ghost images on the facades since they are not geometrically reconstructed and thus not considered in the occlusion handling. A quite advanced solution is presented in [17] which could be integrated in the future.

Acknowledgements. This paper was supported by a grant (HE 2459/21-1) from the Deutsche Forschungsgemeinschaft (DFG).

References

1. Blender. http://www.blender.org
2. Boykov, Y., Veksler, O., Zabih, R.: Fast approximate energy minimization via graph cuts. IEEE Trans. Pattern Anal. Mach. Intell. **23**(11), 1222–1239 (2001)
3. Chauve, A.L., Labatut, P., Pons, J.P.: Robust piecewise-planar 3D reconstruction and completion from large-scale unstructured point data. In: Proceedings of CVPR, pp. 1261–1268 (2010)
4. Cohen-Steiner, D., Alliez, P., Desbrun, M.: Variational shape approximation. In: Proceedings of ACM SIGGRAPH 2004 Papers, pp. 905–914 (2004)
5. Cornelis, N., Leibe, B., Cornelis, K., Gool, L.: 3D urban scene modeling integrating recognition and reconstruction. Int. J. Comput. Vis. **78**(2), 121–141 (2007)
6. Furukawa, Y., Curless, B., Seitz, S.M., Szeliski, R.: Manhattan-world stereo. In: Proceedings of CVPR, pp. 1422–1429 (2009)
7. Furukawa, Y., Curless, B., Seitz, S.M., Szeliski, R.: Reconstructing building interiors from images. In: Proceedings of ICCV, pp. 80–87 (2009)
8. Furukawa, Y., Ponce, J.: Accurate, dense, and robust multi-view stereopsis. IEEE Trans. Pattern Anal. Mach. Intell. **32**(8), 1362–1376 (2010)
9. von Gioi, R.G., Jakubowicz, J., Morel, J.M., Randall, G.: LSD: a Line Segment Detector. Image Process. On Line **2**, 35–55 (2012)
10. Ikehata, S., Yang, H., Furukawa, Y.: Structured indoor modeling. In: Proceedings of ICCV, pp. 1323–1331 (2015)
11. Isack, H., Boykov, Y.: Energy-based geometric multi-model fitting. Int. J. Comput. Vis. **97**, 123–147 (2012)
12. Krähenbühl, P., Koltun, V.: Efficient inference in fully connected CRFS with Gaussian edge potentials. In: Shawe-Taylor, J., Zemel, R.S., Bartlett, P.L., Pereira, F., Weinberger, K.Q. (eds.) Advances in Neural Information Processing Systems 24, pp. 109–117. Curran Associates Inc. (2011)
13. Martinovic, A., Knopp, J., Riemenschneider, H., Van Gool, L.: 3D all the way: semantic segmentation of urban scenes from start to end in 3D. In: Proceedings of CVPR, pp. 4456–4465 (2015)
14. Sinha, S.N., Steedly, D., Szeliski, R.: Piecewise planar stereo for image-based rendering. In: Proceedings of ICCV, pp. 1881–1888 (2009)
15. Strecha, C., von Hansen, W., Gool, L.J.V., Fua, P., Thoennessen, U.: On benchmarking camera calibration and multi-view stereo for high resolution imagery. In: Proceedings of CVPR (2008)
16. Teboul, O., Kokkinos, I., Simon, L., Koutsourakis, P., Paragios, N.: Parsing facades with shape grammars and reinforcement learning. IEEE Trans. Pattern Anal. Mach. Intell. **35**(7), 1744–1756 (2013)
17. Waechter, M., Moehrle, N., Goesele, M.: Let there be color! Large-scale texturing of 3D reconstructions. In: Fleet, D., Pajdla, T., Schiele, B., Tuytelaars, T. (eds.) ECCV 2014, Part V. LNCS, vol. 8693, pp. 836–850. Springer, Heidelberg (2014)
18. Werner, T., Zisserman, A.: Model selection for automated architectural reconstruction from multiple views. In: Proceedings of the British Machine Vision Conference, pp. 53–62 (2002)
19. Xiao, J., Fang, T., Zhao, P., Lhuillier, M., Quan, L.: Image-based street-side city modeling. In: ACM SIGGRAPH Asia 2009 Papers, pp. 114:1–114:12 (2009)

Stereo Visual Odometry Without Temporal Filtering

Joerg Deigmoeller[(✉)] and Julian Eggert

Carl-Legien-Strasse 30, 63073 Offenbach am Main, Germany
joerg.deigmoeller@honda-ri.de

Abstract. Visual Odometry is one of the key technology for navigating and perceiving the environment of an autonomous vehicle. Within the last ten years, a common sense has been established on how to implement high precision and robust systems. This paper goes one step back by avoiding temporal filtering and relying exclusively on pure measurements that have been carefully selected. The focus here is on estimating the ego-motion rather than a detailed reconstruction of the scene. Different approaches for selecting proper 3D-flows (scene flows) are compared and discussed. The ego-motion is computed by a standard P6P-approach encapsulated in a RANSAC environment. Finally, a slim method is proposed that is within the top ranks of the KITTI benchmark without using any filtering method like bundle adjustment or Kalman filtering.

1 Introduction

For autonomously navigating platforms it is indispensable to use some kind of odometry to travel along a planned path or to relocate itself in a known environment. One possibility is wheel odometry, which is the combination of measured revolutions of a platforms wheel plus steering angle if available. This method suffers from slip and also heavy drift in position which increases over time. Similar problems occur with an IMU (Inertial Measurement Unit) that usually incorporates accelerometers, gyroscopes and sometimes GPS within a strap-down algorithm. This requires an intensive and complex filtering to compensate errors from GPS plus huge drifts from the accelerometers. In the end, such a system can become very expensive and slow in terms of reaction time on sudden changes in movement.

On the other side, visual odometry has become a serious alternative because of decreasing camera costs and the fast developing market of small powerful integrated low cost processors. Still, problems like drift over time remain. Nevertheless, the accuracy is in a much lower range than wheel odometry (also because the slip problem is avoided) and it opens the possibility for many other applications that make use of cameras, like collision avoidance, lane keeping or sign recognition. Also very powerful is the combination of visual odometry with gyroscopes which can have very accurate rotation rates [15].

In this paper, the focus is on visual odometry with a stereo camera. This is the easiest vision set-up to implement and the one that currently leads to

© Springer International Publishing AG 2016
B. Rosenhahn and B. Andres (Eds.): GCPR 2016, LNCS 9796, pp. 166–175, 2016.
DOI: 10.1007/978-3-319-45886-1_14

the most accurate results. In contrast, a mono camera set-up is per se not able to estimate the real 3D-translation (only up to scale) because of the missing real world relation. To overcome this, a ground plane estimation with known distance of the camera above ground could be used to compute the missing scale. This brings in new errors of inaccurate or even false measures. The most straightforward and accurate way is to get the scale factor from a calibrated stereo set-up.

Further, the drift inherent to purely visual odometry system could be reduced by applying VSLAM-techniques (Visual Simultaneous Localization and Mapping) which relocate the moving platform to previously visited places. The main interest of this work is going back to the starting point of a VSLAM-system - the pure visual odometry - and to take maximal advantage of the process to achieve a high precision with a simple as possible approach.

2   Related Work

The term visual odometry appeared for the first time in the publication [14]. A very comprehensive overview of state of the art visual odometry can be found in [7,17]. The key message from their tutorial for a stereo system is to compute the relative rotation and translation by minimizing the re-projection error on the image plane (Perspective from n Points, PnP). In contrast, minimizing the error of 3D-points is inaccurate because of increasing uncertainties with increasing depth. Additionally, a filtering method like bundle adjustment should be applied to reduce the drift over time.

Thanks to publicly available benchmarks like the well-known KITTI benchmark [8], visual odometry methods are now comparable in their precision. Nearly all of the top ranked methods on the KITTI benchmark apply the minimization of the re-projection error. The top ranked visual odometry submission [4] first estimates the rotational motion and subsequently the translation. Features are matched by a combination of SAD and NCC plus geometric constraints. They are tracked over time and pixel positions are refined in a predictor-corrector manner. Long life features are preferred against shortly tracked features. A similar approach of tracking long life features has been used in [1]. Again, they refine tracked features in a prediction-correction framework called "integrated features". [16] uses standard visual odometry processes like feature tracking and multi-window bundle adjustment in a carefully built system motivated from monocular visual odometry. A different approach is presented by [5] which performs a photometric alignment based on depth maps. Depth is computed along the stereo baseline (Static Stereo) and the movement baseline (Temporal Stereo). Correspondence measures are tracked over time and search ranges are constrained from previous estimates. Camera positions are finally optimized in a pose-graph using key frames and loop closures are done if the cameras are close to a previously visited location.

Some work also analyzed the influence of features at different depth on the pose estimation. For example [13] uses features at infinity distance (infinity according to the pixel raster of the image sensor) for rotation estimation and close features for translation. [11] make use of the bucketing technique - known from robust regression methods - to indirectly pick features at different depths for a better pose estimation. For pose optimization, they use an Iterated Sigma Point Kalman Filter (ISPKF).

In contrast to the previously mentioned publications, this work does not use any temporal filtering, neither bundle adjustment nor any predictor-corrector like filtering. The system is built in a way that as few as necessary processing steps are used and poses are concatenated from pure measurements. This reduces the implementation effort drastically as already a proper feature tracking requires indexing and complex managing over time.

The advantage of the proposed system is its fast reaction time which is important for applications like collision avoidance or for drastically changing movements. Still, the approach is competing with the top ranked methods on the KITTI benchmark and currently on rank 8 under the stereo vision methods (see Chap. 6 for more details).

3   System Overview

Assuming that the stereo images are already rectified, the system consists of two parts. First, the 3D-flow (scene flow) computation and second, the pose estimation.

The scene flow computation is a combination of disparity and optical flow computation using standard Harris corner detector [9] with subsequent pyramidal Lucas & Kanade optical flow computation [2].

The pose estimation is a simple P6P-method (Perspective from 6 Points) encapsulated in a RANSAC (Random Sample Consensus) framework.

The idea was to use available standard methods (e.g. from OpenCV) to first extract the crucial points of visual odometry. In a later step - which is not part of this paper - specializations of the core parts are planned.

In the remainder of this paper, the focus is on the comparison of different constraints on the scene flow estimations in Sect. 4. The pose estimation - discussed in Sect. 5 - is not modified and runs with parameters that have been determined in previous optimizations. Finally, experimental results are shown on the KITTI benchmark data.

4   Scene Flow Estimation

The scene flow is always computed by two consecutive stereo image pairs $\{I_i^l, I_i^r\}$ and $\{I_{i+1}^l, I_{i+1}^r\}$. Initially, standard Harris corners are estimated by first computing the partial image derivatives:

$$Q(x) = \sum_W \begin{bmatrix} I_x^2 & I_x I_y \\ I_x I_y & I_y^2 \end{bmatrix} \tag{1}$$

and then extracting the corner response $H(x,y)$ by:

$$H(x) = \lambda_1 \lambda_2 - k(\lambda_1 + \lambda_2)^2 \qquad (2)$$

where λ_1 and λ_2 are the eigenvalues of $Q(x)$. W is the neighbourhood around a pixel position $x = (x,y)^T$. The parameter k influences the "cornerness" of a feature. W is a 7×7 window, with the size determined by optimization using an extensive parameter grid search. 4000 features are initially computed and sorted by their corner response value.

Additionally, the integer pixel position of the Harris feature is refined to sub-pixel accuracy. That means, x is recalculated with the help of gradient information in its neighbourhood [3].

After the feature extraction, the Lucas & Kanade optical flow is computed for pairwise combinations of the input images $\{I_i^l, I_i^r, I_{i+1}^l, I_{i+1}^r\}$, where i, $i+1$ denote subsequent images in time and l, r denote left and right images of the stereo set-up. The Lucas & Kanade optical flow is the perfect counterpart to the Harris corner, because its correlation measure results in the same partial image derivatives multiplied by a vector containing the temporal derivatives:

$$\begin{pmatrix} u \\ v \end{pmatrix} = \sum_W \begin{bmatrix} I_x^2 & I_x I_y \\ I_x I_y & I_y^2 \end{bmatrix}^{-1} \begin{bmatrix} -\sum_W I_x I_t \\ -\sum_W I_y I_t \end{bmatrix} \qquad (3)$$

where $v = (u,v)^T$ is the optical flow. As v is only valid in a local neighbourhood the pyramidal approach has been used to propagate optical flows from down-sampled images to the highest resolution. 5 pyramid levels have been used and for W a window of 9×9 has been chosen, also determined from previous parameter optimization.

Lucas & Kanade optical flows are very fast to compute but tend to get stuck in local minima. Therefore, further checks are required to limit the measurements to a reliable set. On the other hand, wrong checks can remove features that might be important for the visual odometry. This sensitive issue is tackled more in detail in the following by different experiments on the KITTI training data.

On the KITTI website an evaluation software and ground truth poses for 11 sequences are available [8]. For every sequence, the translation error and rotation error is calculated. All following experiments refer to this error measure.

For scene flow estimation, the disparity between $\{I_{i+1}^l, I_{i+1}^r\}$ and the optical flow between $\{I_i^l, I_{i+1}^l\}$ (see Fig. 1) are computed by the Lucas & Kanade method. This is the minimal processing effort as the poses are optimized on the re-projection error, i.e. 3D positions from $\{I_{i+1}^l, I_{i+1}^r\}$ and 2D correspondences from $\{I_i^l, I_{i+1}^l\}$ are sufficient (see Sect. 5).

The first consistency check is a forward/backward check. That means, if the optical flow or disparity from the end point back to the starting point deviates more than a threshold t_{fb}, then the feature is rejected. Table 1 shows the translation errors and rotation errors for different t_{fb}. As a threshold of $t_{fb} = 5$ pixels gives the best result, this value is used for further experiments. On the other hand, switching the forward/backward check off leads to a significant drop of the performance.

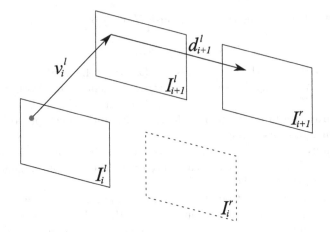

Fig. 1. Computation of the disparity d_{i+1}^l and the optical flow v_i^l for a Harris corner feature initialized in I_i^l.

Table 1. Influence of backwards check on overall performance

	$t_{fb} = 1$	$t_{fb} = 2$	$t_{fb} = 5$	fb off
translation error [%]	1.3426	1.3314	1.3070	2.4815
rotation error [deg/m]	0.0063	0.0065	0.0062	0.0175

The second consistency check is on the disparity measure only. Since for disparity measure a standard optical flow method is used, all vectors that have a y-component greater than zero pixels are theoretically not possible because a perfect rectification aligns both images in a way that the epipolar lines are horizontal. In practice, rectifications are never perfect and hence a threshold to remove disparities with a larger y-component than a threshold t_d is introduced. Additionally, disparities that have a positive x-component are obviously also invalid measurements, because disparities should only have negative signs (measured from the left to the right image). Therefore, positive disparities are also rejected. Based on Table 2, a threshold of $t_d = 1$ is chosen for future tests.

Table 2. Influence of check for y-disparity component on overall performance

	$t_d = 1$	$t_d = 2$	$t_d = 5$
translation error [%]	1.3070	1.3424	1.3663
rotation error [deg/m]	0.0062	0.0066	0.0067

So far, tests were made with a Harris corner response factor k close to zero. This means that as many features as possible are kept to leave the decision of rejection on the subsequent checks. In the next experiment the k value is

Table 3. Influence of k on overall performance

	$k = 0.0$	$k = 0.01$	$k = 0.02$
translation error [%]	1.3070	1.3209	1.3532
rotation error [deg/m]	0.0060	0.0064	0.0064

increased to check the influence of the "cornerness" on the overall performance. A value of $k = 0.0$ means that the features can also be edges and with increasing k features more and more resemble corners.

From Table 3, it can be seen that a value of $k = 0.0$ gives the smallest translation error. This shows that a high corner response is probably not the best indicator for a good feature for visual odometry estimation with combined optical flow and disparity. Definitely, a corner has sufficient structure to allow an optical flow measure and avoid the aperture problem. On the other hand, using stereo images and consecutive images allows for more meaningful outlier rejection checks by using geometric constraints.

The last consistency check is a circle check to identify outlier. This circle check computes the flows between left and right images in time as well as the disparities between first and second image pairs (see Fig. 2). Only if all concatenated pixel measurements end up at the same position in image I^r_{i+1} with an error less than a threshold t_{cc}, the feature is kept.

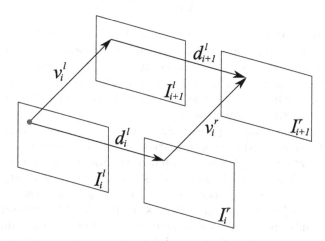

Fig. 2. Circle check: only if all measurements end up at the same position in I^r_{i+1} the feature is kept.

As can be seen in Table 4, the circle check does not significantly improve the performance compared to the previous version (1.3070 % against 1.3048 %). Additionally, it requires double computation effort compared to the version

Table 4. Influence of circle check on overall performance

	$t_{cc} = 1.0$	$t_{cc} = 2.0$	$t_{cc} = 5.0$
translation error [%]	1.3453	1.3124	1.3048
rotation error [deg/m]	0.0064	0.0064	0.0062

without circle check. Therefore, the previous version without circle check is used as final method.

5   Pose Estimation

The pose estimation is a standard P6P-approach minimizing the re-projection error on the image plane as follows:

$$\arg \min_{T_i} \sum_j \left\| \hat{x}_{i,j}^l - \frac{1}{[0\ 0\ 1]T_i\hat{X}_{i+1,j}^l} T_i\hat{X}_{i+1,j}^l \right\|^2 \tag{4}$$

where T_i is the transformation matrix from time step $i + 1$ to time step i containing rotation and translation:

$$T_i = \begin{pmatrix} r_1 & r_2 & r_3 & t_x \\ r_4 & r_5 & r_6 & t_y \\ r_7 & r_8 & r_9 & t_z \end{pmatrix}$$

$\hat{X}_{i+1,j}^l$ is the homogeneous 3D-position in the second image estimated from d_{i+1}^l and the values from rectification for focal length, principal point and baseline. $\hat{x}_{i,j}^l$ are the Harris corner positions converted to homogeneous coordinates (cf. Fig. 1). T_i is computed from $i + 1$ to i to directly get the ego-motion of the vehicle. Computing from i to $i+1$ would return the coordinate transformations, which is obviously the inverse ego-motion.

After a first estimation of T_i using Singular Value Decomposition (SVD), R and T are refined by non-linear optimization on the geometric error [12,17].

The computation of T_i is encapsulated in the robust regression framework RANSAC [6,10]. The inlier/outlier-ratio has been set to a conservative value of 0.5 to avoid run-time optimizations at too early stage. The most crucial parameter is the re-projection error that defines the threshold for the census set t_r. The feature points are at such a high precision that the re-projection error can be set below 1 pixel. Table 5 shows the influence of the re-projection threshold. The overall performance drastically increases with decreasing t_r. A threshold of $t_r = 0.1$ pixel finally lead to the best results on training and testing set.

6   Experimental Results

In the previous chapters different methods have been evaluated on the KITTI benchmark training data. In this chapter, the results of the testing data are

Table 5. Influence of the re-projection error threshold on overall performance

	$t_r = 0.5$	$t_r = 0.3$	$t_r = 0.1$
translation error [%]	1.8953	1.6104	1.3070
rotation error [deg/m]	0.0113	0.0090	0.0060

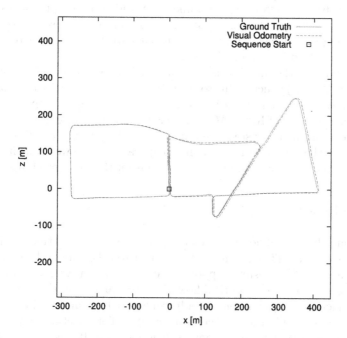

Fig. 3. Reconstructed path of sequence 13 and ground truth path from the KITTI benchmark.

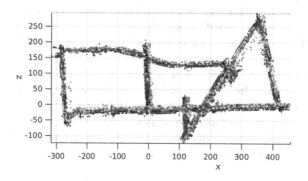

Fig. 4. Reconstructed path of sequence 13 (red dots) and 3D-reconstruction along the driven path (gray dots). (Color figure online)

presented. In summary, the algorithm computes 3D positions from $\{I_{i+1}^l, I_{i+1}^r\}$ and 2D correspondences from $\{I_i^l, I_{i+1}^l\}$ (no circle check). Additionally, a forward/backward check is applied with $t_{fb} = 5$ pixels, a disparity rejection if $t_d > 1$ pixel and a Harris corner response factor of $k = 0.0$. The RANSAC applies a re-projection threshold of $t_r = 0.1$ pixel.

Uploading this version gives a translation error of 1.17% and a rotation error of 0.0035 [deg/m], which ranks 8th under the vision approaches (NOTF, 5th April 2016) and 11th in overall ranking (including laser approaches).

Figure 3 depicts ground truth poses and the computed poses by the NOTF algorithm. Figure 4 depicts the same path but with the reconstructed features that have been used for the ego-motion estimation.

At the moment, the run-time is comparably high (440 ms on a Core i5-4460, 1 core used at 3.2 GHz) which is due to the fact that the parameters are chosen very conservatively; many more iterations than required for e.g. sub-pixel refinement and random sampling of RANSAC. This has been a deliberate decision so as not to optimize at an too early stage. In a next step, the parameters will be adapted in a way that the performance remains comparable at a lower run-time, which will be expected to be in a range of 100–150 ms on the same machine.

7   Conclusion

A simple and slim visual odometry method has been proposed that is within the top ranks of the KITTI benchmark. In contrast to other methods, no temporal filtering is applied. The results support the conclusion that with a proper outlier rejection, raw and unfiltered optical flow measures can deliver the same precision as current methods applying bundle adjustment or Kalman filtering.

The presented study tackled the problem of outlier rejection by purely varying geometric constraints on the optical flow measure. It has been shown that such constraints have a high influence on the performance. Choosing the right combination is a balancing act between keeping as many accurate features as possible and rejecting imprecise measures.

The pose estimation has not been modified, which is a topic remaining for future work. Probably, there will be a higher precision if the selection of measurements in the RANSAC framework is done with more prior knowledge instead of pure random sampling.

Still unclear is if there will be a performance boost by applying filtering methods. This will also be an open question for future investigations.

Further improvement is expected if a real 1D disparity measure is applied for 3D features instead of standard optical flow with subsequent feature rejection. Probably, a significant number of disparities gained by the optical flow procedure are wrong measures, because a full search is applied.

References

1. Badino, H., Yamamoto, A., Kanade, T.: Visual odometry by multi-frame feature integration. In: 2013 IEEE International Conference on Computer Vision Workshops (ICCVW) (2013)
2. Bouguet, J.Y.: Pyramidal implementation of the Lucas Kanade feature tracker. Intel Corporation, Microprocessor Research Labs (2000)
3. Bradski, G., Kaehler, A.: Learning OpenCV: Computer Vision with the OpenCV Library (2008)
4. Cvisic, I., Petrovic, I.: Stereo odometry based on careful feature selection and tracking. In: European Conference on Mobile Robots (ECMR) (2015)
5. Engel, J., Stueckler, J., Cremers, D.: Large-scale direct SLAM with stereo cameras. In: International Conference on Intelligent Robot Systems (IROS) (2015)
6. Fischler, M.A., Bolles, R.C.: Random sample consensus: a paradigm for model fitting with applications to image analysis and automated cartography. Commun. ACM **24**, 381–395 (1981)
7. Fraundorfer, F., Scaramuzza, D.: Visual odometry part II: matching, optimization and applications. IEEE Robot. Autom. Mag. Robustness **19**, 78–90 (2012)
8. Geiger, A., Lenz, P., Stiller, C., Urtasun, R.: Kitti vision benchmark suite (2015)
9. Harris, C., Stephens, M.: A combined corner and edge detector. In: Proceedings of Fourth Alvey Vision Conference (1988)
10. Hartley, R., Zisserman, A.: Multiple View Geometry in Computer Vision (2003)
11. Kitt, B., Geiger, A., Lategahn, H.: Visual odometry based on stereo image sequences with RANSAC-based outlier rejection scheme. In: IEEE Intelligent Vehicles Symposium (2010)
12. Ma, Y., Soatto, S., Kosecka, J., Sastry, S.: An Invitation to 3-D Vision (2001)
13. Mair, E., Burschka, D.: Z(inf) - monocular localization algorithm with uncertainty analysis for outdoor applications. In: Mobile Robots Navigation (2010)
14. Nister, D., Naroditsky, O., Bergen, J.: Visual odometry. In: Proceedings of the 2004 IEEE Computer Society Conference on Computer Vision and Pattern Recognition, CVPR 2004, vol. 1, pp. 652–659. IEEE (2004)
15. Nuetzi, G., Weiss, S., Scaramuzza, D., Siegwart, R.: Fusion of IMU and Vision for Absolute Scale Estimation in Monocular SLAM (2010)
16. Persson, M., Piccini, T., Felsberg, M., Mester, R.: Robust stereo visual odometry from monocular techniques. In: IEEE Intelligent Vehicles Symposium (2015)
17. Scaramuzza, D., Fraundorfer, F.: Visual odometry part I: the first 30 years and fundamentals. IEEE Robot. Autom. Mag. **18**, 80–92 (2011)

Learning II

Large-Scale Active Learning
with Approximations of Expected Model
Output Changes

Christoph Käding[1,2(✉)], Alexander Freytag[1,2], Erik Rodner[1,2],
Andrea Perino[3,4], and Joachim Denzler[1,2,3]

[1] Computer Vision Group, Friedrich Schiller University Jena, Jena, Germany
[2] Michael Stifel Center Jena, Jena, Germany
[3] German Centre for Integrative Biodiversity Research (iDiv) Halle-Jena-Leipzig,
Leipzig, Germany
[4] Institute of Biology, Martin Luther University Halle-Wittenberg,
Halle (Saale), Germany
christoph.kaeding@uni-jena.de

Abstract. Incremental learning of visual concepts is one step towards
reaching human capabilities beyond closed-world assumptions. Besides
recent progress, it remains one of the fundamental challenges in computer
vision and machine learning. Along that path, techniques are needed
which allow for actively selecting informative examples from a huge pool
of unlabeled images to be annotated by application experts. Whereas a
manifold of active learning techniques exists, they commonly suffer from
one of two drawbacks: (i) either they do not work reliably on challenging
real-world data or (ii) they are kernel-based and not scalable with the
magnitudes of data current vision applications need to deal with. Therefore, we present an active learning and discovery approach which can deal
with huge collections of unlabeled real-world data. Our approach is based
on the expected model output change principle and overcomes previous
scalability issues. We present experiments on the large-scale MS-COCO
dataset and on a dataset provided by biodiversity researchers. Obtained
results reveal that our technique clearly improves accuracy after just a
few annotations. At the same time, it outperforms previous active learning approaches in academic and real-world scenarios.

1 Introduction

Over the past years, we observed striking performance leaps in supervised learning tasks due to the combination of linear models and deep learnable image

This research was supported by grant DE 735/10-1 of the German Research Foundation (DFG).

Electronic supplementary material The online version of this chapter (doi:10.
1007/978-3-319-45886-1_15) contains supplementary material, which is available to
authorized users.

B. Rosenhahn and B. Andres (Eds.): GCPR 2016, LNCS 9796, pp. 179–191, 2016.
DOI: 10.1007/978-3-319-45886-1_15

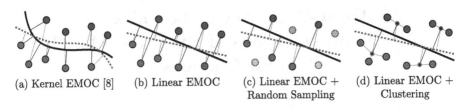

(a) Kernel EMOC [8]   (b) Linear EMOC   (c) Linear EMOC +   (d) Linear EMOC +
                                                Random Sampling   Clustering

Fig. 1. Visualization of the expected model output change (EMOC) criterion and our approximations thereof. Classification boundaries in a two-class scenario are marked as thick lines before (solid) and after a model update (dashed). Model outputs are denoted as thin lines. In [10], all output changes of a kernelized model are computed (a). A linear model reduces complexity of model evaluations (b). Evaluating output changes only on a random subset (c) or on cluster centroids (d) reduces computational complexity further

representations. However, the demand for annotated data grew in the same frequency of newly published accuracy records. On the other hand, our ability to provide increasing labeled datasets is limited. Similarly intuitive is the observation that not all labeled images are equally informative for a given task. The area of active learning tackles this observation: by designing algorithms which estimate the gainable information of unseen examples, annotation costs can be reduced by labeling only the most informative ones.

While active learning has been an active area of research for more than 20 years [6], the majority of algorithms have been evaluated on synthetic or small scale datasets (*e.g.,* [6,14,16,18,27]). Undoubtedly, these algorithms achieve reasonable results in the presented benchmarks. However, it is unclear whether their performances with respect to computation time, memory demand, and classification accuracy scale sufficiently to large real-world datasets. However, especially due to the increasing availability of large unlabeled datasets, today's active learning algorithms have to have "large-scale abilities". In this paper, we follow this observation by presenting an active learning technique which is able to deal with large-scale datasets as well as unseen classes.

Our approach is based on the expected model output change (EMOC) criterion by Freytag et al. [10], which we transfer to linear models and approximate appropriately. Hence, the contribution of this paper is two-fold:

1. we present a realization of EMOC for regularized linear least square regression and derive efficient closed-form solutions for score computation and model update, and
2. we introduce and analyze approximations of resulting scores to reduce computational burdens even further.

The combination of both complementary aspects overcomes limitations of previous approaches and enables active learning with sophisticated selection criteria for large sets of unlabeled data. A schematic overview of our approaches is given in Fig. 1. We evaluate our techniques on the challenging MS-COCO dataset [21] and provide evidence for the technique's suitability in large-scale scenarios. Finally, we present results on a real world dataset from biodiversity researchers who are particularly interested in classifying large collections of unlabeled images.

2   Related Work

Active learning is a widely studied field which aims at reducing labeling efforts. The general goal of active learning is to optimally select examples for annotation, which ultimately reduces the error of the classifier as fast as possible. A detailed summary of active learning techniques was presented by Settles [26]. In the following, we only review the most prominent and most relevant techniques.

Established Approaches for Active Learning. The early work of Roy and McCallum [24] presented approximations of estimated error reduction. Since the resulting algorithm is still computationally expensive, a majority of follow-up work has been based on surrogate functions, *e.g.,* [2,5,9,15,16,18,26,27]. A common strategy is the selection of examples the current classifier is most uncertain about [15,16,18,27]. This strategy is for example also used by [7,29] and further extended to query whole batches of unlabeled data. Complementary is the idea of rapidly exploring the space [2,18] which is purely data-driven. A third example is the preference of examples which leads to large changes of model parameters [5,9,26]. However, these concepts miss a clear connection to the reduction of errors, which is the ultimate goal of learning.

Related Work on Large-Scale Active Learning. The necessity for dealing with large datasets is a well-known problem for active learning. A simple yet efficient solution is to sample batches of data for evaluation, as presented by Hoi et al. [13] and Fu and Yang [11]. Similarly, the data can be pre-clustered [1]. Alternatively, models need to be applied which scale well to large datasets, *e.g.,* the probabilistic k-nearest neighbors approach by Jain et al. [15]. Another challenge is the growing number of classes. By only taking a subset of possible updates into account, Ertekin et al. [8] showed how this can be handled efficiently. Although these approaches scale nicely to large datasets, they still miss a clear connection to the reduction of errors.

Approaches Using Expected Output Changes. In contrast to the previous approaches, selecting examples which lead to large estimated model output changes approximates the expected reduction of errors. Motivated by Vezhnevets et al. for the task of semantic segmentation [28], it was later presented by Freytag et al. [10] from a general perspective. The authors initially focused on specific realizations for binary classification with Gaussian process models. Later on, they extended their approach to multi-class scenarios with unnameable instances [17]. Although the reported results lead to impressive accuracy gains in challenging scenarios, the authors were limited to medium-scale datasets due to the choice of kernel classifiers. In this work, we show how to overcome these limitations using two complementary aspects: (i) by transferring the EMOC criterion to linear models and (ii) by approximating involved expectation operations. The approach of [4] proposes to estimate an optimal mix based on expected model output changes of passive and arbitrary active learning techniques. The idea of their method is orthogonal to ours and can be used in addition to the techniques presented in our paper.

3   Expected Model Output Changes in a Nutshell

In this paper, we aim at extending the recently proposed expected model output changes (EMOC) criterion to large-scale scenarios. We start with a short review of the underlying idea and its multi-class variant as presented in [10,17].

The EMOC Principle. In [10], Freytag et al. introduced EMOC as an approximation to the estimated reduction of expected risk. In contrast to previous approaches, the criterion favors only those examples $\mathbf{x}'$ which lead to largest output changes after re-training – averaged over any possible label $y' \in \mathcal{Y}$:

$$\Delta f(\mathbf{x}') = \mathbb{E}_{y' \in \mathcal{Y}} \, \mathbb{E}_{\mathbf{x} \in \Omega} \left(\mathcal{L}(f(\mathbf{x}), f'(\mathbf{x})) \right). \tag{1}$$

Here, f' refers to the updated model after including the unlabeled example $\mathbf{x}'$ with the estimated label y' to the current training set. The output changes are calculated with a loss function $\mathcal{L}$, e.g., using an L_1-loss as suggested in [10]. However, note that Eq. (1) is not computable in practice for realistic settings due to the expectation over the input space Ω.

Similar to the transfer from expected risk to empirical risk, the authors of [10] proposed to rely on the empirical data distribution induced by the labeled data $\mathcal{L}$ and unlabeled data $\mathfrak{U}$. For classification scenarios, we further note that labels are discrete. Combining both aspects leads to the final EMOC criterion for arbitrary classification scenarios with finite data:

$$\Delta f(\mathbf{x}') = \sum_{y' \in \mathcal{Y}} \left(\frac{1}{|\mathcal{L} \cup \mathfrak{U}|} \sum_{\mathbf{x} \in \mathcal{L} \cup \mathfrak{U}} \mathcal{L}(f(\mathbf{x}), f'(\mathbf{x})) \right) p(y'|f(\mathbf{x}')). \tag{2}$$

As it turned out, this active learning criterion is more robust compared to expected risk minimization and achieves state-of-the-art results.

EMOC for Multi-class Scenarios with Unnameable Instances. Besides the theoretical derivation of EMOC, [10] contained efficient realizations only for Gaussian process models in binary classification tasks. Later on, the authors extended their results to multi-class scenarios by specifying appropriate loss functions and estimators for multi-class classification probabilities [17]. Furthermore, they investigated scenarios where unlabeled data contains so-called "unnameable instances". Unnameable instances refer to examples for which an oracle can not provide a proper label. These instances, also termed "noise" examples, will not lead to any improvement of the classifier and should thus be avoided during selection. The work of [17] shows that this can be achieved by (1) density reweighting and (2) predicting unnameable instances by learning their distribution over time. In this paper, we apply these modifications to deal with multi-class scenarios containing unnameable instances.

The reported results in [17] clearly demonstrate the benefit of EMOC in realistic scenarios with unnameable instances. However, the choice of Gaussian process models limits its applicability to scenarios with only several thousands of examples. In the following, we are interested in transferring their approach to linear models which will allow us to tackle significantly larger data collections.

4   EMOC for Linear Models and Large Datasets

In the following, we provide two complementary contributions to overcome the previous drawbacks of EMOC on large-scale scenarios. First of all, we present how EMOC can be applied to linear least square regression, including efficient evaluations of the criterion and efficient update rules (Sect. 4.1). In addition, we show how to approximate involved expectation operations to reduce computational burdens (Sect. 4.2).

4.1   EMOC for Linear Least Square Regression

Given the expressive power of deep learnable representations, replacing kernel methods with linear pendants can be well justifiable. For binary scenarios, a general linear model can be written as $f(\mathbf{x}) = \mathbf{w}^{\mathrm{T}}\mathbf{x}$ where the bias can be included into $\mathbf{w}$ by augmenting $\mathbf{x}$ with a constant dimension. The optimal solution for $\mathbf{w} \in \mathbb{R}^D$ depends on the chosen loss function. Well-known examples are logistic regression, linear SVMs, and least-square regression, which follow from minimizing the logistic loss, the hinge loss, or the quadratic loss on the training data set. Classification decisions are obtained by thresholding $f(\mathbf{x})$, *e.g.*, against zero.

For multi-class scenarios, a simple and common extension is the combination of class-specific one-vs-all models. Thereby, a binary classifier f_c is trained for each class c and the classifier with largest response on new data $\mathbf{x}$ determines the classification result. In the following, we focus on regularized least-square regression due to the resulting closed-form solutions (denoted as LSR in the remainder of the paper). Note that this directly corresponds to the linear version of Gaussian process regression as used in [17]. In this case, the hyperplanes $\mathbf{w}_c \in \mathbb{R}^D$ can be obtained as $\mathbf{w}_c = \mathbf{C}_{\mathrm{reg}}^{-1}\mathbf{X}\mathbf{y}_c$, where the matrix $\mathbf{X} \in \mathbb{R}^{D \times N}$ holds the N training examples with feature dimension D and $\mathbf{y}_c$ is the vector of binary one-vs-all labels for class c. Furthermore, the regularized covariance matrix of the data $\mathbf{C}_{\mathrm{reg}}$ is obtained by $\mathbf{C}_{\mathrm{reg}} = \mathbf{X}\mathbf{X}^{\mathrm{T}} + \sigma_n^2\mathbf{I}$. The parameter σ_n^2 controls the degree of regularization and is related to the idea of weight decay [3].

When transferring the general EMOC criterion in Eq. (2) to LSR models, we obtain the following estimate. A detailed derivation is given in the supplementary material (see Sect. S1) and is purely based on applying linear algebra [22].

$$\Delta f_{mc}(\mathbf{x}') = \frac{1}{1 + \mathbf{x}'^{\mathrm{T}}\mathbf{C}_{\mathrm{reg}}^{-1}\mathbf{x}'} \cdot \sum_{y' \in \mathcal{Y}} \left(p(y'|\mathbf{x}') \frac{1}{|C|} \sum_{c \in C} |\mathbf{w}_c^{\mathrm{T}}\mathbf{x}' - y_c'| \right)$$

$$\cdot \frac{1}{|\mathcal{L} \cup \mathcal{U}|} \sum_{\mathbf{x}_j \in \mathcal{L} \cup \mathcal{U}} |\mathbf{x}_j^{\mathrm{T}}\mathbf{C}_{\mathrm{reg}}^{-1}\mathbf{x}'|. \tag{3}$$

Since $\mathbf{C}_{\mathrm{reg}}$ and $\mathbf{w}$ are of fixed size, the memory demand as well as required computation times remain constant for increasing training set sizes. Hence, we can evaluate the EMOC score efficiently over time (denoted by LSR-EMOC).

The second important issue for a successful active learning system is the possibility for online learning. Thereby, labeled data can be incrementally added and learning from scratch is avoided. Intuitively, this aspect gains importance for increasing dataset sizes. For the choice of one-vs-all LSR models, we can derive the following closed-form update rules which lead to efficient online learning abilities using the Sherman-Morrison-formula [23]. For a detailed derivation please also refer to Sect. S1:

$$\mathbf{w}_c' = \mathbf{w}_c + \mathbf{C}_{\mathrm{reg}}^{-1}\mathbf{x}' \left(\frac{y_c' - \mathbf{x}'^{\mathrm{T}}\mathbf{w}_c}{1 + \mathbf{x}'^{\mathrm{T}}\mathbf{C}_{\mathrm{reg}}^{-1}\mathbf{x}'} \right), \tag{4}$$

$$\mathbf{C}_{\mathrm{reg}}^{-1}{}' = \left(\mathbf{C}_{\mathrm{reg}} + \mathbf{x}'\mathbf{x}'^{\mathrm{T}} \right)^{-1} = \mathbf{C}_{\mathrm{reg}}^{-1} - \frac{\mathbf{C}_{\mathrm{reg}}^{-1}\mathbf{x}'\mathbf{x}'^{\mathrm{T}}\mathbf{C}_{\mathrm{reg}}^{-1}}{1 + \mathbf{x}'^{\mathrm{T}}\mathbf{C}_{\mathrm{reg}}^{-1}\mathbf{x}'}. \tag{5}$$

We denoted with $\mathbf{w}_c'$ the new weight vector for class c after adding $\mathbf{x}'$ with corresponding binary label y_c'. Similarly, $\mathbf{C}_{\mathrm{reg}}'$ denotes the updated covariance matrix. Note that the inverse of $\mathbf{C}_{\mathrm{reg}}$ has to be computed only once and can be updated incrementally (see Eq. (5)). Since all required variables in Eqs. (4) and (5) are available, the entire update requires only $\mathcal{O}(D^2)$ operations. Similar rules based on the Cholesky decomposition [25] can be derived as well.

4.2   Approximating the Expectation Operation

Based on our previous derivations, we can directly apply the LSR-EMOC criterion to large unlabeled datasets. However, evaluating the criterion is still moderately costly due to the involved expectation operation with respect to all available data (second sum in Eq. (3)). To overcome this issue, we can approximate the expectation operation, *e.g.*, using Monte-Carlo-like sampling.

The simplest approximation is to use a randomly drawn subset $\mathcal{S}_r \subset \mathcal{L} \cup \mathcal{U}$ when estimating model output changes. If examples in $\mathcal{S}_r$ are drawn i.i.d. from all available data, we can expect that the resulting dataset statistics will be comparable. Hence, the expectation remains unchanged:

$$\Delta f_{\mathrm{mc}}(\mathbf{x}' \mid \mathcal{L} \cup \mathcal{U}) \approx \Delta f_{\mathrm{mc}}(\mathbf{x}' \mid \mathcal{S}_r), \tag{6}$$

where we used the notation of $\Delta f_{\mathrm{mc}}(\mathbf{x}' \mid \mathcal{S}_r)$ to denote that the LSR-EMOC score for example $\mathbf{x}'$ is computed using only the subset $\mathcal{S}_r$. In the following, this approximation is referred to as LSR-EMOC$^{\mathrm{r}-|\mathcal{S}_r|}$.

Although the property in Eq. (6) seems beneficial, a mere random selection can likely sample redundant data. We can explicitly avoid this effect by clustering all examples in advance and approximating the expectation using the set $\mathcal{S}_c$ of cluster centroids only. Thereby, diversity is explicitly enforced which can be beneficial for focusing on underrepresented regions of space. We call this approximation LSR-EMOC$^{\text{c-}|\mathcal{S}_c|}$. Nonetheless, the equality of expectations as in Eq. (6) is no longer given.

As third alternative, we could aim at selecting an optimal subset $\mathcal{S}_{\text{opt}} \subset \mathfrak{L} \cup \mathfrak{U}$ which leads to the closest approximation of scores:

$$\mathcal{S}_{\text{opt}} = \underset{\mathcal{S}_* \subset \mathfrak{L} \cup \mathfrak{U}}{\arg\max} |\Delta f_{\text{mc}}\left(\mathbf{x}' \mid \mathfrak{L} \cup \mathfrak{U}\right) - \Delta f_{\text{mc}}\left(\mathbf{x}' \mid \mathcal{S}_*\right)|. \qquad (7)$$

Unfortunately, determining the optimal subset leads to a combinatorial problem similarly complex as active learning itself. Hence, it is only theoretically feasible. In the following experimental evaluations, we provide evidence that the first two approximations are well suited for large-scale active learning tasks.

5 Experiments

In the following, we present a detailed evaluation of our LSR-EMOC approach, where we especially focus on active class discovery. Furthermore, we show the benefits of active learning for the real-world application of camera trap analysis.

5.1 Large-Scale Active Learning for Object Classification

The first part of our evaluations is concerned with the applicability of our introduced approaches to the challenging dataset MS-COCO and relevant subsets thereof. We use the MS-COCO-full-v0.9 dataset [21] and follow the evaluation protocol of [17]. Thus, we add "noise" examples which reflect the scenario that certain examples are unnameable even for experts. In contrast to [17], we use L_2-normalized `relu7` features of the BVLC AlexNet [20]. This consistently increases the accuracy in our experiments for all active learning techniques. We optimize hyperparameters (e.g., the regularization weight for LSR) on a hold-out set and keep the values fixed for all experiments.

Our approaches are compared against the baseline presented in [17], i.e., EMOC on GP-regression with a linear kernel. Furthermore, we compare against several established methods: GP-Var and GP-Unc by Kapoor et al. [18], 1-vs-2 by Joshi et al. [16], and PKNN by Jain and Kapoor [15]. We use the parameter configuration schemes as in [17]. Finally, we include an upper bound which results from having all unlabeled data as labeled training examples available.

MS-COCO Animals Dataset. For a sanity-check evaluation, we follow [17] and use the subset of MS-COCO which corresponds to animal categories (10 categories in total). As in [17], we apply Geodesic Object Proposals [19] to obtain 3824 samples as well as 4574 image patches as training data and "noise" samples. Additionally, a hold-out set of 750 samples is used as validation set. Each

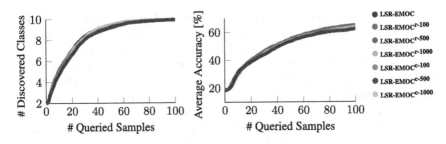

Fig. 2. Comparing approximations of LSR-EMOC on MS-COCO Animals

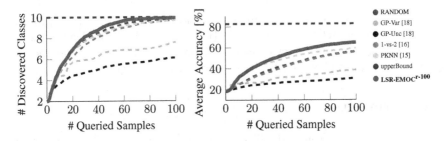

Fig. 3. Comparison of active learning methods on MS-COCO Animals

experiment starts with 10 randomly chosen examples for each of 2 randomly chosen classes. All remaining data of the training set is used as unlabeled pool. We conduct 100 experiments with different random initializations to obtain reliable results. In each experiment, we conduct 100 queries. Learned models are evaluated after every query on a hold-out test set which is randomly drawn from the validation set and which consists of 30 samples per class.

First of all, we were interested in a comparison between EMOC of LSR models and our proposed approximations thereof. Note that LSR-EMOC leads to the same results as EMOC with GP-regression and linear kernels as used in the corresponding evaluation in [17]. Since both approaches only differ in required resource for computing scores an additional comparison regarding accuracy is not required here. Instead, we present results for LSR-EMOC and our approximation techniques in Fig. 2.

It can clearly be seen that the EMOC approach for LSR models as well as the proposed approximation techniques lead to almost identical results. Hence, we conclude that approximating EMOC calculations is possible without a notable loss in accuracy. Although the dataset is moderately small, we already obtain a speedup of 2.1 (LSR-EMOC $\approx$ 12.1 s and LSR-EMOC$^{r\text{-}100}$ $\approx$ 5.7 s for a whole query selection). Furthermore, it can be seen that pre-clustering of data yields no advantage over mere random selection. Hence, we conclude that the random selection should be preferred due to smaller computational costs. For the datasets used in the following evaluations, we performed similar comparisons

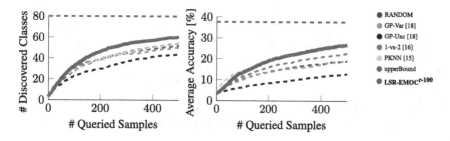

Fig. 4. Comparison of active learning methods on MS-COCO

which lead to comparable findings. Due to the lack of space, the results are shown in the supplementary material (see Sect. S3). In the following evaluations, we only show the fastest of our approximations, *i.e.*, random sampling with 100 samples (LSR-EMOC^{r-100}).

As a second experiment on the dataset, we compared our proposed method with several active learning baselines. Results are shown in Fig. 3. As can be seen, LSR-EMOC approach performs best with respect to both performance measures. Note that these results are comparable to the ones reported in [17]. However, our choice of LSR-EMOC offers scalability to larger unlabeled pools.

MS-COCO Dataset. Since we are interested in large-scale scenarios, we also use the entire MS-COCO dataset which can not be processed by the method of [17] in reasonable time. Image patches are obtained by using the ground truth annotations provided by the dataset. We use each box which is at least 256 × 256 pixel of size. Thereby, we obtain a training set of 36212 image patches with 80 categories that consist of three to 10632 examples. Similarly, we obtain a validation set with 46485 patches and three to 15986 examples per category. To keep the same ratio of unnameable instances in the unlabeled pool, we add 20000 randomly selected patches with a maximal intersection over union score of 0.25 to any ground truth bounding box. We start with three initially known classes and 10 randomly chosen examples per category. All remaining data of the training set is used as unlabeled pool. We evaluate performances on 30 randomly selected validation samples per class. For robustness of our evaluations, we average results of nine random initialization. Since not all classes provide enough samples for the hold-out test set, we evaluate models on a fixed set which consists of 2304 examples. In each experiment, we perform 500 query steps. All other setup parameters are kept unchanged compared to the previous section. Note further that EMOC on GP regression (*i.e.*, kernelized regularization LSR) is not longer applicable in this setting due to memory consumption and computation time. Results are shown in Fig. 4.

Again, it can clearly be seen that our method performs best with respect to the number of discovered classes. Considering accuracy, PKNN and our approach achieve comparable results. The performance drop in the beginning can

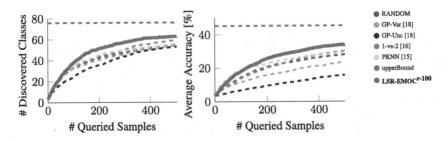

Fig. 5. Comparison of active learning methods on MS-COCO with a balanced class distribution.

be attributed to the imbalanced nature of MS-COCO. A corresponding visualization can be found in the supplementary material (see Sect. S2) as well as a runtime comparison (see Sect. S4). Note that a fast increase of accuracy can also be achieved by explicitly searching for rare classes as presented in [12]. However, rare class discovery is especially challenging in the presence of unnameable instances and not within the scope of this paper.

MS-COCO with a Balanced Class Distribution. We were finally interested in a comparison for a setting where classes are better balanced. Therefore, we use the previous setup and ignore categories having more than 1000 samples in the training set. These classes are person (10632 samples), dining table (3979 samples), bed (1400 samples) and cat (1020 samples). Thereby, we obtain a training set with 19181 samples from 76 categories and a test set with 25060 examples. After randomly selecting 30 validation samples per class, we evaluate the methods on a test set of 2184 samples. To augment the data with unnameable instances, 10000 bounding boxes are randomly drawn as described previously. The remaining setup is unchanged. Results are shown in Fig. 5.

As can be seen, our method leads to superior results compared to all competitors. In direct comparison with the runner-up (PKNN), we obtain the same accuracy with only two thirds of the requested annotations. We thus conclude that our method is well suited for active learning on large-scale datasets.

5.2 Active Learning for Camera Trap Image Analysis

In the second part of our evaluations, we are interested in applying active learning to a task which arises in biodiversity assessments. Biodiversity researchers are interested in quantitative analysis of animal abundance, species composition and site occupancy. One way to treat this challenging task is to place camera traps in the wild and to record short sequences of images if any movement is detected. Thereby, researchers are faced with huge amounts of unlabeled data which can to date only be analyzed manually. One task is to differentiate among "background" and "contains-objects". Using active learning, we aim at training classifiers with few labeled data to solve this task.

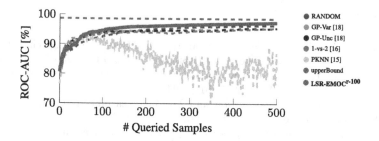

Fig. 6. Results on labeling camera trap images as either "background" or "contains-objects" with only a small number of annotations

Fig. 7. Example queries from the biodiversity dataset

To evaluate the benefits of active learning, we obtained a medium-scale dataset which was labeled by application experts. It consists of 2931 frames from which 2088 show animals. Similar to the previous evaluation, we randomly select three examples from both categories and allow 500 queries. As feature representation, we use normalized `relu7` features from the BVLC AlexNet calculated on the entire image. We repeat the random initialization 10 times to obtain reliable results. Accuracy is measured on the whole dataset after every step. Note that this is exactly the scenario which is desired by application experts: to obtain labels for the entire dataset as reliable as possible while manually labeling only few examples thereof. Results can be found in Fig. 6.

Again, our method leads to superior results compared with all competitors. In particular, we obtain the same accuracy as random selection with only 52 % of required annotations. Surprisingly, the performance of PKNN is dropping over time, which we attribute to the fact that the metric learning could not cope with the variations in the data. Qualitative results can be seen in Fig. 7 as well as in Sect. S5. According to application experts, the results already lead to a valuable reduction of annotation costs.

6   Conclusion

We presented an active learning technique able to cope with large-scale data. Our technique is based on the principle of expected model output changes and builds on two complementary aspects: the effectiveness of linear models as well as careful approximations of necessary computations. We provided empirical evidence that our approach is capable of performing well even on challenging imbalanced datasets. Furthermore, we presented real world experiments for biodiversity data analysis which finally show the applicability and effectiveness of our method.

References

1. Alajlan, N., Pasolli, E., Melgani, F., Franzoso, A.: Large-scale image classification using active learning. IEEE Geosci. Remote Sens. Lett. **11**(1), 259–263 (2014)
2. Baram, Y., El-Yaniv, R., Luz, K.: Online choice of active learning algorithms. J. Mach. Learn. Res. (JMLR) **5**, 255–291 (2004)
3. Bishop, C.M.: Pattern Recognition and Machine Learning. Information Science and Statistics. Springer, New York (2006)
4. Bouneffouf, D.: Exponentiated gradient exploration for active learning. Computers **5**(1), 1 (2016)
5. Cai, W., Zhang, Y., Zhou, S., Wang, W., Ding, C., Gu, X.: Active learning for support vector machines with maximum model change. In: Calders, T., Esposito, F., Hüllermeier, E., Meo, R. (eds.) ECML PKDD 2014, Part I. LNCS, vol. 8724, pp. 211–226. Springer, Heidelberg (2014)
6. Cohn, D., Atlas, L., Ladner, R.: Improving generalization with active learning. Mach. Learn. **15**(2), 201–221 (1994)
7. Demir, B., Bruzzone, L.: A novel active learning method in relevance feedback for content-based remote sensing image retrieval. IEEE Trans. Geosci. Remote Sens. **53**(5), 2323–2334 (2015)
8. Ertekin, S., Huang, J., Bottou, L., Giles, L.: Learning on the border: active learning in imbalanced data classification. In: ACM Conference on Information and Knowledge Management, pp. 127–136 (2007)
9. Freytag, A., Rodner, E., Bodesheim, P., Denzler, J.: Labeling examples that matter: relevance-based active learning with Gaussian processes. In: Weickert, J., Hein, M., Schiele, B. (eds.) GCPR 2013. LNCS, vol. 8142, pp. 282–291. Springer, Heidelberg (2013)
10. Freytag, A., Rodner, E., Denzler, J.: Selecting influential examples: active learning with expected model output changes. In: Fleet, D., Pajdla, T., Schiele, B., Tuytelaars, T. (eds.) ECCV 2014, Part IV. LNCS, vol. 8692, pp. 562–577. Springer, Heidelberg (2014)
11. Fu, C., Yang, Y.: A batch-mode active learning SVM method based on semi-supervised clustering. Intell. Data Anal. **19**(2), 345–358 (2015)
12. Haines, T.S.F., Xiang, T.: Active rare class discovery and classification using dirichlet processes. Int. J. Comput. Vision (IJCV) **106**(3), 315–331 (2014)
13. Hoi, S.C., Jin, R., Lyu, M.R.: Large-scale text categorization by batch mode active learning. In: ACM International Conference on World Wide Web, pp. 633–642 (2006)
14. Huang, S.J., Jin, R., Zhou, Z.H.: Active learning by querying informative and representative examples. In: Neural Information Processing Systems (NIPS), pp. 892–900 (2010)
15. Jain, P., Kapoor, A.: Active learning for large multi-class problems. In: IEEE Conference on Computer Vision and Pattern Recognition (CVPR), pp. 762–769 (2009)
16. Joshi, A., Porikli, F., Papanikolopoulos, N.: Multi-class active learning for image classification. In: IEEE Conference on Computer Vision and Pattern Recognition (CVPR), pp. 2372–2379 (2009)
17. Käding, C., Freytag, A., Rodner, E., Bodesheim, P., Denzler, J.: Active learning and discovery of object categories in the presence of unnameable instances. In: IEEE Conference on Computer Vision and Pattern Recognition (CVPR), pp. 4343–4352 (2015)

18. Kapoor, A., Grauman, K., Urtasun, R., Darrell, T.: Gaussian processes for object categorization. Int. J. Comput. Vision (IJCV) **88**, 169–188 (2010)
19. Krähenbühl, P., Koltun, V.: Geodesic object proposals. In: Fleet, D., Pajdla, T., Schiele, B., Tuytelaars, T. (eds.) ECCV 2014, Part V. LNCS, vol. 8693, pp. 725–739. Springer, Heidelberg (2014)
20. Krizhevsky, A., Sutskever, I., Hinton, G.E.: Imagenet classification with deep convolutional neural networks. In: Neural Information Processing Systems (NIPS), pp. 1097–1105 (2012)
21. Lin, T.-Y., Maire, M., Belongie, S., Hays, J., Perona, P., Ramanan, D., Dollár, P., Zitnick, C.L.: Microsoft COCO: common objects in context. In: Fleet, D., Pajdla, T., Schiele, B., Tuytelaars, T. (eds.) ECCV 2014, Part V. LNCS, vol. 8693, pp. 740–755. Springer, Heidelberg (2014)
22. Plackett, R.L.: Some theorems in least squares. Biometrika **37**(1/2), 149–157 (1950)
23. Press, W.H.: Numerical Recipes: The Art of Scientific Computing, 3rd edn. Cambridge University Press, Cambridge (2007)
24. Roy, N., McCallum, A.: Toward optimal active learning through sampling estimation of error reduction. In: International Conference on Machine Learning (ICML), pp. 441–448 (2001)
25. Seeger, M.: Low rank updates for the cholesky decomposition. Technical report, University of California, Berkeley (2004)
26. Settles, B.: Active learning literature survey. Computer Sciences Technical Report 1648, University of Wisconsin-Madison (2009)
27. Tong, S., Koller, D.: Support vector machine active learning with applications to text classification. J. Mach. Learn. Res. (JMLR) **2**, 45–66 (2002)
28. Vezhnevets, A., Buhmann, J.M., Ferrari, V.: Active learning for semantic segmentation with expected change. In: IEEE Conference on Computer Vision and Pattern Recognition (CVPR) (2012)
29. Yang, Y., Ma, Z., Nie, F., Chang, X., Hauptmann, A.G.: Multi-class active learning by uncertainty sampling with diversity maximization. Int. J. Comput. Vision (IJCV) **113**(2), 113–127 (2014)

A Convnet for Non-maximum Suppression

Jan Hosang[(✉)], Rodrigo Benenson, and Bernt Schiele

Max-Planck Institute for Informatics, Saarbrücken, Germany
jhosang@mpi-inf.mpg.de

Abstract. Non-maximum suppression (NMS) is used in virtually all state-of-the-art object detection pipelines. While essential object detection ingredients such as features, classifiers, and proposal methods have been extensively researched surprisingly little work has aimed to systematically address NMS. The de-facto standard for NMS is based on greedy clustering with a fixed distance threshold, which forces to trade-off recall versus precision. We propose a convnet designed to perform NMS of a given set of detections. We report experiments on a synthetic setup, crowded pedestrian scenes, and for general person detection. Our approach overcomes the intrinsic limitations of greedy NMS, obtaining better recall and precision.

1 Introduction

The bulk of object detection pipelines are based on three steps: (1) propose a set of windows (via sliding window or object proposals), (2) score each window via a trained classifier, (3) remove overlapping detections (non-maximum suppression). DPM [8] and R-CNN [11,12,25] follow this approach. Both object proposals [14] and detection classifiers [28] have received enormous attention, while non-maximum suppression (NMS) has been seldom addressed. The de-facto standard for NMS consists of greedily merging the higher scoring windows with lower scoring ones if they overlap enough (e.g. intersection-over-union $IoU > 0.5$), which we call GreedyNMS in the following.

GreedyNMS is popular because it is conceptually simple, fast, and for most tasks results in satisfactory detection quality. Despite its popularity, it has important shortcomings. GreedyNMS trades off precision versus recall. If the IoU threshold is too large (too strict) then not enough surrounding detections are suppressed, high scoring false positives are introduced and precision suffers. If the IoU threshold is too low (too loose) then multiple true positives are merged together and the recall suffers. For any IoU threshold, GreedyNMS is sacrificing precision or recall (as shown experimentally in Sect. 4). One can do better than this by leveraging the full signal of the score map (statistics of the surrounding detections) rather than blindly applying a fixed policy everywhere in the image.

Current object detectors are becoming surprisingly effective on both general (e.g. Pascal VOC, COCO) and specific object detection (e.g. pedestrians, faces).

Electronic supplementary material The online version of this chapter (doi:10. 1007/978-3-319-45886-1_16) contains supplementary material, which is available to authorized users.

B. Rosenhahn and B. Andres (Eds.): GCPR 2016, LNCS 9796, pp. 192–204, 2016.
DOI: 10.1007/978-3-319-45886-1_16

The oracle analyses for "perfect NMS" from [14, Table 5] and [23, Fig. 12] both indicate that NMS accounts for almost a quarter of the remaining mistakes.

Instead of doing hard pruning decisions as GreedyNMS, we design our network to make soft decisions by re-scoring (re-ranking) the input detection windows. Our re-scoring is final, and no post-processing is done afterwards, thus the resulting score maps must be very "peaky". We call our proposed network "Tyrolean network", abbreviated Tnet. (Tyrolean because "it likes to see peaks".)

Contribution. We are the first to show that a convnet can be trained and used to overcome the limitations of GreedyNMS. Our experiments demonstrate that, across different occlusion levels, the Tyrolean network (Tnet) performs strictly better than GreedyNMS at *any* IoU threshold.

As an interesting scenario for NMS, we report results for crowded pedestrian scenes and general person detection. Our Tnet can operate solely over detection boxes (like GreedyNMS), and does not use external training data. Furthermore, Tnet provides better results than auto-context [37]. We consider our results a proof of concept, opening the door for further exploration.

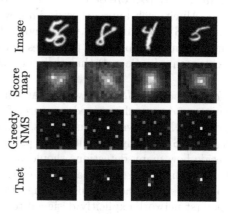

Fig. 1. GreedyNMS produces false positives and prunes true positives, while our proposed Tnet correctly localize even very close digits. First to last row: oMNIST image, input score map, GreedyNMS IoU > 0.3, and Tnet IoU & S (1, 0 → 0.6).

1.1 Related Work

Clustering Detections. The decade old greedy NMS (GreedyNMS) is used in popular detectors such as V&J [39], DPM [8], and is still used in the state-of-the-art R-CNN detector family [11,12,25]. Alternatives such as mean-shift clustering [5,42], agglomerative clustering [2], and heuristic variants [30] have been considered, but they have yet to show consistent gains. Recently [27,35] proposed principled clustering approaches that provide globally optimal solutions, however the results reached are on par, but do not surpass, GreedyNMS.

Linking Detections to Pixels. The Hough voting framework enables reasoning amongst conflicting detections by linking the detections to local image evidence [1,17,18,41]. Hough voting itself, however, provides low detection accuracy. [4,44] refine detections by linking them with semantic labelling; while [43] side-steps NMS all-together by defining the detection task directly as a labelling problem. These approaches arguably propose a sound formulation of the detection problem, however they rely on semantic labelling/image segmentation. Our system operates directly on bounding box detections.

Co-occurrence. To better handle dense crowds or common object pairs, it has been proposed to use specialized 2-object detectors [22,29,34], which then require a careful NMS strategy to merge single-object with double-object detections. Similarly, [26] adapts the NMS threshold using crowd density estimation. Our approach is directly learning based (no hand-crafted 2-objects or density estimators), and does not use additional image information.

Auto-context re-score detections using local [3,37] or global [38] image information. Albeit such approaches do improve detection quality, they still require a final NMS processing step. Our convnet does re-score detections, but at the same time outputs a score map that does not require further processing. We provide experiments (in Sect. 4) that show improved performance over auto-context.

Convnets and NMS. Few works have linked convnets and NMS, detection convnets are commonly trained unaware of the NMS post-processing step. [40] proposed an NMS-aware training loss, making the training truly end-to-end. The used NMS is greedy and with fixed parameters. [32] proposes to use an LSTM to decide how many detections should be considered in a local region. The detections amongst the regions are then merged via traditional NMS. In contrast, our convnet requires no post-processing. To the best of our knowledge our Tnet is the first network explicitly designed to replace the final NMS stage.

In Sect. 2 we describe our base network, Sect. 3 explores its use in a synthetic setup. Then Sect. 4 reports results over DPM [8] detections in crowds datasets (small scale variance), and finally results over FasterRCNN [25] on Pascal VOC people [7].

2   Base Tyrolean Network

The main intuition behind our proposed Tyrolean network (Tnet) is that the score map of a detector together with a map that represents the overlap between neighbouring detections contains valuable information to perform better NMS than GreedyNMS (see Fig. 1, second row). Our network is a traditional convnet but with access to two slightly unusual inputs (described below), namely score map information and IoU maps. Figure 2 shows the overall network. In our base Tnet the first stage applies 512 11×11 filters over each input layer, and 512 1×1 filters are applied on layers 2 and 3. ReLU non-linearities are used after each layer but the last one. Neither max-pooling nor local normalization is used.

The base network is trained and tested in a fully convolutional fashion. It uses the same information as GreedyNMS, and does not access the image pixels directly. The required training data are only a set of object detections (before NMS), and the ground truth bounding boxes of the dataset. We focus on the single class case and consider exploiting multi-class information future work.

Input Grid. As preprocessing all detections in an image are mapped into a 2d grid (based on their centre location). If more than one detection falls into the same

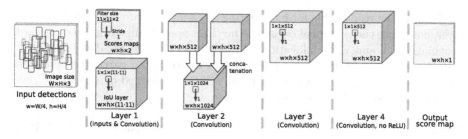

Fig. 2. Base architecture of our Tyrolean network (Tnet). Each box is a feature map, its dimensions are indicated at its bottom, the coloured square indicates the convolutional filters size, the stride is marked next to the downward arrow. (Color figure online)

cell, we keep only the highest scoring detection. Each cell in the grid is associated with a detection bounding box and score. We use cells of 4×4 pixels, thus an input image of size $W \times H$ will be mapped to input layers of size $w \times h = W/4 \times H/4$. Since the cells are small, mapping detections to the input grid has minimal impact on the NMS procedure. In preliminary experiments we validated that: (a) we can at least recover the performance of GreedyNMS (applying GreedyNMS over the input grid provides the same results as directly applying GreedyNMS), (b) the detection recall stays the same (after mapping to the input grid the overall recall is essentially identical to the raw detections).

This incarnation of Tnet can handle mild changes in scale amongst neighbouring detections. Section 4 reports experiments with detections over a $3\times$ scale range. In Sect. 4 we also explain how to adapt our approach to general person detection (Pascal VOC [7]), with large scale and aspect ratio variance.

IoU Layer. In order to reason about neighbouring detection boxes (or segments) we feed Tnet with IoU values. For each location we consider a $11 \times 11 = 121$ neighbourhood, thus the input IoU layer has $w \times h \times 121$ values. Together the cell size and neighbourhood size should provide the Tnet with sufficient information about surroundings of a detection, where this choice depends on the object sizes in the image and the expected object density and thus are application dependent.

Score Maps Layer. To reason about the detection confidence, we feed Tnet with the raw detection score map (once mapped to the input grid). The NMS task involves ranking operations which are not easily computed by linear and ReLU $(\max(\cdot, 0))$ operators. To ease the task we also feed the Tnet with score maps resulting from GreedyNMS at multiple IoU thresholds. All score maps are stacked as a multi-channel input image and feed into the network. $S(\tau)$ denotes a score map resulting from applying GreedyNMS with $IoU \geq \tau$, $S(\tau_1, \tau_2)$ denotes a two channels map ($S(\tau_1)$ and $S(\tau_2)$ stacked). Note that $S(1)$ returns the raw detection score map. Our base Tnet uses $S(1, 0.3)$ which has dimensionality $w \times h \times 2$ (see Fig. 2). The convolutional filters applied over the score maps input have the same size as the IoU layer neighbourhood (11×11 cells).

Tnet is then responsible for interpreting the multiple score maps and the IoU layer, and make the best local decision. Our Tnet operates in a fully feed-forward convolutional manner. Each location is visited only once, and the decision is final. In other words, for each location the Tnet has to decide if a particular detection score corresponds to a correct detection or will be suppressed by a neighbouring detection in a single feed-forward path.

Parameter Rules of Thumb. Figure 2 indicates the base parameters used. Preliminary experiments indicated that removing top layers has a clear negative impact on the network performance, while the width of these layers is rather insensitive. Having a high enough resolution in the input grid is critical, while keeping a small enough number of convolutions over the inputs allows to keep the number of model parameters under control. During training data augmentation is necessary to avoid overfitting. The training procedure is discussed in Sect. 2.1, while experimental results for some parameters variants are reported in Sect. 4.

Input Variants. Experiments in the next sections consider multiple input variants. The IoU layer values can be computed over bounding boxes (regressed by the sliding window detector) or over estimated instance segments [24]. Similarly, for the score maps we consider different numbers of GreedyNMS thresholds, which changes the dimensionality of the input score map layer.

In all cases we expect the Tnet to improve over a fixed threshold GreedyNMS by discovering patterns in the detector score maps and IoU arrangements that enable to do adaptive NMS decisions.

2.1   Training procedure

Typically detectors are trained as classifiers on a set of positive and negative windows, determined by the IoU between detection and object annotation. When doing so the spatial relation between detector outputs and the annotations is neglected. We adopt the idea from [32] of computing the loss by matching detections to annotations, and train the network to predict new detection scores that are high for matched detections and low everywhere else. In contrast to the conventional wisdom of training the detector to have a smooth score decrease around positive instances, we declare a detection right next to a true positive to be a negative training sample. Processing detections *independently* would hurt generalisation, but Tnet has access to neighbouring detections circumventing this problem. This is necessary because our network must itself perform NMS.

Training Loss. Our goal is to reduce the score of all detections that belong to the same person, except exactly one of them. To that end, we match every annotation to the highest scoring detection that overlaps at least 0.5 IoU. This determines the set of positives, while all other detections are negative training examples. This yields a label y_p for every location p in the input grid (see previous section). Since background detections are much more frequent than true positives, it is necessary to weight the loss terms to balance the two. We use the weighted logistic loss and choose the weights so that both classes have the same weight per frame. We also consider setting weights to balance classes across the full dataset and giving lower weights for highly occluded samples, see Sect. 4.1.

The model is trained from scratch, randomly initialized with MSRA [13], and optimized via Adam [16]. All experiments are implemented with Caffe [15]. See supplementary material for details of the training loss and training parameters.

As pointed out in [20] the threshold for GreedyNMS requires to be carefully selected on the validation set of each task, the commonly used default IoU > 0.5 can severely underperform. Other NMS approaches such as [27,35] also require training data to be adjusted. When maximizing performance in cluttered scenes is important, training a Tnet is thus not a particularly heavy burden. Training our base Tnet on un-optimized CPU and GPU code takes a day.

3   Controlled Setup Experiments

NMS is usually the last stage of an entire detection pipeline. Therefore, in an initial set of experiments, we want to understand the problem independent of a specific detector and abstract away the particularities of a given dataset.

If objects appeared alone in the images, NMS would be trivial. The core issue for NMS is deciding if two local maxima in the detection score map correspond to one or multiple objects. To investigate this core aspect we create the oMNIST ("overlapping MNIST") toy dataset. This data does not aim at being particularly realistic, but rather to enable a detailed analysis of the NMS problem.

Each image is composed of one or two off-centre MNIST digits with IoU $\in$ [0.2, 0.6]. We mimic a detector by generating synthetic perturbed score maps. Albeit noisy, the detector is "ideal" because its detection score remains high despite strong occlusions. The supplementary material and Fig. 1 show examples of the generated score maps and corresponding images. By design GreedyNMS will have difficulties handling such cases (at any IoU threshold). We generate a training/test split of 100k/10k images (fix across experiments).

Other than score maps our convnet uses IoU information between neighbouring detections (like GreedyNMS). Our experiments cover using the perfect segmentation masks for IoU (ideal case), noisy segmentation masks, and the sliding window bounding boxes.

3.1   Results

Results are summarised in Fig. 3. Curves are scored via AR; the average recall on the precision range [0.5, 1.0]. The evaluation is done using the standard Pascal VOC protocol, with IoU > 0.5 [7].

GreedyNMS. As can be seen in Fig. 3 varying the IoU thresholds for GreedyNMS trades off precision and recall. The best AR that can be obtained with GreedyNMS is 60.2 % for IoU > 0.3. Example score maps for this method can be found in Fig. 1, third row.

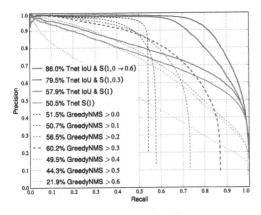

Legend (in figure):
- 86.0% Tnet IoU & S(1,0 → 0.6)
- 79.5% Tnet IoU & S(1,0.3)
- 57.9% Tnet IoU & S(1)
- 50.5% Tnet S(1)
- 51.5% GreedyNMS > 0.0
- 50.7% GreedyNMS > 0.1
- 56.5% GreedyNMS > 0.2
- 60.2% GreedyNMS > 0.3
- 49.5% GreedyNMS > 0.4
- 44.3% GreedyNMS > 0.5
- 21.9% GreedyNMS > 0.6

Fig. 3. oMNIST test set detection results.

Table 1. PETS val. set results. Base Tnet is underlined.

Method	AR
GreedyNMS	
bboxes IoU > 0.3	54.3 %
DeepMask segments	52.0 %
Tnet variants	
IoU & S $(1, 0 \rightarrow 0.6)$	*59.6 %*
IoU & S $(1, 0.3)$	57.9 %
IoU & S (1)	36.5 %
S (1)	33.9 %

Upper Bound. As an upper bound for any method relying on score map information we calculate the overlap between neighbouring hypotheses based on perfect segmentation masks (available in this toy scenario). With perfect overlaps and perfect scores GreedyNMS returns perfect results. Based on our idealized but noisy detection score maps the upper bound reaches 90.0 % AR. In Sect. 4 we report experiments using segmentation masks estimated from the image, which results in inferior performance.

Base Tnet. Using the same information as GreedyNMS with bounding boxes, our base Tnet reaches better performance for the entire recall range (see Fig. 3), S $(1, 0.3)$ indicates the score maps from GreedyNMS with IoU > 0.3 and ≥ 1, i.e. the raw score map. In this configuration Tnet obtains 79.5 % AR, clearly superior to GreedyNMS. This shows that, at least in a controlled setup, a convnet can indeed exploit the available information to overcome the limitations of the popular GreedyNMS method.

Instead of picking a specific IoU threshold to feed Tnet, we consider IoU & S $(1, 0 \rightarrow 0.6)$, which includes S $(1, 0.6, 0.4, 0.3, 0.2, 0.0)$. As seen in Fig. 3, not selecting a specific threshold results in the best performance; 86.0 % AR. If we remove GreedyNMS score maps and only provide the raw score map (IoU & S (1)) performance decreases significantly. As soon as some ranking signal is provided (via GreedyNMS score maps), our Tnet is able to learn how to exploit best the information available. Qualitative results are presented in Fig. 1, bottom row.

Auto-context. Importantly we show that IoU & S (1) improves over S (1) only. (S (1) is the information exploited by auto-context methods, see Sect. 1.1). This shows that the convnet is learning to do more than simple auto-context. The detection improves not only by noticing patterns on the score map, but also on how the detection boxes overlap.

4   Person Detection Experiments

After the proof of concept in a controlled setup, we move to a realistic pedestrian detection setup. We are particularly interested in datasets that show diverse occlusion where NMS is non-trivial. We decided for the PETS dataset [9], which exhibits diverse levels of occlusion and provides a reasonable volume of training and test data. We use 5 sequences for training, one sequence for validation and testing (23k, 4k, 10k annotations respectively, see supplementary material for details). PETS has been previously used to study person detection [36], tracking [21], and crowd density estimation [33]. Additionally we test the generalization of the trained model on the ParkingLot dataset [31], and the applicability to general person detections on Pascal VOC [7]. Figure 6 shows example frames.

Standard pedestrian datasets such as Caltech [6] or KITTI [10] average less than two pedestrians per frame, making close-by detections a rare occurrence. In PETS and ParkingLot > 50 % of pedestrians have some occlusion, and about ∼ 20 % have significant occlusion ($IoU > 0.4$). Pascal presents fewer occlusion cases, people being the class where it is most frequent. See supplementary material for details on these datasets.

Person Detector. In this work we take the detector as a given. For the PETS experiments we use the baseline DPM detector from [36]. We are not aware of a detector (convnet or not) providing better results on PETS-like sequences (we considered some of the top detectors in [6]). Importantly, for our exploration the detector quality is not important per-se. As discussed in Sect. 3 GreedyNMS suffers from intrinsic issues, even when providing an idealized detector. In fact Tnet benefits from better detectors, since there will be more signal in the score maps. We thus consider our DPM detector a fair detection input. We use the DPM detections after bounding box regression, but before any NMS processing.

Person Segments. In Sect. 4.1 we report results using segments estimated from the image content. We use our re-implementation of DeepMask [24], trained on the Coco dataset [19]. See supplementary material for details and qualitative results. We use DeepMask as a realistic example of what can be expected from modern techniques for instance segmentation.

4.1   Results

Our PETS results are presented in Table 1 (validation set) and Fig. 4 (test set). Qualitative results are shown in Fig. 6. The supplementary material provides additional val & test results.

Boxes. Just like in the oMNIST case, the GreedyNMS curves in Fig. 4 have a recall versus precision trade-off. We pick $IoU > 0.3$ as a reference threshold.

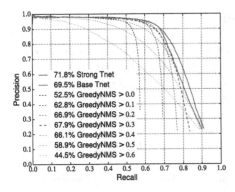
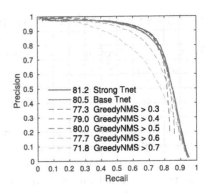

Fig. 4. Detection results on PETS test set. Our approach is better than any GreedyNMS threshold and better than the upper envelope of all GreedyNMS curves.

Fig. 5. Persons detection results on Pascal'12 test set. Tnet improves over all GreedyNMS thresholds.

Segments. GreedyNMS should behave best when the detection overlap is based on the visible area of the object. We compute DeepMask segments over DPM detection, feed these in GreedyNMS, and select the best IoU threshold for the validation set. Table 1 shows results slightly below the bounding boxes case. Although many segments are rather accurate, they drop in quality when heavier occlusion is present. In theory using segments should improve GreedyNMS, in practice they hurt more than they help.

Auto-context. For the S (1) entry in Table 1 only the raw detection score map is feed to Tnet (same nomenclature as Sect. 3.1). Since performance is lower than other variants (e.g. IoU & S (1)), this shows that our approach is exploiting available information better than just doing auto-context over DPM detections.

Tnet. Both in validation and test set our trained network with IoU & S (1, 0.3) input provides a clear improvement over vanilla GreedyNMS. Just like in the oMNIST case, the network is able to leverage patterns in the detector output to do better NMS than the de-facto standard GreedyNMS method.

Table 1 reports the results for a few additional variants. IoU & S (1, 0 → 0.6) shows that it is not necessary to select a specific IoU threshold for the input score map layer. Given an assortment (S (1, 0.6, 0.4, 0.3, 0.2, 0.0)) the network will learn to leverage the information available.

Using a relaxed loss that decreases weight of hard examples (peaks on the background and strong occlusions) helps further improve the results, moving from 57.9 % to 58.9 % AR. Weighting classes equally over the full dataset (global weighting) instead of frame-by-frame gives a mild improvement from 57.9 % to 58.0 % AR. See supplementary material for details on these loss variants.

Strong Tnet. We combine the best ingredients identified on the validation set into one strong model. We use IoU & S(1, 0 → 0.6), relaxed loss, and global weighting. Figure 4 shows that we further improve over the base Tnet from 59.5 % to 71.8 % AR on the PETS test set. The gap between base Tnet and GreedyNMS is smaller on the test set than on validation, because test set has lighter occlusions. Still our strong Tnet provides a consistent improvement over GreedyNMS.

In the supp. material we experimentally show that Strong Tnet improves GreedyNMS for all occlusions levels. Our network does not fit to a particular range of occlusions, but learns to handle all of them with comparable effectiveness.

At test time Tnet takes ∼200 milliseconds per frame (all included).

ParkingLot Results. To verify that our Tnet can generalize beyond PETS, we run the same DPM detector as on the PETS experiment over the ParkingLot sequence and do NMS using the networks trained on PETS training set only. Results show that Tnet improves from 80.3 % to 83.3 % AR over the best GreedyNMS threshold of IoU > 0.3. Even though Tnet was not trained on this sequence we see a similar result as on the PETS dataset. Not only does our Strong Tnet improve over the best GreedyNMS result, but it improves over the upper envelope of all GreedyNMS thresholds (similar trend as Fig. 4). See see detailed curves in supplementary material and qualitative results in Fig. 6.

(a) GreedyNMS   (b) Strong Tnet

Fig. 6. Qualitative detection results of GreedyNMS and Strong Tnet (both operating at same recall). Tnet is able to suppress false positives as well as recover recall that is lost with GreedyNMS. See supp. material for additional results.

Pascal Results. Pascal VOC [7] contains less occlusion but is more challenging with respect to appearance, scale, and aspect ratio variance. We focus on the "people" class which offers the highest diversity in occlusion. As a base detector we use the publicly available FasterRCNN [25]. The small variance in performance of the GreedyNMS swipe in Fig. 5 shows that this data contains fewer occlusions than PETS.

Tnet is trained on Pascal '07 trainval and tested on the test set. To adapt the Tnet to multiple scales and aspect ratio we switch from the fully convolutional approach to a detection-centric representation. Instead of a fixed-size neighbourhood grid we adapt its scale and aspect ratio to each detection box being re-scored. We also use the image features. See details in the supplementary material. After tuning the training parameters, Base Tnet matches the best GreedyNMS with 80.5 % AP (Fig. 5). Strong Tnet matches the upper envelope of all GreedyNMS thresholds, improving the results to 81.2 % AP.

5   Conclusion

We have discussed the limitations of GreedyNMS in detail and presented experiments showing its recall versus precision trade-off. For the sake of speed and simplicity GreedyNMS disregards most of the information available in the detector response. Our proposed Tyrolean network (Tnet) mines the patterns in the score map values and bounding box arrangements to surpass the performance of GreedyNMS. On the person detection task, our final results show that our approach provides, compared to any GreedyNMS threshold, both high recall and improved precision. These results confirm that Tnet can overcome the intrinsic limitations of GreedyNMS, while keeping practical test time speeds. We consider the reported results a proof of concept, opening the door for further extensions.

Current detection pipelines consist of a convnet and a hard-coded NMS procedure. Replacing the NMS with a Tnet opens the possibility of true end-to-end training of object detectors and we reckon that significant improvements can be obtained by replacing NMS with a Tnet.

References

1. Barinova, O., Lempitsky, V., Kholi, P.: On detection of multiple object instances using Hough transforms. PAMI **34**, 1773–1784 (2012)
2. Bourdev, L., Maji, S., Brox, T., Malik, J.: Detecting people using mutually consistent poselet activations. In: Daniilidis, K., Maragos, P., Paragios, N. (eds.) ECCV 2010, Part VI. LNCS, vol. 6316, pp. 168–181. Springer, Heidelberg (2010)
3. Chen, G., Ding, Y., Xiao, J., Han, T.X.: Detection evolution with multi-order contextual co-occurrence. In: CVPR (2013)
4. Dai, J., He, K., Sun, J.: Convolutional feature masking for joint object and stuff segmentation. In: CVPR (2015)
5. Dalal, N., Triggs, B.: Histograms of oriented gradients for human detection. In: CVPR (2005)

6. Dollár, P., Wojek, C., Schiele, B., Perona, P.: Pedestrian detection: an evaluation of the state of the art. PAMI **34**, 743–761 (2012)
7. Everingham, M., Eslami, S.M.A., Van Gool, L., Williams, C.K.I., Winn, J., Zisserman, A.: The Pascal visual object classes challenge: a retrospective. IJCV **111**, 98–136 (2015)
8. Felzenszwalb, P., Girshick, R., McAllester, D., Ramanan, D.: Object detection with discriminatively trained part-based models. PAMI **32**, 1627–1645 (2010)
9. Ferryman, J., Ellis, A.: Pets 2010: dataset and challenge. In: AVSS (2010)
10. Geiger, A., Lenz, P., Urtasun, R.: Are we ready for autonomous driving? The kitti vision benchmark suite. In: CVPR (2012)
11. Girshick, R.: Fast R-CNN. In: ICCV (2015)
12. Girshick, R., Donahue, J., Darrell, T., Malik, J.: Rich feature hierarchies for accurate object detection and semantic segmentation. In: CVPR (2014)
13. He, K., Zhang, X., Ren, S., Sun, J.: Delving deep into rectifiers: surpassing human-level performance on imagenet classification. In: ICCV (2015)
14. Hosang, J., Benenson, R., Dollár, P., Schiele, B.: What makes for effective detection proposals? PAMI **38**, 814–830 (2015)
15. Jia, Y., Shelhamer, E., Donahue, J., Karayev, S., Long, J., Girshick, R., Guadarrama, S., Darrell, T.: Caffe: Convolutional architecture for fast feature embedding. In: ACM International Conference on Multimedia (2014)
16. Kingma, D., Ba, J.: ADAM: a method for stochastic optimization. In: ICLR (2015)
17. Kontschieder, P., Rota Bulò, S., Donoser, M., Pelillo, M., Bischof, H.: Evolutionary Hough games for coherent object detection. CVIU **116**, 1149–1158 (2012)
18. Leibe, B., Leonardis, A., Schiele, B.: Robust object detection with interleaved categorization and segmentation. IJCV **77**, 259–289 (2008)
19. Lin, T.-Y., Maire, M., Belongie, S., Hays, J., Perona, P., Ramanan, D., Dollár, P., Zitnick, C.L.: Microsoft COCO: common objects in context. In: Fleet, D., Pajdla, T., Schiele, B., Tuytelaars, T. (eds.) ECCV 2014, Part V. LNCS, vol. 8693, pp. 740–755. Springer, Heidelberg (2014)
20. Mathias, M., Benenson, R., Pedersoli, M., Van Gool, L.: Face detection without bells and whistles. In: Fleet, D., Pajdla, T., Schiele, B., Tuytelaars, T. (eds.) ECCV 2014, Part IV. LNCS, vol. 8692, pp. 720–735. Springer, Heidelberg (2014)
21. Milan, A., Roth, S., Schindler, K.: Continuous energy minimization for multitarget tracking. PAMI **36**, 58–72 (2014)
22. Ouyang, W., Wang, X.: Single-pedestrian detection aided by multi-pedestrian detection. In: CVPR (2013)
23. Parikh, D., Zitnick, C.: Human-debugging of machines. In: NIPS WCSSWC (2011)
24. Pinheiro, P.O., Collobert, R., Dollar, P.: Learning to segment object candidates. In: NIPS (2015)
25. Ren, S., He, K., Girshick, R., Sun, J.: Faster R-CNN: towards real-time object detection with region proposal networks. In: NIPS (2015)
26. Rodriguez, M., Laptev, I., Sivic, J., Audibert, J.Y.: Density-aware person detection and tracking in crowds. In: ICCV (2011)
27. Rothe, R., Guillaumin, M., Van Gool, L.: Non-maximum Suppression for Object Detection by Passing Messages Between Windows. In: Cremers, D., Reid, I., Saito, H., Yang, M.-H. (eds.) ACCV 2014. LNCS, vol. 9003, pp. 290–306. Springer, Heidelberg (2015)
28. Russakovsky, O., Deng, J., Su, H., Krause, J., Satheesh, S., Ma, S., Huang, Z., Karpathy, A., Khosla, A., Bernstein, M., Berg, A.C., Fei-Fei, L.: ImageNet large scale visual recognition challenge. IJCV **115**, 211–252 (2015)

29. Sadeghi, M.A., Farhadi, A.: Recognition using visual phrases. In: CVPR (2011)

30. Sermanet, P., Eigen, D., Zhang, X., Mathieu, M., Fergus, R., LeCun, Y.: Overfeat: integrated recognition, localization and detection using convolutional networks. In: ICLR (2014)

31. Shu, G., Dehghan, A., Oreifej, O., Hand, E., Shah, M.: Part-based multiple-person tracking with partial occlusion handling. In: CVPR (2012)

32. Stewart, R., Andriluka, M.: End-to-end people detection in crowded scenes (2015). arXiv:1506.04878

33. Subburaman, V.B., Descamps, A., Carincotte, C.: Counting people in the crowd using a generic head detector. In: AVSS (2012)

34. Tang, S., Andriluka, M., Schiele, B.: Detection and tracking of occluded people. In: BMVC (2012)

35. Tang, S., Andres, B., Andriluka, M., Schiele, B.: Subgraph decomposition for multi-target tracking. In: CVPR (2015)

36. Tang, S., Andriluka, M., Milan, A., Schindler, K., Roth, S., Schiele, B.: Learning people detectors for tracking in crowded scenes. In: ICCV (2013)

37. Tu, Z., Bai, X.: Auto-context and its application to high-level vision tasks and 3D brain image segmentation. PAMI **32**, 1744–1757 (2010)

38. Vezhnevets, A., Ferrari, V.: Object localization in imagenet by looking out of the window. In: BMVC (2015)

39. Viola, P., Jones, M.: Robust real-time face detection. IJCV **57**, 137–154 (2004)

40. Wan, L., Eigen, D., Fergus, R.: End-to-end integration of a convolutional network, deformable parts model and non-maximum suppression. In: CVPR (2015)

41. Wohlhart, P., Donoser, M., Roth, P.M., Bischof, H.: Detecting partially occluded objects with an implicit shape model random field. In: Lee, K.M., Matsushita, Y., Rehg, J.M., Hu, Z. (eds.) ACCV 2012, Part I. LNCS, vol. 7724, pp. 302–315. Springer, Heidelberg (2013)

42. Wojek, C., Dorkó, G., Schulz, A., Schiele, B.: Sliding-windows for rapid object class localization: a parallel technique. In: Rigoll, G. (ed.) DAGM 2008. LNCS, vol. 5096, pp. 71–81. Springer, Heidelberg (2008)

43. Yan, J., Yu, Y., Zhu, X., Lei, Z., Li, S.Z.: Object detection by labeling superpixels. In: CVPR (2015)

44. Yao, J., Fidler, S., Urtasun, R.: Describing the scene as a whole: joint object detection, scene classification and semantic segmentation. In: CVPR (2012)

Image Analysis

Occlusion-Aware Depth Estimation Using Sparse Light Field Coding

Ole Johannsen, Antonin Sulc$^{(\boxtimes)}$, and Bastian Goldluecke

University of Konstanz, Konstanz, Germany
{ole.johannsen,antonin.sulc,bastian.goldluecke}@uni-konstanz.de

Abstract. Disparity estimation for multi-layered light fields can robustly be performed with a statistical analysis of sparse light field coding coefficients [7]. The key idea is to explain each epipolar plane image patch with a dictionary composed of atoms with known disparity values. We significantly improve upon their approach in two ways. First, we reduce the number of necessary dictionary atoms, improving descriptive quality of each and reducing time complexity by an order of magnitude. Second, we introduce a way to explicitly handle occlusions, which is the main drawback in the previous work. Experiments demonstrate that we thus achieve substantially better results on both Lambertian as well as multi-layered scenes.

1 Introduction

Light fields have been shown to be a promising representation for a successful 3D analysis of complex scenes [4–6,11–14]. In contrast to a simple 2D image, a 4D light field captures a dense collection of views with view points parallel to a common image plane. The connection to scene structure becomes visible on the epipolar plane images (EPIs), which are slices through the light field across horizontal or vertical lines in the center view, see Fig. 1. In fact, each 3D point is projected into multiple views, and the projections lie on a common line in the EPI, whose slope encodes disparity.

The pioneering work in EPI analysis [1] performs gradient-based slope estimation to infer scene depth. Similarly, [14] uses the first order structure tensor for orientation estimation, but in addition enforce global consistency to increase robustness. An approach based on the idea of stereo matching is proposed in [5]. They formulate a variational framework for efficiently matching all sub-aperture views with the reference view. Robust PCA as a matching term for stacked sub-aperture views is proposed in [4]. The ubiquitous problem of narrow baseline present in hand-held light field cameras was addressed in [6], where subaperture views are matched using the phase-shift theorem.

One of the key problems in depth estimation are occlusions, which often lead to erroneous estimates with patch-based methods. Current state-of-the-art therefore explicitly handles these cases [13]. Here, an edge prior and photo-consistency is used to segment patches into occluded and non-occluded regions.

© Springer International Publishing AG 2016
B. Rosenhahn and B. Andres (Eds.): GCPR 2016, LNCS 9796, pp. 207–218, 2016.
DOI: 10.1007/978-3-319-45886-1_17

Fig. 1. *Epipolar plane images (EPIs).* The center view of the light field is parameterized with image coordinates x and y. The EPIs below and to the right correspond to the slices through the white lines in the center view, where s and t describe the varying view point coordinates. 3D scene points are projected to straight lines in the EPI, whose slope of is inversely proportional to the distance of the point [1].

In [12], a specialized convolution kernel encodes scale and depth of a set of rays, whose variance is used to detect occlusions.

A remaining limitation of the above methods is the inability to deal with reflections, transparencies or specularities, as they are based on the assumption of a Lambertian scene. Specularity removal was addressed in [11] by modelling light source color and removing the light component contribution. In [8], they propose an additive model for non-Lambertian patches in a variational framework similar to [4], where one of the two factors is sparse and the other is low-rank. These models, however, cannot handle partially transparent or strongly reflective surfaces, which lead to multi-layered scenes and thus EPIs, see Fig. 2. In [15], this case was analyzed with the second order structure tensor to compute two super-imposed orientations.

Contributions. Our work is a direct improvement of [7], which also deals with super-imposed scenes. They propose a robust method for multi-layered disparity estimation, using sparse coding of EPI patches via a dictionary composed of patches with known disparity. We significantly improve upon their work in

Fig. 2. *Light field with two disparity layers.* The image shows part of an EPI of the *laptop2* light-field [15] with a reflecting surface and reflection layer, each of which has different disparity.

two ways. First, we propose a way to reduce the number of necessary atoms in the dictionary. This not only increases computational efficiency by an order of magnitude, the results are also more accurate as responses by remaining atoms are more meaningful and reliable. Second, we introduce explicit occlusion handling into the method, where we separately encode upper and lower parts of EPIs, and merge the contributions by the different channels in accordance with occlusion orientation. Our proposed framework substantially improves accuracy at occlusion boundaries. In summary, we obtain a method whose accuracy is on par with current state-of-the-art for Lambertian scenes, and in addition able to more accurately detect and deal with multi-layered regions.

2   Sparse Light Field Coding for Disparity Estimation

In this section, we will briefly recap the concepts of how sparse coding can be used to analyze scene structure from light fields. We will keep to the notation introduced by [7], and quickly summarize their key contributions. Their main idea is to encode every patch p of an EPI as a sparse linear combination $p = a_1 D_1 + \cdots + a_n D_n$, where the D_k are the atoms of an overcomplete dictionary. The twist is that the dictionary is designed in a way that each element of the dictionary is constructed to ideally match a known disparity. The coefficients a_k of the expansion are found by solving a standard l^1-*sparse coding* or Lasso problem [10]. The individual atoms of the dictionary as well as the EPI patches are normalised to zero-mean and constant variance. This is similar to performing a structure-texture-decomposition. For more details on how to construct the dictionary, we refer to Sect. 3, the illustration in Fig. 3, and of course [7].

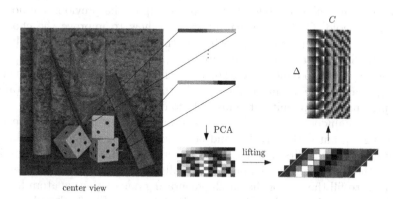

center view

Fig. 3. *Creating the dictionary.* First, 1D patches are extracted from center view by sliding along each horizontal and vertical line in the image. Then, PCA is applied on the 1D grayscale patches in order to obtain an orthonormal patch basis. The first elements in order of decreasing singular value are picked as *generators* to build the dictionary. For each generator C and disparity value L, we obtain a final atom by shearing the generator along the patch, offsetting by the disparity when moving to the next view.

Disparity for Lambertian Surfaces. We aggregate the coding coefficients a_k corresponding to the same disparity value across all color channels and atoms in a single vector of disparity responses α_i. If we disregard occlusions, then for a Lambertian light field the orientation across a small patch of an EPI varies slowly, and corresponds to the disparity of the center pixel. In the Lambertian case, the non-zero responses α_i should thus be clustered closely around a single value, which is the patch disparity. This is one key idea behind [7]. However, they show that one can do much more, and also analyze multi-layered scenes.

Reconstructing Multi-layered Sscenes. In case of multi-layered scenes, the luminosity captured at a certain pixel is the superposition of two different surfaces, the reflecting surface and the reflection, or the transparent surface and the object behind, respectively. As these two surfaces are at different distances to the camera, the EPI shows two super-imposed line patterns with two different orientations. See Fig. 2 for an illustration.

As shown in [7], the response of sparse coding can also be used to model these superimposed patterns and estimate the respective orientations. Using statistical analysis of the coefficients, they compute a mask to identify the multi-layered regions, and identify the two clusters of coefficients corresponding to the different disparity values of the super-imposed surfaces. They show that this approach already yields a significant improvement over existing methods based on second-order structure tensor [15]. While we do not change the underlying method for statistical analysis, we will show in Sect. 5 that our improved dictionary also improves the results for multi-layered scenes.

3   Optimized Dictionaries for Sparse Light Field Coding

We now present our contributions to improve upon the previous method [7], which are twofold. On the one hand, we show how to improve the choice of dictionary, resulting in a dictionary which both yields more accurate results and is much smaller, and thus faster to apply in sparse coding. On the other hand, we introduce a way to handle occlusions and thus improve accuracy to the level of current state-of-the-art in Lambertian depth estimation, while also retaining and improving the capability of being able to deal with multiple layers.

In the remainder of this section, we discuss how to perform sparse light field coding [7], but with a smaller and occlusion-aware dictionary. Building the dictionary starts with first finding a set of vectors C whose linear combinations represent the center line of each patch - we call them *generators*. The generators are sheared to fill the rest of the patch, generating one dictionary atom for each disparity value in the set Δ of given disparity labels, see Fig. 3. The idea is that this way, one obtains a dictionary to code every EPI patch in the light field.

Obviously, the critical question is how to choose the set of generators. In [7], they employed dictionary learning on (normalized) patches of the center view to determine C. Additional research shows that this procedure is not optimal, as it turns out that overcompleteness for reconstructing the center lines is unnecessary. Instead, for the dictionary generators, it is more important to only use the most meaningful vectors to capture the patch structure, and achieve overcompleteness by shearing with a large number of disparity labels. As a consequence, we propose to choose the generators as the most important principal components of the set of all 1D center view patches. As typically the patches have only 13 pixels, we have less than 13 generators - indeed, as we will see later in Fig. 8, optimum performance is achieved for only $9-10$ of them. The result is a significant speed-up of the method, as well as an improvement in accuracy. We will give an in-depth analysis in Sect. 5.

Furthermore, occlusions are a main source of error for depth estimation. This is not different for the idea of sparse coding to determine patch orientation. One observation we made at occlusion boundaries is that although the detected boundaries are sharp, they are shifted by a few pixels with a bias to increase the size of foreground objects. A main reason for this is that after normalization, the contrast between foreground object and background is frequently larger than that of the structure within the objects, and thus the dominant factor in orientation analysis, see Fig. 4. Sparse coding optimizes the choice of elements to account for this contrast, and thus selects dictionary elements that explain the occlusion boundary, corresponding to the disparity of the foreground element.

Due to the small baseline in light fields, when looking at a single patch of an EPI, occlusion boundaries intersect the center pixel line only either on the top or on the bottom part of the patch. Thus, we propose to split the dictionary, and code top and bottom part of each EPI patch separately. Dictionary elements are still weighted according to their horizontal contrast at the line corresponding to the center view, which is however not in the patch center anymore. The splitting of the dictionary leads to four different disparity estimates for each center view pixel if one also takes into account horizontal and vertical EPIs. The next section shows how we optimally merge these four channels into a single disparity map for the center view in agreement with the occlusion boundary orientation.

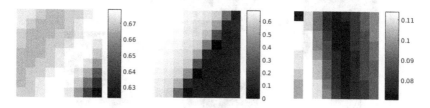

Fig. 4. *Patches depicting an occlusion boundary (center) and adjacent patches of the surface (left,right)* All patches are taken from red channel of the *buddha* dataset. The center patch shows a region with an occlusion boundary. As the contrast between the foreground (left part of patch) and the background (right part) is large, the only visible structure after normalisation corresponds to the occlusion boundary. Note that the right most column of the left patch is the same as the left most of the center patch, similar for the center and right patch. After normalisation, the values are stretched such that the structure within the region is visible, please refer to the color axis of the different patches.

4   Occlusion-Aware Disparity Map Optimization

Our final algorithm for occlusion aware depth estimation using sparse coding proceeds in three steps. First, an initial depth map is aggregated from the four disparity channels (combinations of top or bottom patch, and horizontal or vertical EPI). Second, we estimate an occlusion map with oriented occlusion boundaries. Finally, we refine the disparity estimate within the occlusion area by choosing the contribution from the optimum channel according to the direction of occlusion. The complete procedure is visualized in Fig. 5. In the following, we will describe it in more detail.

Step 1: generating the initial depth map. As an initial disparity estimate u_0, we aggregate the four channels into a single disparity map using just a point-wise weighted average. Intuitively, patches with more structure give more reliable estimates, so we choose to compute the weight w_j for each channel $j = 1, \ldots, 4$ using the coefficients α_{ji} from the channel's dictionary expansion according to $w_j = \sum_i |\alpha_{ji}|$. To improve the initial estimate and make it fully dense, we denoise it and complete regions where the weight is below a certain threshold τ for all channels in a joint TGV-L^1 inpainting step, where we compute

$$\underset{u}{\mathrm{argmin}} \left\{ TGV(u) + \int_\Omega 1_{\{\tau \leq \sum_j w_j\}} |u - u_0| \, \mathrm{d}x \right\}, \tag{1}$$

with the primal-dual algorithm [2]. This initial depth map is already precise for areas without occlusions.

Step 2: detecting occlusion region and orientation. Occlusion areas are related to strong disparity gradients, or edges in the initial disparity map u. Thus, we

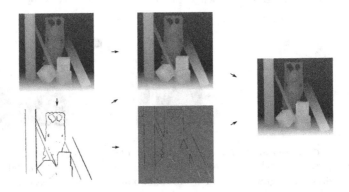

Fig. 5. *Pipeline for occlusion handling based on occlusion boundary orientation.* First, the initial depth map is calculated in step 1 (top left). In step 2, the occlusion mask below is calculated based on disparity gradients, and the orientation of the occlusion boundaries determined. Inside the occlusion region, the values are chosen optimally according to this orientation estimate (step 3, bottom center). Combining this estimate with the initial depth outside (top center) yields the final disparity map (right).

Fig. 6. *Visualization of patches for different EPI orientation around occlusions.* The patches to the right correspond to different EPI orientations and locations around an occlusion (left). The main patch of size 9×5 is split into two 5×5 patches corresponding to the upper and lower part, visualized by the black squares. The patches parallel to the occlusion boundary show the correct disparity for foreground (green) or the background (yellow), respectively, correctly depending on their location. In contrast, if the EPI orientation is chosen perpendicular to the occlusion orientation, the foreground disparity dominates as orientation is estimated for the contrast change between foreground and background. Thus, for occlusions parallel to the axis, it is optimal to choose patches oriented in the same direction as the occlusion. (Color figure online)

compute the first order structure tensor of u and define as occlusion region the set of pixels where at least one Eigenvalue is larger than a certain threshold. The occlusion orientation is defined as the direction with the strongest increase, i.e. the Eigenvector associated with the largest Eigenvalue. Note that the orientation direction thus points from background to foreground.

Step 3: improving disparity in occlusion regions. In the final pass, we improve the disparity estimate in the occlusion regions by selecting the estimate from the optimal channel j according to occlusion orientation. The key idea is that in each pixel, we select the source channel such that the disparity estimate of the encoded patch is not biased by the occlusion boundary. Figure 6 illustrates this idea and shows that in general, the source EPI orientation should be similar to the occlusion orientation.

To achieve this, we bin the orientations into eight classes corresponding to compass directions N, NE, ..., assigned clockwise with "N" pointing towards the top of the center view. If occlusion orientation is one of $\{N, E, S, W\}$, it is regarded as aligned with either horizontal or vertical EPI, and both upper and lower part should give the correct disparity estimate. We thus assign the weighted average of both. Otherwise, there is no optimal choice for EPI orientation, and we choose the weighted average of the upper/lower patches corresponding to the smaller disparity for each to counter the bias towards enlarged foreground regions. The following table summarizes the choice of source disparity channels depending on occlusion boundary orientation (Fig. 7).

Note that the above selection process is only performed within the estimated occlusion region. Some pixels might still be missing due to unreliable information, for example, if the necessary choice of source channels have an associated

gradient direction	N	NE	E	SE	S	SW	W	NW
source disparity	HT HB	HT VB	VT VB	HT VT	HT HB	HB VT	VT VB	HB VB

Fig. 7. *Choice of correct source disparity for each possible orientation of the occlusion edge.* The final disparity is the weighted average of two channels, encoded by a combination of horizontal (H) or vertical (V) EPI and top (T) or bottom (B) patch, respectively.

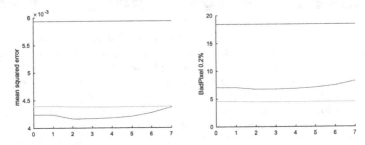

Fig. 8. *Comparison between the original method (blue), the original method with the proposed reduced dictionary (red) and the complete occlusion-aware method (yellow) for different sizes of generator sets.* Errors are compared for removing the least important 0 to 7 elements of the full generator set. Our proposed method to choose the generator yields an overall improvement in accuracy of around 30 % for the mean squared error as well as three quarters for the bad pixel ratio. Occlusion handling improves fine details and boundaries significantly, while very slightly increasing mean error due to having less regularization. (Color figure online)

weight below the threshold for reliability. Thus, we perform a final denoising and inpainting optimization pass equivalent to (1), with the disparities in the occlusion region replaced by the updated ones.

5   Results

We perform our experiments with a Matlab implementation of our method, using a Lasso solver from the SPAMS toolbox [9].

Effect of Generator Size and Comparison to Previous Method. First, we compare our method against the original method as published in [7] on the ray-traced *buddha* data set of the HCI Light Field Benchmark [17], which is fully Lambertian. As our proposed method allows to reduce the size of the dictionary and select the most important patches of the generator, we additionally evaluate the impact of the number of generator atoms. EPI patch size is 5×5, or 9×5 for the full occlusion aware pipeline, respectively.

In general, choosing the PCA over the original dictionary learning approach yields more accurate results, with an improvement of up to 30 % in terms of MSE and reduction of the number of bad pixels to one quarter of the previous amount. Occlusion handling substantially reduces the number of bad pixels, with a however slightly increased MSE. Reducing the number of the elements in the generator by a small number leads to a slight improvement in quality as well as runtime. For the occlusion aware depth estimation this effect is very minor and peaks at around 5 removed elements. The runtime for dictionary learning per channel and EPI orientation ranges from around 3 s for the complete PCA patch generator set to 1.3 s when removing 7 elements. In comparison, the original method took 70 s per channel and EPI orientation.

Evaluation on Lambertian Surfaces. In a second set of experiments, we compare to other methods on the complete synthetic benchmark data sets in [17], see Fig. 9. Competing methods are [3], which is based upon analysing EPIs and enforces consistent depth labeling at occlusions (EPI_C), as well as [16], which combines horizontal and vertical EPIs in a globally optimal labeling scheme (EPI_G). We also include the multi view stereo methods ST_S and ST_G, which compute a cost volume on the center view based on a point-wise color consistency matching cost [17]. ST_S smoothes the point-wise optimum, while in ST_G global optimization with a continuous multi-label method is performed. For a detailed description, we refer to [17]. On average, our method is the most accurate among all the competing methods.

To test performance with regard to occlusion handling and fine details, we evaluate the *bad pixel percentage*, which is largely influenced by sharpness and precision of occlusion boundaries. We compare the bad pixel percentage for an outlier threshold of 1 %, 0.5 % and 0.2 %. Finer precision can not be evaluated as the depth resolution in the ground truth data is not high enough. Our method is very competitive, achieving better or similar results compared to state-of-the-art (Fig. 10).

lightfield	EPI_C	EPI_G	ST_S	ST_G	DL	IDL
buddha	0.55	0.62	0.78	0.90	0.57	**0.37**
buddha2	0.87	0.89	1.05	**0.68**	1.08	0.72
horses	2.21	2.67	1.85	**1.00**	3.26	1.31
medieval	1.10	1.24	0.91	**0.76**	0.84	0.87
monasRoom	0.82	0.93	1.05	0.79	0.65	**0.48**
papillon	2.52	2.48	2.92	3.65	1.85	**1.40**
stillLife	**2.61**	3.37	4.23	4.04	2.95	3.00
couple	**0.16**	0.19	0.24	0.30	0.42	0.33
cube	0.82	0.87	**0.51**	0.56	0.51	0.49
maria	**0.10**	0.11	0.11	0.11	0.11	**0.10**
pyramide	**0.38**	0.39	0.42	0.42	0.48	0.39
statue	0.29	0.35	**0.21**	**0.21**	0.62	0.24
average	1.04	1.18	1.19	1.12	1.11	**0.81**

Fig. 9. *Comparison of different methods for disparity estimation.* Datasets are from the HCI light field benchmark [17]. The numbers show mean squared disparity error for different competing methods summarized in Sect. 5 (EPI_C to ST_G), the method DL from [7] which we build upon, as well as our proposed improved method IDL. All numbers are multiplied by 100 for easier reading. Best results in each row are bold-faced. We achieve the best result on 5 of the data sets, and are first place on average.

Method / Dataset	[4]			[5]			[6]			[12]			Ours		
Error percentage	1.0%	0.5%	0.2%	1.0%	0.5%	0.2%	1.0%	0.5%	0.2%	1.0%	0.5%	0.2%	1.0%	0.5%	0.2%
buddha	-	-	5.03	2.12	3.91	8.37	-	-	4.69	1.2	-	-	**0.94**	**1.53**	4.48
monasRoom	-	-	12.75	2.08	4.66	12.90	-	-	8.91	2.4	-	-	**1.95**	**3.87**	11.19

Fig. 10. *Evaluation of occlusion handling.* Numbers in the table show percentage of pixels where depth error is larger than 1%, 0.5% and 0.2%, respectively. We compare on those datasets of [17] for which [4–6,12] provided results. On the *buddha* and *monasRoom* datasets, our method outperforms previous state-of-the-art in two of the percentiles, while being competitive or better than three approaches in the third. This demonstrates that our method can recover fine details and precise occlusion boundaries.

Evaluation on Multi-layered Scenes. In addition, we evaluate our method on data sets exhibiting reflective and transparent surfaces. Here, the original method [7] which we build upon already outperforms existing methods. For this reason, we only compare to [7]. Our proposed approach again improves accuracy for detecting multi-layered regions, and substantially reduces the error of disparity estimation for both layers, see Fig. 11.

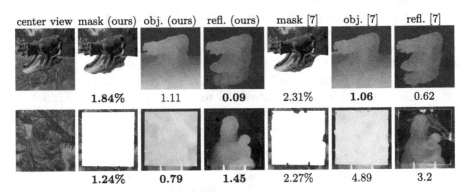

Fig. 11. *Accuracy evaluation of two-layer disparity reconstruction.* We compare our method to [7] on the ray-traced *Tiger* dataset (top) with a reflective plane, and a data set captured with a gantry (bottom), for which ground truth was acquired with a laser scanner [15]. The disparity maps and multi-layer masks are visually much better, confirmed by a better mean squared disparity error below each depth map (multiplied by 100). The error of the masks is calculated as the percentage of incorrect pixels.

6   Conclusion

In this paper, we propose improvements for disparity estimation in multi-layered light fields based on the sparse coding ideas in [7]. As a first contribution, our approach uses an orthonormal set of 1D center view patches instead of an overcomplete dictionary. The most meaningful generators for dictionary lifting are chosen as the first few principal components. Thus, we reduce the number of necessary dictionary atoms and drastically improve run-time. In addition, the generators have better descriptive quality, thus we obtain more accurate results on synthetic benchmarks for Lambertian and multi-layered scenes.

A second contribution is occlusion handling. We make use of the fact that even in the presence of occlusions, certain combinations of upper and lower parts of the horizontal and vertical EPI patches still estimate the correct disparity, and select the optimum patch based on the estimated orientation of the occlusion boundary. After refinement in a variational framework, this approach substantially increases accuracy at occlusion boundaries.

Acknowledgements. This work was supported by the ERC Starting Grant "Light Field Imaging and Analysis" (LIA 336978, FP7-2014).

References

1. Bolles, R., Baker, H., Marimont, D.: Epipolar-plane image analysis: an approach to determining structure from motion. Int. J. Comput. Vis. **1**(1), 7–55 (1987)
2. Chambolle, A., Pock, T.: A first-order primal-dual algorithm for convex problems with applications to imaging. J. Math. Imaging Vis. **40**(1), 120–145 (2011)
3. Goldluecke, B., Wanner, S.: The variational structure of disparity and regularization of 4D light fields. In: Proceedings of the International Conference on Computer Vision and Pattern Recognition (2013)
4. Heber, S., Pock, T.: Shape from light field meets robust PCA. In: Proceedings of the European Conference on Computer Vision (2014)
5. Heber, S., Ranftl, R., Pock, T.: Variational shape from light field. In: International Conference on Energy Minimization Methods for Computer Vision and Pattern Recognition, pp. 66–79 (2013)
6. Jeon, H., Park, J., Choe, G., Park, J., Bok, Y., Tai, Y., Kweon, I.: Accurate depth map estimation from a lenslet light field camera. In: Proceedings of the International Conference on Computer Vision and Pattern Recognition (2015)
7. Johannsen, O., Sulc, A., Goldluecke, B.: What sparse light field coding reveals about scene structure. In: Proceedings of the International Conference on Computer Vision and Pattern Recognition (2016)
8. Hosseini Kamal, M., Favaro, P., Vandergheynst, P.: A convex solution to disparity estimation from light fields via the primal-dual method. In: Tai, X.-C., Bae, E., Chan, T.F., Lysaker, M. (eds.) EMMCVPR 2015. LNCS, vol. 8932, pp. 350–363. Springer, Heidelberg (2015)
9. Mairal, J., Bach, F., Ponce, J., Sapiro, G.: Online learning for matrix factorization and sparse coding. J. Mach. Learn. Res. **11**, 19–60 (2010)
10. Olshausen, B., Field, D.: Sparse coding with an overcomplete basis set: a strategy employed by V1? Vis. Res. **37**(23), 3311–3325 (1997)
11. Tao, M.W., Wang, T.-C., Malik, J., Ramamoorthi, R.: Depth estimation for glossy surfaces with light-field cameras. In: Agapito, L., Bronstein, M.M., Rother, C. (eds.) ECCV 2014 Workshops. LNCS, vol. 8926, pp. 533–547. Springer, Heidelberg (2015)
12. Tosic, I., Berkner, K.: Light field scale-depth space transform for dense depth estimation. In: Computer Vision and Pattern Recognition Workshops (CVPRW), pp. 441–448 (2014)

13. Wang, T., Efros, A., Ramamoorthi, R.: Occlusion-aware depth estimation using light-field cameras. In: Proceedings of the IEEE International Conference on Computer Vision, pp. 3487–3495 (2015)
14. Wanner, S., Goldluecke, B.: Globally consistent depth labeling of 4D light fields. In: Proceedings of the International Conference on Computer Vision and Pattern Recognition, pp. 41–48 (2012)
15. Wanner, S., Goldluecke, B.: Reconstructing reflective and transparent surfaces from epipolar plane images. In: Weickert, J., Hein, M., Schiele, B. (eds.) GCPR 2013. LNCS, vol. 8142, pp. 1–10. Springer, Heidelberg (2013)
16. Wanner, S., Goldluecke, B.: Variational light field analysis for disparity estimation and super-resolution. IEEE Trans. Pattern Anal. Mach. Intell. **36**(3), 606–619 (2014)
17. Wanner, S., Meister, S., Goldluecke, B.: Datasets and benchmarks for densely sampled 4D light fields. In: Vision, Modelling and Visualization (VMV) (2013)

Joint Object Pose Estimation and Shape Reconstruction in Urban Street Scenes Using 3D Shape Priors

Francis Engelmann[(✉)], Jörg Stückler, and Bastian Leibe

Computer Vision Group, Visual Computing Institute,
RWTH Aachen University, Aachen, Germany
engelmann@vision.rwth-aachen.de

Abstract. Estimating the pose and 3D shape of a large variety of instances within an object class from stereo images is a challenging problem, especially in realistic conditions such as urban street scenes. We propose a novel approach for using compact shape manifolds of the shape within an object class for object segmentation, pose and shape estimation. Our method first detects objects and estimates their pose coarsely in the stereo images using a state-of-the-art 3D object detection method. An energy minimization method then aligns shape and pose concurrently with the stereo reconstruction of the object. In experiments, we evaluate our approach for detection, pose and shape estimation of cars in real stereo images of urban street scenes. We demonstrate that our shape manifold alignment method yields improved results over the initial stereo reconstruction and object detection method in depth and pose accuracy.

1 Introduction

Object-level shape priors are arguably important components for object pose estimation and 3D reconstruction from images. Shape priors provide strong regularization cues for these problems which are highly ill-posed in a purely data-driven manner. In this paper, we propose a novel approach that uses shape priors for segmenting objects and estimating their shape and pose from stereo images. This knowledge about objects is useful in applications such as autonomous driving or augmented/virtual reality. For autonomous driving, shape and pose can be vital for navigation in order to judge free-space or possible collisions. Accurate 6-DoF pose from single stereo pairs can also be useful for tracking applications.

It is often not feasible to match all possible instances of an object class to images directly using explicit CAD models. Thus, we take the approach to learn compact shape manifolds that represents the intra-class object variance. We find objects, e.g. cars, in the stereo images using a state-of-the-art 3D object detection method (3DOP, [3]) and align the reconstruction with our shape manifold. Our

Electronic supplementary material The online version of this chapter (doi:10.1007/978-3-319-45886-1_18) contains supplementary material, which is available to authorized users.

© Springer International Publishing AG 2016
B. Rosenhahn and B. Andres (Eds.): GCPR 2016, LNCS 9796, pp. 219–230, 2016.
DOI: 10.1007/978-3-319-45886-1_18

method provides shape in occluded areas or regions where vision or laser-based methods often fail, such as textureless, reflective, or transparent surfaces. It also provides a segmentation of the object instance in the image.

In experiments, we assess the performance of our approach for detection, pose and shape estimation of cars in stereo images of urban street scenes using the popular KITTI benchmark [5]. We demonstrate superior pose estimation performance compared to the baseline 3D object detection approach (3DOP). Our method also provides shape reconstructions that improve on the initial stereo reconstruction.

In summary, we make the following contributions: (1) We propose a method that recovers shape and pose of objects from stereo images using class-specific 3D shape priors. Our registration method directly operates on the 3D stereo reconstruction from a single stereo pair. (2) We combine our shape matching method with a state-of-the-art 3D object detection approach to accurately detect objects, determine their 3D pose and shape, and segment them in stereo images. This approach improves the initial stereo reconstruction, especially at farther ranges or textureless and specular surfaces where purely stereo-based reconstructions are inherently limited in reconstruction quality. It also excels in pose accuracy compared to the initial 3D object detection approach.

2   Related Work

Traditionally, multi-view stereo approaches use local surface-based priors to regularize depth reconstruction [6,10,17,23]. SPS-Stereo [23], for instance, uses a piecewise planarity assumption within superpixels for joint stereo reconstruction, segmentation, and optical flow. Recently, several methods have been proposed that incorporate semantic and appearance-based priors that model surface properties of object classes. Saxena et al. [20] demonstrated that depth can be estimated from monocular images using a discriminatively-trained Markov random field model on appearance cues. Sun et al. [21] use random forests to cast votes for object detection, pose and 3D shape of objects in monocular images. A similar method has been proposed by Thomas et al. [22] which transfers depth from training image patches to a detected object using a patch-based implicit shape model detector. Haene et al. [9] propose a variational framework for joint 3D reconstruction and class segmentation in a multi-view stereo setup. The method uses trained object class-specific local surface priors for depth reconstruction. Joint semantic segmentation and 3D reconstruction has also been investigated by Kundu et al. [11] who pose this problem in a higher-order conditional random field to jointly estimate semantic segmentation and 3D occupancy in a volumetric map. Guney and Geiger [8] start from a sparse reconstruction and a semantic segmentation to perform CRF-based dense reconstruction with semantic priors. They impose local shape priors on the superpixels in a semantic segment.

Several semantic SLAM methods have been proposed that include objects through rigid 3D shape templates into the mapping and localization process [7, 18]. Some recent depth reconstruction and SLAM methods also use 3D shape priors. The priors model the shape variation of an object class more generically as manifolds of 3D models. One key difference in such methods is how the object shape manifold is modeled and how the objects can be detected and their pose recovered. Bao et al. [2] create shape and appearance-based shape priors that model the object shape as a deformable template whose shape depends on a set of anchoring 2D interest points. Implicit shape models based on a truncated signed distance function (TSDF) are used in [16]. This method applies GP-LVMs [12] for manifold learning on the TSDF and recovers segmentation, 3D pose and reconstruction in a level-set formulation. However, the level-set segmentation also requires a pre-trained random forest regressor for inside and outside probabilities on the specific target object, which is obtained through manual initialization on a video. Sandhu et al. [19] use kernel PCA and a region-based level-set formulation instead. Dame et al. [4] take the GP-LVM shape priors in [16] one step further into a monocular dense SLAM system. While we evaluate our method on stereo data from urban scenarios, the above methods are demonstrated in small-scale monocular settings. Closer to our data scenario, [25] detect objects similar to a few annotated examples in TSDF maps that are integrated from stereo depth obtained in urban street scenes. They propose a method to learn PCA shape priors on the detected objects and demonstrate the models to improve reconstruction quality. In contrast, we estimate the shape from a single stereo pair observation in order to be able to align shape priors also with dynamic objects. Furthermore, we use an object proposal method that is trained on a larger set of training examples and provides a coarse 3D pose estimate. Zia et al. [26] use a shape prior encoded by linear embedding of CAD wireframe models to estimate the 3D pose and shape of objects such as cars and bicycles in monocular images. They train a detector for the wireframe vertices and propose an optimization procedure that fits the wireframe shapes to the detected vertices. This shape prior is also used by Menze et al. [14] to jointly estimate object pose and shape together with scene flow from stereo images. Our shape priors represent surface implicitly using TSDFs and, hence, do not require correspondence of wireframe vertices and edges between example instances.

Related to our work are also 3D object detection methods. In 3DOP [3], objects are detected using a selective search approach in SPS-Stereo reconstructions. First, a large set of object proposals is generated in an energy minimization framework that finds potential objects according to a set of shape and appearance based features in a reduced volumetric search space. Each proposal is then classified as part of an object class using a convolutional neural network. The network also regresses the orientation of the object. We use 3DOP for initial 3D object detection and refine the detections using shape prior matching. The work of Zheng et al. [24] focuses on improving an object proposal method with shape priors. Different to our method, it uses a GP-LVM shape prior to sample shapes and render additional training images for a state-of-the-art object proposal approach.

3   Our Method

Our approach to 3D shape recovery and pose estimation aligns a 3D manifold of shapes with noisy stereo reconstructions of objects. We learn this 3D shape

1.Input Depth   2.Car Detections   3.Initialization   4.Optimization   5.Our Result

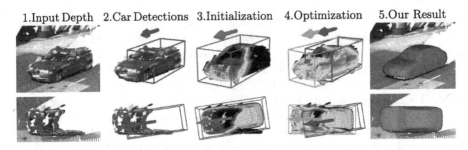

Fig. 1. Overview of our pipeline: from stereo images, we estimate depth using a stereo reconstruction method (e.g. SPS-Stereo [23]) and compute object detections (blue bounding boxes) using 3DOP [3]. We then optimize the shape and the pose of the detected object by solving an energy-minimization problem. The red bounding box shows the initialization that we determine from the 3DOP result and the object segment, the optimization result is shown in green. On the right, we display the optimized shape and pose superimposed on the initial stereo reconstruction. (Color figure online)

prior from a database of CAD models of an object class (for instance, cars). We use a local optimization method that determines shape and pose concurrently in an energy minimization framework. In order to align a shape model to each object in a scene (see Fig. 1), we first detect the objects in stereo data using the state-of-the-art 3D object detection approach from [3]. The method also provides us with a coarse pose initialization, which we subsequently refine with our shape matching method.

3.1   Shape Modelling and Manifold Learning

We learn 3D shape priors using linear subspace analysis (PCA) on a TSDF representation of objects in a class. We use TSDFs, as shapes of object instances can be homogeneously approximated in a shared voxel grid representation. Using a multi-view rendering pipeline, we transform a CAD model database of various object shapes into volumetric TSDF grids. The coordinate frame origin of each instance is placed at the center of gravity and at ground level height, while the axes are aligned with forward, sideward, and upward directions. Figure 2 illustrates example shapes on a learned manifold of cars.

More formally, a TSDF $\Phi(\mathbf{x}, \mathbf{z})$ yields the truncated signed distance at point $\mathbf{x} \in \mathbb{R}^3$ towards the object surface. Hence, the surface is implicitly represented as the zero-level set of the TSDF. The TSDF is approximated through trilinear interpolation of TSDF values $\tilde{\phi}_i(\mathbf{z})$ at vertices $i \in \mathcal{N}(\mathbf{x})$ in a voxel grid. The vertex set $\mathcal{N}(\mathbf{x})$ corresponds to the corners of the voxel that point $\mathbf{x}$ falls into. The TSDF voxel grid values are embedded in the linear subspace through the mapping

$$\mathbf{z}\left(\tilde{\phi}\right) = \mathbf{V}^\top \left(\tilde{\phi} - \boldsymbol{\mu}_{\tilde{\phi}}\right), \tag{1}$$

Fig. 2. Example shapes in our learned shape manifold of cars. The center shape corresponds to the mean shape.

where $\widetilde{\phi}$ is stacked from all vertex distances and $\boldsymbol{\mu}_{\widetilde{\phi}}$ is its mean over all examples in the training set (i.e., the mean shape). The subspace projection matrix $\mathbf{V}^{\top}$ is obtained through eigen decomposition $\boldsymbol{\Sigma} = \mathbf{V}\mathbf{D}\mathbf{V}^{\top}$ of the covariance

$$\boldsymbol{\Sigma} = \frac{1}{M-1} \left(\widetilde{\boldsymbol{\Phi}} - \boldsymbol{\mu}_{\widetilde{\phi}}\right)^{\top} \left(\widetilde{\boldsymbol{\Phi}} - \boldsymbol{\mu}_{\widetilde{\phi}}\right) \tag{2}$$

where $\widetilde{\boldsymbol{\Phi}}$ is the design matrix stacked from the TSDF vertex distances $\widetilde{\phi}^{\top}$ of the M examples. Given an encoding $\mathbf{z} \in \mathbb{R}^{K}$, the corresponding TSDF can be reconstructed using $\widetilde{\phi}(\mathbf{z}) = \mathbf{V}\mathbf{z} + \boldsymbol{\mu}_{\widetilde{\phi}}$.

3.2 Object Detection and Segmentation

We detect objects in a scene using 3DOP [3]. We observed that the 2D bounding boxes in the image domain are more accurate then the rather coarse bounding box estimates in 3D. Since we use stereo reconstructions (obtained with libELAS [6] or SPS-Stereo [23] in our experiments), the points $\mathcal{X}$ on an object may not fall inside the 3D bounding box due to disparity noise. Thus, we segment the points on the object that project into the 2D bounding boxes and find points that are close to the estimated 3D center position. As an additional segmentation cue in our urban street scene setting, we remove points on and below the road plane which is found by the same approach as used in 3DOP. Finally, we redetermine the 3D bounding box of the segmented points and determine a pose estimate $\boldsymbol{\xi}_0 := \left(\theta_0 \ \mathbf{t}_0^{\top}\right)^{\top}$ from the rotation obtained by the 3D bounding box of 3DOP. For the translation we try both the center of the 3D bounding box of the segmented points and the center of the 3DOP bounding box, and pick the best scoring one in terms of energy. We additionally apply a verification step by pruning detections that have an unreasonably sized bounding box, i.e. where the bounding box extent in each dimension is unreasonably small.

3.3 Concurrent Shape and Pose Alignment

We optimize concurrently for shape and pose of the detected objects using the segmented object points $\mathcal{X}$. The pose estimate is initialized from the detected pose $\boldsymbol{\xi}_0$, while the shape estimation is started from the mean shape $\mathbf{z}_0 := \mathbf{0} \in \mathbb{R}^{K}$. Our energy function corresponds to the negative logarithm of the a-posteriori probability of the stereo reconstruction given the reconstructed shape and pose estimate,

$$E(\mathcal{X}, \boldsymbol{\xi}, \mathbf{z}) = -\frac{1}{N} \left(\sum_{i=1}^{N} \log \left[p\left(\mathbf{x}_i \mid \boldsymbol{\xi}, \mathbf{z} \right) \right] \right) - \log p(\mathbf{z}) - \log p(\boldsymbol{\xi}), \qquad (3)$$

where N is the number of object points. Using our TSDF shape representation, the observation likelihood depends on the distance from the surface,

$$\log p\left(\mathbf{x}_i \mid \boldsymbol{\xi}, \mathbf{z} \right) = \text{const.} - \frac{1}{2\sigma_d^2} \rho \left(\phi \left(R(\theta) \mathbf{x}_i + \mathbf{t}, \mathbf{z} \right) \right). \qquad (4)$$

Instead of an outlier-sensitive quadratic norm corresponding to a Gaussian distribution $(\rho(y) = \|y\|_2^2)$, we use the robust Huber-norm $\rho(y) = \|y\|_\epsilon$ on the residuals. The shape prior penalizes deviations from the mean shape through

$$\log p(\mathbf{z}) = \text{const.} - \frac{1}{2} \sum_{j=1}^{K} \left(\frac{z_j}{\sigma_j} \right)^2, \qquad (5)$$

where σ_j^2 is the eigen value of the j-th principal component. For the pose prior, we can exploit domain knowledge. In the case of cars in urban street scenes, we model that the object should stand on the ground, i.e.,

$$\log p(\boldsymbol{\xi}) = \text{const.} - \frac{1}{2\sigma_y^2} \left(t_y - g(t) \right)^2, \qquad (6)$$

where $g(t)$ is the estimated road height at position t. In this setting, we also only need to estimate the rotation of the car around the vertical direction. The noise parameters σ_d and σ_y implement a trade-off between observation likelihood $p(\mathbf{x}_i \mid \boldsymbol{\xi}, \mathbf{z})$, shape prior and pose prior. We optimize for pose and shape alternatingly until convergence. The terms are optimized using gradient descent for which we employ the Ceres solver [1].

4   Experiments

We evaluate our method on the popular KITTI dataset [5]. Specifically, we use the KITTI Stereo 2015 training dataset [15], as it focuses mainly on cars in urban and rural scenes. This dataset consists of 200 stereo frames that contain semantic segmentations of 431 vehicles. The stereo images have a resolution of 1242×375 px each and a baseline of 0.54 m. The vehicle segments are also annotated with dense depth from manually fitted CAD models. We added manual ground truth pose annotations for the vehicles on the first 50 frames of the dataset in order to evaluate pose accuracy. For this, we fitted 3D models from Google Warehouse to the data. Throughout our experiments we use a bin size of 0.1 m for the TSDF voxel grids and a truncation distance of ±0.2 m. We empirically determine the noise parameters as $\sigma_d^2 = 0.03$ and $\sigma_y^2 = 3$. As stereo reconstruction inputs we use libELAS [6] and SPS-Stereo [23]. For libELAS, we remove noisy points whose normals are perpendicular to the viewing direction. For 3DOP we use an up-sampling factor of 2.415.

4.1   Pose Estimation Accuracy

We evaluate pose estimation accuracy for 3DOP as our baseline method and variants of our own approach that use stereo reconstructions from libELAS, SPS-Stereo, and the ground truth depth annotation as 3D input for shape and pose alignment. Figure 3, top row, shows the pose accuracy results obtained with these approaches on the 50 pose-annotated frames of the KITTI Stereo 2015 training dataset. It can be seen that our approach is able to improve pose accuracy in translation as well as orientation. Our method even achieves better accuracy at larger distances where the input stereo depth is more noisy.

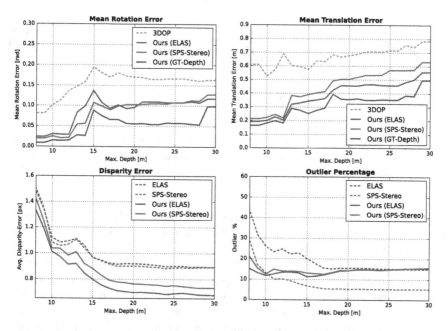

Fig. 3. Upper row: pose estimation results. Both the translation and rotation exhibit significant improvements compared to the baseline method (3DOP, [3]). Bottom row: depth reconstruction results. See text for details.

4.2   Shape Estimation Accuracy

We also assess the quality of the matched shapes using the ground-truth depth annotations on the KITTI Stereo 2015 dataset. To this end, we compare the initial stereo reconstructions by libELAS and SPS-Stereo with improved reconstructions obtained by our method using both initial stereo methods. To obtain the stereo depth maps, we backproject our estimated 3D shapes into the stereo images. To this end, we determine the zero-level set surface represented by the optimized TSDF using the marching cubes algorithm [13]. The results in the bottom row of Fig. 3 show that on average our method can achieve better accuracy in disparity, especially at larger distances. Note, that the outlier rate is

Table 1. Ablation study on shape reconstruction error averaged over all points. We show the effectiveness of each component in our method by enabling them step by step. Note the improvements in score with each step. Figure 4 visualizes the TSDF distance.

Pipeline components	TSDF distance (avg.±std.dev. [m])		
	libELAS [6]	SPS-Stereo [23]	Ground Truth
3DOP + init. pose + mean shape	0.136±0.044	0.134±0.044	0.105±0.032
3DOP + init. pose + optimized shape	0.133±0.045	0.131±0.045	0.086±0.035
3DOP + optimized pose + mean shape	0.127±0.050	0.130±0.048	0.079±0.044
3DOP + optimized pose + optim. shape	**0.124±0.051**	**0.127±0.049**	**0.063±0.040**

Fig. 4. Estimated pose and shape using different input depths. From left to right: libELAS [6], SPS-Stereo [23], ground truth depth. Points are color-coded by TSDF distance i.e. the Euclidean distance between a point and the zero-level set of the TSDF.

slightly larger for our method, but comparable with libELAS. One reason for this is that pose misalignments cause pixels in the background to be set onto the matched foreground shape.

Table 1 shows shape matching results in terms of mean and std. dev. of the TSDF distance of the points in the object segments. The results demonstrate how much the individual steps in our pipeline contribute to the improvements of the shape alignment. Shape as well as pose optimization improve the alignment. Note that when using stereo depth as input, the distances also include the noise of the stereo depth. Hence, we also give the distances for the ground truth as input in order to assess the shape reconstruction quality isolated from the stereo depth estimation algorithm. We show several qualitative examples of shape matching results in Fig. 4. The examples demonstrate that our method can well align TSDFs through shape and pose optimization to input stereo reconstructions. We also provide a result when using ground truth as input to demonstrate our method on clean inputs.

Figures 5 and 6 show qualitative shape matching results in whole image context using libELAS and SPS-Stereo inputs to our method. The results in Fig. 5 and the left column in Fig. 6 demonstrate that the aligned shapes in these images capture the shape of the objects well. In the upper right image of Fig. 6, it can be seen that for occlusions or far-distance measurements our method can yield misaligned results, but it still captures the coarse pose and shape of the objects in this example. In the middle right image, 3DOP cannot provide good object

Fig. 5. Qualitative Results From top to bottom, every set of four rows shows: Input image with 2D 3DOP detections and back-projected inferred shapes (first row). Input image with 3D 3DOP detections and 3D view of inferred shapes (second row). libELAS depth map with applied normal filtering and our improved depth map (third row). SPS-Stereo depth map and our improved depth map (fourth row). Depth encoded from small (red) to large (blue) values. (Color figure online)

Fig. 6. Example depth reconstruction and segmentation results for libELAS depth input. Disparity encoded from small (red) to large (blue) values. Right column shows problematic examples for our method. See text for a detailed discussion. (Color figure online)

detections on the parked cars on the right street side. Finally, in the lower right image, a suboptimal matching result is obtained for a truck vehicle which is not represented in our shape manifold. Additional qualitative results are shown in the supplementary material.

5 Conclusions and Future Work

In this paper, we have presented a method for detecting objects of a given class and for concurrently estimating their shape and pose in stereo images from urban street scenes. Our method employs a state-of-the-art 3D object detection approach which coarsely estimates the pose of the objects. We learn a 3D TSDF shape manifold of instances of an object class using a model database. We propose an energy-minimization approach to align stereo reconstructions with object pose and shape within the manifold.

In experiments, we have demonstrated that our method is able to yield improved poses for cars on the KITTI Stereo 2015 dataset compared to [3]. The shape estimated by our method also yields improved depth compared to the input stereo reconstruction methods such as libELAS and SPS-Stereo.

We have demonstrated that our approach works well for cars in urban street scenes. Cars are rigid objects that can be well represented using the linear subspace embedding method. In future work, we want to further investigate the suitability of embedding methods to model deformable or articulated objects in our pipeline.

Acknowledgements. This work has been supported by ERC Starting Grant CV-SUPER (ERC-2012-StG-307432).

References

1. Agarwal, S., Mierle, K.: Ceres solver. http://ceres-solver.org
2. Bao, S.Y., Chandraker, M., Lin, Y., Savarese, S.: Dense object reconstruction with semantic priors. In: Proceedings of the IEEE International Conference on Computer Vision and Pattern Recognition (CVPR) (2013)
3. Chen, X., Kundu, K., Zhu, Y., Berneshawi, A., Ma, H., Fidler, S., Urtasun, R.: 3D object proposals for accurate object class detection. In: Proceedings of Neural Information Processing Systems (NIPS) (2015)
4. Dame, A., Prisacariu, V.A., Ren, C.Y., Reid, I.D.: Dense reconstruction using 3D object shape priors. In: Proceedings of the IEEE International Conference on Computer Vision and Pattern Recognition (CVPR) (2013)
5. Geiger, A., Lenz, P., Urtasun, R.: Are we ready for autonomous driving? the KITTI vision benchmark suite. In: Proceedings of the IEEE International Conference on Computer Vision and Pattern Recognition (CVPR) (2012)
6. Geiger, A., Roser, M., Urtasun, R.: Efficient large-scale stereo matching. In: Kimmel, R., Klette, R., Sugimoto, A. (eds.) ACCV 2010, Part I. LNCS, vol. 6492, pp. 25–38. Springer, Heidelberg (2011)
7. Geiger, A., Wang, C.: Joint 3D object and layout inference from a single RGB-D image. In: Gall, J., et al. (eds.) GCPR 2015. LNCS, vol. 9358, pp. 183–195. Springer, Heidelberg (2015). doi:10.1007/978-3-319-24947-6_15
8. Güney, F., Geiger, A.: Displets: resolving stereo ambiguities using object knowledge. In: Proceedings of the IEEE International Conference on Computer Vision and Pattern Recognition (CVPR) (2015)
9. Häne, C., Zach, C., Cohen, A., Angst, R., Pollefeys, M.: Joint 3D scene reconstruction and class segmentation. In: Proceedings of the IEEE International Conference on Computer Vision and Pattern Recognition (CVPR). pp. 97–104 (2013)
10. Hirschmüller, H.: Stereo processing by semiglobal matching and mutual information. IEEE Trans. Pattern Anal. Mach. Intell. (PAMI) **30**(2), 328–341 (2008)
11. Kundu, A., Li, Y., Dellaert, F., Li, F., Rehg, J.M.: Joint semantic segmentation and 3D reconstruction from monocular video. In: Fleet, D., Pajdla, T., Schiele, B., Tuytelaars, T. (eds.) ECCV 2014, Part VI. LNCS, vol. 8694, pp. 703–718. Springer, Heidelberg (2014)
12. Lawrence, N.: Probabilistic non-linear principal component analysis with Gaussian process latent variable models. J. Mach. Learn. Res. (JMLR) **6**, 1783–1816 (2005)
13. Lorensen, W.E., Cline, H.E.: Marching cubes: a high resolution 3D surface construction algorithm. In: Proceedings of SIGGRAPH (1987)
14. Menze, M., Heipke, C., Geiger, A.: Joint 3D estimation of vehicles and scene flow. In: Annals of the Photogrammetry, Remote Sensing and Spatial Information Sciences (2015)
15. Menze, M., Geiger, A.: Object scene flow for autonomous vehicles. In: CVPR (2015)
16. Prisacariu, V.A., Segal, A.V., Reid, I.: Simultaneous monocular 2D segmentation, 3D pose recovery and 3D reconstruction. In: Lee, K.M., Matsushita, Y., Rehg, J.M., Hu, Z. (eds.) ACCV 2012, Part I. LNCS, vol. 7724, pp. 593–606. Springer, Heidelberg (2013)
17. Ranftl, R., Gehrig, S., Pock, T., Bischof, H.: Pushing the limits of stereo using variational stereo estimation. In: Proceedings of the Intelligent Vehicles Symposium (2012)

18. Salas-Moreno, R.F., Newcombe, R.A., Strasdat, H., Kelly, P.H., Davison, A.J.: SLAM++: simultaneous localisation and mapping at the level of objects. In: Proceedings of the IEEE International Conference on Computer Vision and Pattern Recognition (CVPR) (2013)
19. Sandhu, R., Dambreville, S., Yezzi, A., Tannenbaum, A.: A nonrigid kernel-based framework for 2D-3D pose estimation and 2D image segmentation. IEEE Trans. Pattern Anal. Mach. Intell. **33**(6), 1098–1115 (2011)
20. Saxena, A., Chung, S.H., Ng, A.Y.: Learning depth from single monocular images. In: Proceedings of Neural Information Processing Systems (NIPS) (2005)
21. Sun, M., Bradski, G., Xu, B.-X., Savarese, S.: Depth-encoded hough voting for joint object detection and shape recovery. In: Daniilidis, K., Maragos, P., Paragios, N. (eds.) ECCV 2010, Part V. LNCS, vol. 6315, pp. 658–671. Springer, Heidelberg (2010)
22. Thomas, A., Ferrari, V., Leibe, B., Tuytelaars, T., Van Gool, L.: Depth-from-recognition: inferring meta-data by cognitive feedback. In: Proceedings of the IEEE International Conference on Computer Vision (ICCV) (2007)
23. Yamaguchi, K., McAllester, D., Urtasun, R.: Efficient joint segmentation, occlusion labeling, stereo and flow estimation. In: Fleet, D., Pajdla, T., Schiele, B., Tuytelaars, T. (eds.) ECCV 2014, Part V. LNCS, vol. 8693, pp. 756–771. Springer, Heidelberg (2014)
24. Zheng, S., Prisacariu, V.A., Averkiou, M., Cheng, M.-M., Mitra, N.J., Shotton, J., Torr, P.H.S., Rother, C.: Object proposals estimation in depth image using compact 3D shape manifolds. In: Gall, J., et al. (eds.) GCPR 2015. LNCS, vol. 9358, pp. 196–208. Springer, Heidelberg (2015). doi:10.1007/978-3-319-24947-6_16
25. Zhou, C., Güney, F., Wang, Y., Geiger, A.: Exploiting object similarity in 3D reconstruction. In: Proceedings of the IEEE International Conference on Computer Vision (ICCV) (2015)
26. Zia, M., Stark, M., Schiele, B., Schindler, K.: Detailed 3D representations for object recognition and modeling. IEEE Trans. Pattern Anal. Mach. Intell. (PAMI) **35**, 2608–2623 (2013)

Motion and Tracking

Joint Recursive Monocular Filtering of Camera Motion and Disparity Map

Johannes Berger[(⊠)] and Christoph Schnörr

Image and Pattern Analysis Group, Heidelberg University, Heidelberg, Germany
johannes.berger@iwr.uni-heidelberg.de, schnoerr@math.uni-heidelberg.de
http://ipa.math.uni-heidelberg.de

Abstract. Monocular scene reconstruction is essential for modern applications such as robotics or autonomous driving. Although stereo methods usually result in better accuracy than monocular methods, they are more expensive and more difficult to calibrate. In this work, we present a novel second order optimal *minimum energy filter* that *jointly* estimates the camera motion, the disparity map and also higher order kinematics recursively on a product Lie group containing a novel *disparity group*. This mathematical framework enables to cope with non-Euclidean state spaces, non-linear observations and high dimensions which is infeasible for most classical filters. To be robust against outliers, we use a *generalized Charbonnier energy function* in this framework rather than a quadratic energy function as proposed in related work. Experiments confirm that our method enables accurate reconstructions on-par with state-of-the-art.

Keywords: Minimum energy filter · Monocular reconstruction · Camera motion estimation · Lie groups

1 Introduction

1.1 Overview

Reconstruction of the scene structure of images and videos is a fundamental building block in computer vision and is required for plenty of applications, e.g. autonomous driving, robot vision and augmented reality. Although stereo methods usually lead to exact reconstruction and work fast, they require calibration of the camera setup and, due to the second camera, these systems are more expensive than single camera systems. Therefore, in this work, we will focus on the monocular approach that consists of reconstructing the scene structure based on the data gained by a *single* moving camera. In contrast to the stereo setting, this problem is ill-posed because of the unknown motion parallax. On the other hand, monocular approaches enable cheaper hardware costs.

J. Berger–Support by the German Research Foundation (DFG, GRK 1653) is acknowledged.

B. Rosenhahn and B. Andres (Eds.): GCPR 2016, LNCS 9796, pp. 233–244, 2016.
DOI: 10.1007/978-3-319-45886-1_19

To increase accuracy and robustness of the monocular reconstruction, we want to use temporal information for smoothing and propagation. Thus, we will introduce a mathematical framework based on *non-linear* filtering equations which describe the behavior of latent variables and the dependency between latent variables and observations. Since, in this scenario, the state variables, e.g. camera motion, do not evolve on an Euclidean space but a more general Lie group, we cannot use classical filters, such as *extended Kalman* filters [14]. Moreover, other state-of-the-art non-linear filters, such as *particle filters* [11], that can be applied to specific Lie groups [17], cannot be easily extended to high dimensional problems [8]. Due to these mathematical problems we will use the novel *minimum energy filter* on compact Lie groups [25] that minimizes a quadratic energy function to penalize deviations of the filtering equations by means of optimal control theory. This filter was shown to be superior to extended Kalman filters on the low dimensional Lie group SE_3 [3]. We will demonstrate that this approach can also be successfully applied to high dimensional problems, enabling *joint* optimization of camera motion and disparity map. As in [3], we will also incorporate higher order kinematics of the camera motion. To be robust against outliers, we will extend the approach of [25] from quadratic energy function to a generalized Charbonnier energy function.

1.2   Related Work

Plenty of methods for depth or disparity map estimation were published during the last decade. We distinguish between stereo methods (that benefit from the additional information gained from the calibrated camera setup) and monocular methods. Recognized stereo methods include [16,22,27] that use the known distance of the cameras (baseline) for accurate triangulation of the scene. These methods also enable reducing the computational effort by using epipolar geometry and by combining local and global optimization schemes. Monocular methods [1,5,9,12,13,19,20] benefit from less calibration effort in comparison to stereo methods, but suffer from a peculiarity of the mathematical setup that prevents to reconstruct the scale of the scene uniquely. To increase the robustness and the accuracy of the reconstruction, modern methods incorporate multiple consecutive frames into the optimization procedure. Well-known is bundle adjustment [26] which optimizes a whole trajectory but cannot be used in online approaches such as sliding window [2] or filtering methods [1,5]. Filtering methods usually require a suitable modeling of the unknown *a posteriori* distribution. However, they suffer from the drawback that the definition of probability densities on non-Euclidean spaces, such as Lie groups, is complicated, although successful strategies to find a solution to this problem have been developed [6,7,17]. Zamani et al. [29] introduces so-called *minimum energy filters* for linear filtering problems for compact Lie groups based on optimal control theory and the recursive filtering principle of Mortensen [18]. This approach was generalized to (non-)compact Lie groups in [25] and applied to a *non-linear* filtering problem on SE_3 for camera motion estimation [4].

1.3   Contributions

Our contributions in this paper add up

- to provide a mathematical filtering framework for *joint* monocular camera motion and disparity map estimation including higher order kinematics,
- to introduce a *novel disparity Lie group for inverse depth maps* which avoids additional positive depth constraints such as barrier functions,
- to solve the corresponding challenging *non-linear* and *high-dimensional* filtering problem on a *product Lie group* by using novel *minimum energy filters*,
- to provide a *generalized Charbonnier* energy function instead of a quadratic energy function [25], which results in robustness against outliers.

1.4   Notation

We use the following spaces: real vector space $\mathbb{R}^n$, special orthogonal/Euclidean group SO_3, SE_3, with their corresponding Lie algebras $\mathfrak{so}_3, \mathfrak{se}_3$, as well as $\mathcal{G}$ for a general Lie group with Lie algebra $\mathfrak{g}$. Tangent spaces at a point x of $\mathcal{G}$ are denoted by $T_x\mathcal{G}$. A tangent vector $\eta \in T_x\mathcal{G}$ can be expressed in terms of a tangent vector ξ on the Lie algebra $\mathfrak{g}$ by using the tangent map of the left translation L_x evaluated at the identity element Id of the Lie group, denoted by $\eta = T_{\mathrm{Id}}L_x\xi$. We also use the shorthand $x\xi := T_{\mathrm{Id}}L_x\xi$. We use the $*$−symbol to indicate dual spaces and operators with respect to the Riemannian metric that can be defined by the tangent map as $\langle x\eta, x\xi \rangle_x := \langle \eta, \xi \rangle_{\mathrm{Id}}$ for $\eta, \xi \in \mathfrak{g}$. The dual of the tangent map is $T_{\mathrm{Id}}L_x^*\eta =: x^{-1}\eta$. We denote by $\mathrm{vec}_{\mathfrak{g}} : \mathfrak{g} \to \mathbb{R}^n, \mathrm{mat}_{\mathfrak{g}} : \mathbb{R}^n \to \mathfrak{g}$ the vectorization and its inverse operation, respectively, where the underlying Lie group $\mathcal{G}$ has dimension n. These operations allow representing the Lie algebra $\mathfrak{g}$ in a compact form. $\mathbf{D}f$ denotes the differential of a function, whereas $\mathbf{D}f(x)[\eta] := \langle \mathbf{D}f(x), \eta \rangle_x$ indicates the directional derivative for a specific direction η. For compactness, we write $\mathbf{D}_i f(x, y, z)$ for the differential of the function f respective the i−th component, whereas $\mathbf{D}_y f(x, y, z)$ directly addresses a specific variable. Hess $f[\cdot]$ stands for the Riemanian Hessian on the considered Lie group; the calculation of the latter requires the Riemannian connection ∇ that can be expressed in terms of a connection function ω on the Lie algebra $\mathfrak{g}$.

2   Model

In this section we will introduce the mathematical framework of joint monocular camera motion and disparity map estimation from the point of view of (stochastic) filtering. Note, that we will use the notion *disparity map* for the inverse of the depth map in this work without using the baseline that is required in stereo settings. In classical filtering theory one wants to determine the most likely state of an unknown process $x = x(t)$ modeled by a perturbed differential equation $\dot{x}(t) = f(x(t)) + \delta(t)$ based on prior perturbed observations $y(s) = h(x(s)) + \epsilon(s)$ for $s \leq t$, which results in a *maximum a posteriori* problem. In this work, we require the state space of x to be a Lie group $\mathcal{G}$ which we need to describe non-Euclidean expressions such as camera motions. Using the expressions $\delta = \delta(t)$ and $\epsilon = \epsilon(t)$ to represent model noise and observations noise, respectively, the resulting filtering equations can be written as

$$\dot{x}(t) = x(t)\big(f(x(t)) + \delta(t)\big), \quad x(t_0) = x_0, \tag{1}$$
$$y(t) = h(x(t)) + \epsilon(t). \tag{2}$$

The state Eq. (1) is modeled on a Lie Group $\mathcal{G}$ by means of the tangent map of the left translation at identity and functions $f, \delta \in \mathfrak{g}$ such that $\dot{x}(t) \in T_x \mathcal{G}$. In the following sections we will introduce the state space of x, the propagation functions f and the observation function h.

2.1   State Space

The camera motion is modeled on the Special Euclidean group $SE_3 := \{\left(\begin{smallmatrix} R & w \\ 0 & 1 \end{smallmatrix}\right) | R \in SO_3, w \in \mathbb{R}^3\}$, and we also use a higher order kinematics (e.g. acceleration of camera) modeled by a vector $v \in \mathbb{R}^6$. The disparity map can be represented by a large vector $d_i \in \mathbb{R}^{|\Omega|}$, resulting in an own dimension for each pixel in the image. However, the depth must always be positive and we want to avoid additional constraints within our optimization. Therefore, we introduce a novel Lie group for the inverse of the depth, denoted by $(0,1)^{|\Omega|}$ which is defined as follows:

Definition 1 (Lie group $(0,1)^n$ (Disparity group)). *By denoting* $d_i(z,t) := \frac{1}{d(z,t)} \in (0,1)$ *the inverse of the depth we define the Lie group* $(0,1)^n$ *with group action for* $x, y \in (0,1)^n$ *as*

$$x \circ y \mapsto \big((x^{-1} - 1) \cdot (y^{-1} - 1) + 1\big)^{-1} = \frac{xy}{1 - x - y + 2xy}.$$

The (Lie group inverse) can be computed as $i(x) := 1 - x$. *This results in the identity element* $\mathrm{Id} = \frac{1}{2}$, *i.e. a vector full of* $1/2$. *The exponential map* $\mathrm{Exp}_{(0,1)^n} : \mathbb{R}^n \to (0,1)^n$ *and the logarithmic map* $\mathrm{Log}_{(0,1)^n} : \mathbb{R}^n \to (0,1)^n$ *are given through*

$$x \mapsto \frac{e^{4x}}{1+e^{4x}} \text{ and } x \mapsto \frac{1}{4}\log\left(\frac{x}{1-x}\right), \text{ respectively.}$$

Using SE_3 for the camera motion, $\mathbb{R}^6$ for the acceleration of the camera and the Lie group given through Definition 1 for the disparity map, we find the product Lie group $\mathcal{G}$ for our state space, i.e.

$$\mathcal{G} := SE_3 \times \mathbb{R}^6 \times (0,1)^{|\Omega|}. \tag{3}$$

2.2   Propagation of the Camera Motion

For propagation of the camera we will use a second order kinematic model that can be expressed as second order differential equation on SE_3 as in [3], which is

$$\dot{E}(t) = E(t)\,\mathrm{mat}_{\mathfrak{se}}(v(t)), \quad E(t_0) = E_0, \tag{4}$$
$$\dot{v}(t) = \mathbf{0}, \quad v(t_0) = v_0,$$

where $E = E(t) \in SE_3$ and $v = v(t) \in \mathbb{R}^6$.

Remark 1. Since E describes the local camera motion from frame to frame, a first order model $\dot{E}(t) = \mathbf{0}$ corresponds to a constantly moving camera, i.e. with constant velocity. Thus, the model (4) describes a constant acceleration in the global camera frame.

2.3   Discrete Propagation of the Disparity Map

The propagation consists of mapping the image grid forward by an estimate of the motion $\hat{E} = (\hat{R}, \hat{w})$, by cubic interpolation of the depth on the irregular grid and back-projection of the resulting scene points. This leads to the following algorithm, which is also depicted in Fig. 1.

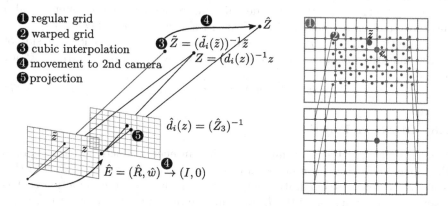

Fig. 1. Discrete propagation of the disparity map

1. Start with the disparity map d_i on regular image grid in camera $(I, 0)$.
2. Warp the image grid forward into next image (camera estimate $\hat{E}(t)$) by using current disparity map d_i to get a grid with points $\tilde{z} = \pi(\hat{R}\left(\begin{smallmatrix} z \\ 1 \end{smallmatrix}\right)(d_i(z))^{-1} + \hat{w})$, where $\pi : \mathbb{R}^3 \to \mathbb{R}^2$ is given through $(z_1, z_2, z_3)^\top \mapsto (z_3)^{-1}(z_1, z_2)^\top$.
3. Perform cubic interpolation on the warped grid $\tilde{z}$ given the values $(z, d_i(z))$ which gives the new depth map $(\tilde{z}, \tilde{d}_i(\tilde{z}))$ in frame $(I, 0)$.
4. Move $\tilde{Z} = \left(\begin{smallmatrix} \tilde{z} \\ 1 \end{smallmatrix}\right)(\tilde{d}_i(\tilde{z}))^{-1}$ to second camera to obtain $\hat{Z} = \hat{R}^\top(\tilde{Z} - \hat{w})$.
5. Recognize the propagated disparity map as third component, $\hat{d}_i(z) = (\hat{Z}_3)^{-1}$.

2.4   Camera Motion and Disparity Map Induced Optical Flow

Since the state space $\mathcal{G}$ consists of the camera motion $E(t)$ and the disparity map $d_i(\cdot, t)$ (inverse of depth map), we require observations that depend on both variables. It is well-known that from a given disparity map and a given camera motion the correspondences between a pair of consecutive images expressed as *optical flow* can be uniquely determined if the scene is static. To be precise, the dependency between the optical flow vector $u(z, t)$ at a position $z \in \Omega$ can be expressed with the following *non-linear* relation, where we denote by $R(t) \in SO_3$

and $w(t) \in \mathbb{R}^3$ the rotational and translational component of the camera motion $E(t) = (R(t), w(t)) \in SE_3$, respectively. For details see [1, Eq. (6)].

$$u(z,t) + z = \pi\Big(R(t)\,(\tfrac{z}{1})\,(d_i(z,t))^{-1} + w(t)\Big). \tag{5}$$

2.5 Overall Filtering Model

The function $f(x(t)) : \mathcal{G} \to \mathfrak{g}$ in (1) can now be defined as follows:

$$f(x(t)) := (f_E(x(t)), f_v(x(t)), f_{d_i}(x(t))), \tag{6}$$

with component functions $f_E(x(t)) := \mathrm{mat}_{\mathfrak{se}}(v(t))$, and $f_v(x(t)) := \mathbf{0_6}$ as in (4) as well as $f_{d_i}(x(t)) := \mathbf{0}_{|\Omega|}$. Beside this continuous propagation step we also incorporate discrete updates of the disparities as described in Sect. 2.3.

By setting $y_z(t) := u(z,t) - z$ and $h_z : \mathcal{G} \to \mathbb{R}^2$, as the right hand side of (5), we find the following observation equations by adding noise $\epsilon_z(t) \in \mathbb{R}^2$ for all $z \in \Omega$.

$$y_z(t) = h_z(x(t)) + \epsilon_z(t), \qquad z \in \Omega. \tag{7}$$

2.6 Objective Function

Minimum energy filtering requires to define an energy function that penalizes the model and observation noise. In contrast to [24], that we will follow in this work, we will not use quadratic energy functions but an energy function that is a smooth approximation of the L^1−norm. The reason is that we want to reduce the influence of outliers in the observations that may cause numerical problems because the gradient grows linearly. The norm of the gradient of the proposed L^1 penalty function is bounded. A smooth approximation to the non-differentiable L^1−norm is the generalized charbonnier penalty function that is smooth (C^∞) and has linear growth, such that we use it for ϕ, i.e. $\phi(x) := (x + \nu)^\beta - \nu^\beta$. With this notation and the shorthand $\|x\|_Q^2 := x^\top Q x$ the energy function reads

$$\mathcal{J}(\delta, \epsilon, x; t) := \tfrac{1}{2}\|x - x_0\|_{R_0^{-1}}^2 + \int_{t_0}^{t}\Big(\tfrac{1}{2}\|\mathrm{vec}_{\mathfrak{g}}(\delta(\tau))\|_{R^{-1}}^2 + \sum_{z \in \Omega}\phi(\tfrac{1}{2}\|\epsilon_z(\tau)\|_{Q_z^{-1}}^2)\Big)d\tau, \tag{8}$$

where Q_z, R_0 and R are symmetric and positive definite matrices.

2.7 Optimal Control Problem

After replacing the observation noise $\epsilon_z(t)$ by the residual $\epsilon_z(t) = \epsilon_z(x(t), t) := y_z(t) - h_z(x,t)$ in (8) we want to minimize the energy function $\mathcal{J}(\delta, x, x(t_0); t) = \mathcal{J}(\delta, \epsilon(x), x(t_0); t)$ regarding the model noise $\delta(t)$ with respect to the differential Eq. (1) yielding the *value function*

$$\mathcal{V}(x(t), t, x(t_0)) := \min_{\delta|_{[t_0, t]}} \mathcal{J}(\delta, x; t) \quad \text{subject to (1).} \tag{9}$$

Calculation of the value function requires to introduce the time-varying (left-trivialized) Hamiltonian function $\tilde{\mathcal{H}} : \mathcal{G} \times \mathfrak{g}^* \times \mathfrak{g} \times \mathbb{R} \to \mathbb{R}$ that is given through

$$\tilde{\mathcal{H}}(x,\mu,\delta,t) := \left(\tfrac{1}{2}\|\mathrm{vec}_\mathfrak{g}(\delta(t))\|_{R^{-1}}^2 + \sum_{z\in\Omega} \phi(\tfrac{1}{2}\|y_z(t) - h_z(x(t)))\|_{Q_z}^2)\right)$$
$$- \langle \mu, f(x(t)) + \delta(t)\rangle_{\mathrm{Id}}. \tag{10}$$

Owing to the *Pontryagin minimum principle* [21] we find the minimizing argument of the value function (9) by minimizing the Hamiltonian $\tilde{\mathcal{H}}$ with respect to δ. Since the Hamiltonian is convex in δ we obtain a unique minimum $\delta^* = \mathrm{mat}_\mathfrak{g}\left(R\,\mathrm{vec}_\mathfrak{g}(\mu)\right)$ resulting in the optimal Hamiltonian $\mathcal{H}(x,\mu,t) : \mathcal{G}\times\mathfrak{g}^*\times\mathbb{R} \to \mathbb{R}$ given through $\mathcal{H}(x,\mu,t) := \tilde{\mathcal{H}}(x,\mu,\delta^*,t)$ such that

$$\mathcal{H}(x,\mu,t) = -\langle\mu, f(x(t))\rangle_{\mathrm{Id}} - \tfrac{1}{2}\|\mathrm{vec}_\mathfrak{g}(\mu)\|_R^2 + \sum_{z\in\Omega}\left(\phi(\tfrac{1}{2}\|y_z(t) - h_z(x(t))\|_{Q_z}^2)\right).$$

In the case of a linear-quadratic control problem this optimal Hamiltonian satisfies the (left-trivialized) Hamilton-Jacobi-Bellman equation, i.e.

$$\frac{\partial}{\partial t}\mathcal{V}(x,t) - \mathcal{H}(x, x^{-1}\mathbf{D}_1\mathcal{V}(x,t),t) = 0. \tag{11}$$

Here, $\mathbf{D}_1\mathcal{V}(x,t) \in T_x^*\mathcal{G}$ is an element of the cotangent space.

Remark 2. Note that our control problem has neither *linear control dynamics* nor a *quadratic* energy function. Thus, we have no guarantee that the HJB equation is a necessary *and* sufficient condition for optimality. Instead we require a good initialization to gain an optimal reconstruction. However, we will show that a fairly general initialization will lead to good reconstructions.

2.8 Recursive Filtering Principle and Truncation

Computation of the total time derivative of the necessary condition

$$\mathbf{D}_1\mathcal{V}(x,t,x(t_0)) = \mathbf{0},$$

and insertion of the HJB Eq. (11) leads to the following lemma that gives a recursive description of the optimal state $x^* = x^*(t)$ (cf. [25, Eq. (37)]).

Lemma 1. *The evolution equation of the optimal x^* state is given through*

$$\dot{x}^*(t) = x(t)\left(f(x^*(t)) - \hat{Z}(x^*(t),t)^{-1} \circ x^{-1}(\mathbf{D}_1\mathcal{H}(x^*(t),0,t))\right), \tag{12}$$

where $\hat{Z} : \mathfrak{g} \to \mathfrak{g}^*$ is the left-trivialized Hessian of the value function given through

$$\hat{Z}(x^*,t) \circ \eta = (x^*)^{-1}\,\mathrm{Hess}\,\mathcal{V}(x^*(t),t,x(t_0))[x^*\eta], \quad \eta \in \mathfrak{g}. \tag{13}$$

Because the non-linear filtering problem is infinite dimensional we will replace the exact operator $\hat{Z}$ by an approximation $Z : \mathfrak{g} \to \mathfrak{g}^*$ which can be obtained by truncation of the full evolution equation of Z. But still the operator $Z(x^*, t)$ on $\mathfrak{g}$ is complicated such that we introduce a matrix representation $P(t)$ that is defined through the relation $\mathrm{vec}_{\mathfrak{g}}(Z(x^*, t)^{-1} \circ \eta) =: P(t)\,\mathrm{vec}_{\mathfrak{g}}(\eta)$.

Lemma 2. *The matrix representation of the approximation of the operator $\hat{Z}$ evolves regarding the following matrix Riccati equation*

$$\dot{P}(t) = R + C(x^*, t)P(t) + P(t)C(x^*, t)^\top - P(t)H(x^*, t)P(t), \qquad (14)$$

where the matrix R is the weighting matrix in the energy function (8) and the matrices C and H are given for $\eta \in \mathfrak{g}$ through

$$C(x^*, t)P(t)\,\mathrm{vec}_{\mathfrak{g}}(\eta) := \mathrm{vec}_{\mathfrak{g}}\big((x^*)^{-1}\mathbf{D}_2(\mathbf{D}_1\mathcal{H}(x^*, \mathbf{0}, t))[Z(x^*, t) \circ \eta]\big)$$
$$+ \mathrm{vec}_{\mathfrak{g}}(\omega^{\overleftarrow{*}}_{\mathbf{D}_2\mathcal{H}(x^*, 0, t)} \circ Z(x^*, t) \circ \eta) + \mathrm{vec}_{\mathfrak{g}}(\omega^*_{(x^*)^{-1}\dot{x}^*} \circ Z(x^*, t) \circ \eta),$$
$$H(x^*, t)\,\mathrm{vec}_{\mathfrak{g}}(\eta) := \mathrm{vec}_{\mathfrak{g}}\big((x^*)^{-1}\,\mathrm{Hess}_1\,\mathcal{H}(x^*, \mathbf{0}, t)[x\eta]\big).$$

Here, $x\omega_\xi\eta := \nabla_{x\xi}x\eta$ denotes the connection function on the Lie algebra $\mathfrak{g}$ of the Levi-Civita connection $\nabla\cdot$ for $\xi, \eta \in \mathfrak{g}$ and $x \in \mathcal{G}$, and $\omega^{\overleftarrow{*}}_\xi$ is the dual of the "swaped" connection function $\omega^{\overleftarrow{}}_\xi\eta := \omega_\eta\xi$ (cf. [24]).

By insertion of the expression P into (12) and by evaluation of the expressions in Lemma 1 and 2 we obtain the final minimum energy filter that consists of continuous propagation of the states with a discrete update of the disparity map.

Theorem 1. *The second order minimum energy filter with additional discrete propagation step for the disparity map is given through the following evolution equations of the optimal state $x^* \in \mathcal{G}$ as well as the second order operator $P \in \mathbb{R}^{(12+|\Omega|) \times (12+|\Omega|)}$.*

$$\dot{x}^*(t) = x^*(t)\big(f(x^*(t)) - \mathrm{mat}_{\mathfrak{g}}(P(t)\,\mathrm{vec}_{\mathfrak{g}}(G(x^*(t), t)))\big), \qquad (15)$$
$$\dot{P}(t) = R + C(x^*, t)P(t) + P(t)C(x^*, t)^\top - P(t)H(x^*, t)P(t), \qquad (16)$$

with initial conditions $x^*(t_0) = x_0$ and $P(t_0) = R_0$, where R_0 is the matrix in (8). $G(x^*, t) = (G_E(x^*), \mathbf{0}, G_{d_i}(x^*)) \in \mathfrak{g}$ denotes the Riemannian gradient of the Hamiltonian in (12) with components G_E and G_{d_i}.

The numerical integration of these equations between the time steps t_{k-1} and t_k correspond to the update step of a filter, where the updates are assumed to be piecewise constant. After each update step the disparity map is propagated forward using the procedure in Fig. 1 that result in the final filter.

Remark 3. The expressions for $C(x^*, t), H(x^*, t)$ and $G(x^*, t)$ can be calculated explicitly but require matrix calculus and differential geometry. The resulting expressions become involved such that we refer the interested reader to the supplemental material[1].

---

[1] http://hciweb.iwr.uni-heidelberg.de/people/johannesberger.

Remark 4. The optimal state can be calculated by geometric numerical integration of the ordinary differential Eqs. (15) and (16), e.g. Crouch-Grossman methods (cf. [15]). During numerical integration it is important to keep the matrix P sparse, therefore we set the off-diagonal entries of the lower right part of P (that addresses the disparities) after each iteration to zero.

3 Experiments

Preprocessing. As stated above, our method requires precise optical flow as input. Since we propose a monocular method we also demand that the optical flow is computed from two consecutive image frames without stereo information. For this reason we used the well-known *EpicFlow* approach [23]. The matches are computed with *Deep Matching* [28]; the required edges are from [10].

Choice of the Weighting Matrices. Monocular methods suffer from the fact that observations that appear close to the epipole (focus of expansion) are orthogonal to the camera motion such that these regions cannot be reconstructed correctly. Therefore we use the weighting term from [1, Eq. (14)] for the weighting matrix Q that decreases the influence of the data term in regions close to the epipole.

Outlier Detection. To remove outliers, we computed the backward flow from frame i to $i + 1$ as well as the forward flow from frame $i + 1$ to i. In regions where these flows are not consistent with each other, we decreased the weight of the term R such that the filter has less ability to fit to the data and the discrete disparity map propagation from Sect. 2.3 reduces the error.

Scale Correction. As monocular approaches cannot estimate the scale of a scene without prior knowledge about invariants in the scene, we corrected the scale by calculating of the pixel-wise quotient of the disparities and taking its median as scale $s := \text{median}\{d_i^{\text{gt}}(z,t)/d_i^{\text{est}}(z,t)|z \in \Omega^*\}$, where Ω^* denotes the image domain without points which are close to the epipole (< 50 pixel distance).

3.1 Qualitative Results

In Fig. 2 we compared the reconstruction of the disparity map of our method with the results from [1] and the ground truth. One can recognize that our method preserves small details and depth discontinuities better than [1] and returns sharper edges.

3.2 Quantitative Results

We evaluated the mean amount of pixels in Ω^* with a disparity error larger than three pixel for both occluded and not occluded scenarios in Table 1. We are slightly inferior towards Becker et al. [1]; however, unlike [1] we do not have spatial regularization within our optimization which explains the differences.

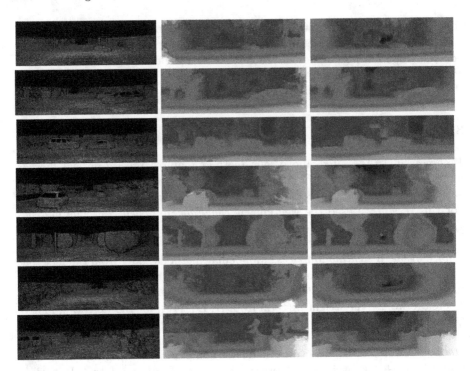

Fig. 2. *Best viewed in color.* Reconstruction of the disparity maps; left column: ground truth from the KITTI stereo benchmark, middle column: monocular method of Becker et al. [1], right column: reconstruction with our monocular method. Although in the quantitative evaluation both methods perform equally, one can recognize that our method results in sharper corners. Due to spatial regularization [1] reconstructs regions close to the epipole better.

Table 1. Evaluation of the mean disparity errors.

	$p_{3px}[\%]$ (occ)	$p_{5px}[\%]$ (occ)	$p_{3px}[\%]$ (noc)	$p_{5px}[\%]$ (noc)
Becker et al. [1]	17.74	10.82	17.63	10.72
our approach	19.24	10.69	19.14	10.59

4   Conclusion

We provided a sound mathematical filtering framework for monocular scene reconstruction based on novel minimum energy filters, extending the classical quadratic energy function from Saccon et al. [25] to a generalized Charbonnier energy function. We demonstrated that the proposed filter copes with challenging mathematical issues, such as a non-Euclidean state space, non-linear filtering equations based on projections, as well as high dimensions; in fact, these difficulties are infeasible for most classical stochastic filters. The introduced *disparity group* enables filtering without additional constraints making the model relatively compact. Our experiments confirmed that the proposed filter is almost as accurate as other state-of-the-art monocular and recursive methods without having an own regularization within the model.

References

1. Becker, F., Lenzen, F., Kappes, J.H., Schnörr, C.: Variational recursive joint estimation of dense scene structure and camera motion from monocular high speed traffic sequences. IJCV **105**, 269–297 (2013)
2. Bellavia, F., Fanfani, M., Pazzaglia, F., Colombo, C.: Robust selective stereo SLAM without loop closure and bundle adjustment. In: Petrosino, A. (ed.) ICIAP 2013, Part I. LNCS, vol. 8156, pp. 462–471. Springer, Heidelberg (2013)
3. Berger, J., Lenzen, F., Becker, F., Neufeld, A., Schnörr, C.: Second-Order Recursive Filtering on the Rigid-Motion Lie Group SE(3) Based on Nonlinear Observations (2015). ArXiv, preprint arXiv:1507.06810
4. Berger, J., Neufeld, A., Becker, F., Lenzen, F., Schnörr, C.: Second Order Minimum Energy Filtering on SE$_3$ with Nonlinear Measurement Equations. In: Aujol, J.-F., Nikolova, M., Papadakis, N. (eds.) SSVM 2015. LNCS, vol. 9087, pp. 397–409. Springer, Heidelberg (2015). doi:10.1007/978-3-319-18461-6_32
5. Bourmaud, G., Mégret, R.: Robust large scale monocular visual SLAM. In CVPR, pp. 1638–1647 (2015)
6. Bourmaud, G., Mégret, R., Arnaudon, M., Giremus, A.: Continuous-discrete extended Kalman filter on matrix lie groups using concentrated Gaussian distributions. J. Math. Imaging Vis. **51**(1), 209–228 (2015)
7. Chikuse, Y.: Statistics on Special Manifolds, vol. 174. Springer, Heidelberg (2012)
8. Daum, F., Huang, J.: Curse of dimensionality and particle filters. In: Aerospace Conference (2003)
9. Davison, A.J., Reid, I.D., Molton, N.D., Stasse, O.: MonoSLAM: real-time single camera SLAM. PAMI **29**(6), 1052–1067 (2007)
10. Dollár, P.: Piotr's Computer Vision Matlab Toolbox (PMT). http://vision.ucsd.edu/pdollar/toolbox/doc/index.html
11. Doucet, A., Freitas, N., Gordon, N.: An introduction to sequential Monte Carlo methods. In: Doucet, A., Freitas, N., Gordon, N. (eds.) Sequential Monte Carlo Methods in Practice, pp. 3–14. Springer, New York (2001)
12. Engel, J., Schöps, T., Cremers, D.: LSD-SLAM: large-scale direct monocular SLAM. In: Fleet, D., Pajdla, T., Schiele, B., Tuytelaars, T. (eds.) ECCV 2014, Part II. LNCS, vol. 8690, pp. 834–849. Springer, Heidelberg (2014)
13. Engel, J., Sturm, J., Cremers, D.: Semi-dense visual odometry for a monocular camera. In: ICCV, pp. 1449–1456. IEEE (2013)
14. Frogerais, P., Bellanger, J., Senhadji, L.: Various ways to compute the continuous-discrete extended Kalman filter. IEEE Trans. Autom. Control **57**, 1000–1004 (2012)
15. Hairer, E., Lubich, C., Wanner, G.: Geometric Numerical Integration, vol. 31. Springer, Heidelberg (2006)
16. Hirschmüller, H.: Stereo processing by semiglobal matching and mutual information. PAMI **30**(2), 328–341 (2008)
17. Kwon, J., Choi, M., Park, F.C., Chun, C.: Particle filtering on the Euclidean group: framework and applications. Robotica **25**(6), 725–737 (2007)

18. Mortensen, R.E.: Maximum-likelihood recursive nonlinear filtering. J. Opt. Theory Appl. **2**(6), 386–394 (1968)
19. Neufeld, A., Berger, J., Becker, F., Lenzen, F., Schnörr, C.: Estimating vehicle ego-motion and piecewise planar scene structure from optical flow in a continuous framework. In: Gall, J., Gehler, P., Leibe, B. (eds.) GCPR 2015. LNCS, vol. 9358, pp. 41–52. Springer, Heidelberg (2015). doi:10.1007/978-3-319-24947-6_4
20. Pizzoli, M., Forster, C., Scaramuzza, D.: REMODE: probabilistic, monocular dense reconstruction in real time. In: ICRA, pp. 2609–2616. IEEE (2014)
21. Pontryagin, L.S., Boltyanskii, V., Gamkrelidze, R., Mishchenko, E.: The Mathematical Theory of Optimal Processes. Interscience Publishers Inc., New York (1962)
22. Psota, E.T., Kowalczuk, J., Mittek, M., Perez, L.C.: MAP disparity estimation using hidden Markov trees. In: ICCV, pp. 2219–2227 (2015)
23. Revaud, J., Weinzaepfel, P., Harchaoui, Z., Schmid, C.: EpicFlow: edge-preserving interpolation of correspondences for optical flow. In: CVPR (2015)
24. Saccon, A., Trumpf, J., Mahony, R., Aguiar, A.P.: Second-order-optimal filters on lie groups. In: CDC (2013)
25. Saccon, A., Trumpf, J., Mahony, R., Aguiar, A.P.: Second-order-optimal minimum-energy filters on lie groups. IEEE TAC **PP**(99), 1 (2015)
26. Triggs, B., McLauchlan, P.F., Hartley, R.I., Fitzgibbon, A.W.: Bundle adjustment – a modern synthesis. In: Triggs, B., Zisserman, A., Szeliski, R. (eds.) ICCV-WS 1999. LNCS, vol. 1883, pp. 298–372. Springer, Heidelberg (2000)
27. Vogel, C., Schindler, K., Roth, S.: 3D scene flow estimation with a piecewise rigid scene model. IJCV **115**(1), 1–28 (2015)
28. Weinzaepfel, P., Revaud, J., Harchaoui, Z., Schmid, C.: Deepflow: large displacement optical flow with deep matching. In: ICCV, pp. 1385–1392 (2013)
29. Zamani, M., Trumpf, J., Mahoney, M.: A second order minimum-energy filter on the special orthogonal group. In: Proceedings of ACC (2012)

From Traditional to Modern: Domain Adaptation for Action Classification in Short Social Video Clips

Aditya Singh$^{(\boxtimes)}$, Saurabh Saini, Rajvi Shah, and P.J. Narayanan

Center for Visual Information Technology, IIIT Hyderabad, Hyderabad, India
aditya.singh@research.iiit.ac.in

Abstract. Short internet video clips like *vines* present a significantly wild distribution compared to traditional video datasets. In this paper, we focus on the problem of unsupervised action classification in wild vines using traditional labeled datasets. To this end, we use a data augmentation based simple domain adaptation strategy. We utilize semantic *word2vec* space as a common subspace to embed video features from both, labeled source domain and unlabled target domain. Our method incrementally augments the labeled source with target samples and iteratively modifies the embedding function to bring the source and target distributions together. Additionally, we utilize a multi-modal representation that incorporates noisy semantic information available in form of hash-tags. We show the effectiveness of this simple adaptation technique on a test set of vines and achieve notable improvements in performance.

1 Introduction

Action classification is an active field of research due to its applications in multiple domains. The last decade has seen a significant paradigm shift from model-based to data-driven learning for this task. Over the years, increasingly complex and challenging action recognition datasets such as UCF101, HMDB, Hollywood, etc. have been introduced [2,10,12,13,17,18,24]. However, with growing popularity of social media platforms and mobile camera devices, there is unprecedented amount of amateur footage that is significantly wilder and complex than curated datasets. In this paper, we analyze this problem on a particular distribution of short video clips shared on the social media platform vine.co, known as *vines*. Vines are six second long, often captured by hand-held or wearable devices, with cuts and edits, and present a significantly wilder and more challenging distribution. The action classifiers trained using traditional distributions such as UCF, HMDB, etc. cannot generalize or adapt to wild distributions like vines [7,25,26]. Recent methods that use increasingly complex features from large-scale dictionaries and Convolutional Neural Networks (CNN) are showing promise in building more generalizable systems. However, these methods require supervised training with large-scale labeled data. Moreover, data from Internet sources, like vines, is ever increasing and manually labeling such data is tedious

© Springer International Publishing AG 2016
B. Rosenhahn and B. Andres (Eds.): GCPR 2016, LNCS 9796, pp. 245–257, 2016.
DOI: 10.1007/978-3-319-45886-1_20

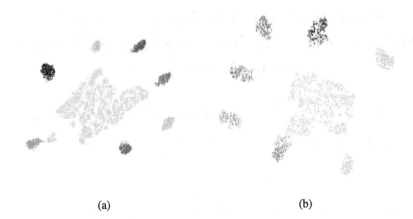

(a)   (b)

Fig. 1. t-SNE Visualization of semantic embedding of UCF and Vines before and after iterative training. The crosses represent auxiliary (UCF) samples and are color-coded according to their class labels. The yellow triangles represent unlabeled target training samples (vines). After iterations, many more vines merge with the clusters formed by the auxiliary samples. The leftover vines possibly belong to none of the action classes and hence do not merge into any cluster. Please see this visualization in color. (Color figure online)

and expensive. A better approach is to expand the scope of existing datasets and classifiers.

We present a simple incremental approach to transfer knowledge from a traditional labeled source dataset to a wilder unlabeled target dataset. The class of methods that try to mitigate the bias/shift between different distributions/datasets fall under the category of *transfer learning* methods. Recent approaches along these lines include works on dataset bias shift [20,26], domain adaptation [6,11,21], zero-shot learning [9,23], heterogeneous/multimodal transfer [14] and other transfer learning methods [1,3,19,33]. However, most of these methods work on image/object category problems or text-data problems and their application to web-scale wild video distributions remain untested. [30] use hierarchical category taxonomy tree, designed by professional linguists, to categorize Youtube videos. However, this approach cannot be extended for action classification as it is difficult to hand-craft a generalized taxonomy for actions. [25] propose a feature encoding that accounts for the bias introduced by dataset specific backgrounds for video classification. However, this method requires both source and target videos to be labeled.

We propose a simple, unsupervised approach that iteratively adapts the base classifiers trained on a labeled training set UCF50 to an unseen, unlabeled set of vines, by incrementally augmenting the training set with vines. Adopting the terminology of domain adaptation and transfer learning literature, we call the UCF50 labeled set an *auxiliary training set* and the unlabeled vines a *target training set*. We leverage a semantic space *word2vec* [15] as a common reference space to bring together the auxiliary and the target domains. To embed video features in this space, we learn a neural-network based embedding function [23]. We first learn this embedding using labeled samples of the auxiliary set and project both labeled and unlabeled samples from auxiliary and target sets into the semantic space. Figure 1(a) shows a t-Distributed Stochastic Neighbor Embedding (t-SNE) visualization of seven classes after projection into the semantic space. The auxiliary samples are represented by crosses, color-coded as per their class labels; the target samples are represented by yellow triangles. It can be clearly seen that the auxiliary and target domains are disparate. While auxiliary training samples (UCF) form separable clusters, most target training samples (vines) are cluttered and inseparable in the semantic space. Though it is not possible to reliably classify all target samples in this space, we use a multi-modal scoring function to select a few vine samples from the target that can be classified with high confidence. Our multi-modal scoring function also incorporates the knowledge from user-given hash-tags for classification. We add these samples to the labeled auxiliary training set, and retrain the embedding function using the augmented auxiliary training set. After several iterations of this process, auxiliary set is augmented with sufficient samples from the target distribution. Figure 1(b) shows the t-SNE visualization of the embedding after several iterations of augmentation and retraining. It can be seen that, after iterations, many more target samples merge with the clusters formed by the auxiliary samples.

A recent work [32] also leverages semanatic embedding for recognizing new action categories in a zero-shot learning framework for traditional datasets (UCF and HMDB). However, the focus of our work is on learning cross-domain action classification for wild social web-videos. Also, our method incrementally relearns the neural network allowing more non-linearity in the embedding function and utilizes multi-modal features that include motion features and hash-tags. The nature of this work is experimental and exploratory. We perform experiments for 7 action classes of UCF50 dataset and show that this surprisingly simple strategy works effectively and yields precision, recall, and F-measure improvement of 2 % to 10 % on an unseen vines test set. Please visit our web-page for more information and research resources, https://cvit.iiit.ac.in/projects/actionvines/.

2   Our Approach

The distribution of vines is widely different from traditional action classification datasets in terms of appearance, quality, content, editing, etc. For a classifier to work well for vines, it needs to be trained on a labeled set of vines. Except, manually annotating such ever-altering web data is tedious and impractical. Vines do come with user-given tags, and description but such tags cannot be considered reliable labels. Figure 2 shows stills from vines retrieved for two action words 'cycling' and 'diving' as queries. Though both sets of vines are hash-tagged with their respective action words, some vines are only related to the concept and not the human action, while some vines are completely unrelated to either the concept or the action. We tackle the problem of improving action classification

Fig. 2. Stills from sample vines (short video clips) retrieved for two queries, 'cycling' (top) and 'diving' (bottom). The vines in the red boxes are semantically related concepts to the query words but are negative examples for the query human action. The vines in the green boxes are positive examples for the respective human actions. The high intra-class variability is worth noting. (Color figure online)

Table 1. Number of samples in auxiliary and target sets across classes. For some classes the true positives are less than 25 % of the total samples in the target train set. This imbalance indicates the fact that 'hash-tags' can only provide noisy labels and other modalities need to be utilized for effectively labeling target training vines.

Action class		Billiards	Cycling	Diving	Golfswing	Horseride	Kayaking	Push up
Target domain (vines)	Train (total)	267	280	258	268	233	284	286
	Train (true +ves)	100	92	133	151	106	73	178
	Test	24	27	39	34	29	16	40
Auxiliary domain (UCF)		129	119	124	120	169	129	90

for vines by utilizing labeled samples from an auxiliary domain and unlabeled samples from a target domain with noisy and weak semantic information. In the following subsections, we provide details of data collection, multi-modal feature representation, and iterative training.

2.1 Data Collection and Statistics

We work on seven of the fifty action categories of UCF50 action recognition dataset. These seven classes are selected based on the sufficient availability of related videos on vine.co. The labeled samples of UCF50 belonging to these seven classes form our auxiliary domain/ auxiliary set and the vines form our target domain/ target set. To collect relevant vines for each action category, we use the action term as the query word and download the top 450 retrieved vines per category (restricted by the vine API). The retrieval of vines is based on the occurrence of the query word in either the corresponding 'hash-tags' or the description. We discard the vines that do not have the action category word as one of the hash-tags. Thus, we have a total of 2357 vines with the associated tags.

This forms our target domain. We divide this set into a target training set and a test set. Our incremental and iterative training for augmenting the auxiliary domain operates on the target training set and we report the performance of the final classifier on the test set. All the retrieved vines are manually annotated by three human operators but we never use the labels of the target training set in anyway for our training but only to gather data statistics, making our approach completely unsupervised.

Table 1 shows the distribution of samples across classes and auxiliary, target train, and test sets. Since, the hash-tags are noisy, many vines in the target set do not have the respective action (false positives). The test set is pruned to remove all such false positives. However, since our training is unsupervised, we do not alter the target train set. The first two rows in Table 1 shows the total samples in the target train set and the number of true positives for each class. We provide this statistic to demonstrate the fact that hash-tags are extremely noisy labels. This fact can also be observed from leftover vines in Fig. 1.

2.2   Feature Representation

Many feature representations based on spatio-temporal constructs [2,16,31], appropriate human body modeling [4,5], successful image features [8,22,29], etc. are proposed in action recognition literature. Our approach leverages multi-modal feature representation to reliably augment the auxiliary set with target samples. We use motion features, semantic embedding features, and tag-distribution features in our method. We explain these features and the related terminology in this section. More details on parameters and code are given in Sect. 3.

Motion Features: Motion encoding is the most preferred feature representation for action recognition training. We compute the fisher vector encoded improved dense trajectories (IDT) [27] for samples of both auxiliary and target sets. IDT features include histogram of oriented gradients (HoG), histogram of optical flow (HoF), and motion boundary histogram (MBH) descriptors across frames. To classify these features, we use linear support vector machines (SVM).

Semantic Features: Mikolov et al. [15] provide a mechanism to represent a word as a vector in a 300-dimensional vector space, commonly known as *word2vec* space. Socher et al. [23] proposed a neural network based supervised method to learn a non-linear function that embeds visual (image) features into the word2vec space based on the corresponding object category words. We use this framework and learn a semantic embedding function that projects motion features (fisher vectors) into the word2vec space corresponding to the action word. We call the resulting 300-dimensional representation, embedded semantic features, or simply semantic features.

Tag Features: Hash-tags can be seen as noisy semantic labels of a video provided by the users. We assume that similar videos will have similar tags. Tagged words are usually slangs which are used to describe a video in an informal manner and hence do not strictly adhere to the word2vec representation of word space. Hence, we utilize tag features in a separate framework. First, we collect all tags associated with the vines in our target dataset and perform stemming to obtain cleaner, non-redundant set of tag-words. We then create a histogram of all tag-words and form a tag dictionary by removing all singleton words. A tag feature for a vine is simply a binary vector of the dimension of the dictionary (1048 in our experiment), such that the value in i^{th} position indicates whether the ith tag in the dictionary is associated with the vine or not.

2.3 Iterative Training

Figure 3 shows a block diagram of the proposed iterative training method. Each step of this method is explained in detail here. We first describe the notations used, then discuss the strategy for initialization and incremental updation of the training set, followed by explanation of these updation rules, and sampling choices.

Notation: We denote the set of action categories as $\mathbb{C} = \{c_i \mid i \in [1,7]\}$, where $c_1 - c_7$ represent the seven action categories 'billiards', 'cycling', 'diving', 'golf', 'horseriding', 'kayaking', and 'pushups'. The negative label corresponding to an action category c_i is represented as $\tilde{c}_i$. The SVM classifiers for fisher vectors and embedded semantic features are denoted respectively by H_{FV} and H_{WV}. The auxiliary set features are represented as $\mathbb{A}$. The training set at k^{th} iteration for learning the classifiers for category c_i is denoted by $\mathbb{T}_k^{c_i}$. The sets of positive and negative examples in $\mathbb{T}_k^{c_i}$ are denoted respectively as $\mathbb{P}_k^{c_i}$ and $\mathbb{N}_k^{c_i} = \bigcup_{j \neq i} P_k^{c_j}$. The target set of unlabeled vines with hash-tag c_i are represented as $\mathbb{U}^{c_i}$. At k^{th} iteration, the set of remaining unlabeled vines is $\mathbb{U}_k^{c_i}$, $\mathbb{U}_k^{c_i} \subset \mathbb{U}^{c_i}$.

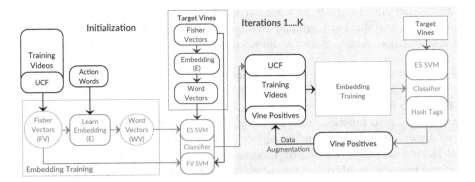

Fig. 3. Block representation of our iterative training approach. Left block shows the specifics of the initialization step and the right block shows the process for iterative updates. The embedding training sub-block (blue) is the same for both initialization and iteration steps (depicted in detail for only initialization step). (Color figure online)

Initialization: The initial training of classifiers for class c_i is performed using the auxiliary set (UCF50 examples) as the training set. At this point, all vines in the target set are unlabeled. Hence, for the 0th iteration,

$$\mathbb{T}_0 = \mathbb{A},\ \mathbb{P}_0^{c_i} = \mathbb{A}^{c_i},\ \mathbb{N}_0^{c_i} = \mathbb{A}^{\tilde{c}_i},\ \mathbb{U}_0^{c_i} = \mathbb{U}^{c_i}$$

For each class, we train the SVM classifiers H_{FV} and H_{WV} using samples from the initial training set $\mathbb{T}_0$. The SVM classifier for each class return a confidence score $\in [0, 1]$ for each target sample. The two SVM scores are multiplied to yield a combined confidence score for every vine sample in the unlabeled target set $\mathbb{U}_0^{c_i}$. The multiplicative scoring function penalizes the overall score when any of the two scores is low and helps to ensure that only the samples with highest confidence are labeled. We pick the top-K scoring vines as potential positive samples, where K is emperically selected to be 10% of the auxiliary positive set ($|\mathbb{P}_0^{c_i}|$) at every iteration. We update the negative set for a class c_i by adding the newly labeled positives of other classes as labeled negatives for c_i. The auxiliary set size can be fixed or modified incrementally as explained later. The positives and negatives in iteration k for the class c_i are denoted as $\mathbb{L}_k^{c_i}$ and $\mathbb{L}_k^{\tilde{c}_i} = \bigcup_{j \neq i} \mathbb{L}_k^{c_j}$. Note, we don't use tag based scoring in the initialization due to unavailability of tags for the initial auxiliary set.

Iterative Training and Update: The training set for class c_i at iteration $k > 0$ is formed by augmenting the newly labeled vines to the auxiliary set.

$$\mathbb{T}_k^{c_i} = \mathbb{T}_{k-1}^{c_i} \cup \mathbb{L}_{k-1}^{c_i} \cup \mathbb{L}_{k-1}^{\tilde{c}_i}, \qquad \mathbb{P}_k^{c_i} = \mathbb{P}_{k-1}^{c_i} \cup \mathbb{L}_{k-1}^{c_i}, \qquad \mathbb{N}_k^{c_i} = \mathbb{N}_{k-1}^{c_i} \cup \mathbb{L}_{k-1}^{\tilde{c}_i}$$

The parameters of the embedding function are re-estimated using the augmented training set. Our hypothesis is that by incrementally adding more vines to the training set, in each iteration, we slowly modify the initial embedding that worked well for the auxiliary set to adapt for the target set (vines). As we are not altering the fisher vector space, we drop the motion feature classifier (H_{FV}) after the initial iteration. The tag score for a target vine in iteration k is the average number of co-occurring tags between given vine and positively labeled vines in the previous iterations. The tag-score s_t is computed as follows,

$$s_t(x_t^v) = \frac{1}{|\mathbb{L}^{c_i}|} \frac{1}{\bar{n}_t} \sum_{x_p \in \mathbb{L}^{c_i}} \sum_{i=1}^{N_D} (x_t(i) * x_p(i)), \quad \text{where,} \quad \mathbb{L}^{c_i} = \mathbb{L}_{k-1}^{c_i} \cup \mathbb{L}_{k-2}^{c_i} \cup ... \mathbb{L}_1^{c_i}$$

Here, N_D is the size of the tag dictionary and $\bar{n}_t$ is the average number of tags per vine in the target set (15 in our experiment). The combined score of a target training vine is computed by multiplying the semantic space SVM confidence scores and the tag-score. The tag-score boosts the overall score of the test vines that have many co-occurring tags with the previously labeled positive vines. The tags help in distinguishing samples of different classes retrieved as a result of the hash-tag. For example, Apart from 'diving', 'sky-diving' and 'diving in a pool' will have different accompanying tags which will match accordingly to the currently classified/labeled vines. We stop the iterations when we have labeled approximately 50% of the auxiliary positives, i.e. $P_0^{c_i}$.

Sampling choice for auxiliary set augmentation: In addition to augmenting the auxiliary set, we also perform an experiment where we gradually replace the auxiliary samples by target samples. This approach allows us to diminish the influence of auxiliary samples and provide more priority to target samples. We evaluate the performance of our method for both sampling choices, with and without replacement in Sect. 3.

3 Experiments and Results

In this section, we explain the experimental setup, establish the baseline performance, and report the results of our method. In the next section, we present analysis and interpretation of these results.

3.1 Experimental Setup

Here, we explain the code setup and parameters used for feature computation and classifier training. To extract the motion features, we compute the improved dense trajectory descriptors [27, 28] for all videos using the code[1] by the authors. For fisher vector computation, the experimental parameters are same as [28] and the GMM parameters are estimated over UCF samples of 50 action classes. The fisher vectors thus computed are of 101,376 dimensions. For computing the semantic features, we embed the fisher vectors into the 300 dimensional word2vec space. For learning the embedding function, we use publicly available implementations of word2vec[2] and zero-shot learning[3]. For initializing the embedding function we use 400 hidden nodes and limit the maximum iterations to 1000. For computing the dictionary of tag-words, we first perform stemming – a commonly used trick in NLP applications to reduce the related forms of a word to its root form. From the remaining words we remove the singletons. The tag feature for a vine is a binary vector of the size of the tag dictionary such that each 0/1 element indicates whether that tag in the dictionary occurs with this vine or not. We use linear SVMs for fisher vector and semantic features classification in our iterative training. For SVMs we fix $C = 1$ and the weight for the positive class to be 7 times more than the negatives to compensate for fewer positive samples as compared to the negatives being added in each iteration.

3.2 Performance Evaluation

We evaluate the performance of our approach by classifying a test set using the semantic embedding learned in the final iteration. We compare the performance of our method with the baseline classifiers trained on the auxiliary dataset (UCF50) for semantic and motion features. We report precision, recall, and F-score for classification of the test dataset using all methods in Table 2 and the

---

[1] https://lear.inrialpes.fr/people/wang/improved_trajectories.

[2] https://code.google.com/p/word2vec/.

[3] https://github.com/mganjoo/zslearning.

Table 2. Comparison table for our methods with the baselines.

Class	Iterative training (ours)						Baseline methods					
	With-replacement			Without-replacement			FV_svm			ES_knn		
	Prec.	Rec.	F-score	Prec.	Rec.	F-score	Prec.	Rec.	F-score	Prec.	Rec.	F-score
Billiards	.750	.875	.807	73.3	.916	**.814**	1.00	.166	.285	1.00	.250	.400
Cycling	.956	.814	**.880**	.884	.851	.867	.585	.888	.705	.621	.851	.718
Diving	.750	.538	.626	.814	.564	**.666**	.645	.512	.571	.620	.461	.529
Golf-Swing	.909	.588	.714	1.00	.588	**.740**	.641	.735	.684	.638	.676	.657
Horseriding	.634	.896	.742	70.2	.896	.787	.857	.827	**.842**	.857	.827	**.842**
Kayaking	.388	.875	**.538**	.361	.812	.500	.407	.687	.511	.333	.750	.461
Pushups	.967	.750	.845	.969	.800	**.876**	.846	.825	.835	.891	.825	.857

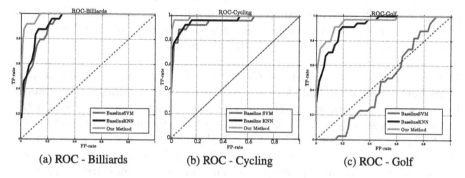

(a) ROC - Billiards   (b) ROC - Cycling   (c) ROC - Golf

Fig. 4. ROC comparison of our iterative training method (without replacement) with baseline FV+SVM and ES+NN.

ROC-curves for three classes are shown in Fig. 4. The two baseline classifiers trained on the auxiliary dataset are represented as, (i) Motion-only (FV+SVM), and, (ii) Semantic-only (ES+NN).

For Motion-only baseline, we train 7 one-vs-rest linear SVM classifiers and assign the labels based on the highest decision value of the corresponding classifiers. For Semantic-only baseline, we train an embedding function using the auxiliary set and use it to project the test samples to the semantic space. We classify the samples to the nearest class in the word2vec space using L_2 distance. The semantic embedding function learnt using our iterative approach is also evaluated in a similar fashion (ES+NN). We evaluate our final semantic embedding for both sampling choices, when (i) the auxiliary set videos are replaced by the newly labeled vines (with replacement), (ii) the auxiliary set is only augmented by the newly labeled vines (without replacement).

4 Analysis

Iterative Relearning of Embedding Function. In Fig. 5, we show the effect of relearning the embedding function by t-SNE visualization of the test samples.

In 0th iteration, we see UCF samples forming separate clusters but vines forming an inseparable distribution. This shows that the embedding function learnt solely using auxiliary set is insufficient to classify the test set. However, after iterations we see that the embedding function projects most of the test samples around their class labels and close to the corresponding UCF samples. This observation supports our hypothesis of incrementally modifying the embedding function using augmented training set. If this hypothesis was faulty then the embedding function would degrade performance of the test classification after iterations (see Fig. 5 and Table 2). In supplementary material we show additional details and visualizations per iteration.

Comparision of Baseline Classifiers. Table 2 shows that the baseline methods, FV+SVM and ES+NN, have comparable performances. However, ES+NN operates in a significantly lower dimensional space (101376 vs. 300) and has much lower time complexity serving as a better alternative.

Without-replacement vs. Baseline Classifiers. This sampling method outperforms both baseline methods for all classes except 'Horseriding' & 'Kayaking'. For Horseriding we obtain a higher recall, however due to fall in precision the overall performance decreases. Though our method performs better than ES+NN but falls short on precision against FV+SVM. Kayaking contains the least ratio of true positives ($<25\%$) in the target set (Table 1). Incremental addition of target samples still helps in improving precision and recall as compared to ES+NN baseline for 'kayaking'.

With-replacement vs. Baseline Classifiers. This sampling method performs significantly better for all classes except 'Horseriding'. For 'Kayaking' our method performs marginally better and as mentioned earlier the improvement is limited due to the lack of positives in the target dataset. For 'Billiards', we achieve an acceptable precision with significantly higher recall against both the baselines which show a highly skewed performance.

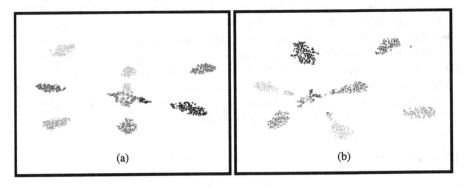

Fig. 5. t-SNE Visualization of semantic embedding of UCF and Vines before and after iterative training. This visualization is best viewed in color. (Color figure online)

With-replacement vs. without-replacement. We experimented with these two sampling choices to see whether diminishing the influence of auxiliary domain will hamper or aid the process of learning the embedding function. It is evident from Table 2, for 5 of the 7 classes without-replacement performs better and for the other two classes the difference is marginal. This result suggests that augmenting the auxiliary domain by target domain without replacement has a positive influence on iterative learning.

5   Conclusion and Future Work

In this paper we explored the problem of improving the performance of action classification for an unseen unlabeled wild domain by utilizing labeled examples from a simpler source domain. We presented a simple iterative technique that improves semantic embedding of video features into a structured reference space to bring together the disparate auxiliary and target domains. We showed the effectiveness of this iterative technique on the task of action classification for 7 classes in vines. We also experimented with two sampling choices for augmenting the auxiliary domain and presented detailed analysis of results. In future, we would like to explore the application of this method for annotation and tag enrichment applications.

References

1. Gong, B., Shi, Y., Sha, F., Grauman, K.: Geodesic flow kernel for unsupervised domain adaptation. In: 2012 IEEE Conference on Computer Vision and Pattern Recognition (CVPR), pp. 2066–2073 (2012)
2. Gorelick, L., Blank, M., Shechtman, E., Irani, M., Basri, R.: Actions as space-time shapes. Trans. Pattern Anal. Mach. Intell. **29**(12), 2247–2253 (2007)
3. Daume III, H.: Frustratingly easy domain adaptation. In: Proceedings of the 45th Annual Meeting of the Association of Computational Linguistics, pp. 256–263 (2007)
4. Ikizler, N., Duygulu, P.: Histogram of oriented rectangles: a new pose descriptor for human action recognition. Image Vis. Comput. **27**(10), 1515–1526 (2009)
5. Jhuang, H., Gall, J., Zuffi, S., Schmid, C., Black, M.J.: Towards understanding action recognition. In: IEEE International Conference on Computer Vision (ICCV), pp. 3192–3199 (2013)
6. Jiang, J., Zhai, C.X.: A two-stage approach to domain adaptation for statistical classifiers. In: Proceedings of the Sixteenth ACM Conference on Information and Knowledge Management, CIKM 2007, pp. 401–410 (2007)
7. Khosla, A., Zhou, T., Malisiewicz, T., Efros, A.A., Torralba, A.: Undoing the damage of dataset bias. In: Fitzgibbon, A., Lazebnik, S., Perona, P., Sato, Y., Schmid, C. (eds.) ECCV 2012, Part I. LNCS, vol. 7572, pp. 158–171. Springer, Heidelberg (2012)
8. Klser, A., Marszaek, M., Schmid, C.: A spatio-temporal descriptor based on 3d-gradients. In: BMVC 2008 (2008)
9. Kodirov, E., Xiang, T., Fu, Z., Gong, S.: Unsupervised domain adaptation for zero-shot learning. In: 2015 IEEE International Conference on Computer Vision (ICCV), pp. 2452–2460 (2015)

10. Kuehne, H., Jhuang, H., Garrote, E., Poggio, T., Serre, T.: HMDB: a large video database for human motion recognition. In: 2011 IEEE International Conference on Computer Vision (ICCV), pp. 2556–2563 (2011)

11. Kulis, B., Saenko, K., Darrell, T.: What you saw is not what you get: domain adaptation using asymmetric kernel transforms. In: 2011 IEEE Conference on Computer Vision and Pattern Recognition, pp. 1785–1792 (2011)

12. Laptev, I., Marszalek, M., Schmid, C., Rozenfeld, B.: Learning realistic human actions from movies. In: IEEE Conference on Computer Vision and Pattern Recognition, 2008. CVPR 2008, pp. 1–8 (2008)

13. Liu, J., Luo, J., Shah, M.: Recognizing realistic actions from videos in the wild. In: IEEE Conference on Computer Vision and Pattern Recognition, 2009. CVPR 2009, pp. 1996–2003 (2009)

14. Mansour, Y., Mohri, M., Rostamizadeh, A.: Domain adaptation with multiple sources. In: Koller, D., Schuurmans, D., Bengio, Y., Bottou, L. (eds.) Advances in Neural Information Processing Systems, vol. 21, pp. 1041–1048 (2009)

15. Mikolov, T., Chen, K., Corrado, G., Dean, J.: Efficient estimation of word representations in vector space. CoRR, abs/1301.3781 (2013)

16. Niebles, J.C., Wang, H., Fei-Fei, L.: Unsupervised learning of human action categories using spatial-temporal words. Int. J. Comput. Vis. **79**(3), 299–318 (2008)

17. Niebles, J.C., Chen, C.-W., Fei-Fei, L.: Modeling temporal structure of decomposable motion segments for activity classification. In: Daniilidis, K., Maragos, P., Paragios, N. (eds.) ECCV 2010, Part II. LNCS, vol. 6312, pp. 392–405. Springer, Heidelberg (2010)

18. Over, P., Awad, G., Michel, M., Fiscus, J., Kraaij, W., Smeaton, A.F., Quenot, G., Ordelman, R.: TRECVID 2015 - an overview of the goals, tasks, data, evaluation mechanisms and metrics. In: Proceedings of TRECVID 2015 (2015)

19. Pan, S.J., Yang, Q.: A survey on transfer learning. IEEE Trans. Knowl. Data Eng. **22**(10), 1345–1359 (2010)

20. Ponce, J., et al.: Dataset issues in object recognition. In: Ponce, J., Hebert, M., Schmid, C., Zisserman, A. (eds.) Toward Category-Level Object Recognition. LNCS, vol. 4170, pp. 29–48. Springer, Heidelberg (2006)

21. Qiu, Q., Patel, V.M., Turaga, P., Chellappa, R.: Domain adaptive dictionary learning. In: Fitzgibbon, A., Lazebnik, S., Perona, P., Sato, Y., Schmid, C. (eds.) ECCV 2012, Part IV. LNCS, vol. 7575, pp. 631–645. Springer, Heidelberg (2012)

22. Scovanner, P., Ali, S., Shah, M.: A 3-dimensional sift descriptor and its application to action recognition. In: Proceedings of the 15th International Conference on Multimedia, pp. 357–360 (2007)

23. Socher, R., Ganjoo, M., Sridhar, H., Bastani, O., Manning, C.D., Ng, A.Y.: Zero-shot learning through cross-modal transfer. CoRR, abs/1301.3666 (2013)

24. Soomro, K., Zamir, A.R., Shah, M.: UCF101: a dataset of 101 human actions classes from videos in the wild. CoRR, abs/1212.0402 (2012)

25. Sultani, W., Saleemi, I.: Human action recognition across datasets by foreground-weighted histogram decomposition. In: 2014 IEEE Conference on Computer Vision and Pattern Recognition (CVPR), pp. 764–771 (2014)

26. Torralba, A., Efros, A.A.: Unbiased look at dataset bias. In: 2011 IEEE Conference on Computer Vision and Pattern Recognition (CVPR), pp. 1521–1528 (2011)

27. Wang, H., Schmid, C.: Action recognition with improved trajectories. In: 2013 IEEE International Conference on Computer Vision (ICCV), pp. 3551–3558 (2013)

28. Wang, H., Oneata, D., Verbeek, J., Schmid, C.: A robust and efficient video representation for action recognition. Int. J. Comput. Vis. 1–20 (2015)

29. Wang, J., Liu, Z., Wu, Y., Yuan, J.: Mining actionlet ensemble for action recognition with depth cameras. In: 2012 IEEE Conference on Computer Vision and Pattern Recognition, pp. 1290–1297 (2012)
30. Wang, Z., Zhao, M., Song, Y., Kumar, S., Li, B.: Youtubecat: Learning to categorize wild web videos. In: The Twenty-Third IEEE Conference on Computer Vision and Pattern Recognition, CVPR 2010, pp. 879–886 (2010)
31. Weinland, D., Ronfard, R., Boyer, E.: Free viewpoint action recognition using motion history volumes. Comput. Vis. Image Underst. **104**(2), 249–257 (2006)
32. Xu, X., Hospedales, T., Gong, S.: Semantic embedding space for zero-shot action recognition. In: 2015 IEEE International Conference on Image Processing (ICIP), pp. 63–67 (2015)
33. Yang, J., Yan, R., Hauptmann, A.G.: Cross-domain video concept detection using adaptive SVMs. In: Proceedings of the 15th International Conference on Multimedia (2007)

Poster Session

Discrete Tomography by Continuous Multilabeling Subject to Projection Constraints

Matthias Zisler[(✉)], Stefania Petra, Claudius Schnörr, and Christoph Schnörr

Heidelberg University, Heidelberg, Germany
`zisler@math.uni-heidelberg.de`

Abstract. We present a non-convex variational approach to non-binary discrete tomography which combines non-local projection constraints with a continuous convex relaxation of the multilabeling problem. Minimizing this non-convex energy is achieved by a fixed point iteration which amounts to solving a sequence of convex problems, with guaranteed convergence to a critical point. A competitive numerical evaluation using standard test-datasets demonstrates a significantly improved reconstruction quality for noisy measurements from a small number of projections.

1 Introduction

Computed tomography [14] deals after spatial discretization in an algebraic set-up with the reconstruction of 2D- or 3D-images $u \in \mathbb{R}^N$ from a small number of noisy measurements $b = Au + \nu \in \mathbb{R}^m$. The latter correspond to line integrals that sum up all absorptions over each ray transmitted through the object. A given projection matrix $A \in \mathbb{R}^{m \times N}$ encodes this imaging geometry. Applications range from medical imaging [3] to natural sciences and industrial applications, like non-destructive material testing [7]. Many situations require to keep the number of measurements as low as possible, which leads to a small number of projections and hence to a severely ill–posed reconstruction problem.

To cope with such problems, a common assumption in the field of *discrete tomography* [8] concerns knowledge of a *finite* range of $u \in \mathcal{L}^N$, $\mathcal{L} := \{c_1, ..., c_K\} \subset [0,1]$, that is, u represents a piecewise constant function. Our main concern in this paper is to effectively exploit the additional prior knowledge in terms of $\mathcal{L}$, besides the projection constraints, in order to solve the *discrete reconstruction problem*

$$Au = b \quad \text{s.t.} \quad u_i \in \mathcal{L}, \quad \forall i = 1, \ldots, N, \tag{1}$$

which generally is a NP-hard problem.

Related work on discrete tomography considers either *binary* or *non-binary* (multivalued) problems. The latter ones are considerably more involved.

Electronic supplementary material The online version of this chapter (doi:10. 1007/978-3-319-45886-1_21) contains supplementary material, which is available to authorized users.

B. Rosenhahn and B. Andres (Eds.): GCPR 2016, LNCS 9796, pp. 261–272, 2016.
DOI: 10.1007/978-3-319-45886-1_21

Regarding *binary discrete tomography*, Weber et al. [21,29] proposed to combine a quadratic program with a non-convex penalty which gradually enforces binary constraints. More recently, Kappes et al. [9] showed how a binary discrete graphical model and a sequence of s-t graph-cuts can be used to take into account the affine projection constraints and to recover high-quality reconstructions.

Regarding *non-binary discrete tomography*, an extension of the latter approach is not straightforward due to the nonlocal projection constraints. Weber [27, Chap. 6] proposed a non-convex term for non-binary discrete tomography that we derive in a natural way in the present work. However, Weber's approach differs with respect to the data term for the projection constraints, regularization and optimization, and additionally requires parameter tuning.

Because u is assumed to be piecewise constant, an obvious approach is to consider sparsity promoting priors. The authors of [23] proposed a dynamic programming approach for minimizing the ℓ_0-norm of the gradient. However, the set $\mathcal{L}$ of feasble intensities is not exploited. In the convex setting, the integrality constraints are dropped and priors like the ℓ_1-norm or the total variation (TV) are used [5,6,22], with a postprocessing step to round the continuous solution to a piecewise constant one. This approach connects discrete tomography and the fast evolving field of *compressive sensing* with corresponding recovery guarantees [5]. Again, however, the prior information of the range of the image to be reconstructed is not involved in the optimization process. We focus next on methods that make use of the set $\mathcal{L}$ during the reconstruction process.

Tuysuzoglu et al. [25] casted the non-binary discrete reconstruction problem into a series of submodular binary problems within an α-expansion approach by linearizing the ℓ_2-fidelity term around an iteratively updated working point. This local approximation discards a lot of information, and a significantly larger number of projections is required to get reasonable reconstructions. Maeda et al. [12] suggested a probabilistic formulation which couples a continuous reconstruction with the Potts model. Alternating optimization is applied to maximize the *a posteriori* probability locally. However, there is no guarantee that these alternating continuous and discrete block coordinate steps converge.

Ramlau et al. [10] investigated the theoretical regularization properties of the piecewise constant Mumford-Shah functional [13] applied to linear ill-posed problems. In earlier work [19], they considered discrete tomography reconstruction using this framework. The difficult geometric optimization of the partition is carried out by a level-set approach and additionally the intensities $\mathcal{L}$ were estimated in an alternating fashion. By contrast, our approach is based on a convex relaxation of the perimeter regularization and the set $\mathcal{L}$ is assumed to be known beforehand.

Varga et al. [26] suggested a heuristic algorithm which is adaptively combing an energy formulation with a non-convex polynomial in order to steer the reconstruction towards the feasible values. Batenburg et al. [2] proposed the *Discrete Algebraic Reconstruction Technique (DART)* algorithm which starts with a continuous reconstruction by a basic algebraic reconstruction method, followed by thresholding to ensure a piecewise constant function. These steps interleaved with smoothing are iteratively repeated to refine the locations where u jumps. This heuristic approach yields good reconstructions in practice but cannot be characterized by an objective function that is optimized.

We regard [2,26] as state-of-the-art approaches for the experimental comparison.

Contributions. We present a novel variational approach to the discrete tomography reconstruction problem in the general non-binary case. Contrary to existing work, we utilize both the non-local projection constraints and the feasible set of intensities $\mathcal{L}$ in connection with an established convex relaxation of the multilabeling approach with a Potts prior. We show how the resulting non-convex overall energy can be optimized efficiently by a fixed-point iteration which requires to solve a convex problem at each step. In this way, the derivation of our non-convex data and its local updates arise naturally. We also propose a suitable rounding procedure as post-processing step, because the integrality constraints are relaxed. A comprehensive numerical evaluation demonstrates the superior reconstruction performance of our approach compared to related work.

2   Reconstruction by Constrained Multilabeling

In this section, we first reformulate the discrete reconstruction problem (1) as a constraint combinatorial multilabeling problem. Then we derive a tractable variational approximation and suggest a proper rounding procedure.

2.1   Constrained Multilabeling Problem

We assume that there are less measurements than pixels $m \ll N$ and hence that the discrete reconstruction problem (1) is ill-posed and requires regularization. A common choice is the Potts model [18], $R(u) = \|\nabla u\|_0 := |\{i \mid (\nabla u)_i \neq 0\}|$ for sparse gradient regularization which favours piecewise constant images. In presence of noisy measurements b, we use the more general constraints $\underline{b}(\epsilon) \leq Au \leq \overline{b}(\epsilon)$ instead of $Au = b$, where ϵ is an upper bound of the noise level. As a result, the discrete reconstruction problem can be rewritten as

$$E(u) = \lambda \cdot \|\nabla u\|_0 \quad \text{s.t.} \quad \underline{b}(\epsilon) \leq Au \leq \overline{b}(\epsilon) \quad \wedge \quad u_i \in \mathcal{L} \quad \forall i = 1...N. \quad (2)$$

We refer to problem (2) as a *constrained multilabeling problem* with Potts regularization but point out that, from the viewpoint of graphical models, the system of affine inequalities induces (very) high-order potentials. This high-order interaction induced by the non-local constraints results in a non-standard labeling problem which becomes intractable for discrete approaches and larger problem sizes. We adopt, therefore, the strategy of solving a sequence of convex relaxations in order to minimize a non-convex energy, which properly approximates the original problem.

2.2   Approximate Variational Problem

Our starting point is the established convex relaxation of the multilabeling problem [11,17,30]. Minimizing the energy in (3a) below with respect to z over the set of relaxed indicator vectors (3b) assigns to each given image pixel from u^0 a label of the set $\mathcal{L} = \{c_1, \ldots, c_K\}$. The discretized total variation, weighted by λ, and the simplex constraints G constitute a basic convex relaxation of the integrality constraints with respect to z.

$$E(z, u^0) = \sum_{i=1}^{N} \sum_{k=1}^{K} z_{ik} \left(u_i^0 - c_k \right)^2 + \lambda \sum_{k=1}^{K} \| \nabla z_k \|_1 \tag{3a}$$

$$\text{s.t.} \quad z \in G := \left\{ z \in [0,1]^{N \times K} : \sum_{k=1}^{K} z_{ik} = 1, \ \forall i = 1, \ldots, N \right\}. \tag{3b}$$

Regarding the notation, we denote by z_k, $k \in \{1, \ldots, K\}$ the k-th *column vector* of z and by $z_{ik} = (z_k)_i$ the entries of the *matrix* z.

Next, we add the projection constraints $\underline{b} \leq Au \leq \overline{b}$ to the relaxed energy (3a) by transforming the indicator variables z back to their corresponding intensities with the linear operator $W : G \to \mathbb{R}^N$, $z \mapsto \sum_{l=1}^{K} c_l z_l$ which preserves convexity of the resulting energy

$$E(z, u^0) = \sum_{i=1}^{N} \sum_{k=1}^{K} z_{ik} \left(u_i^0 - c_k \right)^2 + \lambda \sum_{k=1}^{K} \| \nabla z_k \|_1$$
$$+ \delta_{\mathbb{R}_+^m}(AWz - \underline{b}) + \delta_{\mathbb{R}_-^m}(AWz - \overline{b}) + \delta_G(z). \tag{4}$$

Note that the constraints $\underline{b} \leq AWz \leq \overline{b}$ and $z \in G$ are implemented by indicator functions $\delta_{\mathbb{R}_+^m}$ and $\delta_{\mathbb{R}_-^m}$.

In tomography, no image u^0 is given, however. Therefore, we cannot drop the unary data term in Eq. (4), since the constraints are feasible for all convex combinations of prototypes c_k. In other words, the constraints only constrain the value of a pixel but do not indicate how the indicator variables should realize this value (similar to estimating a vector given only its magnitude).

A straightforward approach would be to start with some initial guess u^0, e.g. computed using some another reconstruction method, followed by iteratively applying this approach above. This gives the fixed point iteration

$$z^{n+1} = \arg \min_z E(z, Wz^n). \tag{5}$$

At every iteration a convex problem has to be solved whose solution updates the unary data term. This raises the question whether the iteration converges and which overall energy is actually optimized?

To address these questions, we first eliminate u^0 in a principled way. Note that $E(z, \cdot)$ in (4) is differentiable with respect to the second argument. We invoke Fermat's (first order) optimality condition $u^* = Wz$ which says that the optimal u^* must be equal to the weighted average of the labels c_k. Substituting this optimality condition back into the energy (4) results in the final version of the proposed energy which only depends on z,

$$
E(z) = \sum_{i=1}^{N} \sum_{k=1}^{K} z_{ik} \left((Wz)_i - c_k \right)^2 + \lambda \sum_{k=1}^{K} \| \nabla z_k \|_1 \\
+ \delta_{\mathbb{R}_+^m} (AWz - \underline{b}) + \delta_{\mathbb{R}_-^m} (AWz - \overline{b}) + \delta_G(z). \tag{6}
$$

This new energy function, Eq. (6), is non-convex because of the products in the first term which measures the discreteness of z. We call this term *phase data term* and denote it by

$$
D(z) := \sum_{i=1}^{N} \sum_{k=1}^{K} z_{ik} \left((Wz)_i - c_k \right)^2. \tag{7}
$$

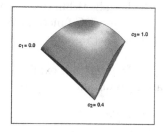

Fig. 1. Visualization of the phase data term $D(z)$ for $N = 1$ over the probability simplex G, the vertices correspond to the values $\mathcal{L} = \{0.0, 0.4, 1.0\}$. Note that the minimum is attained at the vertices of the simplex which correspond to unit vectors.

Using the notation introduced after Eq. (3), the i-th summand of (7) reads

$$
\sum_{k=1}^{K} z_{ik} \left(\sum_{l=1}^{K} z_{il} c_l - c_k \right)^2 = \sum_{k=1}^{K} z_{ik} c_k^2 - \left(\sum_{k=1}^{K} z_{ik} c_k \right)^2 \tag{8}
$$

which is concave with respect to the vector z_i. Consequently, $D(z)$ given by (7) is concave as well. Figure 1 shows a plot of $D(z)$. Weber [27, Chap. 6] proposed this term for discrete tomography which arises here in a natural way, whereas his overall approach differs with respect to data term for the projection constraints, regularization and optimization.

3   Optimization

In this section, we reformulate the objective function (6) as a DC program [15] and work out a corresponding optimization algorithm.

DC Programming. A large subclass of non-convex optimization problems are DC functions (difference of convex functions) which can be solved by DC Programming [15]. This generalizes subgradient optimization of convex functions to local optimization of DC functions. Accordingly, basic concepts of convex optimization like duality and KKT conditions were extended to DC functions [24]. The basic form of a DC program is given by

$$z^* = \arg\min_z g(z) - h(z), \tag{9}$$

where $g(z)$ and $h(x)$ are proper, lower semicontinuous, convex functions. There exists a simplified version of the DC algorithm [16] for minimizing (9) which guarantees convergence to a critical point by starting with $z^0 \in \mathrm{dom}(g)$ and then alternatingly applying the updates

$$v^n \in \partial h(z^n) \qquad \text{and} \qquad z^{n+1} \in \partial g^*(v^n) \tag{10}$$

until a termination criterion is reached, where g^* denotes the Legendre-Fenchel conjugate [20] of g. To apply the DC algorithm to our non-convex energy $E(z)$ in (6), we rewrite $E(z) = g(z) - h(z)$ as a DC function. We set $h(z) = -D(z)$ since the phase data term (7) is concave by (8), and we denote by $g(z)$ the remaining convex terms from Eq. (6).

In order to make the step $z^{n+1} \in \partial g^*(v^n)$ explicit, we apply the subgradient inversion rule of convex analysis to obtain

$$z^{n+1} \in \partial g^*(v^n) \quad \Leftrightarrow \quad v^n \in \partial g(z^{n+1}) \quad \Leftrightarrow \quad 0 \in \partial g(z^{n+1}) - v^n \tag{11}$$

which is equivalent to the convex optimization problem

$$z^{n+1} = \arg\min_z g(z) - \langle v^n, z \rangle. \tag{12}$$

Because h is differentiable, the first step of (10) reads

$$v^n \in \partial h(z^n) \quad \Leftrightarrow \quad v^n = -\nabla D(z^n), \tag{13}$$

where the gradient of D at z for pixel i and label c_k is given by (see Lemma 1 from the supplementary material)

$$(\nabla D(z))_{ik} = \frac{\partial D(z)}{\partial z_{ik}} = ((Wz)_i - c_k)^2, \qquad i = 1, \dots, N, \quad k = 1, \dots, K. \tag{14}$$

Combining equations (13) and (14) and inserting into equation (12) yields

$$z^{n+1} = \arg\min_z E(z, Wz^n) = \arg\min_z g(z) + \sum_{i=1}^{N} \sum_{k=1}^{K} z_{ik} ((Wz^n)_i - c_k)^2. \tag{15}$$

We notice that the DC algorithm, summarized as Algorithm 1 below, agrees with the iteration (5), and hence *proves its convergence*. We apply the primal dual (PD) algorithm proposed by [4] to solve each convex subproblem (16).

Algorithm 1. DC Fixed Point Algorithm

---

1. Initialization: choose any $z^0 \in \mathbb{R}^{n \times k}$
2. Generate a sequence $(z^n)_{n \in \mathbb{N}}$ by solving the convex problems

$$z^{n+1} = \arg\min_z E(z, Wz^n) \tag{16}$$

   until a termination criterion is met.

Rounding Step. Recall that the data term $D(z)$ of (6) only steers the solution to the finite set of feasible values $\mathcal{L}$. As a consequence, for vanishing regularization parameter λ, the minimizer z will correspond to indicator vectors z_i that assign a unique label to each pixel i. For larger values of λ which are more common in practice, however, the minimizing vectors z_i will not be integral in general. Therefore, a post-processing step for rounding the solution is required.

Given the minimizer z^* of (6), we propose to select a label for each pixel i as a post-processing step by solving the local problems

$$\hat{u}_i^* = \arg\min_{c \in \mathcal{L}} |(Wz^*)_i - c|, \qquad i = 1, \ldots, N. \tag{17}$$

Note that this method differs from the common rounding procedure of multilabeling approaches which select the label c_k if $z_{ik} = \max\{z_{i1}, \ldots, z_{iK}\}$.

4 Numerical Experiments

Set-up. In this section, we compare our approach to state-of-the-art approaches for non-binary discrete tomography in limited angles scenarios. Specifically, we considered the Discrete Algebraic Reconstruction Technique ($DART$) [2] and the energy minimization method from Varga et al. [26] (*Varga*). As multivalued test-datasets we adapted the binary phantoms from Weber et al. [28] to more labels, shown as phantom 1,2 and 3 by Fig. 2. Phantom 5 in Fig. 2 was taken from [2] and phantom 4 is the well-known Shepp-Logan phantom. We created noisy scenarios by applying Poisson noise to the measurements b with a signal-to-noise ratio of $SNR = 20$ db. The geometrical setup was created by the ASTRA-toolbox [1], where we used parallel projections along equidistant angles between 0 and 180 degrees. Each entry a_{ij} of the matrix A corresponds to the length of the line segment of the i-th projection ray passing through the j-th pixel in the image domain. The width of the sensor-array was set 1.5 times the image size, so that every pixel intersects with a least a single projection ray.

Implementation Details. Each subproblem of Algorithm 1 was approximately solved using the primal dual (PD) algorithm [4] limited to 1000 iterations or until the primal dual gap drops below 0.1. The outer iteration was terminated if the change of the energy between two subsequent iterations, normalized by the number of pixels, was smaller than 10^{-5} in the noiseless case and 10^{-4} in the

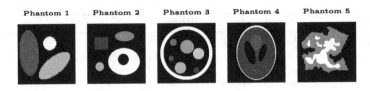

Fig. 2. The 5 different phantoms used for the numerical evaluation.

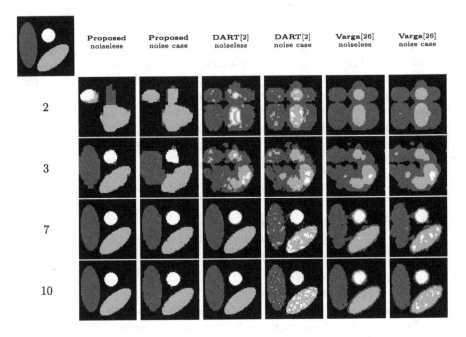

Fig. 3. Visual results of experiment phantom 1.

noisy case. Additionally, we limited the number of outer iterations to 20. For DART we used the publicly available implementation included in the ASTRA-toolbox [1] and for the method of Varga [26] we used our own implementation in MATLAB since no public code was available. We tried to use the default parameters of the competing approaches as proposed by their authors. However, since the test-datasets differ in size, we slightly adjusted the parameters in order to get best results for every algorithm and problem instance.

Performance Measure. For the evaluation we measured the relative pixel error, that is the relative number of erroneously reconstructed pixels as compared to the groundtruth.

Results. Figure 4 shows all results of the numerical evaluation. For each test-datasets (phantoms 1 - 5), the left plot displays the relative pixel error for increasing numbers of projection angles. On the right, the corresponding runtime is

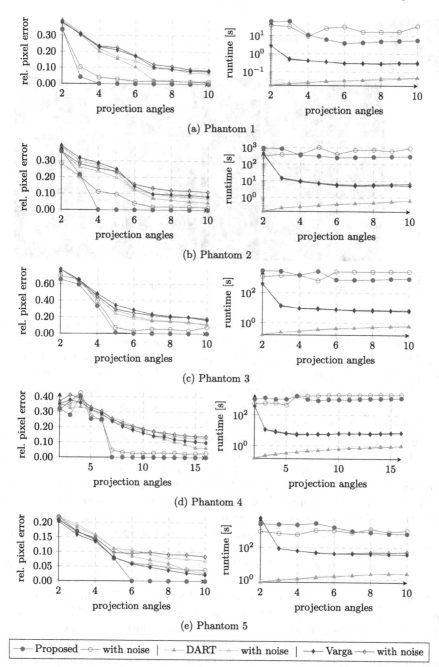

(a) Phantom 1

(b) Phantom 2

(c) Phantom 3

(d) Phantom 4

(e) Phantom 5

| —●— Proposed —○— with noise | —▲— DART —△— with noise | —◆— Varga —◇— with noise |

Fig. 4. Numerical evaluation of the approaches for the different test-datasets and increasing (but small) numbers of projections, in the noiseless case (filled markers) and in the noisy case (non-filled markers), with noise level $SNR = 20$ db. The relative pixel error is shown. The proposed approach gives perfect reconstructions with the least number of projection angles in the noiseless case and also returns high-quality reconstructions in the presence of noise, compared to the other approaches.

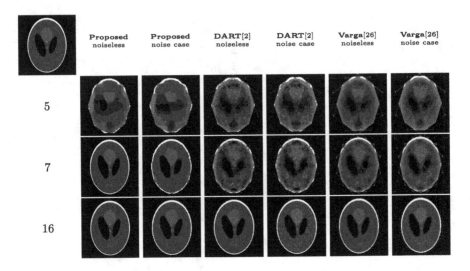

Fig. 5. Visual results of experiment phantom 4.

shown as log-scaled plot. For each algorithm two curves are drawn: filled markers correspond to the noiseless case and non-filled markers correspond to the noisy case. The results show that the proposed approach returns a perfect reconstruction with the least number of projection angles in the noiseless case among all approaches. In the scenarios, the proposed algorithm is performing better, too. In the noiseless case phantom 1 can be almost perfectly reconstructed from only 3 projection angles and fully from 4 by the proposed approach whereas DART needs 7 projection to get an almost perfect reconstruction and the method of Varga needs at least 7 projections to get a reasonable reconstruction. These visual differences can be seen in Fig. 3. This ranking of the performance of the approaches is similar for phantoms 2,3 and 5, except for the phantom 5 in the noiseless case where the approach of Varga performs better than DART. Figure 5 shows the results for phantom 4, where our approach is able to fully reconstruct from merely 7 projections in the noiseless case and returns a good piecewise-constant result in the noisy case. Due to a lack of space, we refer to Appendix B of the supplementary material for the visualization of the results for all test-datasets.

Regarding the runtime (right plots from Fig. 4), DART is the fastest approach, Varga is in between DART and the proposed approach, which is clearly consuming more runtime to return more accurate solutions. However, if computational performance is important, the proposed approach could be easily parallelized and implemented e.g. in CUDA to run on modern graphics cards.

5   Conclusion and Future Work

We presented a novel non-convex variational approach for solving the discrete tomography reconstruction in the general non-binary case. The approach combines a convex relaxation of the multilabeling problem with Potts prior and the non-local tomographic projection constraints. The feasible set of labels is taken into account by a non-convex data term which naturally emerges when the function to be reconstructed is represented as a convex combination of these values. A DC algorithm reliably minimizes the overall objective function and provably converges. The reconstruction performance turned out to be superior to the state of the art.

In future work, we plan to improve the running time and focus on the theoretical aspects of this approach. The proposed data term (7), in particular, fits nicely into spatially continuous variational formulations and thus may indicate ways for further improvement.

References

1. Aarle, W., Palenstijn, W., Beenhouwer, J., Altantzis, T., Bals, S., Batenburg, K., Sijbers, J.: The ASTRA toolbox: a platform for advanced algorithm development in electron tomography. Ultramicroscopy **157**, 35–47 (2015)
2. Batenburg, K., Sijbers, J.: DART: a practical reconstruction algorithm for discrete tomography. IEEE Trans. Image Proc. **20**(9), 2542–2553 (2011)
3. Bushberg, J., Seibert, J., Leidholdt, E., Boone, J.: The Essential Physics of Medical Imaging, 3rd edn. Wolters Kluwer, Philadelphia (2011)
4. Chambolle, A., Pock, T.: A first-order primal-dual algorithm for convex problems with applications to imaging. J. Math. Imaging Vis. **40**(1), 120–145 (2011)
5. Denitiu, A., Petra, S., Schnörr, C., Schnörr, C.: Phase transitions and cosparse tomographic recovery of compound solid bodies from few projections. Fundamenta Informaticae **135**, 73–102 (2014)
6. Goris, B., Broek, W., Batenburg, K., Mezerji, H., Bals, S.: Electron tomography based on a total variation minimization reconstruction technique. Ultramicroscopy **113**, 120–130 (2012)
7. Hanke, R., Fuchs, T., Uhlmann, N.: X-ray based methods for non-destructive testing and material characterization. Nucl. Instrum. Methods Phys. Res. Sect. A Accelerators, Spectrometers, Detectors Assoc. Equip. **591**(1), 14–18 (2008)
8. Herman, G., Kuba, A.: Discrete Tomography: Foundations, Algorithms and Applications. Birkhäuser, Basel (1999)
9. Kappes, J.H., Petra, S., Schnörr, C., Zisler, M.: TomoGC: binary tomography by constrained graphcuts. In: Gall, J., Gehler, P., Leibe, B. (eds.) GCPR 2015. LNCS, vol. 9358, pp. 262–273. Springer, Heidelberg (2015)
10. Klann, E., Ramlau, R.: Regularization properties of mumford-shah-type functionals with perimeter and norm constraints for linear ill-posed problems. SIAM J. Imaging Sci. **6**(1), 413–436 (2013)
11. Lellmann, J., Becker, F., Schnörr, C.: Convex optimization for multi-class image labeling with a novel family of total variation based regularizers. In: Proceedings of the IEEE Conference on Computer Vision (ICCV 2009) Kyoto, Japan, vol. 1, pp. 646–653 (2009)
12. Maeda, S., Fukuda, W., Kanemura, A., Ishii, S.: Maximum a posteriori X-ray computed tomography using graph cuts. J. Phys. Conf. Ser. **233**, 012023 (2010)
13. Mumford, D., Shah, J.: Optimal approximations by piecewise smooth functions and associated variational problems. Commun. Pure Appl. Math. **42**(5), 577–685 (1989)

14. Natterer, F.: The Mathematics of Computerized Tomography, 1 edn. Society for Industrial and Applied Mathematics, Philadelphia (2001). http://epubs.siam.org/doi/abs/10.1137/1.9780898719284
15. Dinh, T.P., Bernoussi, S.: Algorithms for solving a class of nonconvex optimization problems. methods of subgradients. In: Hiriart-Urruty, J.B. (ed.) Fermat Days 85: Mathematics for Optimization. North-Holland Mathematics Studies, vol. 129, pp. 249–271. North-Holland, Amsterdam (1986)
16. Dinh, T., Hoai An, L.: Convex analysis approach to D.C. programming: theory, algorithms and applications. Acta Math. Vietnamica 22(1), 289–355 (1997)
17. Pock, T., Chambolle, A., Cremers, D., Bischof, H.: A convex relaxation approach for computing minimal partitions. In: IEEE Conference on Computer Vision and Pattern Recognition, CVPR 2009, pp. 810–817, June 2009
18. Potts, R.B.: Some generalized order-disorder transformations. Math. Proc. Camb. Phil. Soc. 48, 106–109 (1952)
19. Ramlau, R., Ring, W.: A mumford-shah level-set approach for the inversion and segmentation of X-ray tomography data. J. Comput. Phys. 221(2), 539–557 (2007)
20. Rockafellar, R.T., Wets, R.J.B.: Variational Analysis, vol. 317. Springer, Heidelberg (2009)
21. Schüle, T., Schnörr, C., Weber, S., Hornegger, J.: Discrete tomography by convex-concave regularization and D.C. programming. Discrete Appl. Math. 151(13), 229–243 (2005)
22. Sidky, E.Y., Pan, X.: Image Reconstruction in Circular Cone-Beam Computed Tomography by Constrained, Total-Variation Minimization. Phys. Med. Biol. 53(17), 4777 (2008)
23. Storath, M., Weinmann, A., Frikel, J., Unser, M.: Joint image reconstruction and segmentation using the potts model. Inverse Probl. 31(2), 025003 (2015)
24. Toland, J.F.: Duality in nonconvex optimization. J. Math. Anal. Appl. 66(2), 399–415 (1978)
25. Tuysuzoglu, A., Karl, W., Stojanovic, I., Castanon, D., Unlu, M.: Graph-cut based discrete-valued image reconstruction. IEEE Trans. Image Process. 24(5), 1614–1627 (2015)
26. Varga, L., Balázs, P., Nagy, A.: An energy minimization reconstruction algorithm for multivalued discrete tomography. In: 3rd International Symposium on Computational Modeling of Objects Represented in Images, Rome, Italy, Proceedings, pp. 179–185. Taylor & Francis (2012)
27. Weber, S.: Discrete tomography by convex-concave regularization using linear and quadratic optimization. Ph.D. thesis, Ruprecht-Karls-Universität, Heidelberg, Germany (2009)
28. Weber, S., Nagy, A., Schüle, T., Schnörr, C., Kuba, A.: A benchmark evaluation of large-scale optimization approaches to binary tomography. In: Kuba, A., Nyúl, L.G., Palágyi, K. (eds.) DGCI 2006. LNCS, vol. 4245, pp. 146–156. Springer, Heidelberg (2006)
29. Weber, S., Schnörr, C., Hornegger, J.: A linear programming relaxation for binary tomography with smoothness priors. Electron. Notes Discrete Math. 12, 243–254 (2003)
30. Zach, C., Gallup, D., Frahm, J., Niethammer, M.: Fast global labeling for real-time stereo using multiple plane sweeps. In: Proceedings of the Vision, Modeling, and Visualization Conference 2008, VMV 2008, Konstanz, Germany, 8–10 October 2008, pp. 243–252 (2008)

Reduction of Point Cloud Artifacts Using Shape Priors Estimated with the Gaussian Process Latent Variable Model

Jens Krenzin[(⊠)] and Olaf Hellwich[(⊠)]

Computer Vision & Remote Sensing, TU Berlin, Berlin, Germany
{jens.krenzin,olaf.hellwich}@tu-berlin.de

Abstract. We present a method that removes point cloud artifacts like noisy points, missing data and outliers from a point cloud using a learned shape prior. The shape prior is learned with the Gaussian Process Latent Variable Model from a set of reference objects. As input data our method uses the estimated object pose from an object detector and a segmented point cloud. We show that the estimated shape prior is capable of modeling fine details to a certain degree. We also show that after applying our method the measured accuracy and completeness is increasing.

1 Introduction

Traditional multi-view stereo approaches like [6,7] are able to estimate a 3D point cloud from a set of images, but do not use prior knowledge about the object classes in the scene for this process. Consider the case that we already know the object classes and the poses for each object in the scene by using an object detector like [5]. If we want to estimate the surface of a cup for example, we as a human already know that a cup has a handle, has a cylindric form, is hollow, one side closed and the other side is open. We as a human can use such prior knowledge to decide intuitively how the surface of an instance from the class *cup* should look like. If we can teach a machine how an object of a specific class is shaped, we could use this knowledge to enhance the accuracy or the completeness of the estimated 3D surface.

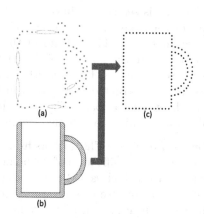

Fig. 1. (a) Erroneous point cloud (Green: Noisy points, Blue: Holes, Red: Outliers). (b) Shape prior. (c) Corrected point cloud (Color figure online)

The focus of this work is to correct three types of point cloud artifacts: noise, outliers and missing data using the prior knowledge about the object class. In Fig. 1 this problem is visualized, where Fig. 1a shows a measured erroneous point

B. Rosenhahn and B. Andres (Eds.): GCPR 2016, LNCS 9796, pp. 273–284, 2016.
DOI: 10.1007/978-3-319-45886-1_22

cloud of a cup. The point cloud has several holes (marked in blue) and outliers (marked in red). Also the point cloud consists of several noisy points (marked in green). The aim of this work is to correct these point cloud artifacts using a Shape Prior. The Shape Prior is shown in Fig. 1b and the corrected Point cloud is shown in Fig. 1c.

2   Related Work

The idea of using prior knowledge from object detection to support the 3D reconstruction process is known as *Semantic 3D* in the literature [16]. In this section we want to give an overview of several data driven surface reconstruction approaches which can solve the problem defined in Sect. 1. Data driven reconstruction algorithms use a predefined database of shapes from an object class. Non-data driven algorithms like [12] can also solve the problem defined in Sect. 1, but do not use a prior knowledge about the object class. Similar to [3] we divide the data driven algorithms into multiple subgroups:

Inpainting: In [18] a method was proposed which first obtains a 3D model from incomplete surface scans and uses a database of 3D shapes to provide geometric priors for regions of missing data. It then retrieves and warps suitable models to conform with the input data and merges the warped model with the input data to obtain the final shape.

Rigid retrieval: In [24] the 3D information is given with an RGB-D image. First this image is segmented into a set of regions with semantic labels. The depth data of each semantic region is then matched with a set of 3D models from a given database. The 3D model that fits best the depth data is then rigidly transformed to the position of the depth image and represents one object in the reconstructed scene. The algorithm iterates over all segmented regions. At the end the reconstructed scene will consist of several rigidly transformed objects from the given database. The main difference to [18] is that the scene consists only of the rigidly transformed shapes.

Non-rigid retrieval: The authors from [17] present an approach where they alternate between classification of the point cloud and non-rigidly fitting a deformable template to each classified part of the point cloud. The deformed templates are then used to resolve classification ambiguities. This is a key difference to [24], where classification and template fitting are working separately.

Part composition: In [25] the authors use a number of labeled 3D models to compose a new 3D shape from the parts of the given models. The process is guided by the spatial layout of the parts. The idea is similar to [8] where the reconstructed surface is also composed of multiple parts.

Model-based SFM: The authors of [2] use a set of training data which consists of multiple 3D scans of an object class. They first learn a mean shape and a set of weighted anchor points for a specific object class. The mean shape captures the commonality of shapes across the class and the anchor points encode similarities between the instances. Then the measured input point cloud is used to find the position of these anchor points for the current measurement. They use these points to warp the mean shape to a modified shape. At the end they use several points of the point cloud to model several details into the modified shape.

Retrieval based on GP-LVM: The GP-LVM is a dimension reduction method and is described in Sect. 3.3 in more detail. In the literature the GP-LVM has been used to estimate a 3D shape prior for object reconstruction from single monocular images [4,21,26] and also object segmentation and tracking [20,22]. The authors of [4] merge the shape prior estimated using the GP-LVM with a scene reconstructed from a monocular SLAM system. To find the pose of the object in the scene they used the DPM object detector [5]. They have shown that using the shape prior estimated from the GP-LVM they are able to reduce the noise in the reconstructed surface and to reduce the reconstruction error.

3   Theoretical Background

3.1   Signed Distance Function

The signed distance function (SDF) is an implicit representation of an object shape S where, at each point p, we know the distance from that point to the closest point on the object surface [11]. The domain Ω_S of a SDF consists of 3 parts: The region inside the object Ω_S^-, the region outside the object Ω_S^+ and the region on the object surface $\partial\Omega_S$. The formula for the SDF is given with

$$\phi(p) = \begin{cases} -d(p), & \text{if } p \in \Omega_S^- \\ 0, & \text{if } p \in \partial\Omega_S \\ d(p), & \text{if } p \in \Omega_S^+, \end{cases} \tag{1}$$

where the distance $d(p)$ is given by

$$d(p) = \min_{\widetilde{p} \in \partial\Omega_S} (|p - \widetilde{p}|). \tag{2}$$

In Fig. 2 an example for the signed distance function is shown for a 2D shape. The white filled circle in Fig. 2a represents the shape and Fig. 2b shows the corresponding signed distance function as a surface. To compute the signed distance function we use the algorithm [15].

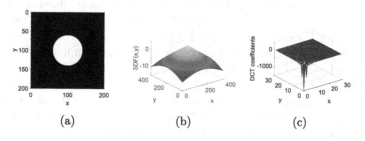

Fig. 2. (a) 2D shape. (b) Signed distance function. (c) DCT coefficients

3.2 Discrete Cosine Transform

The discrete cosine transform (DCT) [1] is a numerical transformation which transforms a time domain signal to a frequency domain signal. It is mostly used for the compression of audio or image data. In this work we use the DCT to compress the SDF. An example is shown in Fig. 2, where Fig. 2b shows the SDF and Fig. 2c shows the corresponding DCT coefficients for this SDF. In this example the signal for the SDF has a size of 400×400. After applying the DCT, the actual information about the shape is stored in the first 15×15 DCT coefficients. The information about the general shape is stored in the lower frequency bands and the fine details of a shape are stored in the upper frequency bands. Since this shape represents just a circle the upper frequency bands are nearly 0. The approach of compressing the SDF using the DCT was also used in [4, 20–22, 26].

3.3 Gaussian Process Latent Variable Model

The following section gives an introduction to mathematical aspects of the Gaussian Process Latent Variable Model [13]. We will refer to this as GP-LVM in the following sections. Consider an observed dataset $Y = [y_1, ..., y_N]^T$ with D dimensions and N observations. We now want to find a mapping $M : Y \to X$, where $X = [x_1, ..., x_N]^T$ is a set with $q < D$ dimensions and N observations. This task is commonly known as dimension reduction, where one possible solution to this task would be the Principal Component Analysis (PCA) [9, 19]. We will refer to the inverse mapping as $M^{-1} : X \to Y$. During the dimension reduction step we lose information stored in Y, which leads to

$$M^{-1}(M(y_i)) = y'_i = y_i + \delta_E, \tag{3}$$

where $\delta_E \in \mathbb{R}^D$ is the estimation error caused by the dimension reduction. Here an example: In the PCA a set of D eigenvectors and D eigenvalues are calculated. By omitting the eigenvectors which correspond to the smallest eigenvalues and using the remaining eigenvectors to project a data point y_i to a latent point x_i we will lose information stored in Y. If we project x_i back to the data space Y, we will get $y'_i = y_i + \delta_E$. The error δ_E will increase if we use less eigenvectors to project a data point y_i to a latent point x_i.

A *Latent Variable Model* (LVM) relates a set of lower dimensional latent variables $X \in \mathbb{R}^{N \times q}$ to a set of observed variables $Y \in \mathbb{R}^{N \times D}$. The relation is given through a set of m parameters $\theta \in \mathbb{R}^m$ [13]. A Latent Variable Model can be defined probabilistically [13]. We describe the mapping function for a Latent Variable Model (LVM) as $M_{LVM}^{-1} : X, \theta \to Y$. In Fig. 3a an example for a Latent Variable Model (LVM) with $N = 1$ observation is shown. From the latent point x_1 a mapping is shown, where the mapping to the observed point y_1 has the highest probability $p = 0.70$. A *Gaussian Process* (GP) specifies a distribution over a function space [13]. Consider the case that several points x_i are known where the function $f(x)$ should go trough. An example is shown

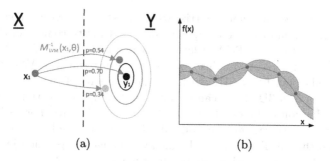

(a)   (b)

Fig. 3. (a) Visualization for a Latent Variable Model (LVM) with the latent space X and the observed space Y. The probability for each mapping is marked in red. (b) Visualization of the distribution over a function space for a Gaussian Process (GP). The points x_i where the function $f(x)$ should go trough are marked in red, the mean function is marked in green. The function space where a possible function can go trough is marked in blue (Color figure online)

in Fig. 3b. A distribution over the function space focuses around the points x_i and widens when no point is given. Since the mean and variance of this distribution changes for every x it is necessary to define a mean function $\mu(x)$ and a covariance function $K(x) = \sigma^2(x)I$ for the distribution over the function space. We refer to a function $f(x)$, which is modelled with a Gaussian Process as $f(x) \sim \mathcal{N}\left(\mu(x), \sigma^2(x)I\right)$, where I is the identity matrix.

The Gaussian Process Latent Variable Model (GP-LVM) is a Latent Variable Model where the mapping function from a latent space X to an observed space Y is modelled with a Gaussian Process. It is used to reduce the dimensionality of the observed data Y. One major advantage to the PCA is that the mapping from X to Y can be non-linear. As stated in [13] the probability for an observation y_j given a latent point x_j is given with

$$p(y_j|x_j) = \mathcal{N}\left(y_j|\mu(x_j), \sigma(x_j)^2 I\right). \tag{4}$$

The mean function $\mu(x_j)$ is defined with

$$\mu(x_j) = Y^T \cdot K^{-1} \cdot k_j \tag{5}$$

and the covariance function $\sigma^2(x_j)$ is defined with

$$\sigma^2(x_j) = \kappa(x_i, x_j) - k_j^T \cdot K^{-1} \cdot k_j. \tag{6}$$

In the Eqs. (5) and (6) a kernel function $\kappa(x_i, x_j)$ is used. In this work we use a RBF kernel:

$$\kappa(x_i, x_j) = \theta_1 \exp\left(-\frac{\theta_2}{2}\|x_i - x_j\|^2\right) + \theta_3 + \theta_4 \delta_{ij}, \tag{7}$$

where θ_{1-4} are the Gaussian Process hyperparameters, which have to be learned for a given set Y. The estimation of these hyperparameters is described in [13].

The matrix K is the covariance matrix, which is estimated with the kernel function $K = \kappa(X, X)$ and the vector $k_j = \kappa(X, x_j)$ is the j-th column of the matrix K. As stated in [13] the GP-LVM leads to a mapping $M^{-1} : X \rightarrow Y$, but not to a mapping $M : Y \rightarrow X$. In this work we are using the GP-LVM to describe the DCT coefficients for a SDF with a small amount of parameters X. The parametrization of a 3D shape can become very complex and thus an effective dimension reduction technique like the GP-LVM is necessary. For each point in the latent space x we can generate one 3D shape, which we later use to remove artifacts from the calculated point cloud. If we change the position in the latent space x, then the corresponding Shape Prior will deform.

3.4   Evaluation Measures

There exist several evaluation methods in the literature to calculate how good the estimation of a 3D surface is in comparison to a ground truth surface. One is the computation of the accuracy and the completeness [10, 23]. For the computation of both metrics the ground truth model and the measurement are represented as a point cloud.

Accuracy: To compute the accuracy we first compute for every point p_i from the measured point cloud the distance $d_{i,min}$ to the closest point of the ground truth point cloud. The accuracy is then the mean value of all distances.

Completeness: To compute the completeness we first compute for every point p_j from the ground truth point cloud the distance $d_{j,min}$ to the closest point of the measured point cloud. The completeness is the percentage of distances which are smaller than a given threshold t_{compl}.

4   Methodology

In this section we describe our method, which we successfully implemented in C++ and Matlab. The framework is divided in 7 subparts. Each of these subparts is part of a pipeline which is shown in Fig. 4.

Building Latent Space for the GP-LVM: To estimate a shape prior we first need a set of reference shapes. In Fig. 5 the first 10 models of our reference shapes are shown. In our experiment we used $N_{Ref} = 50$ reference models. We first

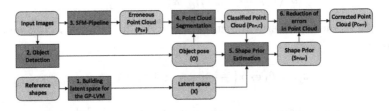

Fig. 4. Pipeline for the reduction of reconstruction errors

align all shapes together using ICP [28], so that all of them have the same scale, translation and rotation. We then compute the SDF for all aligned shapes using the algorithm [15]. After this step we compute the DCT for all shapes and cut out the first K_{DCT} coefficients for every dimension. For each shape we get a cube of DCT coefficients with K_{DCT}^3 scalar values. We then reshape each cube to a vector with K_{DCT}^3 columns and compose all resulting vectors row-wise into the matrix $Y_{Ref} \in \mathbb{R}^{N_{Ref} \times K_{DCT}^3}$. After this step we train our GP-LVM to find a lower dimensional subspace for Y_{Ref} with K_{Lat} dimensions. The observed space is $Y \in \mathbb{R}^{K_{DCT}^3}$ and the latent space is $X \in \mathbb{R}^{K_{Lat}}$.

Object Detection: In our framework we used the DPM object detector [5] to find the object pose O (the position and rotation) in the scene. As stated in [2] the estimated object pose will have an estimation error which we reduce during the Shape Prior Estimation using the ICP algorithm [28].

SFM-Pipeline: In this work we are using VisualSFM [27] as our SFM-Pipeline. We refer to the calculated erroneous point cloud as P_{Err}.

Point Cloud Segmentation: To segment the point cloud into the region of the object $P_{Err,C}$ we are using the SAC-Segmentation. We initialize the segmentation process with positions of the object middle points found by [5].

Shape Prior Estimation: In this step we estimate the shape that fits best to the point cloud $P_{Err,C}$. We later use this shape to fill holes, remove outliers and reduce the noise in the point cloud. To estimate the shape we are minimizing the following energy function:

$$E(\boldsymbol{x}) = \sum_{i=1}^{N} \left(\phi_{S(\boldsymbol{x})}(\boldsymbol{p_i})\right)^2, \tag{8}$$

where $\boldsymbol{x} = (x_1, x_2, ..., x_{K_{Lat}})^T$ is the position in the latent space X, $S(\boldsymbol{x})$ is the corresponding shape for this latent point $\boldsymbol{x}$ and $\boldsymbol{p_i} = (p_{xi}, p_{yi}, p_{zi})^T$ is the position of the i-th point in the 3D point cloud $P_{Err,C}$. To get the SDF $\phi_{S(\boldsymbol{x})}$

Fig. 5. The first 10 shapes from the training data set

(a) n_I=25 (b) n_I=30 (c) n_I=35 (d) n_I=40 (e) n_I=45 (f) n_I=50

Fig. 6. Current shape priors after n_I optimization steps

for a latent point x we compute the vector of DCT coefficients for the current latent point x_{curr} using the mapping $M^{-1} : X \rightarrow Y$ of the trained GP-LVM, reshape the vector into a cube, set the remaining DCT coefficients outside of the cube to 0 and calculate the inverse DCT for the cube of DCT coefficients. After our optimization converged or a maximum number of iterations is exceeded we estimate the triangulated surface of our shape prior. Since the optimization used an SDF, we need to convert this implicit surface into a mesh S_{Prior}. For this step we use the marching cubes algorithm [14]. Figure 6 shows the calculated mesh after n_I iterations. The mesh S_{Prior} is used to reduce the artifacts in the points cloud.

Reduction of Artifacts in Point Cloud: At first we remove the outliers from the point cloud. For this we compute for every point p_i of $P_{Err,C}$ the minimum distance d_{out} to the surface of the Shape Prior S_{Prior}. The points where the distance d_{out} is above a threshold t_{out} are treated as outliers and will be removed from the point cloud. After we removed the outliers from the point cloud, we want to reduce the noise of the remaining points. The points where the minimum distance d_{out} to the surface of the Shape Prior S_{Prior} is under the threshold t_{out} are treated as noisy points and we project them on the surface of the Shape Prior S_{Prior}. In the last step we fill the holes in the point cloud. At first we uniformly sample the surface of the Shape Prior S_{Prior} to get a point cloud version P_{Prior} of the shape prior. For every point of the shape prior we compute the minimum distance d_{dens} to a point from the point cloud $P_{Err,C}$. If the minimum distance d_{dens} is over a threshold t_{dens}, the corresponding point from P_{Prior} is added to $P_{Err,C}$. After this step all holes of the point cloud $P_{Err,C}$ are closed. After these corrections we get the *corrected* version of this point cloud P_{Corr}.

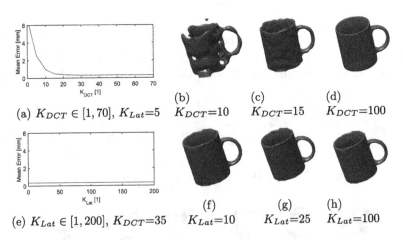

Fig. 7. (a), (e) Mean error for different evaluations. (b)–(d) Variation of K_{DCT} with $K_{Lat} = 5$. (f)–(h) Variation of K_{Lat} with $K_{DCT} = 35$

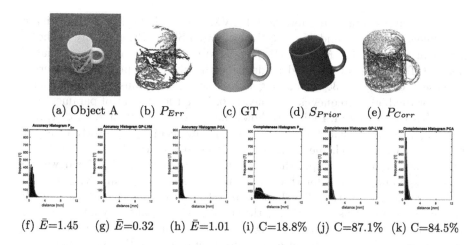

(a) Object A   (b) P_{Err} (c) GT   (d) S_{Prior} (e) P_{Corr}

(f) $\bar{E}$=1.45   (g) $\bar{E}$=0.32   (h) $\bar{E}$=1.01   (i) C=18.8%   (j) C=87.1%   (k) C=84.5%

Fig. 8. Results for Object A

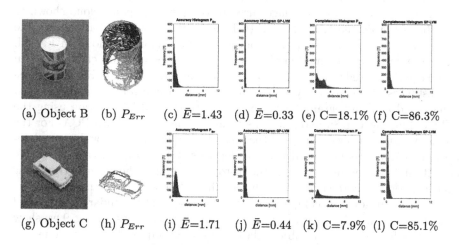

(a) Object B   (b) P_{Err} (c) $\bar{E}$=1.43   (d) $\bar{E}$=0.33   (e) C=18.1%   (f) C=86.3%

(g) Object C   (h) P_{Err} (i) $\bar{E}$=1.71   (j) $\bar{E}$=0.44   (k) C=7.9%   (l) C=85.1%

Fig. 9. Results for Object B and C

5   Results and Discussion

If we want to enhance the accuracy and the completeness of the reconstructed object using a shape prior, then the shape prior must be more accurate and complete than the measurement itself. Only for this case we can profit from the presented method. One question that arises is: How accurate can the estimated Shape Prior be? For this investigation we compare the ground truth model with the estimated shape prior and measure the mean error. For the estimation process we use a perfect point cloud without any noise. Two important parameters for the estimation process are K_{DCT} and K_{Lat}. The amount of parameters that describe our shape is $\mathbb{P} = K_{DCT}^3 + K_{Lat} + N_\theta$, where $N_\theta = 4$ is the number of hyperparameters for the GP-LVM. In the following we investigate the influence of K_{DCT} and K_{Lat} on the estimated Shape Prior. Figure 7a shows the mean accuracy for $K_{DCT} \in [1, 70]$ and $K_{Lat} = 5$. It can be seen that if more DCT coefficients are used to describe the object shape, the mean error decreases. At $K_{DCT} \approx 35$ the curve goes in saturation, because the DCT coefficients for the higher frequencies are nearly 0. Here the amount of parameters is $\mathbb{P} = 35^3 + 5 + 4 = 42884$. Figure 7b shows the mean accuracy for $K_{Lat} \in [1, 200]$ and $K_{DCT} = 35$. It can be seen that the mean accuracy is mostly constant if K_{Lat} is varied, which means that the actual size of the latent space has a smaller impact on the shape, than the DCT coefficients. In Fig. 7b–d we see the corresponding shapes for three different values of K_{DCT} and $K_{Lat} = 5$. In Fig. 7b we clearly see that the shape is mostly destroyed, because not enough DCT coefficients are used. In Fig. 7c the shape is visible, but very uneven at the surface. In Fig. 7d we can see a ringing effect that occurs, because we cut out the first K_{DCT} DCT coefficients in every dimensions and set the remaining DCT coefficients to 0 in the inverse DCT. In Fig. 7f–h we see the corresponding shapes for three different values of K_{Lat} and $K_{DCT} = 35$. The shapes are mostly equal. In Fig. 8a we see one of the images used to compute the point cloud shown in Fig. 8b. In Fig. 8c the ground truth (GT) for this measurement is shown. The shape prior for the reduction of errors in the point cloud is shown in Fig. 8d. After applying our presented method we get the corrected point cloud shown in Fig. 8e. Here we used as parameters $K_{DCT} = 35$ and $K_{Lat} = 5$. In Fig. 8f–i we see the distances of the accuracy and completeness of the erroneous and corrected point cloud as a histogram. In Fig. 8g and j we show the correction using the GP-LVM and in Fig. 8h and k are the results using the standard PCA. For the accuracy histograms we computed the Mean Error ($\bar{E}$) in mm. For the completeness histograms we computed the completeness (C) with $t_{compl} = 1.6\,mm$. We also fitted a gamma function into the histograms to show how the distributions change after the correction. It is shown, that after applying our method the measured accuracy and completeness are increased. The standard PCA could also be used, but delivers a worse accuracy and completeness. In Fig. 9 we show the results for two different object classes. For each object class we have used a dataset of similar objects. Object C has a more complex surface structure and the achieved accuracy after the correction step is slightly worse than for object A or B. The more details a surface from a object class has and the more variation in the class exist, the more difficult it is to create a corresponding training set.

6   Conclusion

We presented a method that removes point cloud artifacts like noisy points, missing data and outliers from a point cloud using a learned shape prior. The shape prior is learned with the Gaussian Process Latent Variable Model from a set of reference objects. As input data our method uses the estimated object pose from an object detector and a segmented point cloud. We have shown that the estimated shape prior is capable of modeling fine details to a certain degree.

We have also shown that after applying our method the measured accuracy and the completeness is increasing. For the future work we could enhance the completeness and accuracy even more if we compose the shape prior of multiple shape parts to handle object classes with a more complex surface.

References

1. Ahmed, N., Natarajan, T., Rao, K.R.: Discrete cosine transfom. IEEE Trans. Comput. **23**(1), 90–93 (1974)
2. Bao, S.Y.Z., Chandraker, M., Lin, Y., Savarese, S.: Dense object reconstruction with semantic priors. In: CVPR, pp. 1264–1271. IEEE (2013)
3. Berger, M., Tagliasacchi, A., Seversky, L.M., Alliez, P., Levine, J.A., Sharf, A., Silva, C.: State of the art in surface reconstruction from point clouds. In: Eurographics STAR (Proceedings of EG 2014) (2014)
4. Dame, A., Prisacariu, V.A., Ren, C.Y., Reid, I.D.: Dense reconstruction using 3D object shape priors. In: 2013 IEEE Conference on Computer Vision and Pattern Recognition, Portland, pp. 1288–1295, 23–28 June 2013
5. Felzenszwalb, P.F., Girshick, R.B., McAllester, D., Ramanan, D.: Object detection with discriminatively trained part based models. IEEE Trans. Pattern Anal. Mach. Intell. **32**(9), 1627–1645 (2010)
6. Furukawa, Y., Curless, B., Seitz, S.M., Szeliski, R.: Towards internet-scale multiview stereo. In: CVPR (2010)
7. Furukawa, Y., Ponce, J.: Accurate, dense, and robust multi-view stereopsis. IEEE Trans. Pattern Anal. Mach. Intell. **32**(8), 1362–1376 (2010)
8. Gal, R., Shamir, A., Hassner, T., Pauly, M., Or, D.C.: Surface reconstruction using local shape priors. In: Belyaev, A., Garland, M. (eds.) Geometry Processing. The Eurographics Association (2007)
9. Hotelling, H.: Analysis of a complex of statistical variables into principal components. J. Educ. Psychol. **24**, 417–441 (1933)
10. Jensen, R., Dahl, A., Vogiatzis, G., Tola, E., Aanæs, H.: Large scale multi-view stereopsis evaluation. In: 2014 IEEE Conference on Computer Vision and Pattern Recognition (CVPR), pp. 406–413. IEEE (2014)
11. Jones, M.W., Baerentzen, J.A., Sramek, M.: 3D distance fields: a survey of techniques and applications. IEEE Trans. Vis. Comput. Graph. **12**(4), 581–599 (2006)
12. Kazhdan, M.M., Hoppe, H.: Screened poisson surface reconstruction. ACM Trans. Graph. **32**(3), 29 (2013)
13. Lawrence, N.D.: Probabilistic non-linear principal component analysis with Gaussian process latent variable models. J. Mach. Learn. Res. **6**, 1783–1816 (2005)
14. Lorensen, W.E., Cline, H.E.: Marching cubes: a high resolution 3D surface construction algorithm. In: SIGGRAPH, pp. 163–169 (1987)
15. Maurer Jr., C.R., Qi, R., Raghavan, V.: A linear time algorithm for computing exact Euclidean distance transforms of binary images in arbitrary dimensions. IEEE Trans. Pattern Anal. Mach. Intell. **25**(2), 265–270 (2003)
16. Moons, T., Gool, L.J.V., Vergauwen, M.: 3D reconstruction from multiple images: Part 1 - principles. Found. Trends Comput. Graph. Vis. **4**(4), 287–404 (2009)
17. Nan, L., Xie, K., Sharf, A.: A search-classify approach for cluttered indoor scene understanding. ACM Trans. Graph. **31**(6), 137:1–137:10 (2012)
18. Pauly, M., Mitra, N.J., Giesen, J., Gross, M., Guibas, L.J.: Example-based 3D scan completion. In: Proceedings of the Third Eurographics Symposium on Geometry Processing. SGP 2005, Eurographics Association, Aire-la-Ville, Switzerland (2005)

19. Pearson, K.: On lines and planes of closest fit to systems of points in space. Phil. Mag. **2**, 559–572 (1901)
20. Prisacariu, V.A., Reid, I.D.: Nonlinear shape manifolds as shape priors in level set segmentation and tracking. In: The 24th IEEE Conference on Computer Vision and Pattern Recognition, CVPR 2011, Colorado Springs, pp. 2185–2192, 20–25 June 2011
21. Prisacariu, V.A., Segal, A.V., Reid, I.: Simultaneous monocular 2D segmentation, 3D pose recovery and 3D reconstruction. In: Lee, K.M., Matsushita, Y., Rehg, J.M., Hu, Z. (eds.) ACCV 2012, Part I. LNCS, vol. 7724, pp. 593–606. Springer, Heidelberg (2013)
22. Ren, C.Y., Prisacariu, V., Reid, I.: Regressing local to global shape properties for online segmentation and tracking. Int. J. Comput. Vision **106**(3), 269–281 (2013)
23. Seitz, S., Curless, B., Diebel, J., Scharstein, D., Szeliski, R.: A comparison and evaluation of multi-view stereo reconstruction algorithms. In: IEEE Computer Society Conference on Computer Vision and Pattern Recognition (CVPR 2006), vol. 1, pp. 519–526. IEEE Computer Society, New York (2006)
24. Shao, T., Xu, W., Zhou, K., Wang, J., Li, D., Guo, B.: An interactive approach to semantic modeling of indoor scenes with an RGBD camera. ACM Trans. Graph **31**(6), 136:1–136:11 (2012)
25. Shen, C.H., Fu, H., Chen, K., Hu, S.M.: Structure recovery by part assembly. ACM Trans. Graph. **31**(6), 180: 1–180: 11 (2012)
26. Wang, Q., Wang, F., Li, D., Wang, X.: Clustering-based latent variable models for monocular non-rigid 3D shape recovery. In: Huang, D.-S., Jo, K.-H., Wang, L. (eds.) ICIC 2014. LNCS, vol. 8589, pp. 162–172. Springer, Heidelberg (2014)
27. Wu, C.: VisualSFM: a visual structure from motion system (2016). http://ccwu. me/vsfm/. Accessed 11 Feb 2016
28. Zhang, Z.: Iterative point matching for registration of free-form curves and surfaces. Int. J. Comput. Vision **13**(2), 119–152 (1994)

Camera-Agnostic Monocular SLAM and Semi-dense 3D Reconstruction

Martin Rünz[✉], Frank Neuhaus, Christian Winkens, and Dietrich Paulus

University of Koblenz-Landau, Mainz, Germany
martin.runz.15@ucl.ac.uk

Abstract. This paper discusses localisation and mapping techniques based on a single camera. After introducing the given problem, which is known as *monocular SLAM*, a new camera agnostic monocular SLAM system (CAM-SLAM) is presented. It was developed within the scope of this work and is inspired by recently proposed SLAM-methods. In contrast to most other systems, it supports any central camera model such as for omnidirectional cameras. Experiments show that CAM-SLAM features similar accuracy as state-of-the-art methods, while being considerably more flexible.

1 Introduction

The term *simultaneous localisation and mapping (SLAM)* denotes the process of creating or refining a map, while determining the own position at the same time. SLAM techniques that rely on vision are referred to as *visual-SLAM* techniques and their performance increased remarkably in the last decade. This work concentrates on *omnidirectional monocular* visual-SLAM systems, which are SLAM systems that deploy a single camera[1] with a wide field of view. Such a vision system would correspond to that of a rabbit or horse, as the eyes of these animals also maximise their field of view at the expense of having monocular vision. There are several reasons for advocating the use of omnidirectional sensors in computer vision. First, many algorithms with applications to robotics detect visual landmarks. These landmarks will be present in many images when an omnidirectional camera is employed, resulting in a higher robustness. Second, a vision system with a high field of view collects more data than a traditional vision system in the same amount of time, although at a lower resolution. This is particularly useful in robotics or when teleconferencing or performing surveillance. The main contribution of this work is the design of a new SLAM system for omnidirectional cameras. In fact, the newly created system makes little assumptions about the camera model and supports traditional, omnidirectional and every single-view camera model[2]. For this reason, it is called *camera-agnostic monocular SLAM –* CAM-SLAM. Furthermore, CAM-SLAM supports arbitrary salient image features and is also capable of reconstructing the environment semi-densely.

---

[1] Or a set of cameras with non-overlapping images.

[2] As long as it is possible to extract and track salient image features.

© Springer International Publishing AG 2016
B. Rosenhahn and B. Andres (Eds.): GCPR 2016, LNCS 9796, pp. 285–296, 2016.
DOI: 10.1007/978-3-319-45886-1_23

1.1 Related Work

A substantial amount of the theoretic principles involved in omnidirectional machine vision has been established during the 1990s [1,9], followed by the implementation of thorough omnidirectional vision systems [2,22]. The first decisive monocular SLAM systems emerged in the subsequent decade and naturally inspired omnidirectional monocular SLAM systems.

In a seminal work [5] Andrew Davison applied EKF-SLAM to the domain of computer vision and his method is able to execute mapping as well as tracking in real-time. The system, however, was limited in map size and required noticeable user interaction. These drawbacks were overcome by Klein and Murray in their seminal PTAM (parallel tracking and mapping) publication [13]. In contrast to previous work, Klein and Murray separate the mapping and tracking task, which allows fast tracking, while the map is refined using bundle adjustment. An alternative approach is to reconstruct a dense 3D map and to use this for tracking, as proposed by Newcombe et al. [21]. Such methods have the advantage that more data of the image is effectively used by the SLAM system and researchers concluded [6,21] that they are more robust as well as more accurate than keypoint-based methods. Both techniques, are still subjects of active research and in the middle of 2015 the state-of-the-art method in terms of accuracy – ORB-SLAM [19] – was a keypoint-based method.

There has been a trend in recent years to compute visual odometry, i.e. to estimate the robot motion, using omnidirectional vision [14,27,28]. The advantage of estimating motion with omnidirectional sensors lies in the computation of the rotational motion component. While rotations are usually a burden when working with traditional cameras, all methods formerly mentioned exploit omnidirectional peculiarities to compute rotation. Although some of the systems, such as the one of Scaramuzza and Siegwart [27], exhibit a high accuracy, their estimation will diverge from the ground truth eventually. This happens because small errors accumulate over time, resulting in an inevitable drift. Furthermore, some of the systems impose strong constraints to the environment.

In contrast to visual odometry approaches, researchers have also adapted full-fledged SLAM systems to the domain of omnidirectional vision, often based on EKF-SLAM [10,23,26] or Fast-SLAM [7]. This might be due to the fact that landmarks are longer visible when an omnidirectional sensor is used. Hence, the drawback that EKF-SLAM scales badly with respect to map size is less prominent. But these methods would not be applicable for a large-scale SLAM system nevertheless. Even though Fast-SLAM performs more efficiently than EKF-SLAM, their processes of tracking and mapping are strongly coupled. This neglects a more profound map optimisation, since tracking has to be executed at framerate. Other methods, again, put strict assumptions on the environment. While Burbridge et al. [3], for example, only maintain a 2D map of the environment, Schoenbein and Geiger [30] assume an urban Manhattan world and Scaramuzza and Siegwart [27] presume planar motion. Maxime Lhuillier presented a generic offline structure from motion system in 2006 [15] that even supports non-central cameras. While its level of abstraction is impressive, it is solving a slightly different problem as no real-time constraint is imposed.

2   System Overview

In order to support consumer quality omnidirectional cameras, CAM-SLAM relies on a parallel tracking and mapping bundle-adjustment strategy inspired by PTAM [13] and ORB-SLAM [19]. It internally creates separate *tracking* and *mapping threads*. An additional *system thread* is created, which handles communication with the user thread and performs some computations in order to unload the tracking thread. Being able to semi-densely reconstruct the environment, CAM-SLAM starts at least one more *reconstruction thread*. When compiled with OpenMP support, which is optional, this number can be increased arbitrarily. Figure 1 illustrates the data flow of a single image frame.

After salient image features were created and assuming that the map is already initialised, the tracking thread takes over new frames. Tracking involves bundle-adjustment of the locally visible map, which is accessible by maintaining a *covisibility graph*, as suggested by Mei et al. [17]. In the case that tracking was successful, the mapping thread may further process the frame by converting it to a keyframe, if required by the system. Here, the decision of the system is based on the conditions proposed by Mur-Artal et al. [19]. Keyframes are used during mapping and are subject to more profound optimisation. In this process, new map points are triangulated, bad ones are removed and existing ones are

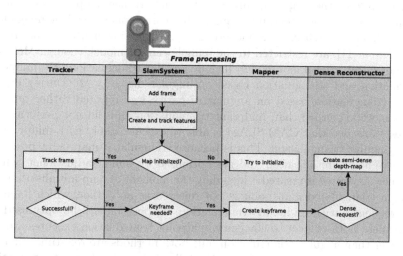

Fig. 1. Frame processing flowchart. While the *Tracker*, *Slam System* and *Mapper* lane each map to one thread in the application, the *Dense Reconstructor* lane maps to at least one thread. New frames arrive in the system thread and are subsequently processed by the tracking, mapping and semi-dense reconstruction thread, according to the system state.

refined with bundle-adjustment. Optionally, the system performs a semi-dense reconstruction of the environment, either online or offline – the latter to increase accuracy.

3   Camera Models

In general, camera models define two projections: From Cartesian 3D coordinates to pixel image coordinates, and vice-versa, from pixel coordinates to a 3D direction. Most visual SLAM systems employ cameras that can be represented with the pinhole camera model. There is, however, a variety of alternative camera models [34] and CAM-SLAM aims at supporting as many models as possible. For this reason it treats the actual camera model as a black-box and solely requires a uniform interface of shared characteristics, namely the aforementioned bidirectional 2D-3D mapping. Additionally, for some camera models one has to implement a function $d : \mathbb{R}^2 \times \mathbb{R}^2 \to \mathbb{R}$ computing the offset between two image space coordinates, which can differ from a simple subtraction. In order to support a wide range of camera models out of the box, CAM-SLAM implements the model by Scaramuzza et al. [29], Mei and Rives [16], an equiangular and cylindrical model, and the pinhole camera model. While optimising, each model is processed in exactly the same way, usually by employing numerical optimisations.

4   Mapping

A central role of the mapping thread is to generate new map points. This is accomplished by identifying and triangulating corresponding salient image features of different keyframes. Some popular triangulation methods, like *linear triangulation* [11], are restricted to the pinhole camera model, though. Methods that allow arbitrary camera models include angular triangulation [25], midpoint triangulation and triangulation based on angular disparity [2]. During experiments, triangulation based on angular disparity was rejected rather quickly, as it is more expensive than midpoint triangulation and did not perform better. Tests revealed that CAM-SLAM is able to execute stably with midpoint as well as angular triangulation. This is because triangulated map-point positions only serve as an initialisation and get optimised by bundle-adjustment, whenever a new keyframe is created – including the moment of map initialisation. As long as a triangulated map point is not rejected as an outlier, which happens more frequently with midpoint triangulation, its position will be optimised by the mapper. With respect to efficiency, midpoint triangulation executes around $60\times$ faster than angular triangulation, but both methods are real-time capable. In order to gain robust triangulation, the following pre- and post-triangulation (distinguished by ◀, ▶) checks are performed for each potential map point:

◀ The angle between the back-projections of both image coordinates that are subject to triangulation, has to be larger than a threshold λ_α. This way, map points with a high depth uncertainty are effectively rejected. An alternative approach is to parametrise map points by their inverse depth, as discussed in [4].

▶ Inspired by ORB-SLAM, the scale consistency is confirmed by verifying that the ratio of distances to both camera centers corresponds to the feature pyramid levels. For instance, when the features are on the same level, the ratio has to be in a range close to 1.

▶ The projection of the newly created map point to both image spaces $u_{1,2}$ has to be valid.

▶ The error between the keypoint positions and $u_{1,2}$ has to be lower than a threshold λ_e which is based on the image-space covariance of the camera model.

Notice that in contrast to regular visual SLAM methods, a maximal reprojection error is enforced instead of the epipolar constraint[3]. Enforcing the epipolar constraint has been avoided, as it would be dependent on a specific camera model and possibly expensive to evaluate.

When CAM-SLAM is newly started or when it lost tracking, it tries to initialise mapping. In the course of this, an essential matrix estimation is performed in a RANSAC-fashion. Even if this approach is less usual than the fundamental matrix estimation, it again offers the advantage of being camera model independent – as long as it is central. The first step of map initialisation is to select a reference keyframe, usually the first input frame. Afterward, each new frame is treated as a potential keyframe and keypoints are matched to the reference keyframe, which is necessary to employ the 8-point algorithm. The matching is based on a feature tracker that locally searches the best matching descriptor in two immediately consecutive frames for each previously matched keypoint of the older frame, and when a match succeeds it is back-propagated to the reference keyframe. This can be understood as a survival of the fittest scheme, as the number of keypoints available for back-tracing is monotonically decreasing. When the number of matches falls below a threshold, a new reference keyframe is selected.

Due to the local search, camera movements should not be too aggressive until being initialised. It is common practice to pre-define a threshold for good features in order to remove outliers. Since this reduces flexibility – thresholds are only valid for one descriptor type and could also be scene dependent – CAM-SLAM follows another strategy. It is assumed that keypoints that were successfully traced back several frames tend to correspond to good matches and that after $\Lambda_i = 4$ consecutive frames without switching the reference keyframe, descriptor distances are approximately normally distributed around a good threshold. Then, after observing Λ_i consecutive frames, the threshold λ_f is learned based on a generous χ^2 test. As soon as the map is initialised, another χ^2 test is performed to refine the threshold. This scheme has been tested successfully with binary ORB and real-valued SURF descriptors.

---

[3] One could argue that this is an implicit epipolar check, since the re-projected position is located on the epipolar line.

When the map is successfully initialised, the mapper performs local bundle-adjustment to optimise map points and keyframe positions. The implementation is based on the g²o graph optimisation framework and adopts a double window approach [32]. As with ORB-SLAM, the optimisation process is performed twice: At a coarse scale first, that is with few Levenberg-Marquardt iterations, and at a finer scale after outliers are removed.

Map points are created whenever a new keyframe is created. This time, point correspondences are found using FLANN [18], and if applicable, also using the tracking method employed during initialisation.

5 Tracking

The tracking-component is responsible for locating the camera in space and has to operate as fast as possible. Should a new image frame arrive before the last one is processed, the new frame is skipped. Initially, the pose of a new frame is estimated using a constant motion model that also incorporates skipped frames. A more sophisticated guess would be possible, for instance with Kalman filtering, but the constant model showed to be sufficient.

Given the initial estimate, feature matching is performed with the currently selected keyframe by projecting available map points to the new frame. This is possible because the keyframe has keypoints associated to map points and map points, as well as the new frame, are already located in 3D space. The distance between the projected and the actual keypoint position has to fall below a threshold however, and the descriptor distance is tested using the threshold learned during map initialisation. If the number of successful matches is lower than the threshold λ_m, the new frame is labeled as untrackable. In this case, the system tries to create a new keyframe as fast as possible, because this could assist future tracking. After receiving Λ_t untrackable frames in a row, tracking is set to be lost. During experiments $\Lambda_t = 1$ was specified. Hence, tracking was lost at the first untrackable frame.

In the case that enough matches are found, bundle-adjustment is performed to refine the initial pose estimate. This process is again divided into two steps – first, before outlier removal; and second, with outlier removal. In contrast to the bundle-adjustment of the mapping-component, map point positions are unaltered and fewer points are used.

Finally, as with ORB-SLAM, the tracker requests a new keyframe when less than $\Lambda_v N_{fk}$ map points associated to the keyframe were found in the frame, where N_{fk} is the number of map points in the keyframe and $0 < \Lambda_v < 1$, here $\Lambda_v = 0.9$. This can be understood as a visual change condition.

5.1   Semi-dense Reconstruction

A comprehensive representation of the environment is crucial for mobile robots and CAM-SLAM implements a semi-dense reconstruction method for this purpose. The procedure is based on the one introduced by Mur-Artal and Tards [20], but a generalised algorithm it presented, which only assumes a central camera model. Given this assumption, epipolar line searches are possible, but the parametrisation of these lines is not predefined. Capturing hyperbolic or parabolic mirrors yields conical epipolar lines, while the cylindrical model results in sinusoid, for instance. Our matching, depth estimation and depth fusion follows the approach of Mur-Artal and Tardos, but the epipolar lines are sampled using a line simplification scheme, following the same principle as the Ramer–Douglas–Peucker [24] algorithm. Given the target keyframe K with the inverse depth range $d_{\min} < d_k < d_{\max}$, a reference keyframe K_i and a pixel coordinate $\boldsymbol{u}$ of interest, the back-projection of $\boldsymbol{u}$ at depth $d_{\min}$ and $d_{\max}$ is projected to the image space of K_i and referred to as $\boldsymbol{v}_{1,2}$. Here, the extremes $d_{\min}$ and $d_{\max}$ are chosen as the 5%- and 95%-quantiles of the depth values of all map points associated with K, which effectively narrows the search and removes outliers. The direct line between $\boldsymbol{v}_1$ and $\boldsymbol{v}_2$ is then sub-sampled by projecting intermediate 3D points of the declared depth range to K_i. Sub-sampling is repeated iteratively until subsequent line-segments are nearly straight or until the length of segments falls below a threshold. After completing the semi-dense inverse depth-map, hole filling and regularisation are applied to improve the quality, similarly as in LSD-SLAM [6]. While LSD-SLAM averages those depth values in the window, however, that are not further away than 2σ from the current one. CAM-SLAM, on the other hand, performs a χ^2 test at 95%, which is effectively the same, but allows to avoid some computational expensive divisions in the implementation. Also, CAM-SLAM checks image intensity consistency during hole filling and regularisation. A result of the triangulation procedure is shown in Fig. 2d.

6 Experiments

In order to evaluate the performance of CAM-SLAM in terms of accuracy, speed and robustness, a variety of comparisons to ground-truth data have been carried out. As flexibility is the major objective of CAM-SLAM, experiments have been executed on diverse datasets and omnidirectional data has explicitly been included. The used datasets are characterised as follows:

1. TUM-RGBD datasets [33]: Pinhole camera, handheld
2. KITTI datasets [8]: Pinhole camera, car-motion
3. Catadioptric RGB-D dataset [31]: Catadioptric camera, car-motion
4. *V360 dataset*: Cylindrical camera, handheld
5. *Room dataset*: Equiangular camera, synthetic images and motion
6. *Mars dataset*: Equiangular camera, synthetic images and motion

While datasets 1–3 are publicly available, sets 4–6 were created within the scope of this work. To capture set 4, a cylindrical camera was rigidly coupled with a marker and externally tracked. Datasets 5 and 6 were generated using the computer graphics software Blender with an equiangular camera model. Synthetic datasets have the advantage of providing perfect ground-truth trajectories, but introduce appearance-related difficulties. For instance, while most real surfaces exhibit structure due to imperfections, synthetic ones can be completely smooth, and hence, featureless. The setup for acquiring set 4, as well as renderings of the synthetic sets are shown in the supplementary thesis.

6.1   Accuracy

Experiments are grouped in two categories: Small- and large-scale experiments. A good measure of performance for the former category is the *absolute trajectory error* (ATE), as described by Sturm et al. [33]. It is computed by determining the absolute differences of camera positions, after aligning the ground-truth with the SLAM-produced trajectory. Here, either a 6D- or 7D-alignment is performed, for example, using the method of Horn [12]. The absolute trajectory error is less suited for large-scale data, however. Imagine a SLAM system always produced the perfect trajectory, but failed in one curve so that every subsequent position had a major offset to the ground truth. Compare this to the case in which a system continuously produces errors, but luckily, did not misinterpret the rotation. In a large-scale scenario, the second system might obtain an ATE which is several orders of magnitude less than the system that made one mistake only. As CAM-SLAM – just like other monocular SLAM-methods – suffers from scale-drift, only segments of large-scale datasets are investigated. For a more profound evaluation on large-scale data, loop-closing would be required, which has not been performed during experiments.

Table 1 compares the *root mean squared* ATE produced by CAM-SLAM to the ones produced by PTAM, LSD-SLAM and ORB-SLAM. Sequences starting with *fr...* belong to the popular TUM-RGBD benchmarking datasets. While the sequences *fr1_xyz* and *fr2_desk* present a static environment with a moving camera, a person is interacting in sequence *fr2_desk_person*. Processing non-static environments is difficult for visual SLAM systems, which is shown in PTAM failing to handle the scene and LSD-SLAM producing large errors. Figures 2b and c

Table 1. Comparison of root mean square absolute trajectory errors in cm, using small-s cale datasets. With the exception of CAM-SLAM measurements, the data is provided by Mur-Artal et al. [19]

	CAM-SLAM	PTAM	LSD-SLAM	ORB-SLAM
fr1_xyz	2.60	1.15	9.00	**0.90**
fr2_desk	3.53	×	4.57	**0.88**
fr2_desk_person	2.29	×	31.73	**0.63**
fr3_long_office	16.83	×	38.53	**3.45**
synth_room	**2.84**	×	×	×
v360 sequence1	**16.21**	×	×	×
v360 sequence2	**14.92**	×	×	×

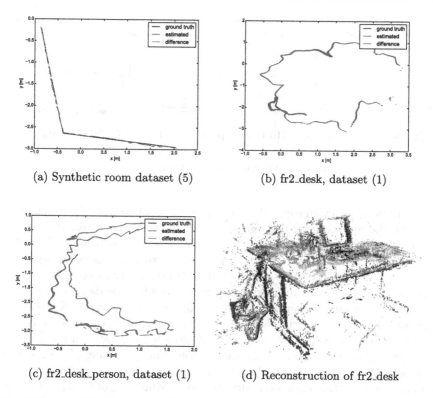

(a) Synthetic room dataset (5)

(b) fr2_desk, dataset (1)

(c) fr2_desk_person, dataset (1)

(d) Reconstruction of fr2_desk

Fig. 2. Plots that highlight the differences between CAM-SLAM estimated trajectories and ground-truth trajectories. While ground-truth trajectories are black, estimated trajectories are blue and differences between associated positions are plotted red. Gaps in the graphs correspond to missing associations, mainly because ground-truth data is missing. Figure (d) shows the result of a semi-dense reconstruction of the environment (Color figure online)

show related plottings of the ground-truth and estimated trajectories as well as their differences.

The results presented in Table 1 show that CAM-SLAM has a comparable performance as state-of-the-art methods. It outperformed LSD-SLAM in all test-sequences and it was robuster than PTAM. ORB-SLAM, on the other hand, consistently produced better results than CAM-SLAM, which is not surprising as it is more finely tuned with respect to the camera model and keypoint descriptors. Furthermore, ORB-SLAM performs loop-closing, while CAM-SLAM did not in the experiments. Nevertheless, CAM-SLAM benefits from its flexibility. Neither of the other methods is able to handle omnidirectional data, while CAM-SLAM performed as well on the omnidirectional synthetic room sequence as on the other sequences. The corresponding trajectory is shown in Fig. 2a.

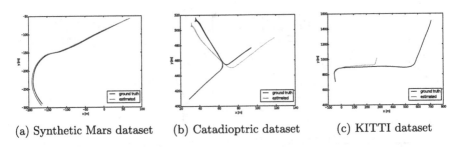

(a) Synthetic Mars dataset   (b) Catadioptric dataset   (c) KITTI dataset

Fig. 3. Plotting of large-scale trajectories

In addition to evaluating the accuracy of CAM-SLAM in small-scale sequences, the applicability to large-scale sequences has been tested. Figure 3 presents the corresponding trajectories, which were generated using three different camera models. The according ground-truth trajectory is evenly approximated by CAM-SLAM, despite a modest drift. Due to the more complex camera movement, a more serious drift occurred in the catadioptric dataset. That the estimated trajectory suffers from a drift in scale becomes clear when observing the pulling in and out of the dead-end road in Fig. 3b. One has to consider, however, that the catadioptric camera is not mounted centrally on the car and that a certain offset is expected for this reason. The remaining plot shown in Fig. 3c resembles experiments with the KITTI dataset that uses a pinhole camera. In this dataset, the most severe drift occurred, which might be related to the shorter visibility of map points. Interestingly, SURF feature matching was more reliable than ORB matching, given catadioptric images. This could be related to the higher degree of distortion, which clearly affects keypoint descriptors, but an in-depth analysis remains future work.

7 Conclusion

This work presented CAM-SLAM, a new monocular SLAM system that focuses on flexibility. It supports any type of central camera model and is also able to perform a semi-dense reconstruction of the environment. Being research software though, CAM-SLAM can still be improved. For instance, the initialisation procedure assumes a non-planar environment. Furthermore, Mur-Artal et al. [19] already realised that their method might profit from representing points at infinity, as described by Civera et al. [4]. The same argumentation holds true for CAM-SLAM: Especially on sequences that exhibit camera transformations with a rotational component only, an inverse depth representation during tracking can stabilise the SLAM execution.

Acknowledgements. Martin Rünz has been partly supported by the SecondHands project, funded from the EU Horizon 2020 Research and Innovation programme under grant agreement No. 643950.

References

1. Baker, S., Nayar, S.K.: A theory of single-viewpoint catadioptric image formation. Int. J. Comput. Vis. **35**(2), 175–196 (1999)
2. Bunschoten, R., Krse, B.: Robust scene reconstruction from an omnidirectional vision system. IEEE Trans. Robot. Autom. **19**(2), 351–357 (2003)
3. Burbridge, C., Spacek, L., Condell, J., Nehmzow, U.: Monocular omnidirectional vision based robot localisation and mapping. In: Proceedings of the TAROS (2008)
4. Civera, J., Davison, A.J., Montiel, J.: Inverse depth parametrization for monocular slam. IEEE Trans. Robot. **24**(5), 932–945 (2008)
5. Davison, A.J.: Real-time simultaneous localisation and mapping with a single camera. In: Proceedings of Ninth IEEE International Conference on Computer Vision, pp. 1403–1410. IEEE (2003)
6. Engel, J., Schöps, T., Cremers, D.: LSD-SLAM: large-scale direct monocular SLAM. In: Fleet, D., Pajdla, T., Schiele, B., Tuytelaars, T. (eds.) ECCV 2014, Part II. LNCS, vol. 8690, pp. 834–849. Springer, Heidelberg (2014)
7. Gamallo, C., Mucientes, M., Regueiro, C.V.: A FastSLAM-based algorithm for omnidirectional cameras. J. Phys. Agents **7**, 12–21 (2013)
8. Geiger, A., Lenz, P., Urtasun, R.: Are we ready for autonomous driving? The KITTI vision benchmark suite. In: Conference on Computer Vision and Pattern Recognition (CVPR) (2012)
9. Geyer, C., Daniilidis, K.: Catadioptric camera calibration. In: The Proceedings of the Seventh IEEE International Conference on Computer Vision, vol. 1, pp. 398–404. IEEE (1999)
10. Gutierrez, D., Rituerto, A., Montiel, J.M.M., Guerrero, J.J.: Adapting a real-time monocular visual slam from conventional to omnidirectional cameras. In: 2011 IEEE International Conference on Computer Vision Workshops (ICCV Workshops), pp. 343–350. IEEE (2011)
11. Hartley, R., Gupta, R., Chang, T.: Stereo from uncalibrated cameras. In: 1992 IEEE Computer Society Conference on Computer Vision and Pattern Recognition. Proceedings CVPR 1992, pp. 761–764, June 1992
12. Horn, B.K., Hilden, H.M., Negahdaripour, S.: Closed-form solution of absolute orientation using orthonormal matrices. JOSA A, **5**(7), 1127–1135 (1988)
13. Klein, G., Murray, D.: Parallel tracking and mapping on a camera phone. In: Proceedings of the 2009 8th IEEE International Symposium on Mixed and Augmented Reality, ISMAR 2009, Washington, DC, pp. 83–86. IEEE Computer Society (2009)
14. Labrosse, F.: The visual compass: performance and limitations of an appearance-based method. J. Field Robot. **23**(10), 913–941 (2006)
15. Lhuillier, M.: Effective and generic structure from motion using angular error. In: 18th International Conference on Pattern Recognition (ICPR 2006), vol. 1, pp. 67–70 (2006)
16. Mei, C., Rives, P.: Single view point omnidirectional camera calibration from planar grids. In: 2007 IEEE International Conference on Robotics and Automation, pp. 3945–3950. IEEE (2007)
17. Mei, C., Sibley, G., Newman, P.: Closing loops without places. In: 2010 IEEE/RSJ International Conference on Intelligent Robots and Systems (IROS), pp. 3738–3744. IEEE (2010)
18. Muja, M., Lowe, D.G.: Fast approximate nearest neighbors with automatic algorithm configuration. In: International Conference on Computer Vision Theory and Application VISSAPP 2009, pp. 331–340. INSTICC Press (2009)

19. Mur-Artal, R., Montiel, J.M.M., Tardós, J.D.: ORB-SLAM: a versatile and accurate monocular SLAM system. Submitted to IEEE Trans. Robot. (2015). arXiv preprint arXiv:1502.00956

20. Mur-Artal, R., Tards, J.D.: Probabilistic semi-dense mapping from highly accurate feature-based monocular slam. In Robotics: Science and Systems (2015)

21. Newcombe, R.A., Lovegrove, S.J., Davison, A.J.: DTAM: dense tracking and mapping in real-time. In: 2011 IEEE International Conference on Computer Vision (ICCV), pp. 2320–2327. IEEE (2011)

22. Peri, V., Nayar, S.K.: Generation of perspective and panoramic video from omnidirectional video. In: Proceedings of DARPA Image Understanding Workshop, vol. 1, pp. 243–245. Citeseer (1997)

23. Phan, K.D., Ovchinnikov, A.V.: Indoor slam using an omnidirectional camera. Middle East J. Sci. Res. **16**(1), 88–94 (2013)

24. Ramer, U.: An iterative procedure for the polygonal approximation of plane curves. Comput. Graph. Image Process. **1**(3), 244–256 (1972)

25. Recker, S., Hess-Flores, M., Joy, K.I.: Statistical angular error-based triangulation for efficient and accurate multi-view scene reconstruction. In: 2013 IEEE Workshop on Applications of Computer Vision (WACV), pp. 68–75. IEEE (2013)

26. Rituerto, A., Puig, L., Guerrero, J.J.: Visual slam with an omnidirectional camera. In: 20th International Conference on Pattern Recognition (ICPR), pp. 348–351. IEEE (2010)

27. Scaramuzza, D., Siegwart, R.: Appearance-guided monocular omnidirectional visual odometry for outdoor ground vehicles. IEEE Trans. Robot. **24**(5), 1015–1026 (2008)

28. Scaramuzza, D.: Omnidirectional vision: from calibration to robot motion estimation. PhD thesis. Citeseer (2008)

29. Scaramuzza, D., Martinelli, A., Siegwart, R.: A toolbox for easily calibrating omnidirectional cameras. In: 2006 IEEE/RSJ International Conference on Intelligent Robots and Systems, pp. 5695–5701. IEEE (2006)

30. Schoenbein, M., Geiger, A.: Omnidirectional 3D reconstruction in augmented manhattan worlds. In: International Conference on Intelligent Robots and Systems, pp. 716–723, Chicago. IEEE, October 2014

31. Schnbein, M., Strauss, T., Geiger, A.: Calibrating and centering quasi-central catadioptric cameras. In: International Conference on Robotics and Automation (ICRA) (2014)

32. Strasdat, H., Davison, A.J., Montiel, J.M.M., Konolige, K.: Double window optimisation for constant time visual slam. In: IEEE International Conference on Computer Vision (ICCV), pp. 2352–2359, November 2011

33. Sturm, J., Engelhard, N., Endres, F., Burgard, W., Cremers, D.: A benchmark for the evaluation of RGB-D slam systems. In: Proceedings of the International Conference on Intelligent Robot Systems (IROS), October 2012

34. Sturm, P.: Camera models and fundamental concepts used in geometric computer vision. Found. Trends Comput. Graph. Vis. **6**(1–2), 1–183 (2010)

Efficient Single-View 3D Co-segmentation Using Shape Similarity and Spatial Part Relations

Nikita Araslanov[(✉)], Seongyong Koo, Juergen Gall, and Sven Behnke

Computer Science Institute, University of Bonn, Bonn, Germany
araslanov@uni-bonn.de, koosy@ais.uni-bonn.de, gall@iai.uni-bonn.de,
behnke@cs.uni-bonn.de

Abstract. The practical use of the latest methods for supervised 3D shape co-segmentation is limited by the requirement of diverse training data and a watertight mesh representation. Driven by practical considerations, we assume only one reference shape to be available and the query shape to be provided as a partially visible point cloud. We propose a novel co-segmentation approach that constructs a part-based object representation comprised of shape appearance models of individual parts and isometric spatial relations between the parts. The partial query shape is pre-segmented using planar cuts, and the segments accompanied by the learned representation induce a compact Conditional Random Field (CRF). CRF inference is performed efficiently by A^*-search with global optimality guarantees. A comparative evaluation with two baselines on partial views generated from the Labelled Princeton Segmentation Benchmark and point clouds recorded with an RGB-D sensor demonstrate superiority of the proposed approach both in accuracy and efficiency.

1 Introduction

As humans, we generally feel comfortable interacting with objects of diverse shapes that can belong to the same semantic category. Mugs, for example, take a variety of shapes, though their functions of containing liquid and drinking are not impeded. It takes us little effort to associate handles of different mugs despite these shape variations. This ability allows us to seamlessly generalise our limited experience to all other objects of similar type that we encounter later in life.

We define the object correspondence problem in terms of co-segmentation. In contrast to a pointwise correspondence, co-segmentation seeks to establish a semantic correspondence between object *parts* by modelling the object structure based on part appearance and topological part relations. We understand parts to fulfill a certain function within the working of the whole shape, such as legs of a chair for stability, or a handle of a vase for grasping. We argue that this formulation lends itself well for many practical applications where high shape discrepancies between same-category objects and partial views make it difficult to estimate a full deformation model.

© Springer International Publishing AG 2016
B. Rosenhahn and B. Andres (Eds.): GCPR 2016, LNCS 9796, pp. 297–308, 2016.
DOI: 10.1007/978-3-319-45886-1_24

2   Related Work

3D shape co-segmentation is closely related to shape correspondence with some of the classical approaches surveyed by van Kaick et al. [38].

The cornerstone of supervised co-segmentation methods [13,15] is the representation of the object surface mesh with a Conditional Random Field (CRF), inspired by similar models in computer vision [29,33]. The unary data terms in the CRF model geometric similarity of individual faces in the mesh, whereas the pairwise term is learned to differentiate between segment boundaries and their interior. Van Kaick et al. [13] also added an "intra-edge" term to distinguish between different shape parts based on their geometric similarity. Good performance of these methods hinges on the size and diversity of the training data.

In an unsupervised setting, a coherent segmentation is sought over a group of shapes simultaneously. The scores of normalised cuts guided agglomerative clustering [8,20] and a tree structure was used [14] to exploit the hierarchy of object structures. Like [14], Sidi et al. [34] computed diffusion maps, but applied spectral clustering instead. Single features or a concatenation thereof were used to establish correspondence between mesh faces [8,13,15], segments [34], supervoxels [20] or corresponding indicator functions [11,23,40], while Hu et al. [9] also clustered each feature independently in their own subspace and fused the result. A rigid pre-alignment was crucial to establish the initial correspondence in [8,14], whereas non-rigid variability of the reference model [1,25,44] or a template structure of primitive shapes [16,42,45] drove the co-analysis itself, very much by analogy with deformable models in images [37]. Huang et al. [10] formulated the problem as a quadratic integer program that jointly optimises over individual segmentation and its consistency with the other shapes in the group. They and Hu et al. [9] applied relaxation techniques, but combinatorial optimisation [13,15], alternating schemes [20] and greedy strategies [16] were also employed to efficiently solve the non-convex objective.

All discussed methods exhibit a number of practical limitations. Most notably, it is the heavy reliance on holistic and contextual features which make them suitable only for closed manifold models [11,13,15,31,32]. At the same time, the potential of structural constraints remains largely untapped [16,21]. Also, unsupervised co-analysis is inherently unable to exploit the ground-truth segmentation: The user might want to identify specific parts of a known model on the novel shape. Kim et al. [16] and the semi-supervised approach of Wang et al. [41] allow mechanisms for a progressive refinement of the segmentation, albeit by means of manual intervention of the user.

Encouraged by the success of part-based models in the context of object detection [2,7], as well as recent advances in classification [5,26,28] and shape retrieval [22,24,35], we propose to revise the classical co-segmentation approach. We learn a part-based representation from a single CAD model or a physical object and expect the query shape to be provided only as a partial point cloud. Our model is also flexible enough for encoding structural constraints between parts in a natural manner. In this work, we demonstrate one such possibility.

3   Method

In the real world, objects can be observed only partially from any given view angle of the sensor. Therefore, we train a model of the given reference shape using the feature vectors extracted from a set of single views (see Fig. 1). The provided query shape is pre-segmented in an unsupervised fashion to obtain part candidates. Note that the partitioning may oversegment object parts. Our choice of the pre-segmentation algorithm is driven by the intention to avoid fine over-segmentation while keeping track of potential model parts at the same time. This makes it compatible with the learned model and allows structure constraints to be incorporated at the level of shape parts as opposed to segment boundaries. The co-segmentation problem ultimately reduces to an efficiently solved inference in a moderately-sized Conditional Random Field.

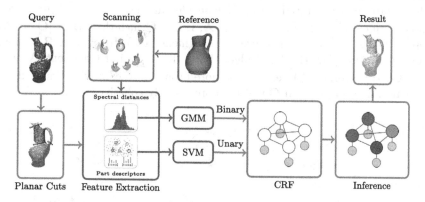

Fig. 1. Overview of our approach. A segmented mesh of the reference shape is used for training. The query is a point cloud of a similar partially observed shape.

3.1   Model

In the context of pointwise shape correspondence, Bronstein et al. [3] developed a shape embedding framework based on the notions of *intrinsic* and *extrinsic* similarity. While isometric deformations do not affect the intrinsic similarity, it is prone to topology changes. By contrast, extrinsic similarity is topologically stable, yet does not exhibit isometric invariance. We integrate these notions of similarity in a part-based representation by minimising the discrepancy in the part shape appearance and the inter-part isometric distortion.

We assume the reference $\mathcal{S} := \bigcup_i \mathcal{S}_i$ and the query $\mathcal{T} := \bigcup_i \mathcal{T}_i$ shapes to be collections of segments formed by points in the Euclidean space $\mathbb{E}^3$. We define a label function $\ell : \mathcal{S} \to L_{\mathcal{S}}$ mapping shape segments $\mathcal{S}_i$ to the label space $L_{\mathcal{S}} \subset \mathbb{Z}$ and let ℓ_i denote the label of segment $\mathcal{S}_i$ for short. The probability $p(\ell_i \mid \mathcal{T}_j)$ is related to appearance similarity of the segment $\mathcal{T}_j$ with the segments in $\mathcal{S}$ labelled ℓ_i. Similarly, we model probability $p(\ell_i, \ell_j \mid \mathcal{T}_i, \mathcal{T}_j)$ to measure the degree of isometric distortion between each pairwise assignment. Our objective can be formulated as a maximum likelihood estimate of the form:

$$\underset{\ell}{\text{minimize}} \quad - \sum_i \overbrace{\log p(\ell_i \mid \mathcal{T}_i)}^{\text{extrinsic similarity}} - \sum_{i,j} \overbrace{\log p(\ell_i, \ell_j \mid \mathcal{T}_i, \mathcal{T}_j)}^{\text{intrinsic similarity}}. \tag{1}$$

3.2 Segmentation

We base the construction of segment candidates on the recently introduced Constrained Planar Cuts (CPC) method [30]. The algorithm finds planar cuts through concave regions that define segment boundaries. In our preliminary experiments, we found that multiple cuts in the regions with high concentration of concave points frequently yield a number of small fragments which are subsequently merged with neighboring segments according to size. The suboptimality of this approach is illustrated in Fig. 2a. Consider an imaginary object profile segmented with cuts ① and ② into parts **A**, **B** and **C** such that $|\mathbf{B}| < |\mathbf{C}| < |\mathbf{A}|$, where $|\cdot|$ is a segment size measure (e.g. segment area). If segment **B** is small enough to be merged, the CPC algorithm will assign it to segment **A** since $|\mathbf{A}| > |\mathbf{C}|$. However, cut ① exhibits a more pronounced concavity than cut ② and, hence, merging **B** with **C** will be more visually cohesive.

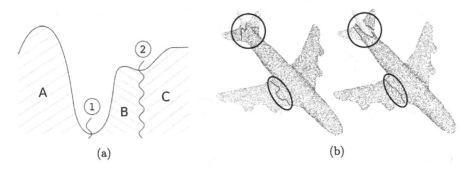

(a)   (b)

Fig. 2. Our modification of the CPC segmentation: **(a)** Illustration of the problem; **(b)** Example segmentation without (left) and with (right) modification.

To address this problem, we merge segments in the ascending order of concavity scores computed as the fraction of concave points on the boundary. Recall that for neighbouring supervoxels with centroids $\mathbf{x}_1$ and $\mathbf{x}_2$ and normals $\mathbf{n}_1$ and $\mathbf{n}_2$ the connection is concave if $\mathbf{n}_1 \cdot \mathbf{d} - \mathbf{n}_2 \cdot \mathbf{d} < 0$, where $\mathbf{d} = (\mathbf{x}_1 - \mathbf{x}_2)/\|\mathbf{x}_1 - \mathbf{x}_2\|$. A comparative example in Fig. 2b demonstrates that an arbitrary order of merging the shape fragments leads to the jagged segment boundaries on the wing and tail of the airplane, whereas agglomeration of the fragments in the increasing order of concavity results in a more natural segmentation. We quantitatively summarise the effectiveness of our modification in comparison with the original version in Table 1.

3.3   Shape Appearance

We represent appearance of each object part using "shape words" derived from a generative model of the underlying feature space spanned by the local shape descriptors. In this work, we contrast the frequency-counting Bag-of-Words (BoW) paradigm with the second-order statistics gathered by the Fisher vectors (FV) [12].

For each view v and shape part with label ℓ, we extract a set of 3D point clusters $\mathcal{P}_{\ell,v}$ with uniformly sampled centres. From every set of point clusters we draw an equal number of randomly sampled fixed-sized subsets $\mathcal{P}_{\ell,v,i} \subset \mathcal{P}_{\ell,v}$, or *feature packets* for short. By construction, the feature packet does not rely on complete visibility of the shape part present in the training data. Furthermore, the effect of the disparity in the surface area of each shape part is mitigated, since every feature packet comprises the same number of point clusters.

Let $M_{\ell,v} = \{\mathbf{m}_{\ell,v,t} \mid \mathbf{m}_{\ell,v,t} \in \mathbb{R}^D, \forall t = 1, ..., T\}$ denote the set of T shape feature vectors with label $\ell \in L_S$ visible from view angle $v \in V$. We model the union of the feature vectors over all labels and views $\bigcup_{\ell \in L_S, v \in V} M_{\ell,v}$ by the Gaussian mixture model (GMM):

$$p(\mathbf{m}_{\ell,v,t}) = \sum_{i=1}^{K} w_i \mathcal{N}(\mathbf{m}_{\ell,v,t}|\boldsymbol{\mu}_i, \Sigma_i), \tag{2}$$

where $\mathcal{N}(\mathbf{m}_{\ell,v,t}|\boldsymbol{\mu}_i, \Sigma_i)$ is a multinomial normal distribution with mean $\boldsymbol{\mu}_i$ and diagonal covariance matrix Σ_i.

A BoW vector $\mathbf{f}_{BoW}(p_{\ell,v}) \in \mathbb{R}^K$ for each cluster in the feature packet $\rho_{\ell,v,i} \in \mathcal{P}_{\ell,v,i}$ can be constructed as:

$$f_{\text{BoW}}^{(k)}(\rho_{\ell,v,i}) = \frac{w_k}{|\rho_{\ell,v,i}|} \sum_t \mathcal{N}(\mathbf{m}_{\ell,v,t}|\boldsymbol{\mu}_k, \Sigma_k), \tag{3}$$

where $\mathbf{m}_{\ell,v,t} \in \rho_{\ell,v,i}$, $|\rho_{\ell,v,i}|$ is the number of low-level feature descriptors and $f_{\text{BoW}}^{(k)}(\cdot)$ is the kth dimension of vector $\mathbf{f}_{\text{BoW}} \in \mathbb{R}^K$. We vectorise each feature packet by taking the average over the BoW vectors of the clusters it contains.

To construct the Fisher vector, we compute the gradients $G_{\boldsymbol{\mu}_k}(\rho_{\ell,v,i}) := \frac{\partial \log p(\rho_{\ell,v,i}|\lambda)}{\partial \boldsymbol{\mu}_k}$ and $G_{\boldsymbol{\sigma}_k}(\rho_{\ell,v,i}) := \frac{\partial \log p(\rho_{\ell,v,i}|\lambda)}{\partial \boldsymbol{\sigma}_k}$ for every point cluster $\rho_{\ell,v,i}$ of the feature packet $\mathcal{P}_{\ell,v,i}$ extracted from a segment with label ℓ in view v:

$$G_{\boldsymbol{\mu}_k}(\rho_{\ell,v,i}) = \frac{1}{|\rho_{\ell,v,i}|\sqrt{\omega_k}} \sum_{t=1}^{|\rho_{\ell,v,i}|} \gamma_{\ell,v,t}(k) \left(\frac{\mathbf{m}_{\ell,v,t} - \boldsymbol{\mu}_k}{\sigma_k} \right), \tag{4}$$

$$G_{\boldsymbol{\sigma}_k}(\rho_{\ell,v,i}) = \frac{1}{|\rho_{\ell,v,i}|\sqrt{2\omega_k}} \sum_{t=1}^{|\rho_{\ell,v,i}|} \gamma_{\ell,v,t}(k) \left(\frac{(\mathbf{m}_{\ell,v,t} - \boldsymbol{\mu}_k)^2}{\sigma_k^2} - 1 \right), \tag{5}$$

where vector division is element-wise, $\sigma_i := \mathbf{diag}(\Sigma_i)$ and

$$\gamma_{\ell,v,t}(k) = \frac{\omega_k u_k(\mathbf{m}_{\ell,v,t})}{\sum_{j=1}^{K} \omega_j u_j(\mathbf{m}_{\ell,v,t})}, \quad \mathbf{m}_{\ell,v,t} \in \rho_{\ell,v,i} \tag{6}$$

is the soft assignment of descriptor $\mathbf{m}_{\ell,v,t}$ to the Gaussian centre k. The Fisher vector is formed by concatenating the gradients (4) and (5) of each Gaussian centre:

$$\mathbf{f}_{\mathrm{FV}}(\rho_{\ell,v,i}) = (G_{\boldsymbol{\mu}_1}^T(\rho_{\ell,v,i}), ..., G_{\boldsymbol{\mu}_K}^T(\rho_{\ell,v,i}), G_{\boldsymbol{\sigma}_1}^T(\rho_{\ell,v,i}), ..., G_{\boldsymbol{\sigma}_K}^T(\rho_{\ell,v,i}))^T. \quad (7)$$

The inherent sparsity of $2KD$-dimensional Fisher vectors is detrimental to their discriminative properties when used in conjunction with the common L2-distance. As a remedy, we apply the power normalisation that uniformly rescales the vector by applying the following function element-wise [26]: $f(z) = sign(z)|z|^\alpha$.

The computed vectors $\mathbf{f}_{BoW}(\cdot)$ and $\mathbf{f}_{FV}(\cdot)$ along with the corresponding labels of the shape parts they represent, form the training dataset of the shape appearance model. We use the Support Vector Machine (SVM) with an RBF kernel for BoW vectors and a linear SVM for Fisher vectors. The trained classifier is used for label prediction of each segment on the query shape.

3.4 Isometric Spatial Relations

The distribution of spectral distances can be used as a measure of shape similarity [4]. Moreover, we could also apply this principle to segment pairs of the same shape, i.e. we can extract the distances between a pair of point sets and compare the distribution to that derived from another pair. To support our intuition, an example with histograms of two partially visible vases is shown in Fig. 3. In addition to providing insights into the shape topology, the histograms also insinuate the normal distribution.

In order to account for distance variation in partial views and intrinsic shape symmetries, we propose to learn a multinomial distribution of distances extracted from every pair of shape parts $D_S(\ell_i, \ell_j) := \{d_S(s_i, s_j) \mid s_i \in \mathcal{S}_i, s_j \in \mathcal{S}_j\}$. Note, that by construction $D_S(\ell_i, \ell_j) = D_S(\ell_j, \ell_i)$ and we allow $i = j$ since the distance distribution is also informative within a single segment.

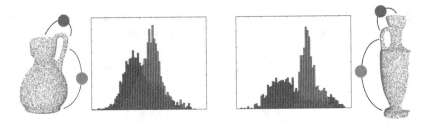

Fig. 3. Comparison of spectral distances between two pairs of segments. The distribution of the commute time distances between pairs of points on the base and the handle (green) and on the handle and the neck (red) are shown. Despite shape discrepancy, the histograms still capture the key features of the shape topology: The base is "farther away" to the handle than the neck. (Color figure online)

Denoting by $\ell_{i\sim i'}$ the assignment of label i' to segment $\mathcal{T}_i$ of the query shape, we compute the likelihood estimate of the data given a pairwise assignment as

$$p\big(D_S(\mathcal{T}_i, \mathcal{T}_j) \mid \ell_{i\sim i'}, \ell_{j\sim j'}\big) = \sum_n \sum_k \omega_k^{i'j'} \mathcal{N}(\mu_k^{i'j'}, \sigma_k^{i'j'} \mid d_S(t_{in}, t_{jn})). \quad (8)$$

Assuming any given pairwise assignment to be equiprobable, its probability estimate is computed using the Bayes rule:

$$p\big(\ell_{i\sim i'}, \ell_{j\sim j'} \mid D_S(\mathcal{T}_i, \mathcal{T}_j)\big) = \frac{p\big(D_S(\mathcal{T}_i, \mathcal{T}_j) \mid \ell_{i\sim i'}, \ell_{j\sim j'}\big)}{\sum_{i'',j''} p\big(D_S(\mathcal{T}_i, \mathcal{T}_j) \mid \ell_{i\sim i''}, \ell_{j\sim j''}\big)}. \quad (9)$$

To compute the distance $D_S(\cdot, \cdot)$, we use the eigenfunctions of the Laplace-Beltrami operator applied directly to the point cloud. We estimate it using the Moving Least Squares (MLS) approximation [17] and define $d_S(x, y)$ as the commute time distance [4], $d_S^2(x, y) = \sum_i \frac{1}{\lambda_i}(\phi_i(x) - \phi_j(y))^2$, where λ_i and $\phi_i(\cdot)$ is the i-th eigenvalue and eigenfunction of the operator.

3.5 Inference

Our resulting model is a small to medium-sized CRF with fully connected label nodes and the energy defined by (1). We extract the same number of feature packets on the query shape $\bigcup_j \mathcal{T}_j$ whose segments were generated in the pre-segmentation step. The scores obtained from predictions of the individual feature packets are averaged over complete segments and the result of the prediction of the label assignment ℓ_i to the segment $\mathcal{T}_j$ is naturally interpreted as $p(\ell_i \mid \mathcal{T}_j)$. We let $p(\ell_i, \ell_j \mid \mathcal{T}_i, \mathcal{T}_j) := p(\ell_{i\sim i'}, \ell_{j\sim j'} \mid D_S(\mathcal{T}_i, \mathcal{T}_j))$ define the distance measure between the two segments. We also add "hard" constraints that penalise part neighbourhoods not observed in the reference shape [13,15].

We observe that our compact model is not dissimilar to the one used by [2] for object part detection. Their study revealed that for small graphs, A^*-based inference often outperformed other algorithms, such as (Loopy) Belief Propagation [43] and the Tree Reweighted Belief Propagation [39] not only in the optimality but also in the runtime. This insight and the equivalence of our models supports our choice of the A^*-search for the inference technique.

4 Evaluation

In two experiments, we evaluate our approach and compare its performance to the baseline derived from the state-of-the-art [13,15]. In our implementation of these methods, we only omitted volumetric and global feature descriptors which do not scale to partial shapes, also corroborated by the failure of the author's original C++/Matlab implementation of [15]. In the first quantitative experiment, we evaluated variants of our approach on the Labelled PSB dataset [15]. In the second qualitative experiment, we used point cloud data of two watering cans recorded with an RGB-D camera. This experiment demonstrates the practical aspects and efficiency of our approach in real-world scenarios.

Table 1. Average accuracy on the LPSB dataset, in percent

	Ant	Airplane	Armadillo	Bearing	Bird	Bust	Chair	Cup	Fish	Fourleg	Glasses	Hand	Human	Mech	Octopus	Plier	Table	Teddy	Vase	Overall
[13]	58.8	62.7	35.2	43.2	58.1	43.5	59.6	81.6	84.2	**60.1**	78.1	52.2	41.3	81.3	82.0	33.7	71.6	71.9	64.3	61.2
[15]	58.9	62.0	35.6	43.4	57.0	43.2	59.6	81.8	**84.4**	59.4	**78.6**	52.7	41.6	81.7	**82.8**	32.5	70.9	71.1	65.5	61.2
SHOT+BoW	66.2	59.2	42.2	52.1	57.4	43.8	60.6	90.0	72.1	51.1	75.4	53.4	35.8	82.4	76.5	70.5	**88.9**	64.5	70.6	63.8
FPFH+BoW	69.9	57.5	48.9	55.7	55.3	40.8	54.5	88.9	75.9	51.6	60.7	54.1	38.0	80.2	66.0	69.5	84.1	72.5	69.2	62.8
SHOT+BoW+ISO	65.6	57.0	39.9	50.5	52.0	43.6	56.7	87.6	71.7	48.1	75.5	46.8	34.2	84.4	75.0	57.3	87.5	69.4	65.3	61.5
SHOT+BoW+ISO*	63.9	58.8	41.2	52.1	53.4	44.0	57.4	89.6	73.2	48.3	74.0	49.7	37.0	84.3	76.8	70.5	86.5	68.1	69.4	63.0
FPFH+FV	**77.7**	64.0	**54.9**	52.2	58.5	44.6	60.2	88.7	78.4	54.9	74.1	56.0	43.7	84.1	69.6	**71.9**	85.4	76.4	70.3	66.6
FPFH+FV (CPC)	77.2	60.4	43.8	49.4	57.8	40.6	58.2	**90.9**	77.9	50.3	69.2	**56.2**	41.2	**85.8**	71.3	70.8	85.5	75.3	68.9	64.8
FPFH+FV (L2)	74.6	63.3	52.2	54.5	57.2	44.8	60.3	88.2	77.8	54.2	73.8	56.0	41.6	82.3	68.2	68.2	85.7	76.4	66.2	65.6
SHOT+FV	72.1	**64.7**	52.5	**57.6**	**60.3**	42.5	**64.1**	90.4	79.0	59.0	75.6	56.0	**45.7**	79.0	79.9	71.8	87.9	76.5	**72.8**	**67.8**
FPFH+FV+ISO	74.1	60.0	51.5	51.2	53.6	**45.0**	55.5	87.5	77.7	50.6	73.4	49.6	40.4	84.6	69.8	58.8	84.1	**77.0**	63.8	63.6

4.1 Quantitative Results

For each category in the Labelled PSB dataset [15], we generated a dataset of *valid* random views. To retain object diversity, a random view was considered valid if at least 20 % of each shape part is visible. We created a uniform grid of view points on a sphere enclosing the shape and proved each for the validity criterion. In order to obtain distinctive shapes, we selected randomly only eight viewpoints with the maximum spread. The dataset is publicly available[1].

For every category, we ran "one-vs-all" co-segmentation scheme with every *compatible* pair of shapes. The pair counts as compatible if the query doesn't contain labels not present on the reference shape. Hence, we performed co-segmentation for at most $20 \times 8 \times 19 = 3040$ object pairs in each category (the runs against own partial views were excluded).

For benchmarking, we adopted the evaluation metrics proposed by [6], namely the Hamming distance, Rand index[2], the Global and Local Consistency Error (GCE and LCE) and the accuracy. We compared a number of configurations of our approach based on either Bag-of-Words (BoW) or Fisher vector (FV) representations. Two shape descriptors were used for the underlying feature space: FPFH [27] and SHOT [36]. To assess the influence of the binary term, we also ran experiments with and without the isometric spatial relations abbreviated ISO.

The accuracy results per category are summarised in Table 1. We observe that our approach shows higher accuracy in 14 out of 19 categories and on average. However, our isometric context did not improve the results. In fact, the

---

[1] http://www.ais.uni-bonn.de/data/alroma.
[2] Reported as one minus Rand index, by convention.

accuracy is worse on average and per category, with the exception of Bust, Mech and Teddy. We attribute this fact to a better pre-segmentation quality of these shapes which did not lead to a significant distortion of the distribution of spectral distances. In some categories, the hard constraints further exacerbated the performance. Dropping them (configuration SHOT+BoW+ISO*) particularly improved the segmentation of Plier, where the failure to segment out the pivot, previously led to a violation of the hard constraint "handles–nose".

Another insight is the better accuracy obtained with SHOT descriptors wrt. FPFH. However, the memory demands become impractical for commodity hardware if Fisher vectors are used ($\sim$10 times more than FPFH). The L2-normalisation of Fisher vectors [26] did not improve the results (FPFH+FV (L2)) which is in line with the expectation that the original motivation for using it does not apply (i.e. there is no background to neglect). Also, the original CPC algorithm (FPFH+FV (CPC)) yielded a lower accuracy on average. This is expected since our modification aimed only at refining segment boundaries.

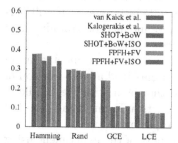

(a) Evaluation on the criteria [6].

	van Kaick et al.	FPFH+FV
Training	259.6	581.0
Learning CRF	506.5	-
Total	766.1	**581.0**
Pre-segmentation	-	34.2
Inference	290.15	16.1
Total	290.15	**50.3**

(b) Average time per object pair, in seconds.

Fig. 4. Quantitative evaluation results.

Our method exhibits a sharp decrease of GCE and LCE as seen in Fig. 4a. While the baselines tend to produce segmentations with many local inconsistencies, our method assigns labels to a few large segments. The results in Fig. 4a also agree with those in Table 1: The configuration based on the Fisher vectors achieves best scores overall while the isometric context exacerbates the performance.

4.2   Qualitative Results

In the second experiment, we evaluated our configuration FPFH+FV on real data by comparing its efficiency and qualitative accuracy with the baseline [13].

We supplied both algorithms with a manually labelled reference shape obtained from an RGB-D sensor. Since the baseline [13] only works with meshes, we computed a fast triangulation [19] from a representative partial view cloud.

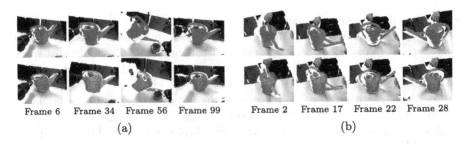

Frame 6   Frame 34   Frame 56   Frame 99   Frame 2   Frame 17   Frame 22   Frame 28

(a)   (b)

Fig. 5. Test sequences from an RGB-D sensor. **Top row:** van Kaick et al. [13]; **Bottom row:** Ours (FPFH+FV). (a) Same query shape as the reference; (b) A novel query shape.

Our approach, by contrast, was able to learn the model from a small number of labelled single-view point clouds extracted from a sequence of training frames.

The first test sequence is a recording of the original model in a previously unseen action. From a representative selection of frames in Fig. 5a, we conclude that although our approach failed to detect the handle in Frame 99, it still performed well in other frames. By comparison, the baseline method [13] identified only patches of the handle throughout the sequence.

In a more challenging setup, both algorithms had to co-segment a novel instance of a watering can. The baseline method misclassified a large fraction of the container in the first two frames and confused the spout with the handle in the last two (Fig. 5b). Our approach mixed up the parts in Frame 2 and detected only part of the handle in Frame 22, but otherwise performed well.

Time benchmarking was conducted in the first part of the experiment using a laptop with Intel Core i7 CPU and 8 GB RAM. The code was parallelised for face- and pointwise operations (e.g. normals and curvatures). The timing results are summarised in Fig. 4b. Despite the additional pre-segmentation step, our co-segmentation was almost six times faster than the baseline implementation.

5   Conclusions

We presented a new approach to the co-segmentation problem that addresses practical limitations of the existing state-of-the-art methods. Our algorithm is readily applicable to point clouds captured from real sensors and does not require a complete object model both for the reference and the query shape. The generality of our pipeline suggests a number of configurations and we have investigated only a subset of them. In future, we plan to experiment with other feature encoding schemes, such as spatial sensitive Bag-of-Words [24] and improve the contextual features using other approximations of diffusion distances [3,18] and spatial relations.

Acknowledgements. This work was supported by German Research Foundation (DFG) under grant BE 2556/12 ALROMA in priority programme SPP 1527 Autonomous Learning.

References

1. Alhashim, I., Xu, K., Zhuang, Y., Cao, J., Simari, P., Zhang, H.: Deformation-driven topology-varying 3D shape correspondence. TOG **34**(6), 236 (2015)
2. Bergtholdt, M., Kappes, J., Schmidt, S., Schnörr, C.: A study of parts-based object class detection using complete graphs. IJCV **87**(1–2), 93–117 (2010)
3. Bronstein, A.M., Bronstein, M.M., Kimmel, R., Mahmoudi, M., Sapiro, G.: A Gromov-Hausdorff framework with diffusion geometry for topologically-robust non-rigid shape matching. IJCV **89**(2–3), 266–286 (2010)
4. Bronstein, M.M., Bronstein, A.M.: Shape recognition with spectral distances. PAMI **33**(5), 1065–1071 (2010)
5. Chatfield, K., Lempitsky, V.S., Vedaldi, A., Zisserman, A.: The devil is in the details: an evaluation of recent feature encoding methods. In: BMVC (2011)
6. Chen, X., Golovinskiy, A., Funkhouser, T.: A benchmark for 3D mesh segmentation. ACM TOG **28**, 73 (2009)
7. Felzenszwalb, P.F., Girshick, R.B., McAllester, D., Ramanan, D.: Object detection with discriminatively trained part-based models. PAMI **32**(9), 1627–1645 (2010)
8. Golovinskiy, A., Funkhouser, T.: Consistent segmentation of 3D models. Comput. Graph. **33**(3), 262–269 (2009)
9. Hu, R., Fan, L., Liu, L.: Co-segmentation of 3D shapes via subspace clustering. CGF **31**, 1703–1713 (2012)
10. Huang, Q., Koltun, V., Guibas, L.: Joint shape segmentation with linear programming. ACM TOG **30**, 125 (2011)
11. Huang, Q., Wang, F., Guibas, L.: Functional map networks for analyzing and exploring large shape collections. TOG **33**(4), 36 (2014)
12. Jaakkola, T., Haussler, D., et al.: Exploiting generative models in discriminative classifiers. In: NIPS, pp. 487–493 (1999)
13. van Kaick, O., Tagliasacchi, A., Sidi, O., Zhang, H., Cohen-Or, D., Wolf, L., Hamarneh, G.: Prior knowledge for part correspondence. CGF **30**, 553–562 (2011)
14. van Kaick, O., Xu, K., Zhang, H., Wang, Y., Sun, S., Shamir, A., Cohen-Or, D.: Co-hierarchical analysis of shape structures. TOG **32**(4), 69 (2013)
15. Kalogerakis, E., Hertzmann, A., Singh, K.: Learning 3D mesh segmentation and labeling. ACM TOG **29**, 102 (2010)
16. Kim, V.G., Li, W., Mitra, N.J., Chaudhuri, S., DiVerdi, S., Funkhouser, T.: Learning part-based templates from large collections of 3D shapes. TOG **32**(4), 70 (2013)
17. Liang, J., Lai, R., Wong, T.W., Zhao, H.: Geometric understanding of point clouds using Laplace-Beltrami operator. In: CVPR, pp. 214–221 (2012)
18. Liu, Y., Prabhakaran, B., Guo, X.: Point-based manifold harmonics. VCG **18**(10), 1693–1703 (2012)
19. Marton, Z.C., Rusu, R.B., Beetz, M.: On fast surface reconstruction methods for large and noisy datasets. In: ICRA, Kobe, Japan, 12–17 May 2009
20. Meng, M., Xia, J., Luo, J., He, Y.: Unsupervised co-segmentation for 3D shapes using iterative multi-label optimization. CAD **45**(2), 312–320 (2013)
21. Mitra, N.J., Wand, M., Zhang, H., Cohen-Or, D., Kim, V., Huang, Q.X.: Structure-aware shape processing. In: Eurographics Report. ACM (2014)
22. Ohbuchi, R., Osada, K., Furuya, T., Banno, T.: Salient local visual features for shape-based 3D model retrieval. In: SMA, pp. 93–102. IEEE (2008)
23. Ovsjanikov, M., Ben-Chen, M., Solomon, J., Butscher, A., Guibas, L.: Functional maps: a flexible representation of maps between shapes. TOG **31**(4), 30 (2012)
24. Ovsjanikov, M., Bronstein, A.M., Bronstein, M.M., Guibas, L.J.: Shape Google: a computer vision approach to isometry invariant shape retrieval. In: ICCV Workshops, pp. 320–327. IEEE (2009)

25. Ovsjanikov, M., Li, W., Guibas, L., Mitra, N.J.: Exploration of continuous variability in collections of 3D shapes. TOG **30**(4), 33 (2011)
26. Perronnin, F., Sánchez, J., Mensink, T.: Improving the fisher kernel for large-scale image classification. In: Daniilidis, K., Maragos, P., Paragios, N. (eds.) ECCV 2010, Part IV. LNCS, vol. 6314, pp. 143–156. Springer, Heidelberg (2010)
27. Rusu, R.B., Blodow, N., Beetz, M.: Fast point feature histograms (FPFH) for 3D registration. In: ICRA, pp. 3212–3217. IEEE (2009)
28. Sánchez, J., Perronnin, F., Mensink, T., Verbeek, J.: Image classification with the fisher vector: theory and practice. IJCV **105**(3), 222–245 (2013)
29. Schnitman, Y., Caspi, Y., Cohen-Or, D., Lischinski, D.: Inducing semantic segmentation from an example. In: Narayanan, P.J., Nayar, S.K., Shum, H.-Y. (eds.) ACCV 2006. LNCS, vol. 3852, pp. 373–384. Springer, Heidelberg (2006)
30. Schoeler, M., Papon, J., Wörgötter, F.: Constrained planar cuts-object partitioning for point clouds. In: CVPR, pp. 5207–5215 (2015)
31. Shapira, L., Shalom, S., Shamir, A., Cohen-Or, D., Zhang, H.: Contextual part analogies in 3D objects. IJCV **89**(2), 309–326 (2010)
32. Shapira, L., Shamir, A., Cohen-Or, D.: Consistent mesh partitioning and skeletonisation using the shape diameter function. VC **24**(4), 249–259 (2008)
33. Shotton, J., Winn, J., Rother, C., Criminisi, A.: Textonboost for image understanding: multi-class object recognition and segmentation by jointly modeling texture, layout, and context. IJCV **81**(1), 2–23 (2009)
34. Sidi, O., van Kaick, O., Kleiman, Y., Zhang, H., Cohen-Or, D.: Unsupervised cosegmentation of a set of shapes via descriptor-space spectral clustering. ACM TOG **30**, 126 (2011)
35. Toldo, R., Castellani, U., Fusiello, A.: Visual vocabulary signature for 3D object retrieval and partial matching. In: Proceedings of the 3DOR Conference, pp. 21–28 (2009)
36. Tombari, F., Salti, S., Di Stefano, L.: Unique signatures of histograms for local surface description. In: Daniilidis, K., Maragos, P., Paragios, N. (eds.) ECCV 2010, Part III. LNCS, vol. 6313, pp. 356–369. Springer, Heidelberg (2010)
37. Toshev, A., Shi, J., Daniilidis, K.: Image matching via saliency region correspondences. In: CVPR, pp. 1–8 (2007)
38. Van Kaick, O., Zhang, H., Hamarneh, G., Cohen-Or, D.: A survey on shape correspondence. CGF **30**, 1681–1707 (2011)
39. Wainwright, M.J., Jaakkola, T.S., Willsky, A.S.: Map estimation via agreement on trees: message-passing and linear programming. IEEE Trans. Inf. Theor. **51**(11), 3697–3717 (2005)
40. Wang, F., Huang, Q., Ovsjanikov, M., Guibas, L.J.: Unsupervised multi-class joint image segmentation. In: CVPR, pp. 3142–3149 (2014)
41. Wang, Y., Asafi, S., van Kaick, O., Zhang, H., Cohen-Or, D., Chen, B.: Active co-analysis of a set of shapes. TOG **31**(6), 165 (2012)
42. Xu, K., Li, H., Zhang, H., Cohen-Or, D., Xiong, Y., Cheng, Z.Q.: Style-content separation by anisotropic part scales. TOG **29**(6), 184 (2010)
43. Yedidia, J.S., Freeman, W.T., Weiss, Y.: Constructing free-energy approximations and generalized belief propagation algorithms. IEEE Trans. Inf. Theor. **51**(7), 2282–2312 (2005)
44. Zhang, H., Sheffer, A., Cohen-Or, D., Zhou, Q., Van Kaick, O., Tagliasacchi, A.: Deformation-driven shape correspondence. CGF **27**, 1431–1439 (2008)
45. Zheng, Y., Cohen-Or, D., Averkiou, M., Mitra, N.J.: Recurring part arrangements in shape collections. CGF **33**, 115–124 (2014)

Fast and Accurate Micro Lenses Depth Maps for Multi-focus Light Field Cameras

Rodrigo Ferreira and Nuno Goncalves[✉]

Institute of Systems and Robotics - University of Coimbra, Coimbra, Portugal
rodrigotoste@isr.uc.pt, nunogon@deec.uc.pt

Abstract. Light field cameras capture a scene's multi-directional light field with one image, allowing the estimation of depth. In this paper, we introduce a fully automatic fast method for depth estimation from a single plenoptic image running a RANSAC-like algorithm for feature matching. The novelty about our approach is the global method to back project correspondences found using photometric similarity to obtain a 3D virtual point cloud. We then use lenses with different focal-lengths in a multiple depth map refining phase and their reprojection to the image plane, generating an accurate depth map per micro lens. Tests with simulations and real images are presented and show a good trade-off between computation time and accuracy of the method presented. Our method achieves an accuracy similar to the state-of-the-art in considerable less time (speedups of around 3 times).

1 Introduction

Plenoptic or light field cameras (PLF) are cameras that acquire the plenoptic function, that is to say that they know, for each pixel, the amount of light traveling in all directions. These cameras have received a lot of interest in the few last years since they inherently allow for multiple view geometry. Although formalized earlier (about 100 years ago), PLF cameras were commercially built only in the last decade. These cameras are built by placing a micro-lens array behind the major optical lens of the system. This construction allows for the formation of an array of smaller images that compose the 4D light field and by easily sampling it. It is then straightforward to estimate the scene's depth due to the redundancy created by the same point being imaged several times.

The concept behind plenoptic cameras was first addressed in 1908 by Lippmann [7] where he suggests the placement of an array of lenses between the camera's main lens and the film. This approach allows the camera to capture the light field of a scene. The concept was later refined by Ives [4] in 1930 but, due to the lack of computational power or existence of digital image sensors, little could be done to extract information from the light field. Now with digital image sensors, this technology has several possible applications such as robotics, face recognition, photography and filmography, augmented reality, depth reconstruction, industrial inspection and more.

B. Rosenhahn and B. Andres (Eds.): GCPR 2016, LNCS 9796, pp. 309–319, 2016.
DOI: 10.1007/978-3-319-45886-1_25

Concerning depth estimation from plenoptic images we are able to achieve the scene depth with only one raw image, which is also essential for image rendering.

In 2004 Dansearau and Bruton [2] proposed a method for depth estimation using 2D gradient operations. They were able to define the light field direction and thus the depth of the corresponding elements within the light field. The areas where the depth could not be estimated were filled by applying region growing. Since plenoptic cameras are not immune to spatial aliasing, which can result on depth estimation errors, in 2009 Bishop and Favaro [1] applied a different approach to compensate the present aliasing, allowing them to recover the depth map from the multiple views provided by the 4D light field.

Wanner and Goldluecke [14] presented in 2012 a technique for depth estimations for 4D light fields, using dominant directions on epipolar plane images. By assuming that the 4D light field can be sliced onto 2D dimensions they started to locally estimate the depth of the epipolar plane images and then labeled the local estimations, integrating them on the global depth maps by imposing spatial constraints. Recently, Fleischmann and Koch [3] approach the depth estimation paradigm with disparity between neighbor lenses. Their method requires a very dense sampling of the light field. The micro-lens depth maps are fused using a semi-global regularization process. They further incorporate a semi-global coarse regularization for insufficiently textured scenes.

In a different approach, Tao et al. [12] used a focal stack to estimate depth in a depth-from-defocus approach, by simultaneously using defocus and correspondences. They combine both cues using a Markov random field framework. Going deeper into the focus, Lin et al. [6] proposed, most recently, an approach based on the symmetry of the focal stack to estimate depth. They prove that the focal stack is symmetric centered in the in-focus slice, for non-occluded pixels. Occlusions are also studied by Wang et al. [13]. They identify the occlusion edges, most useful for object segmentation and, hence, to improve the depth estimation quality. They prove that points in the edge of objects in different depth planes do not meet the standard photometric consistency equation and they derive new expressions for these points.

As for the image rendering, it consists in converting the plenoptic image into a focused image the same way as a conventional camera would see the world. Although the works presented by Ng et al. [9] and Lumsdaine and Georgiev [8] are fast, they present many artifacts and low resolution. Another approach and the one that achieves the best results for multi-focus LF cameras is proposed by Perwass and Wietzke [11]. Having a scene dense depth map it is possible to back trace each pixel onto the image plane. This method allows the render of a high resolution image with few artifacts which can be achieved with a multi-focus plenoptic camera. The major drawback is the high computational power required to process the dense depth map and the image rendering.

In this paper we present a novel fully automatic algorithm to estimate a dense depth map from a single image of a multi-focus plenoptic camera. Our algorithm rely on a robust search for photometric similarity between micro-lenses and by smart mixing images with different levels of blur. The obtained point cloud is then filtered to improve the final depth map. We achieve very good results when compared to the state of the art in a considerable less computational time.

2   Multi-focus Plenoptic Cameras

A multi-focus plenoptic camera has a micro-lens array placed in front of the image sensor where each micro-lens have a different focal length from its neighbor lenses. In this paper we are interested in the model presented in [11] and which is represented in Fig. 1a. For this type of cameras a real world object X_1 (Fig. 1a) is projected through the camera's main lens onto a virtual image Y_1. This virtual image is then projected through the micro-lens array into the image plane, capturing multiple views of the object. There are lenses with three different focal length, allowing to obtain a larger depth of field. Lenses with different focal lengths will present different blurs for the same depth and will be in focus for different depth ranges. The most common lens type arrangement is hexagonal, as illustrated by the top image of Fig. 1b. The bottom image of Fig. 1b shows a sample of a scene at a constant depth where it is possible to identify different lens types through blur.

To clarify the different types of depth maps, notice that we define three different concepts: (1) sparse depth map - it is the raw depth map obtained by projecting the 3D virtual points to the image plane and attributing a depth value for each projected pixel, (2) coarse depth map - it is the depth map obtained by attributing a single depth value for each micro-lens - it is a dense map, since all pixels have a depth value, but it is not dense in a conventional camera point of view (it is not a scene's depth map) and (3) dense depth map - it is the scene's depth map obtained by synthesizing the image and attributing a depth value for each pixel, as if the camera were a conventional pinhole one.

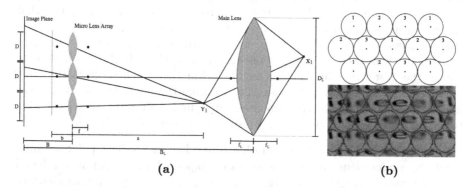

Fig. 1. (a) Plenoptic camera model. (b top) Hexagonal layout of lenses where the lens type is identified by a number. (b bottom) Sample from a Raytrix dataset with different blurs in different lens types.

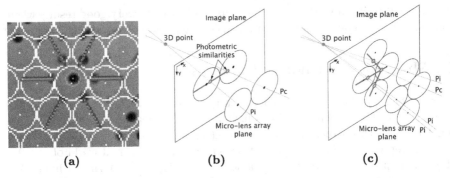

Fig. 2. (a) Model tested by the RANSAC-like algorithm. The green circle is the salient point and the red, green and blue lines are the epipolar band where we search for correspondences. The green epipolar line is the main test line while the red and blue lines represent the ±1 pixel tolerance. (b) and (c) 3D representation of the epipolar geometry between two and four micro-lenses respectively. The green line is the epipolar line, the green circles are best photometric similarities and the red dot it the estimated 3D point for the detected similarities. (Color figure online)

2.1   Feature Detection and Depth Estimation

Our algorithm to estimate a sparse depth map is based on photometric similarities between pairs of micro-lens images. Fleischmann and Koch [3] use a similar approach, based on photometric similarity. We use SIFT to search for salient points in the image (as a whole). This method allows us to obtain the most significant points in the image only by adjusting threshold parameters. Regard that we use SIFT features for simplicity and since they have good discriminatory capabilities, however, any salient points detection can replace the use of SIFT. Having the salient points, neighboring lenses are then searched for photometric correspondences, by relying on stereo epipolar geometry (notice that salient points obtained in non useful areas, for instance areas between microlenses images, are discarded). Since we are provided a big number of salient points and their respective correspondences, we apply a RANSAC-method to obtain the best 3D point cloud. Our algorithm then back projects the pairs of correspondences. Notice that the distance from the micro-lens array and the image plane is provided by the camera manufacturer (calibration data), allowing to obtain a sparse 3D point cloud. We summarize our method as follows:

- **Step 1 - Selection of the epipolar lines.** For each salient point within a reference micro-lens image I_a, a subset of epipolar lines are considered based on a group of target micro-lens images $I_{a_1}, ..., I_{a_n}$ (neighbor micro-lenses). The n epipolar lines for a point x in the reference image are given by $L_i = \{x + tv : t \in \mathbb{R}\}$ with $v = (c_{a_i} - c_a)/2r$ [3], where c_{a_i} and c_a are the coordinates of the center of the target micro-lens a_i with $i \in \{1, ..., n\}$ and the reference micro-lens a with r radius respectively. See Fig. 2a.

– **Step 2 - Find a correspondence.** Photometric similarities are searched within the target micro-lenses along the n epipolar lines for possible disparities $dj \in [0, d_{max}], d_{max} < 2r$. So, it is calculated the sum of absolute differences (SAD) (of Eq. (1)) [3] between local neighborhoods $\Omega(x)$, in the reference image, and $\Omega(x - d_j v)$, in the target image.

$$SAD(x, d_j; a, a_i) = \frac{1}{A(x, v, d_j)} \sum_{u \in \Omega(x)} |I_a(u) - I_{a_i}(u - d_j v)|(u - d_j v). \quad (1)$$

with

$$A(x, v, d_j) = \sum_{u \in \Omega(x)} (u - d_j v). \qquad (x) = \begin{cases} 1 & \text{if } ||x|| < r \\ 0 & \text{else} \end{cases}.$$

By minimizing the SAD through Eq. (2) it is obtained the pixel coordinates for the best photometric similarity within each epipolar line of the neighbor micro-lenses.

$$X(a, a_i) = \underset{x}{\text{argmin }} SAD(x, d_j; a, a_i), \quad s.t. \ X(a, a_i) \in I_{a_i} \qquad (2)$$

– **Step 3 - Estimation of the 3D virtual points.** A subset of lines are defined, representing one pixel tolerance for the epipolar line (Fig. 2a), and are grouped two by two. For each pair it is computed the 3D point that minimizes the distance (in 3D) between lines P_i and P_c (Fig. 2b). The final 3D point has the median of their coordinates

– **Step 4 - Testing the model.** Having an hypothetical 3D point obtained in the previous step, we now need to test the hypothesis for this virtual point. The chosen error measurement is the average distance of the virtual candidate points to the correspondent lines obtained in the previous step.

– **Step 5 - Assessment of the model.** A threshold on the measure defined on the previous step is defined so that only the best estimations are selected. This allows to assume which lines are suited to add to the model (inliers). If there is more than one outlier, the hypothetic model is discarded and we go back to step 1.

– **Step 6 - Re-estimations of the 3D virtual point.** This step is similar to step 3. We re-estimate all 3D virtual points using only the inliers. These lines are again grouped two by two and the 3D point for every combination is the point that minimizes the distance between them. The final 3D point is the median coordinates of all points generated by every line combination.

– **Step 7 - Error metrics.** In this step we evaluate the model in terms of error. It is a mean error from the inliers's distances obtained in step 3, as well as the number of neighbor micro-lenses where a correspondence is found. This will be further discussed on Sect. 2.2.

– **Step 8 - Repeat steps 1–7 for every salient point.**

The output of the previous algorithm is a 3D point cloud of virtual points as projected by the main lens of the camera to their virtual image. At a final stage, a coarse regularization method will reproject the 3D points of the cloud to the micro-lens images and, thus, attribute an average depth for every micro-lens.

As for the lens pattern used in step 1 (where neighbor lenses are searched for replications of a given salient point) we use different combinations of lenses. Knowing that for a multi-focus plenoptic camera there are lenses with different types, we define lens groups based on the lens type and the distance to the central lens. Figure 3 shows these configurations. We do a smart mixture of lens groups that, even mixing different blurs due to the different focal lengths, is able to optimize the depth estimated throughout the scene's depth ranges. Notice that the depth accuracy depends on the stereo baseline, which is smaller for farther scene depths. Our smart adaptive mixture of micro-lens is able to adjust baseline and range. The neighborhood is limited to R_5 because there is no major correspondences beyond this distance to the center lens (about $3.5D$). Table 1 summarizes all lens patterns studied in our work, where D is the lens diameter.

2.2   Depth Improvement

Assume z as the virtual depth of a generic point of the captured scene. As stated by Perwass and Wietzke [11], the maximum radius (R_{max}) that determines the number of micro-lenses that replicate a certain feature is given by Eq. (3), where B is the distance between the micro-lens plane and the image plane and D is the micro-lens diameter (in pixels). Consequently, the closer a point is to the camera (higher virtual depth), the more lenses will replicate it. Figure 4 is an example for both close and far features on a raw image. When using the R_0 lens pattern (see Fig. 3) the algorithm searches adjacent lenses with different types for feature matching, being adequate for farther depth ranges. On the other hand, the R_1 configuration is always adequate since it searches lenses of the same type (same focal length). Notice that, as for the R_5 pattern, although the number of correspondences obtained is much lower, their baseline is much higher and, therefore, the back projection of its correspondences is more stable. Our

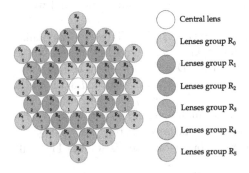

Fig. 3. Illustration of the lens neighborhood, with every group labeled from R0 to R5, and lens type from 0 to 2.

Table 1. Table summarizing the lens pattern parameters (assumes that the central lens type is 0).

Lense patterns	# of Lenses	Lenses types	Distance to central micro-lens
R_0	6	1, 2	D
R_1	6	0	$\sqrt{3} \times D$
R_2	6	1, 2	$2 \times D$
R_3	12	1, 2	$\sqrt{7} \times D$
R_4	6	0	$3 \times D$
R_5	6	0	$2\sqrt{3} \times D$

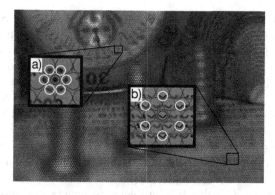

Fig. 4. Salient point replication on neighbor lenses: (a) feature replication for a low z value sample. (b) feature replication for a high z value sample

algorithm then presents an adaptive mixture of micro-lens patterns, by using as many information as possible, and selecting the more stable configurations when available.

$$R_{max} = \frac{|z| \times D}{2 \times B} \tag{3}$$

Lens Selection. On seeking a more precise reconstruction of the depth map we propose the aggregation of both R_0, R_1, R_4 and R_5 depth data points by quartile sectioning and weight attribution. Our work focuses on the usage of R_0, R_1, R_4 and R_5 lens configuration since they produce the majority and most consistent results of all configurations. Since correspondences in R_4 and R_5 are not always available (only for very close points relative to the camera position) and their blur is similar to the blur of correspondences in R_1, we mention the union of both configurations as $R_1 + R_4 + R_5$. For the fusion of R_0 and $R_1 + R_4 + R_5$ depth maps we consider a linear combination of their estimated depths, given by Eq. (4), where α is the weight parameter, varying between 0 and 1 based on the depth of the corresponding depth point. We divided the depth map range (from the sparse point cloud) into quartiles so that the first quartile represents the closer depth data points and the fourth quartile the farther depth data points relative to the camera position. For the first quartile the depth data points are extracted from the $R_1 + R_4 + R_5$ depth map, being $z = z_{R_1+R_4+R_5}$. The same applies for the fourth quartile, being $z = zR_0$. For the second and third quartile we use a linear weight of both depth maps.

$$z = \begin{cases} z_{R_1+R_4+R_5}, & \text{if } \hat{z} \in Q1 \\ (1-\alpha)z_{R_0} + \alpha z_{R_1+R_4+R_5}, & \text{if } \hat{z} \in Q2 \cup Q3 \\ z_{R_0}, & \text{if } \hat{z} \in Q4 \end{cases} \tag{4}$$

where $\hat{z} = \frac{z_{R_0}+z_{R_1+R_4+R_5}}{2}$.

Detection and Correction of Highly Blurred Areas. Some plenoptic images might contain sections where none of the lens types can focus. In these cases it is more favorable to assume $z = z_{R_1+R_4+R_5}$ rather than use highly blurred lenses for the final depth map. The texture in these far depth sections is blurred and it is hard to find salient points since they highly depend on texture detail. Then, the algorithm might detect salient points and correspondences for a minimum solution of the RANSAC-like algorithm (when only two correspondences are detected), which will result in a less accurate depth map. For these cases the estimated depth points are not consistent and assume a noisy representation (overfitting). For a non-minimum solution (when more then two correspondences are used) the depth map is not dense enough for a sufficiently dense reconstruction. To solve this problem we generate a minimum solution depth map and we cross it with the non-minimum (robust) solution depth map of the same plenoptic image. For the lack of space we omit the details.

2.3   Coarse Depth Map

For the reconstruction of the dense depth map we use a coarse depth map, having one depth per micro-lens. This process is related with the reprojection of the sparse map points from the source virtual object onto the image plane through the center of the micro-lenses. First, we have to identify which features of the sparse point set are projected through each micro-lens. Even though we do not have the focal length value for each micro-lens, since the distance between image plane and micro-lens array is known, we project every feature within the cone centered on every micro-lens and with radius R_{lens} (Fig. 5). This is of key importance since even without calibration of the lenses we are able to reconstruct depth. The lens depth is estimated by averaging the depth values of the point set projected into its R_{lens} radius. Notice that a point can be projected through several micro-lens depending on its virtual depth. For each set of points projected into each micro-lens a fine filter is applied. This filter allows a more robust estimation for the depth of each micro-lens, being this depth the averaging of every point's color intensity that follows Eq. (5) for a local median $\hat{p}$ and standard deviation σ_p of $P(n)$ (local point set with n points)

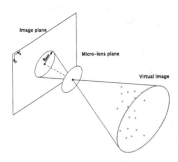

Fig. 5. R_{lens} projection cone for one micro-lens and features that fall inside it.

where Ω_p is the point set domain. We then obtain a single depth per micro-lens given by $Z(a_i)$.

$$P_{filtered} = \{P(n) : P(n) \in [\hat{p} - \sigma_p, \hat{p} + \sigma_p], n \in \Omega_p]. \tag{5}$$

To densely fill every micro-lens without depth we propagate its neighbor lens's depth value. The propagated depth is an averaging of the neighbor lenses depth (assuming a robust region growing with three or more neighbor lenses).

2.4 Dense Depth Map

As for the rendering of the dense depth map we use, as basis information, the coarse depth map. This algorithm is based on the synthesization method of Perwass and Wietzke [11] with a modification at the micro-lens selection for the depth estimation. Instead of selecting the micro-lenses inside the R_{max} radius based on their effective resolution ratio (since we avoid to use the focal length of micro lenses), we use all the lenses inside R_{max}. The final depth (or intensity) value is the weighted mean of the depth (or intensity) of the selected micro-lenses, where the weight accounts for the vignetting effect on lenses (notice that, as stated by [5,10], the micro-lenses have a considerable vignetting effect).

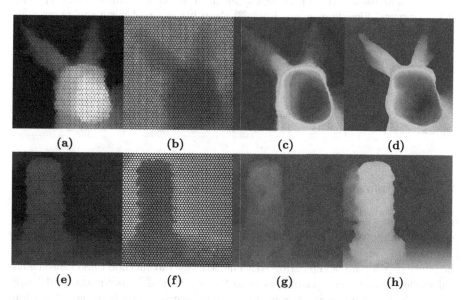

Fig. 6. Excerpts of ours, ground truth and Raytrix's results. (a–e) our coarse depth estimation, (b–f) Fleischmann and Koch's disparity estimation, (c–g) our dense depth estimation, (d) depth ground truth, (h) Raytrix's results.

3   Results

We compare our results to the method of Fleischmann and Koch [3]. We measure the computational time and the mean absolute error (MAE) for both methods, as shown on Table 2. These measurements where performed on synthetic datasets and on real world datasets provided by Raytrix. Our algorithm achieves comparable results to those of [3] with less computation time for the micro-lens coarse map, and additionally estimating a dense depth map. Since Fleischmann and Koch do not produce a dense depth map, we present the root mean square error (RMSE) between our dense depth map and the depth ground truth of the synthetic datasets (Table 2). The RMSE for the synthetic datasets is considerably low but, since Raytrix do not provide the depth ground truth, we present a visual comparison with Raytrix's results, shown in Fig. 6. Since these images are not immune to aliasing effects due to resize, we present excerpts of the scenes. Detailed full resolution images can be found on the supplementary material. The color pallet we used on our dense depth map is different from Raytrix's. Since we don't know the color pallet used by Raytrix, we applied the OpenCV "colormap_jet" pallet to the scene's depth. Results on several additional datasets are also present in supplementary material.

Table 2. Computational time (in seconds) and mean absolute disparity error (in pixels) for both our and Fleischmann and Koch [3] algorithm and root mean square error for our dense depth map.

Datastes	Computation time					MAE		RMSE
	Our sparse est.	Our coarse est.	Our dense est.	Our total	F&K total	Our coarse est.	F&K est.	Our dense est.
Bunny	368 s	710 s	77 s	**1155 s**	3874 s	0.497	**0.195**	3.4 %
Bolt	450 s	855 s	80 s	**1385 s**	4473 s	0.271	**0.174**	2.9 %
4plane	556 s	1109 s	85 s	**1750 s**	4300 s	0.230	**0.178**	2.5 %

4   Conclusion

In this paper we propose a light weight algorithm to estimate the depth of a plenoptic image based on detected features for a multi-focus plenoptic camera. Our method uses a coarse map with one depth value per micro-lens to estimate the dense depth map of the captured scene. We test our method on synthetic and real world datasets, comparing them to the method of Fleischmann and Koch [3]. This is an accuracy vs. computation time comparison where our algorithm achieves comparable results in substantial less time. Although our algorithm presents higher error measurements but relatively close to [3], the achieved error values are lower than half of a pixel size. The computation time of our algorithm can still be improved with GPU parallel processing.

References

1. Bishop, T.E., Zanetti, S., Favaro, P.: Light field superresolution. In: Proceedings of IEEE International Conference on Computational Photography, ICCP, pp. 1–9 (2009)
2. Dansearau, D., Bruton, L.: Gradient-based depth estimation from 4D light field. In: Proceedings of International Symposium on Circuits and Systems, vol. 3, pp. III-549–552 (2004)
3. Fleischmann, O., Koch, R.: Lens-based depth estimation for multi-focus plenoptic cameras. In: Jiang, X., Hornegger, J., Koch, R. (eds.) GCPR 2014. LNCS, vol. 8753, pp. 410–420. Springer, Heidelberg (2014)
4. Ives, H.E.: Optical properties of Lippman lenticulated sheet. J. Opt. Soc. Am. **21**, 171 (1930)
5. Liang, C.K., Ramamoorthi, R.: A light transport framework for lenslet light field cameras. ACM Trans. Graph. (TOG) **34**(2), 16 (2015)
6. Lin, H., Chen, C., Bing Kang, S., Yu, J.: Depth recovery from light field using focal stack symmetry. In: Proceedings of the IEEE International Conference on Computer Vision, pp. 3451–3459 (2015)
7. Lippmann, G.: Épreuves réversibles. Photographies intégrals. C. R. Acad. Sci. **146**, 446–451 (1908)
8. Lumsdaine, A., Georgiev, T.: Full resolution lightfield rendering. Indiana University and Adobe Systems, Technical report (2008)
9. Ng, R.: Digital light field photography. Ph.D. thesis, Stanford University (2006)
10. Ng, R., Levoy, M., Bredif, M., Duval, G., Horowitz, M., Hanrahan, P.: Light field photography with a hand-held plenoptic camera. Comput. Sci. Tech. Rep. CSTR **2**(11), 1 (2005)
11. Perwass, C., Wietzke, L.: Single lens 3D-camera with extended depht-of-field. In: Proceedings of SPIE Human Vision and Electronic Imaging (2012)
12. Tao, M., Hadap, S., Malik, J., Ramamoorthi, R.: Depth from combining defocus and correspondence using light-field cameras. In: Proceedings of the IEEE International Conference on Computer Vision, pp. 673–680 (2013)
13. Wang, T.C., Efros, A.A., Ramamoorthi, R.: Occlusion-aware depth estimation using light-field cameras. In: Proceedings of the IEEE International Conference on Computer Vision, pp. 3487–3495 (2015)
14. Wanner, S., Goldlueck, B.: Globally consistent depth labeling of 4D light fields. In: Proceedings of 2012 IEEE Conference on Computer Vision and Pattern Recognition, pp. 41–48 (2012)

Train Detection and Tracking in Optical Time Domain Reflectometry (OTDR) Signals

Adam Papp[1(✉)], Christoph Wiesmeyr[1], Martin Litzenberger[1], Heinrich Garn[1], and Walter Kropatsch[2]

[1] Digital Safety and Security Department,
Austrian Institute of Technology GmbH, Vienna, Austria
{adam.papp.fl,christoph.wiesmeyr}@ait.ac.at
[2] Pattern Recognition and Image Processing Group,
Vienna University of Technology, Vienna, Austria

Abstract. We propose a novel method for the detection of vibrations caused by trains in an optical fiber buried nearby the railway track. Using optical time-domain reflectometry vibrations in the ground caused by different sources can be detected with high accuracy in time and space. While several algorithms have been proposed in the literature for train tracking using OTDR signals they have not been tested on longer recordings. The presented method learns the characteristic pattern in the Fourier domain using a support vector machine (SVM) and it becomes more robust to any kind of noise and artifacts in the signal. The point-based causal train tracking has two stages to minimize the influence of false classifications of the vibration detection. Our technical contribution is the evaluation of the presented algorithm based on two hour long recording and demonstration of open problems for commercial usage.

1 Introduction

Railway safety is an important task, as millions of people and cargo being transported every day. Conventional tracking is often achieved by bidirectional communication between train and track equipment. Other systems need detectors to be installed next to the railway and they deliver a signal when a train passes through the detector. In this paper we investigate a different technique, by the use of an *optical time-domain reflectometry* (OTDR) instrument. It injects a series of light pulses into a fiber cable and measures the scattered or reflected light (Rayleigh backscatter) at the same end of the cable. The refractive index change due to pressure change on the cable is the major cause for scattering, which can be measured with a positional resolution down to 0.5 m [1]. The interested reader on different type of OTDR devices and their physical principle is referred to the survey of Bao and Chen [1]. OTDR devices can be used to detect break points in fiber cable (e.g. underwater cable reparation), for intrusion detection [3,6,10,13] or even for rock slide detection [2].

Vibrations of train movements nearby the railway track can be monitored using an OTDR device, where in most cases fiber cables are already installed

© Springer International Publishing AG 2016
B. Rosenhahn and B. Andres (Eds.): GCPR 2016, LNCS 9796, pp. 320–331, 2016.
DOI: 10.1007/978-3-319-45886-1_26

for communication purposes. The OTDR is an active measurement device as it injects light pulses into the fiber cable. The optical fiber at the railway track can be considered as passive, since trains do not need to communicate with the OTDR device. Several methods for train tracking using OTDR signals have been proposed in the literature [12,20]. However, these algorithms were not evaluated for longer recordings with many trains crossing. We will review the existing literature and describe the problem in detail in the following section. All the algorithmic details, as well as a discussion of the accuracy of the proposed method will be given in the later sections. We will further provide an outlook for future work and improvements.

2 Problem Description and Related Work

Our datasets were acquired with an OTDR device [8] and stored as a matrix, where each row is the measurements of the optical cable characteristics measured with one laser pulse. The dimension of the matrix is determined by the number of cable segments and the duration of the recording. The fiber cable consist of a fixed number of segments in each recording and a segment has a length of 0.68 m. The monitored section has two parallel railway tracks, includes a number of stops and a shunting yard. Figure 1 visualizes both input datasets. Although in this contribution the data along the complete time axis are available, the detection and tracking have been implemented for online processing using only a given chunk of measurements at a time.

Given the raw OTDR measurements $m(x, t)$ we want to detect and track trains, i.e. for each train that passes through the monitored stretch of railway tracks we want to automatically detect tuples with positions and times denoting the positions of the train at a given time. The quality of the tracking algorithm is then measured based on two main criteria: correct detection of all the trains passing the monitored track and the accuracy of the individual tracks. The rest of this section will be devoted to the discussion of the algorithms for OTDR signal processing and related motion tracking that can be found in the literature.

2.1 Signal Processing in OTDR

OTDR signals have been used in many different fields and many different signal processing techniques have been applied to these signals. In the following we provide an overview of the literature available.

For intrusion detection averaging methods were used [3,6], where the latest measurement is subtracted from the average. Averaging methods are accurate enough for intrusion detection where the position of the optical fiber can be chosen such that an event causes a large signal. For train vibration detection these methods proved not to be accurate enough due to the highly varying signal to noise ratio (SNR).

Qin et al. [14] introduced wavelet denoising in Φ-OTDR signal processing by thresholding the wavelet coefficients. They point out, that wavelet denoising

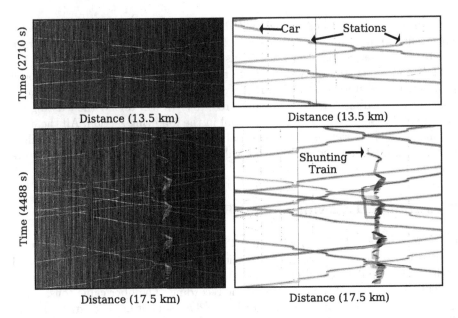

Fig. 1. The left side shows the input datasets, where each second of measurement is aggregated into one pixel. The pixel intensity is the energy of frequency coefficients between 50 and 150 Hz. The left-top data were taken with 4 kHz and the left-bottom were taken with 2 kHz. The right side shows the detection and tracking, where each tracked object is encoded with a different color. For clarification we labeled a tracked car, a shunting train and two of the stations. The two datasets were recorded with one minute offset to change the parameters of the recording device (Color figure online).

allows to remove noise that is present across all the frequencies while other frequently used methods (e.g. moving average) often only remove high frequency content from the signal. Wavelet denoising was applied by Peng et al. for pipeline intrusion detection [13] and for train detection [12]. To obtain locations of rising and falling edge of train signals normalized sliding variance was applied.

Using a spectral decomposition of the signal different authors have tried to distinguish between different events detected in OTDR signals. Kong et al. [9] have presented a method to detect events in OTDR signals based on Short-time Fourier Transformation (STFT) and correlation matching. Wu et al. [22] presented a method based on phase space matrix construction, eigenvalue decomposition and neural network classification to process signals from Φ-OTDR signals. Timofeev et al. [21] applied Gaussian Mixture Model (GMM) with Support Vector Machine (SVM) kernel to distinguish between different events (e.g. a walking man, a truck moving) in signals acquired with C-OTDR device. The (GMM-SVM) method was introduced by You et al. [24] for speaker recognition. The feature values they use are built using Linear-Frequency Spaced Filterbank Cepstrum Coefficients (LFCC) from 200 to 3000 Hz. Timofeev [19] applied

(GMM-SVM) also to detect activities (e.g. soil digging with excavator or working with crowbar) nearby the railway track in signals from C-OTDR devices.

We propose a Fourier transformation based method, as our tests have shown that it is possible to extract features to distinguish between vibration and background signals even with low SNR. Other methods such as wavelet denoising and averaging methods have been considered for our problem, but these need thresholds, which may vary under different circumstances. We found GMM not suitable for our problem since the two clusters for background and vibration signals do not have the shape of a Gaussian distribution. It is important to point out that we normalize the Fourier coefficients before classification, therefore the energy of the signal is not relevant for the classification. We have seen considerable variance of the energy of the signal present in the different cable segments.

2.2 Motion Tracking

This section gives an overview on motion tracking between image frames based on the survey of Yilmaz et al. [23] and we discuss the possibilities of point-tracking, kernel-tracking and silhouette-tracking for our purpose. Point-tracking relies on an external mechanism that detects objects in every frame. Deterministic methods solve the correspondence between consecutive frames by defining a cost between tracked points. Minimization of the cost can be formulated as a combinatorial problem [5, 15–17]. Stochastic methods, e.g. Kalman filter [7], solve the correspondence by taking the measurement and model uncertainties into account. A Kalman filter can be only applied for one object, multiple objects need multiple Kalman filters.

Kernel-tracking e.g. mean-shift clustering proposed by Comaniciu and Meer [4] or KLT tracker proposed by Shi and Tomasi [18] are based on maximizing or comparing the similarity of appearance between consecutive frames by defining a feature vector for each tracked object or region. The proposed feature vectors extracted in this contribution are not reliable enough to apply kernel-tracking.

Silhouette-tracking is based on tracking objects e.g. hands by a complex descriptor of the region. Train signals acquired by an OTDR device after classification form in ideal case rectangular signals and do not require complex descriptors. Signal edges can be detected and a point-tracking mechanism can be adapted. It is essential to handle entry and exit of objects as trains are entering and leaving the measurement range. Multiple data association must be handled also, as multiple trains can appear in one time frame.

3 Algorithm

In the following we will describe our algorithm for train tracking, which is carried out in two main steps. In the first step, the beginning and end points of trains for a given second of time in the raw data are detected. In the second step these points are used for extracting attributes from trains i.e. position, speed and length for the given second.

3.1   Point Detection

The first step of the point detection is to classify points in time and space where vibration is present in the cable. To extract feature values for classification, Fourier transformation is used. For each cable segment we compute the Fourier transform for each second to receive a high dimensional feature vector $d_{i,j}(k)$, where i denotes the cable segment, j denotes the position in time (in seconds) and k denotes the frequency channel of the Fourier transform. The applied transformation can be seen as a sparse Short-Time Fourier transformation on the complete signal. It is important to note that, even for cable segments which provide a noisy signal, the Fourier transform has a typical pattern when vibrations of a train are present, see Fig. 2, therefore detection can be also applied on segments with low SNR.

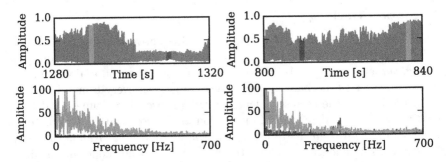

Fig. 2. The top-left and top-right images are part of raw input signals, where the top-left has high SNR and top-right has low SNR. From both signals two one second signals have been selected, one for train signal (encoded with red) and one for background signal (encoded with blue). The corresponding FFTs of the selected signals are visualized with the same color in the bottom images, where it can be seen that vibration can be detected even in signals with low SNR (Color figure online)

Using all Fourier coefficients as feature vectors would be expensive and many coefficients would be redundant or carry no information about the signal, therefore feature vector reduction is performed by scalar quantization. Each Fourier coefficient is assigned to a distinct bin and the reduced feature vector contains the normalized sum of the corresponding coefficients for each bin, where the normalization divider is the sum of all coefficients and the bins are linearly spaced. Principal Component Analysis (PCA) is then used to further reduce the feature vector. The reduced feature vectors are classified using a Support Vector Machine (SVM). The SVM was trained to make binary decisions between background-signal and vibration-signal using a Radial Basis Function (RBF) kernel. By an abuse of mathematical notation we can write the complete event detection process as the composition of the following steps: $r_{i,j} = \text{SVM} \circ \text{PCA} \circ \text{QUANT} \circ \mathcal{F}$. The complexity of the detection is linear in both time (seconds) and space (number of segments), while due to Fourier transformation it has logarithmic complexity with respect to the sampling rate of the OTDR device.

The classification for each second of the original measurements results in a vector of binary classification $r_{i,j}$, where i denotes the cable segment and j denotes the position in time (in seconds). For a given second in time, the classifications of the last 10 s are summed along the time axis resulting in a vector describing the number of positive classifications in one cable segment within the time window. On this vector Gaussian filtering is performed along the space axis. Thresholding this vector leads to a filtered binary classification along space for a given second. Finally, the beginning (rising) and end (falling) points of trains are detected by taking the first derivative of the filtered results. Figure 3 visualizes the filtering steps.

3.2   Motion Tracking

Motion tracking is solved between two consecutive seconds as an optimization problem. The tracking is modeled in two stages. First, the beginning and end points of trains are tracked. These points can disappear when a train stops or when the trajectory of two trains are overlapping, therefore a second stage is defined for train tracking. Point tracking and train tracking are both solved as an optimization problem, where the following vertex sets are defined:

- V_{np} represents the new points detected after filtering of the classification results. This vertex set is redefined every second.
- V_{tp} represents the tracked points. Insertion and deletion in this set can be done in each second after solving the optimization problem.
- V_{tt} represents the tracked trains. Insertion and deletion in this set can be done in each second after solving the optimization problem.

For tracking in the two stages the following complete weighted undirected bipartite graphs are defined:

- $\mathcal{G}_p(V_p, E_p, w_p)$, where $V_p = V_{np} \cup V_{tp}$, $E_p = \{\{v_{np}, v_{tp}\} : v_{np} \in V_{np}, v_{tp} \in V_{tp}\}$
- $\mathcal{G}_t(V_t, E_t, w_t)$, where $V_t = V_{tp} \cup V_{tt}$, $E_t = \{\{v_{tp}, v_{tt}\} : v_{tp} \in V_{tp}, v_{tt} \in V_{tt}\}$.

To set up the optimization problems we define the following functions for vertices in the defined vertex sets:

- $u(v) \in \{-1, +1\}$ for $v \in V_{np} \cup V_{tp}$, determines if a point is rising (beginning of train) or falling (end of train).
- $p(v) \in \{0, ..., K\}$ for $v \in V_{np} \cup V_{tp} \cup V_{tt}$, denotes the position (segment), where K is the number of segments.
- $c_{tp}(v) \in [0, 1]$ for $v \in V_{tp}$, denotes the confidence of a tracked point, which is computed from the weighted sum of valid observations in time, the weights are forming a normalized exponential probability distribution function.
- $c_{tt}(v) \in [0, 1]$ for $v \in V_{tt}$, denotes the confidence of a tracked train, which is computed from weighted average of tracked point confidence observations. It also takes into account the number of rising/falling points.

- $s_{tp}(v) \in \mathbb{R}^+$ for $v \in V_{tp}$, determines velocity of tracked point, which is computed from the slope of the position of the last 10 s.
- $s_{tt}(v) \in \mathbb{R}^+$ for $v \in V_{tt}$, determines velocity of tracked train, which is computed from weighted average of tracked point velocity observations.
- $\Delta_T(v) \in \mathbb{N}^+$ for $v \in V_{tt}$, denotes the number of seconds since last update of tracked train.
- $\Delta(v_1, v_2) = p(v_1) - p(v_2) \ v_1, v_2 \in V_{np} \cup V_{tp} \cup V_{tt}$, is a function that computes the distance between two vertices in the same graph.
- $\Delta_E(v) = p(v) + s(v) \ v \in V_{tp}$, is a function that computes the expected distance between the current and the next position of the tracked point.
- $\sigma_{\mathcal{G}_p}(v)$ gives the set of all incident edges for a vertex $v \in V_p$ in graph $\mathcal{G}_p$.
- $\sigma_{\mathcal{G}_t}(v)$ gives the set of all incident edges for a vertex $v \in V_t$ in graph $\mathcal{G}_t$.

The weights for the edges $e_p \in E_p$ and $e_t \in E_t$ are computed as:

- $w_p(e_p) = w_p(\{v_{np}, v_{tp}\}) = c_e(v_{tp}) * \frac{1}{1+|\Delta(v_{np}, v_{tp}) - \Delta_E(v_{tp})|} \in [0, 1]$, which denotes the weight of an edge in $\mathcal{G}_p$, where $e_p = \{v_{np}, v_{tp}\} \in E_p$.
- $w_t(e_t) = w_t(\{v_{tp}, v_{tt}\}) = c_p(v_{tt}) * c_e(v_{tp}) * (a + (\frac{1}{\Delta_T(v_{tt}) * |\Delta(v_{te}, v_{tt})|})) \in [0, 2]$, which denotes the weight of an edge in $\mathcal{G}_t$, where $e_t = \{v_{tp}, v_{tt}\} \in E_t$ and $a = 1$ if both tracked point and tracked train moves in the same direction.

For the two graphs two separate Binary Integer Programs (BIP) are defined, where the objective functions are maximized. For each edge e in one of the two defined graphs we associate a binary variable x_e. For $e \in E_p$, the variable x_e is set to 1 if the corresponding new point is associated with the tracked point. Similarly, for $e \in E_t$, the variable x_e is set to 1 if the corresponding tracked point is associated with the tracked train.

Point tracking

$$\max \sum_{e \in E_p} w_p(e) x_e \ s.t. \tag{1}$$

$$\sum_{e \in \sigma_{\mathcal{G}_p}(v)} x_e \leq 1 \quad \forall v \in V_p \tag{2}$$

$$x_e u(v_{np}) = x_e u(v_{tp}) \\ \forall e = \{v_{np}, v_{tp}\} \in E_p \tag{3}$$

$$x_e \, \text{sgn}(s_{tp}(v_{tp})) = x_e \, \text{sgn}(\Delta(v_{np}, v_{tp})) \\ \forall e = \{v_{np}, v_{tp}\} \in E_p \tag{4}$$

$$x_e \in \{0, 1\} \quad \forall e \in E_p \tag{5}$$

Train tracking

$$\max \sum_{e \in E_t} w_t(e) x_e \ s.t. \tag{6}$$

$$\sum_{e \in \sigma_{\mathcal{G}_t}(v_{tp})} x_e \leq 1 \quad \forall v_{tp} \in V_{tp} \tag{7}$$

$$x_e c_{te}(v_{tp}) \geq 0.5 x_e \\ \forall e = \{v_{tp}, v_{tt}\} \in E_t \tag{8}$$

$$x_e \Delta(v_{tp}, v_{tt}) \leq 1500 \\ \forall e = \{v_{tp}, v_{tt}\} \in E_t \tag{9}$$

$$x_e \in \{0, 1\} \quad \forall e \in E_t. \tag{10}$$

In the following we will discuss the roles of the constraints in the linear programs. Constraint 2 ensures that each tracked point and each new-point can have only one association. Constraint 3 ensures that rising and falling points

Table 1. Cross-validation of train tracking with ground truth.

Train (ID)	23468	29515	2330	73	23488	Avg	Min	Max
LOOCV (meter)	38.24	4.89	37.76	64.92	48.11	38.78	4.89	64.92

cannot be associated. Constraint 4 ensures that the sign of $\Delta(e)$ and the tracked point velocity must be the same. Constraint 7 ensures that each tracked point can only be association with one tracked train, but multiple tracked points can be assigned to a tracked train. This serves as a noise filter, since points can appear from classification noise and no new trains should be constructed. False-positive edges often have a confidence lower than 0.5, therefore constraint 8 ensures that tracked points only with confidence higher than 0.5 are considered. Constraint 9 ensures that tracked points with large distance cannot be associated.

The BIPs are solved with greedy heuristics and the result is a list of tracked trains, each with the following attributes: position, confidence, velocity and length. The complexity of the greedy solution is derived from the complexity of the sorting algorithm in terms of the number of edge weights within the graph. The visualization in Fig. 3 shows an example of the tracking algorithm. The length of a train is computed by the standard deviation of tracked point position observations. Entry and exit of objects are handled as:

- new points $v_{np} \in V_{np}$ without association are promoted to vertex set V_{tp},
- if a tracked point $v_{tp} \in V_{tp}$ has no association, an empty-edge is assigned to decrease confidence,
- if a tracked point $v_{tp} \in V_{tp}$ reaches the confidence zero, it is removed from vertex set V_{tp},
- tracked points $v_{tp} \in V_{tp}$ without association are promoted to vertex set V_{tt},
- if a tracked train $v_{tt} \in V_{tp}$ has no association and the position is close either to the beginning or the end of the measurement range, it is removed from vertex set $V_{tt} \in V_{tt}$.

4   Evaluation

In the first step, parameters of the classification were investigated. We have received two datasets for the research with a total of around 169 million samples. For training and testing input data 10000 background and 10000 train samples were annotated by hand within the first dataset. To ensure non-overlapping samples, training data was taken from the first half of the dataset and testing data were taken from the second half of the dataset. Accuracy of the SVM classifier has been computed as (TP+TN)/(TP+TN+FP+FN). Frequency intervals from 1, 25, 50, 75, 100 to 200, 300, ..., 900, 1000 with bin count 5, 10, ..., 35, 40 were considered. Table 2 shows that as the beginning of the frequency interval increases, the number of TP decreases. Low frequency vibrations are present in a wider vicinity of a moving train than its high frequency vibrations. Leaving out

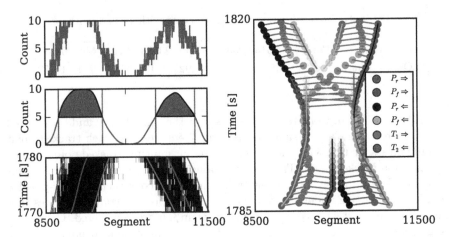

Fig. 3. The detection of begin/end points is visualized on the left side. The left-bottom image shows a 10 s window of the classification result. The left-top image shows the result of summation along the time axis as a one dimensional signal representing the count of positive classifications. The left-middle image shows the Gaussian filtering along the space axis. On the same image the filled section shows where threshold is exceeded, as well as the corresponding point detection, where green is the rising edge and red is the falling edge. On the left-bottom image the blue lines are the middle of trains and red lines are the head and tail of trains. The image on the right shows the train tracking graphs when the trajectories of two trains are crossing each other. Points (V_{tp}) are noted as P, the subscript represents rising/falling. Trains (V_{tt}) are noted as T, the subscript has no effect on the algorithm. Arrows represent the direction of points and trains. After time 1789 the points in the middle are not detectable any more and their confidence is starting to decrease, which is encoded as the alpha channel in the visualization. When their confidence is lower than 0.5, they are not associated to the trains and the confidence of the trains are decreasing also. In the middle of the image, the points change direction and new points are inserted to the set of tracked points. When the confidence of these points reaches 0.5, they are associated to the trains. At the top of the image, the points in the middle are tracked again and the confidence of the trains reaches 100 % again. (Color figure online)

low frequency bins from classification allows to locate trains with higher positional accuracy. The decline in accuracy without quantization shows that the implicit averaging of quantization is important. Reduction using PCA slightly decreases accuracy, but Table 2 shows a positive impact on the processing speed and using two eigenvectors the data can be reconstructed 87 %. Table 2 also shows that applying PCA directly to the Fourier transform is slower than using quantization first. The speed of the SVM classification is not only depending on the number of feature values, but also on the number of support vectors. The speed tests of the Python implementation were executed on a single core of an Intel(R) E5-1620 v3 CPU and the processing speed for one second data from both datasets were processed in around 2 s. We concluded from visual evaluation that false positive classifications have more negative impact on the point detection than false negatives.

Table 2. Accuracy and speed results of different parameters, where SVM was used for classification. FFT was executed on 5000 samples/segment. We show for each frequency interval the highest accuracy results. Note that quantization includes normalization.

Accuracy	TN	FP	FN	TP	FFT	Quant	PCA	SVM	Frequency	Bins	Reduction
%	Count				ns/segment				Hz	Count	Type
99.61	9970	30	47	9953	110.5	2.3	0.0	20.5	25-995	10	None
99.60	9970	30	50	9950	111.1	2.5	0.1	15.6	25-995	10	PCA
99.58	9969	31	53	9947	108.7	2.5	0.0	51.0	1-701	25	None
99.50	9967	33	66	9934	108.2	2.3	0.1	27.8	1-701	25	PCA
99.42	9972	28	88	9912	126.1	2.5	0.0	47.9	50-500	10	None
97.82	9981	19	417	9583	123.7	2.2	0.0	55.6	75-500	10	None
97.67	9974	26	440	9560	109.4	7.8	0.0	4647	1-701	700	None
97.28	9951	49	494	9506	111.0	8.1	3.6	139.1	1-701	700	PCA

The tracking algorithm was evaluated using cross-validation with ground truth data, see also [11]. Leave-one-out cross-validation (LOOCV) was used where a time offset was computed from $n - 1$ trains and using this offset an absolute average of distances was computed as the validation value. From Table 1 the conclusion was made that the absolute average difference of the tracking is 38.78 m. Figure 1 shows the detection and tracking results. We find important to point out that all trains were found and tracked correctly. The detection algorithm was not trained to distinguish between cars and trains, therefore a car was tracked by the motion tracking algorithm. The data shown in Fig. 1 include the rail section of a shunting-yard at around kilometer 11 and tracking of trains are not satisfactory at that location. The average processing speed of the tracking algorithm for each second of data was around 10 ns.

5   Conclusion

In this paper a novel method was proposed to extract feature vectors from OTDR signals to distinguish between background-signal and vibration-signal. The algorithm is not dependent on the signal energy but classifies only based on the shape of the spectral distribution. From the given datasets train-signals were classified with an accuracy larger than 98 %. The algorithm is designed to work in real-time and processes raw data of one second in each step. Due to filtering of the classification the algorithm has a delay of 5 s in the current implementation.

Based on the classification a tracking algorithm has been presented that is able to automatically detect and track trains with an average of 38.8 m. To our knowledge this is the first algorithm that is reliably able to track trains automatically with crossings over a long period of time. In our data trains are tracked reliably up to a section with a shunting yard. The overlapping trains in that section lead to errors in the tracking algorithm therefore these cases have to be investigated in more detail. We plan to improve robustness of the tracking method by including spatio-temporal features and eliminating parameters for train beginning/end detection, furthermore we plan to investigate if the tracking model can be simplified by tracking the center of trains in a single-stage manner.

Acknowledgements. The data used for the work presented in this paper have been collected in the research project *Sensorsystem für Bahnstrecken* funded by the Austrian Research Agency FFG under contract number 840448. We especially acknowledge Wolfgang Zottl (ÖBB Infrastruktur GmbH) for approving the measurements and Günther Neunteufel (Fiber Cable Technologies GmbH) for providing the data.

References

1. Bao, X., Chen, L.: Recent progress in distributed fiber optic sensors. Sensors **12**(7), 8601–8639 (2012)
2. Chen, C., Chen, R., Wei, F., Wu, D.H.: Experimental and application of spiral distributed optical fiber sensors based on OTDR. In: 2011 International Conference on Electric Information and Control Engineering (ICEICE), pp. 5905–5909. IEEE (2011)
3. Choi, K.N., Juarez, J.C., Taylor, H.F.: Distributed fiber optic pressure/seismic sensor for low-cost monitoring of long perimeters. In: AeroSense 2003. International Society for Optics and Photonics, pp. 134–141 (2003)
4. Comaniciu, D., Ramesh, V., Meer, P.: Kernel-based object tracking. IEEE Trans. Pattern Anal. Mach. Intell. **25**(5), 564–577 (2003)
5. Jiang, H., Fels, S., Little, J.J.: A linear programming approach for multiple object tracking. In: 2007 IEEE Conference on Computer Vision and Pattern Recognition, CVPR 2007, pp. 1–8. IEEE (2007)
6. Juarez, J.C., Maier, E.W., Choi, K.N., Taylor, H.F.: Distributed fiber-optic intrusion sensor system. J. Lightwave Technol. **23**(6), 2081 (2005)
7. Kalman, R.E.: A new approach to linear filtering and prediction problems. J. Basic Eng. **82**(1), 35–45 (1960)
8. Kanellopoulos, S., Shatalin, S.: Detecting a disturbance in the phase of light propagating in an optical waveguide, 11 September 2012, US Patent 8,264,676. https://www.google.com/patents/US8264676
9. Kong, H., Zhou, Q., Xie, W., Dong, Y., Ma, C., Hu, W.: Events detection in OTDR data based on a method combining correlation matching with STFT. In: Asia Communications and Photonics Conference, pp. ATh3A–148. Optical Society of America (2014)
10. Kumagai, T., Sato, S., Nakamura, T.: Fiber-optic vibration sensor for physical security system. In: 2012 International Conference on Condition Monitoring and Diagnosis (CMD), pp. 1171–1174. IEEE (2012)
11. Papp, A., Wiesmeyr, C., Litzenberger, M., Garn, H., Kropatsch, W.: A real-time algorithm for train position monitoring using optical time-domain reflectometry. In: IEEE International Conference on Intelligent Rail Transportation (accepted) (2016)
12. Peng, F., Duan, N., Rao, Y.J., Li, J.: Real-time position and speed monitoring of trains using phase-sensitive OTDR. IEEE Photonics Technol. Lett. **26**(20), 2055–2057 (2014)
13. Peng, F., Wu, H., Jia, X.H., Rao, Y.J., Wang, Z.N., Peng, Z.P.: Ultra-long high-sensitivity ϕ-OTDR for high spatial resolution intrusion detection of pipelines. Opt. Express **22**(11), 13804–13810 (2014)

14. Qin, Z., Chen, L., Bao, X.: Wavelet denoising method for improving detection performance of distributed vibration sensor. IEEE Photonics Technol. Lett. **24**(7), 542–544 (2012)
15. Rangarajan, K., Shah, M.: Establishing motion correspondence. In: 1991 Proceedings of IEEE Computer Society Conference on Computer Vision and Pattern Recognition, CVPR 1991, pp. 103–108. IEEE (1991)
16. Sethi, I.K., Jain, R.: Finding trajectories of feature points in a monocular image sequence. IEEE Trans. Pattern Anal. Mach. Intell. **1**, 56–73 (1987)
17. Shafique, K., Shah, M.: A noniterative greedy algorithm for multiframe point correspondence. IEEE Trans. Pattern Anal. Mach. Intell. **27**(1), 51–65 (2005)
18. Shi, J., Tomasi, C.: Good features to track. In: 1994 Proceedings of IEEE Computer Society Conference on Computer Vision and Pattern Recognition, CVPR 1994, pp. 593–600. IEEE (1994)
19. Timofeev, A.V.: Monitoring the railways by means of C-OTDR technology. Int. J. Mech. Aerosp. Ind. Mechatron. Eng. **9**(5), 701–704 (2015)
20. Timofeev, A.V., Egorov, D.V., Denisov, V.M.: The rail traffic management with usage of C-OTDR monitoring systems. World Acad. Sci. Eng. Technol. Int. J. Comput. Electr. Autom. Control Inf. Eng. **9**(7), 1492–1495 (2015)
21. Timofeev, A., Egorov, D.: Multichannel classification of target signals by means of an SVM ensemble in C-OTDR systems for remote monitoring of extended objects. In: MVML-2014 Conference Proceedings, vol. 1 (2014)
22. Wu, H., Li, X., Peng, Z., Rao, Y.: A novel intrusion signal processing method for phase-sensitive optical time-domain reflectometry (ϕ-OTDR). In: OFS2014 23rd International Conference on Optical Fiber Sensors. p. 91575O. International Society for Optics and Photonics (2014)
23. Yilmaz, A., Javed, O., Shah, M.: Object tracking: a survey. ACM Comput. Surv. (CSUR) **38**(4), 13 (2006)
24. You, C.H., Lee, K.A., Li, H.: GMM-SVM kernel with a Bhattacharyya-based distance for speaker recognition. IEEE Trans. Audio Speech Lang. Process. **18**(6), 1300–1312 (2010)

Parametric Dictionary-Based Velocimetry for Echo PIV

Ecaterina Bodnariuc[1]([⊠]), Stefania Petra[1], Christian Poelma[2], and Christoph Schnörr[1]

[1] Image and Pattern Analysis Group, University of Heidelberg, Heidelberg, Germany
ecaterina.bodnariuc@iwr.uni-heidelberg.de
[2] Laboratory for Aero and Hydrodynamics, Delft University of Technology, Delft, The Netherlands

Abstract. We introduce a novel motion estimation approach for Echo PIV for the laminar and steady flow model. We mathematically formalize the motion estimation problem as a parametrization of a dictionary of particle trajectories by the physical flow parameter. We iteratively refine this unknown parameter by subsequent sparse approximations. We show smoothness of the adaptive flow dictionary that is a key for a provably convergent numerical scheme. We validate our approach on real data and show accurate velocity estimation when compared to the state-of-the-art cross-correlation method.

1 Introduction

Ultrasound techniques are widely used to measure blood flow in clinical applications. They enable noninvasive measurements that can be applied to opaque flows. Echo PIV [8,11] is a velocimetry technique that applies optical PIV analysis algorithms to sequential ultrasound images and has been developed to improve blood flow analysis using clinical ultrasound machines. Echo PIV involves two steps: an imaging step and a motion estimation step. While the imaging step is rapidly evolving [13–15], the motion estimation step has been adopted from traditional laser-based imaging [2] and employs cross-correlation techniques prevailing in different fields of experimental fluid dynamics [1,12]. These techniques have been optimized during the last decade and are widely used by research groups and also as commercial software packages by industry[1]. However, they do not take advantage of *physical motion properties* of the underlying flow in order to effectively regularize flow velocimetry under adverse imaging conditions, as in the case of Echo PIV. Highly accurate motion estimation is of pivotal importance, because subsequent steps of flow analysis, like wall shear stress measurements, rely on *flow derivatives*.

In this paper, we adopt and elaborate a radically different approach [3] for the motion estimation step in Echo PIV. The approach is based on the Poiseuille

---

[1] See, e.g. http://www.lavision.de/en/products/davis.php.

© Springer International Publishing AG 2016
B. Rosenhahn and B. Andres (Eds.): GCPR 2016, LNCS 9796, pp. 332–343, 2016.
DOI: 10.1007/978-3-319-45886-1_27

model for flows in a pipe which yields a one-dimensional parametrization of physically plausible flows. While this model could be refined [16] and even more steps towards the incompressible Navier-Stokes flow model on corresponding bounded domains could be made [7], such additional degrees of freedom quickly turn out to be detrimental for accurate flow estimation under adverse imaging conditions. A second key property exploited by [3] concerns the *sparsity* of microbubbles that are used to seed and to image real flows, as this enables to apply established techniques for sparse estimation and optimization.

Contribution. Our new approach significantly simplifies the approach from [3] and is computationally less expensive. We mathematically formalize the parametrization of a high-dimensional dictionary of particle trajectories by the physical flow parameter. This is exemplified by two corresponding mappings that are continuous and continuously differentiable, respectively. Such properties are key to *provably convergent numerical optimization*, but are missing in [3]. Different established optimization techniques can then be reliably applied, depending on the degree of smoothness of the mapping. Unlike in [3], our approach is validated on *in vitro measurements* of real data, at the limit of standard PIV methods corresponding to low micro-bubble seeding and high flow velocities.

Overall, our approach consistently integrates a basic physical flow model and an adaptively generated trajectory dictionary into a sparse reconstruction framework. This results in a *global spatio-temporal* velocimetry technique that extracts information from the entire given video sequence and therefore is highly accurate and robust. It thus provides a viable alternative to the established (semi-) local cross-correlation techniques.

Organization. In Sect. 2 we give an overview of the proposed method. In Sect. 3 we describe and characterize in detail the dependency of the flow trajectory matrix on the flow model parameter. Section 4 is devoted to the optimization approach. The method is validated on real data in Sect. 5. We conclude in Sect. 6.

2   Proposed Approach

In Fig. 1 we briefly sketch the basic Echo PIV set-up and refer to [3,11] for further details.

Let f denote the input data, which is a sequence of N_t consecutive images at subsequent time steps merged together as shown in Fig. 2. We assume that f is well-approximated by a sparse superposition of trajectory atoms from a flow dictionary $A(v_m^*)$, introduced in Sect. 3. Hence

$$f \approx A(v_m^*)u(v_m^*), \tag{2.1}$$

where $u(v_m^*)$ is an indicator vector selecting active trajectories in $A(v_m^*)$. If we would know the maximal velocity v_m^* of the flow profile, then we could trace particles along trajectories by determining the indicator vector $u(v_m^*)$ via a sparse reconstruction

$$u(v_m^*) = \arg \min_{u \in [0,1]^N} \|A(v_m^*)u - f\|_2^2 + \lambda\|u\|_1, \tag{2.2}$$

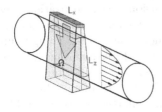
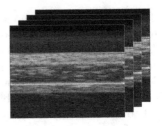

Fig. 1. A schematic representation of the Echo PIV setup (*left*), adapted from [11]. In a rigid cylindrical tube of inner radius $R = L_z/2$ flows a liquid seeded with microbubbles contrast agents. A linear transducer array is placed along the tube axis, above an observation area of size $L_x \times L_z$, and emits a sound pulse into inhomogeneous medium. The same transducer records the back scattered RF (radio frequency) signal. After the signal processing steps, which consists of the Hilbert transform, envelope detection and log-compression, a 2D image is obtained, also knows as B-mode image. A sequence of images (*right*) is recorded at a fixed frame rate Δt^{-1}. In the state-of-the-art method, particle image velocimetry (PIV) analysis, the velocity field is estimated by cross-correlating consecutive pairs of B-mode images.

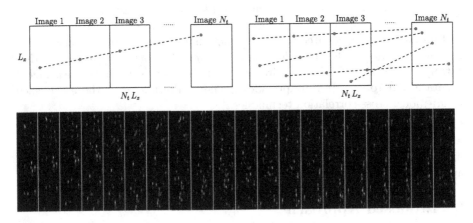

Fig. 2. Each column in the dictionary $A(v_m)$ describes a possible trajectory for a single particle seen in N_t consecutive images concatenated along the tube axis (*top left*, adapted from [3]). The input data f is given by all N_t images, which usually contain several particles (*top right*, adapted from [3]). The Poiseuille flow model (3.1) leads to straight line particle trajectories. This can be also observed in the real data example (*bottom*) with $N_t = 20$ images. The problem is to *sparsely* match particles to trajectories in $A(v_m^*)$ parametrized by the unknown maximal velocity v_m^* based on the input data f.

provided $A(v_m^*)$ is nearly an isometry on the class of sparse signals [5]. However v_m^* is unknown and has to be determined from the input data f. Our ansatz is to include the estimation of the unknown parameter v_m^* in the reconstruction step. To this end we denote the non-negative parameter v_m by $v \in \mathbb{R}_+$ and we consider the function

$$g(v) = \min_{u \in [0,1]^N} \|A(v)u - f\|_2^2 + \lambda\|u\|_1, \tag{2.3}$$

which will be minimized in order to decrease the "distance" of the input data f to our unknown parametric linear model $A(v_m^*)u(v_m^*)$. In other words, we are estimating the unknown parameter v_m^* by adapting a trajectory dictionary $A(v)$ to our image sequence. A convergent numerical scheme for minizing g is developed in Sect. 4.

3   Flow Dictionary

3.1   Poiseuille Flow Model

The laminar and steady flow in a straight cylindrical tube of radius R is governed by the following equations of motion:

$$\begin{cases} x(t) = x(t') + (t - t')\,v_m\,\alpha(z) \\ z(t) = z(t') = const. \end{cases} \tag{3.1}$$

where $z \in [0, 2R]$, $\alpha(z) = 1 - (R - z)^2/R^2$ and $t, t' \geq 0$. The non-negative parameter v_m is the maximal flow velocity - the velocity of particles moving along the tube axis. Subsequently we will omit index m and denote v_m by v.

3.2   Trajectory Matrix $A(v)$

We further detail the construction of the space-time trajectory dictionary $A(v)$, which depends on the maximal flow velocity introduced in (3.1). Let $\Omega := [0, L_x] \times [0, L_z] \subset \mathbb{R}^2$ denote a fixed field of view in the x/z-plane, see Fig. 1. We uniformly discretize Ω into $N_x N_z$ rectangular cells

$$\Omega_{i,j} := [(i - 1)\,\Delta x, i\,\Delta x] \times [(j - 1)\,\Delta z, j\,\Delta z], \qquad i \in [N_x], \quad j \in [N_z] \tag{3.2}$$

of size $\Delta x \Delta z$ with $\Delta x = L_x/N_x$, $\Delta z = L_z/N_z$. Using the continuous B-spline basis function of degree one, $\psi\colon \mathbb{R} \to \mathbb{R}$, or the continuously differentiable B-spline basis function of degree two, $\varphi\colon \mathbb{R} \to \mathbb{R}$, given by

$$\psi(t) := \begin{cases} 2t, & 0 \leq t < \frac{1}{2}, \\ 2 - 2t, & \frac{1}{2} \leq t \leq 1, \\ 0, & \text{otherwise}, \end{cases} \tag{3.3}$$

$$\varphi(t) := \begin{cases} \frac{9}{2}t^2, & 0 \leq t < \frac{1}{3}, \\ -\frac{3}{2}(1 - 6t + 6t^2), & \frac{1}{3} \leq t < \frac{2}{3}, \\ \frac{9}{2}(1 - 2t + t^2), & \frac{2}{3} \leq t \leq 1, \\ 0, & \text{otherwise}, \end{cases} \tag{3.4}$$

we define for every $(x_i, z_j) = ((i - 1/2)\Delta x, (j - 1/2)\Delta z)$ where $(i, j) \in \{0, \ldots, N_x + 1\} \times \{0, \ldots, N_z + 1\}$ the cell-centered 2-dimensional basis functions

$$\psi_{i,j} : \mathbb{R}^2 \to \mathbb{R}, \quad (x, z) \mapsto \psi_{i,j}(x, z) := \psi\left(\frac{x - x_i}{2\,\Delta x} + \frac{1}{2}\right)\psi\left(\frac{z - z_j}{2\,\Delta z} + \frac{1}{2}\right), \quad (3.5)$$

$$\varphi_{i,j} : \mathbb{R}^2 \to \mathbb{R}, \quad (x, z) \mapsto \varphi_{i,j}(x, z) := \varphi\left(\frac{x - x_i}{3\,\Delta x} + \frac{1}{2}\right)\varphi\left(\frac{z - z_j}{3\,\Delta z} + \frac{1}{2}\right), \quad (3.6)$$

which form a partition of unity of Ω. Figure 3a illustrates this construction for quadratic function (3.4) in 1D-domain $[0, L_x]$ with $L_x = N_x = 5$ and $\Delta x = 1$. Note that $N_x + 2$ basis functions are required and, accordingly, $(N_x + 2)(N_z + 2)$ basis functions in the 2D case.

The following discussion is developed for the quadratic functions (3.6), and can be easily extended to piecewise linear functions (3.5) by substituting $\varphi_{i,j}$ with $\psi_{i,j}$.

A *point particle* located at $(x_0, z_0) \in \Omega$ in a 2D-fluid is *mathematically* represent as a Dirac measure $\delta(x_0, z_0)$ with unit mass. The *discretized representation* is given by the coefficients

$$c_{i,j} = \int_{\mathbb{R}^2} \delta(x_0 - x', z_0 - z')\varphi_{i,j}(x', z')\mathrm{d}x'\mathrm{d}z' = \varphi_{i,j}(x_0, z_0), \quad (3.7)$$

with $i \in \{0, \ldots, N_x + 1\}$, $j \in \{0, \ldots, N_z + 1\}$ and the corresponding function

$$\delta(x_0, z_0) \approx \hat{\delta}_{(x_0, z_0)}(x, z) = \sum_{i=0}^{N_x+1} \sum_{j=0}^{N_z+1} \varphi_{i,j}(x_0, z_0)\varphi_{i,j}(x, z). \quad (3.8)$$

Figure 3b–c illustrate in the 1D scenario of Fig. 3a the coefficients and the functions corresponding to two point particles. Note that the mass of $\hat{\delta}_{(x_0, z_0)}(x, y)$ is no longer concentrated at (x_0, z_0) but "smeared over"

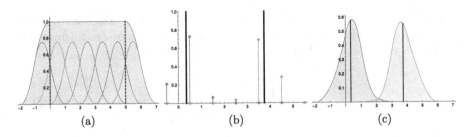

(a)   (b)   (c)

Fig. 3. (a) Partition of unity of the domain $[0, 5]$ using the functions (3.4). (b) Two unit-mass Dirac measures located at x_1 and x_2, respectively, indicated by the two black lines. The corresponding coefficients $\varphi_i(x_1)$ and $\varphi_i(x_2)$, for $i \in \{0, \ldots, 6\}$ are indicated by the blue and yellow points, respectively, located at the cell centroids $i - 1/2$. (c) The two functions $\hat{\delta}_{x_1}(x), \hat{\delta}_{x_2}(x)$ resulting from the basis expansion are used for the representation and matching of real particles. Black lines indicate the centroid position which exactly recover x_1 and x_2. (Color figure online)

$$\text{supp} \left(\hat{\delta}_{(x_0,z_0)}(x,z) \right) = \bigcup_{\substack{i-1 \leq i' \leq i+1 \\ j-1 \leq j' \leq j+1}} \Omega_{i',j'} \quad \text{if} \quad (x_0,z_0) \in \Omega_{i,j}, \tag{3.9}$$

that is over the cell containing the location (x_0, z_0) of the point particle and all adjacent cells. Yet, the representation is still exact in that the point particle can be recovered in terms of its location, which is given by the centroid

$$\begin{pmatrix} x_0 \\ z_0 \end{pmatrix} = \int_{\mathbb{R}^2} \begin{pmatrix} x \\ z \end{pmatrix} \hat{\delta}_{(x_0,z_0)}(x,z) \mathrm{d}x \mathrm{d}z. \tag{3.10}$$

This larger, but still focused, support of functions representing point particles is a favorable property for matching observed point particles in image sequences of experimental fluids.

Regarding the latter matching task, we set up a dictionary of discretized particle trajectories, based on the flow model (3.1). Specifically, we consider a sequence of N_t frames imaging the flow within the region Ω at time $t_k = (k-1)\Delta t$, $k \in [N_t]$. The dictionary is composed of all particle trajectories that meet the center positions $(x_i, z_j) = ((i-1/2)\Delta x, (j-1/2)\Delta z) \in \Omega_{i,j}$ of all cells given by (3.2). Let us look at a single such trajectory, shown in Fig. 4, traced by the particle $\hat{\delta}_{(x_i,z_j,t_k)}(x,z,t)$ that meets the location (x_i, z_j) at time point t_k, $k \in [N_t]$. Due to the flow model (3.1), it moves at each t_l, $l \in [N_t]$ to the space-time points

$$\mathcal{T}_{i,j,k} := \left\{ \left(x_i + (t_l - t_k) v\alpha(z_j),\ z_j,\ t_l \right) : l \in [N_t] \right\}. \tag{3.11}$$

The union of all such sampled trajectories defines the set of space-time positions

$$\mathcal{T} := \bigcup_{i \in [N_x], j \in [N_z], k \in [N_t]} \mathcal{T}_{i,j,k}. \tag{3.12}$$

Let $x_{il} = x_i + (t_l - t_k) v\alpha(z_j)$, then each space-time position $(x_{il}, z_j, t_l) \in \mathcal{T}_{i,j,k} \subset \mathcal{T}$ corresponds to a particle $\delta(x_{il}, z_j, t_l)$, which for the purpose of numerical matching is approximated by

$$\hat{\delta}_{(x_{il},z_j,t_l)}(x,z,t) = \sum_{i'=0}^{N_x+1} \sum_{j'=0}^{N_z+1} \varphi_{i',j'}(x_{il},z_j,t_l) \varphi_{i',j'}(x,z), \tag{3.13}$$

according to (3.8). Note that in the present context of space-time trajectories, it is convenient to index the coefficients $\varphi_{i',j'}(x_{ik}, z_j, t_l)$ also by time, even though only spatial discretization is performed and hence the basis functions (3.6) do not depend on time.

The final step concerns the definition of a matrix A which collects the coefficients $\varphi_{i',j'}(x_{il}, z_j, t_l)$ corresponding to all functions (3.13) indexed by $\mathcal{T}$ of (3.12). We first define the auxiliary function

$$\text{ind}: (i,j,k) \mapsto (k-1)N_x N_z + (j-1)N_x + i, \quad i \in [N_x],\ j \in [N_z],\ k \in [N_t] \tag{3.14}$$

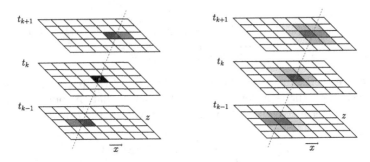

Fig. 4. Particle trajectory intersecting the region Ω at consecutive time steps and the "smeared over" support of functions representing point particles via (*left*) piecewise linear (3.5) or (*right*) quadratic (3.6) B-spline basis functions. The figures also illustrate the sparse nature of the matrix $A(v)$.

which indexes the collection of N_t cell-discretized domains Ω corresponding to the frames of a given image sequence. We now define the matrix

$$A_{\mathrm{ind}(i',j',l),\mathrm{ind}(i,j,k)} := \varphi_{i',j'}(x_{il}, z_j, t_l) \tag{3.15}$$

based on (3.13). In a similar way, we define the matrix A for piecewise linear functions (3.5), that is,

$$A_{\mathrm{ind}(i',j',l),\mathrm{ind}(i,j,k)} := \psi_{i',j'}(x_{il}, z_j, t_l). \tag{3.16}$$

In words, each column of A corresponds to the coefficients of the particle approximations (3.13) at locations given by $\mathcal{T}_{i,j,k}$ of (3.11). We refer to Fig. 4 for an illustration.

Lemma 1. *Let $v \in \mathbb{R}_+$ be a non-negative variable representing the flow parameter v_m in (3.1). Then (3.15)/(3.16) defines a mapping*

$$v \mapsto A(v) \in \mathbb{R}_+^{N \times N}, \quad N = N_x N_z N_t, \tag{3.17}$$

which is continuously differentiable/continuous.

Proof. Each entry of A defined by (3.15)/(3.16) is given by a C^1-function/ C-function of the form (3.6)/(3.5), which in turn is given by (3.4)/(3.3). By (3.11), the first argument of the right-hand side of (3.15)/(3.16) linearly depends on v, and so does the first factor of (3.6)/(3.5). $\qquad\square$

4   Optimization

4.1   Parametric Optimization

We recast (2.3) as a parametric optimization problem and consider

$$(P_v) \qquad \min_{u \in \mathbb{R}^N} J(u, v) \qquad \text{s.t.} \quad u \in F(v), \tag{4.1}$$

where $J(u,v) : \mathbb{R}^N \times \mathbb{R} \to \mathbb{R}$, $J(u,v) := \|A(v)u - f\|_2^2 + \lambda \|u\|_1$ and $F(v) := [0,1]^N$ is the *constant* feasible set and thus independent of v. Then g from (2.3) is the *optimal value function* of (4.1), given by $g(v) = \min\limits_{u \in F(v)} J(u,v)$. We denote by $S(v) = \arg\min\limits_{u \in F(v)} J(u,v)$ the optimal solution set and investigate continuity of $v \mapsto g(v)$ and the associated set valued mapping $v \rightrightarrows S(v)$. Continuity of g is a minimal requirement for reliable numerical optimization. The constraints and the regularization make the minimization of $J(u, \cdot)$ non-smooth, unless the minimum would be an interior point. But this cannot be expected to hold since constraints will be active and the minimizer will lie on the boundary.

Theorem 1. *([4, Proposition 4.4]) Let $v_0 \in \mathbb{R}$ be an arbitrary point in the parameter space. Suppose that*

(i) the function $(u,v) \mapsto J(u,v)$ is continuous on $\mathbb{R}^N \times \mathbb{R}$,
(ii) the multifunction $v \rightrightarrows F(v)$ is closed,
(iii) there exist an $\alpha \in \mathbb{R}$ and a compact set $K \subset \mathbb{R}^N$ such that for every v in a neighborhood of v_0, the level set

$$\mathrm{lev}_\alpha J(\cdot, v) := \{u \in F(v) : J(u,v) \le \alpha\} \tag{4.2}$$

is nonempty and contained in K,
(iv) for any neighborhood $\mathcal{V}_u$ of the set $S(v_0)$ there exists a neighborhood $\mathcal{V}_v$ of v_0 such that $\mathcal{V}_u \cap F(v) \ne \varnothing$ for all $v \in \mathcal{V}_v$.

Then the optimal value function $g(v)$ is continuous at $v = v_0$, and the multifunction $v \rightrightarrows S(v)$ is upper semi-continuous at v_0.

Corollary 1. *The optimal value function g from (2.3) is continuous on $\mathbb{R}$.*

Proof. We apply Theorem 1. *(i)* holds since J is continuous in both arguments in view of the definition of J and the continuity of $v \mapsto A(v)$ by Lemma 1. *(ii),(iv)* hold automatically since the feasible set $F(v) = [0,1]^N$ is constant and closed. Finally *(iii)* holds since for any $v \in \mathbb{R}$ the solution set $S(v)$ is nonempty in view of the compactness of the feasible set and continuity of $J(\cdot, v)$. Hence $\forall \alpha \ge g(v) \in \mathbb{R}$ we have $\emptyset \ne S(v) \subset \mathrm{lev}_\alpha J(\cdot, v) \subset [0,1]^N =: K$. $\qquad\square$

4.2   Optimizing the Optimal Value Function

A straightforward way of approximating the minimizer of g from (2.3) in a range of interest $a \le v \le b$ would be to evaluate the function at a fine grid of points in $[a,b]$ and choose the one corresponding to the lowest value, compare Fig. 5. However, this is a slow and computationally expensive method.

In [9] Mifflin and Strodiot proposed a rapidly converging five-point algorithm closely related to the well-known bisection method [10, Chap. 3] for *continuous* univariate functions, which uses function evaluations, but no derivatives. The method uses function values at five points, denoted and ordered such that

$$\hat{v}_- < v_- < v_0 < v_+ < \hat{v}_+, \tag{4.3}$$

to construct quadratic and polyhedral approximations to the function and then choose a point among the minimizers of the approximating functions via rules that do not require additional function evaluations. This property is significant since every evaluation of g requires the solution of the ℓ_1-regularized box-contrained least-squares problem (2.2). For further details we refer to the original paper [9]. Results are reported in Sect. 5.

5   Experiments

We applied our method to two challenging in vitro datasets with different flow velocities that follow the Poiseuille flow model assumptions, Sect. 3.1. The first one corresponds to a slow flow, depicted by very noisy B-mode images, henceforth called data set (a). The second data set (b) corresponds to a very fast flow at the limit of Poiseuille flow assumptions. For each data set we merge $N_t = 10$ consecutive images (corresponding to the tube interior) to represent the vector f. In Table 1 we summarize relevant parameters corresponding to both data sets and refer for an illustration to Fig. 1.

To estimate the maximal velocity v_m^* we perform univariate minimization of $v \mapsto g(v)$ as described in Sect. 4.2. The more involved step is the evaluation of g. This requires the evaluation of the sparse trajectory matrix $A(v)$ of size $N \times N$, $N = N_x N_z N_t$, but also requires solving the constrained convex optimization problem in (2.3) for certain v values. These evaluations are performed using CVX [6]. The number of function evaluations is kept low by using the fast converging five-point algorithm [9]. The convergence of this algorithm is illustrated in Fig. 5 along with the graph of g. We refer for results and discussions to Figs. 5, 6 and Table 1.

Table 1. The columns on the *left* show the data set parameters used in the experiments. The columns on the *right* present the results for maximal velocity v_m^* (in cm/s) estimated by the proposed approach and compared to the heuristic for minimizing g on a fine grid (lines 2 & 3) and the cross-correlation results which has been validated against flow meter estimates in previous studies [11].

	data set (a)	data set (b)		data set (a)	data set (b)
$L_z = 2R$	0.5 cm	0.5 cm	Cross Correlation, Fig. 6	12.76	73.83
L_x	4 cm	4 cm	**Ours**, heuristic, L. B-spline, Fig. 5	13.90	77.00
Δt	1/128 s	1/128 s	**Ours**, heuristic, Q. B-spline, Fig. 5	13.90	77.50
N_t	10	10	**Ours**, exact, L. B-spline, Fig. 5	13.73	77.00
$N_x \times N_z$	64 × 331	64 × 231	**Ours**, exact, Q. B-spline	13.72	77.49

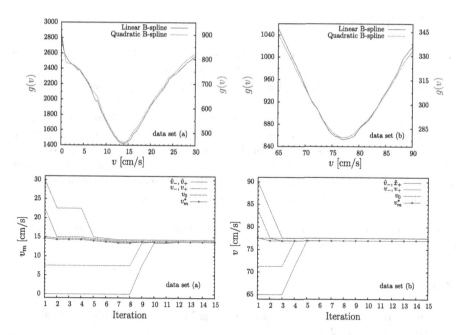

Fig. 5. Velocity estimation via parametric optimization for data sets (a), l.h.s., and (b), r.h.s. The *top row* plots the parametric function $g(v)$ defined via the trajectory matrix $A(v)$ and the corresponding sparse reconstruction. For the data set (a) we set $\lambda = 0$ and for date set (b) we set $\lambda = 0.1$ The coefficients of $A(v)$ are defined by either piecewise linear (3.16) or quadratic (3.15) B-spline basis functions. The maximal flow velocity v_m^* is attained at the minimum of $g(v)$. The *bottom row* illustrates the performance of the five-point algorithm [9] applied to the two data sets using matrix $A(v)$ given by (3.16). The five points $\hat{v}_- < v_- < v_0 < v_+ < \hat{v}_+$ are shown at each iteration step k with pointed (for v_0), dashed (for v_-, v_+) and continuous (for $\hat{v}_-$, $\hat{v}_+$) lines. In both cases they accurately converge to v_m^*, which is shown in red. (Color figure online)

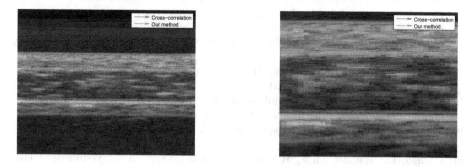

Fig. 6. Illustration of the velocity field estimated via the cross-correlation method (blue arrows) and our approach (red) for the data set (b). Both methods perform similarly. For numbers we refer to Table 1. The *right* image shows a zoom-in of the result on the left and highlights the poor resolution and noisy nature of B-mode images. (Color figure online)

6 Conclusion

We have formulated, analyzed and tested on real data the velocity estimation problem in Echo PIV for laminar and steady flows as a parametric sparse reconstruction problem. The sparsifying dictionary consists of space-time trajectories of individual particles, which is adaptively updated during the iterative process and robustly refines the unknown velocity information. We obtain a convergent numerical scheme based on a carefully designed flow dictionary. The comparison with cross-correlation results, demonstrates the robustness of our approach. In addition, our method is completely transparent and not a black-box depending on many fine-tuned parameters. Further work will concentrate on defining the trajectory dictionary using the more general pulsatile blood flow model [16].

Acknowledgements. EB, SP and CS thank the German Research Foundation (DFG) for its support via grant GRK 1653.

References

1. Adrian, R.J., Westerweel, J.: Particle Image Velocimetry. Cambridge University Press, Cambridge (2011)
2. Adrian, R.J.: Twenty years of particle image velocimetry. Exp. Fluids **39**(2), 159–169 (2005)
3. Bodnariuc, E., Gurung, A., Petra, S., Schnörr, C.: Adaptive dictionary-based spatio-temporal flow estimation for echo PIV. In: Tai, X.-C., Bae, E., Chan, T.F., Lysaker, M. (eds.) EMMCVPR 2015. LNCS, vol. 8932, pp. 378–391. Springer, Heidelberg (2015)
4. Bonnans, J.F., Shapiro, A.: Perturbation Analysis of Optimization Problems. Springer, Heidelberg (2000)
5. Foucart, S., Rauhut, H.: A Mathematical Introduction to Compressive Sensing. Birkhäuser, Basel (2013)
6. Grant, M., Stephen Boyd, S.: CVX: Matlab Software for Disciplined Convex Programming, version 2.1, March 2014. http://cvxr.com/cvx
7. Heywood, J., Rannacher, R., Turek, S.: Artificial boundaries and flux and pressure conditions for the incompressible Navier-Stokes equations. Int. J. Numer. Meth. Fluids **22**, 325–352 (1996)
8. Kim, H., Hertzberg, J., Shandas, R.: Development and validation of echo PIV. Exp. Fluids **36**(3), 455–462 (2004)
9. Mifflin, R., Strodiot, J.J.: A rapidly convergent five-point algorithm for univariate minimization. Math. Program. **62**, 299–319 (1993)
10. Minoux, M.: Mathematical Programming, Theory and Algorithms. Wiley, New York (1989)
11. Poelma, C., van der Mijle, R.M.E., Mari, J.M., Tang, M.X., Weinberg, P.D., Westerweel, J.: Ultrasound imaging velocimetry: toward reliable wall shear stress measurements. Eur. J. Mech. - B/Fluids **35**, 70–75 (2012)
12. Raffel, M., Willert, C., Wereley, S., Kompenhans, J.: Particle Image Velocimery - A Practical Guide. Springer, Heidelberg (2007)
13. Rodriguez, S., Deschamps, M., Castaings, M., Ducasse, E.: Guided wave topological imaging of isotropic plates. Ultrasonics **54**(7), 1880–1890 (2014)

14. Rodriguez, S., Jacob, X., Gibiat, V.: Plane wave echo particle image velocimetry. In: Proceedings of Meetings of Acoustics, POMA 19 (2013)
15. Schiffner, M.F., Schmitz, G.: Fast image acquisition in pulse-echo ultrasound imaging using compressed sensing. In: 2012 IEEE International Ultrasonics Symposium (IUS), pp. 1944–1947. IEEE (2012)
16. Womersley, J.: Method for the calculation of velocity, rate of flow and viscous drag in arteries when the pressure gradient is known. J. Physiol. **127**, 553–563 (1955)

Identifying Individual Facial Expressions by Deconstructing a Neural Network

Farhad Arbabzadah[1], Grégoire Montavon[1], Klaus-Robert Müller[1,2], and Wojciech Samek[3(✉)]

[1] Machine Learning Group, Technische Universität Berlin, Berlin, Germany
farhadarb@gmail.com
[2] Department of Brain and Cognitive Engineering, Korea University, Seoul, Korea
[3] Machine Learning Group, Fraunhofer Heinrich Hertz Institute, Berlin, Germany
wojciech.samek@hhi.fraunhofer.de

Abstract. This paper focuses on the problem of explaining predictions of psychological attributes such as attractiveness, happiness, confidence and intelligence from face photographs using deep neural networks. Since psychological attribute datasets typically suffer from small sample sizes, we apply transfer learning with two base models to avoid overfitting. These models were trained on an age and gender prediction task, respectively. Using a novel explanation method we extract heatmaps that highlight the parts of the image most responsible for the prediction. We further observe that the explanation method provides important insights into the nature of features of the base model, which allow one to assess the aptitude of the base model for a given transfer learning task. Finally, we observe that the multiclass model is more feature rich than its binary counterpart. The experimental evaluation is performed on the 2222 images from the 10k US faces dataset containing psychological attribute labels as well as on a subset of KDEF images.

1 Introduction

Deep Convolutional Networks (ConvNets) [15] are the architecture of choice for many practical problems such as large-scale image recognition [9,11]. Typically, these networks have millions of free parameters that are learned from large datasets. The great success of ConvNets and an abundance of hardware and software frameworks [10] has led to the availability of a set of pre-trained models for specified tasks. Retraining these pre-trained models to a new task allows to successfully use ConvNets also in small sample settings [6,24]. This procedure is an instance of the transfer learning paradigm [5]. In a nutshell, a model is trained on a domain related to the problem at hand, then adapted to the target domain with only few data points.

In this contribution a pre-trained deep neural network trained for gender and age classification [17] is used and subsequently retrained to predict psychological attributes such as attractiveness, happiness, confidence and intelligence from face photographs. Since most labelled attribute datasets are rather small,

© Springer International Publishing AG 2016
B. Rosenhahn and B. Andres (Eds.): GCPR 2016, LNCS 9796, pp. 344–354, 2016.
DOI: 10.1007/978-3-319-45886-1_28

we use a pre-trained model and thus harvest from the rich representation that the neural network has learned on a related problem. If the tasks are sufficiently similar, we can transfer the knowledge acquired by the pre-trained model from one domain, e.g., age or gender, to another, e.g., happiness or attractiveness. Our study is based on the 10k US faces dataset [4]. Note that only a subset of 2222 images in that dataset are labelled with the needed attributes. Therefore we retrain the neural network [17] to reproduce the human assessment labels from the Bainbridge dataset. However, our focus is not primarily the excellent prediction of these attributes as such, but the explanation thereof. So, we focus on the question of *what* makes the neural network assign certain attractiveness, happiness scores etc. to a novel test image and whether this assignment corresponds to what we as humans expect. For this we apply a recently proposed explanation method termed Layer-wise Relevance Propagation (LRP) [2] that allows a better understanding of what a neural network is using as decisive features on a single sample basis. We visualize the rationale of the trained predictors using this method, study its robustness and relate the results to human expectations.

2   Understanding Neural Networks

The explanation method we are going to use in the following experiments is Layer-wise Relevance Propagation (LRP) [2]. The basic idea is to perform a backward pass of the final score for a given image x through the neural network, such that one finds a mapping between the score and the images input pixels, which reflects the *relevance* R_p of the respective pixels p of the image x for the network's decision. The first proposition of the LRP method is the conservation of relevance between layers. Let (l) and $(l + 1)$ be adjacent layers, then the conservation of relevance is expressed as:

$$\sum_i R_i^{(l)} = \sum_j R_j^{(l+1)}, \tag{1}$$

where the sums run over all neurons in respective layers. The conservation principle ensures that the network's output $f(x)$ is redistributed to the input domain such that $f(x) = \sum_p R_p$. The relative distribution of the relevance scores on the input domain reflects the importance of the respective pixels for the overall score. We call the image of the pixel-wise relevance scores a *heatmap*, which can be visualized and interpreted (see Fig. 1).

The individual assignment of relevance scores can be done using two methods. Let $z_{ij} = a_i^{(l)} w_{ij}^{(l,l+1)}$ be the weighted activation of neuron i onto neuron j in the following layer. The first rule assigns a weighted average of weighted activations z_{ij} to each node. Mathematically, this rule can be written as

$$R_i^{(l)} = \sum_j \frac{z_{ij}}{\sum_{i'} z_{i'j} + \epsilon \cdot \text{sign}(\sum_{i'} z_{i'j})} R_j^{(l+1)}. \tag{2}$$

The parameter ϵ in the first rule is only relevant if the denominator in the above expression is zero. Then setting $\epsilon > 0$ will ensure, that there is no division by zero.

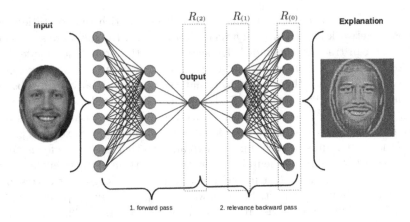

Fig. 1. Illustration of the Layer-wise Relevance Propagation (LRP) for happiness classification. The first step of the procedure is a regular forward pass (blue nodes) that yields the classification score $f(x) = R_{(2)}$, the first red node. The second step is a backward pass (red nodes) that passes through the network in a reverse order. In the backward pass the score $R_{(2)}$ is redistributed layer by layer (indicated by the red rectangles). Each node at the lower layer will receive a relevance score relative to the activations a_j of each node based on one of the rules in Eq. (2) or (3). (Color figure online)

Note that by setting $\epsilon \neq 0$ the conservation of relevance between layers will no longer hold. In this case one can add an additional renormalization step before the next LRP-pass, which will ensure that the sum of relevances is preserved.

The second rule is based on the weighted average rationale as well. However, in the second rule the positive and negative weighted activations z_{ij}^+ and z_{ij}^- are treated separately and weighted by two additional parameters α and β, which force a certain ratio between positive and negative contributions.

$$\sum_i R_i^{(l)} = \sum_j \left(\alpha \cdot \frac{z_{ij}^+}{\sum_{i'} z_{i'j}^+} + \beta \cdot \frac{z_{ij}^-}{\sum_{i'} z_{i'j}^-} \right) R_j^{(l+1)}. \tag{3}$$

Here, z_{ij}^+ and z_{ij}^- denote the positive and the negative part of z_{ij} respectively, such that $z_{ij}^+ + z_{ij}^- = z_{ij}$. For $\alpha + \beta = 1$ the relevance conservation property holds.

An empirical comparison of different explanation methods can be found in [21]. For a more theoretical view on LRP we refer the reader to [18] and for applications beyond image classification to [1,23]. An implementation of LRP can be found in [14] and downloaded from www.heatmapping.org. The following heatmaps were obtained using Eq. (3) with $\alpha = 2$ and $\beta = -1$.

3   Experimental Evaluation

We retrain the models for age and gender by [17] on the 10k US faces dataset [4] to predict individual ratings of attractiveness, happiness, confidence and intelligence for the 2222 images with these scores in the dataset. The retraining happens for each base model (age, gender) in two modes. In the first mode only the dense layers of the network are retrained for the new target scores. In the second mode the entire network including the convolution units are retrained. The presented subject faces are only those, that are part of the subset of 48 faces of the Bainbridge dataset [4], which are licensed for publishing.

3.1 Preprocessing and Setup

The individual image rating scores (1 to 9) are rescaled to the output domain [0, 1]. The input images are rescaled to fit the input format of the network (227x227 pixels and 3 color channels). A labelled subset of 2222 images of the 10k US faces dataset is used to train the different networks. The 2222 images are randomly split into training and test set, each with 1111 samples. In total, we use 16 different networks. Half of them with the age model as a base model and the other half with the gender model as the base model. Then each of the networks is either completely retrained or only the dense layers are adapted.

The images are composed of a white frame that contains an oval central region with the face. We train the model using stochastic gradient descent with a learning rate of 0.001 using a Nesterov momentum of 0.9 [16]. The weights are initialized for each of the base models to those provided by Levi [17]. The annotated dataset is split equally into a test and training set.

3.2 Performance and Analysis of Base Models

Table 1 lists the mean absolute error (MAE) for the prediction of scores versus the average score assigned by the human test group in the original dataset [4]. The error is given in terms of the human scaling from 1 to 9 points. Interestingly, the gain of retraining the full model for the attractiveness assessment, does not yield a high improvement on the MAE, while the computational cost of retraining a full ConvNet are significantly higher than solely retraining the dense layers.

In transfer learning we want to select a base model that already captures as many as possible relevant features for the new task [20]. In case of our two base models, we would need to make a choice, whether to take the gender base model or the age base model. In the following we demonstrate that explanation methods, such as the LRP algorithm, are helpful in making an educated guess about which model to use as the basis for the transfer learning task.

Table 1. Overview of mean absolute error of the 16 models.

Base	Retraining	Attractiveness	Happiness	Confidence	Intelligence
Age	Dense Only	0.43	0.41	0.37	0.33
	Full	0.42	0.42	0.34	0.31
Gender	Dense Only	0.47	0.36	0.34	0.35
	Full	0.43	0.38	0.52	0.29

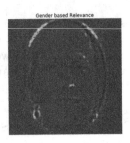

Fig. 2. Left: Raw input image. Middle: Heatmap for a test-subject for the gender based model. Right: Heatmap for the age based model.

Figure 2 illustrates for one sample image the difference of features that are picked up by the two models, if we use the same scale. It turns out that the age model picks up a lot more facial details, while the gender model is more sensitive to the overall shape of the face. The edges of the face seem to provide already quite a lot of information about the subject's gender. Note that the gender model is a binary classifier (female or male), while the age model is a multi-class classifier placing the subject into one of many possible age groups. The multi-class structure of the age model might be the reason for it's feature richness. Wrinkles, for example, are only relevant for higher age groups, while teeth are universally relevant.

3.3   Rate of Convergence

The learning curves in Fig. 3 show that the dense retrained models based on gender are learning slower than the models based on age. Thus, the above interpretation of the LRP heatmaps in terms of feature richness of the model correlates with the slower rate of convergence of the training error. Therefore, we conclude that the age based model captures more of those relevant features and thus the network based on the age model learns faster, both if we retrain the whole model or just the fully connected layers, as we can see from Fig. 3.

This confirms that we can use the LRP method for the assessment of the aptitude of a base model for a given transfer learning task, especially if we possess additional knowledge about the structure of the problem (e.g., set of psychologically relevant features). If a model assigns the bulk of relevance to this significant feature subset, then we conjecture that the network applies a more *human-like* strategy as opposed to a model that is responding random artifact which happens to correlate with the task.

3.4   Explanation for Happiness

The 10k US faces dataset does not contain the same face in a different emotional state. Therefore, we have taken another dataset, the Karolinska directed emotional faces (KDEF) [8], which contains the same adult person with different

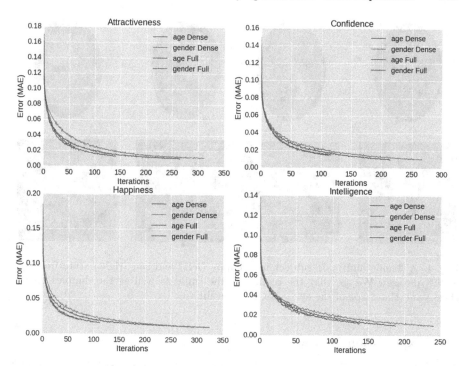

Fig. 3. Training errors for attractiveness, happiness, confidence and intelligence ratings. The four curves correspond to the two base models and the two training modes (dense layers or full model retraining).

emotional states for the following analysis. We applied the same preprocessing as described above.

Figure 4 depicts the heatmaps of a female and a male subject in a happy and an unhappy state. The heatmaps of the female subject have three principal regions of interest. Number one, pointed at by indicator arrow (c), is the mouth. Here we see that for the happy face the smile and the teeth are important. While the heatmap for the unhappy face also shows the teeth, they are not as relevant as in the happy case. Region number two, see indicator arrow (b), are the nostrils and the cheeks. The nostrils are wider compared to the sad state. Furthermore, the cheeks are lifted up forming dimples. Lastly, the outline of the eyebrows, as shown by indicator arrow (a), is marked relevant for both, the happy and unhappy face. However, the roundish shape of the outline for the happy face has more relevance assigned to it than the straight counterpart of the sad face. For the male counterpart we make similar observations. Firstly, the shape of the lips seems to matter. Secondly, a smile showing the subject's teeth indicates happiness. Thirdly, the dimples matter too. In these examples most relevance is assigned to gender unspecific features such as smiles and dimples, however, some relevance is also assigned to the outline of the eyebrows which can be gender specific.

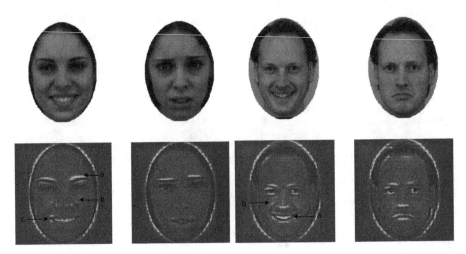

Fig. 4. A female and male subject in a happy (left) and sad (right) state from the KDEF dataset. We see that the teeth and the smile as well as the dimples on the cheeks and the shape of the eyebrows are relevant.

3.5   Explanation for Age

The test subjects in Fig. 5 show three basic features, that according to the model are indicative for advanced age. Indicator arrow (a) in left image shows that the earlobe is seen as evidence for advanced age. Furthermore, indicator arrow (b) points at a significant wrinkle around the eye region. Wrinkles around the eye are indeed indicators of advanced age. However, the most dominant feature indicating advanced age are saggy eyelids.

Gray hair is partially identified as relevant, but not always as the most relevant indicator. Wrinkles, for example, are a more reliable indicator of age.

Fig. 5. Two old test subjects and the corresponding heatmaps. Indicator arrows are showing areas of high relevance. For the first individual these are the right earlobe (a), the wrinkle below the birthmark (b) and the upper eye bags (c). The second old test-subject has upper eye bags (a) as well as saggy eyelids as the most relevant features that indicated a high age.

3.6   Explanation for Attractiveness

Figure 6 shows two individuals that have been classified as attractive. In both cases, a lot of relevance is assigned to the eyes. Furthermore, straight lines appear in both heatmaps. A possible interpretation is that these are indicators of symmetry. The heatmap of the female shows a straight line below the nose, indicating

Fig. 6. The test subjects have been classified as attractive. For the woman the important features are the eyes (c), the nose (b) and the teeth (a); for the man the hair and the shapes of the eyebrows and the nose.

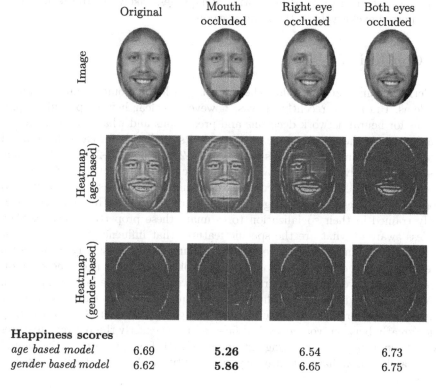

	Original	Mouth occluded	Right eye occluded	Both eyes occluded
Happiness scores				
age based model	6.69	**5.26**	6.54	6.73
gender based model	6.62	**5.86**	6.65	6.75

Fig. 7. Sample subject occluded in various ways shown next to the heatmap and happiness score for the two considered models. Mouth occlusion causes the happiness scores to decrease for both models, and the heatmap values in the mouth region to drop as well.

symmetry of this part. Furthermore, the female person possesses a large space between the eyes and the eyebrows that is considered relevant.

The straight lines in the male example in Fig. 6 correspond to the nose, the eyes and partially to the mouth. Asymmetric deviation of the mouth appears to be less relevant. The vertical texture of the man's hair is also assessed as relevant.

3.7   Occlusion Tests

We validate the insights obtained from the analysis of heatmaps by an experiment that analyzes how the model and the heatmaps react to selective occlusions. Figure 7 shows a sample subject where various facial features are occluded: mouth, right eye, and both eyes. We use the skin color for occlusion in order to reduce visual artefacts (e.g. the apparition of strong unnatural edges). Below each image, we show the heatmap and prediction score for two models of happiness: one pretrained on the age model and one pretrained on the gender model.

It can be observed in both cases that only the mouth occlusion is causing the happiness score to decrease significantly. On the other hand, removing the eyes sometimes even increases the perception of happiness, likely due to the attention being ported exclusively to the mouth region.

4   Conclusion

Modern learning machines allow the modeling of highly complex and nonlinear problems. Until very recently, it was, however, unclear how to provide explanations for neural network decisions and predictions and what exactly in terms of inputs made the learning machine provide its prediction for each single novel data point. Explanation methods such as [3, 7, 12, 13, 19, 22, 25–27] have been able to successfully solve this important open problem. The present contribution has applied LRP to a particularly complex domain, namely assessing multifaceted properties in images, such as age, gender, attractivity etc. Humans are excellently trained in their socialization to estimate these properties, perhaps they are less aware of what are the specific features that influence their judgement when distinguishing between an elderly or a younger person. Clearly, wrinkles vs. a general percept of freshness would help to holistically guess age. The state-of-the-art convolutive neural nets trained in this work also have a holistic approach to accurately predict age, but the interesting question is, what are the features that are of use for them to come up with this good prediction. Obviously, they differ greatly between young and old faces and it is exactly the relevant features *specific per image* that are being extracted by LRP from the convolutive neural net. In addition, we have qualitatively and quantitatively shown their robustness under occlusion.

In that sense we can probe the artificial neural network on its percept of age, gender, attractivity etc. Future research will aim to relate to psychophysical studies in human perception. After having established basic convolutive neural network models (with state-of-the-art performance) for predicting certain data rich properties, we could reuse these models and adapt them to data poorer properties such as attractivity by transferring the neural network representation and using only few data point for retraining. While this has been done in a very straight forward manner, it will be a subject of future research to consider how to do this transfer in an optimal manner, also it is interesting to study whether a generative neural network will be better suited to include prior representation knowledge from one prediction task to the other. We would like to stress that the focus of this paper has been to open the black box of a complex learning model that has successfully learned a task where the optimal prediction strategy pursued by the artificial system has been so far somewhat unclear. In particular we are also enabled to judge whether the generalization properties yielding a good out of sample predictor are based on artifacts in a data set or on an appriopriate problem decomposition strategy.

Acknowledgement. This work was supported by the German Ministry for Education and Research as Berlin Big Data Center BBDC (01IS14013A), the Deutsche Forschungsgesellschaft (MU 987/19-1) and the Brain Korea 21 Plus Program through the National Research Foundation of Korea funded by the Ministry of Education. Correspondence to KRM and WS.

References

1. Arras, L., Horn, F., Montavon, G., Müller, K.R., Samek, W.: Explaining predictions of non-linear classifiers in NLP. In: Proceedings of the Workshop on Representation Learning for NLP at Association for Computational Linguistics Conference (ACL), pp. 1–7 (2016)
2. Bach, S., Binder, A., Montavon, G., Klauschen, F., Müller, K.R., Samek, W.: On pixel-wise explanations for non-linear classifier decisions by layer-wise relevance propagation. PLoS ONE **10**(7), e0130140 (2015)
3. Baehrens, D., Schroeter, T., Harmeling, S., Kawanabe, M., Hansen, K., Müller, K.R.: How to explain individual classification decisions. J. Mach. Learn. Res. **11**, 1803–1831 (2010)
4. Bainbridge, W.A., Isola, P., Oliva, A.: The intrinsic memorability of face photographs. J. Exp. Psychol. Gen. **142**(4), 1323 (2013)
5. Caruana, R.: Multitask learning. Mach. Learn. **28**(1), 41–75 (1997)
6. Donahue, J., Jia, Y., Vinyals, O., Hoffman, J., Zhang, N., Tzeng, E., Darrell, T.: DeCAF: a deep convolutional activation feature for generic visual recognition (2013). arXiv preprint. arXiv:1310.1531
7. Dosovitskiy, A., Brox, T.: Inverting visual representations with convolutional networks (2015). arXiv preprint. arXiv:1506.02753
8. Goeleven, E., De Raedt, R., Leyman, L., Verschuere, B.: The Karolinska directed emotional faces: a validation study. Cogn. Emot. **22**(6), 1094–1118 (2008)
9. He, K., Zhang, X., Ren, S., Sun, J.: Deep residual learning for image recognition. (2015). arXiv:1512.03385
10. Jia, Y., Shelhamer, E., Donahue, J., Karayev, S., Long, J., Girshick, R., Guadarrama, S., Darrell, T.: Caffe: Convolutional architecture for fast feature embedding. In: Proceedings of the ACM International Conference on Multimedia, pp. 675–678. ACM (2014)

11. Krizhevsky, A., Sutskever, I., Hinton, G.E.: Imagenet classification with deep convolutional neural networks. In: Advances in Neural Information Processing Systems, pp. 1097–1105 (2012)
12. Landecker, W., Thomure, M.D., Bettencourt, L.M.A., Mitchell, M., Kenyon, G.T., Brumby, S.P.: Interpreting individual classifications of hierarchical networks. In: IEEE Symposium on Computational Intelligence and Data Mining (CIDM), pp. 32–38 (2013)
13. Lapuschkin, S., Binder, A., Montavon, G., Müller, K.R., Samek, W.: Analyzing classifiers: fisher vectors and deep neural networks. In: Proceedings of the IEEE Conference on Computer Vision and Pattern Recognition (CVPR), pp. 2912–2920 (2016)
14. Lapuschkin, S., Binder, A., Montavon, G., Müller, K.R., Samek, W.: The layerwise relevance propagation toolbox for artificial neural networks. J. Mach. Learn. Res. 17(114), 1–5 (2016)
15. Le Cun, B.B., Denker, J.S., Henderson, D., Howard, R.E., Hubbard, W., Jackel, L.D.: Handwritten digit recognition with a back-propagation network. In: Advances in Neural Information Processing Systems (1990)
16. LeCun, Y.A., Bottou, L., Orr, G.B., Müller, K.-R.: Efficient backprop. In: Montavon, G., Orr, G.B., Müller, K.-R. (eds.) Neural Networks: Tricks of the Trade, 2nd edn. LNCS, vol. 7700, pp. 9–48. Springer, Heidelberg (2012)
17. Levi, G., Hassner, T.: Age and gender classification using convolutional neural networks. In: Proceedings of the IEEE Conference on Computer Vision and Pattern Recognition Workshops, pp. 34–42 (2015)
18. Montavon, G., Bach, S., Binder, A., Samek, W., Müller, K.R.: Explaining nonlinear classification decisions with deep taylor decomposition (2015). arXiv:1512.02479
19. Nguyen, A., Yosinski, J., Clune, J.: Multifaceted feature visualization: Uncovering the different types of features learned by each neuron in deep neural networks. arXiv preprint (2016). arXiv:1602.03616
20. Pan, S.J., Yang, Q.: A survey on transfer learning. IEEE Trans. Knowl. Data Eng. 22(10), 1345–1359 (2010)
21. Samek, W., Binder, A., Montavon, G., Bach, S., Müller, K.R.: Evaluating the visualization of what a deep neural network has learned (2015). arXiv:1509.06321
22. Simonyan, K., Vedaldi, A., Zisserman, A.: Deep inside convolutional networks: visualising image classification models and saliency maps. In: ICLR Workshop (2014)
23. Sturm, I., Bach, S., Samek, W., Müller, K.R.: Interpretable deep neural networks for single-trial eeg classification (2016). arXiv:1604.08201
24. Yosinski, J., Clune, J., Bengio, Y., Lipson, H.: How transferable are features in deep neural networks? In: Advances in Neural Information Processing Systems, pp. 3320–3328 (2014)
25. Yu, W., Yang, K., Bai, Y., Yao, H., Rui, Y.: Visualizing and comparing convolutional neural networks. arXiv preprint (2014). arXiv:1412.6631
26. Zeiler, M.D., Fergus, R.: Visualizing and understanding convolutional networks. In: Fleet, D., Pajdla, T., Schiele, B., Tuytelaars, T. (eds.) ECCV 2014, Part I. LNCS, vol. 8689, pp. 818–833. Springer, Heidelberg (2014)
27. Zintgraf, L.M., Cohen, T.S., Welling, M.: A new method to visualize deep neural networks (2016). arXiv preprint. arXiv:1603.02518

Boundary Preserving Variational Image Differentiation

Yosra Mathlouthi[1], Amar Mitiche[1], and Ismail Ben Ayed[2(✉)]

[1] Institut National de la Recherche Scientifique (INRS-EMT), Montreal, QC, Canada
[2] École de Technologie Supérieure (ETS), Montreal, QC, Canada
Ismail.BenAyed@etsmtl.ca

Abstract. The purpose of this study is to investigate image differentiation by a boundary preserving variational method. The method minimizes a functional composed of an anti-differentiation data discrepancy term and an L^1 regularization term. For each partial derivative of the image, the anti-differentiation term biases the minimizer toward a function which integrates to the image up to an additive constant, while the regularization term biases it toward a function smooth everywhere except across image edges. A discretization of the functional Euler-Lagrange equations gives a large scale system of nonlinear equations that, however, is sparse, and "almost" linear, which directs to a resolution by successive linear approximations. The method is investigated in two important computer vision problems, namely optical flow and scene flow estimation, where image differentiation is used and ordinarily done by local averaging of finite image differences. We present several experiments, which show that motion fields are more accurate when computed using image derivatives evaluated by regularized variational differentiation than with conventional averaging of finite differences.

1 Introduction

Image derivatives appear in the formulation of a variety of computer vision problems and applications, particularly motion analysis where they are the ground for image motion computation, detection, tracking, and three-dimensional interpretation [8].

As pointed out long ago [12], image derivative estimation is an ill-posed problem because small image variations can lead to arbitrary errors in the computed derivatives. In general, prior filtering to dampen image noise is unproductive because it does not specifically address ill posedness [3]. In contrast, regularization affords rigorous problem statements which can be effective [3,12,13]. However, computer vision studies have usually computed image derivatives as locally averaged finite image differences. For instance, the following formulas [7] have been commonly used in motion analysis:

© Springer International Publishing AG 2016
B. Rosenhahn and B. Andres (Eds.): GCPR 2016, LNCS 9796, pp. 355–364, 2016.
DOI: 10.1007/978-3-319-45886-1_29

$$I_x(r,c) \approx \frac{1}{4} \sum_{\Delta r=0}^{1} \{ I_0(r+\Delta r, c+1) - I_0(r+\Delta r, c)$$

$$+ I_1(r+\Delta r, c+1) - I_1(r+\Delta r, c) \}$$

$$I_y(r,c) \approx \frac{1}{4} \sum_{\Delta c=0}^{1} \{ I_0(r+1, c+\Delta c) - I_0(r, c+\Delta c)$$

$$+ I_1(r+1, c+\Delta c) - I_1(r, c+\Delta c) \}$$

$$I_t(r,c) \approx \frac{1}{4} \sum_{\Delta r=0}^{1} \sum_{\Delta c=0}^{1} \{ I_1(r+\Delta r, c+\Delta c)$$

$$- I_0(r+\Delta r, c+\Delta c) \}, \tag{1}$$

where I_x, I_y, I_t represent the estimated spatiotemporal derivatives of the image, I; $\Delta r, \Delta c$ are, respectively, row r and column c displacements; I_0 and I_1 are the current and next frames of the image sequence.

Several studies have addressed variational derivative estimation from approximate measurements of one-dimensional functions. The objective functional typically contains a data conformity term and a regularization term [3,5,6,9]. The formulation of [3] used a natural definition of the derivative in the data term of the objective functional: the derivative of a function integrates to the function up to an additive constant. This *anti-differentiation* characterization of the image derivative term simply biases the functional minimizer to produce a function which, when, integrated gives the image up to an additive constant. The regularization term imposes regularity to the minimizer.

The study in [9] used an anti-differentiation data term and Tikhonov regularization, by which the computed derivative is smooth everywhere over the image domain. The purpose of this study is to extend the formulation to a boundary preserving objective functional using an L^1 regularization function. Therefore, this generalization will seek image derivatives as functions which, when integrated, give back the input image, and which are smooth everywhere on the image domain except across image edges.

There are three basic reasons for using L^1 regularization for boundary preservation: (1) its ability to preserve sharp edges while penalizing oscillations, (2) in practice, it can be implemented by computationally effective approximations without affecting the accuracy of results in a noticeable way and, (3) there is a significant literature in its support [13].

A discretization of the objective functional Euler-Lagrange equations gives a large-scale sparse system of non-linear equations, which can be solved efficiently by successive linear approximations. We confront the algorithm to two important computer vision applications that extensively use image derivatives, namely estimation of *optical flow*, the (two-dimensional) field image motion vectors over the image domain, and its three-dimensional generalization to *scene flow*, the field over the image domain of the visible environmental surfaces three-dimensional motion. We use the *Middlebury* dataset to evaluate the scheme on optical flow estimation, and the test images of [9] for scene flow estimation.

2   Regularized Image Differentiation

Let $I : \Omega \subset \mathbb{R}^2 \to \mathbb{R}$ be an image and I_x, I_y its spatial partial derivatives. We will describe the method for estimating I_x. For I_y, one can apply the same process to the transpose of I. Because only two images of the sequence are used, I_t can be computed using the local averages of image finites differences given in the previous section. The functional to minimize with respect to the image spatial derivative function f is:

$$E(f) = \frac{1}{2} \int_\Omega \left(\|Af - I\|^2 + \alpha \|\nabla f\| \right) dx dy, \tag{2}$$

where A is the anti-differentiation operator w.r.t x:

$$Af(x,y) = \int_0^x f(z,y)dz, \tag{3}$$

α is a weighting factor to control the relative contribution of the smoothness term in the functional, $\nabla f = (f_x, f_y)$ and

$$\|\nabla f\| = \left(f_x^2 + f_y^2 \right)^{\frac{1}{2}}. \tag{4}$$

The first term of the objective function, the anti-differentiation term, will bias the solution toward a derivative that is a function integrating to the image up to an additive constant. The second term is the L^1 regularization, to bias the solution toward a derivative estimate that is smooth everywhere except across image edges. The corresponding Euler-Lagrange equations are given by:

$$A^*(Af - I) - \alpha \frac{\partial}{\partial x} \frac{f_x}{\left(f_x^2 + f_y^2 \right)^{\frac{1}{2}}} - \alpha \frac{\partial}{\partial y} \frac{f_y}{\left(f_x^2 + f_y^2 \right)^{\frac{1}{2}}} = 0, \tag{5}$$

where A^* is the adjoint operator of A:

$$A^* f(x,y) = \int_x^l f(z,y)dz. \tag{6}$$

To avoid the non-differentiability due to the denominators in (5), in practice, we can replace these denominators by $\left(f_x^2 + f_y^2 + \epsilon \right)^{\frac{1}{2}}$, where ϵ is a small positive value. In general, this operation does not affect the computational outcome in any significant way.

The Euler-Lagrange equations can be solved effectively by successive linear approximations: at the current iteration, the nonlinear terms computed at the preceding iteration are used as data, which gives a linear equation to solve. Specifically, at current iteration k, the following equation is considered:

$$A^*(Af^k - I) - \frac{\alpha}{\left((f_x^{k-1})^2 + (f_y^{k-1})^2 + \epsilon \right)^{\frac{1}{2}}} \nabla^2 f^k = 0, \tag{7}$$

We discretize Ω according to a regular grid where points i are listed top-down and left to right. Let $N = n \times n$, for an image of size $n \times n$. For $i = 1, ..., N$, let f_i be function f evaluated at point i, and $\mathbf{f} \in \mathbb{R}^N$ the corresponding vector of size N. For notational convenience, we use the same symbol A and A^* of the linear operators in (7) for their $N \times N$ matrices. We apply the approximation of the composite trapezoid quadrature rule for integrals to define matrix A:

$$
\begin{aligned}
A(sn + i, sn + 1) &= \tfrac{1}{2}; & i &= 2, ..., n; \ s = 0, ..., n - 1 \\
A(sn + i, sn + i) &= \tfrac{1}{2}; & i &= 2, ..., n; \ s = 0, ..., n - 1 \\
A(sn + i, sn + i - j) &= 1; & i &= 3, ..., n; \ j = 1, ..., i - 2; \ s = 0, ..., n - 1.
\end{aligned}
$$

All the other matrix elements are equal to zero. A is sparse and block diagonal with $n \times n$ diagonal blocks. In the same way we define matrix A^* by:

$$
\begin{aligned}
A^*(i, i) &= \tfrac{1}{2}; & i &\in [1, n^2], \ i \neq sn, \ s = 1, ..., n \\
A^*(sn + i, (s + 1)n) &= \tfrac{1}{2}; & i &= 1, ..., n - 1; \ s = 0, ..., n - 1 \\
A^*(sn + i, sn + i + j) &= 1; & i &= 1, ..., n - 1; \ j = 1, ..., n - i - 1; \ s = 0, ..., n - 1.
\end{aligned}
$$

In practice, the Laplacian term in (7) is discretized, at point i and iteration k, as a fixed proportion of:

$$
\sum_{j \in \mathcal{N}_i} (f_j^k - f_i^k), \tag{8}
$$

Discretization of (7) produces, at each iteration k, a large-scale sparse system of non-linear equations which can be effectively solved by an iterative method such as Gauss-Seidel [4].

3 Experimental Evaluation

Quantitative and qualitative evaluations of the image derivatives by our L^1 regularized anti-differentiation are carried out in this section. We investigate the method within the context of two major motion analysis problems, where image spatial derivatives are significantly implied: (a) standard optical flow (2D) estimation with the variational formulation of Horn and Schunck [7,8,11], where we use the benchmark *Middlebury* database; and (b) scene flow (3D) estimation from a monocular images sequence as in [9]. We further report additional experiments over a synthetic image with known partial derivatives. The results of our tests demonstrate that the L^1 regularized differentiation offers better performances when compared to the averaged finite differences technique and to the L^2 regularized differentiation, especially on the boundaries of motion.

3.1 Synthetic Example

This example uses the synthetic image depicted in Fig. 1 (first row, leftmost image) and its noisy version computed by adding a white Gaussian noise, with a signal-to-noise ratio of 1 (second row, leftmost image). The ground-truth derivative for this image is known. We applied L^1 and L^2 regularized differentiations,

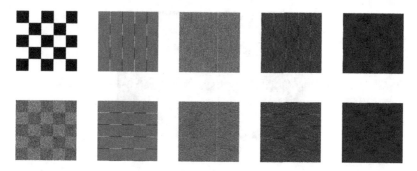

Fig. 1. *Noisy Chessboard.* First column: Chessboard image (first row) and its noisy version with SNR = 1 (second row). Second column: the ground truth of partial derivatives: I_x (first row) and I_y (second row). Third column: estimated partial derivatives using L^1 regularized differentiation with $\alpha = 1$: I_x (first row) and I_y (second row). Fourth column: estimated partial derivatives using L^2 regularized differentiation with $\alpha = 1$: I_x (first row) and I_y (second row). Fifth column: estimated partial derivatives using standard averaged finite differences: I_x (first row) and I_y (second row).

as well as local averaged finite differences (1) to the noisy version of the image. We will not depict the results for the noiseless case because locally averaged finite differences and regularized differentiation yield similar results, as one would expect. Figure 1 illustrates the results for the noisy version, which show that the values computed by L^1 regularized differentiation are closer to the actual derivatives than those computed by the other methods. Table 1 lists the mean squared errors and the standard deviation errors between the estimated derivatives and the ground truth. L^1 regularized differentiation performs much better throughout the image and on the edges. Smoothness parameter α was fixed equal to 1 for all the tests in this example, and the initial values of the partial derivatives were all set to zero.

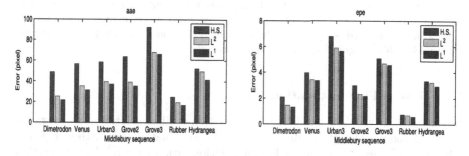

Fig. 2. *Middlebury* database: average angular error *aae* (left) and endpoint error *epe* (right) for different sequences of the database. Both errors were computed using the estimated optical flow and the ground truth. $\alpha = 1$. (Color figure online)

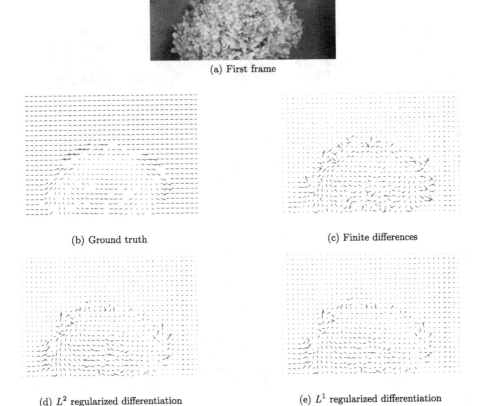

(a) First frame

(b) Ground truth   (c) Finite differences

(d) L^2 regularized differentiation   (e) L^1 regularized differentiation

Fig. 3. *Hydrangea sequence.* (a) The first of the two input images; (b) optical flow ground truth; (c) optical flow computed with averaged finite differences in (1); (d) optical flow computed with L^2 regularized differentiation ($\alpha = 1$); (e) optical flow computed with L^1 regularized differentiation scheme ($\alpha = 1$).

3.2   Optical Flow Estimation

In this section, we show the benefit of variational differentiation over averaged finite differences (1) in the context of optical flow estimation. We further show the advantage of using L^1 regularized differentiation rather than L^2. Our evaluation can use any optical flow algorithm based on image derivatives. We used the standard algorithm of Horn and Schunck [7,8,11]. Hence, we will compare the accuracy of estimated optical flows with and without variational differentiation, in the cases of L^1 and L^2 regularization.

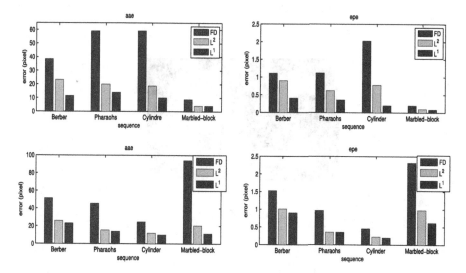

Fig. 4. Scene flow estimation: average angular error *aae* (left) and endpoint error *epe* (right) for different sequences ($\alpha = 1$). The first row plots the errors computed over the whole image domain, whereas the second plots errors on motion boundaries.

Table 1. Quantitative evaluations on the noisy Chessboard image (SNR = 1): mean square errors (MSE) and standard deviation errors (SDE) for L^1 regularized differentiation (L^1), L^2 regularized differentiation (L^2) and averaged finite differentiation (FD). The errors were evaluated over the whole image domain (second row) and on 5×5 windows throughout the boundaries (third row).

Method	error	L^1	L^2	FD
Noised Chessboard (image)	MSE	0.06	0.14	0.41
	SDE	0.09	0.13	0.31
Noised Chessboard (boundaries)	MSE	0.02	0.03	0.06
	SDE	0.07	0.09	0.16

We used the sequences of the benchmark database *Middlebury* [1] for which the ground-truth flow is given[1]. These sequences include (i) real scenes with non rigid motion, (ii) complex synthetic sequences and (iii) stereo sequences that are modified versions of real static scenes. We used two standard error measures to evaluate optical flow [1]: the average angular error (aae) and the endpoint error (epe). Figure 2 plots both average errors (aae and epe) for different sequences ($\alpha = 1$), showing that our L^1 regularized differentiation (bars in red) yielded the lowest errors.

---

[1] http://vision.middlebury.edu/flow/.

(a) First frame

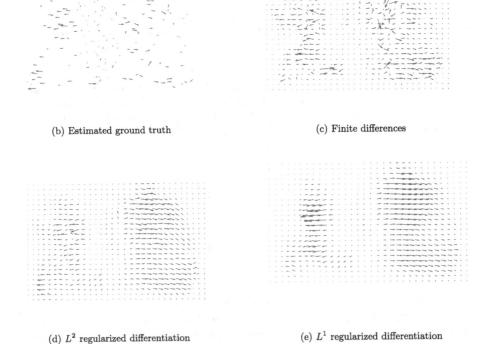

(b) Estimated ground truth

(c) Finite differences

(d) L^2 regularized differentiation

(e) L^1 regularized differentiation

Fig. 5. A vector representation of the scene flow induced optical flow for the Pharaohs figurines movement: (a) the first of the two input images; (b) computed ground truth flow; (c) flow when using averaged finite differences for image derivatives; (d) flow when using the L^2 regularized differentiation scheme; (e) flow when using the L^1 regularized differentiation scheme.

Figure 3 depicts an example (sequence *Hydrangea*), where our L^1 regularized differentiation yielded an optical flow that is visually consistent with the actual (ground-truth) motion. This includes motion boundaries.

3.3 Scene Flow Estimation

In this section, we consider the problem of dense scene flow and depth estimation from a monocular image sequence [9]. Scene flow is the three-dimensional velocity field of the visible surfaces in a scene, and its estimation involves image partial derivatives. We compare scene flows obtained using three different image derivative estimations: L^1 regularized differentiation, differentiation based on L^2 smoothness [9], as well as standard finite differences (1). We used the data set in [9], which presents some challenges: Weak variations in spatio-temporal intensity, presence of shadows and complex real motions. Since we do not have a scene flow ground truth, we evaluated the results indirectly using optical flow fields corresponding to projections of the obtained scene flows.

Figure 4 plots the aae and epe errors for the used sequences throughout the whole image domain and on the edges. The L^1 regularized differentiation yielded better performances than those based on L^2 regularized differentiation and local averaged finite differences. These evaluations point to the practical advantage of regularized differentiation, in particular, L^1 based, in the context of motion estimation. For a visual (qualitative) evaluation, we present results using *Berber* sequence (Fig. 5). One can see that the motion fields computed with a variational approach yielded a better consistency with the ground truth than standard finite differences, particularly in the L^1 case.

4 Conclusion

This study investigated a boundary preserving variational method to compute image derivatives. The objective functional contained a data term and an L^1 regularization. The data term used an anti-differentiation definition of a derivative to constrain the solution toward a derivative estimate which integrates to the image up to a scale factor. The discretization of the Euler-Lagrange equations produced a large sparse non-linear system of equations which was effectively solved using progressive linear approximations. We tested the impact of this method on two important computer vision problems, namely optical flow and scene flow estimation. Our results showed that the optical flow, and the scene flow, computed using derivatives resulting from the L^1 regularized differentiation method were more accurate than those resulting from an L^2 regularized differentiation method, or traditional methods which approximate the derivatives locally by averaged finite differences. It would be interesting to investigate optimization of our functional with stat-of-the-art solvers for non-smooth problems [2,10].

References

1. Baker, S., Scharstein, D., Lewis, J., Roth, S., Black, M.J., Szeliski, R.: A database and evaluation methodology for optical flow. Int. J. Comput. Vision **92**(1), 1–31 (2011)
2. Chambolle, A., Pock, T.: A first-order primal-dual algorithm for convex problems with applications to imaging. J. Math. Imaging Vision **40**(1), 120–145 (2011)
3. Chartrand, R.: Numerical differentiation of noisy, nonsmooth data. ISRN Appl. Math. **2011**, 1–11 (2011). (Article ID 164564)
4. Ciarlet, P.G.: Introduction a l'analyse numerique matricielle et a l'optimisation. Masson, Paris (1988)
5. Cullum, J.: Numerical differentiation and regularization. SIAM J. Numer. Anal. **8**, 254–265 (1971)
6. Hanke, M., Scherzer, O.: Inverse problems light: numerical differentiation. Am. Math. Mon. **108**(6), 512–521 (2001)
7. Horn, B., Schunck, B.: Determining optical flow. Artif. Intell. **17**, 185–203 (1981)
8. Mitiche, A., Aggarwal, J.: Computer Vision Analysis of Image Motion by Variational Methods. Springer, Heidelberg (2013)
9. Mitiche, A., Mathlouthi, Y., Ben Ayed, I.: Monocular concurrent recovery of structure and motion scene flow. Frontiers in ICT (2015)
10. Pock, T., Cremers, D., Bischof, H., Chambolle, A.: An algorithm for minimizing the Mumford-Shah functional. In: IEEE International Conference on Computer Vision (ICCV), pp. 1133–1140 (2009)
11. Sun, D., Roth, S., Black, M.J.: Secrets of optical flow estimation and their principles. In: IEEE Conference on Computer Vision and Pattern Recognition (CVPR), pp. 2432–2439 (2010)
12. Terzopoulos, D.: Regularization of inverse visual problems involving discontinuities. IEEE Trans. Pattern Anal. Mach. Intell. **4**, 413–424 (1986)
13. Vogel, C.R.: Computational methods for inverse problems. Front. Appl. Math. (2002)

A Prediction-Correction Approach
for Real-Time Optical Flow Computation
Using Stereo

Maxime Derome[(✉)], Aurelien Plyer, Martial Sanfourche, and Guy Le Besnerais

ONERA - The French Aerospace Lab, Palaiseau, France
{maxime.derome,aurelien.plyer,martial.sanfourche,
guy.le_besnerais}@onera.fr

Abstract. Estimating the optical flow robustly in real-time is still a
challenging issue as revealed by current KITTI benchmarks. We propose
an original two-step method for fast and performant optical flow estimation from stereo vision. The first step is the prediction of the flow due
to the ego-motion, efficiently conducted by stereo-matching and visual
odometry. The correction step estimates the motion of mobile objects.
Algorithmic choices are justified by empirical studies on real datasets.
Our method achieves framerate processing on images of realistic size, and
provides results comparable or better than methods having computation
times one or two orders of magnitude higher.

1 Introduction

Estimating the dense temporal matching between two consecutive images —also
called *Optical Flow* (OF)— is a well know problem in computer vision. From
a single camera, it provides a clue on the motion and the 3D structure of the
scene. From a stereorig, although the 3D structure can be directly estimated
by stereo-matching, computing the OF is still necessary to provide dynamic
scene perception and estimate moving objects displacement. In this context,
estimating OF together with depth maps allows to compute the 3D motion
field—called *Scene Flow* (SF), which essentially summarizes all the information
about ego-motion, 3D structure and moving objects.

Recent works on stereo matching have lead to both accurate and fast algorithms [7,9,10,19]. As for the OF estimation, numerous progress have been made
concerning robustness to outliers and illumination change [22] and large displacements: through multi-scale or pyramidal approaches [1] or using feature matching
to drive the OF estimation [2,23]. However, compared to the significant efforts
made to improve the accuracy of OF, we feel that little attention has been paid
to the real-time capability of OF algorithms [16,25]. If we look at the KITTI
ranking for OF [8], we notice that the few algorithms that achieve video rate
computation give significantly lower performances than top-ranking methods.
We also observe that these top-ranking methods make use of stereo information
[14,20] or epipolar geometry [24].

© Springer International Publishing AG 2016
B. Rosenhahn and B. Andres (Eds.): GCPR 2016, LNCS 9796, pp. 365–376, 2016.
DOI: 10.1007/978-3-319-45886-1_30

In fact, most of these algorithms estimate the SF and use an advanced modelization of the scene [20] or of the objects [14] to improve the accuracy of the results. Such approaches achieve leading performances but are computationally expensive and require several minutes to perform. Algorithms proposed in [24] perform one or two orders of magnitude faster but they are still too slow for real-time application on KITTI's image dimensions and, moreover, they rely on the assumption of a static scene.

1.1 Contributions

In contrast with previous approaches that use stereo, our main purpose is not to improve the OF's accuracy but to reach the shortest processing time while keeping a good estimation performance. Our approach is in the line to the work of Wedel et al. [21] which decouples the stereo and the OF problems and first estimates the disparity map to bootstrap SF estimation. Here we intend to benefit as much as possible from the geometric information we can get from a stereorig, and go even further in the decoupling by using a visual odometer to estimate the camera motion. This can be related to Muller et al. [15] which uses ego-motion information obtained from an inertial sensor to support the OF estimation and avoid the *staircase effects* induced by the total variation regularization. But, again, our goal here is to reduce computation time, not improve OF estimation.

Note that, although we consider a stereovision context, we focus on OF rather than SF estimation. Let us first note that having estimated the OF and knowing the depth maps at the two time instants, SF computation essentially reduces to a change of coordinate frame. As shown by the literature review, the main computational bottleneck then lies in the OF estimation, which motivates the present work. Besides, there are reactive tasks in vision-based robotics which can exploit information deduced from the OF without calling for SF estimation. A sparse representation of the scene, where moving objects are reduced to a bounding box with a mean 3D velocity, can be sufficient for designing an obstacle avoidance system, and requires much less computation than the full SF derivation.

Our contribution is two-fold. First, we present a simple prediction-correction approach that exploits geometric information obtained by grayscale stereo images to improve the OF estimation. Second, by carefully selecting the best trade-off between computational efficiency and performance for the algorithms involved in each step (stereo-matching, visual odometry, optical flow), we demonstrate framerate processing (10 Hz) while achieving good results on KITTI datasets.

2 Prediction-Correction of Computation in Stereo

The main idea behind our approach is to split the OF estimation into two steps: (i) estimate the static part of the OF, which amounts to *predict* the optical flow between two time instants from 3D structure and camera motion; (ii) *correct* the OF to account for moving objects.

The static part of the OF can be deduced from the disparity map and the ego-motion respectively computed by stereo and visual odometry algorithms. Thanks to the epipolar constraint, the estimation of disparity with calibrated stereo images boils down to a 1D search whereas OF requires a 2D search. Besides, unlike OF algorithms, stereo algorithms handle well boundaries. Recovering the ego-motion by visual odometry is a 6-parameters estimation problem that can be solved efficiently even in presence of moving objects, using a robust estimation procedure such as RANSAC [6].

The correction step mainly aims at estimating the part of the OF due to moving objects. It also corrects errors in the depth map propagated by the prediction step. In many situations, the associated residual OF is of low magnitude and good results can be obtained from fast local OF estimation algorithms. Local problems can be encountered when dealing with fast moving objects, though.

Before presenting the prediction and the correction stages of the proposed Prediction-Correction OF (PCOF) approach, we briefly define the notations used in this paper.

2.1 Convention and Notations

We consider the pinhole camera model for the left camera frame which is taken as reference.

- I_t, left camera (grayscale) image at time instant t
- f, camera focal in pixel
- b, stereorig baseline
- (x, y), pixel location
- (x_0, y_0), coordinates of the optical center projection into the image plane
- (u, v), optical flow between I_t and I_{t+1}
- d_t, disparity map at time instant t
- X_t, 3D coordinates in (left) camera frame at time instant t
- $X_t(x, y, d) = -\frac{b}{d(x,y)}(x - x_0, y - y_0, f)$, the triangulation function at t
- Π, the projection operator which maps a 3D point to the image plan
- R and T, the camera rotation and translation between t and $t + 1$ such that $X_{t+1} = RX_t + T$ for a static point.

2.2 Prediction Stage

The predicted OF (u_{pred}, v_{pred}) is computed by assuming that the scene static between t and $t + 1$:

$$\begin{pmatrix} u_{pred} \\ v_{pred} \end{pmatrix}(x, y) = \xi_{t+1}^{pred}(x, y, d_t) - \begin{pmatrix} x \\ y \end{pmatrix}, \tag{1}$$

where $\xi_{t+1}^{pred}(x, y, d_t)$ is the predicted position in I_{t+1}, of a point located in (x, y) in I_t:

$$\xi_{t+1}^{pred}(x, y, d_t) = \Pi\big(RX_t(x, y, d_t) + T\big). \tag{2}$$

From the predicted optical flow, one can predict the image that should be observed if there were no moving objects in the scene [5]. This can be done from t to $t+1$ (forward scheme) or from $t+1$ to t (backward scheme). As we intend to estimate the OF in the geometry of image t, we adopt, as in [4], a backward scheme and use $\xi_{t+1}^{pred}(x, y, d_t)$ to warp I_{t+1} into frame t. Another advantage of the backward scheme is that the predicted image I_t^{pred} can be synthesized by a simple interpolation starting from a regular grid

$$I_t^{pred}(x, y) = I_{t+1}(\xi_{t+1}^{pred}(x, y, d_t)). \tag{3}$$

while the forward scheme leads to an irregular interpolation.

2.3   Correction Stage

For the sake of comparison we present two different correction strategies that respectively use the predicted OF (u_{pred}, v_{pred}) and the predicted image I_t^{pred}.

Prediction Warping Optical Flow (PWOF). A natural way to compensate the camera motion is to initialize an OF algorithm with (u_{pred}, v_{pred}) and run it on one pyramid level only. This strategy is similar to the one of Revaud et al. [17], who initialize a TV-L1 OF algorithm with a flow obtained by the interpolation of sparse set of matches. Here the initial warping corresponds to the static part of the optical flow, hence in a non-pyramidal approach, the motion of fast moving objects might be difficult to estimate.

Prediction Correction Optical Flow (PCOF). Another option is to compute the OF $(\delta u, \delta v)$ between I_t and I_t^{pred}. In this context the brightness consistency equation writes:

$$I_t(x, y) = I_t^{pred}(x + \delta u(x, y), y + \delta v(x, y)). \tag{4}$$

By definition (cf. Eq. 3), I_t^{pred} writes:

$$I_t^{pred}(x, y) = I_{t+1}(x + u_{pred}(x, y), y + v_{pred}(x, y)) \tag{5}$$

Thus, by combining Eqs. 4 and 5, we obtain the final OF estimate (u,v) after correction:

$$u(x, y) = \delta u(x, y) + u_{pred}(x + \delta u(x, y), y + \delta v(x, y)) \tag{6}$$
$$v(x, y) = \delta v(x, y) + v_{pred}(x + \delta u(x, y), y + \delta v(x, y)) \tag{7}$$

3   Algorithmic Choices: Odometry, Stereo and OF

In this section we present the various algorithms which have been considered and justify our choices by an empirical performance/cost study on KITTI datasets.

3.1   Ego-Motion Estimation

To estimate the camera motion from stereo images, we choose the visual odometer eVO proposed in [18]. Given 2D-3D matchings $\{[x_{t+1}^n, y_{t+1}^n], X_t^n\}$, it minimizes the following reprojection error: .

$$\mathcal{E}(R, T) = \frac{1}{N} \sum_{n=1}^{N} \left\| \begin{bmatrix} x_{t+1}^n \\ y_{t+1}^n \end{bmatrix} - \Pi(RX_t^n + T) \right\|^2 . \tag{8}$$

In [18], feature points extraction and 3D triangulation is done only at keyframes, so as to reduce computation load and reduce drift. Here we only consider two consecutive stereo pairs, so the feature points processing is performed at each frame. Despite this setting, the camera motion can be estimated at 20 Hz on a single CPU. In practice, the optimization of (8) is done within the RANSAC framework [6] to ensure the system robustness in presence of moving objects as long as the major part of the image is covered by static elements.

3.2   Dense Stereo Matching

Dense stereo matching, or dense disparity estimation in our rectified stereo context, has been extensively studied and several fast algorithms are available. They include Semi-Global Matching (SGM) [10] whose implementation on FPGA [7] allows stereo matching at 25 Hz (for 128 disparities and images of 740 × 480 pixels), Efficient Large-scale Stereo (ELAS) [9] running at 20 Hz on a CPU (for KITTI size images, when enabling sub-sampling option) and Adaptive Coarse-to-fine-stereo (ACTF) [19] that reaches 32 Hz on a 240 cores GPU (for 256 disparities and images of 640 × 480 pixels). We choose the last one which offers a remarkable trade-off between speed and accuracy, and is particularly efficient for preserving the boundaries of foreground objects. Yet, as SGM is considered as a reference method in stereovision, we also consider it in Subsect. 4.1 for comparisons purpose — actually, we use the Semi-Global Bloc Matching (SGBM) which is the OpenCV version of SGM that differs by its cost function. Because of the uniquess criterion enforced by the left-right checking, some parts of the disparity map might remain undefined. As done in [19], we fill these parts with the nearest valid pixel disparity found by an horizontal and vertical search.

Regardless of the stereo algorithm used, the disparity map is then regularized by performing the first iteration of the consensus framework introduced in [3]. It essentially fits plane models on the disparity over small overlapping windows—we use 16 × 16 and 32 × 32 overlapping windows. This smoothing preserves the boundaries quite well, while efficiently filtering the map and rejecting outliers. Besides, this algorithm is highly parallelizable and the gain brought seems to worth the small computational overhead.

3.3   Optical Flow

In the following, we consider High Accuracy Optical Flow (HAOF) [1], TV-L1 optical flow [25] and Large Displacement Optical Flow (LDOF) [2] algorithms, that are often cited as references among variational methods derived from the seminal work of Horn and Schunck [11]. We also consider FOLKI [12], an OF algorithm based on Lucas-Kanade paradigm [13], that achieves real-time performances on a GPU [16]. In our experiments, we use LDOF and OpenCV version of HAOF and TV-L1 with default parameters, and FOLKI with: $J = 5$ resolution levels, $K = 4$ iterations, two window radii {8;4} and rank order 4 (more explanations about these parameters can be found in [16]).

4   Results on KITTI Datasets and Processing Time

For the evaluation, we have considered KITTI 2012 [8] and KITTI 2015 [14] datasets, which contain stereo images acquired from a moving car in urban environment. The 2012 dataset presents static scenes, whereas the 2015 dataset focuses on moving objects.

4.1   Comparison of the Correction Approaches and OF Algorithms

Experiments on KITTI 2012 dataset are summarized in Table 1. We compare the performances of both PWOF and PCOF strategies described in Subsect. 2.3, while testing different OF algorithms: FOLKI, HAOF and TV-L1. In all cases, as explained in Subsect. 3.2, we choose ACTF stereo followed by a filtering step, for the dense stereo matching used in the prediction stage.

Table 1 first demonstrates that the PCOF strategy, based on OF estimation on a predicted image, performs equally or better than PWOF whatever the OF method. An illustration is given in Fig. 1 in a case where the prediction is particularly inaccurate because of a visual odometry error. Leading performances are achieved with PCOF and FOLKI optical flow. This might appear surprising at first, since local methods like FOLKI are reputed to be less accurate than variational methods like HAOF and TV-L1. However FOLKI is very robust and converges faster than HAOF and TV-L1. Moreover the higher performance of the latter methods to adaptively smooth the OF are not very relevant here because the sought residual flow is often rather inhomogeneous. Finally the last line of Table 1 shows that using SGBM instead of ACTF stereo slightly increases the results, but at the expense of a computational overhead (cf. Subsect. 4.3).

4.2   Advantages of the Prediction-Correction Approach

Static Environments. In the case of a static environment, Table 1 demonstrates that the prediction step, which exploits ego-motion and the dense stereo matching computation, already performs far better than FOLKI OF. This is partly due to the fact that object boundaries are over-smoothed by window-based OF methods such as FOLKI. Moreover, despite the static environment, the correction stage brings a significant improvement.

Table 1. Optical flow performances on KITTI - 2012 training set in term of percentage of outliers (*Out-*) and average error in pixels (*Avg-*) on the whole image (*-All*) and on the non-occluded area (*-Noc*)

Optical flow	Out-Noc	Out-All	Avg-Noc	Avg-All
FOLKI	21.95 %	31.01 %	5.5 px	11.2 px
Predicted OF	6.70 %	9.85 %	1.2 px	1.7 px
PWOF - HAOF	5.96 %	9.18 %	1.1 px	1.6 px
PWOF - TV-L1	6.66 %	15.59 %	1.2 px	2.3 px
PWOF - FOLKI	8.03 %	11.79 %	1.6 px	2.2 px
PCOF - HAOF	5.92 %	9.18 %	1.1 px	1.6 px
PCOF - TV-L1	7.39 %	10.42 %	1.3 px	1.8 px
PCOF - FOLKI	5.43 %	8.77 %	1.1 px	1.6 px
PCOF-SGBM - FOLKI	5.27 %	8.08 %	1.1 px	1.8 px

Dynamic Environments. In presence of moving objects, the correction stage becomes necessary to estimate the OF which cannot be deduced only from the camera motion and the scene geometry, see Table 2. Figure 2 presents two examples from KITTI 2015 dataset with moving cars. The prediction fails to estimate the OF on moving objects which is provided by the correction step. PCOF significantly improves FOLKI results, but still encounters difficulties with very large motions (cf. Fig. 2, second column) for which LDOF [2] is more suitable (cf. Table 2) but leads to an important computational overhead (cf. Table 5).

Table 2. Optical flow performances improvement brought by the PCOF approach, on KITTI - 2015 training set. Percentages of OF outliers, on the whole image (-all), on the background (e.g. static part, -bg) and the foreground (i.e. on moving objects, -fg)

Optical flow	Fl-bg	Fl-fg	Fl-all
FOLKI	40.10 %	55.53 %	44.57 %
Predicted OF	17.53 %	86.69 %	29.46 %
PCOF	14.46 %	55.55 %	22.62 %
PCOF - LDOF	13.97 %	29.62 %	18.16 %

4.3 Processing Time

Algorithms on CPU. Tests have been done on a workstation with 6 CPUs (Interl Core i7 at 3.2GHz). With 400 feature points, the visual odometer [18] runs in 50 ms using a single CPU. Most of the processing time is spent in the feature points extraction and could be significantly speeded up by parallelization. SGBM performs in 730 ms (OpenCV implementation) and appears unfit for framerate processing.

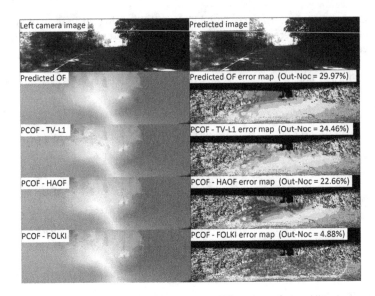

Fig. 1. First row: left camera image (left) and predicted image (right). From second to fifth row: OF (left) and error map (right) displayed using KITTI color convention, for the predicted OF, and PCOF using TV-L1, HAOF, and FOLKI. Blue corresponds to low error on the OF estimation, and orange to high error. *Out-Noc* is also displayed. (Color figure online)

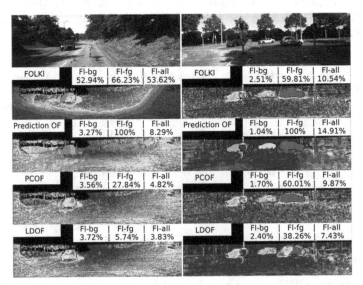

Fig. 2. Error on the estimated OF fields (blue corresponds to low error, and red to high error), and percentage of outliers (i.e. points for which the OF end-point error is > 3 px and > 5 %) for the optical flow (*Fl-all*, *Fl-bg* and *Fl-fg*) on the whole image but also on the background (e.g. static part) and the foreground (i.e. on moving objects). (Color figure online)

Table 3. Average processing time (in ms) on KITTI dataset, with two different GPUs, for each step of our pipeline and for different optical flow algorithms with and without (in brackets) pyramidal approach

	ACTF + filtering	Prediction	FOLKI	HOAF	TV-L1
GTX TITAN (2688 cores)	11 + 7	1	27 (15)	127 (31)	128 (226)
Quadro 2000 (192 cores)	50 + 31	1	150 (113)	843 (283)	703 (1401)

Algorithms on GPU. Except for the ego-motion estimation, every step of PCOF can be done on GPU. We provide in Table 3 runtimes obtained on a high performance GPU (GeForce GTX TITAN) and a standard one (Quadro 2000). Among the OF algorithms tested with PCOF, only FOLKI has proven to be fast enough for framerate processing (10 Hz). HAOF can also be considered using PWOF (i.e. no image pyramid) on the TITAN.

Note that the stereo part (ACTF and consensus filtering) runs on the GPU, in parallel with the visual odometry performed on the CPU in 50 ms. Thus PCOF processing time is around 80 ms with the GeForce GTX TITAN, which fits framerate processing on KITTI sequences (10 Hz).

Table 4. Extract of KITTI 2012 OF ranking, with methods using stereo image (st), epipolar geometry (ms) or more than two temporally adjacent images (mv)

	Method	Setting	Out-Noc	Out-All	Avg-Noc	Avg-All	Runtime
1	PRSM	st mv	2.46 %	4.23 %	0.7 px	1.0 px	300 s
...	...	...	...	...	...	...	...
4	SPS-Fl	ms	3.38 %	10.06 %	0.9 px	2.9 px	11 s
...	...	...	...	...	...	...	...
9	MotionSLIC	ms	3.91 %	10.56 %	0.9 px	2.7 px	11 s
10	CNN-HPM		4.89 %	13.01 %	1.2 px	3.0 px	23 s
...	...	...	...	...	...	...	...
13	PCOF-SGBM	st	5.40 %	8.73 %	1.2 px	2.1 px	0.8
14	PPM-Fast		5.41 %	15.19 %	1.2 px	3.4 px	2.8 s
15	PCOF	st	5.59 %	9.69 %	1.2 px	1.9 px	0.08 s
...	...	...	...	...	...	...	...
49	eFolki		19.31 %	28.79 %	5.2 px	10.9 px	0.026 s
...	...	...	...	...	...	...	...
58	FlowNetS + ft		37.05 %	44.49 %	5.0 px	9.1 px	0.08 s

4.4   KITTI 2012 and 2015 Optical Flow Rankings

Looking at KITTI 2012 and 2015 Optical Flow benchmarks (Tables 4 and 5), we can conclude that the stereo information pays off. On one hand, the proposed approach performs favourably compared to pure OF algorithms. On the

Table 5. Extract of KITTI 2015 OF ranking, with methods using stereo image (st), epipolar geometry (ms) or more than two temporally adjacent images (mv)

	Method	Data	Fl-bg	Fl-fg	Fl-all	Time
1	PRSM	st mv	5.33 %	17.02 %	7.28 %	300 s
...	...	...	...	...	...	...
8	PCOF-LDOF	st	14.34 %	41.30 %	18.83 %	50 s
9	CNN-HPM		18.33 %	24.96 %	19.44 %	23 s
10	MR-Flow		19.42 %	27.65 %	20.79 %	12 s
...	...	...	...	...	...	...
14	PCOF + ACTF	st	14.89 %	62.42 %	22.80 %	0.08 s
15	CPM-Flow		22.32 %	27.79 %	23.23 %	4.2 s
16	MotionSLIC	ms	14.86 %	66.21 %	23.40 %	30 s

other hand, although our approach gives a higher percentage of outliers than SF algorithms that also use stereo information (noted *st*), it runs several order of magnitude faster. Finally, let us emphasize that PCOF is among the only three algorithms able to achieve framerate processing (10 Hz) on the KITTI datasets.

As for the KITTI 2015 ranking, the percentage of OF outliers (Fl-all) is significantly higher, mainly due to the large motions induced by fast moving objects. Using LDOF instead of FOLKI significantly improves the performances in this case, but at the expense of an important computational overhead (cf. PCOF-LDOF and PCOF + ACTF in Table 5).

5   Conclusion

We have proposed to fully exploit stereo information for fast and performant OF estimation. In the prediction step, the static part of the OF is derived from depth and visual odometry. The correction step improves the estimation and estimates the OF associated with moving objects, with corrrect performance except for the fastest ones. Relying on relevant algorithmic choices, we have been able to reach framerate (10 Hz) processing while maintaining high quality OF estimation, as shown by a performance evaluation on KITTI datasets. On-going work concerns the integration of covariance propagation in the prediction/correction process and the application of the proposed pipeline to an obstacle avoidance system for lightweight ground and aerial robots.

Acknowledgment. This work was sponsored by the Direction Générale de l'Armement (DGA) of the French Ministry of Defense.

References

1. Brox, T., Bruhn, A., Papenberg, N., Weickert, J.: High accuracy optical flow estimation based on a theory for warping. In: Pajdla, T., Matas, J.G. (eds.) ECCV 2004. LNCS, vol. 3024, pp. 25–36. Springer, Heidelberg (2004)
2. Brox, T., Malik, J.: Large displacement optical flow: descriptor matching in variational motion estimation. PAMI **33**(3), 500–513 (2001)
3. Chakrabarti, A., Xiong, Y., Gortler, S.J., Zickler, T.: Low-level vision by consensus in a spatial hierarchy of regions. In: CVPR (2015)
4. Derome, M., Plyer, A., Sanfourche, M., Le Besnerais, G.: Real-time mobile object detection using stereo. In: ICARCV (2014)
5. Derome, M., Plyer, A., Sanfourche, M., Le Besnerais, G.: Moving object detection in real-time using stereo from a mobile platform. Unmanned Syst. **3**(4), 253–266 (2015)
6. Fischler, M.A., Bolles, R.C.: Random sample consensus: a paradigm for model fitting with applications to image analysis and automated cartography. ACM **24**(6), 381–395 (1981)
7. Gehrig, S.K., Eberli, F., Meyer, T.: A real-time low-power stereo vision engine using semi-global matching. In: Fritz, M., Schiele, B., Piater, J.H. (eds.) ICVS 2009. LNCS, vol. 5815, pp. 134–143. Springer, Heidelberg (2009)
8. Geiger, A., Lenz, P., Stiller, C., Urtasun, R.: Vision meets robotics: the KITTI dataset. Int. J. Robot. Res. **32**(11), 1231–1237 (2013)
9. Geiger, A., Roser, M., Urtasun, R.: Efficient large-scale stereo matching. In: Kimmel, R., Klette, R., Sugimoto, A. (eds.) ACCV 2010, Part I. LNCS, vol. 6492, pp. 25–38. Springer, Heidelberg (2011)
10. Hirschmller, H.: Stereo processing by semiglobal matching and mutual information. Pattern Anal. Mach. Intell. **30**(2), 328–341 (2008)
11. Horn, B.K., Schunck, B.G.: Determining optical flow. Artif. Intell. **17**, 185–203 (1981)
12. Le Besnerais, G., Champagnat, F.: Dense optical flow by iterative local window registration. In: ICIP (2005)
13. Lucas, B.D., Kanade, T.: An iterative image registration technique with an application to stereo vision. In: IJCAI, pp. 674–679 (1981)
14. Menze, M., Geiger, A.: Object scene flow for autonomous vehicles. In: CVPR (2015)
15. Müller, T., Rannacher, J., Rabe, C., Franke, U.: Feature- and depth-supported modified total variation optical flow for 3D motion field estimation in real scenes. In: CVPR (2011)
16. Plyer, A., Le Besnerais, G., Champagnat, F.: Massively parallel Lucas Kanade optical flow for real-time video processing applications. J. Real-Time Image Proc. **11**(4), 713–730 (2016)
17. Revaud, J., Weinzaepfel, P., Harchaoui, Z., Schmid, C.: EpicFlow: edge-preserving interpolation of correspondences for optical flow. In: CVPR (2015)
18. Sanfourche, M., Vittori, V., Le Besnerais, G.: eVO: a realtime embedded stereo odometry for MAV applications. In: IROS (2013)
19. Sizintsev, M., Kuthirummal, S., Samarasekera, S., Kumar, R., Sawhney, H.S., Chaudhry, A.: GPU accelerated realtime stereo for augmented reality. In: 3DPVT (2010)
20. Vogel, C., Schindler, K., Roth, S.: 3D scene flow estimation with a piecewise rigid scene model. Int. J. Comput. Vis. **115**, 1 (2015)

21. Wedel, A., Brox, T., Vaudrey, T., Rabe, C., Franke, U., Cremers, D.: Stereoscopic scene flow computation for 3D motion understanding. Int. J. Comput. Vis. **95**(1), 29–51 (2011)
22. Wedel, A., Pock, T., Zach, C., Bischof, H., Cremers, D.: An improved algorithm for TV-L^1 optical flow. In: Cremers, D., Rosenhahn, B., Yuille, A.L., Schmidt, F.R. (eds.) Statistical and Geometrical Approaches to Visual Motion Analysis. LNCS, vol. 5604, pp. 23–45. Springer, Heidelberg (2009)
23. Weinzaepfel, P., Revaud, J., Harchaoui, Z., Schmid, C.: Deepflow: large displacement optical flow with deep matching. In: ICCV (2013)
24. Yamaguchi, K., McAllester, D., Urtasun, R.: Efficient joint segmentation, occlusion labeling, stereo and flow estimation. In: Fleet, D., Pajdla, T., Schiele, B., Tuytelaars, T. (eds.) ECCV 2014, Part V. LNCS, vol. 8693, pp. 756–771. Springer, Heidelberg (2014)
25. Zach, C., Pock, T., Bischof, H.: A duality based approach for realtime TV-L^1 optical flow. In: Hamprecht, F.A., Schnörr, C., Jähne, B. (eds.) DAGM 2007. LNCS, vol. 4713, pp. 214–223. Springer, Heidelberg (2007)

Weakly-Supervised Semantic Segmentation by Redistributing Region Scores Back to the Pixels

Josip Krapac[(✉)] and Siniša Šegvić

Faculty of Electrical Engineering and Computing,
University of Zagreb, Zagreb, Croatia
josip.krapac@fer.hr

Abstract. We address the problem of semantic segmentation of objects in weakly supervised setting, when only image-wide labels are available. We describe an image with a set of pre-trained convolutional features and embed this set into a Fisher vector. We apply the learned image classifier on the set of all image regions and propagate the region scores back to the pixels. Compared to the alternatives the proposed method is simple, fast in inference, and especially in training. The method displays very good performance of on two standard semantic segmentation benchmarks.

1 Introduction

Semantic segmentation is one of the most challenging computer vision tasks with wide range of applications in scene and image understanding, class-specific attention, robot perception and autonomous navigation and planning. The goal of semantic segmentation is to assign a label to each pixel, where the label corresponds to an object class, *e.g.* "cat", "sofa" or "person". Semantic segmentation is difficult because the set of semantic concepts is very diverse, and objects may be located across a wide range of scales and poses. The segmentation model training in strongly supervised setting assumes that each image pixel is accompanied with its target class label. At test time the learned model is used to infer class labels for each pixel in a given input image. The main drawback of the strongly-supervised approach is the need for pixel-level annotations, because the acquisition of such precise labels is costly and requires substantial effort and time. A complex image may require more than 15 min of human attention. The best results are obtained with models based on deep convolutional nets which are known to be especially data hungry.

This is one of the main reasons for recent interest in approaches that relax the annotation effort [13–15,17,26]. These can be grouped into two main categories: weakly- and semi-supervised approaches. Weakly-supervised approaches learn the classification models without any pixel-level training data, which can be done by relying on bounding-box and image-wide annotations. Semi-supervised approaches assume that the bulk of the training data is weakly-supervised or unsupervised while a small part of the training dataset is annotated on the pixel-level. Due to the need to leverage weakly-supervised data, each semi-supervised

© Springer International Publishing AG 2016
B. Rosenhahn and B. Andres (Eds.): GCPR 2016, LNCS 9796, pp. 377–388, 2016.
DOI: 10.1007/978-3-319-45886-1_31

approach is typically built on top of a weakly-supervised engine. This justifies further research in weakly-supervised approaches even though semi-supervised approaches are able to offer better performance.

In this paper we are concerned with semantic segmentation in the weakly-supervised setting, where we have access only to image-wide labels. The training phase requires only images annotated with image-wide labels, while at test time one should predict a class label for each pixel. Our method relies on a single per-class hyper-parameter $m(c)$ which modulates the extent of background in the processed images. The recent surge of interest for this very challenging problem is motivated by excellent performance of convolutional neural networks on related computer vision tasks: image categorization [10], object detection [19] and strongly-supervised semantic segmentation [12]. Convnets have significantly improved state-of-the-art in weakly-supervised semantic segmentation, but methods that employ them require either large amounts of weakly-annotated images [17] or suffer from computationally complex training [13] and inference [26].

We propose a simple yet very effective method for weakly-supervised semantic segmentation. The method is based on Fisher vector embedding of pre-trained convolutional features and linear classifiers learned from image-wide labels. We apply the learned classifier to all image regions, and employ a novel method to aggregate region-level scores into pixel-level decisions. To determine the class-specific hyper-parameters for the model we use a few tens of bounding box annotations per object class. The method requires only a hundreds of weakly-annotated images and a few tens bounding box annotations per class and displays fair performance and fast execution. The results are competitive compared to state-of-the-art methods as displayed by performance on standard and challenging semantic segmentation benchmarks.

2   Related Work

Most approaches to semantic segmentation operate in a strongly supervised context where training images are densely annotated on the pixel-level [2,5,21]. Impressive results in this context have recently been obtained using fully convolutional neural networks [12]. However, strongly-supervised approaches require pixel-level labels that are costly to obtain. Much recent interest has therefore been directed towards relaxing the annotation effort. This work can be grouped into two main categories: weakly-supervised approaches [13–15,17,26] and semi-supervised approaches [9,13,14,24]. Weakly supervised approaches relax the extent of supervision from ground-truth segmentation masks to image-level [13,14,17] or box-level [6,13,14,24] labels.

Much semantic segmentation work relies on bottom-up segmentation, since similar neighboring pixels are likely to share the common class. Some of these approaches score the segments indirectly, by averaging pixel-based evidence, and redistribute the scores back to the pixels [5,26]. This often improves the results by regularizing the semantic segmentation and aligning it with the natural image boundaries. However, most recent bottom-up segmentation approaches have been trained on pixel-level annotations [1,23], which makes the weakly-supervised qualification questionable.

Many recent approaches improve weakly supervised segmentation results by fitting various hyper-parameters. For example, one can set the relative size of the objects with respect to the background [13,14], or the inherent difficulty of the particular class (per-class thresholds of pixel scores [17]). Setting these hyper-parameters requires cross-validation on a pixel-level annotated validation set [17] or an insight into inherent dataset bias [13,14].

Most semantic segmentation approaches smooth the produced segmentation masks with some kind of a conditional random field (CRF) [13,14,26]. The CRF parameters can be learned from the image-wide labels [26] or from a small held-out set of fully-annotated images [13].

Advanced weakly-supervised approaches train semantic segmentation models exclusively with image-wide labels [13–15,17,26]. One way to tackle this problem is to leverage the information recovered with a multi-label image classification model [17]. Fisher vector image representation [20] offers interesting opportunities along these lines due to capability to relate an image-wide classification model to the contributions at the patch-level [5,25]. Applications of Fisher vectors to semantic segmentation have so for been researched only in the strongly-supervised setting and with SIFT features [5]. Here, following [3], we use Fisher vectors in conjunction with convolutional features and use the learned object classification models for weakly-supervised semantic segmentation.

3   Method

Here we describe the proposed method for weakly-supervised semantic segmentation. First, we explain the Fisher vector embedding and the advantages over embedding given by deep neural nets. Next, we describe how to infer pixel-level predictions from a set of region scores obtained by applying the learned classifier to all image regions. Finally, we show how to convert multi-label pixel predictions to multi-class pixel predictions.

3.1   Learning the Image Classifier

The task of image classifier is to learn the mapping from a set of images $\mathcal{X}$ into a set of class labels $\mathcal{Y}$. This mapping is learned from a set of images associated with class labels $\{(\boldsymbol{X}_i, \boldsymbol{y}_i)\}_{i=1}^N$. Each image is represented by a set of local descriptors $\boldsymbol{X}_i = \{\boldsymbol{x}_{i,1}, \cdots, \boldsymbol{x}_{i,N_i}\}$, *e.g.* convolutional features extracted from an inner layer of convolutional net. In the remainder of the paper we call *patch* the central part of convolutional feature's receptive field. Label vector $\boldsymbol{y}_i$ has 1 on positions corresponding to the classes that are present in the image. We assume a general multi-label setting where labels are not mutually exclusive, so $\boldsymbol{y}_i$ can have more than one non-zero entry. Recently it has been shown that Fisher vector embedding of image represented with a set of convolutional features in conjunction with linear classifiers yields very good classification performance, comparable to the performance of embedding produced by a fully-connected (FC) part of the net [3]. In this approach a patch descriptor x is first explicitly embedded in a higher-dimensional space defined by the parameters of a pre-trained generative model via function Φ. Next, all patch embeddings are averaged by spatial pooling into the global image representation $\Phi(X_i)$:

$$\Phi(X_i) = \frac{1}{N_i} \sum_{j=1}^{N_i} \Phi(x_{ij}), \tag{1}$$

where N_i is the number of patches in the image X_i. The additivity of patch Fisher vectors along with linearity of the learned one-vs-all classifier entails the additivity of patch scores $s(c|\cdot)$ for class c:

$$s(c|X_i) = w_c^\top \Phi(X_i) = w_c^\top \sum_{j=1}^{N_i} \Phi(x_{ij}) = \sum_{j=1}^{N_i} s(c|x_{ij}). \tag{2}$$

Thus the score of an image $s(c|X)$ is given as the sum of patch scores. This allows us to determine the contribution of each patch to the image score, and therefore propagate the image score back to the patches, which is the main advantage of Fisher vector embedding over the FC part of the net. We use a logistic regression classifier so the posterior for a class is $p_c(c = 1|X_i) = \sigma(s(c|X_i))$. Note that we do not use improved Fisher vector [16], since preliminary experiments have shown only a marginal classification performance improvement, and using non-linear normalizations would break linearity of the image score $w.r.t.$ patch scores.

3.2   From Image-Level Predictions to Pixel-Level Predictions

The classifier learned on the full images is then applied to image regions. We consider two settings: in the first setting regions correspond to patches, while in the second setting we consider all rectangular regions in the image. We first normalize region descriptor by the number of patches the region contains, and then apply the classifier learned on full images. This classifier score is computed at the resolution of convolutional feature maps and upsampled using nearest neighbor interpolation to the resolution of the full image. In the first setting the classifier learned on images is applied to patches. In case of general object classes displayed against complex backgrounds this setting is not likely to produce good results. In the second setting one has to arrive at patch scores from a set of region scores. We do this by considering the scores of all regions that contain the patch. To efficiently compute the scores for all image regions and all classifiers we use integral images, as in [11]. The score for each pixel is then computed as:

$$p_c(c = 1|x, m) = \prod_{k=1}^{M} p_c(c = 1|Z_k)^{\frac{m}{M}} \tag{3}$$

where Z_i is the Fisher vector of the ith out of M regions that contain image patch described by x. The scoring is illustrated in Fig. 1. When $m = M$ we

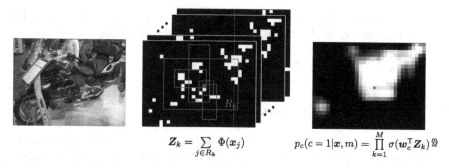

$$Z_k = \sum_{j \in R_k} \Phi(x_j) \qquad p_c(c = 1|x, m) = \prod_{k=1}^{M} \sigma(w_c^{\mathsf{T}} Z_k)^{\frac{m}{M}}$$

Fig. 1. Illustration of pixel scoring based on the regions that contain it. First the convolutional features x are extracted and embedded in the Fisher vector $\Phi(x)$. Then, Fisher vector is computed for each R_k that contains location of feature x, using integral images. Finally, the class prediction for the pixel at location of feature x is computed by combining the predictions of all regions that contain it.

assume that the region descriptors are independent, which is clearly invalid as region overlap contains at least region descriptor x, so we alleviate this by setting $m < M$. For smaller objects we would like to put more weight on independent decisions of regions, which means that we expect that higher m yields better performance. For larger objects we would like to put more weight on the interplay of overlapping regions, which means that we expect that smaller m yields better performance. In the remainder of the section we leave out dependence on m.

3.3 From Multi-label to Multi-class Pixel Predictions

Class posteriors that we propagate from an image to the pixels are based on learned one-vs-all classifiers, which are learned in multi-label setting, so in general $\sum_{c=1}^{C} p_c(c = 1|x) \neq 1$. On the other hand, the semantic segmentation is a multi-class problem since each pixel belongs to only one semantic class. Thus, we need to arrive at probability distribution over $C + 1$ class labels for each pixel. To this end we couple the predictions of one-vs-all classifiers by first determining the probability that a pixel belongs to the background via noisy-and model [18]:

$$p_b(b = 1|x) = \prod_{c=1}^{C} 1 - p_c(c = 1|x), \tag{4}$$

and then we normalize the probabilities to obtain class posteriors for each pixel:

$$p_C(C = c|x) = \frac{p_c(c = 1|x)}{\sum_{c=1..C,b} p_c(c = 1|x)} \tag{5}$$

The use of noisy-and model discourages assignment of a pixel to the background if any of one-vs-all classifiers has high class posterior. In other words, pixel can have high background posterior $p_b(b = 1|\boldsymbol{x})$ only if all C classifiers have low $p_c(c = 1|\boldsymbol{x})$. Finally, we determine the class for each pixel using MAP:

$$\hat{c}(\boldsymbol{x}) = \arg\max_{c=\{1..C,b\}} p_C(C = c|\boldsymbol{x}) \tag{6}$$

4   Experimental Evaluation

We perform evaluation on two standard semantic segmentation benchmarks: Pascal VOC 2007 (VOC'07) and Pascal VOC 2012 (VOC'12) [8]. When training the classifier we also include the image-wide labels from the objects designated as "difficult" and "truncated", since Cinbis *et al.* [4] showed that this improves the results of weakly-supervised localization. Both datasets contain 20 same classes, VOC'07 contains 9963 images, divided in approximately equal train and test splits. VOC'12 is around two times the size of VOC'07. We report intersection-over-union (IoU) averaged over all classes as the standard performance measure for semantic segmentation [8].

4.1   Experimental Setup

We used convolutional features from the conv5.4 layer of the 19-layer convolutional network VGG-E [22] pre-trained on ImageNet [7]. The number of feature maps in the selected convolutional layer is $d = 512$ which corresponds to the dimensionality of the feature vector. Each feature in the output map has a receptive field of 252×252 pixels, but we consider that a feature vector is mostly influenced by a small central patch. The patch size is determined from the number of max-pooling layers and the size of the pooling region: there are 4 2×2 max pooling layers up to 5th convolutional layer net, so a pixel in the selected feature map corresponds to the patch of size 16×16 in the input image. The maximal size of images in both datasets is 500×500 pixels so the size of the largest feature map is 32×32. Unlike [3] we use just one scale. Preliminary results showed that classification performance with single scale features drops only slightly, while significantly reducing the run-time per image. We use convolutional part of the net just as local pre-trained feature extractor and do not perform any fine-tuning.

We use the Fisher vector embedding instead of fully-connected layers and use the same setting as in [3]: GMM with $K = 64$ components with diagonal covariance matrices. We also noticed that PCA on convolutional features yields lower classification performance, so we do not perform any pre-processing of convolutional features. This yields $D = K(1 + 2d)$ dimensional Fisher vectors for each image patch. Following standard Fisher vector classification pipeline [16] these are pooled by mean pooling into an image representation. We use additive normalization (zero-mean) and multiplicative normalization with the inverse of the Fisher matrix, which we assume diagonal. However we do not use non-linear normalizations of improved Fisher vector [16], to be able to keep additivity of the patch classification scores into the image classification score. Differently from [3], we use logistic regression instead of SVM, as our method requires class posterior estimates, as described in Sects. 3.2 and 3.3.

4.2   Results

Our first set of experiments quantitatively explores the influence of parameter m on results. Figure 2 shows the influence of m on the performance for particular classes. In Fig. 3 we display segmentations for different values of m. Parameter m influences the spatial extent of the segmented object: for small objects a higher value of m yields better performance, while for larger objects a lower m is better. High value of m yields high precision, indicating that classifier assigns high scores to class-specific patches. However, a classifier assigns low scores to large non-specific object parts, which for high m results in poor recall. Our region scoring allows propagation of scores from small class-specific parts to the greater spatial extent, increasing thus recall.

In Table 1 (left) we demonstrate the influence of region scoring on the results. When pixels' class posteriors are determined from a limited spatial extent corresponding to the the patch that covers it, the performance is poor. The performance is improved by including image level prior (ILP), as in [17]: the classes not detected in the image are downweighted, so the number of false positives is reduced.

From Fig. 2 it is clear that the best m depends on the class. For each class we determine the value $m(c)$ that maximizes segmentation IoU by treating a the bounding boxes from VOC'07 dataset as ground-truth segmentations. However, setting the determined $m(c)$ for each class in each image would yield different ranges of estimated class posteriors $p_c(c = 1|\mathbf{x})$. This would adversely

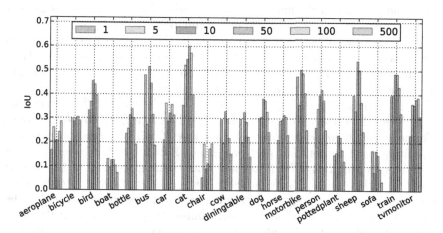

Fig. 2. Semantic segmentation performance on VOC'07 when varying the value of parameter m. Optimal value of m depends on the object class: classes with smaller objects *e.g.* airplanes and tv monitor benefit from higher m, while bigger objects benefit from low value of m *e.g.* motorbikes and buses.

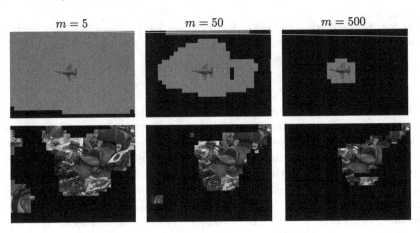

Fig. 3. The demonstration of different values of parameter m to the semantic segmentation. High m suppresses the influence of the regions with low prediction of the class. Therefore the parts of the sky, although highly correlated with airplane are removed when more weight is put on the contribution of smaller regions and individual patches. On the other hand, objects that cover large parts of the image benefit from the interplay of many larger object regions to propagate the decision from class-specific object parts to full spatial extent of the object, benefiting from lower values of parameter m.

influence segmentation performance because it introduces a bias towards classes with smaller $m(c)$. To this end we propose that m is determined per-image in inference as expectation over the classes, where the distribution over the classes is estimated by full image classifier: $\hat{m}(\mathbf{X}) = \mathbb{E}[m|\mathbf{X}] = \sum_c p_C(C = c|\mathbf{X})m(c)$.

For each class we randomly select the same number of bounding boxes, and explore the influence of the number and the random box sampling on segmentation performance by reporting mean and standard deviation. Using more boxes results in significantly better performance, so in the remainder of the paper we use per-class values of m determined from 20 training bounding boxes. We think that annotating 20 bounding boxes per class presents a modest effort compared to the benefit of improved segmentation performance.

In Table 1 (right) we compare our method to the state-of-the-art on challenging VOC'12 dataset. We use per-class m values that give best segmentation performance for 20 bounding boxes per class on VOC'07. We already achieve very competitive result without any post-processing. Pinheiro and Collobert [17] uses 760000 images from ImageNet (76x more than training set of VOC'12) to learn the segmentation model. Their model is trained in multi-class setting, which assumes one object per image, our training works in a more general multi-label setting. The per-class thresholds are determined from the ground-truth annotations of the VOC'12 train split. Finally, to improve precision, they use bottom up segmentation for post-processing. Their best results are achieved with costly multiscale combinatorial grouping (MCG) [1] segmentation. When superpixel segmentation is used, the proposed model outperforms their method, even

Table 1. *Left*: Results on VOC'07 show the proposed region voting significantly improves the segmentation performance. As little as 5 bounding boxes per class are sufficient for good performance. *Right*: Results on VOC'12: the proposed method gives comparable performance to the state-of-the-art methods that use more data, are more computationally complex and apply post-processing steps. Per-class performance is available at Pascal submission server.

Patch scores	IoU × 100
Patches only	10.63
Patches + ILP	18.66

Region scores (bboxes/class)	IoU × 100
5	32.24 ± 0.80
10	33.17 ± 0.65
20	33.59 ± 0.32

Method	IoU × 100
[17] with superpixel	36.6
[17] with MCG	42.0
[13] with CRF	39.6
Region score pooling (our)	38.0

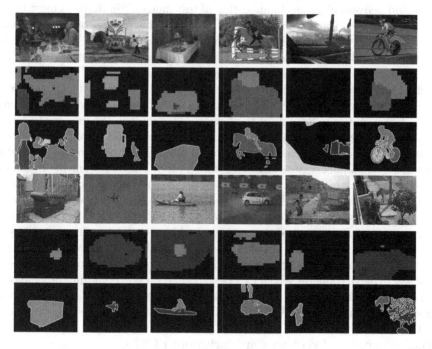

Fig. 4. Examples of segmentation produced by the proposed method.

though we do not perform any post-processing. We also achieve results comparable to the ones of Papandreou *et al.* [13] trained on the same data. Their method employs costly iterative training to fine-tune network weights, and a conditional random field (CRF) for post-processing.

In Fig. 4 we show some successful segmentations and some failure cases. The method is able to segment multiple objects in the image, either when they belong to the same of different classes. In some cases our method detects the objects that are not in ground-truth segmentations, *e.g.* part of the bottle that is seen through the glass. The main failure cases are due to the weak response of classification model which causes misdetections and due to the context of the object that occurs frequently with the object, *e.g.* water is not frequently seen in images that do not contain boats, and characteristic horseback-riding obstacles are not seen in images that do not contain horses. The problem of over and under segmentation is mostly due to the use of inappropriate value of parameter m indicating that better results can be obtained with better selection of hyper-parameters.

5   Conclusion

We have presented a simple and effective method for semantic segmentation of objects a in weakly supervised setting. Our method learns from image-wide labels and delivers pixel-level annotation of test images. Similarly to most other recent computer vision approaches, we build on the success of convolutional features learned on large image collections such as ImageNet. The novelty in our method addresses the heart of the weakly supervised segmentation problem: relating the pixel-level class posterior with a model trained on image-wide labels. Many previous works address that problem by aggregating independent pixel-level evidence. However, such formulation results in many false positives and relies an image-level prior to alleviate this problem. We propose to relate the pixel-level posterior with the posteriors of all encompassing regions as determined by the image-wide classification model: a pixel is considered foreground if most of encompassing regions classify as foreground. This requirement effectively reduces the problem of both false positives and false negatives and significantly improves the performance. The proposed approach requires fast calculation of region-level classification scores, which we solve efficiently by using linear classifiers on top of Fisher embedding and integral images. The main advantages of our approach are conceptual simplicity and the capability to deliver competitive results without any kind of post-processing. The resulting method has only one per-class hyper-parameter which can be validated on few bounding box annotations. Experiments show competitive semantic segmentation performance on the standard test datasets of PASCAL VOC 2007 and 2012. Interesting directions for the future work include integration of information from multiple scales at region and pixel level via binary and higher-order CRFs.

Acknowledgement. This work has been fully supported by Croatian Science Foundation under the project I-2433-2014.

References

1. Arbeláez, P., Pont-Tuset, J., Barron, J., Marques, F., Malik, J.: Multiscale combinatorial grouping. In: CVPR (2014)
2. Boix, X., Gonfaus, J.M., van de Weijer, J., Bagdanov, A.D., Gual, J.S., Gonzàlez, J.: Harmony potentials - fusing global and local scale for semantic image segmentation. IJCV (2012)
3. Cimpoi, M., Maji, S., Kokkinos, I., Vedaldi, A.: Deep filter banks for texture recognition, description, and segmentation. IJCV 1–30 (2016)
4. Cinbis, R.G., Verbeek, J., Schmid, C.: Weakly supervised object localization with multi-fold multiple instance learning. In: PAMI (2016)
5. Csurka, G., Perronnin, F.: An efficient approach to semantic segmentation. IJCV (2011)
6. Dai, J., He, K., Sun, J.: BoxSup: exploiting bounding boxes to supervise convolutional networks for semantic segmentation. In: ICCV (2015)
7. Deng, J., Dong, W., Socher, R., Li, L.J., Li, K., Fei-Fei, L.: ImageNet: a large-scale hierarchical image database. In: CVPR (2009)
8. Everingham, M., Gool, L., Williams, C.K., Winn, J., Zisserman, A.: The pascal visual object classes (VOC) challenge. IJCV (2010)
9. Hong, S., Noh, H., Han, B.: Decoupled Deep Neural Network for Semi-supervised Semantic Segmentation. CoRR abs/1506.04924 (2015)
10. Krizhevsky, A., Sutskever, I., Hinton, G.E.: ImageNet classification with deep convolutional neural networks. In: NIPS (2012)
11. Lampert, C.H., Blaschko, M.B., Hofmann, T.: Efficient subwindow search: a branch and bound framework for object localization. In: PAMI (2009)
12. Long, J., Shelhamer, E., Darrell, T.: Fully convolutional networks for semantic segmentation. In: CVPR (2015)
13. Papandreou, G., Chen, L., Murphy, K.P., Yuille, A.L.: Weakly- and semi-supervised learning of a deep convolutional network for semantic image segmentation. In: ICCV (2015)
14. Pathak, D., Krähenbühl, P., Darrell, T.: Constrained convolutional neural networks for weakly supervised segmentation. In: ICCV (2015)
15. Pathak, D., Shelhamer, E., Long, J., Darrell, T.: Fully convolutional multi-class multiple instance learning. In: ICLR Workshop (2015)
16. Perronnin, F., Sánchez, J., Mensink, T.: Improving the Fisher Kernel for large-scale image classification. In: Daniilidis, K., Maragos, P., Paragios, N. (eds.) ECCV 2010, Part IV. LNCS, vol. 6314, pp. 143–156. Springer, Heidelberg (2010)
17. Pinheiro, P.O., Collobert, R.: From image-level to pixel-level labeling with convolutional networks. In: CVPR (2015)
18. Ramachandran, S., Mooney, R.J.: Revising Bayesian network parameters using backpropagation. In: ICNN (1996)
19. Ren, S., He, K., Girshick, R.B., Sun, J.: Faster R-CNN: towards real-time object detection with region proposal networks. In: NIPS (2015)
20. Sánchez, J., Perronnin, F., Mensink, T., Verbeek, J.J.: Image classification with the fisher vector: theory and practice. IJCV (2013)
21. Shotton, J., Winn, J.M., Rother, C., Criminisi, A.: Textonboost for image understanding: multi-class object recognition and segmentation by jointly modeling texture, layout, and context. IJCV (2009)
22. Simonyan, K., Zisserman, A.: Very deep convolutional networks for large-scale image recognition. In: ICLR (2015)

23. Uijlings, J.R.R., van de Sande, K.E.A., Gevers, T., Smeulders, A.W.M.: Selective search for object recognition. IJCV (2013)
24. Xu, J., Schwing, A.G., Urtasun, R.: Learning to segment under various forms of weak supervision. In: CVPR (2015)
25. Zadrija, V., Krapac, J., Verbeek, J.J., Segvic, S.: Patch-level spatial layout for classification and weakly supervised localization. In: GCPR (2015)
26. Zhang, W., Zeng, S., Wang, D., Xue, X.: Weakly supervised semantic segmentation for social images. In: CVPR (2015)

Learning a Confidence Measure for Real-Time Egomotion Estimation

Stephanie Lessmann[1,3]([✉]), Jens Westerhoff[1,2], Mirko Meuter[1], and Josef Pauli[3]

[1] Delphi Electronics and Safety, Wuppertal, Germany
stephanie.lessmann@delphi.com
[2] University of Wuppertal, Wuppertal, Germany
[3] University of Duisburg-Essen, Duisburg, Germany

Abstract. This paper presents a method to generate a meaningful confidence measurement during online real-time egomotion estimation of a vehicle using a monocular camera. This confidence measurement should give the information whether the signal fulfills a certain accuracy range in all parameters or not. For that reason features from an optical flow field incorporating the egomotion error are determined and a confidence measurement is learned using ground truth egomotion data that we obtain from an offline bundle adjustment before. We show that our confidence measurement gives reliable results and can further be used to filter the egomotion estimation using a Kalman filter. Incorporating the knowledge of the egomotion accuracy determined by the confidence we are able to update the confidence measure for the filtered results. This leads to an improved system availability.

1 Introduction

Many system-components in the field of driver assistance systems have a certain probability to fail. As the outputs should be further used for subsequent system components it is mandatory to get additional information about the quality of the signal. This information should not only reflect the correctness of the signal but also give an accuracy bandwidth in which the signal can be trusted. In particular egomotion estimation via a monocular camera requires such an additional quality estimate, as the output is used for online camera calibration or for egomotion compensation in tracking applications like lane markings, vehicle tracking or pedestrian tracking. A false signal can lead to degraded or completely false output signals of these modules which leads to false reactions in the vehicle actuation, e.g. for lane marking. In general the additional quality estimate is termed as confidence. However, the meaning of the term confidence is often not well defined.

In this paper we present a new approach to generate a well-founded confidence measurement for monocular camera egomotion estimation. In general confidence measurements are often given on the continuous interval $[0 \ldots 1]$, like in [17] for the optical flow computation. As we want to decide if the estimated egomotion parameters are correct or not, a binary confidence measurement is

© Springer International Publishing AG 2016
B. Rosenhahn and B. Andres (Eds.): GCPR 2016, LNCS 9796, pp. 389–401, 2016.
DOI: 10.1007/978-3-319-45886-1_32

an appropriate solution. Thus, we treat the binary confidence measure generation as a classification problem. In general it is also possible to use regression and binarize in a second step. However, as mentioned in other fields of machine learning regression is not necessarily better than just classification [11]. Thus we also compare to a regressor. For the training of our approaches we incorporate ground truth data which we compute offline using sparse bundle adjustment [13,25], while in the online mode a real-time egomotion estimation is working.

In addition we use the confidence signal within a temporal fusion algorithm based on a Kalman filter [16]. If the filter is consistent we can output a new confidence measurement related to the filtered egomotion. This improves the system wide availability of the egomotion result.

1.1   Related Work

In the literature many approaches to compute the vehicle egomotion from a monocular camera exist. To mention only a few, we refer to [10,15,18,23,27, 31]. Some of these approaches incorporate a confidence map of an optical flow field directly into the estimation of the egomotion parameters [15,23], e.g. as a weighting factor. But all of these approaches do not tackle the problem to generate a confidence measure for the egomotion parameters. If we consider the field of stereo vision we can also find some approaches. In [1], for example, eigenvalues are determined to give a confidence measure for the accuracy of depth values. Approaches which learn a confidence measure for stereo matching can be found in [12,21]. However, to the best of our knowledge, the problem to learn a confidence measure for the estimated vehicle egomotion parameters for monocular camera has not been tackled so far.

1.2   Paper Structure

For the remainder of this paper we proceed as follows. In Sect. 2 we describe how our confidence measurement is trained. After the description of our setup (Subsects. 2.1 and 2.2) we give a short definition what confidence means to us and how we create the ground truth using bundle adjustment (Subsect. 2.3). In Sect. 2.4 we define features using an optical flow field and the estimated egomotion. Furthermore, we use our confidence measurement in a temporal Kalman filter for the egomotion estimation in Subsect. 2.5. We present the obtained training results in Sect. 3.1 and filtering results in Sect. 3.2.

2   Confidence Training

2.1   Video Setup

For the egomotion estimation as well as for our confidence training and testing, the videos were recorded using a forward looking camera with a resolution of 1024×512 pixels at 30fps. The camera is mounted in a truck as this provides dynamic egomotion also in the roll and pitch angles. For further information about the vehicle coordinate system we refer to [26]. We determine the intrinsic calibration parameters including the distortion parameters of the lens. We also have access to the data from the vehicle velocity and yaw rate sensor via CAN-Bus.

2.2 Egomotion Setup

In the egomotion module we compute translational parameters $T \in \mathbb{R}^3$ and rotation parameters $\Omega \in \mathbb{R}^3$ called yaw,pitch and roll using a previously computed optical flow field. We generate the optical flow field with a pyramidal implementation of the KLT feature tracker [3] for two consecutive images of the video respectively. To provide real time capabilities our optical flow field has a sparse resolution of 39×28 optical flow vectors. Using the vehicle velocity sensor optical flow vectors with inappropriate length can further be filtered out. We indicate the j-th optical flow feature point in the first image with $x_j \in \mathbb{R}^3$ and the corresponding point in the second image with $x'_j \in \mathbb{R}^3$. The coordinates we use are undistorted and normalized before with the help of the intrinsic calibration.

The objective which is minimized during egomotion estimation is the first order geometric error, the so-called Sampson distance [13] which is based on the epipolar constraint. The Sampson distance is defined as

$$S := \sum_j (\psi_j(R, T))^2 \tag{1}$$

with

$$\psi_j(R, T) := \frac{(x'_j)^T \widehat{T} R x_j}{\left\| \left[(\widehat{T} R x_j)_1, (\widehat{T} R x_j)_2, ((\widehat{T} R)^T x'_j)_1, ((\widehat{T} R)^T x'_j)_2 \right]^T \right\|_2}. \tag{2}$$

The rotation matrix $R \in SO(3)$ is parameterized by the rotation parameters Ω. The notation $\widehat{(\cdot)}$ indicates the cross product in terms of a skew-symmetric matrix. As the translation can be obtained only up to scale it is necessary to restrict the translation vector to a certain length during optimization, e.g. assume the third component to be -1 (points translate into negative direction during forward motion). The vector length can be refined later using the information of the vehicle velocity.

A classic way of minimizing the objective S is a Levenberg-Marquardt minimization [19,20]. Due to computational limitations in real-time systems we have chosen another way and solve for rotation and translation iteratively [18]. As initial parameters for the nonlinear minimization we choose a straightforward motion. In order to handle outliers we embed the optimization procedure into an M-estimator sample consensus (MSAC) framework [28] which is an expansion of the well-known random sample consensus (RANSAC) [9]. Here we use 100 MSAC iterations. The result is further refined using an M-Estimator [14], the Huber-k-Estimator.

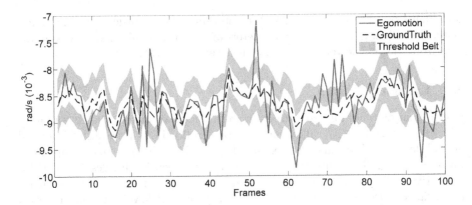

Fig. 1. Confidence Ground truth definition showing Bundle Adjustment results, real-time egomotion and the threshold belt for one of the five egomotion parameters. The confidence is defined as 1 if the egomotion lies within the threshold belt for all egomotion parameters.

2.3   Confidence Definition and Ground Truth

We want to classify the egomotion into two classes depending on how good the parameters are estimated compared to a ground truth. If the egomotion fulfills a certain egomotion accuracy for every parameter, the estimation is termed as "correct" and we refer to it as "confidence is 1" else the "confidence is 0". In order to train a confidence signal for the vision based egomotion, a definition is needed defining when the egomotion is correct or not.

The definition can be made with the help of ground truth data obtained by an inertial measurement unit (IMU), e.g. a 9-axis sensor or, like in our case, with the help of approaches which promise more accurate vision based parameter estimation. For that reason we use Sparse Bundle Adjustment [13,25] on a video data set of 37458 Frames in 64 Video with the video setup mentioned before. If other moving objects appear in the scene we label them with a bounding box and perform the bundle adjustment only on features which are not in the labeled regions. This allows us to get a reasonable ground truth. Our Bundle Adjustment results are further filtered with the help of a yaw rate sensor reducing the noise in the ground truth data. On the training set each output signal of the camera based motion sensor is separated into one of two classes, (true positives (TP) and true negatives (TN)) depending on how good the estimated parameters fit to the ground truth data. In order to get more TN, we reduce the amount of iterations of the RANSAC algorithm in the egomotion estimation. We define the egomotion to be correct if the error is lower than 1σ. Additionally, we use threshold belt areas as visualized in Fig. 1 to avoid unsecure data at the boundaries of the threshold and neglect all data which lie inside of these threshold belt areas.

2.4 Features

By classifying into two distinguished sets, we can clearly define a correct signal and a false signal on our training data. We now want to generalize the definition for unknown data during runtime. For the confidence training and classification we define a feature set, which makes use of the optical flow data which is generated before the egomotion estimation. The feature set which we want to test within this paper constists of an inlier histogram, a localized inlier histogram and an histogram of relative median optical flow vector length.

The inlier histogram should give the discretized information of the distribution of the egomotion error. For every optical flow feature pair (x_j, x'_j) we evaluate the objective $\psi_j(R, T)$ from which we already computed the egomotion. For the histogram bins B_i, we define consecutive, non-overlapping intervals E_i of the egomotion error range, whereby the index i denotes the related feature bin. The optical flow feature pair (x_j, x'_j) is then counted to the pre-defined histogram bin B_i if $\psi_j(R, T)$ lies in the interval E_i. The histogram bins are further normalized using the amount of all optical flow feature pairs M

$$B_i = \frac{|\{j|\psi_j(R, T) \in E_i, j = 1, \ldots, M\}|}{M}. \tag{3}$$

If we consider regions in the image we can give localized versions of the histogram mentioned above. Here we divide the image into four regions of identical magnitude and compute the histogram for every region. This approach can be continued successively to get smaller regions (more levels). We decided to divide the image in the center into four parts of equal size. An example for an inlier histogram for both confidence classes is given in Fig. 3 based on optical flow vectors as also given in Fig. 7. In this figure every bin of the inlier histogram has a different color.

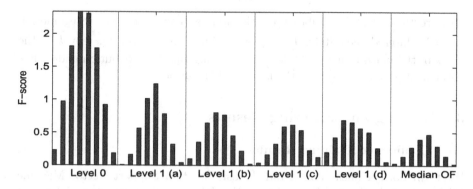

Fig. 2. Computed F-Scores in every histogram bin for different feature types. Here Level 0 denotes the global inlier histogram and Level 1 the local inlier histogram, whereby (a)–(d) are the different image regions (upper left, upper right, down left, down right). Median OF is the relative median optical flow feature.

For the histogram of relative median optical flow vector length we calculate the ration of median of the optical flow vector length for every egomotion error bin to the median optical flow vector length in the whole image.

In order to select the best features for our training we computed the F-Measure [6] of all features, see Fig. 2. This F-measure can only give a rough impression which features should be selected as dependencies among features are missing. For our case the eight "inner" bins of every histogram give the best results.

2.5 Egomotion Filtering and Confidence Propagation

This chapter tackles the problem of filtering the egomotion results in a Kalman filter. The confidence signal is used here to decide, whether the input egomotion signal is applicable for subsequent filtering and the confidence accuracy belt used in the definition also gives information about the egomotion accuracy of the signal. The egomotion accuracy can be used for the filter as measurement covariance information, which is required by a Kalman filter. Furthermore, by defining additional confidence levels by extending the classification problem to different accuracy belts, one could also feed the raw signal into the filter with different measurement covariance values. We implement a linear Kalman filter with a constant velocity model for every parameter, as also used in [22]. The confidence measure is used in such a way that egomotion measurements are rejected if the input is determined as false. If the whole filter is consistently defined we can generate a new confidence signal in a second step using the confidence and signal inputs. For that we evaluate the filter estimate covariance.

$$\widetilde{\mathrm{conf}_k} = \begin{cases} 1 & if \ \wedge_i \left(n_i \cdot det(\widehat{\boldsymbol{P}}^i_{k|k-1}) < \alpha_i\right) \\ 0 & otherwise \end{cases}. \qquad (4)$$

Here the index i describes the i-th filter, as parameters of the egomotion could be filtered separately. $\widehat{\boldsymbol{P}}^i_{k|k-1}$ is the filter covariance, whereby k is the index of the video frame. α_i is determined using the χ^2 distribution and n_i is a normalization factor given by the normal distribution.

3 Training and Filtering Results

3.1 Confidence Training Results

We train both a linear and a radial basis function Support Vector Machine (SVM) [2,7,29] using n-fold cross validation following the instructions in [5] and also compare to a support vector regression (SVR). For the SVR we apply the regression to every egomotion parameter and combine the outputs with thresholding afterwards. As we have an imbalanced data set, we use a weighting factor

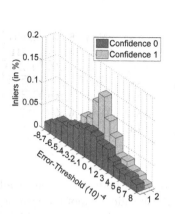

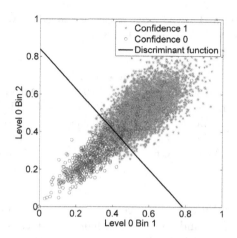

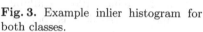

Fig. 3. Example inlier histogram for both classes.

Fig. 4. Example classes for a trained linear SVM with only two bins of the global inlier histogram.

in the SVM training to reduce the imbalance. All features used are normalized on the interval $[0, 1]$. The typical used accuracy measurement of the classifier is an inappropriate quality measure for an imbalanced data set. We exchange this using a balanced accuracy (5) as described in [4]

$$\text{BalAcc} := 0.5 \cdot \frac{\text{TP}}{\text{TP} + \text{FN}} + 0.5 \cdot \frac{\text{TN}}{\text{TN} + \text{FP}}. \tag{5}$$

The balanced accuracy results for the different feature combinations can be found in Table 1. We can reach the best results with all features reaching an accuracy of 88.9 % (linear) or 89.3 % (RBF), while the Median OF feature alone only gets an accuracy value of 73.5 % (linear) or 74 % (RBF). In Fig. 4 we show, how good the classes can be separated using two sample bins of the inlier histogram, even if only two bins of the histogram are used as features. The SVR is more prone to noise in the groundtruth data which is also mirrored in the results. Moreover the parameter handling is more complex for the regression as five SVR have to be trained instead of one SVM.

We also present the receiver operator characteristic also known as ROC-curves [8] to give a more general performance evaluation (Fig. 5) and computed the area under the curves (ROC-AUC). The ROC-AUC values are presented in Table 1. As we can see the use of the RBF-kernel function has only a minor advantage. Thus, we choose a linear SVM for our system.

Table 1. ROC-AUC Values of trained SVM (left) and Balanced Accuracy Values of trained SVM and SVR (right)

	Linear	RBF		SVM Linear	SVM RBF	SVR Linear	SVR RBF
All Features	0.91	0.948	**All Features**	0.889	0.893	0.566	0.8189
Level 0 and 1	0.912	0.947	**Level 0 and 1**	0.888	0.889	0.678	0.793
Level 0	0.913	0.935	**Level 0**	0.886	0.887	0.799	0.717
Level 1	0.913	0.946	**Level 1**	0.889	0.889	0.599	0.758
Median OF	0.796	0.805	**Median OF**	0.735	0.74	0.624	0.659

With the classification we have to find the balance between system availability and correct confidence classification in the specific egomotion accuracy bandwidth. In the extreme case, without classification, we have 100 % availability of our egomotion system but all erroneous estimations are taken as good. As the system confidence output is 1 in the positive cases, the System Availability SAv can be defined as the ratio between all positives and all positive/negative data

$$SAv := \frac{TP + FP}{TP + FP + TN + FN}. \tag{6}$$

The problem to find the correct balance between System Availability and false positiv detections can be transferred to the problem to find the "good" position on the ROC-curve, as the ROC curve represents the true positive rate against the false positive rate. In our case we shift the discriminant function such that more false egomotion states are detected according to a point with lower false positive rate on the ROC-curve.

3.2 Filtering Results

To test the filtering we choose a scene with moving objects which has not been used in the confidence training. In Fig. 7 one frame of this scene is depicted.

We let our online egomotion estimation run on the whole unlabeled scene. Everything combined together, optical flow and egomotion estimation, the algorithm needs 11.72ms on a Intel Core i7-3770 CPU @3.40 GHz. In some frames the egomotion estimation does not work properly, e.g. during overtaking another vehicle. As we can see (Fig. 6) the confidence classifier can detect the most obviously false states and the filtering benefits from this additional input. This can also be seen in the System Availability which increases from 93.9 % before filtering to 95.9 % after filtering on the whole scene.

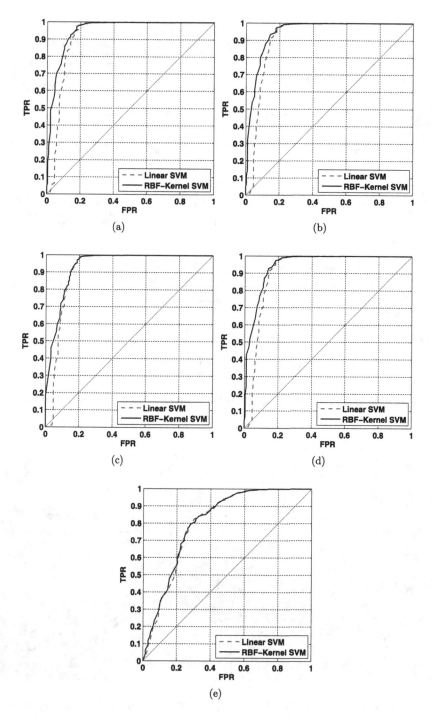

Fig. 5. ROC-curves using (a) all features, (b) global and local inlier histogram, (c) global inlier histogram, (d) local inlier histogram, (e) optical flow feature.

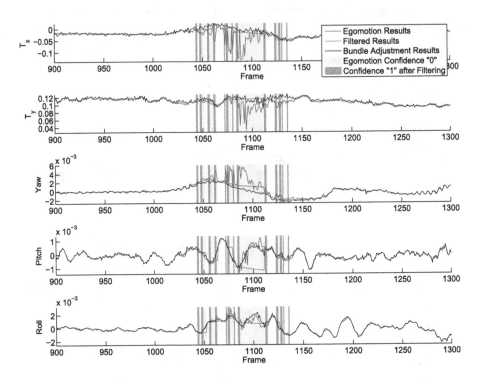

Fig. 6. Kalman filtered egomotion using additional confidence information.

Fig. 7. Scene used for the filtering example. Different bins of inlier histogram are visualized in several colors. (Colour figure online)

4   Conclusion and Outline

In this paper we presented a trained confidence measurement for an egomotion estimation which has a direct relationship to the estimation error of the ego-motion. The classfier can detect false estimates whereby the false negative rate remains low which is a necessary condition to ensure a high system availability.

The confidence measurement can further be used in a filter environment. Here, due to the properties of a linear Kalman filter, one can give a new confidence output for the filtered results, if the filter is designed such that it is consistent.

For future development we want to test additional features. The ground truth generation can be enhanced using a sensor which is independent from the video image. Using a sensor avoids laboriously labeling of other moving objects in the video scene and thus allows to integrate more video files into the data set for training and testing. As the motion of a vehicle has a limited degree of freedom we will also try out a more sophisticated filter model, like in [24,30].

References

1. Agrawal, A., Chellappa, R.: Robust ego-motion estimation and 3-D model refinement using surface parallax. IEEE Trans. Image Process. **15**(5), 1215–1225 (2006)
2. Boser, B.E., Guyon, I.M., Vapnik, V.N.: A training algorithm for optimal margin classifiers. In: Proceedings of the Fifth Annual Workshop on Computational Learning Theory, pp. 144–152. ACM (1992)
3. Bouguet, J.Y.: Pyramidal implementation of the affine lucas kanade feature tracker description of the algorithm. Intel Corporation **5**, 1–10 (2001)
4. Brodersen, K.H., Ong, C.S., Stephan, K.E., Buhmann, J.M.: The balanced accuracy and its posterior distribution. In: 20th International Conference on Pattern Recognition (ICPR), pp. 3121–3124. IEEE (2010)
5. Chang, C.C., Lin, C.J.: Libsvm: a library for support vector machines. ACM Trans. Intell. Syst. Technol. (TIST) **2**(3), 27 (2011)
6. Chen, Y.W., Lin, C.J.: Combining SVMs with various feature selection strategies. In: Guyon, I., Nikravesh, M., Gunn, S., Zadeh, L.A. (eds.) Feature Extraction, pp. 315–324. Springer, Heidelberg (2006)
7. Cortes, C., Vapnik, V.: Support-vector networks. Mach. Learn. **20**(3), 273–297 (1995)
8. Fawcett, T.: An introduction to ROC analysis. Pattern Recogn. Lett. **27**(8), 861–874 (2006)
9. Fischler, M.A., Bolles, R.C.: Random sample consensus: a paradigm for model fitting with applications to image analysis and automated cartography. Commun. ACM **24**(6), 381–395 (1981)
10. Goecke, R., Asthana, A., Pettersson, N., Petersson, L.: Visual vehicle egomotion estimation using the fourier-mellin transform. In: 2007 IEEE Intelligent Vehicles Symposium, pp. 450–455. IEEE (2007)
11. Guo, G., Fu, Y., Dyer, C.R., Huang, T.S.: Head pose estimation: classification or regression?. In: 19th International Conference on Pattern Recognition, ICPR 2008, pp. 1–4. IEEE (2008)

12. Haeusler, R., Nair, R., Kondermann, D.: Ensemble learning for confidence measures in stereo vision. In: Proceedings of the IEEE Conference on Computer Vision and Pattern Recognition, pp. 305–312 (2013)
13. Hartley, R.I., Zisserman, A.: Multiple View Geometry in Computer Vision, 2nd edn. Cambridge University Press, Cambridge (2004). ISBN: 0521540518
14. Huber, P.J.: Robust estimation of a location parameter. Ann. Math. Stat. **35**(1), 73–101 (1964)
15. Jaegle, A., Phillips, S., Daniilidis, K.: Fast, robust, continuous monocular egomotion computation. arXiv preprint (2016). arXiv:1602.04886
16. Kalman, R.E.: A new approach to linear filtering and prediction problems. Trans. ASME-J. Basic Eng. **82**(Series D), 35–45 (1960)
17. Kondermann, C., Kondermann, D., Jähne, B., Garbe, C.S.: An adaptive confidence measure for optical flows based on linear subspace projections. In: Hamprecht, F.A., Schnörr, C., Jähne, B. (eds.) DAGM 2007. LNCS, vol. 4713, pp. 132–141. Springer, Heidelberg (2007)
18. Lessmann, S., Siegemund, J., Meuter, M., Westerhoff, J., Pauli, J.: Improving robustness for real-time vehicle egomotion estimation. In: Intelligent Vehicles Symposium (2016)
19. Levenberg, K.: A method for the solution of certain non-linear problems in least squares. Q. Appl. Math. **2**(2), 164–168 (1944). JSTOR
20. Marquardt, D.W.: An algorithm for least-squares estimation of nonlinear parameters. J. Soc. Ind. Appl. Math. **11**(2), 431–441 (1963)
21. Motten, A., Claesen, L., Pan, Y.: Binary confidence evaluation for a stereo vision based depth field processor SoC. In: 2011 First Asian Conference on Pattern Recognition (ACPR), pp. 456–460. IEEE (2011)
22. Musleh, B., Martin, D., de la Escalera, A., Guinea, D.M., Garcia-Alegre, M.C.: Estimation and prediction of the vehicle's motion based on visual odometry and Kalman filter. In: Blanc-Talon, J., Philips, W., Popescu, D., Scheunders, P., Zemčík, P. (eds.) ACIVS 2012. LNCS, vol. 7517, pp. 491–502. Springer, Heidelberg (2012)
23. Neufeld, A., Berger, J., Becker, F., Lenzen, F., Schnörr, C.: Estimating vehicle ego-motion and piecewise planar scene structure from optical flow in a continuous framework. In: Gall, J., Gehler, P., Leibe, B. (eds.) GCPR 2015. LNCS, vol. 9358, pp. 41–52. Springer, Heidelberg (2015). doi:10.1007/978-3-319-24947-6_4
24. Pink, O., Moosmann, F., Bachmann, A.: Visual features for vehicle localization and ego-motion estimation. In: 2009 IEEE Intelligent Vehicles Symposium, pp. 254–260. IEEE (2009)
25. Snavely, N., Seitz, S.M., Szeliski, R.: Photo tourism: exploring photo collections in 3D. In: ACM transactions on graphics (TOG), vol. 25, pp. 835–846. ACM (2006)
26. Society of Automotive Engineers. Vehicle Dynamics Committee: Vehicle Dynamics Terminology: SAE J670e: Report of Vehicle Dynamics Committee Approved July 1952 and Last Revised July 1976. Handbook supplement, Society of Automotive Engineers (1978)
27. Stein, G.P., Mano, O., Shashua, A.: A robust method for computing vehicle egomotion. In: Proceedings of the IEEE Intelligent Vehicles Symposium, IV 2000, pp. 362–368. IEEE (2000)
28. Torr, P.H., Zisserman, A.: MLESAC: a new robust estimator with application to estimating image geometry. Comput. Vis. Image Underst. **78**(1), 138–156 (2000)
29. Vapnik, V.N., Vapnik, V.: Statistical Learning Theory, vol. 1. Wiley, New York (1998)

30. Weydert, M.: Model-based ego-motion and vehicle parameter estimation using visual odometry. In: 2012 16th IEEE Mediterranean Electrotechnical Conference (MELECON), pp. 914–919. IEEE (2012)
31. Yamaguchi, K., Kato, T., Ninomiya, Y.: Vehicle ego-motion estimation and moving object detection using a monocular camera. In: 18th International Conference on Pattern Recognition, ICPR 2006, vol. 4, pp. 610–613. IEEE (2006)

Learning to Select Long-Track Features for Structure-From-Motion and Visual SLAM

Jonas Scheer[1]([⊠]), Mario Fritz[2], and Oliver Grau[1]

[1] Intel Visual Computing Institute, Saarbrücken, Germany
jonas.scheer@intel-vci.uni-saarland.de
[2] Max-Planck Institute for Informatics, Saarbrücken, Germany

Abstract. With the emergence of augmented reality platforms, Structure-From-Motion or visual SLAM approaches have regained in importance in order to deliver the next generation of immersive 3D experiences. As a new quality is achieved by deployment on mobile devices, computational efficiency plays an important role. In this work, we aim to reduce complexity by limiting the number of features without sacrificing quality. We select a subset of image features, using a learning based approach. A random forest is trained to pick 2D image features which are likely to be significant for a 3D reconstruction. Additionally, we aim for an objective that selects long track features, so that they can be "re-used" in multiple frames. We evaluate our feature selection technique on real world sequences and show a significant reduction of image features and the resulting decreased computation time is not effecting the accuracy of the 3D reconstruction.

1 Introduction

A fundamental problem in computer vision is the estimation of extrinsic camera parameters (position and orientation) from a sequence of images. One classic approach is structure-from-motion (SfM) [3]: From a set of corresponding 2D features, the problem can be formulated by estimating 3D points corresponding to the 2D features and the camera pose per image. The method of choice is bundle adjustment [3,18]. More recent classes of Simultaneous Localization and Mapping (SLAM) algorithms separate out the problem of mapping, that basically solves the SfM problem from camera pose estimation, in order to achieve real-time capabilities of the system [8]. In particular, for real-time applications one has to find a compromise between number of 2D/3D features and accurate pose estimation so to match the computational resources of the target hardware.

The core idea of this work is to select image features which are important for SfM or SLAM and at the same time visible in many frames (long track-length), so that computation amortizes better and the associated optimization problems of the bundle adjustment stays small. Figure 1 shows two images with SIFT features and their correspondences[1]. Most features are correctly matched

---

[1] We acknowledge Hartmann et al. for providing their PARK datasets.

© Springer International Publishing AG 2016
B. Rosenhahn and B. Andres (Eds.): GCPR 2016, LNCS 9796, pp. 402–413, 2016.
DOI: 10.1007/978-3-319-45886-1_33

Fig. 1. Two images [4] of the same scene, with marked geometrically correct *(green)* and wrong *(red)* SIFT matches (only 3 example matches are highlighted). There are wrong correspondences for different parts of the roof as well as on different trees. (Color figure online)

(green circles), but there are quite a few wrong correspondences (red circles). We built on the ideas of Hartmann et al. [4], by using a learning base approach to reduce the number of features. We train a random forest classifier, optimized for retaining image features that are significant for SfM and SLAM in terms of visibility across frames, and correct matches (Fig. 1 green circles). Additionally, the features should have a long track-length, thus they can be found across – potentially distant – frames. The last criterion makes the retained image features more reusable such that they can be used for camera tracking for a long period of time. In our evaluation we show reduction in the number of image features as well as the benefits in computation time while retaining reconstruction quality. In fact, we achieve a slightly improved accuracy of the resulting 3D reconstruction compared to our baseline methods which we attribute to an outlier removal achieved by our method.

2   Related Work

Several approaches have been introduced to speed-up computation time for SfM or visual SLAM. In [8], real-time performance was achieved by utilising multiple threads and FAST [11] image features. Although detection and matching of features like [9,11,12] is very efficient, SIFT [10] is still a reference in feature matching and also used as the basis in this work. In [20], features are ranked according to their observability, as defined in [6], such that only features with a high observability score will be used. Nevertheless, to compute the observability score, all features have to be extracted and matched and also are kept for further updates. For this reason, no significant feature reduction is achieved. Hauagge and Snavely [5] select important features for SfM, by exploit symmetry properties of images. However, their assumptions are only true for symmetric structures as in buildings. Furthermore, Hauagge et al. can only use the full potential of their method, if the symmetric main object resides in the middle of the image. Khan et al. [7] also perform image feature reduction, but they focus on improving bag of words for large scale image datasets. Although the time used for feature matching in SfM or visual SLAM can also be speeded up by using Kd-Trees [13] and hashing techniques [2], Hartmann et al. [4] already showed the benefits of a learning based approach. By predicting SIFT correspondences across frames, the computation time of a SfM matching procedure is decreased significantly and hence the classification overhead is negligible. In this work, we build on the idea of [4] by utilising a classifier for feature reduction. [4] optimizes the SIFT matching probability, which works on a 2D image level. We are going a step further and also take the underlying 3D structure of a scene into account. Our main contribution is a new optimization criterion for training a SfM or SLAM classifier. We explain, how this criterion can be realized by existing learning methods. Furthermore, we investigate evaluation methods explicitly suited for SfM and SLAM, e.g. by looking at the track-length of features.

3   Learning to Select Long-Track Features

In this section we explain our learning objective. We present the employed training procedure and dataset as well as discuss the processing pipeline which is used to annotate the training data according to our training objective.

3.1   Preliminaries

We use SIFT [10] features, represented by their descriptors. A SIFT descriptor is a vector of length 128 holding integer values $\in \{0..255\}$. As described in [10], SIFT features match, if their descriptors have an euclidean distance, smaller than some threshold. To define geometrically correct matches, we use the pinhole camera model as described in [3] to project a 3D scene point onto a 2D image.

Geometrically Correct Matches: Given two images with features $feat_1 \in I_1$ and $feat_2 \in I_2$ as well as two camera projections P_1 and P_2 (3D to 2D). If $feat_1$ and $feat_2$ are valid matches and there exists a 3D scene point P, such that P_1 projects it onto $feat_1$ and P_2 projects it onto $feat_2$, then $feat_1$ and $feat_2$ are Geometrically Correct Matches.

3.2   Optimization Criterion

After extracting SIFT features, we can distinguish between different types of features, as already shown in Fig. 1. While some features have a correspondence in another image which belongs to a different part of the scene, other features have no match at all. We propose the following separation of features:

- *All*: All available SIFT features.
- *Matchable*: Features with valid SIFT matches, according to [10]
- *Geo*: Features with Geometrically Correct Matches
- *LT*: *Geo* features visible in multiple images

This definition leads to the following inclusions:

$$All \supseteq Matchable \supseteq Geo \supseteq LT \qquad (1)$$

If we set the amount of camera views for LT to 2 we get:

$$Geo = LT \qquad (2)$$

In order to reconstruct a 3D point out of 2D points, we need at least two images with different camera poses. There is no specific definition of the number of camera views for LT. Depending on the captured images we have to choose the track-length, such that LT features come from images with a wide camera baseline. Especially slow camera movements or high frame rates require long tracks, due to many images capture the same part of a scene. For this reason, the camera poses of LT features undergo a noticeable transformation. While the training procedure has to be done only once, a slightly higher effort to find an appropriate track-length is justified. Classification itself, does not depend on a certain frame rate or camera motion. The classifier selects features which are likely to fulfill the LT property, hence can be found in camera views with a wide baseline.

Hartmann et al. are optimizing the SIFT matching criterion, what leads to: Hartmann $\approx Matchable$.

One of the main purposes of SfM and SLAM is to reconstruct the surrounding 3D world as well as use the reconstruction to track the camera pose. For this reason, a SfM or SLAM classifier should be optimized for Geo features, not for $Matchable$. Focusing on the accurate tracking of a camera in real-time, LT can be utilized. Due to LT features are visible in multiple frames, they can be reused during camera tracking. While $short$-$track$ features quickly disappear, LT features are of use for a longer period of time. For this reason, a classifier, optimized for retaining LT features should be used to reduce the amount of data for SfM or vSLAM.

3.3   Feature Selection Model

Data: We use the PARK dataset of [4] for training. The original dataset contains 121 images with a resolution of 3024×2016. The images are captured with a DSLR camera and most of the images are taken using a wide baseline. This means, the distance of two consecutive images is approximately more than one meter. Hence, by using a track-length greater than 3, not enough common features across images can be found to create a reconstruction of the scene. Due to this fact, given the wide basline dataset, LT features with track-length 3 are sufficient. Figure 2 shows three consecutive images from PARK.

Learning: To learn LT features, we have to label the training data as *positive* or *negative*. According to our optimization criterion, it holds: positive $= LT$ and negative $= All \setminus LT$. This means, given a set of features, we have to separate the ones, which belong to a 3D reconstruction to obtain LT. Our adjusted version of

Fig. 2. Three consecutive images of the used training dataset [4].

Theia [17] creates a 3D model and outputs for every 3D point the corresponding SIFT features together with their descriptors. Additionally, only the 3D points are considered, for which a certain number of camera views exist. Although in the training images the main object is localized mainly in the image center, this does not influence our random forest. SIFT features contain only local spatial information, not global spatial information. Finally, the labeled SIFT features are used to train a random forest, which leads to our feature selection model. We use a random-forest with 25 trees and a depth of 25. The splitting criterion used in [15], is the gini-impurity as in [1].

Implementation Details: Our processing pipeline consists of a customized version of the structure from motion libraries Theia [17] and Bundler [14]. Feature extraction is done by, VLFeat [19]. We adapt the framework of Hartmann et al. for the feature selection. The random forest classification is based on [15]. We use these mixture of different tools, to mimic the pipeline of [4]. In order to ensure reproducibility of the results, we will make our code available at time of publication.

4   Experiments

In the following, we present the test image datasets, the used baseline methods as well as the pipeline we were using to generate the results. Afterwards we check, to what extend our objective of preserving features in LT is achieved. Therefore we analyze if we can indeed select a significantly smaller set of features which has high track-length. Thus, we measure the amount of reduced features, their track-length as well as the accuracy of the reconstructed 3D models. Furthermore, the runtime for bundle-adjustment and feature matching are measured. Additionally, we visualize the outcome of our classifier by showing point cloud reconstructions and the features distribution within an image.

4.1   Evaluation Scenario

To test our feature selection technique, we use two image sequences (Herz-Jesu-P25, Fountain-R25) from [16]. Both sequences contain 25 images, captured by a Canon D60 camera. They have a pixel resolution of 3072 × 2048 and with the

Fig. 3. 3 images of the Herz-Jesu-P25 sequence and the Fountain-R25 sequence of the test dataset [16] respectively. The surrounding buildings in Fountain-R25 are not visible in every image.

default vlFeat SIFT settings, we can find an average number of 93, 641 features per frame. Three images of each sequence are shown in Fig. 3. In the Herz-Jesu-P25 sequence, the images are captured by moving from the left side of a church to the right side. In the Fountain-R25 sequence, a fountain is the main scene object and is visible in every camera view. However, there are also many elements with a lot of structure in the background. The images in the Fountain-R25 sequence are captured by moving from right to left. We compare our trained classifier (*lt-cl*) to the method of [4] (*match-cl*). We also report no feature reduction at all, to assure an improvement by any of the classification methods. Additionally, we present results by adjusting the SIFT parameters with an increased DoG threshold (*hDoG*). By doing so, features will be retained in highly textured regions. At the beginning, SIFT features are extracted using VLFeat [19] and reduced with on of the three methods (*match-cl, hDoG, lt-cl*). Afterwards, the obtained feature sets are processed by Theia [17] and a 3D reconstruction of the captured scene, including camera poses for each image, is created. The both learning based methods *lt-cl* and *match-cl* support regression. Consequently, adjusting thresholds will lead to a varying number of features. A reconstruction is valid, if all 25 camera poses can be estimated. If one of the reduction methods is too restrictive, discards a lot of features and is not able to register one of the camera poses anymore, a reconstruction might become invalid.

4.2   Feature Reduction

Table 1 shows the set of remaining features after classification. The total amount of features for a given scene is shown in the first column. The second column shows the average number of features per frame and the third column the number of 3D points for a resulting reconstruction. While *lt-cl* achieves the highest feature reduction, the mean reprojection error (right column) of the 3D model decreases. Thus, we can create a more accurate model with fewer features.

Table 1. Our classifier achieves the highest feature reduction with lowest mean reprojection error.

Herz-Jesu-P25 sequence

	Total feature/scene	Avg. feat/frame	3D points	Mean repr. error
All features	2136475	85459	150893	0.4451
hDoG	67543	2701	4624	0.4169
Match-cl ([4])	139986	5599	9129	0.5250
lt-cl (ours)	**31331**	**1253**	**2836**	**0.3513**

Fountain-R25 sequence

	Total feature/scene	Avg. feat/frame	3D points	Mean repr. error
All features	2545581	101823	221311	0.7356
hDoG	50686	2027	4596	0.7460
Match-cl ([4])	39903	1596	2454	0.8421
lt-cl (ours)	**20379**	**815**	**1691**	**0.5748**

Table 2. Our methods registers all cameras, while *hDoG* and *match-cl* register less, even though more features per frame are used.

	Herz-Jesu-P25 sequence			Fountain-R25 sequence		
	3D points	Avg. features	Reg. cameras	3D points	Avg. features	Reg. cameras
hDoG	4043	2397	24	3154	1864	22
Match-cl ([4])	8220	5188	24	1864	1334	24
lt-cl (ours)	**2836**	**1253**	**25**	**1691**	**815**	**25**

lt-cl can achieve a reduction of features of around 50 % with respect to the second best method. While *lt-cl* gives the best reduction performance in both scenes, there is no clear second best method. To demonstrate the limits of the different methods, their thresholds are increased until Theia is not able to register all camera poses anymore. Table 2 shows that *lt-cl* is still able to estimate poses for all 25 views, while fewer features are sufficient. For this reason, we need less data to build a 3D model, when using *lt-cl*. While this is the extreme case, one should lower the thresholds in a real world system. Especially images with little overlap might cause problems for all feature reduction methods.

4.3 Track-Length

After computing a 3D reconstruction, Theia provides statistics about the number of features, with a certain track-length. We only consider image features, which result in a valid 3D point of the corresponding reconstruction. Figure 4 shows, the track-length histograms for both image sequences. *lt-cl* (blue) performs best

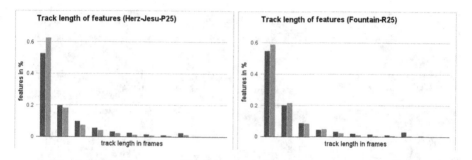

Fig. 4. Track-Length for our classifier (blue) match-cl [4] (red). (Color figure online)

for both of them. *match-cl* (blue) selects more features with a short track-length and therefore has more features in the left part of Fig. 4. In the right part, the bins for *lt-cl* outperform the ones of *match-cl*. This shows, together with the results of Sect. 4.2, the optimization criterion is effective. Our trained classifier selects long track features in *LT*.

4.4   Feature Distribution

After reducing features to a minimum, their distribution within an image is investigated. This is shown in Fig. 5 for the different methods. The left column shows the results for the *hDoG* method which prefers features in highly textured areas. While this seems good in the first place, for most scenes it is not guaranteed, that such areas can be found across the whole scene. In our example sequence, many *hDoG* features (Fig. 5, top left) focus on the center of the fountain, while our long-track classifier spreads the features more across the image (Fig. 5, top right). Consequently, after a highly textured area gets out of view, finding correspondences might become difficult. The classifier of Hartmann (Fig. 5, top middle) also selects features in the center of the fountain, but distributes them more across the fountain. After feature reduction, the two baseline methods, cluster in certain areas, within an image. Our classifier on the other hand selects features all over the image, so you still can features, if a certain region is out of view. However, if you consider the 3D reconstruction, *lt-cl* (Fig. 5 bottom right) mainly preserves features in the fountain region. Scene Fountain-R25 shows that our classifier follows our training objective. As the fountain is visible in every frame, long-track features are more likely in this area and our classifier is able to select them.

4.5   Accuracy of 3D Models

The camera accuracy is measured by comparing a reconstruction with reduced features to the reconstruction that uses all available features. For this reason, using all features is considered as ground truth. Our feature selection method *lt-cl* is applied and a 3D reconstruction is built using the preserved features.

Fig. 5. Distribution of features. Left column: hDoG; Mid column: match-cl; Right column: lt-cl. Top-row: 618 image features each; Mid-row: 826 image features each; Bottom-row: point-clouds with 10591 (hDog) 9678 (match-cl), 6784 (lt-cl) features. hDog and match-cl focus on highly textured areas.

This reduced reconstruction is aligned to the ground truth reconstruction with a similarity transformation. Afterwards, for all camera pairs of both reconstructions, the error of their position and rotation is measured and an average value computed. This procedure is repeated for the baseline methods (*hDoG* and *match-cl*). Consequently, the quality of the preserved features, for each reduction method is measured, with respect to the registration of camera poses. The results are shown in Table 3. Our classifier results in less 3D points, but still achieves a lower position as well as rotation error. This shows that the features which are chosen by *lt-cl* are more valuable for obtaining the pose of a camera. Due to the monocular setting we are using, the reconstructions have no fixed scale. This also means that the position errors are relative to some scaling factor. Nevertheless, this does not change the accuracy of our method.

4.6 Runtime Improvements

To quantify the speed-up of our classifier, the average feature matching time as well as the time needed to perform bundle adjustment was investigated. Theia was executed with two frames only, thus we have a lower bound for the improvement of most SfM and SLAM systems when applying our classifier.

The results are listed in Table 4. Due to the fewer features selected by our classifier we can gain a bundle adjustment speed-up of 67 % compared to the classifier of Hartmann et al. Especially for mobile systems with limited resources, a decrease in computation time from 16.2 ms to 11.0 ms (67 %) for bundle-adjustment and

Table 3. Our classifier gives the lowest rotation & position errors.

Herz-Jesu-P25 sequence

	3D points	Mean position error	Mean rotation error
hDoG	4624	0.0060	0.0049
Match-cl ([4])	9129	0.0065	0.0026
lt-cl (ours)	**3586**	**0.0051**	**0.0018**

Fountain-R25 sequence

	3D points	Mean position error	Mean rotation error
hDoG	4596	0.0335	0.0092
Match-cl ([4])	2454	0.0341	0.0134
lt-cl (ours)	**1691**	**0.0258**	**0.0025**

Table 4. Avg timings (milliseconds) for Herz-Jesu-P25 sequence.

	Features	Feature matching	Bundle adjustment
All features	85459	3477 ms	146 ms
Match-cl ([4])	5263	69.5 ms	16.2 ms
lt-cl (our)	**2107**	**23.9 ms**	**11.0 ms**

from 69.5 ms to 23.9 ms (34 %) for feature matching gives a significant speed-up. Since the computation time for a full bundle adjustment has a cubic influence with respect to the amount of camera views, an even higher speed-up is possible. Table 2 shows, that only our method is able to register all 25 camera views. This means, to include the missing information of the unregistered camera in a SfM process, you need an additional camera, such that there is an sufficient view overlap to register the unregistered one. By utilizing long-track features in visual SLAM, we can construct a keyframe-graph with less camera poses. Thus, SfM as well as vSLAM benefit from a sparser representation of camera views, due to the use of our classifier which is interesting to investigate further.

5   Conclusion

We have proposed a feature selection criterion better suited for SLAM and SfM. With our Long-Track features, we trained a random forest that selects features which are likely to lead to a valid 3D reconstruction and are visible in multiple camera views. A SfM pipeline was used, to generate the training data. Compared to our baseline methods, our classifier reduces the number of image features significantly. We validate that our classifier follows the *Track-Length* criterion, by examine the track-length of the selected features. Together with the distribution properties of long-track features, we show the benefit for SfM and visual SLAM. Our method leads to slightly more accurate 3D models, although less features are used. Additionally, we show runtime improvements for bundle-adjustment and feature matching resulting from our learning method.

References

1. Breiman, L., Friedman, J., Olshen, R., Stone, C.: Classification and Regression Trees. Wadsworth and Brooks, Monterey (1984)
2. Gionis, A., Indyk, P., Motwani, R.: Similarity search in high dimensions via hashing. In: Proceedings of the 25th International Conference on Very Large Data Bases. VLDB 1999, pp. 518–529. Morgan Kaufmann Publishers Inc., San Francisco (1999). http://dl.acm.org/citation.cfm?id=645925.671516
3. Hartley, R.I., Zisserman, A.: Multiple View Geometry in Computer Vision, 2nd edn. Cambridge University Press, Cambridge (2004). ISBN: 0521540518
4. Hartmann, W., Havlena, M., Schindler, K.: Predicting matchability. In: 2014 IEEE Conference on Computer Vision and Pattern Recognition (CVPR), pp. 9–16, June 2014
5. Hauagge, D., Snavely, N.: Image matching using local symmetry features. In: 2012 IEEE Conference on Computer Vision and Pattern Recognition (CVPR), pp. 206–213, June 2012
6. Kalman, R.: On the general theory of control systems. IRE Trans. Autom. Control **4**(3), 110–110 (1959)
7. Khan, N., McCane, B., Mills, S.: Feature set reduction for image matching in large scale environments. In: Proceedings of the 27th Conference on Image and Vision Computing New Zealand, IVCNZ 2012, pp. 67–72. ACM, New York (2012). http://doi.acm.org/10.1145/2425836.2425852
8. Klein, G., Murray, D.: Parallel tracking and mapping for small AR workspaces. In: Proceedings of the Sixth IEEE and ACM International Symposium on Mixed and Augmented Reality (ISMAR'07), Nara, Japan, November 2007
9. Leutenegger, S., Chli, M., Siegwart, R.: BRISK: binary robust invariant scalable keypoints. In: 2011 IEEE International Conference on Computer Vision (ICCV), pp. 2548–2555, November 2011
10. Lowe, D.G.: Distinctive image features from scale-invariant keypoints, vol. 60, pp. 91–110. Kluwer Academic Publishers, Hingham, November 2004. http://dx.doi.org/10.1023/B:VISI.0000029664.99615.94
11. Rosten, E., Drummond, T.W.: Machine learning for high-speed corner detection. In: Leonardis, A., Bischof, H., Pinz, A. (eds.) ECCV 2006, Part I. LNCS, vol. 3951, pp. 430–443. Springer, Heidelberg (2006)
12. Rublee, E., Rabaud, V., Konolige, K., Bradski, G.: ORB: an efficient alternative to sift or surf. In: 2011 IEEE International Conference on Computer Vision (ICCV), pp. 2564–2571, November 2011
13. Silpa-Anan, C., Hartley, R.: Optimised KD-trees for fast image descriptor matching. In: IEEE Conference on Computer Vision and Pattern Recognition, 2008. CVPR 2008, pp. 1–8, June 2008
14. Snavely, N., Seitz, S.M., Szeliski, R.: Photo tourism: exploring photo collections in 3D. ACM Trans. Graph. **25**(3), 835–846 (2006)
15. Stefan, W.: Random-forests (2012). https://github.com/stefan-w/random-forests
16. Strecha, C., von Hansen, W., Van Gool, L., Fua, P., Thoennessen, U.: On benchmarking camera calibration and multi-view stereo for high resolution imagery. In: IEEE Conference on Computer Vision and Pattern Recognition, 2008. CVPR 2008, pp. 1–8, June 2008

17. Sweeney, C.: Theia Multiview Geometry Library: Tutorial & Reference. University of California Santa Barbara
18. Triggs, B., McLauchlan, P.F., Hartley, R.I., Fitzgibbon, A.W.: Bundle adjustment – a modern synthesis. In: Triggs, B., Zisserman, A., Szeliski, R. (eds.) ICCV-WS 1999. LNCS, vol. 1883, pp. 298–372. Springer, Heidelberg (2000)
19. Vedaldi, A., Fulkerson, B.: VLFeat: An open and portable library of computer vision algorithms (2008). http://www.vlfeat.org
20. Zhang, G., Vela, P.A.: Good features to track for visual SLAM, June 2015

Source Localization of Reaction-Diffusion Models for Brain Tumors

Rym Jaroudi[1]([✉]), George Baravdish[1], Freddie Åström[2],
and B. Tomas Johansson[1,3]

[1] Linköping University, Linköping, Sweden
{`rym.jaroudi,george.baravdish`}`@liu.se`, `b.t.johansson@fastem.com`
[2] Heidelberg Collaboratory for Image Processing,
Heidelberg University, Heidelberg, Germany
`freddie.astroem@iwr.uni-heidelberg.de`
[3] Aston University, Birmingham, UK

Abstract. We propose a mathematically well-founded approach for locating the source (initial state) of density functions evolved within a nonlinear reaction-diffusion model. The reconstruction of the initial source is an ill-posed inverse problem since the solution is highly unstable with respect to measurement noise. To address this instability problem, we introduce a regularization procedure based on the nonlinear Landweber method for the stable determination of the source location. This amounts to solving a sequence of well-posed forward reaction-diffusion problems. The developed framework is general, and as a special instance we consider the problem of source localization of brain tumors. We show numerically that the source of the initial densities of tumor cells are reconstructed well on both imaging data consisting of simple and complex geometric structures.

1 Introduction

Brain cancer is one of the most common cancers worldwide. A brain tumor is an abnormal growth of tissue cells partly due to genetic events. Treatment of brain tumors includes surgery, radiotherapy and chemotherapy and is based on a number of factors, with the location in the brain where the tumor formed being of pivotal importance. Studies have been conducted showing that the source of a tumor is correlated with characteristics such as genetic signature [17,30]. These characteristics can influence the behaviour of the tumor including its diffusion and proliferation properties and can therefore be an important marker for diagnosis. The influence of the source location on the diffusion and proliferation properties is herein neglected for simplicity, and future work can focus on incorporating priors on the multimap between the

R. Jaroudi—Support by EU funding under the program ALYSSA (ERASMUS MUNDUS Action 2, Lot 6) is gratefully acknowledged.

F. Åström—Support by the German Science Foundation and the Research Training Group (GRK 1653) is gratefully acknowledged.

© Springer International Publishing AG 2016
B. Rosenhahn and B. Andres (Eds.): GCPR 2016, LNCS 9796, pp. 414–425, 2016.
DOI: 10.1007/978-3-319-45886-1_34

source location and the diffusion and proliferation properties due to genetics. In this work, largely motivated by the potential impact of tumor source localization, we address the problem of reconstructing the source of cell densities evolved within a reaction-diffusion model commonly used to describe tumor growth. Unlike the majority of research done in the area of tumor source localization, which aim at approximating the nonlinear PDE models by systems of ODEs (for example with the Eikonal equation [21]), we propose here a novel and altogether different mathematical approach. We take advantage of the theory of inverse problems to reconstruct initial data in parabolic equations, that is we recast the reconstruction of the source as a backward parabolic problem (for an overview of backward problems, see Chap. 9 in [10]). In doing this, we remove sources of uncertainty introduced when reducing the model to ODEs, i.e., we work with the reaction-diffusion model directly.

Our approach formulates an iterative procedure for solving well-posed forward PDEs at each iteration step, with the aim of adjusting the initial state to match the given data. On an abstract level, this procedure can be seen as a nonlinear Landweber method [23] for an operator equation. The proposed approach assumes that the initial tumor cell density (needed as input data) is measurable; typically it would be extracted from medical imagery.

1.1 Overview

In Sect. 2, we give an overview of some current mathematical models describing tumor growth, i.e., the forward-problem. In Sect. 3, we describe the reaction-diffusion model and state the corresponding inverse problem; the iterative procedure is outlined in Sect. 3.1 together with its connection to the non-linear Landweber method. In Sect. 3.2, some details are given to motivate the well-posedness of the forward problems and the uniqueness of a solution to the inverse problem as well as the convergence of the procedure. In Sect. 4, we describe numerical implementation of the procedure and perform numerical experiments on the Shepp-Logan phantom as well as on MRI data, showing the accuracy of the approach for source localization with different source terms. Finally, some conclusions and remarks are given in Sect. 5.

2 Reaction-Diffusion Models and Related Works

One of the first PDE models for tumor growth was proposed by Murray in the early 1990s [3,5,26]. This model consists of a reaction-diffusion type parabolic PDE with the reaction term representing the proliferation and the diffusion term representing the infiltration [18]:

$$\begin{cases} \partial_t u - \mathrm{div}(D\nabla u) - f(u) = 0 & \text{in } \Omega \times (0,T) \\ u(0) = \varphi & \text{in } \Omega \\ D\nabla u \cdot n = 0 & \text{on } \partial\Omega \times (0,T) \end{cases} \tag{1}$$

Here, u is the tumor cell density at time t at the spatial position x, with D the diffusion tensor for tumor cells and f a reaction term describing the cell growth as a function of the current cell concentration. Different models have been suggested for the proliferation rate f, e.g., $f(u) = \rho u$ referred to as the exponential source term and $f(u) = \rho u(1 - u)$ as the logistic source term where $\rho > 0$, see [27] and [16] for specific applications.[1] The interpretation of the term $\text{div}(D\nabla u)$ in (1) is that it describes the invasion of tumor cells as a diffusive flux along the concentration gradient. The initial tumor cell density φ is given at time $t = 0$, and the boundary condition on $\partial\Omega$ states that tumor cells do not diffuse outside the brain region.

Let us briefly give some works on (1) to show that it is an established model with known and validated parameters.

Clinical imaging data offers the benefit of non-invasive, in vivo and timely measurement of parameters needed in (1). Under the influence of experimental results of Giese et al. [8] regarding the differential motility of tumor cells on grey and white matters, Swanson et al. [25] assumed an infiltrative growth of the tumor cells, while considering differences in cell diffusion in white and gray matter. They suggested that the diffusion tensor D in (1) is spatially dependent: $D = d(x)I$, where I is the identity matrix and $d(x)$ is the diffusion coefficient. Moreover, this diffusion coefficient should only take two different values; in the white matter (myelin) of the brain it is dw, and in the grey matter it is dg, with $dw >> dg > 0$, corresponding to the observation that tumor cells move faster on myelin. Furthermore, in [25] medical images necessary for the diagnosis (CT and MR images) of brain tumors were used to calibrate the parameters ρ and D. Extending the work [25] regarding the differential motility of tumor cells on different tissues, Jbabdi et al. [11] assumed that tumor cells not only move faster on myelin, but also that they follow the white matter fiber tracts that are present in the brain. Simulations using (1) incorporating this extension corroborated well with real tumor growth obtained from MR images.

Other extensions can be done, for example, the invasive nature of tumor growth. Clatz et al. [6] did this by assuming that brain tissue is a linear viscoelastic material.

Let us mention that Konukoglu et al. proposed an altogether different tool for radiotherapy in [13], which extrapolates the extents of the tumor invasion not visible in MR images from the visible part. Based on the reaction-diffusion formalism, they deduced the anisotropic eikonal equation: $\frac{\sqrt{\nabla u \cdot (D\nabla u)}}{\sqrt{\rho u}} = 1$, $u(\partial\Omega) = u_0$, describing the extents of the tumor starting from the visible tumor contour in the MR image. With this, one can obtain ordinary differential equations to solve for the cell density rather than a partial differential equation.

However, as explained above, (1) is well-established for tumor growth, and although challenging to solve due to its nonlinear term, we shall base our reconstruction of the tumor source on this model.

---

[1] Note that the PDE models considered in this work have their origin in ordinary differential equation (ODE) models and the terminology is adopted from ODE models with corresponding source terms as their solution. For example, $u_t = \rho u$ has the *exponential function* $u = Ce^{\rho t}$ as a solution. Furthermore, the logistic equation $u_t = u(1 - u)$ has the *logistic function* $u = 1/(1 + e^{-t})$ as a solution.

3   Source Location

The model (1) describes the tumor cell density u over time. Given knowledge of this density at a fixed time $T > 0$, that is $u = \psi$ at $t = T$, to find the initial distribution (source) amounts to solving

$$\begin{cases} \partial_t u - \operatorname{div}(D(x)\nabla u) - f(u) = 0 & \text{in } \Omega \times (0, T) \\ u(T) = \psi & \text{in } \Omega \\ D\nabla u \cdot n = 0 & \text{on } \partial\Omega \times (0, T) \end{cases} \tag{2}$$

Compared with (1), we have now a final condition imposed (at $t = T$) instead of an initial one (when $t = 0$), and (2) is known as a backward parabolic problem having the additional challenge of being ill-posed with respect to measurement noise in the data, see further [10, Chap. 9] for details on backward problems.

To obtain a regularizing procedure for the stable determination of the initial source φ, we note that the backward problem in (2) can be rewritten as: Determine φ in (1) matching the given data

$$u(x, T) = \psi(x). \tag{3}$$

The determination of φ from this data is our inverse problem (IP) and amounts to solving (2).

3.1   Nonlinear Landweber Method

The inverse problem consisting of finding the initial condition in (1) to match (3) can be reduced to a nonlinear operator equation. This takes the form

$$A(\varphi) = \psi. \tag{4}$$

The definition of $A\varphi$ is $u_T(\varphi)$, with $u_T(\varphi)$ the restriction of the solution of (1) to $t = T$ for a given initial state φ.

Equation (4) inherits the ill-posedness of the backward parabolic problem (2). Therefore, to obtain a stable solution, the nonlinear Landweber method given, for example, in [23] can be applied. In this method, the initial source is updated according to

$$\varphi_{k+1} = \varphi_k - A'^*(A\varphi_k - \psi), \tag{5}$$

where φ_0 is an arbitrary initial guess of the source (belonging to the standard space of square integrable functions, $L^2(\Omega)$), and A'^* is the adjoint of the Fréchet derivative of the operator A. Convergence rates and stability results can be found in [23]. In particular, for noisy data, the iterations has to be ceased at some point otherwise the errors will start to magnify. In the linear case, an approach of this form to find the initial distribution together with a source term, was used in [12]. Thus, it is natural to generalize this to the nonlinear setting.

To calculate the action of the operator A on the element φ_k amounts to solving (1) with data φ_k, resulting in an approximate cell density distribution u_k. Moreover, the action of the operator A'^* on the element $(A\varphi_k - \psi)$ is obtained by solving a corresponding adjoint linear problem to (1).

Lemma 1. *The adjoint linear equation corresponding to the governing equation in (1), that is*

$$\partial_t u - \operatorname{div}(D(x)\nabla u) - f(u) = 0, \tag{6}$$

is given by

$$\partial_t v + \operatorname{div}(D(x)\nabla v) + f_u'(u)v = 0. \tag{7}$$

Proof. Briefly, without entering into full details, the change of sign in Eq. (7) is obtained by multiplying the Eq. (6) by a suitable (test) function v and integrating by parts over the time interval $(0,T)$. Moreover, the linear elliptic part in (7) is obtained by observing that A has a Fréchet derivative, and that the Gateaux derivative of $-\operatorname{div}(D(x)\nabla u) - f(u)$ at u in the direction of v, can be used to evaluate it,

$$\frac{d}{d\varepsilon}[-\operatorname{div}(D(x)(\nabla u + \varepsilon \nabla v)) - f(u + \varepsilon v)]|_{\varepsilon=0} = -\operatorname{div}(D(x)\nabla v) - f_u'(u)v, \tag{8}$$

and the result follows. □

To solve the inverse problem (1) and (3), following the scheme (5), we start by solving

$$\begin{cases} \partial_t u_1 - \operatorname{div}(D(x)\nabla u_1) - f(u_1) = 0, & \text{in } \Omega \times (0,T) \\ \partial_n u_1 = 0, & \text{on } \partial\Omega \times (0,T) \\ u_1(0) = \varphi_0, & \text{in } \Omega \end{cases} \tag{9}$$

Given that u_k, $k \geq 1$, has been constructed, we proceed by solving the linear adjoint problem

$$\begin{cases} \partial_t v_k + \operatorname{div}(D(x)\nabla v_k) + f_u'(u_k)v_k = 0, & \text{in } \Omega \times (0,T) \\ \partial_n v_k = 0, & \text{on } \partial\Omega \times (0,T) \\ v_k(T) = u_k(T) - \psi, & \text{in } \Omega \end{cases} \tag{10}$$

to obtain v_k. Then u_{k+1} is constructed as the solution to

$$\begin{cases} \partial_t u_{k+1} - \operatorname{div}(D(x)\nabla u_{k+1}) - f(u_{k+1}) = 0, & \text{in } \Omega \times (0,T) \\ \partial_n u_{k+1} = 0, & \text{on } \partial\Omega \times (0,T) \\ u_{k+1}(0) = u_k(0) - v_k(0), & \text{in } \Omega \end{cases} \tag{11}$$

We iterate the last two steps until the desired level of accuracy has been obtained.

Using Lemma 1, it is straightforward to verify that the above procedure corresponds to the nonlinear Landweber method (5) for solving (4).

3.2   Well-Posedness of the Forward Problem (1)

It is possible to introduce a weak formulation and with a rather direct approach prove that (1) is well-posed in standard Sobolev spaces for parabolic equations (for such spaces, see [15, Chap. 4.2]). However, to save space, we refer to general theory for abstract parabolic equations and note that (1) can be written

$$\begin{cases} u_t' + Bu = f(u(t)) \\ u(0) = \varphi \end{cases}$$

Equations of this form and further abstractions have been studied in depth in the literature in various spaces, see for example, [29, Chap. 30].

In our case of (1), B is the divergence term, and B generates a semi-group, see [20, Theorem 7.2.5]. From this, and since we work with functions f being at least Lipschitz continuous, we have from [20, Theorem 6.1.2],

Theorem 1. *Let $\varphi \in L^2(\Omega)$. Then there exists a unique (weak or mild) solution $u \in L^2(0, T; H^1(\Omega))$ to the reaction-diffusion problem (1), and this element u depends continuously on the data.*

The similar result holds for classical solutions in spaces of Hölder continuous and differentiable functions, see Theorem 7.4, p. 491, in [14]. The adjoint and linear problem (10) is also well-posed.

More general reaction-diffusion models containing, for example, convection terms and having non-linearities in the divergence term, can be considered, see [22, Chap. 8.6]. Thus, our approach is not limited to (1).

For the reconstructions, it is important to know that there is only one solution to the backward problem (2). Formally, the solution to the backward problem can be represented as

$$u(t) = S(t - T)\psi - \int_t^T S(t - s)f(u(s))\, ds$$

with S being the semi-group generated by the divergence term in (1). Using this representation, one can build on the results for source reconstructions, see [4,7], to obtain that the backward problem has a unique solution. This holds for functions f that are locally Lipschitz, see further [28]. Thus, we can state

Theorem 2. *The backward problem (2) has a unique solution.*

We assume that data are given and compatible such that (2) has a solution.

For the convergence of the nonlinear Landweber type method outlined in the steps (9)–(11), we assume that the initial guess is chosen such that in a neighbourhood of it there is the estimate

$$\|A(\varphi) - A(\varphi_0) - A'(\varphi_0)(\varphi - \varphi_0)\| \le \eta\|A(\varphi) - A(\varphi_0)\|$$

with $0 < \eta < 1/2$, and A from (4). Given this, the nonlinear Landweber method converges, see Theorem 2.4 in [9].

4   Evaluation

We evaluate the proposed solution scheme (9)–(11) on two types of data with synthetically generated tumors obtained via the forward model (2). The parameters values are equal in the forward and backward model.

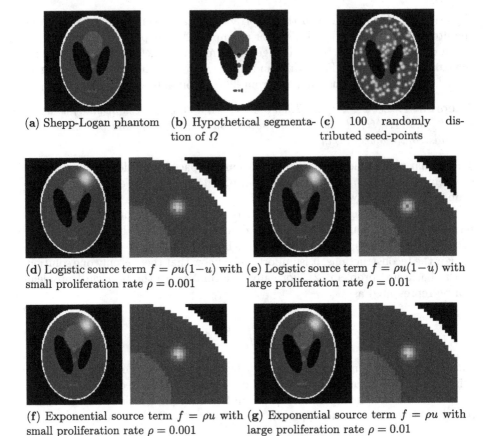

(a) Shepp-Logan phantom

(b) Hypothetical segmentation of Ω

(c) 100 randomly distributed seed-points

(d) Logistic source term $f = \rho u(1-u)$ with small proliferation rate $\rho = 0.001$

(e) Logistic source term $f = \rho u(1-u)$ with large proliferation rate $\rho = 0.01$

(f) Exponential source term $f = \rho u$ with small proliferation rate $\rho = 0.001$

(g) Exponential source term $f = \rho u$ with large proliferation rate $\rho = 0.01$

Fig. 1. Source localization for the Shepp-Logan phantom image with different source terms and proliferation rates: logistic in (d), (e) and exponential source term in (f), (g). In (d)–(g): right figures show the final source location in red and the initial distribution in yellow; left figures show the tumour distribution at time T in yellow and the tumor boundary in green. Panel (c) illustrates the randomly generated seed-points. (Color figure online)

4.1   Discretization

We adopt a generic forward Euler discretization strategy using finite differences approximating derivatives in the parabolic PDEs [19]. Since Ω is the (curved) boundary of the brain (union of white and gray matter segments), special care needs to be taken when computing the Neumann boundary condition on irregular grids. We approach this problem by replicating the boundary pixels in the outward normal direction of Ω sequentially (left-right, up-down, right-left and down-up). Any inconsistency for diagonal flow vectors could not be observed, and this straightforward strategy performs remarkably well.

Table 1. Mean L1 pixel distance and standard deviation for 100 seed-points between the ground truth seed center location and the estimated tumor source for the Shepp-Logan and the MRI images.

Shepp-Logan phantom	$f = \rho u(1-u)$		$f = \rho u$	
ρ	0.001	0.01	0.001	0.01
Landweber	1.35 ± 1.40	2.73 ± 1.56	1.37 ± 1.36	2.67 ± 1.56
Centroid	1.65 ± 2.05	3.16 ± 1.91	1.35 ± 1.37	2.65 ± 1.55
MRI T1				
Landweber	1.54 ± 2.01	3.52 ± 1.84	0.77 ± 0.98	2.17 ± 1.35
Centroid	1.98 ± 2.30	5.34 ± 2.12	0.77 ± 0.98	2.16 ± 1.34

4.2 Evaluation Setup

We use two different settings to evaluate the proposed source reconstruction of tumors: the first is usage of the standard Shepp-Logan phantom [24] describing a comparably simple geometry, the second setting describes a more involved geometry and consists of an MRI T1-weighted brain scan [2] from the Internet Brain Segmentation Repository (IBSR) [1]. In the synthetic setting of the Shepp-Logan phantom, we manually selected hypothetical white and gray matter regions whereas in the second configuration the data has ground truth segmentation provided by experts. These imaging data are illustrated in Figs. 1(a), (b) and 2(a), (b), respectively.

For each of the data, we use 100 seed-points shown in panels (c) of respectively figure. For each seed-point we run the forward model to obtain a synthetic tumor at time a $T > 0$ for a particular parameter configuration. In the Shepp-Logan phantom we used diffusivity speed 1 in the white matter and 0.05 in the gray matter segment. For the MRI image we set diffusivity speed 1 in the white matter region and 0.1 in the gray matter region. In all of the experiments, we let the update step in the Euler scheme be 10^{-1}, ρ either 0.001 or 0.01 influencing the degree of the nonlinearity for the exponential and logistic source terms in the PDE model (1). The forward problem was iterated 100 times for the Shepp-Logan phantom and 500 for the MRI image, these data were used as φ_0 in (9). The problem (9) is iterated 20 times and the resulting u_1 is used as initial data to (10) and (11), each iterated two and one time respectively. Finally, the overall problem (10)-(11) is iterated 10 times. We found no improvement in source localization by performing additional iterations of the outer loop. For comparison, we segment the tumor and compute its centroid (or "center of mass"), and let this point represent a baseline method for source localization. The next section discusses the results.

4.3 Results

Figures 1 and 2 display examples of source localization for the Shepp-Logan phantom and the MRI image in (a). Panel (b) depicts the regions of hypothetical

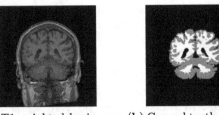

(a) T1-weighted brain scan (b) Ground truth segmenta- (c)   100   randomly   dis-
of MRI data from IBSR   tion provided by experts   tributed seed-points

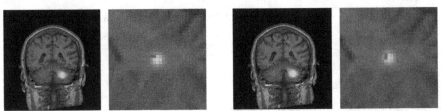

(d) Logistic source term $f = \rho u(1-u)$ with (e) Logistic source term $f = \rho u(1-u)$ with
small proliferation rate $\rho = 0.001$ large proliferation rate $\rho = 0.01$

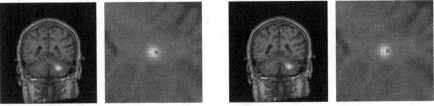

(f) Exponential source term $f = \rho u$ with (g) Exponential source term $f = \rho u$ with
small proliferation rate $\rho = 0.001$ large proliferation rate $\rho = 0.01$

Fig. 2. Panel (a) shows a T1-weighted MRI brain scan from IBSR. Its ground truth
segmentation provided by experts is shown in panel (b). Panel (c) illustrates the randomly generated seed-points and each point constitutes one experiment. (d), (e), (f)
and (g) shows different source localization for different proliferation rates. In (d)–(g):
right figures show the final source location in red and the initial distribution in yellow;
left figures show the tumour distribution at time T in yellow and the tumor boundary
in green. (Color figure online)

white and gray matter regions. In (d)–(f), left panels, show the tumors cell
densities obtained with the forward model and the initial seed-points depicted
in yellow in the right panels. When the tumor density is nearly homogeneous the
source localization works well with a minor error as visualized in the right panels.
If the tumor source is located close to the boundary Ω it is more difficult to
reconstruct as the inverse scheme needs to handle a severely anisotropic growth
pattern.

Both Figs. 1 and 2 show experiments of source localization for the Shepp-
Logan phantom image and the MRI data image with different source terms and

proliferation rates. In panels (d), (e) of Fig. 1 and panels (d), (e) of Fig. 2, we use a logistic source term $f = \rho u(1 - u)$ for a small proliferation rate $\rho = 0.001$ and a larger one $\rho = 0.01$. Moreover, in panels (f) and (g) of Fig. 1 and panels (f) and (g) of Fig. 2, we did the similar simulations but with an exponential source term $f = \rho u$. For both source terms we obtain an accurate estimate of the tumor (or density) source.

Table 1 shows the mean L1 pixel distance of 100 seed-points (illustrated in (c), Figs. 1 and 2) between the ground truth seed center location and the estimated tumor source for the Shepp-Logan image and the MRI T1 image. Since we include two source terms, the logistic and the exponential proliferation, this is also a quantitative evaluation for evaluating the robustness of the scheme for different source terms. The parameter ρ determines the influence of the source term and a larger value yields a tumor cell density which is more anisotropic than with smaller values, making the source localization harder. Therefore, it is expected that the error should increase as the value of ρ increases. We also remark that the source of tumors located close to the boundary will be harder to reconstruct as the proposed regularizing procedure needs to handle a severely anisotropic growth pattern.

5   Conclusion

Motivated by the importance of being able to determine the initial location where a brain tumor formed, we have proposed an iterative regularizing procedure for a nonlinear backward parabolic reaction-diffusion model, and applied it for the stable determination of the initial brain tumor cell density. Mathematical analysis of the procedure, such as well-posedness of the forward problems used in the iterations, were undertaken. Numerical experiments were included on the Shepp-Logan phantom as well as an MRI image for various nonlinear terms in the parabolic equation. These initial experiments show that it is possible to retrieve the initial source in a stable way with the proposed procedure, and with accepted accuracy. Future work includes, for example, other source terms and validation against real data.

References

1. IBSR, Internet Brain Segmentation Repository. www.nitrc.org/projects/ibsr/. Accessed Mar 2016
2. Release Name: Male Subject, T1-Weighted Brain Scan: 788_6. www.nitrc.org/frs/shownotes.php?release_id=2305. Accessed Mar 2016
3. Bellomo, N., de Angelis, E.: Selected Topics in Cancer Modeling Genesis Evolution Immune Competition and Therapy. Springer Science & Business Media, Berlin (2008)
4. Cannon, J.R.: Determination of an unknown heat source from overspecified boundary data. SIAM J. Numer. Anal. 5(2), 275–286 (1968)

5. Chaplain, M.: Avascular growth, angiogenesis and vascular growth in solid tumours: the mathematical modelling of the stages of tumour development. Math. Comput. Model. **23**(6), 47–87 (1996)

6. Clatz, O., Sermesant, M., Bondiau, P.Y., Delingette, H., Warfield, S.K., Malandain, G., Ayache, N.: Realistic simulation of the 3-D growth of brain tumors in MR images coupling diffusion with biomechanical deformation. IEEE Trans. Med. Imaging **24**(10), 1334–1346 (2005)

7. D'haeyer, S., Johansson, B.T., Slodička, M.: Reconstruction of a spacewise-dependent heat source in a time-dependent heat diffusion process. IMA J. Appl. Math. **79**(1), 33–53 (2014)

8. Giese, A., Kluwe, L., Laube, B., Meissner, H., Berens, M.E., Westphal, M.: Migration of human glioma cells on myelin. Neurosurgery **38**(4), 755–764 (1996)

9. Hanke, M., Neubauer, A., Scherzer, O.: A convergence analysis of the Landweber iteration for nonlinear ill-posed problems. Numer. Math. **72**(1), 21–37 (1995)

10. Isakov, V.: Inverse Problems for Partial Differential Equations. Springer, New York (1998)

11. Jbabdi, S., Mandonnet, E., Duffau, H., Capelle, L., Swanson, K.R., Pélégrini-Issac, M., Guillevin, R., Benali, H.: Simulation of anisotropic growth of low-grade gliomas using diffusion tensor imaging. Magn. Reson. Med. **54**(3), 616–624 (2005)

12. Johansson, B.T., Lesnic, D.: A procedure for determining a spacewise dependent heat source and the initial temperature. Appl. Anal. **87**(3), 265–276 (2008)

13. Konukoğlu, E., Clatz, O., Bondiau, P.-Y., Delingette, H., Ayache, N.: Extrapolating tumor invasion margins for physiologically determined radiotherapy regions. In: Larsen, R., Nielsen, M., Sporring, J. (eds.) MICCAI 2006. LNCS, vol. 4190, pp. 338–346. Springer, Heidelberg (2006)

14. Ladyženskaja, O.A., Solonnikov, V.A., Uralceva, N.N.: Linear and Quasilinear Equations of Parabolic Type, vol. 23. American Mathematical Society, Providence (1968). Translated from the Russian by S. Smith. Translations of Mathematical Monographs

15. Lions, J.L., Magenes, E.: Non-homogeneous Boundary Value Problems and Applications, vol. II. Springer, New York, Heidelberg (1972). Translated from the French by P. Kenneth, Die Grundlehren der mathematischen Wissenschaften, Band 182

16. Marušić, M., Bajzer, Ž., Freyer, J., Vuk-Pavlović, S.: Analysis of growth of multicellular tumour spheroids by mathematical models. Cell Prolif. **27**(2), 73–94 (1994)

17. Mueller, W., Hartmann, C., Hoffmann, A., Lanksch, W., Kiwit, J., Tonn, J., Veelken, J., Schramm, J., Weller, M., Wiestler, O.D., et al.: Genetic signature of oligoastrocytomas correlates with tumor location and denotes distinct molecular subsets. Am. J. Pathol. **161**(1), 313–319 (2002)

18. Murray, J.D.: Mathematical Biology II Spatial Models and Biomedical Applications Interdisciplinary Applied Mathematics, vol. 18. Springer, New York (2001)

19. Nocedal, J., Wright, S.: Numerical Optimization. Springer Series in Operations Research and Financial Engineering. Springer, New York (2006)

20. Pazy, A.: Semigroups of Linear Operators and Applications to Partial Differential Equations, Applied Mathematical Sciences, vol. 44. Springer, New York (1983)

21. Rekik, I., Allassonnière, S., Clatz, O., Geremia, E., Stretton, E., Delingette, H., Ayache, N.: Tumor growth parameters estimation and source localization from a unique time point: application to low-grade gliomas. Comput. Vis. Image Underst. **117**(3), 238–249 (2013)

22. Roubíček, T.: Nonlinear Partial Differential Equations with Applications. International Series of Numerical Mathematics, vol. 153. Birkhäuser Verlag, Basel (2005)

23. Schuster, T., Kaltenbacher, B., Hofmann, B., Kazimierski, K.S.: Regularization Methods in Banach Spaces. Radon Series on Computational and Applied Mathematics, vol. 10. Walter de Gruyter GmbH & Co. KG, Berlin (2012)
24. Shepp, L.A., Logan, B.F.: The fourier reconstruction of a head section. IEEE Trans. Nucl. Sci. **21**(3), 21–43 (1974)
25. Swanson, K.R., Alvord, E., Murray, J.: A quantitative model for differential motility of gliomas in grey and white matter. Cell Prolif. **33**(5), 317–329 (2000)
26. Swanson, K.R., Alvord, E., Murray, J.: Virtual brain tumours (gliomas) enhance the reality of medical imaging and highlight inadequacies of current therapy. Br. J. Cancer **86**(1), 14–18 (2002)
27. Tracqui, P.: From passive diffusion to active cellular migration in mathematical models of tumour invasion. Acta Biotheor. **43**(4), 443–464 (1995)
28. Tuan, N.H., Trong, D.D.: On a backward parabolic problem with local Lipschitz source. J. Math. Anal. Appl. **414**(2), 678–692 (2014)
29. Zeidler, E.: Nonlinear Functional Analysis and Its Applications. II/B: Nonlinear Monotone Operators. Springer, New York (1990). Translated from the German by the author and Leo F. Boron
30. Zlatescu, M.C., TehraniYazdi, A., Sasaki, H., Megyesi, J.F., Betensky, R.A., Louis, D.N., Cairncross, J.G.: Tumor location and growth pattern correlate with genetic signature in oligodendroglial neoplasms. Cancer Res. **61**(18), 6713–6715 (2001)

Depth Estimation Through a Generative Model of Light Field Synthesis

Mehdi S.M. Sajjadi, Rolf Köhler, Bernhard Schölkopf, and Michael Hirsch(✉)

Max-Planck-Institute for Intelligent Systems,
Spemannstraße 38, 72076 Tübingen, Germany
{msajjadi,rkoehler,bs,mhirsch}@tuebingen.mpg.de

Abstract. Light field photography captures rich structural information that may facilitate a number of traditional image processing and computer vision tasks. A crucial ingredient in such endeavors is accurate depth recovery. We present a novel framework that allows the recovery of a high quality continuous depth map from light field data. To this end we propose a generative model of a light field that is fully parametrized by its corresponding depth map. The model allows for the integration of powerful regularization techniques such as a non-local means prior, facilitating accurate depth map estimation. Comparisons with previous methods show that we are able to recover faithful depth maps with much finer details. In a number of challenging real-world examples we demonstrate both the effectiveness and robustness of our approach.

1 Introduction

Research on light fields has increasingly gained popularity driven by technological developments and especially by the launch of the Lytro consumer light field camera [25] in 2012. In 2014, Lytro launched the *Illum* follow-up model. While these cameras are targeted to the end-consumer market, the company Raytrix [28] manufactures high-end light field cameras, some of which are also capable of video recording, but aimed for the industrial sector. Both Lytro and Raytrix use an array of microlenses to capture a light field with a single camera.

Prior to the first commercially available light field cameras, other practical methods have been proposed to capture light fields, such as a camera array [34], a gantry robot mounted with a DSLR camera that was used to produce the Stanford Light Field dataset [1] or a programmable aperture which can be used in conjunction with a normal 2D camera to simulate a light field camera [23].

Previously proposed approaches [12,20,32] model a depth map as a Markov Random Field and cast depth estimation as a multi-labelling problem, so the reconstructed depth map consists of discrete values. In order to keep the computational cost to a manageable size, the number of depth labels is typically kept low which results in cartoon-like staircase depth maps.

In contrast, we propose an algorithm which is capable of producing a continuous depth map from a recorded light field and which hence provides more accurate depth labels, especially for fine structures. Before we discuss related

© Springer International Publishing AG 2016
B. Rosenhahn and B. Andres (Eds.): GCPR 2016, LNCS 9796, pp. 426–438, 2016.
DOI: 10.1007/978-3-319-45886-1_35

work in Sect. 3 and present our method in Sect. 4, we lay down our notation and light field parametrization in the following section.

2   Light Field Parametrization

It is instructive to think of a light field as a collection of images of the same scene, taken by several cameras at different positions. The 4D light field is commonly parametrized using the two plane parametrization introduced in the seminal paper by [21]. It is a mapping

$$L : \Pi \times \Omega \to \mathbb{R} \qquad (s, t, x, y) \mapsto L(s, t, x, y)$$

where $\Omega \subset \mathbb{R}^2$ denotes the image plane and $\Pi \subset \mathbb{R}^2$ denotes the focal plane containing the focal points of the different virtual cameras. (x, y) and (s, t) denote points in the image plane and camera plane respectively. In a discretely sampled light field, (x, y) can be regarded as a pixel in an image and (s, t) can be regarded as the position of the camera in the grid of cameras. We store the light field as a 4D object with $\dim(L) = (S, T, X, Y)$.

For the discrete case, also called *light field photography*, each virtual camera is placed on a cross-section of an equispaced $n \times n$ grid providing a view on the same scene from a slightly different perspective. Two descriptive visualizations of the light field arise if different parameters are fixed. If $s = s^*$ and $t = t^*$ are fixed, so-called *sub-aperture images* I_{s^*,t^*} arise. A sub-aperture image is the image of one camera looking at the scene from a fixed viewpoint (s^*, t^*) and looks like a normal 2D image. If $(y = y^*, t = t^*)$ or $(x = x^*, s = s^*)$ are kept fixed, so-called *epipolar plane images* (EPI) [4] E_{y^*,t^*} or E_{x^*,s^*} arise.

An interesting property of an EPI is that a point P that is visible in all sub-aperture images is mapped to a straight line in the EPI, see Fig. 2b. This characteristic property has been employed for a number of tasks such as denoising [9,15], in-painting [15], segmentation [22,40], matting [8], super-resolution [3,37, 38] and depth estimation (see related work in Sect. 3). Our depth estimation algorithm also takes advantage of this property.

3   Related Work and Our Contributions

Various algorithms have been proposed to estimate depth from light field images. To construct the depth map of the sub-aperture image I_{s^*,t^*} a structure tensor on each EPI E_{y,t^*} $(y = 1, \ldots, Y)$ and E_{x,s^*} $(x = 1, \ldots, X)$ is used by [36] to estimate the slopes of the EPI-lines. For each pixel in the image I_{s^*,t^*} they get two slope estimations, one from each EPI. They combine both estimations by minimizing an objective function. In that objective they use a regularization on the gradients of the depth map to make the resulting depth map smooth. Additionally, they encourage that object edges in the image I_{s^*,t^*} and in the depth map coincide. A coherence measure for each slope estimation is constructed and used to combine the two slope estimations. Despite not using the full light field but only the sub-aperture images $I_{s^*,t}$ $(t = 1, \ldots, T)$ and I_{s,t^*} $(s = 1, \ldots S)$ for a given (s^*, t^*), they achieve appealing results.

In [20] a fast GPU-based algorithm for light fields of about 100 high resolution DSLR images is presented. The algorithm also makes use of the lines appearing in an EPI. The rough idea for a 3D light field is as follows: to find the disparity of a pixel (x, s) in an EPI, its RGB pixel value is compared with all other pixel values in the EPI that lie on a slope that includes this pixel. They loop over a discretized range of possible slopes. If the variance in pixel color is minimal along that slope, the slope is accepted. For a 4D light field not a line is used, but a plane. [33] note that uniformly colored areas in the light field form not lines but thick rays in the EPI's, so they convolve a Ray-Gaussian kernel with the light field and use resulting maxima to detect areas of even depth.

In [32] the refocusing equation described in [26] is used to discretely sheer the 4D ligthfield in order to get correspondence and defocus clues, which are combined using a Markov random field. A similar approach is used by [12]. [35] build on [32] by checking edges in the sub-aperture images for occlusion boundaries, yielding a higher accuracy around fine structured occlusions. [24] estimate the focal stack, which is the set of images taken from the same position but with different focus settings and also apply Markov random field energy minimization for depth estimation.

[41] introduce a generative model from binary images which is initialized with a disparity map for the binary views and subsequently refined step by step in Fourier space by testing different directions for the disparity map. [17] suggest an optimization approach, which makes use of the fact that the sub-aperture images of a light field look very similar: sub-aperture images are warped to a reference image by minimizing the rank of the set of warped images. In their preceding work [18] the same authors match all sub-aperture images against the center view using a generalized stereo model, based on variational principles. [29] uses a multi-focus plenoptic camera and calculates the depth from the raw images using triangulation techniques. [2] uses displacement estimation between sub-aperture image pairs and combines the different estimations via a weighted sum, where the weights are proportional to the coherence of the displacement estimation.

Contributions of this paper: While a number of different approaches for depth estimation from light field images exists, we derive to the best of our knowledge for the first time a fully generative model of EPI images that allows a principled approach for depth map estimation and the ready incorporation of informative priors. In particular, we show

1. a principled, fully generative model of light fields that enables the estimation of *continuous* depth labels (as opposed to discrete values),
2. an efficient gradient-based optimization approach that can be readily extended with additional priors. In this work we demonstrate the integration of a powerful non-local means (NLM) prior term, and
3. favourable results on a number of challenging real-world examples. Especially at object boundaries, significantly sharper edges can be obtained.

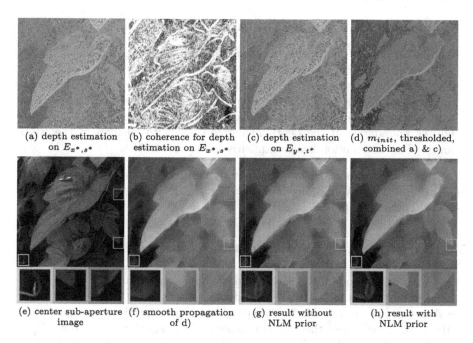

(a) depth estimation on $E_{x*,s*}$ (b) coherence for depth estimation on $E_{x*,s*}$ (c) depth estimation on $E_{y*,t*}$ (d) m_{init}, thresholded, combined a) & c)

(e) center sub-aperture image   (f) smooth propagation of d)   (g) result without NLM prior   (h) result with NLM prior

Fig. 1. Overview of our method on an image by [32], best viewed on screen. Note: each image was normalized to [0,1], so gray values between images may vary. Images (a) and (c) show rough depth maps, computed using the first part of the local depth estimation method of [36], (a) on the EPI $E_{x*,s*}$, and (c) on the EPI $E_{y*,t*}$. (b) Coherence map for the depth estimation on the EPI $E_{x*,s*}$. (d) The two noisy depth maps are thresholded using their corresponding coherence maps and then combined. Evidently, coherent depth values are mainly located at edges while non-coherent depth values (in red) occur in smoother regions. (f) To fill the non-coherent areas, the coherent depth values are propagated using an NLM approach. (g) Our result without a prior shows more details than (f), but also introduces speckles in the depth map. (h) The NLM prior is able to get reduce speckles while preserving fine details, especially on edges. (Color figure online)

4 Overview

Our proposed algorithm computes the depth map of a selected sub-aperture image from a light field. In this paper – without loss of generality – we choose the center sub-aperture image. Our method works in a two step procedure: as a first step, a rough estimation of the depth map is computed locally (Sect. 5). This serves as an initialization to the second step (Sect. 6), in which the estimated depth map is refined using a gradient based optimization approach.

The following implicit assumptions are made by our algorithm:

- All objects in the scene are Lambertian, a common assumption, which is also made by [7,20,30,38].
- There exist no occlusions in the scene. This means that lines in the EPI images do not cross. This is a reasonable assumption, especially for the Lytro camera, as the angular resolution is not very large, as also stated by [9,10].[1]
- Object boundaries in the depth image coincide with changes in the RGB image. This assumption is also explicitly made in [14,27].

Note that these assumptions are not perfectly met in real scenes. Despite relying implicitly on these assumptions, our algorithm works well on real world images as we will demonstrate in Sect. 8.

5   Rough Depth Map Estimation Using NLM

To get an initialization for the depth map, we adopt the initial part of the depth estimation algorithm of [36][2]: the local depth estimation on EPIs. It estimates the slopes of the lines visible in the epipolar image using the structure tensor of the EPI. It only uses the epipolar images of the angular center row (E_{y,t^*} with $t^* = T/2$, $y = \{1, \dots Y\}$) and angular center column (E_{x,s^*} with $s^* = S/2$, $x = \{1, \dots X\}$) and yields two rough depth estimates for each pixel in the center image, see Fig. 1(a, c). Additionally, it returns a coherence map $C(\cdot)$ that provides a measure for the certainty of the estimated depth values (Fig. 1(b)).

This approach returns consistent estimates at image edges but provides quite noisy and unreliable estimates at smoother regions, see Fig. 1(a, c). We take the two noisy depth estimates and threshold them by setting depth values with a low coherence value to *non-defined*. This gives us an initial estimate for the depth values at the edges. After thresholding, the two estimates are combined: if both estimates on E_{y,t^*} and E_{x,s^*} for a pixel in the depth map have coherent values, we will take the depth estimation with the higher coherence value. The result is shown in Fig. 1(d). This rough depth map estimate is denoted by m_{init}.

To propagate depth information into regions of non-coherent pixels (red pixels in Fig. 1(d)), we solve the optimization problem

$$\underset{m}{\arg\min} \sum_{p} \sum_{q \in N(p)} w_{pq} \left[\left(m(p) - m(q) \right)^2 + C(p) \left(m_{init}(p) - m(q) \right)^2 \right] \quad (1)$$

where $w_{pq} \in [0,1]$ is a weighting term on the RGB image that captures the similarity of the color and gradient values of the 3×3 window around p and q (see Sect. 6.1, Eq. (2)). $N(p)$ are the neighboring pixels around p, e.g. in an 11×11 window with p in the center. The term $w_{pq}(m(p) - m(q))^2$ ensures that

---

[1] We discuss the implication of the no-occlusion assumption in more detail in the supplemental material.

[2] We use the given default values $\sigma = 1.0$ and $\tau = 0.5$.

pixels in $N(p)$ have similar depth values as p if they are similar in the RGB image (high w_{pq}). The term $w_{pq}C(p)(m(q) - m_{init}(p))^2$ enforces that a pixel with high coherence $C(p)$ propagates its depth value $m_{init}(p)$ to neighboring pixels q which are similar in the RGB image. Figure 1(f) shows the result of this propagation step. Equation (1) is minimized using L-BFGS-B [6].

6   Refinement Step

The refinement step is based on the observation that the sub-aperture images can be almost entirely explained and predicted from the center image $I := I_{S/2,T/2}$ alone, namely by shifting the pixels from the image I along the lines visible in the

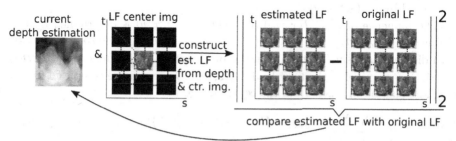

(a) Overview of the refinement step visualized with sub-aperture images, best viewed on screen: The estimated light field (LF) is constructed by shifting pixels from the center sub-aperture image to the other sub-aperture images. The shifting depends on the current depth value of the shifted pixel and the distance to the sub-aperture image. The objective is to minimize the squared L2 distance between the estimated LF and the original LF.

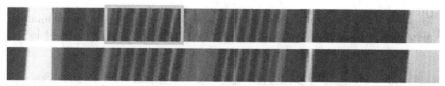

(b) **Top:** Original EPI E_{y^*,t^*} from 7 sub-aperture images using the row in each image, which is highlighted in red above. **Bottom:** Estimated EPI constructed solely from the center row by shifting center row pixels according to their depth values. Note that for better visualization, the EPI's are vertically stretched to twice their heights. Four red lines are overlaid to visualize the emergence of lines in the EPI.

(c) Overview of the refinement step visualized with an EPI.

Fig. 2. Overview of the refinement step. (Color figure online)

epipolar image. This has already been observed by others [16,19,41]. Figure 2c visualizes the case for an EPI E_{y^*,t^*}.

To make full use of the recorded 4D light field, the center image pixels are not only moved along a line, but along a 2D plane. For a fixed s^* or t^* this 2D plane becomes a line visible in the respective EPI views E_{x^*,s^*} or E_{y^*,t^*}. Note that the slopes of the line m_{x_c,y_c} going through the center pixel (x_c, y_c) are the same in E_{y_c,t^*} and E_{x_c,s^*}.

When moving a center image pixel $I(x_c, y_c)$ along the 2D plane with given slope m_{x_c,y_c}, its new coordinates in the sub-aperture image $I_{S/2+d_s,T/2+d_t}$ become $(x_c + m_{x_c,y_c}d_s, y_c + m_{x_c,y_c}d_t)$, where d_s and d_t denote the angular distances from the center sub-aperture image to the target sub-aperture image, formally $d_s = s - S/2$, $d_t = t - T/2$. The estimated light field that arises from shifting pixels from the center sub-aperture image to all other sub-aperture views is denoted by $\widetilde{L}_m(s,t,x,y)$.

The influence of pixel $I(x_c, y_c)$ on pixel $\widetilde{L}_m(s,t,x,y)$ is determined by the distances $x-(x_c+m_{x_c,y_c}d_s)$ and $y-(y_c+m_{x_c,y_c}d_t)$. Only if the absolute values of both distances are smaller than one, the pixel $I(x_c, y_c)$ influences $\widetilde{L}_m(s,t,x,y)$, see Fig. 3. Any pixel in the light field $\widetilde{L}_m(s,t,x,y)$ can thus be computed as the weighted sum of all pixels from the center image I:

$$\widetilde{L}_m(s,t,x,y) = \sum_{x_c}\sum_{y_c} I(x_c,y_c) \cdot \Lambda\big(x - (x_c + m_{x_c,y_c}d_t)\big) \cdot \Lambda\big(y - (y_c + m_{x_c,y_c}d_s)\big)$$

where $\Lambda : \mathbb{R} \to [0,1]$ is a weighting function and denotes the differentiable version of the triangular function defined as

$$\bar{\Lambda}(x) = \begin{cases} 1+x & \text{if } -1 < x < 0 \\ 1-x & \text{if } 0 \le x < 1 \\ 0 & \text{otherwise, i.e. if } |x| \ge 1 \end{cases}$$

To allow for sub-pixel shifts, we use the following bilinear interpolation scheme: As shown in Fig. 3, the intensity value of the pixel $\widetilde{L}_m(s,t,x,y)$ is the

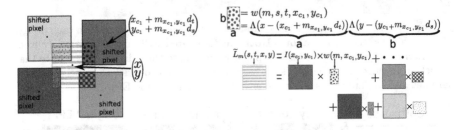

Fig. 3. Modified Bilinear Interpolation: The color of the estimated pixel is determined by using a weighted sum of the shifted pixels that overlap with it. The weight of each pixel is the area of overlap with the estimated pixel. (Color figure online)

weighted sum of all overlapping pixels (the four colored pixels in Fig. 3). The weight of each pixel is the area of overlap with the pixel $\tilde{L}_m(s, t, x, y)$, which is given by the triangular term.

Note that in practice, it is not necessary to iterate over all pixels in the center image for every pixel $\tilde{L}_m(s, t, x, y)$. Instead, the projection of each pixel in the center image is calculated and added to the (up to) 4 pixels in the subview where the overlapping area is nonzero, leading to a linear runtime complexity in the size of the light field. To get a refined depth estimation map we optimize the following objective function:

$$m = \underset{m}{\operatorname{argmin}} \|\tilde{L}_m - L\|_2^2 + \lambda R(m)$$

where $R(m)$ is a regularization term which we will describe in more detail in the remainder of this section.

6.1   Non-local Means Regularization

The NLM regularizer was first proposed in [5] and has proven useful for the refinement of depth maps in other contexts [13]. We define it as

$$R(m) = \sum_p \sum_{q \in N(p)} w_{pq}(m(p) - m(q))^2$$

with $N(p)$ being the search window around a pixel p, e.g. an 11×11 window, and w_{pq} is the weight expressing the similarity of the pixels p and q. We define w_{pq} as

$$w_{pq} = \exp\left(-\sum_{\substack{p' \in N'(p) \\ q' \in N'(q)}} \frac{[I(p') - I(q')]^2}{\sigma_{Color}^2} + \frac{[\nabla_{p,p'} I - \nabla_{q,q'} I]^2}{\sigma_{Grad}^2}\right) \tag{2}$$

where σ_{Color}^2 and σ_{Grad}^2 are the variances in the color and gradient values of the image and $\nabla_{p,p'} I := I(p) - I(p')$ is the image gradient at pixel position p. This encourages edges in the depth map at locations where edges exist in the RGB image and smoothens out the remaining regions. In all experiments, N' was a 3×3 window.

7   Implementation Details

Our implementation is in MATLAB. For numerical optimization we used the MATLAB interface by Carbonetto [6] of the gradient based optimizer L-BFGS-B [42]. The only code-wise optimization we applied is implementing some of the computationally expensive parts (light field synthesis) in C (MEX) using the multiprocessing API OpenMP[3]. Current runtime for computing the depth map from the $7 \times 7 \times 375 \times 375 \times 3$ light field from the Lytro camera is about 270 seconds on a 64bit Intel Xeon CPU E5-2650L 0 @ 1.80 GHz architecture using 8 cores. All parameter settings for the experiments are included in the supplementary and in the source code and are omitted here for brevity. In particular, we refer the interested reader to the supplementary for explanations of their influence to the depth map estimation along with reasonable ranges that work well for different types of images. The code as well as our Lytro dataset is publicly available.[4]

8   Experimental Results

Comparison on Lytro Images. In Fig. 4 we show a comprehensive comparison of our results with several other works including the recent work of [24,35]. The resolution of the Lytro light field is $S \times T = 7 \times 7$, and the resolution of each sub-aperture image is $X \times Y = 375 \times 375$ pixels. We decoded the raw Lytro images with the algorithm by [11][5], whereas others have developed proprietary decoding procedures leading to slightly different image dimensions.

Overall, our algorithm is able to recover more details and better defined edges while introducing no speckles to the depth maps. Depth variations on surfaces are much smoother in our results than e.g. in [35] or [24] while being able to preserve sharp edges. Even small details are resolved in the depth map, see e.g. the small petiole in the lower left corner of the leaf image (second row from the top, not visible in print).

Comparison on the Stanford Light Field Dataset. In Fig. 5 we compare our method on the truck image of the Stanford light field dataset [1]. The light field has a resolution of $S \times T = 17 \times 17$ sub-aperture views. Each sub-aperture image has a resolution of $X \times Y = 1280 \times 960$ pixels. Compared to the already visually pleasing results of [20,36], we are able to recover finer and more accurate details (see closeups in Fig. 5). Additionally, the edges of the depth map match better with the edges of the RGB image. The results on the Amethyst image and further comparisons are shown in the supplementary.

Quantitative Evaluation on Artificial Dataset. We compare our algorithm with the state of the art [35] on the artificial dataset provided by [39]. We could not reproduce the given numerical results, so we used the provided code for the comparison. The average root mean square error on the whole dataset[6] is **0.067** for [35] and **0.063** for our algorithm. The depth maps and further details are given in the supplementary.

---

[3] http://openmp.org
[4] http://webdav.tue.mpg.de/pixel/lightfield_depth_estimation/
[5] The images have neither been gamma compressed nor rectified.
[6] Buddha, buddha2, horses, medieval, monasRoom, papillon, stillLife.

Reference   Our results   [32]   [35]   [24]   [31]   [36]

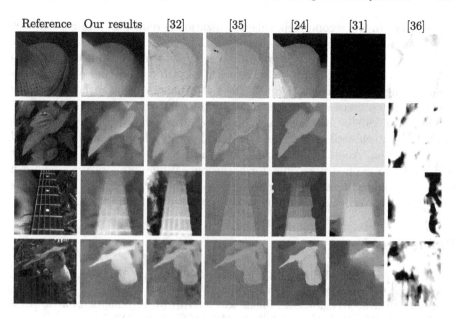

Fig. 4. Comparison on Lytro images taken from [32], best viewed on screen. The results for [31,36] are taken from [24]. Our algorithm is able to recover finer details and produces fewer speckles in the depth map. Note that [31] is originally an optical flow algorithm whose results are included for comparison. (Color figure online)

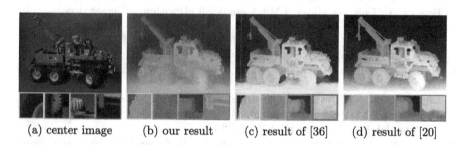

(a) center image   (b) our result   (c) result of [36]   (d) result of [20]

Fig. 5. Comparison on images of the Stanford light field dataset [1], best viewed on screen. We are able to recover finer details and our depth boundaries match better with the RGB image boundaries. The resolution is 1280×960 for all images except for [36], where it is 768×576 as the image is taken from the respective paper. (Color figure online)

9   Conclusion and Future Work

We presented a novel approach to estimate the depth map from light field images. A crucial ingredient of our approach is a generative model for light field images which can also be used for other image processing tasks on light fields. Our approach consists of two steps. First, a rough initialization of the depth map is computed. In the second step, this initialization is refined by using a gradient based optimization approach.

We have evaluated our approach on a light field image from the Stanford dataset [1], on real-world images taken with a Lytro camera and on artificially generated light field images. Despite the Lytro images being rather noisy, our recovered depth maps exhibit fine details with well-defined boundaries.

Our work can be extended and improved in several directions. The algorithm lends itself well to parallelization and seems ideally suited for a GPU implementation. Another interesting direction is to modify our generative light field model to explicitly account for occlusions. While our forward model can be readily adapted to allow for cross-sections in the EPI, optimization becomes more intricate. We leave a solution to this problem for future work.

References

1. The (new) stanford light field archive (2008). http://lightfield.stanford.edu. Accessed 07 Apr 2016
2. Adelson, E.H., Wang, J.Y.A.: Single lens stereo with a plenoptic camera. IEEE Trans. Pattern Anal. Mach. Intell. (PAMI) **14**(2), 99–106 (1992)
3. Bishop, T.E., Favaro, P.: The light field camera: extended depth of field, aliasing, and superresolution. IEEE Trans. Pattern Anal. Mach. Intell. (PAMI) **34**(5), 972–986 (2012)
4. Bolles, R.C., Baker, H.H., Marimont, D.H.: Epipolar-plane image analysis: an approach to determining structure from motion. Int. J. Comput. Vis. **1**(1), 7–55 (1987)
5. Buades, A., Coll, B., Morel, J.M.: A non-local algorithm for image denoising. In: CVPR (2005)
6. Carbonetto, P.: A programming interface for L-BFGS-B in MATLAB (2014). https://github.com/pcarbo/lbfgsb-matlab. Accessed 15 Apr 2015
7. Chai, J.X., Tong, X., Chan, S.C., Shum, H.Y.: Plenoptic sampling. In: ACM SIGGRAPH (2000)
8. Cho, D., Kim, S., Tai, Y.-W.: Consistent matting for light field images. In: Fleet, D., Pajdla, T., Schiele, B., Tuytelaars, T. (eds.) ECCV 2014, Part IV. LNCS, vol. 8692, pp. 90–104. Springer, Heidelberg (2014)
9. Dansereau, D.G., Bongiorno, D.L., Pizarro, O., Williams, S.B.: Light field image denoising using a linear 4D frequency-hyperfan all-in-focus filter. In: IS&T/SPIE Electronic Imaging (2013)
10. Dansereau, D.G., Mahon, I., Pizarro, O., Williams, S.B.: Plenoptic flow: closed-form visual odometry for light field cameras. In: IROS (2011)
11. Dansereau, D.G., Pizarro, O., Williams, S.B.: Decoding, calibration and rectification for lenselet-based plenoptic cameras. In: CVPR (2013)
12. Diebold, M., Goldlücke, B.: Epipolar plane image refocusing for improved depth estimation and occlusion handling. In: Annual Workshop on Vision, Modeling and Visualization: VMV (2013)
13. Favaro, P.: Recovering thin structures via nonlocal-means regularization with application to depth from defocus. In: CVPR (2010)
14. Ferstl, D., Reinbacher, C., Ranftl, R., Rüther, M., Bischof, H.: Image guided depth upsampling using anisotropic total generalized variation. In: ICCV (2013)

15. Goldluecke, B., Wanner, S.: The variational structure of disparity and regularization of 4D light fields. In: CVPR (2013)
16. Gortler, S.J., Grzeszczuk, R., Szeliski, R., Cohen, M.F.: The lumigraph. In: ACM SIGGRAPH (1996)
17. Heber, S., Pock, T.: Shape from light field meets robust PCA. In: Fleet, D., Pajdla, T., Schiele, B., Tuytelaars, T. (eds.) ECCV 2014, Part VI. LNCS, vol. 8694, pp. 751–767. Springer, Heidelberg (2014)
18. Heber, S., Ranftl, R., Pock, T.: Variational shape from light field. In: Heyden, A., Kahl, F., Olsson, C., Oskarsson, M., Tai, X.-C. (eds.) EMMCVPR 2013. LNCS, vol. 8081, pp. 66–79. Springer, Heidelberg (2013)
19. Isaksen, A., McMillan, L., Gortler, S.J.: Dynamically reparameterized light fields. In: ACM SIGGRAPH. ACM (1996)
20. Kim, C., Zimmer, H., Pritch, Y., Sorkine-Hornung, A., Gross, M.H.: Scene reconstruction from high spatio-angular resolution light fields. ACM SIGGRAPH (2013)
21. Levoy, M., Hanrahan, P.: Light field rendering. In: ACM SIGGRAPH. ACM (1996)
22. Li, N., Ye, J., Ji, Y., Ling, H., Yu, J.: Saliency detection on light field. In: CVPR (2014)
23. Liang, C.K., Lin, T.H., Wong, B.Y., Liu, C., Chen, H.H.: Programmable aperture photography: multiplexed light field acquisition. ACM SIGGRAPH (2008)
24. Lin, H., Chen, C., Bing Kang, S., Yu, J.: Depth recovery from light field using focal stack symmetry. In: ICCV (2015)
25. Ng, R.: Digital light field photography. Ph.D. thesis, stanford university (2006). Ren Ng founded Lytro
26. Ng, R., Levoy, M., Brédif, M., Duval, G., Horowitz, M., Hanrahan, P.: Light field photography with a hand-held plenoptic camera. Computer Science Technical Report CSTR 2(11) (2005)
27. Park, J., Kim, H., Tai, Y.W., Brown, M.S., Kweon, I.: High quality depth map upsampling for 3D-TOF cameras. In: ICCV (2011)
28. Perwass, C., Wietzke, L.: The next generation of photography (2010). https://github.com/pcarbo/lbfgsb-matlab. Accessed 15 Apr 2015, Perwass and Wietzke founded Raytrix
29. Perwass, C., Wietzke, L.: Single lens 3D-camera with extended depth-of-field. In: IS&T/SPIE Electronic Imaging (2012)
30. Sebe, I.O., Ramanathan, P., Girod, B.: Multi-view geometry estimation for light field compression. In: Annual Workshop on Vision, Modeling and Visualization: VMV (2002)
31. Sun, D., Roth, S., Black, M.J.: Secrets of optical flow estimation and their principles. In: CVPR (2010)
32. Tao, M.W., Hadap, S., Malik, J., Ramamoorthi, R.: Depth from combining defocus and correspondence using light-field cameras. In: ICCV (2013)
33. Tosic, I., Berkner, K.: Light field scale-depth space transform for dense depth estimation. In: CVPR Workshops (2014)
34. Vaish, V., Wilburn, B., Joshi, N., Levoy, M.: Using plane + parallax for calibrating dense camera arrays. In: CVPR (2004)
35. Wang, T.C., Efros, A.A., Ramamoorthi, R.: Occlusion-aware depth estimation using light-field cameras. In: ICCV (2015)
36. Wanner, S., Goldluecke, B.: Globally consistent depth labeling of 4D light fields. In: CVPR (2012)
37. Wanner, S., Goldluecke, B.: Spatial and angular variational super-resolution of 4D light fields. In: Fitzgibbon, A., Lazebnik, S., Perona, P., Sato, Y., Schmid, C. (eds.) ECCV 2012, Part V. LNCS, vol. 7576, pp. 608–621. Springer, Heidelberg (2012)

38. Wanner, S., Goldluecke, B.: Variational light field analysis for disparity estimation and super-resolution. IEEE Trans. Pattern Anal. Mach. Intell. (PAMI) **36**(3), 606–619 (2014)
39. Wanner, S., Meister, S., Goldluecke, B.: Datasets and benchmarks for densely sampled 4D light fields. In: Annual Workshop on Vision, Modeling and Visualization: VMV (2013)
40. Wanner, S., Straehle, C., Goldluecke, B.: Globally consistent multi-label assignment on the ray space of 4D light fields. In: CVPR (2013)
41. Zhang, Z., Liu, Y., Dai, Q.: Light field from micro-baseline image pair. In: CVPR (2015)
42. Zhu, C., Byrd, R.H., Lu, P., Nocedal, J.: Algorithm 778: L-BFGS-B: fortran subroutines for large-scale bound-constrained optimization. ACM TOMS **23**(4), 550–560 (1997)

Coupling Convolutional Neural Networks and Hough Voting for Robust Segmentation of Ultrasound Volumes

Christine Kroll[1], Fausto Milletari[1(✉)], Nassir Navab[1,2],
and Seyed-Ahmad Ahmadi[3]

[1] Computer Aided Medical Procedures, Technische Universität München,
Munich, Germany
christine.kroll@tum.de
[2] Computer Aided Medical Procedures, Johns Hopkins University, Baltimore, USA
[3] Department of Neurology, Klinikum Grosshadern,
Ludwig-Maximilians-Universität München, Munich, Germany

Abstract. This paper analyses the applicability and performance of Convolutional Neural Networks (CNN) to localise and segment anatomical structures in medical volumes under clinically realistic constraints: small amount of available training data, the need of a short processing time and limited computational resources. Our segmentation approach employs CNNs for simultaneous classification and feature extraction. A Hough voting strategy has been developed in order to automatically localise and segment the anatomy of interest. Our results show (i) improved robustness, due to the inclusion of prior shape knowledge, (ii) highly accurate segmentation even when only small datasets are available during training, (iii) speed and computational requirements that match those that are usually present in clinical settings.

1 Introduction and Related Work

Modern medicine strongly relies on a number of imaging modalities such as computed tomography (CT), magnetic resonance imaging (MRI) and ultrasound (US). Visualising and segmenting body parts enables a variety of new possibilities for medical research studies, diagnosis, monitoring of disease progression, surgical planning and image-guided interventions. For instance, transcranial ultrasound volumes (TCUS) depicting the human midbrain can be segmented in order to perform a differential [28] and early [2] diagnosis of the Parkinson's disease. This task is reportedly challenging even for human experts [18] due to low contrast, low signal to noise ratio, mis-leading patterns and invisible contours of the respective regions. Fully manual delineation in these images is a very time-consuming task that requires an expert to process the volumes slice by slice. Fully automatic, accurate and robust segmentation algorithms can help overcome these challenges and greatly support the daily clinical practice, as long as the constraints regarding computational resources and limited amount of annotated data are met.

© Springer International Publishing AG 2016
B. Rosenhahn and B. Andres (Eds.): GCPR 2016, LNCS 9796, pp. 439–450, 2016.
DOI: 10.1007/978-3-319-45886-1_36

Only few attempts have been made so far to automatically segment brain structures in TCUS volumes. In [14], Hough Forests have been employed to delineate the midbrain in ultrasound volumes using a voting strategy similar to the one proposed in our work. Other approaches build upon deformable models based on active contours [1,6,23], leveraging appearance and shape models to improve robustness.

Recently, deep learning techniques like CNNs have attracted great attention in the area of computer vision. Thereby, voxel-wise classification is widely used to perform a semantic segmentation by labeling each voxel independently, based on the visual content of its surrounding patch. In the medical domain, this approach has been applied to segmentation of various structures like bones [3], blood vessels [12], neuron membranes [5], brain structures [10] and tumors [8].

However, classifying each image patch independently is rather inefficient as it includes many redundant computations. Therefore, a variety of proposals have been made to circumvent these unnecessary computations. One approach is to replace the fully connected layers at the end of the network with convolutional ones and perform semantic segmentation [7,24]. Alternatively, whole 2D images [11,21] or 3D volumes [16] can get processed at once through fully convolutional architectures, which allows for evaluating the whole image in one pass and within a fraction of time compared to the sliding window approaches.

The performance of semantic segmentation algorithms is limited and often produces noisy results, since each pixel is classified independently from its neighbours and therefore lacks spatial consistency. Consequently, many different post-processing methods have been proposed, such as energy based models [13], fully connected conditional random fields [4] or a graph partitioning algorithm [25]. CNNs can also be used as simple feature extractors and thereby serve as a basis for many different segmentation algorithms. Exemplary implementations include the segmentation of retinal blood vessels with a random forest based on CNN features [29] and the segmentation of the hippocampus with an atlas based framework using convolutional independent subspace analysis networks as feature extractors [9].

We propose to solve the task of segmenting the midbrain in transcranial ultrasound volumes (TCUS) by performing a CNN based voxel-wise classification that is combined with a Hough based voting strategy as a post-processing method. This approach is substantially different to the Hough networks proposed by Riegler et al. [20] who perform a simultaneous classification and regression with CNNs for the task of head pose estimation and facial feature localizatio. In comparison, we use an approach based on nearest neighbours retrieval in feature space, which imposes stronger shape priors.

Our Hough-CNN algorithm corresponds to the one presented in [15]. In this work however, we further explore several important parameters of the training setup. We analyze (i) the impact of different neural networks architectures, (ii) optimal patch dimensionality and neighborhood context through patch size and (iii) how classification performance is influenced by the amount of training data. We first vary this amount by extracting increasing number of patches from the maximum available set of training volumes, and then by decreasing the number of overall provided training volumes. In particular, the latter experiment examines the robustness of our method towards less variability in the training set, which is of particular interest due to the involved cost in creating segmentation groundtruth by clinical experts. We additionally investigate other practical aspects of our method that allow better reproducibility of our research.

2 Method

The most straightforward approach of applying CNNs to solve segmentation tasks is to perform semantic segmentation, for which a CNN classifier is trained to correctly classify the centric pixel or voxel of a given image patch. To this end, a set of J training patches $P = \{p_1^i, p_2^i, ..., p_J^i\}$ is extracted from each training volume $t_i \in T = \{t_1, t_2, ..., t_I\}$, for each labeled region l as well as for the background. The respective label annotation is given by the corresponding annotated volumes (i.e. ground truth volumes) $g_i \in G = \{g_1, g_2, ..., g_I\}$.

Segmentation of a previously unseen image volume is obtained by classifying each individual voxel successively with the trained network. However, applying a CNN classifier to the whole image volume in a sliding window fashion is rather inefficient, as it involves many redundant computations that need to be carried out for neighboring patches. More efficiently, identical results can be achieved by convolving the whole volume with respective convolution filters, given that no padding is employed within the network. Similarly, patch-wise processing for pooling layers can be avoided by sliding respective pooling windows over the whole volume in one pass instead. Only fully connected layers require patch-wise processing, as their weights are only defined for the original input map size.

Nevertheless, fully connected layers can be converted to convolutional ones which contain as many convolution kernels as there are neurons in the fully connected layer and whose filter sizes are as big as the original input map. To this end, the weights are simply rearranged such that they preserve the spatial correspondences. In case that a fully connected layer comprised of N neurons is preceded by another one, the resulting convolutional layer contains N convolution kernels of size 1×1. Once no fully connected layer is present within the CNN, the whole image volume can be processed in one pass, classifying multiple voxels at once. Thereby, the resolution of the resulting output map depends on the overall amount of subsampling s that is carried out by the network.

In order to obtain a full resolution segmentation for 2D images, Sermanet et al. [24] propose to pad the input image and to apply the CNN classifier $s \times s$ times to a slightly shifted subimage along the horizontal and vertical axis. This procedure is outlined in Fig. 1 for a subsampling of two. Here, a colored rectangle in the left image marks the area which needs to be processed by the CNN in order to retrieve the classification results of the pixels labeled with the same color in the right image. Even though this method is tied to the condition that no padding is used within the CNN, this small limitation is outweighed by

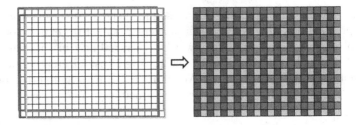

Fig. 1. Processing a sequence of slightly shifted image areas to retrieve a full resolution semantic segmentation when employing a subsampling of two within the CNN. (Color figure online)

the immense speedup of the sliding-window classification. Due to the way we build 2.5D patches from volumetric data (see Sect. 3.2), the problem cannot be translated into a fully convolutional network: 2.5D patches need to be evaluated one by one.

However, a pure semantic segmentation approach has the disadvantage that it neither considers the overall image context nor any shape priors of the regions to be extracted and, therefore, is likely to produce erroneous contours. Thus, our segmentation algorithm, inspired by [14], builds upon the semantic segmentation result but additionally re-uses the output of intermediate CNN layers as feature vectors for a voting strategy framework which introduces implicit prior shape knowledge and thereby imposes global consistency on the final segmentation.

A schematic 2D representation of our Hough-CNN segmentation approach is given in Fig. 2 for the task of segmenting the midbrain within a TCUS volume.

We first train a CNN with patches extracted from the annotated volumes $t_i \in T = \{t_1, t_2, ..., t_I\}$. Applying the trained network to each training volume i, we generate a database entry $q = (f, l, v, idx)$ for each voxel that is classified as foreground. Each entry consists of (i) feature vectors f consisting of the activations of the second last fully connected layer of the network; (ii) a voting vector $v = (\mathbf{x} - \mathbf{c}_l)$ representing the displacement from the position of the patch $\mathbf{x}$ to the anatomy centroid $\mathbf{c}$ of the region l; (iii) the necessary information $idx = (i, \mathbf{x})$ to retrieve a portion of the ground truth segmentation contour from the region surrounding the currently considered foreground patch in the i-th training volume. In this way, we implicitly capture prior knowledge about the localisation and shape of the regions to be delineated.

The evaluation of a previously unseen image volume starts with a CNN based voxel-wise classification (structures marked in red in Fig. 2b) in conjunction with the extraction of the respective feature vector f. Afterwards, the K most similar database entries $\{q_1^o, ..., q_K^o\}$ are identified for each voxel o located at position x_o that is assigned a foreground classification label l by the CNN. For this purpose, a k-nearest neighbor search [17] is performed based on the Euclidean distance ϵ_o^u between the feature vector of the currently processed voxel o and all database entries u that hold the same classification label l. Furthermore, a database entry

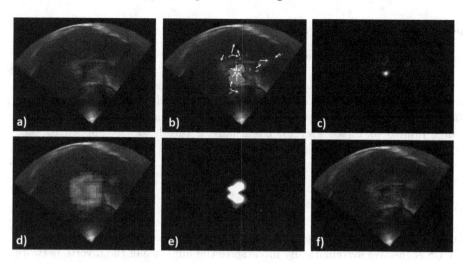

Fig. 2. Outline of Hough-CNN segmentation for one region: (a) image to be segmented, (b) semantic segmentation result (red) and voting vectors (white) for region centroid, (c) vote map, (d) back-projection of segmentation patches, (e) segmentation volume (f) final segmentation contour (red). (Color figure online)

q_k^o is discarded if the respective distance ϵ_o^k exceeds a maximum value ϵ_{max} which is determined empirically.

Next, the vectors v_k of each encountered neighbor q_k are retrieved from the database to vote for the centroid location $x_o + v_k$ of region l (white arrows in Fig. 2b). Thereby all votes dedicated to the centroid of region l are collected in a separate vote map m_l while being weighted with the inverse of the Euclidean distance $\hat{\epsilon}_o^k = \frac{1}{\epsilon_o^k}$. As soon as all votes have been cast, each vote map m_l is smoothed by a Gaussian filter with standard deviation σ in order to eliminate occurring noise. Figure 2c shows an exemplary vote map that clearly identifies the correct location of the midbrain. False positives within the semantic segmentation result vote for random centroid locations and are therefore implicitly rejected.

For experiments in this work, we assume single-instance detection, i.e. each anatomical region can only occur once inside an image volume. Then, the location of the maximum value $\hat{c}_l$ of the feature map m_l is declared as the centroid position of region l. However, an extension of Hough-CNNs to multi-instance detection would be straightforward, if each local maximum in the voting map m_l with a value greater than a specified threshold is considered as a detected location of the respective region type l.

After localizing the individual regions, all elements q_k^o are identified whose voting vectors $x_o + v_k$ contributed to the obtained centroid position of region l, within a certain radius r. Based on the respective index $idx_k = (i, x_k)$ a segmentation patch $\hat{g}_k^o$ of size $\gamma = (\gamma_h \times \gamma_w \times \gamma_d)$ is extracted from the ground truth volume g_i at position x_k and processed such that $\hat{g}_k^o(x) = \begin{cases} 1 & \text{if } x = l \\ 0 & \text{if } x \neq l \end{cases}$.

Each binary segmentation patch gets weighted by $\hat{\epsilon}_o^k$ and reprojected into a segmentation volume ψ_l at position x_o (see Fig. 2d). Once all patches have been accumulated, each segmentation volume is normalized such that its values range from 0 to 1 (see Fig. 2e). Eventually, a threshold θ is applied to each segmentation volume ψ_l in order to retrieve the final segmentation contour of region l (see Fig. 2f).

3   Experiments

In this work, we apply our general segmentation approach presented in Sect. 2 to TCUS scans. We systematically investigate the influence of the diverse network architectures as well as of the number, type and extent of the respective training patches on the resulting segmentation performance of our method.

3.1   Dataset

We employ a total of 162 TCUS scans acquired freehand and compounded into volumes with isotropic resolution of 1 mm, depicting the human midbrain.

The ground truth of each TCUS volume is generated by an expert neuroimage technician. Our dataset features a large variation of image quality and midbrain shape across scans. For our experiments, we split the TCUS data into 40 volumes from 8 subjects for training, eight sweeps from two subjects for validation, and 114 sweeps from 24 subjects for testing.

3.2   Patch Extraction

For the training of the CNN classifier, patches need to be extracted from the annotated datasets. In order to analyze different aspects of applying CNNs to medical segmentation tasks, we create a variety of different training sets.

We investigate three different types of patch dimensionality that are suitable for CNN processing of volumetric images. The most widespread approach is to evaluate 2D intensity patches of size $\rho = (\rho_{width} \times \rho_{height})$ (see Fig. 3a) along one

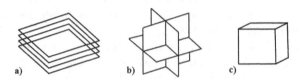

Fig. 3. Patch types for image volumes: (a) 2D patches along one spatial axes, (b) 2.5D patches (2D patches along each spatial axes), (c) 3D patches.

spatial axis. These are fast to process but do not capture the full 3D spatial context [3,5,8,10,13]. The second option is to extract three orthogonal 2D patches of size $\rho = (\rho_{width} \times \rho_{height})$ (see Fig. 3b), marking a compromise between still low computational requirements, while covering at least a limited, planar amount of 3D information. This approach has initially been proposed by Prasoon et al. [19], who process each 2D patch in a separate network path. In this work, however, we follow the adaption of Roth et al. [22]. Here, orthogonal 2D patches are of equal size and get concatenated in third dimension, to form the three channels of a pseudo-colour RGB image. This simplifies the training of the CNN classifier to a 2D scenario, again keeping computational resources low. Finally, the third alternative is to process 3D patches of size $\rho = (\rho_{width} \times \rho_{height} \times \rho_{depth})$ (see Fig. 3c). Capturing the fully 3D spatial context, these patches may improve classification, but at the cost of much higher memory and training time demands, due to the required 3D convolutions [26,27].

The spatial extent of the individual patches defines the anatomic context that can be captured by the CNN, but also influences the amount of computational resources that is required. Thus, we analyze the differences between quadratic or cubic patches with a side length of 31 and 51 voxels, corresponding to a spatial area of about $9 \, cm^2$ or $27 \, cm^3$ and $25 \, cm^2$ or $125 \, cm^3$, respectively.

In order to investigate the influence of varying training set sizes on the performance of the CNNs, we also conduct experiments with different amounts of training patches by extracting up to 1.000 and 5.000 patches per region (including background) and per training volume, yielding around 80.000 and 400.000 training patches in total.

Finally, an experiment is performed which reduces the amount of training volumes to identify the minimum required amount of medical training data. Here, the number of TCUS sweeps per subject is incrementally reduced by one which corresponds to a step size of eight volumes. This investigation is of particular interest for the clinically applicability, as the available amount of training data represents a very limited resource in the medical domain.

3.3   Network Architecture

For our experiments, we consider six different network architectures with varying depth and convolution filter sizes. Each network architecture consists of convolutional ($C_{kernel\ size}^{\#kernels}$), pooling ($P_{window\ size}^{subsampling}$) and fully connected ($F_{\#neurons}$) layers as outlined in Table 1. Thereby all convolutional and fully connected layers employ PReLU activation functions. Besides, drop out is used with a ratio of 0.5 for all fully connected layers except for the last one, in order to prevent the training from overfitting.

4   Results

This section presents the applicability of CNNs for segmenting the midbrain in transcranial ultrasound (TCUS) volumes. For this purpose Figs. 4 and 5 depict

Table 1. CNN architectures

Name	Small Alex		9-7-5-3-3		7-5-3		5-5-5-5-5		3-3-3-3-3		3-3-3-3-3-3-3-3	
Patch size	31	51	31	51	31	51	31	51	31	51	31	51
Network layout	C_{11}^{64}	C_{11}^{64}	C_9^{64}	C_9^{64}	C_7^{64}	C_7^{64}	C_5^{64}	C_5^{64}	C_3^{64}	C_3^{64}	C_3^{64}	C_3^{64}
	P_2^1	P_2^2		P_3^2	P_3^2	P_3^2		P_3^2	P_3^2	P_3^2		P_3^2
	C_5^{64}	C_5^{64}	C_7^{64}	C_7^{64}	C_5^{64}	C_5^{64}	C_5^{64}	C_5^{64}	C_3^{64}	C_3^{64}	C_3^{64}	C_3^{64}
	P_2^1	P_2^1				P_2^2				P_2^2		
	C_3^{64}	C_3^{64}	C_5^{64}	C_3^{64}	C_3^{64}	C_3^{64}	C_5^{64}	C_5^{64}	C_3^{64}	C_3^{64}	C_3^{64}	C_3^{64}
	C_3^{64}	C_3^{64}	C_3^{64}	C_3^{64}			C_5^{64}	C_5^{64}	C_3^{64}	C_3^{64}	C_3^{64}	C_3^{64}
	C_3^{64}	C_3^{64}	C_3^{64}	C_3^{64}			C_5^{64}	C_5^{64}	C_3^{64}	C_3^{64}	C_3^{64}	C_3^{64}
											C_3^{64}	C_3^{64}
											C_3^{64}	C_3^{64}
											C_3^{64}	C_3^{64}
	F_{128}	F_{128}	F_{128}	F_{128}	F_{128}	F_{128}	F_{128}	F_{128}	F_{128}	F_{128}	F_{128}	F_{128}
	F_{128}	F_{128}	F_{128}	F_{128}			F_{128}	F_{128}	F_{128}	F_{128}	F_{128}	F_{128}
	F_{R+1}	F_{R+1}	F_{R+1}	F_{R+1}	F_{R+1}	F_{R+1}	F_{R+1}	F_{R+1}	F_{R+1}	F_{R+1}	F_{R+1}	F_{R+1}

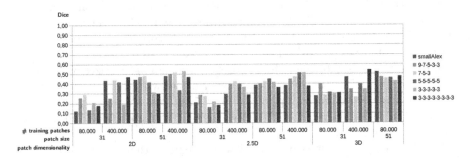

Fig. 4. CNN based semantic segmentation results in terms of average Dice coefficient over 114 TCUS test volumes.

the CNN based semantic segmentation performance and the results of our new Hough-CNN method in terms of average Dice coefficients over all test volumes for varying amount, size and dimensionality of training patches.

Thereby, Fig. 4 shows that the semantic segmentation result improves with higher amounts of training data and larger spatial context for the voxel-wise classification, whereas the CNN network architecture exhibits no systematic influence on final semantic segmentation performance.

In contrast, our Hough-CNN segmentation approach is very robust towards different network architectures, small patch sizes, low patch dimensionalities and little amount of training data while achieving much more accurate results than the pure CNN based voxel-wise classification. As a consequence, our Hough-CNN segmentation enables to use small training dataset size. Furthermore, it is sufficient to classify small 2D intensity patches by the CNNs when post-processing the classification result with our Hough voting strategy, which decreases the required computational resources both in terms of processing time and memory footprint.

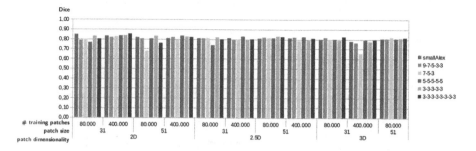

Fig. 5. Hough-CNN segmentation results in terms of average Dice coefficient over 114 TCUS test volumes.

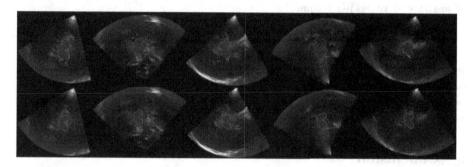

Fig. 6. Slices through TCUS test scans. Ground truth (red area) and semantic (first row) and Hough-CNN (second row) segmentation results (line) obtained by classifying 2D 31 × 31 patches with the "3-3-3-3-3-3-3-3" architecture trained on 400K patches. (Color figure online)

Figure 6 shows several slices through the TCUS test volumes depicting the ground truth (red area) and the obtained segmentation contour (red line) for both the semantic (first row) and our Hough-CNN segmentation method (second row). In general, the Hough-CNN segmentation method localizes and extracts the midbrain very accurately in the TCUS scans and produces very smooth contours, regardless of the bone window quality, the overall visibility of midbrain structures and the occurrence of dropout artifacts or blurring.

The influence of a varying number of training volumes on the semantic and Hough-CNN segmentation performance is shown in Fig. 7 in terms of Dice coefficients that are averaged over all test volumes.

The semantic segmentation performance for the midbrain in TCUS scans continuously improves with an increasing amount of training volumes. Compared to that, Dice overlaps of corresponding Hough-CNN segmentations stabilise as soon as at least 16 volumes are used for training. This demonstrates the capability of the Hough-CNN method to compensate a certain amount of failures of the CNN classification, which in return reduces the number of required training volumes to a clinically feasible amount.

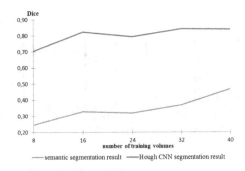

Fig. 7. Comparison of semantic and Hough-CNN segmentation under varying amount of training volumes for CNN architecture "3-3-3-3-3-3" trained with 5.000 2D patches of size 31 × 31 voxels per volume.

Finally, compared to literature, our Hough-CNNs (Dice 0.85 + −0.01) outperform active contours (Dice 0.83 + −0.03 [1]), perform comparable to state-of-the-art using Hough-Forests (Dice 0.85 + −0.03 [14]), observe high robustness on a test set of unprecedented size (114 test volumes vs. 22 [1] and 12 [14]), and segment generally within the range of human error (inter-rater Dice 0.85 [18]).

5   Conclusion

We present a fully automatic approach to perform volumetric segmentation of transcranial ultrasound images depicting the human midbrain. Our approach leverages CNNs to both classify the volume of interest voxel-wise and extract high level features that are representative of patch visual content. The strength of our method is the ability to reject erroneous contributions to the final segmentation contour by using a voting strategy. Through Hough voting, we impose global coherency of the classification results obtained patch-wise, while incorporating implicit shape knowledge. This is also enforced by the segmentation strategy, which allow us to obtain smooth contours resembling the ones seen during training. Our approach was tested on several scans in order to demonstrate its generalisation capabilities and yielded state-of-the-art results and precision comparable to the one of human raters.

Acknowledgements. This study was funded by the Lüneburg Heritage and Deutsche Forschungsgesellschaft (DFG) Grant BO 1895/4-1. We gratefully acknowledge the support of NVIDIA Corporation in donating a Tesla K40 GPU for this study.

References

1. Ahmadi, S.A., Baust, M., Karamalis, A., Plate, A., Bötzel, K., Klein, T., Navab, N.: Midbrain segmentation in transcranial 3D ultrasound for Parkinson diagnosis. Med. Image Comput. Comput. Assist. Interv. **14**(Pt 3), 362–369 (2011)

2. Berg, D., Seppi, K., Behnke, S., Liepelt, I., Schweitzer, K., Stockner, H., Wollenweber, F., Gaenslen, A., Mahlknecht, P., Spiegel, J., Godau, J., Huber, H., Srulijes, K., Kiechl, S., Bentele, M., Gasperi, A., Schubert, T., Hiry, T., Probst, M., Schneider, V., Klenk, J., Sawires, M., Willeit, J., Maetzler, W., Fassbender, K., Gasser, T., Poewe, W.: Enlarged substantia nigra hyperechogenicity and risk for Parkinson disease: a 37-month 3-center study of 1847 older persons. Arch. Neurol. **68**(7), 932–937 (2011)

3. Cernazanu-Glavan, C., Holban, S.: Segmentation of bone structure in X-ray images using convolutional neural network. Adv. Electr. Comput. Eng. **13**(1), 87–94 (2013)

4. Chen, L.C., Papandreou, G., Kokkinos, I., Murphy, K., Yuille, A.L.: Semantic image segmentation with deep convolutional nets and fully connected CRFs. arXiv preprint arXiv:1412.7062 (2014)

5. Ciresan, D., Giusti, A., Gambardella, L.M., Schmidhuber, J.: Deep neural networks segment neuronal membranes in electron microscopy images. In: Advances in Neural Information Processing Systems, pp. 2843–2851 (2012)

6. Engel, K., Toennies, K.D.: Segmentation of the midbrain in transcranial sonographies using a two-component deformable model. In: 12th Annual Conference on Medical Image Understanding and Analysis, pp. 3–7. Citeseer (2009)

7. Farfade, S.S., Saberian, M.J., Li, L.J.: Multi-view face detection using deep convolutional neural networks. In: Proceedings of the 5th ACM on International Conference on Multimedia Retrieval, pp. 643–650. ACM (2015)

8. Havaei, M., Davy, A., Warde-Farley, D., Biard, A., Courville, A., Bengio, Y., Pal, C., Jodoin, P.M., Larochelle, H.: Brain tumor segmentation with deep neural networks. arXiv preprint arXiv:1505.03540 (2015)

9. Kim, M., Wu, G., Shen, D.: Unsupervised deep learning for hippocampus segmentation in 7.0 Tesla MR images. In: Wu, G., Zhang, D., Shen, D., Yan, P., Suzuki, K., Wang, F. (eds.) MLMI 2013. LNCS, vol. 8184, pp. 1–8. Springer, Heidelberg (2013)

10. Lee, N., Laine, A.F., Klein, A.: Towards a deep learning approach to brain parcellation. In: 2011 IEEE International Symposium on Biomedical Imaging: From Nano to Macro, pp. 321–324. IEEE (2011)

11. Long, J., Shelhamer, E., Darrell, T.: Fully convolutional networks for semantic segmentation. In: Proceedings of the IEEE Conference on Computer Vision and Pattern Recognition, pp. 3431–3440 (2015)

12. Melinščak, M., Prentašić, P., Lončarić, S.: Retinal vessel segmentation using deep neural networks. In: VISAPP 2015 (10th International Conference on Computer Vision Theory and Applications) (2015)

13. Middleton, I., Damper, R.I.: Segmentation of magnetic resonance images using a combination of neural networks and active contour models. Med. Eng. Phys. **26**(1), 71–86 (2004)

14. Milletari, F., Ahmadi, S.A., Kroll, C., Hennersperger, C., Tombari, F., Shah, A., Plate, A., Bötzel, K., Navab, N.: Robust Segmentation of Various Anatomies in 3D Ultrasound Using Hough Forests and Learned Data Representations. Medical Image Computing and Computer Assisted Interventions (2015, to appear)

15. Milletari, F., Ahmadi, S.A., Kroll, C., Plate, A., Rozanski, V., Maiostre, J., Levin, J., Dietrich, O., Ertl-Wagner, B., Bötzel, K., et al.: Hough-CNN: deep learning for segmentation of deep brain regions in MRI and ultrasound. arXiv preprint arXiv:1601.07014 (2016)

16. Milletari, F., Navab, N., Ahmadi, S.A.: V-Net: fully convolutional neural networks for volumetric medical image segmentation. arXiv preprint arXiv:1606.04797 (2016)

17. Muja, M., Lowe, D.G.: Scalable nearest neighbor algorithms for high dimensional data. IEEE Trans. Pattern Anal. Mach. Intell. **36**, 2227–2240 (2014)
18. Plate, A., Ahmadi, S.A., Pauly, O., Klein, T., Navab, N., Bötzel, K.: Three-dimensional sonographic examination of the midbrain for computer-aided diagnosis of movement disorders. Ultrasound Med. Biol. **38**(12), 2041–2050 (2012)
19. Prasoon, A., Petersen, K., Igel, C., Lauze, F., Dam, E., Nielsen, M.: Deep feature learning for knee cartilage segmentation using a triplanar convolutional neural network. In: Mori, K., Sakuma, I., Sato, Y., Barillot, C., Navab, N. (eds.) MICCAI 2013, Part II. LNCS, vol. 8150, pp. 246–253. Springer, Heidelberg (2013)
20. Riegler, G., Ferstl, D., Rüther, M., Bischof, H.: Hough networks for head pose estimation and facial feature localization. J. Comput. Vis. **101**(3), 437–458 (2013)
21. Ronneberger, O., Philipp, F., Thomas, B.: U-Net: convolutional networks for bio-medical image segmentation. In: Navab, N., Hornegger, J., Wells, W.M., Frangi, A.F. (eds.) MICCAI 2015. LNCS, vol. 9351, pp. 234–241. Springer, Heidelberg (2015). doi:10.1007/978-3-319-24574-4_28
22. Roth, H.R., Lu, L., Seff, A., Cherry, K.M., Hoffman, J., Wang, S., Liu, J., Turkbey, E., Summers, R.M.: A new 2.5D representation for Lymph node detection using random sets of deep convolutional neural network observations. In: Hata, N., Barillot, C., Hornegger, J., Howe, R., Golland, P. (eds.) MICCAI 2014, Part I. LNCS, vol. 8673, pp. 520–527. Springer, Heidelberg (2014)
23. Sakalauskas, A., Lukoševičius, A., Laučkaitė, K., Jegelevičius, D., Rutkauskas, S.: Automated segmentation of transcranial sonographic images in the diagnostics of Parkinsons disease. Ultrasonics **53**(1), 111–121 (2013)
24. Sermanet, P., Eigen, D., Zhang, X., Mathieu, M., Fergus, R., LeCun, Y.: Overfeat: integrated recognition, localization and detection using convolutional networks. arXiv preprint arXiv:1312.6229 (2013)
25. Song, Y., Zhang, L., Chen, S., Ni, D., Lei, B., Wang, T.: Accurate segmentation of cervical cytoplasm and nuclei based on multiscale convolutional network and graph partitioning. IEEE Trans. Biomed. Eng. **62**(10), 2421–2433 (2015)
26. Turaga, S.C., Murray, J.F., Jain, V., Roth, F., Helmstaedter, M., Briggman, K., Denk, W., Seung, H.S.: Convolutional networks can learn to generate affinity graphs for image segmentation. Neural Comput. **22**(2), 511–538 (2010)
27. Urban, G., Bendszus, M., Hamprecht, F., Kleesiek, J.: Multi-modal brain tumor segmentation using deep convolutional neural networks. In: MICCAI BraTS (Brain Tumor Segmentation) Challenge. Proceedings, Winning Contribution, pp. 31–35 (2014)
28. Walter, U., Dressler, D., Probst, T., Wolters, A., Abu-Mugheisib, M., Wittstock, M., Benecke, R.: Transcranial brain sonography findings in discriminating between parkinsonism and idiopathic Parkinson disease. Arch. Neurol. **64**(11), 1635–1640 (2007)
29. Wang, S., Yin, Y., Cao, G., Wei, B., Zheng, Y., Yang, G.: Hierarchical retinal blood vessel segmentation based on feature and ensemble learning. Neurocomputing **149**, 708–717 (2015)

Author Index

Printed in the United States
By Bookmasters